THE GENDER REVOLUTION

REVOLUTION

& NEW SEXUAL HEALTH

THE GENDER REVOLUTION

& NEW SEXUAL HEALTH

CELEBRATING UNLIMITED DIVERSITY
OF THE HUMAN SEXUALITY HYPERCUBE

FIRST EDITION

FREDERICK L. PETERSON, JILL BLEY, AND RICHELLE FRABOTTA

SAN DIEGO

Bassim Hamadeh, CEO and Publisher
Jennifer Codner, Acquisitions Editor
Michelle Piehl, Senior Project Editor
Alia Bales, Production Editor
Emely M. Villavicencio, Senior Graphic Designer
Stephanie Kohl, Licensing Coordinator
Natalie Piccotti, Director of Marketing
Kassie Graves, Vice President of Editorial
Jamie Giganti, Director of Academic Publishing

3970 Sorrento Valley Blvd., Ste. 500, San Diego, CA 92121

CONTENTS

How to Use This Book...xi

The Authors' Backgrounds and Perspectives xiii

Acknowledgments xvii

A Note About Language and Gender... xix

SECTION I

Let's Measure Your Sexual Mind 1

CHAPTER ONE: Exploring, Measuring, and Honoring Your Sexual Health...........................5

Introduction 5

A Report from the Front Lines of the Revolution 7

Exploring and Validating Your Own Experience and Perspective 9

Making Sense of Your Score for the Self-Assessment of Family Support 17

Consider This.. 18

A New Line of Exploration... 19

The Cost of Low Sexual Literacy... 22

Enhancing Your Sexual Health Through Sexual Literacy........................ 29

References 30

CHAPTER TWO: Measuring Your Sexual Satisfaction... 31

Introduction to the Dimensions of Sexual Health.................................. 31

Potential Benefits of Completing the SHAWS.. 32

Baseline Measure of Satisfaction: Sexual Health and Wellness Satisfaction (SHAWS) 33

Making Sense of Your SHAWS Baseline Scores 38

Real-Life Demonstration of the Scoring and Interpretation of the SHAWS........... 39

The Nature of Satisfaction.. 41

The Relationship Between Satisfaction and Authenticity....................... 43

The Balance of Strategies 45

So, Where to from Here? 50

References 50

CHAPTER THREE: The Big Wheel and Beginnings of the New Sexual Health 51

Introduction 51

What Is Sexual Health? 52

What Is the Big Wheel of Health? 53

Frank's Story 54

Joe's Story 55

The Self-Assessment of Satisfaction for Your Overall Health 57

Completing a Baseline Measure of Overall Health and Well-Being Satisfaction 57

Overall Health and Well-Being Satisfaction Ratings 58

Deeper Questions 62

Some Wise Words on Health and Happiness 63

References 66

CHAPTER FOUR: Success Story: The Clan of Scott (Memorial Day 1986) **67**

Sex and Physical Disability 67

CHAPTER FIVE: Success Story: Alex's Love Story **77**

World Professional Association for Transgender Health Standards of Care 77

Alex: A Navy Seal Who Struggled with Gender Dysphoria 80

References 84

SECTION II

Let's Explore Your sexual Mind 85

CHAPTER SIX: Our Early Sexual Heritage in America 87

Introduction 87

Why Look Deeper into the History of Sex in America? 89

The Good Health Doctrine 90

The Mad History of the Life and Death of Masturbation as Disease 93

The Birth of MAD: Enter the Onanists 95

Sexophrenia: The Legacy of Our Sexual Heritage 99

The Quest for Sexual Literacy, Sexual Health, and Personal Fulfillment 108

References 109

TIMELINE: The Century of the Woman: Significant Events in the American
Experiment in Democracy 111

CHAPTER SEVEN: America's 20th-Century Journey from Sexosophy to Sexology 121

Introduction 121

The Great Transition from Sexosophy to Sexology (Part I): 123

The Great Transition from Sexosophy to Sexology (Part II): 124

The Great Transition from Sexosophy to Sexology (Part III): 128

The Great Transition from Sexosophy to Sexology (Part IV): 129

The Kinsey Years (1940 to 1956)..131

The Masters and Johnson Years: The Golden Years of Sex Research (1954 to 1980) 133

America's Sexual Makeover: Cultural Notes on the 1950s and 1960s...137

The 1970s: The Commercialization and Professionalization of Sex Therapy 140

The 1980s and 1990s—The Medicalization of Sex and the Emergence of the Field of Sexual Health 141

A Final Note to Our Review of the 20th-Century Journey to Sexology 145

References 146

CHAPTER EIGHT: Health Benefits from Sexual Expression 148

Introduction...148

The Relationship Between Sexual Expression and Health—Stories from Doc....................................151

A Case for Celibacy..152

Technical Time-Out: What Exactly Is an Orgasm?...153

The Relationship Between Sexual Expression and Health—The Research 156

The Magnitude of the Problem 168

Conclusion 171

References 173

CHAPTER NINE: Joe and Marie: A Story of Unconsummated Marriage and Training with the Master at the Masters and Johnson Institute **175**

CHAPTER TEN: The Dee Rockwood Story: From Hypermasculine Super-Athlete to the Grandma in the Church Pew Next to You **180**

SECTION III

Let's Blow Your Sexual Mind!...191

CHAPTER ELEVEN: Considering Sexual Identity..193

Introduction...193

What Is Sexuality? 194

What Is Sexual Identity? Results of a Review of College Textbooks 195

Other Important Voices Considered Regarding Sexual Identity..197

Definitions of the Three Basic Components of Sexual Identity 199

Basic Sex Orientation: How Are You So Sure You Are a Man or Woman? 200

The Mathematics of Human Sexual Diversity (Part I)...203

Basic Sexual Orientation: How Are You So Sure You Are Gay, Bi, or Straight? 206

Basic Sex-Role Orientation: How Are You So Sure That You are as Masculine and Feminine as You Believe? 210

Now Back to the Central Question of Sexual Identity 212

A New Definition of Sexual Identity and the Sexual Identity Cube.............................213

The Kicker for the Sexual Identity Cube:

The Mathematics of Sexual Diversity (Part II).............................218

References.............................220

Figure Credit.............................221

CHAPTER TWELVE: Sexual Expression **222**

Introduction.............................222

What Is Sexual Expression?.............................222

Nature Versus Nurture? (The Wrong Question).............................224

A Brief Note on Normalcy.............................225

Lovemaps, Paraphilias, and Sexual Expression.............................227

The Sexual Expression Cube:

Fantasy, Behavior, and Mediators.............................228

Mediators of Sexual Expression: Bioculturally Bound Factors.............................235

The Sexual Tipping Point.............................237

As This Chapter Concludes.............................240

References.............................241

CHAPTER THIRTEEN: Sex and the Fourth Dimension: The Sexual Hypercube **243**

Introduction.............................243

The Fourth Dimension, Hyperspace, and the Sexual Hypercube.............................245

The Sexual Hypercube Model.............................246

Application of the Sexual Hypercube Model.............................249

What Evidence Is There That Sexual Identity and Expression Change?.............................253

Animal Models of Changes in Biological Sex and Expression.............................253

Human Models of Movement Across the Sexual Hypercube.............................255

What Guidelines Govern Changes in Sexual Identity and Expression?.............................259

References.............................261

Figure Credits.............................261

CHAPTER FOURTEEN: The Gage and Devin Story.............................**262**

Introduction.............................262

Gage's Story.............................263

Enter Devin.............................265

Back to the Pageants.............................266

CHAPTER FIFTEEN: The Story of Jane and Eddie Finding a Way Through the Pain....**268**

Introduction.............................268

Sexual Pain.............................269

The Dark Presence Cloaked by the Psychobiology of Trauma.............................270

The Healing Process.............................272

Reflections on Jane's Path to Health 273

References 274

SECTION IV

Putting Your Sexual Mind Into Play...275

CHAPTER SIXTEEN: When Sex Hurts...277
Introduction...277

History of Laws Governing Rape 278

Development of the Diagnosis of PTSD in the Treatment of Rape Victims 295

Diagnosis of Dissociative Identity Disorder (DID) Adapted from DSM-4 300

Sexual Assault Prevention 304

Prevention of Childhood Sexual Abuse 306

Summary of Statistics in Studies on Sexual Abuse 306

References 307

CHAPTER SEVENTEEN: When You Hurt Others and Yourself: Problematic Sexual
Behavior **309**
Introduction...309

What Are Problematic Sexual Behaviors? 310

What Other Names Do PSBs Go By, and Why Do Men Engage in Them? 312

Additional Approaches to Determining If Sexual Behaviors Are Problematic or Not 315

The Recovery Process 316

The Story of Karl: A Demonstration of Men with PSB 318

Key Components of the Recovery Process 324

The Positive Sexuality Recovery Model 326

Illegal PSBs That Hurt Others: Sex Offenses 329

Summary: Final Thoughts of PSB 332

References 333

CHAPTER EIGHTEEN: The Mind Is a Tricky Thing, but the Body Never
Forgets: Kala's Story.. **335**

CHAPTER NINETEEN: Making Sense of All You Have Learned....................................341
The Pleasure of It All...341

The Sexual Communication Exercise 344

A Lifelong Love Story—Angelia and Shelly 347

Sharing Sexual Fantasies 349

Sensate Focus Exercises 353

Sexual Self-Image Exercises 358

References 360

CHAPTER TWENTY: Are There Ever Any Final Thoughts on the Topic of Sex? 361

Introduction 361

"Without You Even Knowing" (A Trip Inside the Psyche) 363

"Without You Even Knowing" (The Academic Explanation) 365

Across the Sexual Hypercube: The Gender Revolution and New Sexual Health 372

Movement Across the Sexual Hypercube: Change of Sexual Identity Throughout the Lifespan 376

Implications of the Sexual Hypercube 378

The End Point: The Sexual Health Challenge 380

References 383

Figure Credit 383

APPENDIX A: Baseline Measure of Satisfaction: Sexual Health and Wellness
Satisfaction (SHAWS) **384**

APPENDIX B: Statistical Consultation Report 390

Glossary 394

References 401

Index..413

HOW TO USE THIS BOOK

The *Gender Revolution & New Sexual Health* comes from a new sexual paradigm based on the sexual science that has driven a complete revolution in how we think of sex and gender in contemporary American culture. This book provides an innovative model of sexuality with a purpose to enhance your sexual health by introducing new sexual concepts and illustrative stories of individuals who have achieved sexual acceptance, satisfaction, and healthy relationships.

The focus of the book is on providing information necessary to enhance your sexual knowledge, comfort, confidence, and sexual practices. The book stands on its own toward these purposes. However, *The Gender Revolution & New Sexual Health* is best used as a complement to the comprehensive knowledge presented in college sexuality textbooks that cover sexual anatomy, physiology, conception, contraception, and other sexuality basics. *The Gender Revolution & New Sexual Health* goes beyond basic sexual information and serves as a guide to transforming knowledge to sexual health. To further extend your capacity to transform knowledge into sexual health, there will be another book of application forthcoming entitled *The Pleasure Playbook*.

The Gender Revolution & New Sexual Health communicates what the authors have shared with people in therapy, university courses, workshops, and sex-advice columns for three decades: practical approaches to overcome challenges people face with their sexuality. Additionally, the book illuminates the interesting world of clinical sexology through stories of success, introduces readers to new concepts (such as a unique model of sexual identity), and motivates readers to develop their own sexual health through proven methods. To better inform readers, research findings are written in plain language to avoid technical jargon. But because new concepts are introduced and some of the terms used in this book will be new to many readers, a glossary is included.

Embedded in the first three chapters are three questionnaires that are to be used as measurements of your satisfaction with 75 different dimensions of your sexual and overall health. You are highly encouraged to take the few minutes necessary to complete these questionnaires to establish a baseline measure of satisfaction. The second of the three questionnaires, the Sexual Health and Wellbeing Satisfaction Scale (SHAWS), is repeated at the end of the book for you to complete as a pre/post-measurement of 25 different key dimensions of satisfaction regarding your present sexual health. Completing the second SHAWS allows you to measure what progress you make as a result of reading this book, participating in therapy, and/or completing a full college course in human sexuality.

The combination of science and clinical application presented in this book represents what the authors have found most useful to clients and students. This approach has a down-to-earth personal and practical style. The numerous real-life examples included throughout the book are based on actual therapy cases with positive outcomes. These stories also represent real people who found their own way, with or without therapy, to overcome personal challenges they faced related to their gender and sexuality. Each were selected not just to inspire and motivate but to demonstrate key principles of gender and sexual health.

THE AUTHORS' BACKGROUNDS AND PERSPECTIVES

I, Docpete, am the primary author of this book and have the privilege of writing with two experts in their fields: Dr. Bley in the sex therapy field and Ms. Frabotta in the field of sex education. While I have written most of this book, I would never attempt to write any text on human sexuality without the perspectives and insights of female collaborators such as reflected through my partnerships with Dr. Bley and Ms. Frabotta. I am not the best writer, sex educator, or sex therapist that I know but I can be pretty damn good on my best days. While I have unique perspectives and insights of my own, I am keenly aware that I am more able to write a better book about complex ideas in the simplest ways through collaboration with Dr. Bley and Ms. Frabotta than I can by myself. In short, you have an improved product.

Dr. Bley is my longtime collaborator and a well-known clinical psychologist in southwest Ohio. She was a founder of Women Helping Women/Rape Crisis Center in 1972 in Cincinnati and taught courses on sex therapy to graduate students in the Clinical Psychology Department at the University of Cincinnati for nearly two decades (1979 to 1997). I first worked with Dr. Bley when she was hired by the Department of Veterans Affairs in the early 1990s to train health care providers on the new concept of sexual health. I later joined her to cowrite a very popular sex-advice column in a Cincinnati newspaper ("Speaking of Sex"), which Dr. Bley already had well established for years. Advertisers would specifically request their ad be placed next to the "Speaking of Sex" column. She then became an Associate Editor (with me) on the 2007 publication of *Innovations in Clinical Practice: Focus on Sexual Health*. Dr. Bley is a Certified Sex Therapist through the American Association of Sex Educators, Counselors, and Therapy (AASECT). As a Certified Sex Therapy Supervisor, she is one of the very few people in Ohio certified to train and supervise other health care professionals who wish to become certified sex therapists. She contributes a valued and insightful perspective into female sexuality and relationship satisfaction. I consider Jill one of the mothers of sex therapy in Ohio and is my go-to-person for all clinical matters of women's sexuality.

Ms. Frabotta is a leading sex educator and is currently completing her PhD at Miami University of Ohio, where she is studying educational leadership. She has been teaching human sexuality in higher education for more than two decades. At the national level, she has served as Chair of Public Relations, Media & Advocacy Steering Committee for AASECT. She also organized moderators for the annual AASECT conferences as Chair of the Moderator Subcommittee. As faculty at Miami University (of Oxford, Ohio), Ms. Frabotta teaches human sexuality and provides comprehensive sex education programs (workshops, training, consultation, and curriculum development) to county boards of developmental disabilities (DD) as well as community-based nonprofits such as Planned Parenthood. She is an AASECT Certified

Sex Educator and Director of Education Services at the Southern Ohio Sexuality Education and Consultation Services (SOSECS). She has taught at rehab centers, prisons, churches and temples, assisted living centers and hospitals, and community events such as Pride. Her clients and students are equally diverse and have included drug and alcohol addicted youth and adults, GL+B+T folks, pregnant and parenting teens, sexual and other violence perpetrators, victims/survivors of trauma, foster care youth and parents and staff, the elderly, and all folks "on the spectrum" of abilities, including those with traumatic brain injuries. These diverse experiences help her be effective in spreading the message that we are all sexual beings with a capacity to learn and grow. Richelle is one of the best sex educators I have ever seen, and I have seen a lot.

By way of my own background, I have had the good fortune to have been trained by several of the best in their fields, including being the last clinical fellow trained by the pioneer sex researcher Dr. William Masters of the Masters and Johnson Institute (1993–1994). Some of my stories of working with the famous Dr. Masters have been included in *Masters of Sex: The Life and Times of William Masters and Virginia Johnson*, which is the basis for the Showtime series *The Masters of Sex*. I was also trained and supervised by Dr. Ron Fox (past president of the American Psychological Association) and Dr. Judy Siefert (past president of the AASECT). I was Director of Medical Education (1987–1997) and Director of the Sexual Health Clinic (1998–2008) at the Veterans Healthcare System of Ohio (Dayton), where I developed a hospital-based holistic model of sex therapy services, which was the only comprehensive hospital-based sex therapy clinic in the Midwest.

I was considered the "sex professor" at Wright State University for two decades (1988–2009) where I had several academic appointments, including at the School of Medicine, School of Professional Psychology, College of Education and Human Services, and College of Business Administration. I am currently on the clinical faculty with the Department of Specialty Medicine, Heritage College of Osteopathic Medicine at Ohio University and have taught human sexuality at several other universities, including the Department of Psychology at the University of Dayton and the Gender, Women's and Sexuality Studies program at the University of Cincinnati.

I previously published many chapters and articles on topics of sexuality and health before I was associate editor of *Innovations in Clinical Practice: Focus on Sexual Health* (published in 2007 with Dr. Bley for health care providers by Professional Resource Press, Sarasota). In 2010, I also co-authored *Joyful Healthy Sex: Fundamental Education* (BK Publications, New Delhi). Teaming up with two of my former students, Dr. Roma Raj and Dr. Mulk Raj, we published this plain-language and culturally sensitive guide for sexual literacy and sexual health for the people of India.

All three authors of this book have decades of experience with research findings, teaching cases, and clinical experiences. All three of us have the professional luxury of writing for interest and personal satisfaction, not because publication is required in a "publish or perish" work setting. We are now at a place in our careers where we have much to say to the general public (from millennials to baby boomers) about gender and sexuality. We hope you enjoy what you are about to learn and would love to hear your thoughts about this book. One thing for sure, you are unlikely to read anything like it.

To contact me, please email Docpete1000@aol.com or though the USPS at **DeLong, Peterson & Associates: Clinical Consulting Specialists**, 131 N. Ludlow Street, Suite 248, Dayton, Ohio 45402. You can also text or phone me at 937-479-0008. Dr. Ron DeLong and I are Clinical Co-Directors of our sister organization and the educational branch of our business, **The Ohio Institute of Sexual Health**.

ACKNOWLEDGMENTS

❖

Thanks to my wife Christy for her help writing this book on sexuality, as she has forgotten more about female sexuality than I will ever know. Thanks to Christy and our extraordinary sons, Dane and Lex, for putting up with all the craziness during the writing of this book (over the last seven years)! Thanks to my two gifted daughters, Claudia and Mackenzie, whose support and love sustained me for many years as well as helped me appreciate what precious life-gifts daughters are. Thanks to my oldest son Joshua, whose birth and youth was the experience that set me on a course as a young father and psychologist of studying sex and gender; and my deep appreciation to Josh for adding Amber and Herschel to my life.

Sincere thanks to my co-author Jill Bley, who once again had the faith to venture into another wild writing project with me. I appreciate Dr. Bley writing several chapters to this text, contributing her insights into female sexuality as well as the wisdom from the early establishment of the field of sex therapy in Ohio. Thanks to my second co-author Richelle Frabotta, who had the curiosity (and smarts) to take on this adventure and contributed several *Featured Stories of Diverse Perspectives and Experiences* stemming from her vast experience as a leading sex educator.

Also, thanks to my many teachers, but especially to Love Mae Bingham (who introduced me to the field of sex therapy), Dr. Ron Fox (my former Dean and past president of the American Psychological Association), Dr. Judy Seifer (former sex therapy supervisor and past president of the American Association of Sex Educators, Counselors, and Therapists), and Dr. William Masters, pioneer sex researcher. It's been a long and winding road well worth traveling.

Thank you to Dr. Jerry Flexman of the Flexman Clinic, who wasn't afraid to have me as the clinic's resident sex therapist the last 25 years. Dr. Flexman was an early leader in the mental health community of Dayton, Ohio, in providing specialized services to men. I also wish to acknowledge my appreciation to Dr. Jerald Kay, an innovative leader in psychiatry and long-time Chair of the Department of Psychiatry at Wright State University School of Medicine, who recommended me as a contributor of a chapter to a book long ago and set me on a path of professional writing.

Thanks to WE (Writers Eclectic) of Yellow Springs, Ohio, for their insights and encouragements along the way of getting a manuscript ready for publication; especially Bomani, Venita, Neil, Mary, Jenny, Shelia, Charles, Kim, and Dee. Mr. Orion Wright contributed his historical and editing expertise to the timeline between Chapters 6 & 7. Mr. Max Flieshman contributed his creative illustrations to capture the new concept of a sexual hypercube. Of course, my strong appreciation extends to the good folks at Cognella Academic Publishing, especially Jennifer Codner, Michelle Piehl, and the entire production team.

Finally, the acknowledgments would not be complete without my deeply felt appreciation to the thousands of clients and students who made this book possible. They shared important lessons about living, loving, and getting along, and some of their best lessons are contained within.

FLP

When I think about the acknowledgments that I have read by other authors, I'm reminded that many mention what a long, laborious task it is to write a book. While it is true that there are days when it felt laborious, the truth is that my part in writing this book has been more pleasure than pain. I owe that to the fact that working with my co-author, Fred (Doc) Peterson, always has been a joyous undertaking. We started writing together about 17 years ago. Our first joint effort was a weekly column, titled "Speaking of Sex," in a local newspaper. Our second was a chapter in a book. Our third was an entire book, *Innovations in Clinical Practice: Focus on Sexual Health*, which we published in 2007. This is our fourth joint writing experience! It has been the easiest for me because when Fred approached me with his idea of writing it, he had already developed an extremely thorough and well-planned outline along with many chapters that he had already written. Not to mention that we have a great mutual respect for each other's talent and professionalism, and we have a shared sense of humor. How could I say, "No"? So my first "thank you" goes to Fred for making this such an easy, joyful, and pleasant experience. And for doing most of the work! I, of course, want also to thank my husband of 57 years for his love, patience, and support. He persevered through many evenings when I had to spend more time in my office causing our dinner together to be delayed another hour or so. He is the love of my life.

JILL BLEY

I thank Drs. Peterson and Bley for inviting me to contribute to this great work. The stories that I wrote, although fiction, have elements of very real life in them. Snippets of these stories are experiences shared with me from friends, students, and colleagues. I thank them and all of us who live, love, and laugh outside of the majority. It takes our sometimes very different ways of navigating relationships to affirm the fact that sexuality is the one thing that we all have in common. :)

A special thanks to the students who contributed their time and efforts during the Fall semester 2017 to field test this publication in my class at Miami University: Amber Simmons, Taylor Svach, and Kaly Snow.

RICHELLE

A NOTE ABOUT LANGUAGE AND GENDER

There are several key points regarding use of language related to gender that the authors care to make special note of at several places within this text.

First, it is important to respect the use of a transgender person's chosen name and any term they use regarding how they identify their sex/gender designation. Therefore, some individuals who have identities other than cisgender and who are featured in this text are referred to by their preferred language (he/she/singular they).

The use of gender-related language of stories within this text has been reviewed by the subjects of the stories and is in alignment with how they prefer to be identified. In some cases, the same individual is described in masculine terms as well as feminine terms within the same story. Some individuals self-identify as male and female, some identify as neither, and some prefer alternative gender-terms (see below).

Transgender is a general and positive term used to describe many types of people who do not feel they fit society's expectations for a designated sex. As referenced in Chapter 20, a recent special issue of *National Geographic* on gender documented a proliferation of terms of self-identification in common use (all related to the umbrella term transgender), including but not limited to:

> trans, transwomen, transman, transboy, bi-gender, nongender, nonbinary, intersex, intersex nonbinary, queer, genderqueer, trans-activist, agender, agender flux, gender fluid, gender nonconforming, gender neutral, pangender

Clinically, individuals who identify as transsexual are more often than not older in age and determined to (or have already undergone) sexual reassignment surgery (SRS). Transsexual people are often proud of the distinction of being transsexual rather than being referred to as transgender. Transsexual is not accurately used as an "umbrella" term.

Generally, the authors most often use the term transgender for its inclusiveness, positivity, and currency. As Nicole Maines is quoted in Chapter 20: "There is an infinite amount of space on the gender spectrum." This short quote is the most accurate verbal description of the unlimited diversity of human sexuality and gender. It is this amazing diversity that propels the use of many terms for sex/gender identification.

It may seem a bit confusing at times, but a little patience and curiosity will help us all better understand each other through our use of these gender-related terms. As science evolves, our understanding of the world around us becomes increasingly complex. So it is true of ourselves. This phenomenon is at the heart of what we are now coming to comprehend: How incredibly complex and diverse we are as human sexual beings. This process is at the heart of this book and the Sexual Hypercube model is a representation of this phenomenon.

LET'S MEASURE YOUR SEXUAL MIND

This book is all about enhancing your sexual health, primarily through becoming more comfortable, confident, and knowledgeable about sexuality, especially your own. It was written to be a companion text to large textbooks used in university-level sexuality courses. Its purpose as a companion textbook on sexual health is to personalize the broad-based comprehensive knowledge college students are introduced to in their first course on sexuality. Although there are many very good general textbooks written on human sexuality, they are really designed to enhance academic knowledge on the subject and are not that helpful in *application* of the knowledge to enhance personal sexual health. This book "stands in the gap" as a guide to applying what we learn from sexual science in a meaningful and personal way.

The book is organized into four primary sections:

1. Section I: Self-assessment of three levels of satisfaction related to childhood sexuality, your current sexual experience, and your overall health and well-being.

1

2. Section II: Understanding our sexual legacy as Americans—moving from what is called sexosophy (the lore, legend, and philosophy of sex) to sexology (the scientific study of sex).
3. Section III: Introduction of new perspectives on sex and gender by way of three new concepts called the Sexual Identity Cube, the Sexual Expression Cube, and the Sexual Hypercube. Implications for this new model of sexual health are discussed for greater self-understanding, acceptance, and satisfaction.
4. Section IV: The darker side of sexuality is addressed in terms of victimization of individuals by sexual trauma. The "dark side" also includes addressing the issues associated with problematic sexual behaviors (PSB—sometimes referred to as sexual compulsivity or sex addiction). The last two chapters of this section bring the focus back to positive sexuality and pathways to sexual health.

To evaluate any increase in personal satisfaction, a second self-assessment using the Sexual Health and Wellbeing Satisfaction Scale (SHAWS) is included to allow comparison of your baseline to your second score on the SHAWS at the end of the book (Appendix A). To further instruct and inspire you, stories of real people who have overcome major challenges to achieve sexual health are highlighted within most of the chapters as well as featured as separate chapters throughout the book (entitled "Success Stories").

As mentioned, Section I contains three self-assessments and the first assessment precedes the others as it is important to evaluate yourself before you are influenced by what follows. Section I is comprised of five chapters, three instructive chapters and two Success Stories. The first three chapters guide you through the "*Total Nine Assessment*" (these three self-evaluations are embedded within each of the three instructive chapters). These three self-assessments are related to

1. what you learned about sex in your family of origin;
2. how much influence your family has had on your sexual development;
3. the level of your satisfaction you currently have regarding the different aspects of your sexual health; and
4. your level of satisfaction with your overall health and how you see your sexual health fitting into your overall health and well-being.

Chapter 1 is intended to expand awareness of the origins of your own personal values related to sexuality. This is achieved via a questionnaire regarding the influences from your family on your sexual development as a child. The results serve as a "snapshot" of yourself at this earlier point in your life. Completing this questionnaire also honors your personal sexual history by acknowledging what you have been through and how you have survived, whether your history involves one of trauma or mostly a walk in the park. Because most Americans arrive at adulthood with low sexual literacy (LSL), several examples of the consequences of LSL are presented. The chapter ends with a story of a beautiful young couple overcoming the sexual aftermath of a motor vehicle accident for the husband and a victory for the wife who was surprised to discover (then correct) the ill effects of negative messages she learned about sex from her family growing up.

Chapter 2 is designed to expand your awareness of the varied dimensions of sexuality and taking a baseline measure of your satisfaction for each dimension of sexual health. Although the questionnaire in Chapter 2 comes from a general set of questions most sex therapists use during an initial clinical assessment, Chapter 2 employs the SHAWS, a specific instrument that I have developed and field tested for several years. A tragic clinical vignette of a physician with a low SHAWS self-rating is included to illuminate the importance of personal satisfaction and authenticity with your sexual self. The chapter concludes with a positive story of a young woman and her family who serves as a model for parents of transgender children.

Chapter 3 completes the section of self-assessment with a health risk assessment for your overall health and well-being from a holistic perspective. The "Big Wheel of Health" is introduced to illustrate the eight most important aspects for your health from a health promotion and disease prevention perspective. This final assessment is necessary because you cannot separate your sexual health from other aspects of health. Each aspect of health (the eight spokes on the Big Wheel) is influenced by the others as well as influences the other areas of health, for better or worse. A "negative-influence scenario" (Frank's story) is presented to show how these mutual influences can devastate a person trying to cope with chronic illness. A "positive-influence scenario" (Joe's story) is also presented using the story of a young Marine returning from war.

The entire set of three assessments (in Chapters 1 to 3) is referred to as the "Total Nine Assessment" (named such after a suggestion of a friend and guru, Sir Thomas Verdon). Each of the three assessments has a scoring system that adds up to a total score of 300 and an accumulative total score of 900. The score of 900 would reflect "complete satisfaction" in every aspect of your sexuality as well as your overall health. The state of complete satisfaction (represented by a 900 score) I have never seen among the thousands of individuals and couples with whom I have consulted in my clinical practice over the past 30 years. Obviously, they seek consultation with me because they have some level of *dissatisfaction* regarding aspects of their health.

I am not saying there are people out there who could not score 900, but I believe they are relatively rare given our self-help culture that stems from pervasive society messages saying, in one way or another, "you are not good enough" (more on this in Chapter 2). That is why I liked Sir Thomas's suggestion for the name of the combined evaluation, "Total Nine Assessment," because there is no "perfect 10."

If you see someone you think is a "perfect 10," then you most likely do not know them well enough to understand their internal imperfections even if they apparently do not show any externally. Yet the eternal search for perfection (whether you are talking about investments or people) has led to the coining of a slang term in the 1980s used to describe a perfect stock ("Bo") based on the 1979 hit movie *10* featuring actress Bo Derek who portrayed the "perfect woman," or "the perfect 10." Besides the illusion of perfection, any numeric rating of people based on their appearance (especially women) is discouraged as it promotes objectification of that individual and a lack of recognition for them as a whole person.

This seems to be the nature of our species. We are not perfect beings even though we may want to be. We may also wish others to be perfect as many people look for the perfect lover. We can also be very hard on ourselves and those we partner up with in these tricky things called relationships.

We either strive toward perfection (being the healthiest we can be) or think it is just too hard so we give up trying at times. My message here is: Be not hard on thyself! Add up your scores from the *Total Nine Assessment* and simply breathe. Remember, the past is the past and there is little to do about changing it. Our personal power lies in what we tell ourselves about the past and present and future. Essentially, our power lies in the personal story that we create in the present. Hopefully, this first section will help you start to better understand your sexual story and see it as more positive and healthy than you may have before reading this book.

The goals of Chapters 4 and 5 are simply to illustrate the overpowering resiliency of the human spirit. The first is through the story of Dr. Scott Redman, a man living with severe disability yet able to find sexual pleasure and complete a doctorate program. His story provides numerous lessons in having meaningful contact with others (including sexually), and even how to face an undiagnosed disease that threatens one's life. Chapter 5 finishes Section I with a story of a particular individual who joins the military to "make him a man" even to the point of becoming a Navy Seal, before finding a path to gender authenticity and greater happiness.

CHAPTER ONE

Exploring, Measuring, and Honoring Your Sexual Health

Written by Frederick Peterson

INTRODUCTION

This book is all about the sex and gender revolution that is dramatically unfolding around us and creating cultural changes that Americans have never seen before. With these changes come revelations about ourselves in terms of how we, as a society, can embrace individuals different than ourselves and accept people loving each other simply based on their love for each other rather than fitting into socially sanctioned categories. This challenges many personal values and religious beliefs but is a necessary expansion of our traditional cultural limits if we are going to live up to our democratic ideals.

Consider the following story. Just about 60 years ago, a couple were sleeping in the privacy of their own home when the police broke into their bedroom and arrested them. Their crime was being married as an interracial couple and violating Virginia's Racial Integrity Act. In 1958, this was a felony in their location. They had married elsewhere and returned to Central Point, Virginia, to raise a family. Richard and Mildred Loving (no kidding, that was their name) were sentenced to one year in prison but their sentence was suspended if they agreed to leave the state and not return for 25 years. They moved to Washington, DC, and appealed the case, which resulted nearly 10 years later in the 1967 Supreme Court decision *Loving v. Virginia* (Stone, 2017). This decision struck down the statute and affirmed an American's right to marry across racial lines (at least heterosexually). Hollywood made a major motion picture of this story, simply entitled *Loving* (Focused Films, 2016).

Beyond the irony of their last name reflecting an expansion of rights to love folks of any color, the irony increases with the 2013 Supreme Court decision striking down the Defense of Marriage Act (DOMA), which defined marriage only between a man and woman (Stone, 2017). It is significant to note that the repeal of DOMA was made by a court of justices that included Clarence Thomas, who is married to a white woman. To add amazement to irony, Justice Thomas voted with the minority in the dissenting opinion against repealing DOMA. That day in 2013 was a personal affirmation for many equal rights activists and sex educators across the country. I remember standing in front of my university sexuality class in 1996 (when DOMA was passed by Congress and signed by President Bill Clinton) and saying: "This law will not stand and you will see it repealed in your lifetime." Back in 1996, many Americans did know that DOMA would fall eventually, but none of us knew it would take 17 years. DOMA "had to" be repealed and same-sex marriage "had to" to be legalized to preserve the notion that we live in a democratic republic and that we can incrementally move forward as a pluralistic nation toward a "more perfect union" of diverse people with diverse opinions.

This book is also about new concepts in sexual diversity and is designed to help individuals undo the damage from the effects of our crazy sexual culture. "Crazy" is the key characteristic of our collective sexual heritage in America, with the word *crazy* used here in the same nonclinical way as in "you're making me nuts." This book illustrates the amazing story of how Americans became so crazy about sex. For example, during most of American history, the medical profession believed that masturbation was a disease that required treatment! And did you know Kellogg's Corn Flakes and Graham crackers were originated as "antimasturbation foods" popular in the 19th century? (Money, 1985; Bley & Peterson, 2007; Ryan & Jetha, 2010).

Here in the early 21st century, Western medicine sees masturbation not only as normal and healthy, but even as a very helpful, some say necessary, skill to develop to achieve sexual satisfaction as an adult (Larson, 1995; LeVay, Baldwin, & Baldwin, 2015; Yarber & Sayad, 2019). As a matter of fact, sex therapists sometimes recommend masturbation exercises to clients (to do, of course, in the privacy of their home). Yet, these historical influences are strong, and their effects are easy to find on a personal basis (such as an individual's discomfort discussing sexual topics) or public basis (such as when President Clinton fired the top physician in America, the Surgeon General, for suggesting masturbation was a safe alternate to interpersonal sex that risks transmission of HIV). Hence, a goal of this book is to heal the sex-negative historical influences by illuminating them and citing many examples of individuals successfully overcoming significant challenges they face regarding their sexual health.

In addition to helping reduce the effects of historic influences, this book endeavors to increase sexual literacy, enhance self-image, resolve sexual conflicts, increase acceptance of sexual identity of oneself and others, and especially improve satisfaction with your sexual self. It starts with accurate information regarding sexuality that is not biased by prejudices and misinformation from our past. However, before discussing formal definitions and concepts of the new sexual health, there are important questions to ask yourself and answer from your own experience.

Before we can tackle new learning, it is important to take a baseline measure of your sexual well-being relative to your experiences growing up in your particular family. This is important for a number of reasons that will be explained shortly. This baseline measure is in the form of a questionnaire presented to you in the next few pages. You will be able to score your questionnaire and interpret the results by a guide that follows. After your baseline measure is completed, there is discussion of how most of us grow up with sexual misinformation and low sexual literacy. The consequences of the misinformation and low sexual literacy are demonstrated in examples from contemporary American culture, including bogus "male enhancement" products pitched to men every day, the little-known background story of Cinderella that supports traditional patriarchy, and the all-too-common story of hate crimes against individuals who are perceived as representing an LGBTQA (lesbian, gay, bisexual, transgender, queer, asexual) sexual minority.

The chapter ends with a positive story of a young couple overcoming their personal obstacles to finding sexual satisfaction. Before we end the chapter on this positive note, let us start with a solemn reminder of how fast things are changing in this gender revolution and why we need to expand our understanding and compassion toward youth who do not feel they fit into our traditional and socially sanctioned organization of society by gender.

A REPORT FROM THE FRONT LINES OF THE REVOLUTION

America is facing the loss of our youth in new, tragic, and preventable ways. This is a story of one anguished teenager (among many) who could not stand her view of how the world is and, in her lonely outlook, could not find a helping hand to guide her to a pathway with any light. She lost all hope that her circumstances would improve. Leelah Alcorn was a desperate teenager who self-identified as a female and whose death attracted international attention at the end of 2014. Her suicide might have been another unfortunate yet little noticed loss in the daily avalanche of media; except that she had posted a suicide note on her Tumblr blog (Alcorn, 2014), in which she railed against how societal attitudes negatively affect the lives of transgender people and expressed the hope that her death would create a dialogue resulting in the improvement of their status (instead of the usual misunderstanding, discrimination, and lack of support they experience as a sexual minority).

In 1997, this teenager was assigned as a male at birth and given the name Joshua Ryan Alcorn. She was raised in a conservative Christian household in southern Ohio near Cincinnati. At age 14, she learned the definition of transgender and for the first time in her life, realized there were others like her, and she knew she wasn't alone. She came out as transgender to her parents, who told her it was just a "phase" she was going through and refused to accept her female gender identity. She became increasingly anxious and depressed, with tensions increasing between Leelah and her disapproving parents.

When she was 16, she requested to undergo counseling to address her symptoms and assist her body to make a smoother transition from male to female. Her parents rebuffed her request and instead sent her to a Christian-based program of conversion therapy. The parents' intention was for the therapist to convince Leelah to reject her female gender identity and accept her male gender as assigned at birth.

After her parents discovered she told her school classmates that she was sexually attracted toward males, her parents removed Leelah from school and revoked her access to social media. She left behind a desperate and altruistic suicide note—not as a plea for help for her own benefit but for all transgender people she was leaving behind. Leelah told of her loneliness, hopelessness, and alienation as key reasons for her decision to end her life. She blamed her parents, religion, and society for causing these feelings. At the age of 17 and a few days after Christmas 2014, Leelah Alcorn committed suicide by walking out in front of oncoming traffic on a nearby highway. Leelah had arranged for her suicide note to be posted online several hours after her death, excerpts from which follow:

> When I was 14, I learned what transgender meant and cried of happiness. After 10 years of confusion I finally understood who I was. I immediately told my mom, and she reacted extremely negatively, telling me that it was a phase, that I would never truly be a girl, that God doesn't make mistakes, that I am wrong. My mom started taking me to a therapist, but would only take me to Christian therapists, (who were all very biased) so I never actually got the therapy I needed to cure me of my depression. I only got more Christians telling me that I was selfish and wrong and that I should look to God for help. I was completely alone for 5 months. No friends, no support, no love. Just my parent's disappointment and the cruelty of loneliness. After a summer of having almost no friends plus the weight of having to think about college, save money for moving out, keep my grades up, go to church each week and feel like shit because everyone there is against everything I live for, I have decided I've had enough. I'm never going to transition successfully, even when I move out. I'm never going to be happy with the way I look or sound. I'm never going to have enough friends to satisfy me. I'm never going to have enough love to satisfy me. I'm never going to find a man who loves me. I'm never going to be happy. Either I live the rest of my life as a lonely man who wishes he were a woman or I live my life as a lonelier woman who hates herself. There's no winning. There's no way out. I'm sad enough already, I don't need my life to get any worse. People say 'it gets better' but that isn't true in my case. It gets worse. Each day I get worse. The only way I will rest in peace is if one day transgender people aren't treated the way I was, they're treated like humans, with valid feelings and human rights. I want someone to . . . say 'that's f*cked up' and fix it. Fix society. Please. (Alcorn, 2014)[1]

This suicide note has touched untold thousands and hopefully aided many distraught youth to find a way to self-preservation. Leelah's heartfelt outpouring is full of confusion, rejection, loneliness, condemnation, cruelty, and sadness. Her suicide involves the basic struggle between two powerful aspects of many people living with depression; two aspects that seemingly are in conflict with one another. First is the voice of pain, futility, and resignation. It is the voice of those living a life without authenticity, almost always a recipe for depression. The second is the voice of life, hope, and self-preservation—a very strong force by nature. The two aspects of Leelah appear to be at odds but in truth, have the same goal. Each force wants to end the pain and feel better (if not for oneself, then most often for someone else who we think would be better off if we weren't around). In Leelah's case, she believed it would be for a better world. So her note is full of resignation that her life would not improve, that she was in a place that had no ray of hope for positive change. Her life force needed support, and there was none for her to find, only condemnation. Essentially the pain and resignation became stronger than the will to live. Without her awareness of available help, she followed her plan with one last desperate plea for a better world.

Leelah Alcorn's suicide soon attracted international attention across mainstream and social media. LGBTQA activists called attention to her death as evidence of the problems faced by transgender youth, and vigils were held in her memory across the United States and as far away as England (Gander, 2014). A month after her suicide, she was referenced in an acceptance speech at the 2015 Golden Globe Awards when Jill Soloway, creator of the television show *Transparent*, held her award up to the audience and stated, "This award is dedicated to the memory of Leelah Alcorn and to many trans people who died too young."

---

1   Source: https://web.archive.org/web/20150101052635/http://lazerprincess.tumblr.com/post/106447705738/suicide-note

Petitions were generated to call for a "Leelah's Law," which would ban the use of conversion therapy in the United States. Both the *New York Times* (Shear, 2015) and the *Washington Post* (Capehart, 2015) covered the story. In April 2015, the *Washington Post* reported: "Obama comes out against 'conversion therapy' to support 'Leelah's Law.'" Within the article, staff writer Jonathan Capehart quoted a spokesperson for the president as saying: "The overwhelming scientific evidence demonstrates that conversion therapy, especially when it is practiced on young people, is neither medically nor ethically appropriate and can cause substantial harm. As part of our dedication to protecting America's youth, this Administration supports efforts to ban the use of conversion therapy for minors" (Capehart, 2015). Within a year, the city of Cincinnati passed an ordinance that criminalized conversion therapy. A proposal has also been introduced in the Ohio legislature to outlaw conversion therapy statewide, similar to the statute passed in California and other bills in more than a dozen states.

Leelah's parents were criticized for referring to Leelah as their son in comments that they made to the media and some LGBTQA rights activists blamed the parents for this child's death. The parents defended their refusal to accept their child's identity and their use of conversion therapy by referencing their Christian beliefs. Leelah Alcorn will be remembered as a martyr who gave her life in hope to advance the acceptance and celebration of all people, including those of sexually diverse backgrounds and those that identify as transgender Americans. It may take a decade or two before there is the political will in Congress, but there will eventually be a ban on the use of conversion therapy in the United States, and it will be called "Leelah's Law."

EXPLORING AND VALIDATING YOUR OWN EXPERIENCE AND PERSPECTIVE

What does the word *sex* mean to you? What feelings and thoughts does this word stimulate inside of you? Would you describe these thoughts and feelings as mostly positive, negative, or neutral? How do you think you developed your responses to the subject of sex? What are all the influences that contributed to your personal perspective on sex? What were the rules you grew up with about talking about sex? What were the rules about seeing family members naked, about showing affection to others, and about dating? Where did these rules originate (who made them up)? What does sexual health mean to you? What does sexual satisfaction mean to you? How do you subjectively determine if you are satisfied with your sexuality?

These questions are being asked now to attempt to clarify and validate your sexual experience thus far in your life. As noted above, we are all subject to misinformation about sex as we develop our personal set of values and beliefs. Accepting this inescapable truth means, to a lesser or greater extent, most of us grew up misinformed about sex and are able to benefit from learning more about it. In fact, "sexperts" agree that the more we know about sex, the more we realize we don't know. Despite how smart we think we are, there are many more questions about sexuality that remain unanswered. For example, one of the top researchers in female sexuality, Dr. Beverly Whipple, is known to tell health care professionals that they should be cautious using the term female sexual dysfunction. This is because we still don't know definitively what normal is for female sexual function, and we are still discovering the amazing range of expression and adaptability of women's sexual responsiveness (Komisaruk, Beyer-Flores, & Whipple, 2006).

This only emphasizes the need to expand our literacy of sexuality as a core experience of being human. However important literacy is, it is still a tricky business. How are you to measure your baseline satisfaction about your own sexual literacy without first being influenced by what you are reading? You may already have detected a particular point of view expressed in just these first few pages and that it may likely differ from your own.

Hence, asking what sexual health means to you and how you define satisfaction at this early stage of your reading is an attempt to explore and honor your experience and personal sense of satisfaction. This doesn't mean your definitions are perfectly accurate or your experiences have all been positive. To measure your personal growth, however, it is helpful to take a baseline measure of your sexual self at this time, as well as at different points in your development. Once new and different information is presented in later chapters, it is hard not to be influenced (positively or negatively) to some degree. Of course, our sense of satisfaction can change over time and, perhaps, changing how you define and achieve satisfaction may be exactly why you are reading this book.

The definition of sexual health and the methods of measuring satisfaction presented in this book come from a particular point of view, which is one of many. However, once new concepts are introduced (whether you love them or hate them), it is too late not to be influenced. This is particularly true for defining sexual satisfaction. How you have defined sexual satisfaction in your past personal life has validity, whether or not it has helped you achieve sexual satisfaction. The empirical approach to defining sexual satisfaction described in later chapters is not intended to replace or to be considered more important than the personal approach you may use to value your sex life. It may just be seen as a different perspective. Hence, before continuing on to more advanced information, take some time to answer the questions presented here.

Please consider actually writing out your responses to the following questions, especially your own definition of sexual satisfaction. It is important to mark where you are now to appreciate the ground you have covered later. Despite any interest in reading on through the chapter or the book, please take some time to wrestle with defining your current sexual values and beliefs as accurately as you can. It may be very difficult to read on and then try to come back to measure where you are now.

The questions that follow are for you to answer, but also to provoke your analytical process and stimulate your memory. It is recommended that you keep your responses in a private secure location until you are ready to review them again sometime in the future or share them with another. Besides privacy concerns, please also be mindful that answering these questions earnestly may bring up unpleasant thoughts or feelings. Should these thoughts and feelings become too uncomfortable, you may want to seek professional support through a counselor or therapist. A qualified professional who is competent to counsel you regarding sexuality issues can be found through visiting the website of the American Association of Sex Educators, Counselors, and Therapists (www.aasect.org).

After all those warnings, you may not want to take the assessment now. But be assured, it is important to your self-understanding and the process of measuring the effects of your childhood experiences on your current sexual health. Take time to think about the question and select the best answer for you.

TABLE 1.1: **The Self-Assessment of Family Support (for Healthy Sexual Development During Childhood/Adolescence)**

Did your parents allow you to discuss sex in your home?	_____
Full discussion was allowed with at least one parent	12 points
Some attempts were made at discussion (some embarrassment)	9 points
Equal amount of encouragement/discouragement for discussion	6 points
Discussion discouraged (with much embarrassment)	3 points
Forget about it! No discussion allowed at all!	0 points
Did you see your parents share public displays of affection (PDA 5 hugs and kisses)?	_____
Yes, they would smooch it up or hug in front of me	12 points
Occasional pecks on the cheek and hugs when arriving/leaving	9 points
PDA was equally encouraged/discouraged	6 points
Rarely saw any PDA—generally absent from daily life	3 points
No way on earth (I still don't know how I was conceived)	0 points
Did you feel comfortable giving and getting hugs and kisses as a child?	_____
Yes, I enjoyed the affection	12 points
Yes, I mostly felt comfortable but occasionally did not	9 points
I felt equally comfortable and uncomfortable, depending on situation	6 points
No, I was mostly uncomfortable giving and getting affection	3 points
No, never liked being touched and I am still that way	0 points
In your family, were you allowed to be partially clothed (or naked) before puberty?	_____
Yes, we ran around naked or shared baths—we never thought much about it	12 points
Yes, to a limited degree (I was a small child for God's sake!)	9 points
Nudity as a child was equally encouraged/discouraged	6 points
Not really, when it happened it was definitely frowned upon	3 points
No, that would never have happened in my family!	0 points

continued ...

Did you feel comforted by your family when others bullied you or made you feel bad? _____

I strongly felt comforted and protected by my family if I was picked on	12 points
Yes, I was usually comforted and protected if I was picked on	9 points
Sometimes I did and other times I did not (or I never got picked on)	6 points
No, I was usually not protected and suffered for it	3 points
I never felt comforted or protected by my family (and suffered a lot for it)	0 points

If any, what messages did you get from school and/or church regarding sex? _____

Overwhelmingly positive messages	12 points
Mostly positive messages	9 points
Equally positive and negative messages (or did not attend school/church)	6 points
Mostly negative messages	3 points
Overwhelmingly negative messages	0 points

What was discussed if you actually received the "birds and bees" talk? _____

Talked about anything I wanted to and given information (like a book)	12 points
Limited discussion of "basics" and was given information	9 points
There was very limited discussion AND very limited information provided	6 points
There was very limited discussion OR very limited information was provided	3 points
No such talk at all AND no information (even when dog was humping my leg)	0 points

Did your family use the anatomically correct names of the genitals (or their parts)? _____

Yes, with little embarrassment (even if they also used pet names)	12 points
Sometimes, but mostly used pet names if they talked about it at all	9 points
Equally used anatomically correct names and pet names	6 points
Mostly used pet names when they felt they had to say something	3 points
No, they just did not go there AT ALL (no use of any names of any sort)	0 points

continued ...

Were you prepared for changes that happened to you in puberty?	_____
I was well informed and not surprised by all the changes	12 points
I was a little prepared from a class in school or from "the talk"	9 points
I was about equally prepared as I was unprepared	6 points
I heard some about puberty but was not really prepared	3 points
I was ambushed—have no idea how I got through	0 points

Was your first period or wet dream a positive experience?	_____
Yes, it was positive and even celebrated	12 points
Yes, it was positive but not really celebrated	9 points
About as positive as it was negative for me	6 points
Not really, it was overall a negative experience	3 points
You have got to be kidding!	0 points

Where did you learn about masturbation?	_____
Got the real story from reliable sources (such as family, books, class)	12 points
Got some information from somewhat reliable sources	9 points
Street corner, locker room, or other unreliable sources	6 points
I learned about masturbation by myself	3 points
I was so scared about what I was told about masturbation that I never tried it	0 points

How did you feel after masturbation?	_____
Felt positive (without shame or embarrassment)	12 points
Felt good but had some concern, guilt, or embarrassment about it	9 points
Felt equally positive and negative about it	6 points
Felt mostly negative about it	3 points
Felt guilt, shame, or like I sinned (or I never masturbated)	0 points

continued ...

As a teenager, did you feel positive about your body? _____

Yes, I felt very positive overall about my body	12 points
I had mostly positive feelings about my body despite some concerns	9 points
I felt equally positive and negative about my body	6 points
No, I did not like my body much while growing up	3 points
No, I could not stand my body's appearance while growing up	0 points

Based on teenage sexual experimentation, did you learn how to achieve orgasm? _____

Pretty much most times (probably at least 90% of the time)	12 points
Most of the time (probably about 70% of the time)	9 points
Hit and miss (inconsistent frequency but on a 50% basis)	6 points
Had a lot of trouble with orgasm (probably 30% or less of the time)	3 points
I never masturbated or never had orgasm when I did	0 points

When you started dating as a teenager, did you discuss your activities with a parent _____

Yes, I felt free to share whatever I wanted with at least one parent	12 points
Yes, for the most part (with some censoring)	9 points
Not really, I censored a lot of what I said but we did talk	6 points
No way! I would have been kicked out of the house!	3 points
I was never allowed to date and/or never chose to date	0 points

How would you describe the first messages you learned about homosexuality? _____

Mostly very positive messages	12 points
Fairly positive messages	9 points
Equally positive and negative messages	6 points
Fairly negative messages	3 points
Overwhelmingly negative messages	0 points

continued ...

Did you ever have questions about your own sexual orientation?	_____
No, I have always been 100% confident of my orientation	12 points
No, not for the most part (at least 80% confidence)	9 points
I have had some question (50% confidence at times) and some turmoil about it	6 points
Yes, but I figured it out with a lot of turmoil at times (30% confidence)	3 points
Yes, and I still don't have it figured out (10% confidence with much turmoil)	0 points
Have you questioned whether you were masculine/feminine enough?	_____
No, I never thought I wasn't masculine/feminine enough	12 points
Not really, I have always been fairly confident that I am masculine/feminine enough	9 points
Yes, but I decided I was okay (masculine/feminine enough)	6 points
Yes, I occasionally think I am not masculine/feminine enough	3 points
Yes, frequently I question whether I am masculine/feminine enough	0 points
Have you ever questioned yourself about being "good enough" as a lover?	_____
No, I always thought I was good enough as a lover	12 points
Not really, I have always been fairly confident that I am good enough as a lover	9 points
Yes, but I decided I was okay (good enough as a lover)	6 points
Yes, I occasionally think I am not good enough as a lover	3 points
I frequently question whether I am good enough as a lover (or I never had sex)	0 points
Were you ever physically abused when you were a child?	---
No, I was never physically abused when I was young	12 points
No, I was never physically abused but I saw/knew of others being abused	9 points
Yes, I was abused but I was given help to heal as a child	6 points
Yes, I was abused and I had to find my own way to heal as a child	3 points
Yes, I was abused and I never did heal as a child	0 points

continued ...

Were you ever sexually abused when you were a child?	---
No, I was never sexually abused when I was young	12 points
No, I was never sexually abused but I saw/knew of others being abused	9 points
Yes, I was sexually abused but I was given help to heal as a child	6 points
Yes, I was sexually abused and I had to find my own way to heal as a child	3 points
Yes, I was sexually abused and I never did heal as a child	0 points
Were you ever involved in an unplanned pregnancy or abortion (as male or female)?	_____
I was never personally involved in an unplanned pregnancy/abortion	12 points
Never personally involved but had unplanned pregnancy/abortion in family	9 points
Had an unplanned pregnancy/abortion and I got through it okay (mild effects)	6 points
Had an unplanned pregnancy/abortion and I had moderate negative effects	3 points
Had an unplanned pregnancy/abortion and I had severe/traumatic effects	0 points
How would you describe your overall feelings and thoughts about sex growing up?	_____
As very positive	12 points
As mostly positive	9 points
As neutral (equally positive/negative)	6 points
As mostly negative	3 points
As very negative	0 points
How would you describe your level of acceptance about your sexuality growing up?	_____
As very accepting	12 points
As mostly accepting	9 points
As neutral (equally accepting/nonaccepting)	6 points
As mostly nonaccepting	3 points
As very nonaccepting	0 points

continued ...

Overall, how do you feel your sexual experiences (or lack of the same) while you were growing up have had an effect on you today? _____

They have had a very positive effect	12 points
They have had a mostly positive effect	9 points
They have had a neutral effect (equally positive/negative or I am not sure)	6 points
They have had a mostly negative effect	3 points
They have had a very negative effect	0 point

MAKING SENSE OF YOUR SCORE FOR THE SELF-ASSESSMENT OF FAMILY SUPPORT

The range of scores is 0 to 300. The scoring is accumulative (so just add up your total score). Generally speaking, the higher the score, the greater the degree of family support you likely experienced for healthy maturation and sexual development as a child and adolescent.

The scoring key is divided into approximate thirds (lower half of range < 150 indicating low support, moderate elevation above the midpoint of 150 indicating moderate level of support, and the highest level of support reflected by scores greater than 225).

This scaling of scores is based completely on clients coming into a specialized sex therapy practice. Hence, statements below should not necessarily be considered generalizable to people who do not go to therapy. Therefore, caution is to be exercised while applying the following descriptive interpretations. In other words, take this measure as a general indication of how you did or did not feel supported as a kid learning about sexuality. A low score does not necessarily suggest an indictment of your family or that your chances of gaining sexual health are a long shot.

> [Authors' Note: In the following paragraphs and rest of the chapter, a new term is used that refers to a feeling of conflict and discomfort about sex. Do not freak out! The term is "sexophrenia" and is used as a nonclinical, nondiagnostic description of the feeling of discomfort many people experience while discussing sex and/or behaving in a sexual manner. The term is more fully described in Chapter 4 (as well as in the glossary), including how our sexophrenic socialization during youth strongly influences most Americans' attitudes toward sexuality.]

1. *Score of 225 and above*: Suggests overall sex-positive development as a child/teenager with a minimal amount of adverse effects from family influences and sexophrenic socialization upon your maturation.
2. *Score between 150 and 225*: Suggests overall sex-neutral or sex-ambivalent development as a child/teenager with a moderate amount of adverse effects from family influences and sexophrenic socialization upon your maturation.
3. *Score below 150*: Suggests overall sex-negative development as a child/teenager with a high amount of adverse effects from family influences and sexophrenic socialization upon your maturation.

CONSIDER THIS

Now those were a lot of questions, but they cover only a small minority of inquiries made during a comprehensive interview for a sexual health evaluation. At this moment, you're probably thinking something like, "Remind me never to participate in a sexual health evaluation." Chances are, you have not been asked some of these questions lately, but that's not the half of it. There are additional qualitative questions you would be asked to further assess the developmental forces pressing and shaping you as you grew up in your family. The following qualitative open-ended questions can help clarify the long-term effects of these forces and your current state of sexual health (if you have had enough questions—skip to the next section):

- What does the word *sex* mean to you today?
- What feelings and thoughts does the word "sex" stimulate inside of you?
- What are the earliest memories you have about the topic of sex?
- What were the rules you grew up with regarding talking about sex?
- What were the rules about being naked or seeing family members naked?
- What were the rules for you about dating?
- Can you (or a relative) identify with whom these rules originated?
- If you had siblings of a different sex, how did the rules of dating differ between you and your siblings?
- What ways, if any, do your religious beliefs affect your sexuality today?
- What other influences contributed to your perspective on sex?
- If you could change anything about your sexuality, what would it be?

You may have felt odd, uncomfortable, or even offended by some of these questions. To explore the origins of that uncomfortable feeling, I ask students to consider the following social experiment that I learned from one of my advanced students, Dr. Eric Sprankle. In a public place, say the following four words out loud (so others can hear): *elbow, foot, penis, clitoris*. When university students are asked to do so in class, they almost always say there is a slight yet definite "shift" in their feelings when they go from the first two words to the last two words. This shift in feeling is sometimes described as awkwardness or a sense of embarrassment. How is this feeling generated? Why is embarrassment such a common experience? Does it have anything to do with how you may have felt "funny" about the list of questions you just reviewed? That "funny feeling" may be the same reason some men do not want to get help for erection dysfunction for fear of having to answer questions about sex with their physician (even though sharing sexual concerns can help lead to the diagnosis of a serious medical condition, such as diabetes or heart disease). Let's explore these possibilities.

A NEW LINE OF EXPLORATION

You may be tired of questions about your sex life, but a bit more patience is requested for three more (in this chapter). The first you have already answered:

- Were you allowed to talk about sex in the home in which you grew up?

(Hold on, let's raise the bar a little.)

- Were you allowed to ask questions about sex at home and get an accurate and honest answer without any reprisals or any other type of negative reaction?

If the answer is yes to this question, consider yourself lucky and in a small minority of the fortunate ones. Whether you wanted to be or not, you were most likely the kid whose friends would feed them questions to ask your parents and then had to play sex educator in the neighborhood or locker room. Based on 30 years of asking this question to university students, usually about 10% of people say "yes" to this question. But saying "yes" to indicate you were *allowed* to ask a question does not necessarily mean that you did! You may have been told you could talk about sex, but actually doing so (talking about sex) is a whole different thing.

If the answer is "no" to the last question, then consider yourself the norm. Most American teenagers would rather stick a needle in their eye than talk about sex with their parents. If you are in the majority of Americans who did not grow up in a family with open communication, then answer this second question.

- Do you remember the day when you were told, "Don't ever talk about or ask a question in this house about sex!"?

There are people who respond yes to this question and do remember being told explicitly not to talk about sex, although they are also in a small minority. One example comes from a hospital clinic for erection dysfunction. A 70-year-old African American man shared the following story.

> As a boy, I was out playing in the neighborhood and some of my friends were sharing the new sex words they had learned from the street corner. I later came home for dinner and found my mother cooking at the stove. I innocently asked, 'Hey mom, what are balls? Do I have balls?' She calmly put down the spoon with which she was stirring a pot of stew, turned around, and slapped me right across the face.

That is an explicit message that there would be no talk of sex in that house. At least that was the message he received—that "balls" must have something to do with sex and "we do not talk about such things."

Now it gets more interesting. If you responded with a "no" to the last question, you are like the majority of college students who also said "no." If you believed you grew up in a home where you could not discuss sex *but* you do not remember being told not to talk about sex, then here is the third question:

- Why did you believe you could not discuss sex (when you were never instructed "do not discuss sex") and how do you explain this apparent contradiction? (Okay, that's a compound question.)

The answer? Most communication is *nonverbal*. Did you ever have an experience of watching TV as a kid with a parent in the room and a sexual topic came up within the TV program? For baby boomers, it could have been as subtle as girls in bikinis in an old Elvis movie. Even less subtle, do you ever remember Elvis the Pelvis swinging his hips around during a televised performance? You probably do not because the camera men (there were no camera women) were strictly instructed to film Elvis only from the waist up.

I am old enough to remember adjusting the rabbit ears on the TV console and sitting three feet away on the floor for the best view of Tina Turner's first national appearance on the *Ed Sullivan Show*. As that young boy's jaw dropped to the floor that fateful Sunday evening in 1970, one of his well-intentioned parents (or perhaps an older sister) put their hands over his eyes to protect him from the rotating hips of *Proud Mary* (this was before the days of remote control). I still don't know whose hands they were as I struggled free because I did not bother looking back in fear of missing one second of viewing time.

If you are younger than age 40, then you may have experienced some version of this story when you first saw Michal Jackson grab his crotch or Britney Spears simulate masturbation on MTV. Even worse, you may have watched any host of the (moronic and ironically titled) "reality" shows that came on television when a parent was sitting in the room. Our contemporary American culture is awash with sexualized content that delivers a message promoting being sexual at increasingly younger ages. It is difficult to avoid such media, unless you perhaps live off the grid.

Your parents may have responded differently, such as frowning, making disparaging comments, or (even worse) actually ask you what you think about what you were seeing. Alternatively, they may have changed the channel, walked out of the room, or tried to distract you from the TV with an obviously bogus conversation or suggestion to go do some activity ("Why do I have to take out the garbage *right now*, mother?").

The point is that, before you ever heard the word and before you ever knew the definition, you were learning America's favorite TABOO. Namely, talking about sex! Taboos serve the function of training us as impressionable children about what is considered improper or unacceptable. Merriam-Webster defines taboo as something that is

1. forbidden to profane use or contact because of what are held to be dangerous supernatural powers;
2. banned on grounds of morality or taste ("the subject is taboo"); or
3. banned as constituting a risk ("the area is still alive with explosives").

Those are some scary and potent descriptions of why your parents most likely did what they did. They were just trying to protect you from what they considered dangerous, immoral, of poor taste, and constituting a risk to your development! They were just trying to preserve your angelic innocence from the influences of adult content (or even Satan's power if that was their persuasion).

Yeah, right! That is, if they really thought about it, and we all know they didn't. More likely the scenario is that they were trying to avoid a topic they did not know how to talk about, that they did not want to talk about, and especially did not want to talk about with you! Many American parents practice the tradition of the bastardized golden rule: "Do unto your kids, as you had done to you."

Many parents may be motivated to (and some actually do) lessen the taboo effect by improving their children's comfort and communication on the topic of sex. If you have done so, you deserve heartfelt and well-deserved congratulations. Yet, most parents tend to do as was done to them, for better or worse, as one of the typical ironic paradoxes we experience in life. There are many paradoxes concerning how we relate to the subject of sexuality in America and their origins are explored in Chapter 6 (along with that specialized form of paradoxical effect named sexophrenia).

As noted, contemporary American culture is flooded with sexualized public content, especially media trying to sell something. These messages typically are based on sexual stereotypes of people and perpetuate misinformation and sexual myths. Even if you raise your child with extraordinary efforts to be comfortable with sexuality, there is little possibility of a child growing up free from other sources that broadcast this taboo. Learning that it is "not proper" to talk about sex comes from years of reinforcement of the taboo in a child's experience from all of society's primary institutions—school, church, family, and society in general.

Messages promoting being sexual are all around us. So we see and hear these messages, but the sexophrenic imperative is that we must not talk about them! The combination of the public perpetuation of sexual myths and stereotypes via the media, along with the numerous obstacles to learning accurate information about sex, results in the majority of us growing up with *low sexual literacy* (LSL).

Typically, Americans do not feel that they grew up with direct opportunity to discuss the facts about sex. We typically do not feel comfortable to ask questions. We often do not get accurate answers if we do. We do not know what changes are going to happen to our bodies in advance of puberty. We typically do not receive support for getting through adolescence with any shred of dignity. We also do not grow up knowing anything about the complexities of relationships that would prepare us for doing anything other than the trial-and-error method to which most of us are so accustomed. Once again, if you are one of the lucky and few (who grew up with the facts of sex), heartfelt and well-deserved congratulations are in order. Let's say you *are* one of the lucky and few. Does that mean you can consider yourself as having "high literacy" regarding sexual health?

"Is this a trick question?" you may ask. Right you are. Just look at some of the considerations of what could constitute *sexual health literacy*:

- ability to understand and be knowledgeable about scientific concepts and research on the topic of human sexuality;
- skills in spoken, written, and online communication concerning sexuality;
- critical interpretation of mass media messages related to sexuality and gender (so as to not fall prey to sexual stereotypes and manipulation);
- ability and knowledge to access and navigate complex health care systems for sexual health information and services; and

- knowledge of cultural and indigenous influences in health decision making related to sexual behavior.

Now that's a curveball, isn't it? Being literate (regarding any topic) is not an either/or dichotomy, but rather should be thought of as on a continuum. We all have sexual literacy to some degree. It is all relative and, most importantly, relative to where you are at present in your own development. Yes, it's good to read a book (especially this one) or take a human sexuality course in college, but there is always more to learn as we go through new stages of life. Each stage has its own unique challenges and changes our perspective on sexuality to some degree.

Another reason the question is a curve ball is that this first chapter focuses on you exploring your own experience thus far in life. This process involves information (such as the topics in the questionnaire you just completed). Information involves literacy. Inevitably, how you measure your satisfaction regarding sexual health literacy will be influenced. Besides, it is important you find this first chapter motivating enough to continue reading and measure your level of sexual health satisfaction as well as overall health (the focus of Chapters 2 and 3, respectively).

At the same time, understanding how sexual misinformation and low sexual literacy (LSL) affect our perspectives is an important objective of this chapter. Hence, three examples of LSL consequences are presented, followed by a real-life story of a couple of beautiful young DINKS (double-income, no kids) overcoming their sexual challenges, including one they didn't know they had.

THE COST OF LOW SEXUAL LITERACY

As the bumper sticker says: "If you think education is expensive, try ignorance." Consequences of LSL are experienced on individual, community, and societal levels. They are also experienced on a continuum from mild to severe. As we examine specific consequences, let us also consider a mass-media example of LSL in action.

The mild-moderate consequences of low sexual literacy include the following:

- Personal embarrassment/taboo about topic of sex
- Negative sexual self-image/self-esteem
- Potential eating disorders, mostly for girls and women
- Lack of confidence/social isolation
- Prejudice and discrimination, including bullying behavior
- Mild-moderate sexual anxiety/dysfunction
- Sexual disease transmission that is treatable and curable
- Financial costs of uncritical interpretation of mass media messages

Case Study of Low Sexual Literacy: Mild to Moderate Consequences

"The Naturally Bogus Male Enhancement Product"

Popularly advertised products claim to "maximize your erection potential and give you the peak enhancement you deserve." They are said to act by enhancing blood flow, thereby producing "firmer and fuller-feeling erections, as well as an increase in energy, confidence, and stamina during sex." A trademark advertisement of this sort was once a leering man (Smiling Bob) whose life was miraculously improved by these sexual magic beans. In an entertaining GQ article called "The Rise and Fall of the Cincinnati Boner King," journalist Amy Wallace reported that the CEO of the manufacturer of this product socked away hundreds of millions as the company had tremendous growth in sales. However, the growth for customers was a big disappointment in the down-under department. In a lawsuit against the company, federal judge Arthur Spiegel concluded the ads for the product were false, the testimonials were made up, the guarantees were phony, and customers' credit cards were automatically billed for pills they never wanted or ordered. Of course, most men were too embarrassed to complain. Judge Spiegel said the company "preyed on perceived sexual inadequacy and vulnerability" of American men. On August 28, 2008, Judge Spiegel sentenced the CEO to prison as the mastermind behind an empire of fraud built on little pills that were supposed to endow men with more than they were given naturally (Wallace, 2009). Of course, hefty fines and prison time are not enough to dissuade others from making all the money they can on the successful manipulation of American male sexual insecurity. If men knew that no pill could extend the length or girth of their penis, knew that size of the penis is not correlated with sexual satisfaction (for him or his partner), and knew their worth as a person was much more than the length of their penis, there would be no "male enhancement" products at all.

Moderate-severe consequences of low sexual literacy include the following:

- Avoidance and aversion about the topic of sex
- Extremely negative self-image/self-esteem
- Serious, even fatal, eating disorders for females (and some men)
- Social isolation leading to depression/exploitation
- Sexual dysfunctions and potential end of relationships
- Sexual disease transmission that is treatable but not curable (HIV)
- Unplanned, unwanted pregnancies (especially for teenagers)
- Hate crime discrimination and violence, including murder
- Financial costs of all above (including lower life expectancy)
- Spiritual trauma related to sexuality leading to self-loathing, self-perception as an "abomination," and even suicide

Case Study of Low Sexual Literacy: Moderate Consequences

Will the Real Cinderella Please Stand Up?

Like men who are manipulated regarding their sexual insecurities, girls and women are certainly not immune to stereotypical sex-role socialization and mass media messages that they are not good enough. Of course, those messages are usually accompanied by advertisement of a product that, for a fee, can buy you an illusion of "more acceptable femininity." Although this process may be a reflection of a free market economy, many feminist authors consider this marketing and sales process a modern expression of our patriarchal society.

Dr. Vera Sonja Maass, a well-known author and sex therapist in Indianapolis, teaches about the dangers to girls and women with low sexual self-esteem and low sexual literacy. LSL results in serious consequences for girls, from negative body image and eating disorders to unplanned pregnancy. Dr. Maass stresses the need to teach girls skills to protect themselves from uncritical acceptance of these messages, which are supported by socially sanctioned cultural scripts for women (in general) and the mythology of the Cinderella fairy tale (in particular). In her book *The Cinderella Test* (Maass, 2009), Dr. Maass asserts that the beloved Disney version of Cinderella is a modern remake of an ancient tale to continue the historical repression of women into lifestyles defined by patriarchy and characterized by sexual submissiveness, domestic servitude, and silent suffering.

After all, Cinderella patiently and defenselessly performed all duties in her domestic exploitation and was rewarded by and/or relied upon a prince coming to save her. Dr. Maass's assertion is well argued as she guides the reader through research of the origins of today's Disney version of Cinderella. Today's popular Cinderella story is an updated version of "Cendrillon," created by 17th-century French poet Charles Perrault (who is credited for adding the glass slipper to the tale). Cendrillon is a millennia-old tale about a powerful heroine fighting for truth and justice. She was aided by the powerful ghost of her deceased mother, who bestowed gifts on Cendrillon to help her triumph over evil. Dr. Maass challenges women with this question: Would you really want the shoe to fit? (Maass, 2009).

Featured Stories of Diverse Perspectives and Experiences

THAT ONE NIGHT IN ORLANDO—RICO AND JON
Written by Richelle Frabotta

People don't notice me much. I'm not a traditional guy, but I'm not effeminate. I'm appropriately "kissed by the Florida sun," but not too dark. I like cotton, free flowing clothes and Converse. It seems that my high cheek bones and haircut often lead others to believe I'm female. That doesn't bother me. I don't have a need for people to know who I am. I know who I am.

I'm just me. My mom and dad have always supported me in my arts and sports endeavors. Is bowling a sport? I was an ace bowler from fourth grade through my early 20s! I macramé and tie a fishing lure with the best of them! I earned my bachelor's and master's degrees from University of Central Florida. I've always preferred reading at home on the veranda while sipping a refreshing cocktail instead of carousing in bars. That made it hard for me to date.

How Rico actually saw me is still a mystery that I ponder daily. Oh, but make no mistake about it, I saw him! His brown skin, dark eyes, and perfectly sculpted body wears a Balani suit like no other Latin man. The Orlando sun and society love him. I love him and I was one of his clerks. Not a good mix, love and workplace.

Rico had an eventful career right out of law school. He took on cases that couldn't be won. Despite the odds, armed with wit, strategic thinking, vast knowledge of case law, he would win anyway. His verbal skills are top notch. Rico can twist a phrase, captivate a jury with engaging monologues, and weave a tale that even the simplest human feels and understands. He is attentive to detail, hardworking, gorgeous, and accomplished.

Don't you think that it's absolute irony that I wanted to date THE most visible and significant lawyer in Orlando? In short, our love affair began when he asked me to dinner at Chatham's Place. Everything was perfect and so romantic. Candlelight, soft piano music, delicious food with impeccable service set the tone. And his beautiful light brown eyes that embraced my every movement let me know I was the only person in the room who mattered. I quit my job the next day.

Rico and I are very different people. We have learned to work together with our complementary skill sets and resources. It's a relief to know that I don't have to handle people, says me and so many other introverts. We compromise on the social aspects. He'll have a glass of wine on the veranda with me while the sun is setting or take me to a quiet dinner on the beach, just the two of us. And I'll accompany him to nightclubs, holiday office parties, and fundraisers occasionally.

Pride month in Orlando is quite the whirlwind of social events, so I knew that the party invites were going to happen en masse. The community really kicks in with the nightclubbing and house partying in June. All the bars have Pride events, but the Pulse nightclub always has the most extravagant. The Pulse has been the community hub for organizing as well as quite an entertainment hot spot. The drag shows and dance boys are top notch! People live life well into the wee morning hours at the Pulse.

Sure enough, Rico put out the request: let's hit Pulse next week for Pride. I found myself a little bit excited to spend time with my lovely celebrating our love in public. I took time to pick our outfits. I got us spa dates and haircuts. We clean up well! I ordered a car and we were off for an evening of being seen—not my favorite, but Rico's excitement was palpable. Extroverts, ha!

When we arrived at the Pulse, the place was lit. So many people. Interesting people at that! Colorful outfits gyrating to pounding energetic beats. The alcohol and laughter were flowing. Rico must have smiled and responded to 30 people before we even got to the patio bar. Me, I just grin, look interested, and kept us moving forward.

We landed in a spot under a huge rainbow light fixture. We danced, talked to folks around us, and I really took a moment to enjoy our community. Everyone was out! I found myself looking around the room and simply appreciating the diversity. No two people looked alike. Everyone was engaged, moving, emoting, and celebrating. A truly joyous Pride!

That three hours went quickly. We eventually made it to our car and drove to a diner for breakfast. No, we didn't close the nightclub and yes, we did not have to wait in line for a table. Rico and I held hands and were same-siders while enjoying our eggs benedict. The coffee was delicious and our server was attentive. A pleasant evening, indeed!

The sirens interrupted our breakfast bliss. We wondered out loud what could be happening. Then Rico's phone blew up with texts. It was hard to piece it together, but there was a shooter at the place we had just enjoyed so much. A shooter was invading our people, our community. It was surreal. It was a tragedy in the making and Rico and I were terrified for all the people with whom we had just spent time.

As the story unfolded over the next few days, we learned about the beautiful individuals who perished because of one man's hate. Lives were altered forever. Rico and I will never be the same. To know we missed this extreme act of violence by 24 minutes leaves us confounded, trembling, and shaking our heads in disbelief. It is our strong bond, united partnership, and resilience that compels us to move forward.

We will not let hate win.

[Authors' Note: At the time, the Pulse nightclub was the site of the largest mass shooting in the United States. It's also the deadliest incident of violence against LGBTQA people on American soil. Prior to this tragedy, it was an entertainment venue, but now its "mission is to create a sanctuary of hope and honor the 49 lives that were taken, the 68 injured victims, the affected survivors and the first responders and health care professionals who cared for the victims."

The following websites have more information about the tragedy:
https://en.wikipedia.org/wiki/Pulse_(nightclub)
https://onepulsefoundation.org/onepulse-foundation/
https://www.facebook.com/pulseorlando/]

Case Example of Low Sexual Literacy: Severest Consequences

Hate Crimes in Junior High School

Unfortunately, hate crimes are far too common anywhere—but especially in a country that was established on the principles of "life, liberty, and the pursuit of happiness." The hate-crime massacre at the gay night club Pulse in Orlando in 2016 is certainly the most horrific example of this. We have a history of discrimination and violence (including murder) being so common against sexual (and other) minorities that we have become somewhat desensitized as Americans by being exposed to incredibly high levels of violence in our society. Only a small percentage of hate crimes catch the attention of the nation such as in Orlando.

Long before the Pulse attack, there was the tragic experience of a little eighth-grader named Lawrence "Larry" King. Because Larry felt different from most boys his age and was not inclined to stay in the closet as society would prefer, Larry was shot by a classmate for being gay on February 12, 2008 (Setoodeh, 2008). Because ignorance is the parent of fear and fear is the parent of violence, this classmate of Larry's felt there were no better options than to take a loaded handgun from his home, pack it in his book bag, and take the life of this boy at point-blank range. This boy's death is another loss of countless deaths from hate crimes but what makes it stand out is that he (and his killer) were both children. The case of Lawrence King can be considered a sad and needless example of LSL because of the perpetrator's lack of knowledge and skills needed to live in a pluralist society (especially in terms of lack of tolerance for others different from him).

There are signs of hope, however. The death of Lawrence King, Matthew Shepard, Gwen Araujo, and many other uncounted LGBTQA people have contributed to the long journey toward greater acceptance of sexual minorities.

For example, top Republican super attorney Ted Olson (best known for winning the 2000 *Bush v. Gore* lawsuit before the Supreme Court) argued the conservative case in support of gay marriage by opposing the passage of Proposition 8, the California law that bans same-sex marriage (Olson, 2010). In addition, the head of the Joint Chiefs of Staff (Admiral Mike Mullen) made an unprecedented statement when he told Congress that overturning "don't ask, don't tell" (DADT) in the military was the right thing to do (Mullen, 2010). When you have the Joint Chiefs of Staff (top military job in America) and one of the most powerful Republican attorneys agree that it's wrong to deny equal rights to people based upon their sexuality, there are strong winds of change blowing. The following year, DADT was officially ended as a policy throughout American military branches, allowing men and women of any political and sexual stripes to openly and proudly serve their country. Five years later, the Supreme Court made the right to same-sex marriage the law of the land (Stone, 2017).

Overcoming Sexual Challenges in a Young Marriage: A Determined Man with Erection Dysfunction and a Smart Woman with Low Sexual Literacy

This is a story about an attractive African American couple in their early 20s, Jill and David (pseudonyms), and is based on their true experiences (with details altered to protect their identities). The purpose of including this story is to stress the importance of sexual health literacy, examining one's own blind spots, and finding pathways to health regardless of the obstacles. (The subject of "blind spots" will be closely examined in Chapter 20.)

Jill and David, both working professionals, are the kind of people you would love to have as neighbors. Both are smart and engaging; David was rugged and handsome, Jill was beautiful and voluptuous. David experienced erection dysfunction (ED) after having pelvic trauma in a motorcycle accident. He reported a history of normal erectile function before his injury two years earlier, but then had tissue trauma to his penis. Doctors initially worked with David on understanding the specific injuries he suffered from having his pelvic bone splintered into to his vascular system and the subsequent scar tissue that developed from surgical removal of bone fragments. At the time of his accident, David and Jill were recently married and still adjusting to married life. The rehabilitation program after the accident lasted nine months as David had to heal and learn to walk again.

David was fortunate to receive care at an excellent medical center that included sexual health as part of his rehabilitation. The physician started David on a first-line treatment of a vacuum constriction device (VCD, aka the pump), which he found satisfactory in terms of helping him get and maintain erections suitable for intercourse. They were happy to be able to continue their sex life together but thought there may be other treatment options they would enjoy more than the VCD, which they found somewhat cumbersome and an interference with the natural flow of their foreplay. Smart and motivated consumers, they looked for a sex therapist to address communication issues common to young married couples, expand their sexual literacy, and get assistance finding the ED treatment option "right for them" (that's how they found me).

David was started on 50 mg. dosage of an oral medication for sexual enhancement but without much effect. He reported some improvement when using 100 mg, the maximum dosage for a 24-hour period. He denied any significant or intolerable side effects. He recalled moving from a satisfaction rating of about "40" for getting and keeping erections, to about "70" with medication. Although the couple was able to have regular sexual intercourse, David still was not satisfied with the overall sexual relationship.

After initial gains in treating the ED, the focus of therapy shifted to resolving communication problems the couple experienced, as they both lacked positive modeling for communication about sex and found it exceedingly difficult to talk about sex. In addition, Jill started to identify aspects of her family history that contributed to a very strict behavioral code about sex and to an overall "sex-negative attitude" about the role sexuality played in their marriage. Not surprisingly, Jill had a very low score on the questionnaire presented earlier in his chapter; her score was 115 on the Self-Assessment for Family Support for Healthy Sexual Development during Childhood/Adolescence (the range of scores is 0–300).

Jill's response to David's improved sexual function became a focus of therapy, especially her mixed emotional response to having sexual relations with David. It was obvious that Jill dearly loved her husband and that she was willing to do about anything sexually to please him. At the same time, she was experiencing mild to moderate feelings of discomfort, and on occasion disgust, when engaged sexually with him.

Jill denied any sexual trauma history nor did she have any lapse in her memory of childhood. Jill slowly started to identify aspects of her socialization as a girl, especially messages from her parents about sex. She began to consider whether these early messages about sex somehow contributed to her adverse visceral response to sex (feelings of nausea and disgust). She always thought that "sex and I are not a good match" and that her negative feelings about sex were part of her particular biology. She simply believed that she was "wired differently" and would never like sex as other women did. Some individual insight-oriented counseling was started to supplement the couple's sex therapy. Individual counseling helped her understand that her socialization contributed to the feelings of being ill. She literally described an "epiphany experience" after a conversation with her husband. David had observed Jill talking to her father on the phone and at one point saying "Oh, Dad!" with exasperation. The father called to invite the couple to vacation with them, but it conflicted with a trip that Jill and David already had planned. When Jill declined her father's invitation, explaining they were going alone on vacation, the father responded with, "Oh, you just want to be alone to do the nasty!" David discovered Jill was not even aware she made the "Oh, Dad" response and was surprised when David asked her about it. She then recalled the conversation and thought nothing of her father's comment. David did, however.

David's conversation with Jill led to her examining how she felt she needed to be a "good girl" when around or talking to her father. Jill said she had changed her college study and career plan for being a teacher (which she always wanted to be) to going into another field, because that would "make Daddy happy." She later realized that she was "transferring" this feeling about herself from her father to her husband, including being taught by her father that sex was something dirty. Jill almost immediately reported feeling empowered in minimizing (and eventually eliminating) her negative feelings to her own sexuality as well as sexual intercourse with David. She concluded that sexophrenic socialization, not her biology, was what made her view sex so negatively.

David wanted to enhance his sexual relationship with Jill, which he described as a bit routine, in part due to Jill's preference for missionary position only. The personal growth Jill experienced in terms of fulfilling more of her own sexual health potential opened up the possibilities for further developing their sexual life together. Jill reported less frequent negative feelings and even started initiating sexual relations—something she never did before because she thought it wasn't part of being a "good girl" (more about "good-girl" training during the discussion on sexophrenia in Chapter 4). David felt his sexual initiatives were more often welcomed by Jill and he was more comfortable exploring other treatment options for his ED.

After reviewing patient health education videos regarding second-line treatment options for ED, David consulted his urologist regarding injection therapy. Using this procedure, David found a double benefit over his use of oral medications. He reported an increase in the rigidity of his erections but also reported increased consistency (reliability) of getting and keeping erections (from 60–70 to 80+) as well as some increase in the lasting duration of erections.

A couple not as open as David and Jill to expanding their sexual literacy nor willing to seek out and accept help would most likely have been at higher risk for ending their marriage in divorce. Instead, this couple's journey together increased not only their satisfaction with sexual relations but also their overall marital relationship. They transcended the challenges that the sexual dysfunction (ED) had presented to their young marriage.

The extra benefit was Jill's transcending the negative (sexophrenic) effects of her socialization about sexuality from family influences. She no longer felt she was somehow missing the physiological capacity to enjoy sex. The couple overcame the obstacles to sexual satisfaction and continued to come to therapy, though less frequently, to discuss family-planning issues and sexual-enhancement possibilities (sharing sexual fantasies and incorporating sex toys into their lovemaking). They soon ended sex therapy when they discovered Jill was pregnant and they turned their attention to becoming a family.

ENHANCING YOUR SEXUAL HEALTH THROUGH SEXUAL LITERACY

Like David and Jill, you may also have had people in your life who have assisted with your general education or mentored you in a specific technical area. Some examples are parents, teachers, elders, and professors who supportively challenged you and said something like, ""I think you could do a little better." Though your general literacy may have thrived and you may even have been seen as a smart person, it is likely your sexual literacy did not develop at the same level of learning. You likely did not have any teachers or mentors say to you, "I'm not sure you are living up to your sexual potential—I think you can do better!"

Not only is there typically an absence of people to assist in becoming literate about sexual health, there were likely many people who put obstacles between you and the sources of information about sexuality (as Jill's father did). As asserted in this chapter, most people grow up with limited opportunity to learn accurate information about sexuality. Fortunately, this is changing slowly. But when we do not have information we need, we do what most people do: We fill in the blanks with sexual myths and misinformation we learn from various sources.

This may be one of the reasons that you are reading this book, to expand your sexual health literacy further by replacing myths and misinformation. Your goal may be to become more informed about sexual health and enhance your overall health and well-being. As you continue to expand your awareness and knowledge, please be comforted by knowing that you do not have to remember everything, and attempting to do so would most likely overwhelm anyone.

The good news is that, today, there are an increasing number of sources for accurate information about sexual health and they are becoming easier to access, especially through the Internet. But although many reliable sources of sexual health information exist (WebMD, the Kinsey Institute, university-affiliated health care centers), even more sources are unreliable and perpetuate misinformation and sexual myths. One of the most respected sources of information on sexuality in America is the Sex Education and Information Counsel for the United States (S.E.I.C.U.S.). They can be contacted at www.siecus.org.

Although learning more about sexual health is important, it does not necessarily result in making you more comfortable with your body or make you better at communicating about sex. Knowledge helps, but actual practice contributes more to an increased sense of comfort. Using positive stories of real people like David and Jill, subsequent chapters will address specific activities that can increase your comfort and satisfaction about your own sexuality.

Remember that sexual health literacy is simply a body of knowledge. In time, you will grow more and more familiar with the specific details and facts about sex. Albert Einstein was quoted as saying, "As our circle of knowledge expands, so does the circumference of darkness surrounding it." As noted earlier, the more you know, the more you know you do not know. Simply said, we know there are areas of sexuality that we just don't know much about. But be not discouraged! You have already started increasing your awareness and expanding your circle of light!

The more you learn, the more informed you are, the better your choices can be about sexual health and the more comfortable you can be as well. In short, become more relaxed being yourself while you learn about the big world of sexuality. You are invited to take the time that is needed to grow in your sexual health, and this starts with your literacy. You have just completed an in-depth reflection of your early sexual development and measured your satisfaction regarding the same. Now get ready to measure how satisfied you currently are with the many dimensions of your present sexual self—more than 20 indices of your personal sexual satisfaction.

REFERENCES

Alcorn, L. (2014). Suicide note. Tumblr. Retrieved from www.dailydot.com/news/leelah-alcorn-transgender-tumblr-suicide-note/

American Association of Sex Educators, Counselors, and Therapists. (2016). Standards for certification. Retrieved from www.aasect.org

Bley, J., & Peterson, F. (2007). Making sexual health a part of your mental health practice. In L. VanderCreek, F. Peterson, & J. Bley (Eds.), *Innovations in clinical practice: Focus of sexual health*. Sarasota, FL: Professional Resources Press.

Capehart, J. (2015, April 10). Obama comes out against "conversion therapy" to support "Leelah's Law." *Washington Post*. www.washingtonpost.com/blogs/post-partisan/wp/2015/04/10/

Gander, K. (2014, December 30). Transgender teenager Leelah Alcorn took her life because "parents would not allow her to transition." *Independent*.

Kavanaugh-Jones, B. (Executive Producer), & Nichols, J. (Director). (2016). *Loving* [Film]. United States: Focused Films.

Komisaruk, B., Beyer-Flores, C., & Whipple, B. (2006). *The science of orgasm*. Baltimore: Johns Hopkins University Press.

Larson, E. (1995). Sex, Race, and Science: Eugenics in the Deep South. Baltimore: Johns Hopkins University Press.

LeVay, S., Baldwin, J., & Baldwin, J. (2015). *Discovering human sexuality* (3rd ed.). Sunderland, MA: Sinauer Associates.

Maass, V. (2009). *The Cinderella test: Would you really want the shoe to fit?* Santa Barbara, CA: Praeger.

Merriam-Webster. (2016). *The Merriam-Webster Dictionary*. Springfield, MA: Author.

Money, J. (1985). *The destroying angel: Sex, fitness, and food in the legacy of degeneracy theory, Graham Crackers, Kellogg's Corn Flakes, and American health history*. Buffalo, NY: Prometheus Books.

Mullen, M. (2010, December 15). Joint Chiefs of Staff testimony to Senate on ending ban on gays in military. 156 Cong. Rec., Pt. 15, 22138.

Olson, T. (2010, January 8). The conservative case for gay marriage. *Newsweek* https://www.newsweek.com/conservative-case-gay-marriage-70923

Ryan, C., & Jetha, C. (2010). *Sex at dawn: How we mate, why we stray, and what it means for modern relationships*. New York: Harper Collins.

Setoodeh, R. (2008, July 8). Young, gay, and murdered. *Newsweek* https://www.newsweek.com/young-gay-and-murdered-junior-high-92787

Shear, M. (2015, April 9). Obama to call for end to conversion therapies for gay and transgender youth. *New York Times*. Retrieved from https://www.nytimes.com/2015/04/09/us/politics/obama-to-call-for-end-to-conversion-therapies-for-gay-and-transgender-youth.html

Stone, G. (2017). *Sex and the Constitution*. New York: Liveright.

Wallace, A. (2009, September 14). The rise and fall of the Cincinnati boner king. *Gentleman's Quarterly* https://www.gq.com/story/smilin-bob-enzyte-steve-warshak-male-enhancement

Yarber, W., & Sayad, B. (2019). *Human sexuality: Diversity in contemporary society* (10th ed.). New York: McGraw-Hill Education.

CHAPTER TWO

Measuring Your Sexual Satisfaction

Written by Frederick Peterson

INTRODUCTION TO THE DIMENSIONS OF SEXUAL HEALTH

Because this book is about enhancing your sexual health, its first goal is to expand your awareness regarding the specific and varied aspects of sexuality. Sexual health is defined as "the integration of the physical, emotional, intellectual, and social aspects of being sexual in ways that are positively enriching and enhance personality, communication, and love" (WHO, 2004). This definition, however, is a general description of some of the primary domains of sexual health and does not get down to the particular components that comprise the total experience of sexuality.

This chapter will illustrate these particular components and in doing so, will address the very first of the many sexual dimensions: sexual health literacy. Whether reading through the first chapter or the entire book, you are expanding your knowledge base of human sexuality. The first three chapters are designed especially to help you develop an under-standing of the "big picture" of sexual health while appreciating the details that follow.

A second goal of this chapter is to complete a baseline measurement of your sexual health satisfaction. Before doing so, however, you have to understand the concepts involved with each dimension (which you will be rating). You are asked to review the areas of sexual life presented in this chapter and determine how satisfied you are with each dimension. Sexual health can be divided into about 25 basic dimensions that are represented by the following four "primary domains":

1. *Sexual self-satisfaction:* Sexual health literacy, sexual self-image, sense of self-love, sexual fantasy, sexual self-pleasure, and access to sexual health services.
2. *Relational sexual satisfaction:* Overall relationship satisfaction, sense of love toward others, sexual activity with a partner, social acceptance of sexuality, and sexual-spiritual satisfaction.

3. *Medical sexual satisfaction:* Sexual disease status, sexual hormone status, sexual pain status, sexual injury status, sexual reproductive status, and sexual compulsivity status.
4. *Sexual identity satisfaction:* Sex orientation (male, female, transgender), sexual orientation (heterosexual, homosexual, bisexual, asexual), and sex-role orientation (traditional masculinity, androgyny, traditional femininity).

POTENTIAL BENEFITS OF COMPLETING THE SHAWS

There are several benefits to completing the questionnaire called the SHAWS (Sexual Health and Wellness Satisfaction). Taking the SHAWS illuminates the many different dimensions of sexual health and expands one's perception of how multifaceted we are as sexual beings. The SHAWS is one of the first measurements of sexual health satisfaction that is based on a comprehensive and holistic conceptualization of sexual health, as defined by the World Health Organization (WHO).

Completing the SHAWS can also stimulate you to pursue different tests of sexual health and add to your knowledge of the working operations of your body. Some of these tests are objective measures of sexual health, such as screening for a sexually transmitted infection (STI) or hormone levels. You will be learning more about the specifics of these objective measures in subsequent chapters. However, the funny thing about these objective measures is that although they are important to know, they do not necessarily determine your satisfaction level. For example, say you find out that you are below the normal range for testosterone (whether you see your sexual identity as female, male, transgender, or any other variation). Having low testosterone may explain low interest in sex, but you may not define your low interest in sex as a problem. In fact, some people are happy they have little interest in sex. Other people may define low interest in sex as a problem and want to take corrective action, such as getting hormone replacement therapy.

Another benefit of working with your health care provider to complete additional measures of sexual health is increased communication about sexual health with your physician, nurse, or mental health professional. The SHAWS was originally developed as an assessment tool in a hospital-based sexual health clinic to facilitate therapist-client communication. It was further expanded to facilitate physician-patient communication about sexual symptoms, which may be important indicators of other serious medical conditions, such as diabetes mellitus.

As discussed in Chapter 1, the sexual heritage of our contemporary American culture makes sex a taboo subject, even today. Sadly, there is much evidence to suggest that many sexual health concerns are ignored in therapy because a person and/or their health care provider are too uncomfortable bringing sex into any discussion (Risen, 2007; Timm, 2009, Grinonneau-Denton, 2018). This is why the SHAWS was originally developed, and the results can contribute to a more comprehensive assessment of your health, whether you or your provider initiates the conversation.

Completing the SHAWS may also serve as a baseline measure of where you are currently in your sexual health development. You can eventually retake it to determine the progress you have made improving your levels of satisfaction. Identifying your areas of low satisfaction can guide you to self-improvement strategies that may be helpful. For example, say you have a very low satisfaction rating in the dimension of sexual self-image. Sex therapists often think of low self-image as "low-hanging fruit" in counseling because there are many helpful strategies to employ to increase a person's self-image. Positive progress can be seen relatively quickly and satisfaction levels increase subsequently. Another copy of the SHAWS is found within Appendix A for the opportunity to complete it a second time for comparison to your baseline measure (which is on the next few pages).

Satisfaction Across the Domains of Sexual Health

Now that you better understand the benefits of completing the SHAWS and have been introduced to the primary domains, you are a step closer to rating your satisfaction. To do so, read the definition of the concept you are rating and answer the questions for each domain. They are based on the assumption that the "more you have of a particular quality, the more satisfaction you have." For example, the more you know about sexuality, the higher your level of satisfaction would be with the dimension of sexual literacy. Remember: rate your satisfaction on a 5-point scale (0, 3, 6, 9, 12), with 0 representing complete or nearly complete dissatisfaction (an absence of satisfaction) and 12 representing complete or nearly complete (or very high) satisfaction.

Please remember this rating is of your satisfaction, which is based on your *perception* of a particular aspect of your sexuality. Your level of satisfaction may change if your perception changes. For example, people may think they know a lot about sexuality and have high satisfaction regarding their sexual health literacy. In fact, people may not understand how little they know or the amount of sexual myth that is part of what they think is their knowledge base. An example of such a myth would be thinking they would know immediately if they had an STI.

Many people do not know they are exposed to STIs or that they actually carry a particular virus or bacteria. Take the striking example of chlamydia, which infects about half of sexually active women by age 30. Nearly three-quarters of infected women (half of infected men) are asymptomatic (LeVay, Baldwin, & Baldwin, 2015). How are they going to know they have chlamydia if they do not have symptoms yet do not get tested for this STI? Hence, a person's rating may change if he or she completed STI screening and discover the infection. Relationship satisfaction is another easy example. The level of satisfaction regarding your relationship may be based on a perception of monogamy. Your satisfaction rating will likely be different if you discover your partner is having an affair.

Therefore, your rating of sexual health satisfaction is based on your perception, and perception is subject to change over time and changing circumstances. At the same time, rating your satisfaction is a valuable strategy in measuring your sexual health, even with these limitations. Hence, the rating you are about to complete is not the only measure of sexual health, but it is a good place to start and then move on to other measures (such as being screened for STIs, for example). Hence, your ratings can be thought of as a "snapshot in time" measure of your current satisfaction.

BASELINE MEASURE OF SATISFACTION: SEXUAL HEALTH AND WELLNESS SATISFACTION (SHAWS)

Read the definition provided to you for each dimension of sexual health. It is provided to help you understand the aspect of your sexuality that you will be rating. Try your best to answer each question regarding your level of satisfaction. For example, even though you may not know something like your hormone level, please rate your satisfaction based upon what you do know ("Well, I've never had a problem in that area") or your general feeling. Use the following rating scale to answer each question:

> 12 = very high satisfaction
> 9 = high level of satisfaction
> 6 = moderate level of satisfaction
> 3 = low level of satisfaction
> 0 = very low level of satisfaction

DNK means you "do not know" your level of satisfaction (think about it and try not to use this option often). Use NA if you feel the question does "not apply" to you, such as if you are asked to rate your satisfaction with a primary relationship and you don't have one. You can either rate the question on your last relationship with a primary partner or just use DNK (or NA if you prefer).

Sexual Self-Satisfaction

Sexual health literacy (knowledge). Accurate information regarding sexuality that is not biased by prejudices and politics.

___ How satisfied are you with your level of knowledge about human sexuality?

Sexual self-image. How you see your own physical appearance, including attractiveness (based on how you see yourself).

___ How satisfied are you with the sexual attractiveness of your body?

Sense of self-love. A tender feeling of kindness, self-care, and acceptance toward yourself, associated with self-respect and positive feeling.

___ How satisfied are you with your ability to love yourself? (This does not mean masturbation, which is the following question.)

Sexual self-pleasuring (sexual function of desire, arousal, and climax through masturbation). Positive feelings resulting from any physical stimulation that makes you sexually interested and aroused (including but not requiring orgasm and not involving another person).

___ How satisfied are you with your ability to experience sexual desire associated with self-pleasure (masturbation)?

___ How satisfied are you with your ability to experience sexual arousal (erections for men and vaginal lubrication for women) associated with self-pleasure (masturbation)?

___ How satisfied are you with your ability to experience sexual climax (orgasm) associated with self-pleasure (masturbation)?

Sexual fantasy. Thinking about sexy things that create or increase sexual feelings (whether or not a person masturbates).

___ How satisfied are you with your ability to enjoy sexual fantasy?

Sexual health service access. Being able to access sexual health services (such as seeing a doctor, getting reproductive services, or getting sex counseling) based on your location and financial status.

___ How satisfied are you in your ability to access sexual health services?

Relational Sexual Satisfaction

Overall relationship satisfaction. Your total satisfaction resulting from all aspects of your relationship with another person (including, but not limited to, emotional, affectionate, sexual, intellectual, financial, spiritual, and safety aspects of your overall relationship).

___ How satisfied are you with the overall relationship with your primary partner? (If you are not in what you consider a "primary relationship" at present, you may respond to this item based on thinking of a particular partner or your last primary relationship. Use NA if it does not apply.)

Overall sexual satisfaction. Your total satisfaction resulting from all SEXUAL aspects of your relationship with another person (including, but not limited to, frequency, duration, climax consistency, and emotional aspects of your overall sexual relationship).

___ How satisfied are you with the overall SEXUAL relationship with your primary partner? (If you are not in what you consider a "primary relationship" at present, you may respond to this item based on thinking of a particular partner or your last primary relationship. Use NA if it does not apply.)

Sense of love for another. A feeling of affection, tenderness, and connection toward a person, often associated with a feeling of passion and a longing for intimacy with that person.

___ How satisfied are you with your ability to experience love toward another person?

Sexual pleasuring with a partner (sexual function of desire, arousal, and climax with another person): Your ability to experience sexual desire, sexual arousal, and orgasm with a sexual partner.

___ How satisfied are you with your ability to experience sexual desire associated with sexual relations with another person?

___ How satisfied are you with your ability to experience sexual arousal (erections for men and vaginal lubrication for women) associated with sexual relations with another person?

___ How satisfied are you with your ability to experience sexual climax (orgasm) associated with sexual relations with another person?

Social acceptance of sexuality. The average amount of acceptance you feel you receive from people in your social networks regarding your sexuality (including an average of support from family, peers, organizational membership, or community as a whole).

___ How satisfied are you with how your sexuality is accepted within your social network (such as family, peers, and community-at-large).

Sexual/spiritual relationship. The degree of alignment between one's spiritual/religious beliefs and one's sexual practices (whether the sexual behaviors are practiced alone or with another person).

___ How satisfied are you with the relationship between your sexuality and your spiritual/religious beliefs? (You can use NA if you do not think this item applies).

Medical Sexual Satisfaction

(Special Note: The previous items are based on the general premise that the more you have (like self-acceptance or ability to have orgasms), the higher your satisfaction. With the exception of the question about fertility, the items in this section are the opposite; the less you have usually means the higher your satisfaction—but not always.)

Sexual pain status. Pain primarily experienced by women (although men can be affected as well) during or immediately after sexual activity (especially sexual intercourse).

___ How satisfied are you with your degree of comfort (absence of pain) during or after intercourse?

Sexual injury status. Sexual trauma or abuse that has been forced upon you by one or more perpetrators against your consent.

___ How satisfied are you that all your sexual relations have been with your consent?

Sexually transmitted infections status (sometimes referred to as sexually transmitted diseases). Related to illness caused by a virus, bacteria, or parasite that has a high probability of transmission between people by means of sexual contact.

___ How satisfied are you with your ability to prevent yourself from getting a sexually transmitted infection? (Please answer regardless of whether or not you actually know if you have a sexually transmitted infection.)

Sexual hormone status. Natural substances produced by the body (primarily testosterone and estrogen), which make a person more interested in sex as well as increasing one's fertility, sense of vitality, and overall health and well-being.

___ How satisfied are you with your status of sexual hormones? (Please answer regardless of whether or not you have actually had your hormone levels measured.)

Problematic sexual behavior status (sexual compulsivity/addiction). When individuals report being unable to control their sexual behavior despite increasingly adverse consequences as a result of their "out-of-control" sexual behavior (consequences such as ruining their health, relationships, and careers).

___ How satisfied are you with your ability to prevent yourself from engaging in problematic sexual behaviors (also referred to as "out-of-control" or "sex addiction" behaviors)?

Sexual reproductive status. The natural capacity to conceive and have children as well as the ability to prevent pregnancy (regardless of one's sexual orientation).

___ How satisfied are you with your fertility (your ability to have children and/or keep from having offspring)?

Sexual Identity Satisfaction

Sex orientation. Physical anatomy and/or traits that most often make people see themselves as male, female, or transgender (transgender defined as a combination of both male and female sex designation).

Please list your identified (designated) sex: _____

(Female, male, transgender, or whatever term you prefer)

___ How satisfied are you with your identified sex (being a man, woman, transgender, or alternative term)?

Sexual orientation. An enduring pattern of emotional, romantic, and/or sexual attraction you have toward men, women, both sexes, or neither sex.

Please list your identified sexual orientation: _____

(Asexual, bisexual, gay, lesbian, heterosexual, or whatever term you prefer)

___ How satisfied are you with your sexual orientation (being asexual, bisexual, gay, lesbian, heterosexual, or alternative term)?

Sex-role orientation. A person's self-description as being traditionally masculine, traditionally feminine, androgynous (having high amounts of both masculine and feminine traits), or a preferred alternative term (such as queer or non–gender conforming).

Please list your identified sex-role orientation: _____

(Traditionally feminine, traditionally masculine, androgynous, or whatever term you prefer)

___ How satisfied are you with your sex-role orientation (androgynous, feminine, masculine, or preferred alternative term)?

Domain and Overall Sexual Health Scoring and Summary

Instructions: This page allows you to summarize your ratings and draw conclusions regarding your sexual health satisfaction.

List how you see your sexual identity:

_____

_____

List your areas of high satisfaction (your highest scores). These can be considered the strengths of your sexual health.

_____

_____

List your areas of low satisfaction (your lowest scores). These are likely to be the areas of your greatest concern and focus of expanding your sexual health.

_____

_____

Add up the sum totals for each section above:

Sexual Self-Satisfaction Indicator	____
Relational Sexual Satisfaction Indicator	____
Medical Sexual Satisfaction Indicator	____
Sexual Identity Satisfaction Indicator	____
Overall Sexual Health Indicator	____

MAKING SENSE OF YOUR SHAWS BASELINE SCORES

The preceding summary page is designed to help you have a better understanding of your areas of satisfaction and, as noted, draw conclusions about what your ratings mean. There is wide variation to the guidelines, so remember that exceptions exist for some of the following generalizations.

Scoring is designed to approximate a continuum of 0 to 300, with 300 representing complete (or nearly complete) satisfaction in all areas of sexual health. A score of 300 represents an ideal model of sexual health. For most people, it is unrealistic to assume they should be anywhere close to a score of 300. People who have been diligently working toward enhancing their sexual health are more likely to be within the 240–270 range. This simple 0–300 "continuum design" is based on several factors:

1. There are 25 dimensions of sexual health you have rated 0–12 for satisfaction (equaling a possible range of scores from 0–300).
2. Two items are subdivided into separate sections (questions 4 and 10 about sexual self-pleasuring and sexual pleasuring with a partner) and they are to be scored as three equal dimensions of sexual function.

3. You are to try your best to give an answer for every area of sexual health. If you cannot, then your total score will be artificially lowered and any missing answer must be taken into account during interpretation.

4. If you responded to any item with "DNK" (do not know) or "NA" (not applicable) because you are not in a primary relationship or a sexual relationship, then adjust your score accordingly. For example, if you used NA one time; your total responses are in relationship to a highest possible total of 288, not 300. Hence, you are not penalized (numerically) for not being in a primary relationship.

5. The following interpretation guidelines for scores are similar to what you used in the first chapter with the Self-Assessment of Family Support.

290–300	Come on, stop fooling yourself!
250–289	Very high satisfaction
200–249	High satisfaction
150–199	Moderate satisfaction
075–149	Low satisfaction
000–075	Stop being so hard on yourself!

The listing of your sexual identity traits simply helps you clarify your core sexual identity for purposes that will be explained later in the book (where you will be asked in Chapter 11 to find yourself within the Sexual Identity Cube). The listing of your areas of highest and lowest levels of satisfaction have specific purposes as well.

Your areas of highest satisfaction are represented by your highest rating (typically a rating of 12). These are the strengths of your sexual health and are important not only in "counterbalancing" your areas of low satisfaction, but possibly in assisting you with strategies to enhance your sexual health satisfaction.

Your areas of lowest satisfaction are represented by your lowest ratings (typically a rating of 0 or 3). These are the areas of your greatest concern and should guide you in focusing your efforts in expanding your sexual health. Pay particular attention to the chapters that focus on increasing your satisfaction in the areas of your lowest ratings.

REAL-LIFE DEMONSTRATION OF THE SCORING AND INTERPRETATION OF THE SHAWS

[Authors' Note: This story is modified to protect confidentiality, and pseudonyms are used.]

Pat, a physician suffering from clinical depression, was referred to a psychiatrist for treatment. Her depression was long-standing and had become very severe. Her depression was so severe it came to the attention of the state licensing board, which required her to receive treatment to practice medicine. The treating psychiatrist discovered that the physician also had sexual issues accompanying her depression, so he referred her for psychotherapy treatment of both her depression and her sexual concerns.

Pat had been previously married and had several children from her marriage. She came from a family described as very conservative WASP (White Anglo-Saxon Protestant) in the Deep South. She also was raised with strong fundamentalist religious training from a grandfather who was a minister. She reported never being able to please her mother and felt that she was always competing for her father's attention while growing up. In college, she began to suffer from depression when she came to believe that she was sexually abused as a teenager.

By all accounts, Pat was an attractive middle-aged woman. However, she did not see herself in a positive light and, in fact, loathed herself for never being "smart enough" to overcome her depression (which she saw as a public sign of her weakness as a person). While married, she had serial affairs, seeking attention and reassurance of her sexual value as a woman. Unfortunately, she contracted an STI and subsequently passed it on to her husband, which was the proverbial "last straw" for the marriage.

Along with standardized psychological testing for anxiety and depression, Pat completed the SHAWS during her initial evaluation. She identified herself as a traditionally feminine heterosexual female (item A on the scoring summary page). She reported several areas of high satisfaction (all rated 12), including her sexual health literacy, her ability to access sexual health services, her ability to experience sexual arousal (alone and with others), being free from sexual pain, and her fertility (as she loved having children and felt in control on avoiding unwanted pregnancy).

Pat's areas of lowest satisfaction caused her considerable misery. Not only did she see herself as unattractive (rated 3), but she also intensely disliked herself and had no allowance for self-love (rated 0). Regarding her satisfaction with the relationship between her spirituality and sexuality, Pat felt she was an "abomination before God" and was full of shame (rated 0). On the "Medical Sexual Satisfaction" domain, she reported low ratings (3) on her satisfaction with her status regarding the STI she contracted (and passed on to her husband), her status of having a history of nonconsensual (abusive) sexual relationships (0), and feeling her sexual promiscuity had risen to the level of sexual compulsive behavior (3).

The total ratings for the four domains of Pat's sexual health are as follow:

Sexual self-satisfaction total score	32/96	(33%)
Relational sexual satisfaction total score	42/96	(44%)
Medical sexual satisfaction total score	42/72	(58%)
Sexual identity satisfaction total score	32/36	(89%)
Overall sexual health total score	148/300	(49%)

Low Satisfaction

Pat came to psychotherapy treatment weekly and attended monthly sessions with the psychiatrist for medication management. She was always on time and friendly, never appearing to resent the mandatory nature of her treatment. Although she seemed to speak honestly about the pain of her past and the regret of her present situation (particularly the fact that her children did not live with her much of the time), she also harbored significant resentment. At times, Pat expressed optimism and encouragement that she would be able to overcome her depression and rebuild the relations with her children. On a superficial level, to someone who did not know Pat, she seemed to have a life of privilege with many positives, including a new fiancé, financial security, good health, and much potential for resolving her traumatic past as well as her disabling depression.

However, Pat never finished her therapy as she succumbed to her depression by killing herself. It was a tragic end to the life of a gifted young woman and talented physician. Additionally, her suicide left a wake of incredible and unmeasured damage in the lives of her family, particularly her children. She left behind much speculation as well. Pat was very intelligent yet trapped by her own brilliance. She could not find her own path out of the labyrinth called depression. Too smart to hold herself to the mere standards of others, she secretly felt irreversibly damaged inside. She was willing to accept the pain but not able to stand the intense sense of being alone with her "secret shame," which she believed no one could ever fully understand.

The system failed in its attempt to save this extraordinary person. The components of the "system" that failed her were the combined professions of medicine, psychiatry, and psychology. The people who knew her best (friends and family) also felt like they did not effectively reach out to her in times of desperation. Her providers were shocked by her death and were left with both a sense of grief and mystery. How could this amazing individual get stuck in her intent for self-destruction and not find her way out? By conforming to medical board–directed treatment, Pat found herself in a classic Catch-22. She had to comply with the requirements of counseling and medication to continue her medical practice. Yet at the same time, she felt compelled to present a persona of "the good patient" to have positive reports sent to the state regulatory board. This was a significant and unfortunate (as well as unforeseen) obstacle to her achieving a basic requirement of psychotherapy—authenticity. Her suicide was another unwanted lesson in the effects of a person's inability to have self-acceptance and authenticity. Without feeling able to express her true self, she could neither share her fears and thoughts of suicide nor discuss effective means of resolving her impulses for self-destruction.

The issue of authenticity and its relationship to personal satisfaction is discussed in greater detail later in this chapter. The SHAWS offered additional insight as to how Pat perceived herself. Unfortunately, in this tragic story, understanding was not enough. The clinical examples presented in the remaining chapters are all stories of positive success. They are of individuals and couples who overcame their personal challenges to get to what most people want so desperately: health and satisfaction, a sense of meaning, and emotionally significant connections with others. Without them, life is not worth living for some.

THE NATURE OF SATISFACTION

As mentioned earlier, satisfaction changes with your perception of how your life changes over time. It changes as you get older and your priorities change, as well as the sexual context you find yourself in (such as being widowed or divorced and being with someone new). Did you know that how you rate your sexual health satisfaction can actually determine whether or not you have a specific diagnosis?

Remember the previous discussion of having low sexual interest? Individuals who complain to their doctor about a lack of sexual interest may be diagnosed with *hypoactive sexual desire disorder (HSDD)*. This diagnosis is characterized by an absence of (or low) interest in sex, but there is a time requirement. The person must have experienced the symptom for at least six months. Additionally, the person (or the partner) has to define the symptom as a problem causing distress, either to one or both of them (American Psychiatric Association, 2013).

People can be disturbed by this absence of sexual interest, or they may not be. Some people who chose not to be sexually active (referred to as celibate) may even welcome the absence of sexual interest. Other people may always have had an absence of sexual interest. Such individuals may call themselves "asexual" and see their absence of sexual interest as normal. In short, people who are celibate, asexual, or have medical conditions that cause an absence of sexual interest may not define low (or absent) sexual interest as a problem.

Here is a key point: If you do not consider the absence of sexual interest a problem, then you may not meet the criteria for a diagnosis of HSDD (see below). It is all about *perception*—and perception determines satisfaction.

That is the funny thing about many diagnosed problems in the area of sexual health—it's a problem only if you define it as one (or sometimes when your partner defines it as a problem). If you have diabetes and deny having it or don't see it as a problem, you still have diabetes. If you have cancer and deny having it or don't see it as a problem, you still have cancer. If you have rapid ("premature") ejaculation, an absence of sexual desire, a lack of vaginal lubrication, no erections, or haven't had an orgasm that you can remember, you actually would not meet the criteria for a sexual disorder diagnosis *unless* you (or your partner, if you have one) were bothered by these symptoms. To phrase this differently, millions of men do not have erections, cannot have intercourse, and do not have the diagnosis of erection dysfunction because they do not perceive the symptom as a problem.

Although satisfaction is a funny (and fuzzy) thing at times, it is incredibly important as an indicator of whether your personal needs are adequately met. Common sense dictates that when our personal needs are met, our satisfaction will be high. But if your *needs* are not fulfilled, you may often be left with a sense of frustration, anxiety, or even depression (or maybe not).

Ah, but how do we define a "need?" One definition of the noun *need* is a "requirement, necessary duty, or obligation" (as in, "*There is no need for you to go there*"); or a lack of something wanted or deemed necessary (as in, "*to fulfill the needs of the assignment*") (Merriam-Webster, 2016). Something we think we need may often be something we just want but can do without. Whether it is a need or a want, the feelings are often the same when we do not get that "something." This is because of our perception. We often do not understand the difference between real needs and our wants.

Needs are things we really cannot live without. Examples are food, water, and a safe environment where we are not in harm's way. Something we just want (but often perceive as a need) represents a mistaken belief that we need it but in reality, we can live without it. Examples are wanting to feel happy, being sexually fulfilled, or having a sense of productivity and a good reputation. These are desirable qualities in our lives and improve our quality of living. We can live without them, although most people strive to achieve these qualities.

Obviously, this difference between needs and wants is incredibly important. Millions, perhaps billions, of people around the world follow spiritual and religious practices that guide them to avoid these "wants" (sometimes referred to as desires or attachments). Islam, Buddhism, Hinduism, Zen, and other ascetic traditions essentially counsel people that their earthly desires are the source of personal unhappiness, interpersonal conflict, and even wars at a societal level. In a sense, success in life is about not getting too attached to it (from this perspective). Recommended readings on this important subject include the writings of Persian Muslim theologian and philosopher Al-Ghazali, particularly *Disciplining the Soul, Refining the Character, and Curing the Sickness of the Heart* (1995) as well as *Breaking the Two Desires* (1995).

The common bit of wisdom used as a cautionary tale in Western culture is "the grass is always greener on the other side of the fence." This piece of common sense speaks to us regarding the difference between needs and wants. The corollary to this saying is, "Yes, the grass is sometimes greener and that's because of all the cow pies you can step in." The Dayton, Ohio, humorist and writer Erma Bombeck said it better with the title of her first book: *The Grass is Always Greener Over the Septic Tank* (Bombeck, 1976).

Take, for example, the person who divorces a spouse to pursue happiness through a new love interest. Often the new relationship does not work out over time. Eventually, that person then reflects about why they thought, "I would not be happy unless I pursued and obtained something I do not have." With the gift of hindsight, this person then may realize that happiness is based within oneself, not externally. But stated differently, experiencing satisfaction (most of the time) frequently depends more on valuing and wanting of what you have. Satisfaction is less often achieved by coveting something you don't have, finally getting it, and realizing it is not what you thought it was at all. Don't get me wrong—external goals (like making a team or getting a college degree) are positive in many ways. But boredom, envy, and restlessness can all be caused by a lack of appreciation. As discussed in Chapter 17 (on Problematic Sexual Behaviors), these emotional triggers can not only be seen as a lack of appreciation but contributing factors in sexual acting-out behavior that can ruin marriages, break up families, or derail careers.

THE RELATIONSHIP BETWEEN SATISFACTION AND AUTHENTICITY

The nature of satisfaction has to do with how much you accept and feel comfortable "being yourself." This is often referred to as being authentic or genuine. How authentic you feel (your degree of authenticity) is much related to this notion of satisfaction, in that a *sufficient level of authenticity is required to have satisfaction*. You must have authenticity for real satisfaction, but authenticity does not necessarily mean you *will* have satisfaction. And you do not have to have satisfaction for authenticity either ("I am being real when I say I don't like this situation").

It is often said that one has to be true to oneself to be happy. If you are living your life for another person, disregarding your own needs and wants, then you have a recipe for dissatisfaction. If you are living with another person (parent, spouse, and/or children) and you feel you cannot be yourself around them, this is also a recipe for dissatisfaction. If you are gay and live a life pretending to be straight, that is a recipe for dissatisfaction. If unresolved over time, all three of these scenarios can lead to clinical depression. The degree you feel you cannot be yourself is the degree you lack authenticity. Generally speaking, there is less satisfaction in a person's life in these types of scenarios just mentioned. At the same time, much of life is about balance.

Authenticity does not mean you can say whatever you want to whomever you want at any time you want (and still keep your job). It does not mean you can answer your door naked any time you want (and not get arrested). It does not mean you can openly express yourself to your same-sex partner in every situation (and always receive acceptance). We are all who we are and the fact that we exercise discretion about how we express ourselves is not necessarily being inauthentic. Discretion often allows us to avoid unnecessary embarrassment, being fired or arrested, having trips to the emergency room, or even being killed. Avoiding these outcomes is a good thing and helps us maintain satisfaction in the long run of our lives.

However, the general guideline is this: *The more you can experience authenticity in your life, the higher your satisfaction.* This is especially true for our sexual health. There is even a body of research that shows people have a tendency to be more authentic as they age. As described below, this aging trend has to do with our sex-role orientation and was perhaps first described as a component of the individualization process as conceptualized by the famous psychoanalyst Carl Jung (Jung, 1971).

When we are children, we learn about what boys and girls are like, and most of us behave in a sex-stereotyped way (at least for a while). As we discussed in Chapter 1, this way of behaving often becomes exaggerated in American culture, which can be described as living in a highly gender-polarized society (girls act sweet and can cry, boys act tough and don't show emotion except anger). Especially when young, most people closely conform to these stereotypes (as part of their building a *persona*, in Jungian terms). Individuals build this persona for many reasons, including being accepted by others into a group of friends, being accepted for a job, dating and mating, and even life-and-death survival. Strict adherence to a code of behavior based on sex-role stereotypes becomes less important to us as we reach middle age and beyond. In a sense, we become more relaxed and are more comfortable being ourselves instead of spending the effort following society's gender-based expectations. This is sometimes thought of as becoming more androgynous and less traditional in terms of one's gender expression.

Jung also referred to this as the "cross-over effect" that occurs in middle age and it is also referred to as "gender-role identity convergence" (Kail & Cavanaugh, 2004). This well-observed phenomenon represents the notion that certain aspects of personality are suppressed in adolescence and young adulthood, only to reemerge and get expressed later in life (Jung, 1960). Remember, this is a general trend across our lifespan. Some people do not "converge," and they are exceptions to the trend. Additionally, there can be times when individuals try to recapture some of our youth (by changing jobs, getting a sports car, or having affairs) and they usually experience significant consequences as a result (such as an absolutely beautiful sports car being driven by an equally attractive middle-aged woman. The vanity plates said "Pd4byX").

This tendency toward authenticity during aging is likely explained by a combination of social and biological factors. For the most part, people generally want to be themselves and are less interested in changing their behavior to please others when they get older. In this sense, it is fair to say that authenticity is promoted by aging because people believe more in the value of authentically being themselves. However, it is acknowledged that many people feel "trapped" in a certain role (such as wife, mother, etc.) and never seem to break out of the expectations of that role to truly be themselves. As noted earlier, this scenario cultivates a lack of authenticity and satisfaction (possibly promoting depression).

A biological factor also contributes to the tendency toward authenticity during aging. Testosterone production begins a slow decline in middle age that continues as we age. As most people know, testosterone is responsible for the sexual desire, a certain amount of energy, and a general sense of vitality people enjoy. What most people do not realize, however, is that symptoms experienced as a result of having too little testosterone are similar to the symptoms of depression. These symptoms mimic each other and, as a result, people who start hormone replacement therapy often report not only an increase in sexual interest, but less fatigue and a sense of greater vitality. In short, some patients report they feel better than they have in a long time. Very often, patients claim to feel like their "old self" again. (Of course, it is important to note that any individual may have medical contraindications for use of products containing hormones.)

The fact of the matter is that most people do not participate in hormone replacement therapy as they age. Most people experience these natural declines in testosterone gradually and get used to a lower level of energy (as well as sexual interest) over several decades, until their lower level of energy and sexual interest becomes their normal experience of day-to-day living. This "shift in normal" is part of the explanation of what Jung called the sex-role convergence (cross-over effect) referred to earlier, and it can happen so gradually that many people do not notice (it occurs outside their awareness). Not only do people have less interest in conforming to a strict code of behavior based on sex stereotypes, people just have less energy to do so than they did 30 to 40 years earlier. With both biological and psychological factors contributing, individuals generally worry less about gender stereotypes, conform less to these stereotypes, and hopefully achieve a greater sense of authenticity as they age. But does that mean a greater sense of satisfaction? It is all about perception, acceptance, and balance.

THE BALANCE OF STRATEGIES

There are two broad approaches to increasing satisfaction. The first is to increase acceptance of oneself—for example, accepting the sexual changes experienced as we age. Most men slow down in how fast they get erections and get to climax. Young men often think it is a bad thing to "slow down" as they see it as a sign of moving past their "sexual peak." As discussed later in the book, being 18 years old is considered a man's sexual peak if you believe "sexual peak" is defined by the age you can ejaculate the longest distance. If men are accepting of changes that occur with aging, they are open to learn the benefits of "slowing down," which results in greater satisfaction for them and for their partners. This begs the question: What is more important—how fast you are going or if you are moving in the right direction toward your goal?

A wonderful old veteran (in his mid-70s) once spoke up during the discussion section of a hospital clinic providing patient education on erection dysfunction. Patients were talking about the dangers of believing the stereotypes about sex and aging, specifically the "slowing down" effects of aging for men in terms of the myth that age itself ends a man's sex life. This particular man was not shy and asked the following question to the entire group of men: "If I have a race around the block with a 25-year-old, I know who is going to win. But that doesn't mean it is not worth going around the block—do you know what I mean?"

The second approach is to increase satisfaction through self-improvement. It is positive self-care to learn to relax and lower your blood pressure, to manage your weight through exercise and healthy eating, or stop smoking to prevent your premature disability and death. Short of getting a new heart, did you know there is no pill, product, or medical procedure you can buy that will reduce the risk of heart attack equal to the health benefits of quitting smoking? It is true. Quitting smoking and not using tobacco for 12 months reduces one's risk for heart attack by about 50 percent. That is not only amazing, but it is considered the "gold standard" of cost-benefit ratios in preventative medicine. Among the many self-help strategies to improve overall health as well as sexual health in particular, smoking cessation is one of the best examples.

Let's take weight management for another example to demonstrate an important point. Losing weight is a national obsession as most Americans are either overweight or obese according to the U.S. Centers for Disease and Prevention (CDC, 2016). There are so many ways to lose weight; it is a billion-dollar industry supplying "new" approaches to eager consumers ready to try the next big thing. Even if you do not achieve your ideal weight, working out can help you feel healthier and, in fact, be healthier. But let's say you do achieve your ideal weight (or get the college degree you want or marry your ideal partner)—it may never be enough.

This is where self-acceptance plays an important relationship to self-improvement. There is an important back-and-forth relationship because one doesn't work well without the other. Even if a person is completely dedicated to self-improvement strategies, you need a healthy dose of self-acceptance. Are you overly critical of yourself and find it difficult to be kind to yourself (have a lack of self-love)? If so, you may find self-help strategies more difficult to employ successfully. Also, exercising (or other strategies) can become obsessive and you can succeed in having a great weight and other indices of good health but feel miserable due to a lack of acceptance (perfectionism when taken to extreme).

The opposite is true as well in terms of the relationship between self-acceptance and self-improvement. You can also have too much self-acceptance. Eating anything in any amount, never exercising, and abusing oneself with alcohol and drugs can be behavior that is driven by self-loathing. It can also be driven by too much self-acceptance, too little self-restraint, and too little emphasis on self-improvement. In terms of good health, it is just not okay to say, "I accept my addiction to alcohol, nicotine, or overeating" and succumb to an early and preventable disability or death. People have the right to say it ("I accept my . . .") and practice overacceptance (or denial), but it is not a model of good health and quality of life.

The right balance of what you can do to help yourself with a good measure of self-acceptance leads to the best outcomes for overall health as well as sexual health satisfaction. However, the strength of both strategies rests upon one thing: authenticity. You have to be comfortable enough with yourself and be honest enough with yourself to accurately assess your level of health and well-being. You don't even need to be an adult to move forward in your life toward greater health and self-acceptance, as the next short story demonstrates so beautifully.

A Report from the Front Lines of the Revolution

LOCAL GIRL AND FAMILY SHOW HOW TO DO IT WELL
Written by Fredrick Peterson

At the elementary school that my two youngest sons used to attend, they once told me of a child who was picked on for wearing girls' clothes. My sons reported that a classmate named Isaiah was picked on by boys who were obsessively concerned about what was masculine and what was not. But they also observed that the girls would accept Isaiah and include him in their class activities. Even at early ages, Isaiah was asked by peers, "Are you a girl or a boy?" With remarkable insight and self-confidence for a seven-year-old, the response was, "I am half boy and half girl and half Native American," or "I'm a human being, that's alright isn't it?" What makes a seven-year-old say something like that, so beyond their few years of experience? It does not happen in a vacuum.

So many times, when families face a serious crisis, it is a dangerous time for all but especially for the most vulnerable family members. All too often, that person is a child or teenager and they pay the greatest price for the family not pulling and working together. Instead, they turn on each other without understanding, without acceptance, or even worse—rejection and violence. This is a different story, showing one exceptional way of how to believe in each other's capacity to grow and, without setting out to, demonstrate a healthy individual and family transition into a whole new life.

By all accounts, the Crawford family started out as pretty typical in most ways: a nuclear family of four with mom a nurse, dad a pilot, and two very cool boys. Over time, they started a remarkable journey of unfamiliar changes and took a direction they never dreamed would be their future. The family's love and support for each other serves as a positive model for family resiliency, raising happy children, and accepting changes in a very complex world.

I first met the child named Zay when she and her parents attended a dinner party at my home to celebrate the birthday of Dee Rockwood (who is the subject of a later chapter). Zay was about 11 years old and understandably was a bit shy at first around new people. The Crawford family was invited as they recently had met Dee at a memorial vigil for Leelah Alcorn and hit it off. Dee and Zay seemed to have an instant connection as advocates for transgender rights, which is pretty remarkable for Zay's tender age.

Zay had already been through many changes that had occurred when she was still using the birth name Isaiah. A growing awareness happened within Isaiah, feelings of strong attraction to all things associated with traditional femininity: dresses, hair, fingernails purses, shopping, and so on. The child rejected all things associated with traditional masculinity: competitive sports, short hair, obsessive talk about male role models (e.g., Han Solo), and so on. Isaiah more and more pushed to wear dresses, paint her nails, and present a feminine self to the world, at home and in public. She loved to identify with Princess Leia, not Han Solo.

Although assertive on the outside, Zay felt hurt inside and was depressed at times when she was called "the gay freak." She explained that she felt like she was "trapped in a cage" and did not know how to get liberated without having to fight for her place in the world.

When Chasilee and Jason (mom and dad) observed Zay's behaviors, statements, and preferences, they were first confused and fearful for their child. After all, many of us fear what we do not understand and fear is the parent of violence. Mom and dad were well aware of the frightening statistics showing how frequent transgender individuals were subject to harassment, depression, violence, homelessness, and even suicide.

Chasilee and Jason were of course protective. They took steps for their child to grow to be who she wanted to be—herself. They started to understand that they had a child who needed to either find a safe way to live with authenticity or live a life of pretending to be somebody she was not. So Chasilee and Jason took many measures important to nurturing and protecting Zay and the entire family. They moved to the small village of Yellow Springs, Ohio, which was known for progressiveness and acceptance of diverse people and attitudes. They talked to school personnel to raise awareness. They allowed their child to join a local Girl Scout troop that actually had extended a personal invitation to Zay. Although the local Girl Scouts in Yellow Springs welcomed Zay, the state level administrators of the Girl Scouts of America said, "Hold on here—you registered your child as a boy and boys don't belong to the Girl Scouts." So the parents attended a conference to discuss the issue and, as Chasilee puts it, "by the end of the meeting, they were fine with it."

The parents also brought their child to LGBTQA-oriented events, such as the memorial vigil to honor the life of Leelah Alcorn. They brought Zay to the Cincinnati-wide LGBTQA prom open to all students in southwest Ohio who did not feel welcome to attend their own school prom—that is if they were to attend as they wish to be, themselves, and/or attend with a same-sex guest.

The gay prom was part of Gay Pride Week Cincinnati 2015. I took my daughter, her friends, and had a great evening. Several hundred (mostly) adults attended a fund-raiser dinner and did some hip-shaking later on that evening, while several hundred kids rocked out in the ballroom downstairss at the Cincinnati Club. Chasilee and Jason sat close by with their daughter who wore a beautiful purple prom gown. It was her first big-time public event with her peers where she got to wear high heels and makeup. She appeared to be glowing with wonder and excitement, and her parents beamed with pride themselves.

It was very cool to see so many young folks enjoying themselves in a space where they did not fear being themselves and at an event that celebrated their differences, rather than feared it. Gender-neutral restrooms were the order of the day and caused little concern. It seems the kids see all the hoopla about "sex-assigned-at-birth" restrooms as just another hang-up of the older generation. Allies of all kinds were an important part of the evening celebrating their grandkids or their friends, or just celebrating another step toward individual freedom in this country.

While Chasilee and Jason were committed to raising their child to be herself, they also did not see any way to completely protect her from the hardships of bullying and discrimination. They were especially concerned about the incredible trauma of puberty, in which her body would slowly become increasingly masculine and her mind rapidly become terribly tormented. One fateful evening, the couple watched a TED talk on what has been referred to as "gender-affirming hormones" to block the natural changes that their child's body would undergo during the onset of puberty.

This is an excellent TED talk by pediatric endocrinologist Norman Spack (of Boston), and I routinely use it as a teaching aid in my university courses on sexual health. Dr. Spack compares the looming and dreaded changes of puberty to when Pinocchio started to slowly change into a donkey, instead of what he wanted to be—a real authentic boy. The parents were encouraged and decided to eventually seek consultation and learn more about helping her daughter's development into a young woman.

When Chasilee and Jason watched the TED Talk, they realized their child had a path forward that could both facilitate her authentic self-development (as a female) as well as save her from adverse and unnecessary changes to her body. In a short film called *Raising Zay*, Chasilee stated she thought—"Oh my gosh, there is hope for my child!" The parents soon were consulting the Gender Clinic at the Children's Medical Center of Cincinnati, one of a growing number of such clinics around the country.

Not long after their first meeting at the Gender Clinic, their daughter Zay had a hormonal implant inserted under the skin to stop the onset of puberty. The procedure is a temporary and reversible measure as it is the first step of a multiple stage process that affords additional time (against the tick, tick, tick of the biologic clock) and allows consideration of additional options. Without the looming pressure of a foreboding puberty, Chasilee described Zay as "finding her place as a thriving, beautiful young lady." Chasilee was a mother renewed, declaring, "It's been so fun to get to know my daughter."

The common sequence of events is that a child demonstrates strong and persistent cross-gender preferences over many years (as Zay did); the child self-identifies as transgender (as Zay did); the parents (hopefully) take the child for consultation at some point to a health care provider who is (hopefully) competent regarding the standards of care for transgender individuals (as Zay's parents did); a psychological evaluation is completed by a (hopefully) competent mental health provider who confirms that the child has a bona fide case of transgender identity (as Zay did); pediatricians then move forward with hormonal interventions that begin to assist the child to have a physical body that matches the gender identity (which Zay began); the child lives full-time as the identified gender (which Zay did for years); legal changes of name and public records begin (as Zay's family did); and then at some point when the child is judged to be medically and psychologically ready to complete the gender reassignment process, surgery is done.

Of course, there are often variations to the order of these steps (based on individual differences) but the general sequence of the steps as outlined above is that recommended within the standards of care set forth by the World Professional Association for Transgender Health (WPATH, 2012). The reason Zay's hormonal measures are considered temporary and reversible is that they are. If a child is not satisfied with said changes from hormonal treatments, there are complications, or the child is otherwise judged to have contra-indications for the final surgery; the "puberty-blocking" hormonal process can be reversed. The hormonal treatments are in two stages: puberty blocking and gender-confirming. Reversals can occur before the initiation of the gender-confirming hormones.

That is not expected with Zay. She seems very happy with these changes that have occurred thus far. So it seems as well with Chasilee and Jason, even though at first they had to mourn the loss of their youngest son. Although they love their new daughter, they may have moments when they miss that boy from time to time but also understand that it is okay to both love Zay and miss what was.

These parents fed their daughter emotional and physical sustenance to build her self-confidence. And this nurturance extended to their son Jeff, brother of Zay and ardent supporter of his sister. Jeff often corrected others regarding appropriate use of pronouns (in the beginning, Jeff was very helpful even to his parents when they used the wrong pronouns). Support also comes from Jeff's friend and the extended family; including grandparents, aunts and uncles, and the whole crew of friends and general supporters from the community.

Many of these supporters came together in May 2016 to celebrate another step in the process so Zay does not have to be referred to by an "old" yet official name on school records. A local judge confirmed a legal change of name from Isaiah Russell Crawford to Zay Irene Crawford. Family and friends gathered in a nearby park in Xenia, Ohio, to eat, drink, and be merry within the continually unfolding story of "Becoming Zay." It is this process by which Zay and her family are confirmed and celebrated.

SO, WHERE TO FROM HERE?

As Zay's story demonstrates—self-acceptance, self-improvement, and a lot of positive support from family, friends, and allies are all important for achieving a sense of authenticity and well-being (it also helps to be smart beyond your years)! We often cannot have all the support from others that Zay did, so it is of key importance that we focus on what we can do for ourselves that results in feeling well, authentic, and affirmed. This is even more important when there is a lot of negativity and rejection that surrounds a person (as with the story of Leelah Alcorn) or that which comes from within (as with the story of Pat).

Going back to the SHAWS; you now have your baseline measure of sexual health satisfaction. Take heart and take time to learn what you need to and move at your own pace through this book. Wherever you are on the continuum of sexual health, let the contents of this book inform and inspire you to keep moving down a path toward well-being and authenticity.

It may sound surprising to hear the following statement from sex educators and therapists (including the authors), but sex is really *not* the most important thing in life, even though you may feel that way in your moments of intense passion! Although this book is dedicated to enhancing your sexual health, the greater context of your *overall health and well-being is really just as important, if not more important!* Take care of the whole you and you will also enhance your sexual life. A key step is to take inventory of your overall health. This third assessment can bring greater clarity to how your sexual health fits into and supports your overall health and well-being.

REFERENCES

Al-Ghazali, A. (1995). *Breaking the two desires.* Book XXIII of *Revival of the religious sciences.* Cambridge, UK: Islamic Texts Society.

Al-Ghazali, A. (1995). *Disciplining the soul, refining the character, and curing the sickness of the heart.* Book XXII of *Revival of the religious sciences.* Cambridge, UK: Islamic Texts Society.

American Psychiatric Association [APA]. (2013). *Diagnostic and statistical manual of mental disorders* (5th ed.). Arlington, VA: American Psychiatric Publishing.

Bombeck, E. (1976). *The grass is always greener over the septic tank.* New York: McGraw-Hill.

Centers for Disease Control and Prevention. (2016). Website from Division of Nutrition, Physical Activity, and Obesity, National Center for Chronic Disease Prevention and Health Promotion. Retrieved from www.cdc.gov/nccdphp/dnpao/index.html

Grinonneau-Denton, A. (2018). Marriage and Family Therapists' Comfort and Willingness to Discuss Sexual Issues of the Couples They Work With. Dissertation in progress at the University of Akron.

Hackett, A. (2016, May 5). Becoming Zay: Growing up trans. *Yellow Springs News.*

Jung, C. (1960). The stages of life. In G. Adler, M. Fordham, & H. Read (Eds.), *The collected works of C. J. Jung: Vol. 8. The structure and dynamics of the psyche.* London, UK: Routledge & Kegan Paul.

Jung, C. (1971). The relations between the ego and the unconscious. In Campbell, J. (Ed.), *The portable Jung.* New York: Viking Press.

Kail, R., & Cavanaugh, J. (2015). *Human development: A life-span view.* New York: Wadsworth.

LeVay, S., Baldwin, J., & Baldwin, J. (2015). *Discovering human sexuality* (3rd ed.). Sunderland, MA: Sinauer Associates.

Merriam-Webster. (2016). *The Merriam-Webster dictionary.* Springfield, MA: Author.

Risen, C. (2007). How to do a sexual health assessment. In L. VanderCreek, F. Peterson, & J. Bley (Eds.), *Innovations in clinical practice: Focus of sexual health.* Sarasota, FL: Professional Resources Press.

Timm, T. (2009). "Do I really have to talk about sex?" Encouraging beginning therapists to integrate sexuality into couples' therapy. *Journal of Couple & Relationship Therapy, 8,* 15–33. doi:10.1080/15332690802626692

Vogel, M. (2015). *Raising Zay* [Film]. Retrieved from www.ciccinnati.com/story/news/2015/02/21/transgender/Cincinnati.

World Health Organization. (2004). *Progress in reproductive health research—A new focus for WHO.* (Pamphlet No. 67). Geneva Switzerland: Author.

WPATH. (2012). *Standards of care for the health of transsexual, transgender, and gender-nonconforming people* (7th ed.). Retrieved from www.wpath.org

CHAPTER THREE

The Big Wheel and Beginnings of the New Sexual Health

Written by Frederick Peterson

INTRODUCTION

David Satcher is the former U.S. Surgeon General serving under Presidents Bill Clinton and George W. Bush from 1998–2002. He is an articulate spokesperson for public health topics, including sexual health. Dr. Satcher published a remarkably progressive study called *The Surgeon General's Call to Action to Promote Sexual Health and Responsible Sexual Behavior* (published in July 2001). Although it has been more than a decade since this publication and some of the figures have changed, it still stands as a beacon calling Americans to understand that sexual health is an important part of overall health and to ignore this fact is to risk the kinds of consequences discussed in the first chapter. To quote Dr. Satcher:

> I was very concerned about the sexual health problems of the country, the fact there are about 12 million cases of sexually transmitted diseases a year and over 3 million of them are among the teenagers. One half of the pregnancies in the United States each year are unplanned and there are more than one million abortions each year. In addition, 22 percent of the women report that they have been sexually assaulted. When you look at the magnitude of the public health problem, I felt it was very important to do a report that was based on public health science, not politics, not religion, not personal opinion. We must as a nation address the significant public health challenges regarding the sexual health of our citizens. (Satcher, 2001)

This is quite a statement from America's top physician only a decade after a former U.S. surgeon general was fired for publicly discussing sexuality and saying the "M" word as a means of avoiding an STI (Jehl, 1994). Dr. Joycelyn Elders not only broke the taboo of publicly talking about masturbation, but made the very practical suggestion that masturbation could be a safe and reasonable alternative to "hooking-up" for teenagers rather than risking pregnancy and sexually transmitted diseases. Fortunately, Dr. Elders did not let getting fired by President Clinton stop her from addressing the new and important perspective on masturbation in the new sexual health, as we will explore in the next few chapters.

The work of both these former surgeon generals prompts the following questions: What is healthy sexuality, and how does it fit into your overall health? This chapter answers these questions and presents a third health assessment. Let us start with an examination of the definition of "sexual health" developed by the WHO (World Health Organization, not the rock and roll band).

WHAT IS SEXUAL HEALTH?

As referenced in the last chapter, the WHO defines sexual health as "a core dimension of being human which includes sex, gender, sexual and gender identity, sexual orientation, eroticism, emotional attachment and love, and reproduction" (WHO, 2004). That's quite a definition and a bit confusing, as most people may not understand all the terms used in this definition. However, if you continue reading, you soon will. The WHO later tried to simplify things by defining sexual health as "an experience of the ongoing process of physical, psychological and socio-cultural well-being related to sexuality." In other words, sexual health encompasses all the areas of your life that are related to being a sexual person and that contribute to your state of overall well-being.

This second definition is a lot shorter but not necessarily easier to understand. Being a governmental entity, the WHO also had to issue an "all-encompassing definition" of sexual health that more explicitly details all the different areas of a person's life that are related to sexuality (2006). See how many domains of life you can count, as it is related to the assessment you will be asked to complete later in this chapter.

> Sexual health is influenced by a complex web of factors ranging from sexual behavior and attitudes and societal factors, to biological risk and genetic predisposition. It encompasses the problems of HIV and STIs, unintended pregnancy and abortion, infertility, and sexual dysfunction. Sexual health can also be influenced by mental health, acute and chronic illnesses, and violence. Addressing sexual health at the individual, family, community or health system levels require integrated interventions by trained health providers and a functioning referral system. It also requires a legal, policy and regulatory environment where the sexual rights of all people are upheld. (WHO, 2006)

Now that's a mouthful, but this comprehensive definition is helpful in better understanding the complexity of sexual health, which is the most recent addition to the health care landscape. It is important to consider sexual health as a distinct and important domain of your overall health.

WHAT IS THE BIG WHEEL OF HEALTH?

Consider your overall health as a "Big Wheel." It represents your overall health and can be separated into eight dimensions, or "spokes." These spokes of the Big Wheel reflect the basic eight areas of your overall health and well-being

1. *Nutrition and health literacy.* These two go together as most people need health literacy (knowing what is important to do to maintain health, especially what to eat) to practice healthy nutrition. Remember, what we do not know, can (and often does) hurt us, so literacy is important!

2. *Medical health.* This includes changes you experience in your body as you grow from one stage of life to another, an absence of diseases, and an ability to have children if you so choose. This area is comprised of cardiovascular, neurological, endocrinological, gastroenterological, respiratory, reproductive, and other aspects of your physical self.

3. *Lifestyle health factors.* This domain primarily involves factors that significantly affect people's health and are so important that they are considered the cornerstone foundations to the disciplines of preventative medicine, health psychology, and health promotion. The key considerations in this domain are related to tobacco and alcohol consumption, drug abuse (prescribed or nonprescribed), and regular health maintenance through exercise, health screenings, and vaccinations.

4. *Environmental health.* Having reliable shelter with clean water and food supply (free of toxins and contagious diseases), living surroundings free of environmental hazards (such as pollutants, secondhand smoke, radiation, etc.), and an environment free of violence and coercion (including domestic violence, gang violence, and war).

5. *Mental health.* Cognitive, emotional, and behavioral factors contributing to personal health, including how you feel about changes experienced as you go through life stages and whether you have a basic positive or negative sense about yourself.

6. *Relational health.* This area includes being able to achieve a significant emotional connection with one or more partner(s), healthy relations with family members (whether that family be biological or a family of choice), maintaining a healthy social network (involving friends and coworkers), and how one defines oneself in relation to the universe (whether or not that includes what is commonly referred to as God).

7. *Work/financial health.* This domain includes how you are able to provide for yourself (and possibly a family), how you define "work" (including volunteering), and how you achieve a sense of productivity or contribution.

8. *Sexual health.* Includes the reciprocal relationships between the previous seven domains and all the dimensions of how you are a sexual being (across all the SHAWS domains of self, relational, and medical aspects of sexuality as well as sexual identity).

The "sexual health" spoke of the Big Wheel is similar to and also different from the rest of the spokes. It is the same in terms of sexual health having a direct effect (either positive or negative) on the other spokes of the Big Wheel. In addition to each spoke of the wheel supporting the other, each dimension of your health contributes (or distracts) from your overall health and well-being.

Communication between you and your health care provider about sexual health issues is exceedingly important to your overall health, as symptoms such as lack of vaginal lubrication or erectile dysfunction may be signs of more serious medical problems such as diabetes or cardiovascular disease. In 2004, the *Journal of the American Medical Association (JAMA)* included a study (Mokdad, Marks, Stroup, & Gerberding, 2004) that reported that almost 1 million Americans die annually from preventable causes, especially the preventable causes represented in the "lifestyle health factors" domain of the Big Wheel.

The *JAMA* report went on to specify that unhealthy personal behaviors are the leading causes of death in the United States. The top three preventable causes of death were an estimated 435,000 American deaths attributable to tobacco use (18%), 365,000 deaths to unhealthy eating habits and physical inactivity (15%), and 85,000 deaths to alcohol abuse (3.5%). In addition, there were 29,000 deaths due to firearms and another 20,000 deaths attributable to unsafe sexual practices. These figures are overwhelming evidence of the paramount importance of considering one's overall health. In addition, these statistics do not include preventable deaths from car accidents, HIV, and other types of drug overdoses.

Think about it—that is nearly 1 million Americans per year who did not have to die prematurely as they did. That's like three jumbo jets crashing every day in this country. Tobacco use, poor diet with lack of exercise, and alcohol abuse are the three primary culprits of preventable causes of death (Mokdad, Marks, Stroup, & Gerberding, 2004). That is why there is such an emphasis on what are called "modifiable risk factors" in preventative medicine—and their associated health promotion interventions such as smoking cessation, healthy eating, regular exercise, weight loss, moderate use of alcohol, and safe sex practices. Let's take a look at two real-world examples of how these statistics play out in the real lives of two Americans—Frank and Joe.

FRANK'S STORY

Consider the following clinical scenario of Frank, a man who developed obesity in his 30s (nutritional and lifestyle domains) and was diagnosed with diabetes in his 40s (medical). Frank was concerned when he began to experience episodic erection dysfunction (sexual) and then felt down about these health declines (emotional). This affected his relationship with his wife because of his irritability and less interest in sex (the latter a symptom of depression as well as low testosterone). Things got worse through his 50s as he considered himself impotent (in a general way as well as sexually) and started a slow sad waltz many couples do called the "avoidance dance." Because he was not able to have intercourse, he started to avoid all sexual relations and even displays of affection with his wife, fearing the reminder of what was missing in the marriage (relational). The more down Frank felt, the less he was able to effectively manage his diabetes by eating right and exercising (partly because of less energy and less motivation but also due to the traveling Frank does for his work).

Frank's diminishing capacity to manage his own health further complicated his diabetes and made him more depressed in a negative spiral. His physical losses began to multiply secondary to his diabetes. Over time, he experienced problems with night vision and his driving had to be restricted for safety reasons (medical). Therefore, he lost his commercial driving license (he drove

0s had to look for alternative employment. Frank's worsening

h risk for circulatory problems, leading to amputation of a toe.

part-time job, he did not find it very meaningful.

olated, partly because he had lost touch with most of his old

trucks over the road. He lost motivation to work (vocational)

ed some mornings. Hence, Frank did not report to his job, lost

financial). His wife was employed but they had grown distant

d increased stress due to living on one income. Consequently,

anhood. He worried about losing his wife as well (relational).

and family would be better off without him. He began thinking

about suicide (spiritual) and may make an attempt if family, friends, or health care professionals do not assist him to feel better. If he does not have access to help or does not accept that he can be helped, Frank very well may be one of the Americans who kill themselves during the time it takes you to read this chapter.

You might be thinking that this example of a negative-spiral loss of health is unusual (or even extreme) and used to demonstrate the interrelations of the eight spokes of the Big Wheel of Health. If you are, then you are half right. Unfortunately, with only minor modifications, this is a common scenario health care professionals see every day. It may be hard to look at, but if we allow ourselves to see them, there are individuals in our neighborhood, at work, at church, and in our family who are a lot like Frank. Of course, the description of this negative health scenario was accelerated and compressed onto one page when it usually takes decades to unfold and it helps to know the history of the person over a few decades to identify the "Franks" around us.

For our purposes in this chapter, Frank's story demonstrates the general point that all the different areas of health affect each other, for better or worse. Sexual health is an important component of overall health and can adversely influence a person's overall health and well-being in devastating ways. Fortunately, the Big Wheel also spins in a positive way for many people. Enter Joe into our consideration.

JOE'S STORY

Joe is a 30-year-old Marine who reported to an appointment with his primary care physician and he filled out a brief questionnaire that showed he was experiencing elevated symptoms of depression and post-traumatic stress disorder (PTSD). Therefore, he was set up with an appointment with the clinical psychologist to talk about whether he wanted help managing his symptoms. At this second appointment, Joe was annoyed to learn that the appointment was with a "shrink" (me) and, during the interview, refused to accept counseling to discuss his PTSD and depressed mood, saying "I'm not crazy, Doc!"

He was told that I didn't think he was crazy and that it was my job to check in with him to see if he wanted any help. I told him when big tough vets (like himself) accept help when they need it, it is a sign of insight and strength, not weakness. While talking to him, I noticed that Joe had a pack of cigarettes in his shirt pocket. I informed him of the smoking cessation class available at the clinic. Although Joe declined counseling for PTSD, he was interested in talking about getting rid of his smoking habit. He and his wife recently had a baby who suffered respiratory infections, ear infections, and colic—all of which are conditions aggravated by the second-hand smoke from the parents (Joe was told this by the pediatrician). So after calling his wife to talk about it, he decided to enroll himself and his wife in the smoking cessation class at the hospital.

Once Joe understood I wasn't there to "shrink" him, he started to open up about his health concerns. At the top of the list was Joe and his wife's use of tobacco (they both smoked one pack a day). Their interest in becoming tobacco-free was primarily due to their concern for the health of their child. Joe talked about his medical history, which included a history of hypertension for which he took medication. He was overweight and admitted his medication caused some problems getting erections and this had increased marital conflict. He also said, with considerable embarrassment, that he was taking an oral medication to have better erections and doesn't like taking them.

Subsequently he and his wife attended the class and stopped smoking. To minimize weight gain when giving up cigarettes, the couple started a walking program and cut out the junk food in their diets. This Marine not only stopped smoking but lost 32 pounds over the course of six months. Both the weight loss and abstaining from smoking lowered Joe's blood pressure. He was then pleased to discover that he was able to discontinue his antihypertensive medication. In turn, Joe experienced a return of his normal erectile function. After one year of being off tobacco, Joe and his wife both cut their risk for heart attack by an amazing 50%!

As previously mentioned, there is no pill that can do the same. In addition, they saved nearly $4,500 in the direct costs alone of smoking and felt good about not exposing their baby to the health risks of second-hand smoke. After one year from our initial meeting, Joe had few symptoms of depression, reported they were getting along well as a couple, and were living a healthier lifestyle than ever (including their child having significantly fewer problems with infections). The kicker to this story is that Joe was still bothered a lot by his PTSD symptoms, although his depression had lessened. After a year and having "proved" our services could be helpful to his family, Joe shared that he was ready to talk about his combat trauma.

This is a true story of a U.S. Marine becoming healthy along with his family. There are many other such stories throughout this book, some directly from the lives of the men and women who have served our country. All the stories use different names and have a few details changed to protect the identity of the individual. Whether short examples such as Joe or a full chapter as you will later read, they are designed to motivate you to put what you are learning (and to a large extent, what you already know) "into play" with regard to your sexual health in specific and your overall health in general.

Sexual health is similar to other aspects of health on the Big Wheel. All the different dimensions of health influence each other and add to (or take away) from your overall health. The way sexual health is different from the other aspects of health and well-being is that it has a heritage of taboo (remember the comments from the former U.S. surgeon general). Consequently, we are not trained to understand or communicate about sex when young. Because of the stigmatized nature of sexuality in our culture (as well as around the world), we have grown up uninformed of most things sexual. What we do learn is often laced with misinformation and stereotypes.

We will delve into this history in the next chapter. But before entertaining you with how crazy we are as a culture about sex, it is time for your third assessment on the topic of your overall health and well-being. If you are the one-in-ten readers who are in great shape and have no concerns about your general health, you can just scan over this next section. For the rest of you, read and heed.

THE SELF-ASSESSMENT OF SATISFACTION FOR YOUR OVERALL HEALTH

The more you learn, the better you are prepared to make choices about your health. The two questionnaires you have already completed helped expand your appreciation of historical influences upon you (from your own personal sexual heritage) and your satisfaction of the state of your current sexual self. Many eye-opening details of America's sexophrenic heritage will be detailed in Chapter 6, and you can decide what factors in your own sexual history and value system have been shaped by our collective sexophrenic history as a nation. This self-assessment measures how satisfied you are with your overall health and is also intended to help expand your appreciation of how your sexual health fits into your overall health.

You cannot separate the two, as demonstrated by the stories of Frank and Joe. Your sexual health is integrated into your overall health. Therefore, to measure your sexual health satisfaction isolated from an assessment of your satisfaction with your overall health would be artificial, would limit your learning, and would not reflect the nature of the new sexual science.

Hence, your patience is again requested before we get into the heart of this book's content. Some of these questions may bear some resemblance to the questions in Chapter 2. However, please remember to keep in mind that you are to respond here concerning your overall health (not just your sexual health). You are asked to answer questions concerning the eight areas of your personal Big Wheel of Health.

COMPLETING A BASELINE MEASURE OF OVERALL HEALTH AND WELL-BEING SATISFACTION

Please read the definitions provided for each of these dimensions of general health (listed below). They are provided to help you understand the aspects of your general health that you will be rating. Try your best to answer each question regarding your level of satisfaction. For example, even though you may not know your blood pressure or cholesterol level, please rate your satisfaction based on what you do know (last available information or a lack of noticeable symptoms).

Unfortunately, as previously mentioned, what you don't know *can* hurt you. Many people do not notice symptoms of diabetes, high cholesterol, or high blood pressure until they are well into the disease process or they have a significant health event such as a stroke or heart attack. Don't let this happen to you! Remember, hypertension is called the "silent killer."

As previously mentioned, satisfaction ratings are important indicators of health, but they do not tell you the actual status of some aspects of your health, such as blood pressure. For example, you may rate your satisfaction with your health status high, not knowing you have hypertension or diabetes. Hence, you are encouraged to get the facts of your actual baseline measures of health by having regular check-ups with your primary care or family medicine provider.

The stakes are higher with your general health than the more specific arena of sexual health. Fortunately, we are not going to die if we don't have sex. Of course, not being accepting about your body image, having difficulty with climax, or just not having sex may be disappointing; but presents no immediate threat to your life. Being overweight, having uncontrolled diabetes, running high blood pressure, and having little regard for what you eat is a recipe for a real health disaster (especially if you don't exercise, experience high stress, and have a family history of heart disease or stroke).

On the other hand, having multiple risk factors for heart disease and stroke does not mean your life is over or that you have to be resigned to live without a high quality of life. That's the funny thing about personal satisfaction: It is individually defined. Individuals with a terrible sexual abuse history, sexual dysfunction, and/or living with AIDS can report high levels of satisfaction with their sexual health or their life in general. People without these challenges in their history, who have good general health, and live a life of privilege can also be completely miserable.

The best approach to health is to be as informed as you can to be better prepared to make health choices. Therefore, if you do not know your blood pressure, buy a home-version blood pressure monitor. If you do not know your blood sugar or cholesterol level, work with your doctor and get the facts. In the meanwhile, complete the following self-assessment as well as you can and use the questions you are stumped by as stimulation for getting with a health coach or your provider to develop a personal health maintenance plan. As before in previous assessments, you can use "NA" for not applicable or "DNK" if you do not know the answer. Please use these options sparingly and adjust your score if necessary.

Satisfaction Ratings Scale: Use the following scale to answer each question:

12 = complete or nearly complete satisfaction

 9 = moderate satisfaction

 6 = equal amount of satisfaction/dissatisfaction

 3 = moderate dissatisfaction

 0 = complete or nearly complete dissatisfaction

OVERALL HEALTH AND WELL-BEING SATISFACTION RATINGS

1. *Nutrition and health literacy.* Nutrition is the specific knowledge related to what, how, and when to eat to provide our bodies a balanced diet of all required nutrients and to aid us in maintaining positive health (including a body weight something close to ideal). Health literacy is knowing what is important to do to maintain our general health across all areas of the Big Wheel.

___ How satisfied are you with how often you eat a daily well-balanced diet that includes several servings of fruits and vegetables, whole grain cereals, and low-fat, low-cholesterol proteins and dairy?

___ How satisfied are you with your body mass index (BMI) in terms of what is recommend for your height and weight?

___ How satisfied are you with your level of knowledge about all that is needed to maintain your overall health and well-being?

2. *Medical health.* Physical health measured on a continuum from optimal body function and an absence of disease to disease and death; it is comprised of cardiovascular, neurological, endocrinological, gastroenterological, respiratory, reproductive, and other aspects of your physical self.

   ___ How satisfied are you with your blood pressure?

   ___ How satisfied are you with your cholesterol level?

   ___ How satisfied are you with being able to avoid a chronic illness such as diabetes, cardio-vascular disease, respiratory disease, and so on? (If you already have been diagnosed with a chronic illness, how satisfied are you in how well you self-manage the illness?)

3. *Lifestyle health factors.* A domain of health involving choices people make that significantly affect their risk for developing chronic disease and are related to tobacco and alcohol consumption, drug abuse (prescribed or nonprescribed), and regular health maintenance through exercise, health screenings, and vaccinations.

   ___ How satisfied are you that you are not exposed to the health risks of using tobacco prod-ucts (cigarettes, cigars, or smokeless tobacco) by your own use or the secondhand smoke of others?

   ___ How satisfied are you that you regularly engage in aerobic exercises (at least of 30 minutes' duration) and exercises that increase your strength and flexibility at least three to four times per week?

   ___ How satisfied are you that you either do not consume alcohol or do so within recommended limits (no more than one drink per day for women and no more than two drinks per day for men ("drink" being considered a 12 oz. beer, 5 oz. of wine, or 1.5 oz. of distilled spirits)?

   ___ How satisfied are you that you regularly engage in health maintenance through recommended health screenings, exams, and vaccinations (including annual dental and vision exams)?

4. *Environmental health.* Having reliable shelter with clean water and food supply (free of toxins and contagious diseases), living surroundings free of environmental hazards (such as pollutants, secondhand smoke, radiation, etc.), and an environment free of violence and coercion (including domestic violence, gang violence, and war).

   ___ How satisfied are you that you have reliable shelter (with little to no risk of being homeless) that has clean water and food supply (free of toxins and contagious diseases)?

___ How satisfied are you that you have living surroundings free of environmental hazards and pollutants, such as asbestos, lead, mercury, radon, radiation, and smog?

___ How satisfied are you that you have a home environment free of violence and coercion (including domestic violence, gang violence, and war)?

5. *Mental health.* Cognitive, emotional, and behavioral factors contributing to personal health, including how you feel about changes experienced as you go through life stages and whether you have a basic positive or negative sense about yourself.

___ How satisfied are you with your ability to have a positive mood and not be overly bothered by depressed feelings?

___ How satisfied are you with your ability to relax and not be overly bothered by worries or anxiety?

___ How satisfied are you with your level of self-esteem?

6. *Relational health.* This area includes being able to achieve a significant emotional connection with others; including primary relationships with one or more partner(s), healthy relations with family members (your biological family or family by choice), maintaining a healthy social network including friends and coworkers, and how you define yourself in relation to the universe (whether or not that includes what is commonly referred to as God).

___ How satisfied are you with your ability to establish and maintain a significant emotional connection in your primary relationship(s) so you feel like part of a "couple?"

___ How satisfied are you with your sense of connection to, and degree of support from, your friends and family?

___ How satisfied are you with your sense of spiritual connection to the world and/or sense of meaning in your life (whether that is through a spiritual belief in a God, higher self, or another entity)?

7. *Work and financial health.* This domain includes how you are able to provide for yourself (and possibly a family), how you define "work," and how you achieve a sense of productivity or contribution.

___ How satisfied are you with what you do for work or the way you support yourself financially?

___ How satisfied are you with a sense of productivity or the contribution you have from your work, volunteering, or hobbies?

___ How satisfied are you with your financial status, including your ability to reliably support yourself (and family?), savings and investments for retirement, and credit rating?

8. *Sexual health.* Includes the reciprocal relationships between the previous seven domains and all the dimensions of how you are a sexual being (across all the SHAWS domains of self, relational, and medical aspects of sexuality).

___ How satisfied are you with your core sexual identity (the combination of sex orientation, sexual orientation, and sex-role orientation)?

___ How satisfied are you with your overall sexual function (the combination of sexual desire, arousal, and orgasm)?

___ How satisfied are you with your overall sexual health (the combination of the self, relational, and medical aspects of your sexuality)?

That's it! Here is some guidance as to how to make sense of your scores. Like the other two questionnaires, just add up your scores and compare them to the range of scores from 0 to 300.

Scores above 225: Congratulations! Your general satisfaction is high (average score of at least 9), which is likely an indication of better-than-average health (assuming you were honest with yourself). Enjoy your good overall health and do all you can to preserve it. You are most likely able to achieve optimal health through your own determination and self-help strategies. However, you still may want the aid of a health coach, personal trainer, or your health care provider to address specific areas of concern regarding your health (such as any individual rating of 0–3). It's always better to have a "team" in your corner.

Scores between 150 and 224: Good work! You reported an average rating in the moderate range of satisfaction with your overall health (average response at least 6), which indicates you have some areas of strength and that you feel good about many areas of your health. The need for professional help is greater, and it is definitely recommended that you work with a health care team. You are recommended to use self-help strategies, but you really need to work with professionals to help get you where you want to go with your health goals. Strongly consider consulting the professionals of your choice who are specialists in the areas of your lowest satisfaction (such as a financial counselor, a minister, health coach, personal trainer, or your health care provider). There are many ways to access these services either free or at little cost.

Scores below 150: Okay, there was a question on this survey about being overly bothered by worry or anxiety. If you scored this low, then you seriously need to be worried! You have reported having pervasive and significant dissatisfaction about many areas of your health, which means there is a good chance you likely have general dissatisfaction with many areas of your life. Your score indicates you may be experiencing important challenges to your health, and there is no question that you need professional assistance to help you find your way back to the days when you actually felt good about yourself, your health, and your life. You may also be suffering from depression, which saps your energy and motivation to make efforts toward positive change. Schedule an appointment for a depression screening today with your primary care provider or counselor!

Please remember, though, your score can be deceiving in two ways. First, this is a rating of your satisfaction only, and you can have high satisfaction partly because you may not be aware of symptoms or a disease process. As mentioned before, one of the purposes of these questionnaires is to prompt you to get the facts on specific health measures in concert with your health care providers, including hormone and cholesterol levels as well as having regular screenings and exams.

Secondly, and although unlikely, you could have scored above 225 and had some low scores (0–3) on most of the questions for the medical and lifestyle health factors. Hence, take a close look at your lowest scores, build a health maintenance plan with your team of health care providers and advisers, and get started in earnest preserving the health you have. Remember, in the domain of sexuality, the general guideline is "use it or lose it." The same can be said of many of the general areas of your overall health that need to be attended to and maintained, such as nutrition, exercise, and relationships.

DEEPER QUESTIONS

This last survey was designed as a general screening of your overall health and well-being. There are many additional questions you could be asked (but will not be) in this book. But if you share a concern with a health care provider about low satisfaction with an area of your health, expect that provider to ask you questions for further follow-up regarding that concern. For example, let's talk about depression. If you did score low (0–3) on the question regarding depression, your provider may ask you some of the following questions:

- Do you feel down and blue more days of the month than days you feel better?
- Are you able to keep from criticizing yourself excessively?
- Do you feel guilty for things you do not have control over?
- Have you had any significant losses recently?
- Have you lost a sense of satisfaction about things you used to enjoy?
- Do you feel hopeless about your future?
- Do you have a sense of purpose and meaning in your daily life?
- Have you had thoughts of hurting yourself, including suicide?
- If you do, do you have a plan for carrying out these thoughts?

Obviously, these are important follow-up questions to your one-item inquiry about depression on the questionnaire. There are similar follow-up questions to most of the other areas on this questionnaire, but these are beyond the scope of this book and take us too far afield from the topic of sexual health. The point is that areas of low satisfaction do need to have follow-up and these areas may have significant impact on your sexual health.

So although this questionnaire was about your overall health, it is also a reminder to put first things first. As in our example, if you are struggling with depression to the degree of thoughts of self-harm, you are instructed at this point to get some help and put your depression in check before focusing on the rest of this book. It's not going to help you or anybody else to discuss how to understand, accept, and celebrate your sexuality if you are intent on ending your life. Of course, people can feel suicidal for many reasons, including having an unresolved history of sexual abuse. Some individuals have not accepted their sexual orientation or gender orientation. They may even think of themselves as an abomination to God or freak of nature. In these cases, sexuality issues may be related to a root cause of the depression. Then continuing to read this book may help. At the same time, medication and a good counselor would likely work better and the book could then be used as a guidepost on the road to recovery.

SOME WISE WORDS ON HEALTH AND HAPPINESS

This chapter on the Big Wheel of Health and well-being would not be complete without relating the topic to an elusive search for something that we all seek but usually only experience in passing periods of time: *happiness*. The relationship between health and happiness was recently brought to wide public attention when U.S. Surgeon General Vivek Murthy provided a TED MED talk for the gratification of all interested around the globe. As a third tip-of-the-hat to the Office of the U.S. Surgeon General, a summary of Dr. Murthy's message follows (Murthy, 2015).

Although happiness is not a typical topic covered by physicians, Dr. Murthy's approach to the subject is innovative and relevant in terms of our discussion here. The good doctor asserts that the obstacles to happiness are also important risk factors to your health! In addition, he identifies three major causes of unhappiness that are unnecessary as well as easily resolved! In his well-studied address, the Surgeon General identified the following three "pot holes" to avoid (or correct) on the road to optimal health:

1. *Social isolation.* This could mean physical isolation (as in becoming a recluse and not having any interaction with other people for extended periods) or emotional isolation even if you are surrounded by people and have some level of interaction. However, this interaction may be quite superficial and not meaningful enough to avoid feeling alone (even if you have people around you). Prospective studies have demonstrated that people who lack social support are at higher risk for cardiovascular disease (Krantz & McCeney, 2002) as well as other medical conditions (Brannon, Updegraff, & Feist, 2018) and that people who have had heart attacks are more likely to have another one that kills them if they live alone (Schmaltz et al., 2007).

2. *A loss or lack of sense of purpose.* If you do not have a sense of purpose in your life, it is hard to avoid hopelessness and thinking, "What does it all matter anyway?" As people, we do our best when we believe, "Yes, what I do does matter" and our activities are a direct reflection of our sense of purpose. Some call this sense of purpose a "life mission" and its clarity is maintained when we re-examined it at different stages throughout the life.

3. *A loss or lack of self-worth.* A person has to believe that they have some worth to feel like they both deserve to be healthy as well as think, "Yes, what I do does matter." Self-worth is often thought of as coming from external praise and reward for the things we do and the ways we help others. That sense of altruism is useful for a sense of self-worth but true self-worth comes from within. This type of self-worth is more intrinsic and associated with the "being" we are as opposed to the things we "do." It doesn't mean we don't feel guilt or regret sometimes for some behavior we did, but intrinsic self-worth is a solid protection against shame about who we are as a person.

Although it is significant that the "Top-Doc" in the country identifies these three social-psychological factors as threats to optimal health, it is even more important to know what to do about these three key health risks. And so Dr. Murthy provides the following behavioral prescriptions to protect one's health:

1. *Gratitude!* Develop an attitude of gratitude for all positives you have in your life. Yes, it sounds overly simple but that is part of the reason being appreciative is so effective. And there

is some good empirical evidence to support this notion, even if it does not solve all your problems. A key point: Don't wait for all your problems to be resolved before you think you can be happy. Each of us can seek to be happy with the imperfections we have and strive to be at peace in the present.

2. *Meditation!* That's right—meditation helps lower harmful effects in your body caused by stress (Krisanaprakornkit, Krisanaprakornkit, Piyavhatkul, & Laopaiboon, 2006; Carmody & Baer, 2008; Goyal et al., 2014). You can practice many forms of meditation that lower your blood pressure and increase your sense of well-being. Many people consider themselves in a meditative mind-set whenever they pray, do yoga, do Tai Chi, or practice mindfulness.

3. *Exercise!* You don't have to be a marathoner to benefit from exercise (thank goodness). Whatever exercise you do is good; you can only get better at it over time (like any skill you practice). Walk, jog, or ride a bike. Can't do those because of hip, leg or feet problems? Get in a pool and swim or do water aerobics. Also consider Tai Chi, a slow movement of the body combined with intentional breathing for relaxation. Tai Chi has been demonstrated to build your balance skills and significantly reduce the frequency of falling for older adults (Jahnke, Larkey, & Etnier, 2010; Leunge, Chan, Tsang, & Jones, 2011; Burschka, Keune, Oy, Oschmann, & Kuhn, 2014).

4. *Connection!* Remember that meaningful social connection with others is the antidote for isolation! It also, very often, helps a person have a greater sense of purpose by being part of something larger than oneself, such as volunteering for your favorite charity or organization (i.e., children's hospital).

That is some solid and amazing counsel regarding being healthy from the Surgeon General, partly because it is not what you would expect to hear from a physician. Medication was not mentioned once. Dr. Murthy's counsel is very consistent with the two final sets of recommendations offered in this chapter on overall health. These recommendations come from a special edition of *Scientific American Mind* (July/August 2016), which focused on the topic of brain health and delaying the common cognitive declines that occur in advanced age. In particular, there was a specific article about building a better brain as we age and how to avoid Alzheimer's disease (Bennett, 2016). What follows is an interpretation of the article's recommendations that are based on the results of dozens of peer-reviewed scientific studies. It appears there are several things you can do to reduce the risk of cognitive decline and developing Alzheimer's dementia (watch out for the first one—it's a doozy):

1. *Pick your parents well!* Make sure you get good genes, a good education, a second language, and music lessons (and avoid emotional neglect).

2. Engage in regular physical activity—walk, swim, Tai Chi, or bicycle! (Anything you can do consistently that is physical.)

3. Engage in regular cognitive activity (like learning a new hobby, language, bee keeping, or going back to school).

4. Strengthen and maintain social ties. Expand your social network of people around you with whom you have meaningful emotional ties.

5. Get out and explore new things (more learning in an active get-out-there-and-see-the-world way).

6. Chill and be happy. Sometimes being relaxed and happy can seem to just happen, but they are two separate yet related states of being which come from skills you can build.
7. Avoid people who are constant downers, including family members if necessary! You can be caring yet have healthy boundaries so their anxiety or problems don't have to be yours!
8. Be conscientious and diligent. Healthy habits go a long way toward contributing to your health and sense of well-being.
9. Spend time engaged in activities that are meaningful and goal-directed. Feel a sense of purpose in your life and live day-to-day serving your purpose and goals.
10. Be heart and brain healthy: It's a twofer! What's good for your heart is good for your brain. So how you eat, exercise, and learn makes a double difference.

This article (Bennett, 2016) also recommends enjoying the MIND diet, which combines two proven diets—the DASH diet and the Mediterranean diet. The MIND diet zeroes in on foods that specifically affect brain health. The emphasis is on eating from 10 brain-healthy food groups: green leafy vegetables in particular, all other vegetables, nuts, berries, beans, whole grains, fish, poultry, olive oil, and a limited consumption of wine. Be mindful of portion sizes! Meanwhile, the MIND diet avoids foods from the five unhealthy groups: red meats, butter or stick margarine, cheeses, pastries and sweets, and fried/fast food. The most hopeful news is that we can build our *cognitive reserve* so that even if one does develop brain lesions/tangles (what causes the symptoms of dementia, such as memory problems), we can compensate and better cope to maintain our function.

The final recommendations come from the Health Promotion and Disease Prevention program of the Department of Veterans Affairs (VA, 2013), one of the largest health care systems in the world. While the VA has its problems as a health care system, it has some outstanding aspects in terms of preventative medicine. These health recommendations are good to include here as a final guide for living. They reflect the VA culture shift from a traditional "find it & fix it" approach to medicine to a health-and-wellness model of care delivery. The recommendations are simple and direct:

- Eat wisely
- Be physically active
- Strive for a healthy weight
- Manage stress
- Limit alcohol
- Be tobacco free
- Be safe
- Be involved in your health care (via partnership with your providers)
- Get recommended screenings, tests, and immunizations

This discussion concludes the largest part of Section I. Now enjoy two inspiring stories of individuals who overcame obstacles to their personal sense of authenticity and happiness. The next two stories (Chapters 4 and 5) illustrate the overpowering resiliency of the human spirit and are about a psychologist named Scott and a Navy Seal named Alex. The story of Scott describes a man living with severe disability yet able to provide incredible life lessons in having meaningful contact with others (including sexually). The last story of Section I is of a person who joins the military to "make him a man" even to the point of becoming a Navy Seal, before finding a path to gender authenticity and greater happiness.

REFERENCES

Bennett, D. (2016). Banking against Alzheimer's. The scientific American mind. *Scientific American*, July/August, 28–37.

Brannon, L., Updegraff, J., & Feist, J. (2018). *Health psychology: An introduction to behavior and health* (9th ed.). Boston: Cengage Learning.

Burschka, J., Keune, P., Oy, U., Oschmann, P., & Kuhn, P. (2014). Mindfulness-based interventions in multiple sclerosis: Beneficial effects of tai chi on balance, coordination, fatigue and depression. *BMC Neurology*, *14*, 165.

Carmody, J., & Baer, R. (2008). How long does a mindfulness-based stress reduction program need to be? A review of class contact hours and effect sizes for psychological distress. Journal of *Clinical Psychology*, *65*(6), 627–638.

Department of Veterans Affairs (VA). (2013). Core messages from the National Center for Health Promotion and Disease Prevention, Office of Patient Care Services. Durham, NC: Author.

Goyal, M., Singh, S., Sibinga, E., Gould, N., Rowland-Seymour, A., Sharma, R., & Haythornthwaite, J. (2014). Meditation programs for psychological stress and well-being: A systematic review and meta-analysis. *JAMA Internal Medicine*, *174*(3), 357–368.

Jahnke, R., Larkey, L., Rogers, C., & Etnier, J. (2010). A comprehensive review of health benefits of qigong and tai chi. *American Journal Health Promotion*, *24*(6), e1–e25.

Jehl, D. (1994, December 10). Surgeon General forced to resign by White House. *New York Times*.

Krantz, D., & McCeney, K. (2002). Effects of psychological and social factors on organic disease: A critical assessment of research on coronary heart disease. *Annual Review of Psychology*, *53*, 341–369.

Krisanaprakornkit, T., Krisanaprakornkit, W., Piyavhatkul, N., & Laopaiboon, M. (2006). Meditation therapy for anxiety disorders. Cochrane Database of Systematic Reviews, Cochrane Art. No: CD004998, DOI: 10.1002/14651858. CD004998.pub2.

Leunge, D., Chan, C., Tsang, H., & Jones, A. (2011). Tai chi as an intervention to improve balance and reduce falls in older adults: A systematic and meta-analytic review. *Alternative Therapies in Health and Medicine*, *17*(1), 40–48.

Mokdad, A., Marks, J., Stroup, D., & Gerberding, J. (2004). Actual causes of death in the United States, 2000. *Journal of American Medical Association*, *291*(10), 1238–1245.

Murthy, V. (2015, June 25). The Surgeon General's prescription for happiness. TED MED Talk [Video]. Retrieved from www.tedmed.com/talks/show?id=527633

Satcher, D. (2001). The Surgeon General's call to action to promote sexual health and responsible sexual behavior. Rockville, MD: Office of Surgeon General/Office of Population Affairs.

Schmaltz, H., Southern, D., Ghali, W., Jelinski, S., Parsons, G., King, K., & Maxwell, C. (2007). Living alone, patient sex, and mortality after acute myocardial infarction. *Journal of General Internal Medicine*, *22*, 572–578.

World Health Organization (WHO). (2004). *Progress in reproductive health research—A new focus for WHO*. (Pamphlet No. 67). Geneva, Switzerland: Author.

World Health Organization. (2006). *Sexual and reproductive health: Defining sexual health*. Geneva, Switzerland: Author.

CHAPTER FOUR

Success Story:

THE CLAN OF SCOTT (MEMORIAL DAY 1986)

Written by Frederick Peterson

SEX AND PHYSICAL DISABILITY

Crossing the Bridge: "What did I get myself into now?" was all I could think as I watched a wild collection of oddballs assemble for the first day at SOPP (School of Professional Psychology at Wright State University). There was no going back to my former master's program at the University of Dayton (UD) as I had burned that bridge.

I had received a letter of acceptance and invitation for the orientation at SOPP the afternoon *before* my statistics final at UD. I didn't plan on making a cavalier escape from the sweltering heat in the classroom on exam day (especially with Jesus looking down at me from his crucifix over the open window), but that's what happened. Something within would not allow me to sit there any longer. I simply wrote on my blue book, "Sorry Dr. Biers, it's really too hot of a day to take this test," and walked to the front of the room where he was sitting, dutifully watching for signs of cheating. Not one of us would have dared to cheat for fear that he would publicly flog us with our own punch cards we had to prepare for the mainframe computer.

This gifted statistics professor, who seemed prepared for every probability, looked up with a stunned expression as if I had identified a secret confound in his statistical design, all in the five minutes since the start of the exam. I simply turned on my heel and walked out of there, while I still could! Of course, he flunked me for the exam but also for the course, as he should have. I really didn't care as I was off on a new adventure at SOPP. I have to admit that I took some twisted pleasure in knowing I was almost certainly the only guy starting the doctorate program who had failed his master's stats course. Little did I know that 20 years later, the good professor would now be the department chair and my boss at UD when I served as their adjunct sex professor. I was fortunate he mellowed and was forgiving. We would just smile at each other, remembering my past foolishness but being treated as an academic colleague.

Having arrived early at the orientation, I sat back and watched a parade of the most eclectic assortment congregate before me. What was it going to be like spending the next five years with these 30 people? Despite their looks, they were supposed to be the best of a talented pool of hundreds who had applied to be part of the first charter class of SOPP. We were also "academic Guineeau pigs" to test the full curriculum design of a new model of preparing professional psychologists—a model that was berated at more traditional research-oriented departments of psychology (like UD).

I thought maybe I had been selected as a "wild card" candidate to test their admission formula, expecting me to get washed out in the mix over the first few quarters. After all, I didn't even have a degree in psychology. I had graduated from Ohio State with an education major and then somehow got into the UD master's program by someone taking pity on me (perhaps Dr. Biers). I applied to SOPP just for "practice"—never expecting to be accepted. My reasoning was I would be a familiar face to them the second time around after graduating from UD and have a better chance of acceptance. If they decided to take me at the first pass, who was I to say no. The few friends I still had at UD said, "You can't do that—everyone knows you first must get your master's and then your PhD." To hell with tradition, I wasn't even going to get a PhD. SOPP was offering a new-fangled "PsyD" (Doctorate of Psychology) as their carrot and no one knew quite if the new degree would be accepted. I just sat there amused with this new adventure unfolding around me.

"Now wait a minute, what the hell is this?" I almost said out loud as the last student to show rolled into the assembly hall. This guy had longer hair than I did, covering the back of his shoulders and circling a round face that seemed to beam a sense of confidence. This was a look I did not expect from a person in a wheelchair who had a personal attendant accompanying him. After all, it was 1980, and you just didn't see that many people in wheelchairs out and about, let alone tackling the rigors of a doctorate program. He casually pulled up to the table across from me just as the orientation began.

The dean welcomed us all and gave a congratulatory address about being the first group in Ohio to go through the entire indoctrination of this new model of training and become this new type of psychologist. Dr. Ron Fox appeared to be an appropriate name for the dean, as he was a svelte guy in his 40s who sported a goatee and cowboy boots. Besides his smart looks, he apparently was clever enough to win a major battle in the state legislature to start this new school. As mentioned, SOPP had many opponents, including those inside academic psychology. I was also impressed at how Dr. Fox took shots at his own field, saying, "Psychologists are the only professionals I know that when attacked from outside, they circle the wagons and shoot toward the center." (This would be an example of what we would come to call a "Foxism").

When the "meet and greet" part of the get-together started, I approached the fellow in the wheelchair, fully aware that part of my draw to him was my ignorance about disabled people as well as my curiosity about what makes him think he could pull off a doctorate degree in his condition. While the dean spoke, I had observed that this guy not only had obvious problems with his legs, but he did not have normal control of his arms either. He was not using the type of wheelchair familiar to me, the kind that one powered through arm rotation. Rather, he used a motorized chair he controlled with a stick on the end of his arm rest, which he moved with his right hand. Seeming to be friendly enough, I approached him.

Extending my hand to greet him, I said, "Hey, I'm Fred Peterson and I guess you are part of this new program also?". He looked up at me with a big smile and brown eyes. "I can't shake your hand, but I am glad to meet you," he said right back with no hesitation. I instantly wanted to evaporate. Although he was gracious about my faux pas, his personal attendant looked at me with an expression like "Did your head have a serious injury or were you just born a screaming idiot?"

"Sit down and have some lunch. My name is Scott." He said as he nodded toward a chair next to him. We became acquainted and learned that we both followed unusual paths to be there that day. Scott had been studying classical guitar at the Conservatory of Music at the University of Cincinnati. He started to notice that he could not play chords that he had already mastered, and his musical talents began to deteriorate. He left the conservatory and switched majors to psychology to try to figure out what was wrong with his nervous system as well as learn how to deal with what was happening to him.

"Did they ever find out what was causing the problem?" I inquired. "No, but they are studying my tissue samples at the Mayo Clinic," he said with a note of pride in his voice. Another fellow joined us named Doug Craig. The three of us soon found ourselves in each other's company on a regular basis, partly by the circumstances of SOPP and partly because of serendipity.

Perhaps by chance (perhaps not), all three of us lived in the UD ghetto. Doug owned a two-story duplex, I lived in the other half, and Scott was a couple blocks over. Doug made the third musketeer of an adventurous trio and I came to learn he was a gentle soul and strong, quiet healer. Our UD neighborhood was a curious mix of poor students, neighborhood old-timers, and transients renting rooms by the week. Through any window came another strange mixture—the pulse of the lives up and down the street. Rushing in were aromas, images, and sounds of the Italian restaurant on the corner, neighbors arguing over the back fence, and the horse barns at the fairgrounds down the street.

Exploring the New World: We started helping each other out by riding to SOPP together as Scott needed a driver and we needed a ride. Doug and I started observing the many ways Scott relied on an attendant to get through his day. At school, the attendant was basically Scott's arms and hands. He got Scott out of his van, helped him in and out of doors, and assisted him getting physically situated in the classroom. He also carried Scott's books, took notes, collected handouts, turned in assignments, and assisted Scott when he had to pee.

Over the first few years in the program, it became apparent that Scott was slowly, yet progressively, losing his physical strength. At his home, he needed assistance getting in and out of bed, using a commode and getting showered, getting dressed and undressed, and preparing and eating his meals. He was losing internal as well as external muscular coordination, so he lost his ability to swallow on his own. Hence, meals became a process of mixing up a blend of protein powder, vitamins, milk, and bananas. This concoction was then poured into a medical drip bag and fed to Scott through a stoma in his abdomen so the nutrition could flow directly into his stomach. So after breakfast, he would hustle off to work like the rest of us and put in a full day at school or the clinic.

A remarkable quality of Scott was his chutzpah to conquer the known world around him despite what others would see as clear limitations and perfect excuses for him not to be fully engaged with society. Scott never let anyone place stereotyped expectations on him in terms of what he could or could not do. That included his parents, friends, professors, the university administration, and especially women who would fall under his spell. He taught everyone around him about what they took for granted as a TAB (temporary able-bodied) and made us realize that *if* we were lucky enough—we would live long enough to join the ranks of the disabled community. It is certainly better than the alternative (being on the other side of the grass).

Scott disarmed people with this "TAB" distinction, eliminating the psychological defense of separating others into "us versus them" and "normal versus disabled" dichotomies. After all, there are many more similarities than differences between Scott and all his TAB friends. Despite the needs he had for physical assistance, he had many more needs that we all have—to be included and validated as a person, to touch and be touched, and to love and be loved. Becoming disabled does not erase these needs of a person. As a matter of fact, able-bodied or not—when do any of us stop needing touch and caring? Through this simple yet radical perspective, he gently showed all of us (who would see him) to emphasize his abilities by taking the "d" off "disabled."

Without being obnoxious about it, he also demonstrated that everybody has certain basic sexual rights like the right to sexual expression, to have privacy to do so, and to develop to one's own highest potential as a sexual being. While serving as his attendant at times, I had the opportunity to watch him teach others (able-bodied or not) that they had the right to receive sexual health information (like about sexually transmitted infections), have access to sexual health services (like contraception), and make one's own decisions about getting married and/or having children. Over time, I learned that Scott had a child with a young woman when he was a teenager and they never married.

Another consequence of Scott losing internal muscular strength was losing control of his swallowing ability to the point attendants had to start using a suction machine to clear the saliva out of his throat. This had to be done about every 20 to 30 minutes (sometimes more) for Scott to avoid choking and allow him to speak clearly. He also took to using a respiration vest to force exhalation strong enough to help him speak with any volume to his voice. These were all activities Doug and I observed as we slowly learned how to be part of the inner circle of Scott's entourage.

The Intensive Course: These duties the personal attendant performed became means of support for a friend as our relationship grew. They were all activities Doug and I (as well as others) learned and repeated hundreds of times a month. Being in the inner circle brought a sense of pride and satisfaction. With Scott, it always felt like a two-way street. We felt we got as much as we gave. Helping out did not seem to be a bother plus it provided learning opportunities that we had never imagined.

One of these learning opportunities was struggling with the question, "At what point during a progressive decline in one's quality of life is it understandable for a person to want to die?" At what point is it fair for someone with nearly no control over his body to request the aid of a close friend to help end his life? Scott felt desperate in many "close calls" from feeling like he could not breathe and fainting to falling out of his chair or having nightmares in which he could not communicate outside his failing body. These questions Scott wrestled with, and so did I.

For several reasons, we both knew that assisted euthanasia was not going to happen from my assistance. I learned that with time, Scott came back to a point of equilibrium balancing his fear of living with the joy he found in life. Later, he usually said that he was glad he was still alive. An important part of the dynamics of equilibrium was his interest in people, meeting new interesting people who would become attendants, and especially the young women who would fall in love with him on multiple levels.

Scott had several attendants "on staff," although only one would be assisting him at any given time. Typically, he would use two or three attendants during the course of a 24-hour period. There would be a day-time attendant and one who would spend the night with him to roll him over to avoid bed scores. Doug and I soon began to "double" as his daytime attendant while we were at school or at training clinics together. However, his favorite attendants were nursing students who needed the work but who also found him fascinating as a person and as a "clinical case." Many of these nursing students were young attractive women who literally fell in love with Scott. Some were married women with their own children who altruistically volunteered as an aid to Scott (which did not make them any less vulnerable to his charms). Their need to mother him was a significant source of support for Scott.

While being attracted to (and falling in love with) someone like Scott may be hard to imagine for many people, there seemed to be no end to the women who wished to be with him, including sexually. One day, Scott was just sitting in his van at the gas station and had the side door open as I filled the gas tank. Two cowgirls from Texas pulled up in a truck next to us, saw Scott, and the next thing I know they were inviting him down to the county fairgrounds for the horse show that brought them to town. Within the hour we were in box seats watching the girls compete. After the show, they spent the evening with Scott and showed him more fun via a private and naked rodeo.

Being with Scott as a sexual partner came with special challenges of course, but that may also have been part of the fascination. Did that special part of his anatomy fail as much of the rest of his body? Fortunately for Scott (and the young women), the penis is not made of the tissue most affected by Scott's affliction.

Scott once described the sheer sense of freedom he felt from the physical constraints of his failing body when he was able to experience orgasm. To Scott, sex was not necessarily the most important thing in the world, but there was nothing quite like it to affirm his sense of worth as a man and help him share a close connection to another human being. This was particularly important as he secretly feared being trapped in a body without means to communicate and dying alone.

Another allure for some of these women was being more physically assertive and active during sex than they were either accustomed to or allowed to be by their former or current lovers. Unless they were cowgirls, many of Scott's lovers were not strong enough to transfer him from his chair to his bed or move this body to the positions preferred for their desired activities. From time to time, another person had to "facilitate" the liaison by being the muscle (to move Scott). Once Scott was on his back in his waterbed, the motion of the ocean was all that was needed for a good time by all.

Occasionally, the creativity of two lovers committed to satisfying their desire is all that is needed. On one trip to his hometown, Scott and his girlfriend found themselves alone in his parents' house with a free hour to kill while his folks, Earl and Alyce, made a run to the airport to pick up some family. His girlfriend spontaneously disrobed at the sound of the door closing and assumed a convenient position on the kitchen table. Scott "bellied up to the bar" by rolling his wheelchair forward to the edge of the table and proceeded to enjoy her breasts and other hotspots. He made her lose count of how many orgasms were possible in the main dining area of a lover's unfamiliar home.

Meanwhile, there was a mix-up at the airport regarding arrival times and Scott's grandparents were waiting on the curb to be picked up. All of a sudden, Scott and his girlfriend both heard the sound of the front door opening and his grandparents calling, "Scotty, where are you?" The girl flew off the table in a single convulsion, grabbed her clothes and ran into the pantry. Scott was left sitting there with the proverbial "Puddy-cat grin" with Tweedy Bird's dangling yellow feathers on his lips. He never expected Granny to say "Bad Puddy-cat!" and she didn't. Instead, she said, "I haven't seen you for ages—give your grandma a big kiss." Once again, Scott faced another particular challenge of not being able to move, including running and hiding.

Hands Across America: On Memorial Day 1986, I woke up to the low thumping of a helicopter flying low over the house. I often listened to that sound as a helicopter landed on the hospital roof just two blocks away. The combination of thumping wings and a siren screaming its way to the Miami Valley Hospital emergency room was enough to make me curious about how busy the ER must be on the holiday. I also wondered what fresh tragedies await the unfortunate ones taking those hurried rides there, by air or ambulance.

This was the ordinary start of what I expected to be an ordinary day. The chopper and siren also woke up my son, and I listened to him run down the hall to pounce upon me. That morning, I wasn't ready for it. The night before was another late party and the world moved in slow motion, except for the boy. Josh, at four, was affectionately referred to as the "wild man" of the neighborhood, or in terms of Newtonian physics: "body + velocity = Josh." He reminded me that we would soon be going over to Scott's house to help clean up the party's aftermath.

It wasn't just another riotous shebang in the ghetto. It was "the Appreciation Party"—the biggest blowout the ghetto had seen in some time. Dreadlocks bounced to a live band as people danced around a bonfire. The party spilled out of the bounds of Scott's place, across Stewart Street and into an early morning stupor.

The party was Scott's idea. We threw a party to say thanks to the people who earlier that day stood in a one-mile line of humanity called "Hands Across America." He was the coordinator for the mile designated to Wright State University, a job he volunteered for just three weeks before the event. In that time, Scott organized enough folks to stand hand in hand for a solid mile. How many is that, you wonder? About 1,400 volunteers who sacrificed an afternoon, drove to a remote location, put up with all the traffic, and baked in the sun while standing in the middle of a road for an hour.

I felt particularly proud to be a part of it all—a feeling of belonging to something much bigger than myself. I was Scott's right-hand man, a major to the general in his goodwill army. Thousands of people who shared a common belief in goodwill were getting together, literally taking a stand against hunger and hopelessness in America. If I was the right-hand man at times, then Doug was Scott's left (and we often switched).

Scott, Doug, and I were right there in the thick of it, making it happen rather than just watching it on the news that night. What we did watch on the news that night was how the event disrupted traffic, annoyed people, and allowed the pessimists to say, "I told you it would never happen." They were right that the human chain did not make it all across the country coast to coast unbroken. They were right that hunger did not vanish in America. While all that was true, it didn't make a damn bit of difference to us. We were in the "right here, right now" feeling and creating our own moment in time. It was like magic, and Scott held the wand. Never mind that he was the handsome "big man on campus." People were attracted to his energy and wanted to join whatever he had going on. And he did—the boy had it going on!

That was what the party was about. It wasn't enough for Scott to pull off such a Herculean task in such an impossible time frame. He enjoyed the challenge. He had to say, "thanks for believing and making it happen" in his own way. To Scott, that meant PARTY. After all, it was the University of Dayton ghetto. Two days before the event, Scott, Doug, and I put together a small flyer in the style of a ransom note complete with letters cut from old magazines. The day before the party he convinced several businesses to donate food, drinks, ice, sound systems—all your basic ingredients for a giant beer blast.

Flyers were passed up and down the line that day in the street, and Scott thought a few scores of folks would come, maybe a hundred. We were more than a little surprised when one head count from the roof topped 300 people, ranging from neighborhood street people to local celebrities. Included in the crowd were Dean Fox and his family. Scott meant a lot to Dean Fox as Scott had received the coveted Dean's Award when he graduated two years earlier. That summer, Scott had continued his education as the school's first postdoctoral intern, specializing in helping gifted and troubled children. That was also the summer Scott had made the cover of the *Ohio Psychologist*, the premier publication of the Ohio Psychological Association.

Evening lapsed into morning. The band played everything they knew three times, and the crowd thinned down to just a handful of regulars. I enjoyed watching people come up to Scott, saying their good-byes. That's the beauty of a circle of friends—watching the love being passed around. I listened to Scott say farewell to another friend through his signature wry smile: "John, endings are always bittersweet." Scott noticed me admiring him. He enjoyed that. He didn't know how he floored me sometimes without even realizing it. That night was a perfect example. He gave me a letter when I came to him to say my good-byes. It said:

> STOP: I will always be your best buddy no matter what simple twists of randomness may cut us asunder. I remember what I promised to you about meeting you on the other side should I die first.
>
> LOOK: You don't have to worry about us being too confluent because we disagree about your friends and bioenergetics.
>
> LISTEN: There's hell of a universe next door. Why don't we go?
>
> Your brother, same soul, different body,
>
> Scott.

I was overwhelmed with surprise and with love. This was the first man in my life with whom I ever had an emotional relationship of real significance. I loved my father and brother, but we always kept that safe, shoulder-to-shoulder distance. Knowing we were blood, it was easy to assume they would always be there. Not so with Scott—he was always right out there with it. I didn't have to assume anything because he always let his feelings be known.

I didn't know what to say about the letter. With a buzzing in my head, I put my hand on one wheel of his chair and sat next to him, just smiling. "This is beautiful. I'm glad you remember and I'll be ready to go someday, but not tonight," I said. He laughed and smiled back, "We'll go when you're ready." He looked as tired as I felt, so I decided to stay and help him get to bed. I assisted him get undressed, unstrap his breathing vest from around his chest and get him transferred onto the side of the bed. Another personal attendant, Rob, assisted me with the move from his wheelchair. Scott was all dead weight, unable to support himself in the least. I prepared his feeding of blended bananas and milk, filled the drip bag and inserted the tube through the stoma in his abdomen.

I helped Scott with his urinal while Rob used the suction machine to clear Scott's throat of saliva. We adjusted Scott's body position in the waterbed to allow the least discomfort while permitting the easiest breathing. This was quite important, as he had not been getting a good oxygen exchange lately (he only used his breathing vest while in his wheelchair). With that, I kissed him on the cheek, took his letter and walked two blocks back to my house.

Walking in the dark, I said a prayer appreciating the many and wondrous gifts in my life, the greatest of which were my loved ones. I quietly celebrated another day as Scott's friend. I and others who knew him marveled at what he would accomplish each day. My mind drifted to a young, intellectually gifted but suicidal kid who the rest of the world saw as another black-leathered hood to throw away. Scott saw past all the bravado. The kid saw past all the medical aids—like the breathing vest that allowed Scott to softly talk heart to heart. This kid would have blown off any conventional therapist in the first session. Scott made the kid curious. Who was going to last longer, he or Scott? The two made a connection. Scott helped him find a way out of his trap of perfectionism, find meaning, and stop running away from himself and his family.

Walking home that night, however, I couldn't help but wonder what Scott's life would have been like if only … if only he had stayed in the UC Conservatory of Music and not changed his study to psychology. If only he never had got sick and baffled the medical scientists with his tissue samples. If only he never progressively lost his ability to walk, dress and toilet himself, use his arms, roll over in bed, swallow, and finally, breathe on his own. What if he didn't have the courage to keep going every time he suffered another loss?

As described earlier, God knows he had enough close calls he did not have to think about suicide. But he did. I wondered how he allowed himself the time to find a way to tolerate the intolerable. What if I had agreed to assist him escape his torment and prevent his worst nightmare? "We would not have had one hell of a party tonight" was all I could answer to such heavy questions on such a short walk.

The rest of the morning passed by like the movement of hummingbirds. I had just lain down, and all of a sudden, I was being pounced upon by a four-year-old dynamo. The sound of glass and trash hitting the bottom of the restaurant dumpster came crashing through the window. The scent of horses running the fairground track followed the crash in, and I knew it was going to be a warm day. The low thumping of the chopper wings and screaming of a siren came in on the tails of the horse scents.

I'll Meet You Here: It was time to walk a familiar path to Scott's, down the greasy alley that passed behind Denny's Restaurant. Josh and I navigated around the trash from the party as we neared Scott's place. "This looks like an all-day job," I said to Josh. We walked through Scott's Victorian front door and into the front room of the house, which had been converted into his bedroom. Rob sat in a chair near the bed where Scott was still in bed sleeping. Rob looked a little strange—not asleep but dazed.

"How was your night, Rob?" No answer. "Rob?" I set my hand on his shoulder as he held his head in his hand. "Not good. I can't wake him up," he mumbled.

I suddenly had a feeling I was performing in a play without knowing the plot or my lines. I sat on the bed next to Scott and felt his face with my hand. He was cold to the touch and—his lips were pale blue.

"Does Scott have a temperature, Daddy?" Josh inquired. "No Joshie, he is sicker than that," I replied. "Scott, Scott—can you hear me?" I pulled up his eyelid and found his usually vibrant brown eyes dilated, vacant.

A warm panic flushed through my body. I picked up the phone and dialed for EMTs. The ambulance was there in just a few moments. Josh, Rob, and I stood there and watched the EMT's move Scott from the bed to the stretcher and out the door in what seemed like seconds. Now I was watching the play from a balcony with time distorted. Initially, it moved slowly, but gained momentum until it was speeding by. I felt myself sit on the waterbed. Josh was unusually quiet, like a small animal sensing something was very wrong.

Past moments of Scott nearly dying flew by like a tornado of sounds and images. These close calls from nearly disastrous situations suddenly seemed too common. He always made it through these tests like he knew it was just a rehearsal. At present, those times didn't matter for Scott. His fire was almost out, if not gone completely.

Scott was off to the hospital. The blasting of the siren surprised me, as the ER was only four blocks away. Wait a minute!

"Scott's parents! What am I going to say to Earl and Alyce?" I wondered aloud. I could not imagine being told my son might be dead, then driving three hours to see him. Scott's mother knew something was wrong just from the tone of my first words. It was now her scene to act out in a play she feared would come every day of her life. Her voice became frantic, "Pete, is he alright?" She was like a second mother to me, and I remembered back on the vacations I shared with them, visiting the ocean and carrying Scott into the waves. Cringing at my lie, I responded, "I think he'll be okay, but I would get down here because it is serious."

Leaving for the hospital, I picked up my son and held him a long time until he squirmed away. As we stepped onto the porch, I was struck by the stark contrast between the empty, quiet house and the flood of people and sound the night before. Just another paradox of Scott's life. His limited physicality facilitated living so fully day to day with an appreciation of every simple thing. And how ironic was the isolating effects of such a dreaded disease yet brought so many people together to create their own community—the "Clan of Scott." Come to think of it, perhaps his appreciation party wasn't just for "Hands Across America" but also an appreciation for the helping hands he had across every aspect of his life. Perhaps it was not just irony that this was Memorial Day.

The next day, I collected the mail and slowly walked to my sitting place next to the open window in my second-story bedroom. Looking out over the neighborhood, I desperately wanted to feel normal and thought about the people I loved with whom I could not be. The street below was unusually silent; there was not even any traffic by the fairgrounds.

Opening the mail, I received a card with no return address. It had a picture of the blue glow of the cosmos on the cover. In the middle of the darkness was a small red arrow pointing to the center of a bright cluster of aqua green stars. I immediately thought of a T-shirt Scott used to wear that had a picture of the galaxy and an arrow that said, "You are here."

Inside, there was no signature. The only printed words were, "I'll meet you here."

CHAPTER FIVE

Success Story:

ALEX'S LOVE STORY

Written by Jill Bley

M ost of the readers of this text probably have not (or have not been aware of having) had any personal contact with someone who has lived with, struggled with, and suffered with the knowledge that their assigned gender at birth or culturally assigned sex role does not fit with who they really are. Therefore, we are going to begin this chapter by explaining how the diagnosis is made and the treatment criteria that therapists should follow when treating this problem that has been labeled as gender dysphoria. Then we are going to present the clinical case history of Alex, an individual who identifies as transsexual.

WORLD PROFESSIONAL ASSOCIATION FOR TRANSGENDER HEALTH STANDARDS OF CARE

The World Professional Association for Transgender Health (WPATH) publishes the manual *Standards of Care for the Health of Transsexual, Transgender, and Gender-Nonconforming People* (2012). The original standards of care (SOC) manual was published in 1979 and was dubbed the Benjamin SOC due to the fact that Harry Benjamin is the man who advocated for those standards in order to set guidelines for the treatment of people who have these issues. WPATH states that all who work with and are charged with the care of clients with gender dysphoria understand that, "a disorder is a description of something with which a person might struggle, not a description of the person or the person's identity.

"Thus, transsexual, transgender, and gender-nonconforming individuals are not inherently disordered" (WPATH, 2012). This is a key point that the authors understand and to which all providers need be sensitive. Clients often seek consultation not because of a problem centered within the individual, but rather because of the problem families and society in general have with tolerating and accepting the individual who identifies as transgender, transsexual, or gender nonconforming.

For many years (and, sadly, even today) people with gender dysphoria are misunderstood and often treated horribly by others, including those who should know better and those who represent, and are responsible to protect the rights of all people. Because of the treatment many people struggling with gender dysphoria receive in our culture, they are often reluctant to tell anyone, even their loved ones, what they are going through. Therefore, it is essential that they can trust that they will find helpful, caring, and informed providers when they take the scary plunge into getting therapeutic help.

Finding the help they need is not easy because all health providers are not trained to provide the requisite care, and because it literally takes a "village" to provide the best care. They need knowledgeable professionals; a primary physician, a psychiatrist, a psychologist, a team of surgeons, nurses, and social workers. They also need supportive loved ones and friends.

Criteria for hormone therapy and surgeries as defined by WPATH (2012) are the following:

1. persistent, well-documented gender dysphoria;
2. capacity to make a fully informed decision and to give consent for treatment;
3. age of majority in a given country (if younger, follow the SOC for children and adolescents); and
4. if significant medical or mental concerns are present, they must be reasonably well controlled.

Because we (the first two authors) are clinical psychologists, we will describe the SOC that should be followed by a clinical psychologist when a person struggling with gender dysphoria comes for help. The first step is to conduct a thorough psychological and social assessment. The assessment is used to aid in understanding what the person's diagnosis and needs may be. The following are definitions of the three categories of gender dysphoria taken from the WPATH 2012 manual:

- *Transsexual*: An individual who seeks to change or who has changed their primary and/or secondary sex characteristics through feminizing or masculinizing medical interventions (hormones and/or surgery), typically accompanied by a permanent change in gender role.

- *Transgender*: A person who crosses or transcends culturally defined categories of gender. The gender identity of transgender people differs to varying degrees from the sex they were assigned at birth. (Bockting, 1999)

- *Gender-nonconforming*: An individual whose gender identity, role, or expression differs from what is normative for their assigned sex in a given culture and historical period.

The assessment is also used to determine if there are other psychological or emotional problems that need to be addressed, such as depression and/or anxiety.

The next step is to develop a treatment plan based on the results of the assessment and to begin the treatment. If the assessment indicates that the person is suffering from concomitant problems, that is, problems that have a high probability of resolving themselves as the person is transitioning, it may not be necessary to address those issues immediately. However, if the problem is related to something as debilitating as post-traumatic stress disorder (PTSD) maybe, then it will be necessary to treat the PTSD first. PTSD is not uncommon among this population for a number of reasons.

The two most likely reasons have to do with childhood abuse that could have been perpetrated against the child and/or adolescent because the people in their family and/or society could not cope with allowing the person to be "different." The second most likely reason is because of the desire (in males, primarily) to "prove" their masculinity to self and others by involving themselves in very dangerous occupations or sports.

Another common problem that the assessment may identify is addiction. Because of the lifelong struggle to come to terms with their gender dysphoria and/or because of the abuse they have had, many have tried to cope through the addictive use of alcohol, drugs, or sex. Therefore, the therapist must be skilled in treating addictions or able to make a referral to a therapist who does have those skills.

If individuals identify as transgender or gender nonconforming, they have probably already been presenting publicly in a variety of ways. Perhaps by cross-dressing, participating in drag shows, binding breasts or penis, enhancing breasts, enhancing buttocks, ridding the body of hair, and so on. The therapist should help the person identify and deal with any behaviors that may be risky, such as anonymous sex and sexual encounters where safe-sex practices are not used.

If the person is transsexual, the treatment is more complex. To begin the process of transitioning toward genital surgery, hormone therapy must begin (unless hormones are not clinically indicated for the individual; WPATH 2012) and, if the person has not already done so, that individual needs to acquire a wardrobe and begin presenting to their world as the gender they wish to be. There are a number of changes to the body that occur when hormone therapy begins, and the person needs to be prepared for the changes. They may want to have electrolysis treatments, breast enhancement (after a minimum of 12 months of hormone therapy so that breast growth has been maximized), or mastectomy that may include the creation of a male chest, shaving of the Adam's apple, and perhaps some facial surgery. The person needs to be fully informed of the medical risks of both feminizing and masculinizing hormone therapies. Therapists should explore with the person issues related to fertility and sexual functioning before the hormone therapy begins and encourage the person to discuss these issues with their intimate partner.

To proceed to the genital surgery the person must be able to provide the surgeon with two referrals from two health care providers. Usually one letter must come from a medical provider and the other from a mental health provider. The reason these letters are required is because up to this point the transition is reversible. One can quit taking the hormones and return to life as it was. Surgeries that remove the gonads and that reconstruct the genitals are not reversible.

If the patient is only going to have surgery to remove the uterus, ovaries, or the testicles, the four criteria listed above must be met along with the following:

- 12 continuous months of hormone therapy as appropriate to the patient's gender goals (unless hormones are not clinically indicated for the individual).

If the person is going to have genital reconstruction surgery, the first five criteria must be met along with the following:

- 12 continuous months of living in a gender role that is congruent with their gender identity.

Although it is not an explicit criterion, most recommend that the patient has scheduled regular visits with a mental health or other medical professional. Of course, the information that has been presented here is only an overview of the treatment process for gender dysphoria. There is much more that providers must know to provide quality, professional, and ethical services for this population.

Now we are going to tell you the story of one case of gender dysphoria treated by the second author of this text. The names and identifying personal information have been changed or altered to protect the privacy of this remarkable person's journey. Her story is told in this book with her permission and with the use of pronouns being reviewed and approved as well.

ALEX: A NAVY SEAL WHO STRUGGLED WITH GENDER DYSPHORIA

When Alex came to my office for the first appointment, he was rather shy. However, as our conversation progressed he began to relax and was able to provide whatever information was asked of him. He was clear that he was very determined and confident about the process that lay ahead of him. He stated, "I want surgery to feel complete. I wore the macho mask for years. I have never dressed as a woman but I do wear a bra for support. I don't know how I will handle some aspects of this, such as my business. I realize this will be a long and difficult road ahead of me, but I want to do it!"

His determination was contagious. From that initial encounter until the end of the time that we met, I knew that he would make the journey to transition and would thrive afterward. He had already told me how many friends he had who were supporting him. In fact, two of those friends did the research to help him find the physician he had seen, who referred him to me for the psychological part of his treatment journey. He had a very kind, gentle, warm, and welcoming aura. Miraculously, he had a wife who was very supportive of his transition. That didn't happen overnight, but his patience and kindness and strong need for the change won her over to the point that she even helped him get a wardrobe during the transitioning.

Developmental History and Evaluation of Alex

Alex was referred by his psychiatrist for a psychological evaluation and psychotherapy. At intake he said that he wanted treatment because he was told that to have a sex change operation he had to see a psychiatrist and a psychologist to "make sure I wasn't crazy." He had already contacted three facilities that provide the genital reconstructive surgery (GRS) and knew what was going to be expected of him. He stated that he was married and that his wife knew about his desire to be a woman and that she was supportive of him doing so. He said that he married a girl he dated in high school. "I tried the gay routine in high school but that wasn't me. I had sex with several women while picturing myself as a woman." He and his wife had never had sex because neither one of them really wanted to. However, they were very affectionate toward one another.

He said that his mother was also aware of his intentions and that she was supportive. He had not told his father and had asked his mother not to tell him yet because he was sure that his father would be angry and verbally abusive toward him if he knew. His father had been verbally and physically abusive toward him during most of his childhood, but not toward his five siblings. His father ridiculed his "sissy" behavior and tried to "make a man" out of him by severely beating him for even small transgressions. He said that he was locked in closets many times by his father. His mother had no authority in the home and appeared helpless to protect him. On occasion he was able to stay with his grandparents who were "extremely good to me." He also reported that he was raped by a female babysitter.

His greatest solace during his childhood was to withdraw into music that he loved to listen to and to play. He said that he could play just about any instrument without taking lessons, just by listening to someone else play.

During the treatment he revealed that from a very young age, probably as early as three or four, he had felt that he was more like his sisters than his brothers. He wanted to play with his sisters, get the same kinds of toys for holiday gifts, and desperately wanted to wear dresses. His first memory of a severe beating from his father was at about age four when his father found him wearing his sister's clothes. He recalled many times during preadolescence daydreaming about being a girl and drawing pictures of himself in girls' clothing. He was terrified of his father's anger about his desire to wear girls' clothes, so he contented himself to make drawings and hide the drawings.

By adolescence he had endured so much pain and humiliation about his "girly" behaviors that he determined to make himself into the strong male that his father, siblings, and friends seemed to need him to be. So he decided to join the military as soon as he was old enough because he kept hearing how the military could make you a man. At age 17 he enlisted in the navy and trained as a Navy Seal. He said that he became a "skilled warrior" and served his country well in Vietnam. Alex was often part of a team that went into enemy territory, sometimes to assassinate a target and other times on rescue missions. He received many honors for his valor. However, his military experiences caused him to have a serious emotional breakdown that required a brief hospitalization.

After the military, he married a woman with whom he had a friendship since he was in the fourth grade. He got a job as a police officer in a small town. He stated that he was a good "peace officer" but realized that his efforts to make everyone believe that he had finally become a man were making him more and more depressed and withdrawn. He quit his job and opened a small business making and selling musical instruments in a large city. He decided that he needed to be in a community where he might find support for and more acceptance of his desire to be a female.

He confided his concerns to some very close friends. They were understanding and empathic. He was amazed that someone understood him. He found a psychiatrist who was willing and able to treat his depression but was not knowledgeable about the treatment of his gender issues. She referred him for the psychological evaluation and treatment. His description of his history indicated a diagnosis of gender dysphoria, transsexual type who was sexually attracted to females. In fact, he stated that he thought that he was probably a lesbian and that "will work well for me and my wife, if she is a lesbian too." He thought that she might have those tendencies but had never "had the nerve to ask her."

The psychological testing indicated that he had no serious pathology; that he was depressed and anxious; that he had a mild to moderate level of post-traumatic stress disorder (PTSD) and that he had many preferences that are typically viewed as feminine. He agreed to work in the therapy to resolve his childhood abuse issues and the traumatic aftermath of his Navy Seal experiences, which included having to kill people, including a woman, during a clandestine attack to rescue some prisoners.

Treatment

During this phase of the treatment he disclosed how killing people had made him feel intense guilt and shame. He worried during that time that he was becoming like his father. He tried to console himself by reminding himself that he was following orders and had chosen to be a part of the military, therefore, he was only doing his duty. He disclosed that after discharge he experienced terrifying, violent nightmares in which he was carrying out a military mission and everyone on the Seal team, including himself, began to scream and yell and kill anyone they saw. All of their faces looked exactly like his father's face, and then he would see his reflection in a puddle, or a mirror, or a pond (depending on the dream) and see that he too looked like his father. He would wake screaming and sobbing and needing his wife to hold and comfort him so that he could become calm.

After consultation with his psychiatrist and his physician, during which a collaborative treatment plan was developed, the treatment began. The first focus of the treatment was on resolving the childhood abuse issues. He was very motivated. He was willing to have two treatment sessions per week. Eye movement desensitization reprocessing (EMDR—this treatment technique is described in Chapter 16) was the primary mode of treatment. He eventually was not only able to talk about his childhood without crying or feeling a lot of anger but was eager to go to his childhood home and tell his father his plans to become a woman.

The confrontation with his father went much better than he expected. He also reported that his siblings were somewhat okay with it too because his mother had talked with each one and asked them to support him. After resolving those family concerns, he was ready to work on the Navy Seal traumas. That work was a little more difficult for him to deal with than the childhood traumas because he felt much grief and sorrow that his attempts to be a "man" led him to kill people (this is a type of PTSD that has been called "moral stress syndrome").

The client's wife attended some of the therapy sessions. She was a very quiet, withdrawn woman, who rarely made eye contact. She was very attached to her spouse and was supportive and encouraging toward him. She stated that she was eager to help him have the surgery he wanted because she knew he would be happier as a woman. She admitted that she had fears about the changes he was making, but she felt confident that the relationship could accommodate to the changes and survive.

The only issues that she had with her spouse were that he didn't do as much around the house as she wanted him to do and that she would like to work part-time. She felt that he did not make enough money since he started his new business, and much of what was earned was being saved to pay for his surgery. They both felt that the money issue would improve as soon as they saved enough for the surgery.

At this point in the treatment I wrote a letter to the client's physician recommending him to begin hormone treatment. He was started on estrogen and an antiandrogenic medication. He also sought out and underwent electrolysis to remove facial hair and cosmetic surgeries to enhance his breasts and remove fatty tissue. As soon as the breast enhancement surgery was completed, he began to dress as a woman publicly. The client emerged as a rather attractive middle-aged woman. Her spouse was complimentary of her and stated that she was a little jealous of her good looks. They used most of their therapy time talking about and figuring out how to deal with the reactions of their friends, families, and neighbors to the gender change.

After about eight months living as a woman, the client selected a surgical facility and made plans to have the complete gender reassignment surgery. Those of us on the treatment team (her psychiatrist, her physician, and I) all wrote letters of recommendation to the surgeon and mental health professional at the surgery facility. Five months after first applying for the surgery she was admitted to the facility and the surgery was performed. The surgery and the recovery period went well. The client and her spouse remained in treatment for six months postsurgery. The general theme of the therapy during those final months was to help the couple adjust to their new relationship. The client's spouse expressed that she was finding herself to be more and more sexually attracted to her partner. At the final session they were experimenting with sexual touching. They were both enjoying it and feeling that the surgery had helped both of them learn to express their lesbian feelings.

Ten years after the treatment was completed, I telephoned Alex. She stated that she was still doing well as far as the gender issues were concerned. However, she was grieving the loss of her wife, who had died the previous summer of cancer and didn't feel that she could talk about it at that time. Later she wrote this to me:

> "I will tell you that my wife and I had a GREAT (sic) life together. We were as one. We loved each other so very much. We hugged and kissed every day and told each other, 'love you.' We never liked being apart even for one day. We were together since 4th grade.
>
> "Our great love and life never changed through the years. We always worked together and helped each other on everything. Our lives were always a success. My business was always good, and she retired from teaching after 30 years. Through sickness and health we were always as one. I held her hand and hugged her until the end, telling her I loved her.
>
> "Dr. B. that is about all I can say. What the future holds is unknown for now. I will work in my shop and keep working at our county airport, where I have been an administrator for many years, and see what happens.
>
> "My wife was a great quilter, and very popular, so I set up a large Memorial Quilt Library in her name at our county airport where her quilt club and friends meet. Hope this little information helps you. I just don't feel like talking right now. ... I miss her."

I was so touched by her love story. How tender, sweet, and rare is that!

Case Discussion

Of course, this case is not the usual way in which these cases unfold. I choose to tell about this client because it was a case that illustrates a motivated, relatively mentally healthy individual who was willing to accept and follow a treatment plan that conforms with the SOC as outlined by the Harry Benjamin International Gender Dysphoria Association and WPATH. Another element of this case that made it a therapist's dream case was that she had a partner who was not only supportive, but who also benefited from the gender change. Plus, they were a couple who truly, dearly loved one another.

My experience is that many of the people who present with a desire to change their gender have been so frustrated by the lack of knowledge, understanding, and acceptance of their issues that they do not want to follow a treatment plan. They may perceive the plan as just another obstacle to getting what they so desperately need. Many others are very ambivalent about what they want to do because of their fears (real and imagined) of what will happen to them in their marriages, their jobs, their extended families, and their communities when people find out about their "secret."

With these cases the first task of therapy is to confront and deal with these issues. The person who is eager to "get it done" has to be able to see the value in taking the time necessary to ensure long-term emotional and psychological health before they have the surgery. The person who is ambivalent because of the perceived repercussions the gender change would have on their life needs to work to resolve those fears by considering all of the options and the consequences of those options.

Multiple forces converge on the therapist who is presented with the challenge and opportunity of working with a client who identifies as lesbian, gay, bisexual, or transgender and who is seeking help with a sexual health concern. Those forces include attitudes, knowledge, and values as they relate to sexual expression, gender expression, relationships, and social context (Haffey, Peterson, Bley, & Glaus, 2007; Yarber & Sayad, 2019).

Standards of ethical practice require knowledge and understanding of the particular issues that impact the lives of the LGBTQA (Lesbian, Gay, Bisexual, Transgender, Queer, Asexual) community (APA, 2015). Many issues addressed in sex therapy remain the same regardless of the orientation or gender identity of the client. However, there are some differences that exist including frequency of certain diagnoses, sexual identity issues, variety of sexual practices (Nichols, 2000), and the effects of oppression on sexual identity. As a caveat, the danger with considering the differences between sex therapy with heterosexual clients and sex therapy with LGBTQA clients is that it may implicitly communicate that heterosexual sexuality is normative and other forms of sexual and gender expression must be understood in relation to heterosexuality.

In contrast to this notion, this book attempts to elucidate those issues that are specific to LGBTQA persons with the assumption that the reader simply may be less familiar with them, not with the assumption that they are defined by points of departure from some heterosexual norm.

REFERENCES

American Psychological Association (APA). (2015). Guidelines for psychological practice with transgender and gender non-conforming people. *American Psychologist, 70*, 832–864.

Bockting, W.O. (1999). From construction to context: Gender through the eyes of the transgendered. *Siecus Report, 28*(1), 3–7.

Haffey, B., Peterson, F., Bley, J., & Glaus, K. (2007). Addressing sexual health concerns of sexual minority clients. Found in L. VanderCreek, F. Peterson, & J. Bley (Eds.), *Innovations in clinical practice: Focus on sexual health*. Sarasota, FL: Professional Resource Press.

Nichols, M. (2000). Therapy with sexual minorities. In S. Leiblum & R. Rosen (Eds.), *The principles and practice of sex therapy* (3rd ed., pp. 335–367). New York: Guilford.

WPATH. (2012). *Standards of care for the health of transsexual, transgender, and gender-nonconforming people* (7th ed.). Retrieved from www.wpath.org

Yarber, W., & Sayad, B. (2019). *Human sexuality: Diversity in contemporary society* (10th ed.). New York: McGraw-Hill.

LET'S EXPLORE YOUR SEXUAL MIND

This section of the book is all about the amazing and little-known early history of sex in America that includes the prescientific understanding of sexuality in the 19th century and the eventual percolation of a new sexual science that developed throughout the 20th century. This new sexual science has been slowly replacing the ignorance, fears, and stereotypes that comprise our sexophrenic heritage in this country. Chapter 6 explores much of this fascinating and crazy history (one you never read about in school). It is important to understand this history to be less vulnerable to the residual cultural influences that affect all of our personal sexual health to one degree or another. Chapter 7 describes the "Great Transition" during the 20th century from the majority of Americans holding religion as the ultimate authority to science being the basis of most decisions, including sexual choices. Between these two chapters that focus on the American history of sex and the cultural shifts that occurred is a historical interlude in the form of a timeline entitled "The Century of the Woman (Significant Events in the American Experiment in Democracy and the Cultural Shift from 19th-Century Sexosophy to 20th-Century Sexology)."

After two chapters of describing our sex-negative and sexophrenic history (Chapters 6 and 7), Chapter 8 details the growing body of literature that documents health benefits of sexual expression. Two chapters finish out Section II with personal success stories to illustrate examples of real people finding their way around significant obstacles to find sexual health and peace of mind. Chapter 9 is about a young beautiful Latinx couple who want to have children but find themselves in a seven-year unconsummated marriage (Latinx is a gender-neutral alternative term for the traditional use of Latina or Latino). Chapter 10 concludes Section II with a remarkable story of old-school gender transformation that might help you understand the secret hypermasculine background of the friendly old lady who may be sitting next to you in church some Sunday.

CHAPTER SIX

Our Early Sexual Heritage in America

Written by Frederick Peterson

INTRODUCTION

Looking back into history is not everybody's favorite pastime, but many people enjoy learning from our collective past. Until recently, American history was primarily written about old white guys—presidents, generals, and captains of industry (that's why they call it "his-story"). American history was recorded with considerable exclusion of women, people of color, and sexual minorities as if they did not make contributions of note. A popular quote about history is from Voltaire, who said the stories of history are the lies the living tell of the dead. But the content that is covered in this chapter is not your father's history lesson. It highlights some of what those forefathers thought was the "science and medi-cine" of the time related to sex; notions and beliefs that may seem absolutely crazy to us today. For example, an adolescent boy's wet dreams were medicalized as a disease called spermatoclemma, an involuntary emission of semen (Robinson, 1934).

Therefore, this chapter and the next are comprised of the abridged highlights of "Sex in America" over the 19th and 20th centuries, with a focus on the beginning (and advance-ments) in sexual science as well as notable events reflecting democratic progress toward greater sexual health as a nation during the period of 1900 to 2000. Between this chapter and the next, there is a timeline to emphasize this progress entitled, "The Century of the Woman (Significant Events in the American Experiment in Democracy and the Cultural Shift from 19th-Century Sexosophy to 20th-Century Sexology)." But before the main focus on the history of sex starts up, let's widen the lens and back up for a bird's-eye view of some BIG history of *Homo sapiens*. This is important background that has a lot to do with how our sexual culture developed over time, a background story even the history teachers weren't taught.

In a well-researched and entertaining book entitled *Sex at Dawn* (2010), psychologist Christopher Ryan and physician Cacilda Jetha lay out a cogent model of sexuality as being a basic struggle between our body's evolutionary biology and today's cultural expectations of restricted sexual behavior. The authors describe the "standard narrative" of our species' past development being characterized as "either monogamous (M-F) or polygyny (M-FF+) with the conclusion normally being that women prefer the former configuration while most men would opt for the latter." Instead, Ryan and Jetha present a significant amount of anthropological evidence that strongly supports a model of "multiple mating" within hunter-gatherer societies. Before the rise of agriculture, everything was expected to be *shared,* including sex (anthropologists call this practice *fierce egalitarianism* where sharing resources was not just expected but mandatory). Hence, small intimate bands would have adults typically engaged in several sexual relationships at the same time; allowing women to have the protection and shared resources of not one male but several who believe they could be the father of any given child in the group.

This all changed with the advent of farming and large-scale agriculture. *Encyclopaedia Britannica* (2018) describes *anatomically modern humans* evolving into their current form some 200,000 years ago, yet they did not begin to engage in agriculture until about 15,000–10,000 years ago. Therefore, the amount of time we have spent in settled agricultural societies is small in comparison with preagricultural development when women played a more egalitarian role in community life. Said differently, humans have evolved our biological nature as hunter-gatherers much longer than we have lived in societies organized by agriculture.

During this great changeover, Ryan and Jetha assert that "the biggest loser (aside from slaves, perhaps) in the agricultural revolution was the human female, who went from occupying a central, respected role in foraging societies to becoming another possession for a man to earn and defend, along with his house, slaves, and livestock (Ryan & Jetha, 2010). The authors also quote Tim Taylor, who wrote *The Prehistory of Sex*: "While hunter-gatherer sex had been modeled on the idea of sharing and complementarity, early agriculturalist sex was voyeuristic, repressive, homophobic, and focused on reproduction" (Taylor, 1996). The repression of sex was limiting to men and women in terms of the development of cultural expectations for heterosexuality but much more severely repressive to women.

William "Will" Durant is considered one of America's most important historians and philosophers, winning a Pulitzer Prize for his work. He is best known for *The Story of Civilization* (an 11-volume series) that was co-written with his wife Ariel Durant and published between 1935 and 1975 (Durant & Durant, 1935–1975). In a collection of his papers called *Heroes of History* (2001), Durant also reminds us that humans have a very long history as a species dating back more than 1 million years of evolution, and he estimates that we only developed agriculture a mere 10,000 years ago. Hence, Durant estimates that humans have lived 25 times longer as hunters than as farmers and our nature has been primarily shaped by this experience. Durant asserts that "inquisitiveness, pugnacity, and ready sexuality" were virtues of survival and comprise the chief nature of humans (Durant, 2001). This is not too surprising that a description of human nature is considered similar to our closest primate cousins. Biologically, we are often compared with the great apes, which is completely incorrect. Actually, we *are* great apes! The great ape family is made of a taxonomic family of primates, including four extant genera: chimpanzees and bonobos (*Pan*), gorillas (*Gorilla*), humans (*Homo*), and orangutans (*Pongo*) (Last, 2013).

So now that the evolutionary biologists have taken notice, let's give the scholars from women and gender studies something to celebrate. Durant goes on to assert that "women are the womb and mainstream of the human race who developed agriculture" while men were out hunting and fighting wars. He described agriculture as the "soil of civilization that promotes cultural creativity. After they developed agriculture, women domesticated the sheep, dog, ass, and pig. The last animal she domesticated was man, but only partially and reluctantly civilized him" (Durant, 2001). Many would agree with Durant that women failed her best efforts to civilize men. With the advent of private property within the rise of agriculture and capitalistic economies, men's perceived need to possess women dramatically increased to "ensure" paternity and inheritances. Men's fears of women's superiority led to a widespread transcultural pattern of subjugation of women historically. That is the BIG history synopsis that provides the backdrop for our "little" history of sex in 20th-century America.

So, back to the history of sex as the antecedent of our contemporary American culture. This brief review begins with a few important developments in Europe that strongly influenced the beginning of American sexual culture. We then focus on how this new societal experiment (called the United States) developed conventions and rules of sex that supported the expansion and domination of society by males of European descent. These rules of sex became codified into social norms through the major institutions of society: law, religion, medicine, education, and public opinion. Before going on to that, another little history lesson is needed that they never taught you in school.

WHY LOOK DEEPER INTO THE HISTORY OF SEX IN AMERICA?

To really appreciate the advances of the "new sexual health" over the past 50 years, we must first take stock of our sexual heritage and its influences on contemporary views of sexuality. Our collective sexual past in America has direct and indirect bearings on our ability to achieve greater degrees of sexual health in 21st-century America.

The perpetuation of sexual myths from the past is a significant barrier to sexual health. Sexual misinformation and myths interfere with real understanding of sexuality, which can adversely affect perceptions of oneself and others. These sexual myths also increase the risk for disease transmission and sexual violence. As depicted in the movie *Kinsey* (Mutrux & Condon, 2004), a young couple once consulted the famous sex professor regarding the young woman's difficulty achieving "satisfaction." Because it was apparent that the young lady could not achieve orgasm by intercourse (which was considered abnormal then), Kinsey suggested that the young man experiment with "oral caressing" his young mate. This suggestion was aggressively rebuffed because of their belief that oral sex caused cancer!

The great Dr. Kinsey tried not to laugh and told the young couple that there was no way oral sex caused cancer. Surprisingly, the newlyweds resisted his counsel by asking the pioneer sex researcher if he had any scientific studies to prove that cancer was not caused by oral sex. Not only was Kinsey shocked by their firm belief in this sexual myth but also by their vigorous defense of it in response to his casually dismissing the idea as nonsense. He was also embarrassed to confess that there were no studies disproving a causal relationship between oral sex and cancer. This experience was part of the young Kinsey's inspiration to launch his obsessive-compulsive search for the truth about the sexual practices of Americans.

That story took place in Bloomington, Indiana, in the 1930s (Brecher, 1979). Fast-forward 80 years and 180 miles east to Yellow Springs, Ohio. After watching the movie *Kinsey*, a beautiful young woman in her 30s shared with me that when she was a girl (in the 1980s), she used to worry about her getting cancer from masturbation! She swears that no one ever talked to her about masturbation and that no one ever suggested that masturbation could or would cause cancer before she had this notion. However, she definitely remembers worrying she might come down with it. Fortunately for her, she had the ovaries to keep at it and decided that if God was going to give her cancer for masturbating, it was probably worth it. These little stories are included here to emphasize the power of sexual mythology and our sexophrenic cultural history, starting with our early American notions of good health and still persisting in residual sexual stereotypes (Peterson, 1999).

THE GOOD HEALTH DOCTRINE

The Good Health Doctrine developed from a long historical line of beliefs regarding what caused physical illness and mental disturbances. Going back to Egyptian medicine and the Greeks, the notion of humors in good balance was believed to be the source of good health. The belief was that four body fluids (black bile, yellow bile, phlegm, and blood) needed to be in balance and that any excess or deficiency would cause illness. This belief system, referred to at times as humorism, dominated the ancient and medieval worlds for 2000 years until the advent of modern medicine and germ theory in the late 1800s (Good, 1994; Oshinsky, 2016).

Infections have been the leading cause of death throughout history from the Black Death pandemic to the Great Influenza; the latter killed 20 to 50 million worldwide in 1918–1919 (Noymer & Garenne, 2000). Not until the discovery of germs and their role in transmission of disease did we really understand how infections spread. Before that was Miasma Theory, which blamed illness on chemical agents from decaying matter such as corpses, rotting vegetation in swamps, and sewer gases (Oshinsky, 2016). The gases given off from this natural decay was thought to collect in dangerous airborne clouds that people inhaled and became ill.

As late as 1888, leading specialists in childhood diseases insisted that diphtheria (a deadly bacterial infection) resulted from inhaling damp gases that arose from city sewers. This is why a common 19th-century "treatment" for illness was "taking a holiday at the seashore" for the fresh air and relaxation. Because we didn't know any better at the time, the Good Health Doctrine developed (the name was coined by sexologist John Money) and dictated that good health was a result of healthy food, exercise, rest with plenty of fresh air, and good sex (meaning only occasional missionary position intercourse strictly for the purpose of baby-making). Any other type of sexual behavior became pathologized, as our in-depth discussion of the history of masturbation will illuminate later in this chapter (Money, 1985; Money, 1986). However, there is a close relationship between how mental health was conceptualized and many nonreproductive sexual behaviors that were seen as undesirable by current morals and conventions of the time. These little stories are included here to emphasize the power of sexual mythology and our sexophrenic cultural history, starting with our early American notions of good health.

Specific to the history of how mental illness was conceptualized, the Babylonians believed possession by demons was the cause whereas ancient Hebrew cultures regarded mental illness as a punishment for sin. Greek philosophers saw mental illness arising from disordered thought process. When early Christianity became established in the fourth century, mental illness was once again blamed on evil spirits. That's why the early Christian Church routinely employed torture and execution as "treatment" for mental illness for more than 300 years (Money, 1998). Many contemporary Christians still hold the belief of demon possession.

Throughout the majority of American history, any sexual behavior other than heterosexual intercourse (within the context of marriage) has been described as unnatural, sinful, selfish, immoral, unhealthy, or a sign of insanity and disease (Money, 1998). In short, the perpetuation of sexual myths not only serves as an obstacle to an individual achieving sexual health but serves many functions. But *what purposes do sexual myths serve?* To answer this question, let's take a brief and deeper look at the persistent sexual myths surrounding the hot topics of the period, especially solo sex (masturbation).

One of the most common myths is that sex is for young people. Consequently, many people believe that you have to be not only young but also beautiful to be attractive to others and sexually happy. Some people reach a certain age and stop being sexually active, not because they don't have sexual feelings and thoughts but because they think something is wrong with being sexual at their age. Youth is a time seen for *sowing one's wild oats* and, in a sense, being reckless. The sexual myth that sex is for the young promotes sexual activity of youth and condemns sexual activity of older folks. The result is more babies.

This particular sexual myth is derived from the primary directive of most world religions, to "go forth, be fruitful, and multiply" (Bley & Peterson, 2007), which is clearly a prescription for procreational sex. The myth that sex is for the young serves the purpose of baby-making. Over the millennia, most (but far from all) societies upheld the primary directive by creating traditions and incentives supporting procreational sex (China is a notable exception). In addition, most (but far from all) instituted significant social sanctions against all other forms of non-procreational sexual expression.

Think about it. Say you were in charge of forming a new society on a new continent 400 years ago. This society was to be built on a new resource-rich continent inhabited by indigenous people but previously unsettled by your culture. If your ultimate goal was to populate this continent, you would have to raise an army, eliminate (or at least dominate) the indigenous people by creating a powerful vision (manifest destiny), and have plenty of labor to exploit in order to expand commerce and manufacturing. How would you do it?

One way (arguably not the best way) would be to do what was done throughout American history: enslave foreign people and import them for generations of servitude, exploit ethnic immigrants into lives of desperate survivorship, and impose strict sexual codes as to what is healthy, what is not, and who can be free to have babies. Your goal would be accomplished by making all non-procreative sexual variations a crime, a sin, and a medical condition. People who did not make babies and were found to be using other forms of sexual expression (than penile-vaginal intercourse) could be put in jail, condemned from the pulpit, or put in an asylum (or otherwise treated for their pathology).

You would also want to create tax incentives to encourage people to get married and have babies. The more babies, the more dependents to claim. Married head of household is more of a deduction than being single. You would want to prevent women from having the right to vote because they might influence the political body that controls their bodies. That is to say, women's voices were unheard with congressional voting calls until just a few decades ago and the overwhelmingly male political body still tries to control women's bodies (legislatively). You would want to outlaw birth control (as it was until nearly 70 years ago). You would want to prevent public sexual education that would allow people to understand how to prevent pregnancies and consider alternative forms of sexual expression (as it was until nearly 50 years ago). You would want to keep gay men and lesbians in the closet and especially in heterosexual marriages where they could occasionally contribute to baby-making (as it was until nearly 40 years ago). You would also want to outlaw abortions (as it was until nearly 40 years ago).

Certainly, intelligent and reasonable people can disagree with this assessment. However, there is overwhelming evidence that society has historically encouraged family formation and baby-making through the tools of societal institutions (tax laws, sodomy laws, medicine, etc.). One could certainly argue that alternative reasons explain why abortion was declared illegal by the government. One could argue that alternative reasons explain why homosexuality was declared illegal and a mental illness by our government. One could argue that masturbation is wrong, is disgusting, and/or promotes illness and moral degeneration. People could argue all these points and be right, but the correctness of their positions would be based on personal values and/or religious beliefs (not science). Let's examine that last one (solo sex) a bit closer.

Perhaps one of the most fascinating examples of society attempting to control sexuality in our American heritage is the case of masturbation, also known at various times in this country as self-abuse, self-vice, self-pollution, and onanism. The last term refers to the Old Testament character Onan, whose story is found in Genesis 38:7−9 and represents the world's first written record of a birth control method called coitus interruptus, or known today as the withdrawal method. This solo-sexual expression has been considered a sin, a crime, and medical disorder for most of American history. As you will see, this historical perspective has changed only recently due to the past 70 years of sexual science. The sexual heritage of the traditional majority culture in America is historically based on the Anglo-Puritan values of Christians (of a Calvinist persuasion) who were so sex sensitive, they covered the legs of furniture with cloth skirts for propriety's sake. However, the early colonial Puritans were not exactly sex-negative as they promoted sex within marriage for reproductive purposes (the primary directive). They were known for being uncompromising and unforgiving of sin, with strict punishments (Beaver, 2015)−especially if a person was believed to be under the influence of the devil.

During the 18th and 19th centuries, the American scientific community (as it was) was heavily influenced by Puritan beliefs and the Good Health Doctrine, as previously mentioned. Heralding back to humoristic notions, excessive loss of semen (through any means but especially masturbation) was a basis for men developing sexual neurasthenia (Money, 1985; Schultz & Schultz, 2008). Even today, the fear of loss of semen and belief in it resulting in a "weakening of the body" is thought to be one reason coaches sometimes advise their athletes not to have sex the night before the big game.

The Good Health Doctrine was present in colonial America with the European settlers and reached its greatest influence from the late 19th century to early 20th century (especially 1880s to

1930s). It was so influential in medicine that even sexual restraint from marital procreational sex was advised as a caution from excessive seminal loss and general overexcitement of the nervous system. Although its heyday was the 19th century, the Good Health Doctrine is still alive and well in many places around the world. When it comes to recreational sex for pleasure and not babies, there is no topic better at flying in the face of the Good Health Doctrine as masturbation.

Before examining the history of masturbation as disease (MAD), one other significant exception to the primary directive of having babies demands attention: the American eugenics movement during the 19th and 20th centuries. This story is well-detailed in a book by Adam Cohen called *Imbeciles: The Supreme Court, American Eugenics, and the Sterilization of Carrie Buck* (Cohen, 2016). The eugenics movement is noted here as another of our dark and cruel practices within the history of sex in America. The origins of eugenics are associated with Francis Galton of England (cousin to Charles Darwin) and dedicated to the promotion of human breeding to produce a highly gifted race of people, partly through a focus on the elimination of "undesirable traits" in the human gene pool. Of course, medicine believed many of these "undesirable traits" were possessed by people who were affected by the practices of onanism (masturbation). "Good well-to-do WASP families" who supported eugenics feared the pollution of the American gene pool by the hordes of immigrants via the reproduction of parents of "inferior stock," which would result in the proliferation of a mental condition eugenic proponents referred to as imbecility. This belief in racial superiority and fear of contamination of the gene pool led to nearly 30 states passing legislation supporting forced sterilization of people displaying "undesirable traits"; most often people who were poor, of color, and/or without education. State-supported sterilization programs were sanctioned in 1927 by the U.S. Supreme Court in *Buck v. Bell* (Cohen, 2016). A few years later, Adolf Hitler in Germany proudly bragged about following the laws of several American states and using the models of American sterilization programs for the prevention of reproduction of the "unfit" (Black, 2003). When the atrocities of the Holocaust became known to the American public, support for the eugenics movement declined and laws slowly changed over several decades to protect reproductive rights. The legacy of these eugenic views is still very much alive in the United States today in various neo-Nazi and white supremist groups.

THE MAD HISTORY OF THE LIFE AND DEATH OF MASTURBATION AS DISEASE

The following brief history of "masturbation as disease" (MAD) will illustrate the origins of myths currently surrounding the subject of masturbation and outlines how our sexual heritage has transitioned since Americans used to view masturbation as a disease. This section of the chapter borrows heavily from a presentation a colleague and I made at the 50th-anniversary annual meeting of the Society for the Scientific Study of Sexuality (SSSS). Dr. Sarah Wright is a clinical psychologist and Coordinator of Human Sexuality Services at the University of South Carolina. She and I co-authored a paper that was presented at that meeting, and what follows are excerpts (Wright & Peterson, 2007).

As mentioned, MAD has been given many names but most often called "onanism," "self-abuse," "self-pollution," and "self-vice" in the medical literature of the day (Robinson, 1934; Gould, 1949). Even a dictionary of sexual terms from the 1980s makes reference to onanism to mean masturbation (Schmidt, 1984). The fact is that until about 70 years ago, masturbation was considered a disease requiring medical treatment in this country. Where did this concept come from? It has deep roots in the ancient notions of the "humors" and the adverse effects of the loss of fluids (going back to the Greek physicians Hippocrates and Galen). However, the more modern major influence of the rise of MAD is credited to Samuel Tissot, a Swiss physician whose writing strongly influenced the "Father of American Medicine," Benjamin Rush.

Tissot became famous in the late 17th century for his assertions that excessive sexual activity ("sexual incontinence"), especially in the form of masturbation, would actually result in physical and mental disability. In 1758, Tissot published "Onania, or a Treatise upon the Disorders Produced by Masturbation." The physical ailments were said to be caused by the loss of semen, and included such problems as loss of eyesight, digestive difficulties, and impotence. Mental problems caused by masturbation were said to include constant fatigue, depression (melancholy), imbecility, loss of sensation, and even insanity. All these worries about masturbation may have gone relatively unnoticed in the New World, accept that Tissot's ideas had significant meaning to Rush, who published one of the first American books on medicine and listed onanism as one of the causes of insanity (Hare, 1962). Hence, several generations of early American physicians were exposed to these teachings.

Tissot claimed to have treated patients who suffered from insanity caused by masturbation. He went on to state that onanism, regardless of frequency, produced seminal weakness, pulmonary consumption, dyspepsia, vertigo, epilepsy, hypochondriasis, loss of memory, and death. As noted, Tissot's writings won favor with Rush, who was well known for his organization of the first medical education system in the United States. Rush is also famous for being one of the signers of the Declaration of Independence and being George Washington's personal physician. As such (and still using the humors understanding of medicine), Rush is also known for bleeding the first president to death in 1799 in an attempt to cure a fever.

Early American physicians accepted the Good Health Doctrine and believed masturbation would lead to a condition known as "sexual neurasthenia." Masturbation was thought to result in a host of dreaded symptoms, ranging from acne and isolating oneself for long periods in the bathroom to general weakness or blindness. Today's sexual myths of too much masturbation causing blindness or making you go crazy were actually the consensus medical opinion of yesteryear (Bley & Peterson, 2007).

Did you know that some of today's common food products were originally invented as "anti-masturbation foods" to prevent the ill effects of the disease of masturbation? Famous health doctrine advocates such as Reverend Sylvester Graham and Dr. John Harvey Kellogg popularized the ideals of good health that excluded sex (except for procreation). The Reverend Graham was so closely associated with this doctrine of good health that some food products today still bear his name, including graham crackers and graham flour (Shprintzen, 2013).

Dr. John Harvey Kellogg and his wife, Ella, originally invented baked flakes of corn as an anti-masturbation food served to the patients of the Sanatorium (the Sans) of Battle Creek, Michigan.

This hospital was considered the Cleveland Clinic of its time and even published its own cookbook for foods to keep you healthy—*Science in the Kitchen* by Ella Kellogg (1892). The story of Dr. Kellogg was popularized in the movie *The Road to Wellville* (Parker, 1994), which described how the wealthy would retreat at the Sans to relieve whatever ailed them. Besides inventing the corn flake as a food to suppress masturbation, the good Dr. Kellogg was famous for publishing a pamphlet entitled *The Thirty-Nine Suspicious Signs of Self-Abuse* (Kellogg, 1888).

Apparently not understanding that many of the same signs of self-abuse were the same signs as something called puberty, Dr. Kellogg warned parents to watch for such "symptoms" as general debility and weakness, sleeplessness, sudden change in mental abilities, untrustworthiness, desire to be alone, shyness, unnatural boldness, weak shoulders, dragging or shuffling the feet while walking, paralysis, lack of breast development, eating clay or paste, use of tobacco, acne, and biting the fingernails (Kellogg, 1888). Of course, treatment at the Sans involved nutritious food (plenty of corn flakes and granola), rigorous exercise, plenty of rest, hydrotherapy, enemas, and no sex (except for what was called "medical message"). Medical message of that day was understood to be the manual stimulation of female genitals to the point of orgasm and had a long history as a treatment of hysteria. It was considered a legitimate medical treatment of the day because the practice was literally "in the hands" (and control) of the male physician and not trusted to be "in the hands" of the woman herself. Of course, in that era, the latter would be seen as a perversion (instead of sexual assault when the physician provided the "procedure") and put the woman at risk for the devastating effects of self-abuse!

THE BIRTH OF MAD: ENTER THE ONANISTS

To review the specific origins of MAD, three related terms need to be defined to describe three different schools of thought that represent how American medicine viewed masturbation over time. These three schools represent the transition of viewing masturbation as a disease to the current effort to normalize this sexual behavior.

1. The term *onanists* is used to describe medical authors who explicitly adhered to the notion that masturbation caused illness.
2. The term *nonanist* is used to describe those medical writers who simply did not mention the practice or only made vague reference to it.
3. The term *contra-onanists* refers to those who openly opposed the notion that masturbation has a detrimental effect on health or those who exposed the health benefits of practicing masturbation. (Wright & Peterson, 2007)

Because masturbation was considered a moral dilemma and up to recently (historically speaking) believed to be a serious health issue, it was dubbed a vice, moral corruption, and something that should be prevented, even if that meant taking extreme measures (Walling, 1904). It was the early 18th century when the ill effects brought on by masturbation were described in a pamphlet titled *The Heinous Sin of Self-Pollution* (the alternative title was *Onania*). The pamphlet was believed to have been written by Tissot, the former clergyman-turned-physician who staunchly believed masturbation to be a vice. His claims were backed by little, if any, medical or scientific knowledge. Despite this, the notion of masturbation as an evil vice that would bring about a slew of negative physical and mental consequences took hold within the medical community. *Onania* even asserted that masturbation resulted in epilepsy, lying, madness, or even drove people to murder or suicide.

A short note is relevant here regarding the wide spread nature and incredible persistence of these beliefs that have survived 300 years as sexual myths into the 21st century. I co-authored a book called *Joyful, Healthy Sex: Fundamental Education* (Raj, Raj, & Peterson, 2010) that was published in India with two former advanced students: Roma Raj (a physician) and Mulk Raj (who has a PhD in military science). To my amazement, the draft of the book asserted that too much masturbation could lead to suicide! I contacted the co-author, Dr. Mulk Raj (a retired brigadier general from the Indian Army), to discuss what I thought was a typo. The good general actually informed me that within Indian military culture, officers were instructed to warn their soldiers against the dangers of masturbation and encouraged liberal use of leave for conjugal visits. Hiding in the historical background of this military policy was an underlining onanistic belief that masturbation was bad for the health of troops and could lead to suicide!

Although the use of the word *onanism* has been inseparably linked with the act of masturbation, the biblical story of Onan does not relate to masturbation. The story of Onan (Gen. 38:7–9) tells the story of Judah's sons, Er and Onan. When Er is slain by God, Onan was obligated to marry Er's widow, Tamar, as required in the Hebrew tradition. Levirate marriage dictated that a woman without children must marry the brother of her deceased husband to carry on the family line. When Onan and Tamar had sex, Onan did not complete the act and "spilled his seed upon the ground." As previously mentioned, the story of Onan is best understood as history's first recorded account of *coitus interruptus* (early withdrawal of the penis from the vagina without ejaculation), not masturbation. For this transgression against levirate law, Onan was then slain by God.

Many have interpreted this story to mean that any semen that is "wasted" and not used for procreation is a sin unto God. This is the reasoning behind the term *onanism*. Because masturbation can result in the loss of semen, it is considered a sin by some religions. This could also potentially explain the focus on the dangers of masturbation in males; women do not waste "the seeds of life" during sexual self-pleasure.

Later in the 18th century, physicians and other health authorities began to write about "evidence" of the dangers of masturbation. Then nearly all publications on the subject of masturbation condemned the act and served as a warning to those who continued its practice. Reasonable people who chose to speak out against the onanists' view of MAD were professionally ostracized and lost patients. This trend persisted into the early 20th century.

Finally, a majority of medical writers and researchers began to state that the claims made against masturbation were unfounded. These were the contra-onanists. Only after significant scientific backing (most notably from the work of Alfred Kinsey, but also others before him) did fact begin to be separated from fiction. Despite this shift toward sexual enlightenment, the stigma of masturbation continues to have a strong general presence in our society today. Fortunately, the belief that "self-harm" through masturbation is waning and the younger generation is less concerned about any physical ill effects. However, today the connection still exists between masturbation and social or religious ramifications ("don't be a wanker;" stigma, guilt, and fear of damnation).

As mentioned, the topic of masturbation was largely ignored in Western society until the pamphlet *Onania* labeled it a moral sin and medical writers started asserting that the practice led to adverse physical outcomes. Onanist writers worked to pathologize masturbation into disease and demonize any dissenters, especially those who were bold enough to suggest masturbation during puberty may be more normal than a disease. This was the experience of G. Stanley Hall, the founder of the American Psychological Association (APA) in 1894 and first to host Freud to lecture in America. Hall was among the first to attempt the systematic study of adolescent sexuality, including masturbation. But in 1904, he was pressured to give up the study of sexuality and a series of public lectures on his book on adolescence for threat of severe professional criticism and loss of reputation (Schultz & Schultz, 2008).

The Medical Treatment of MAD

Countless youth were needlessly tormented by such anti-masturbation home remedies as tying hands to the bedposts at bedtime. One of my older veterans said his mother sometimes poked her head inside his bedroom at night and asked, "Where are your hands, where are your hands?" Medical treatments for masturbation included circumcision (for girls and boys) and even castration. Masturbation and seminal loss were so vilified that even involuntary nocturnal ejaculations (wet dreams) were medicalized as the disease of spermatoclemma according to the *Medical Sex Dictionary* (Robinson, 1933).

Treatment of suspected masturbation ranged from changing the clothing worn so that it was not too tight to circumcision or other physical applications of pain to deter it. Certain foods, tonics, and medicines were also used for both the treatment and prevention of MAD. Some early physicians prohibited consumption of specific foods, such as gravy, alcohol, oysters, salt, pepper, fish, chocolate, ginger, jelly, and coffee as they were expressly forbidden to masturbators. An important component of the Good Health Doctrine was the belief that some foods had the capacity to irritate the nervous system, thus increasing sexual desire.

Dr. Kellogg believed that masturbation was a sin as well as adisease that could lead to a host of disorders and felt that his corn flakes would help prevent such harm. In addition to promoting diet as a means of preventing masturbation, Kellogg suggested that children should have their genitals bandaged and have their hands bound to bedposts at night to prevent masturbation. Other anti-masturbation devices included belts and locks that prevented access to the genitals and even metal mittens that eliminated manual dexterity. Believe it or not, straitjackets were also used to restrict the movement of the arms and hands. Another device consisted of a ring that was worn loosely around the penis. Inside the ring were metal spikes that would stab the penis if it were to become erect. These were just a few of many forms of devices designed to curb masturbation (LeVay, Baldwin, & Baldwin, 2015; Yarber & Sayad, 2019).

Although these treatments and preventative measures may or may not have been effective for their intended purpose, they were flawed in many ways (including ethically) from today's standards. In many instances, more permanent cures were sought. Leeches were used to remove excess blood from the genitals, which was believed to contribute to sexual desire. Castration, circumcision, and clitoridectomies (surgical removal of the clitoris) were among the most extreme measures used to treat masturbation. Burning and blistering the genitals using a hot wire or iron was thought to deaden the nerve endings and reduce one's desire for self-stimulation. In 1934, Dr. Robinson (the popular writer on the topic of youth avoiding the ill effects of onanism) noted, "In two or three cases, I have found it necessary to apply rapidly a red-hot wire to the child's genital; this rather brutal little procedure proved effective; the child ceased to masturbate" (Robinson, 1934). The family reference text, *The Household Physician* (Buffum, Loving, Warren, Small, Thorndike, Smith, & Lyman, 1905) recommended mineral acids, bitters, strychnine, iron, and syrup of hypophosphites. Many medicines and tonics were also used as a cure for MAD and were a virtual parade of nonsense and unnecessary harm to children from today's point of view.

While G. Stanley Hall wrote of masturbation during adolescence in a more humane way than most of his contemporaries, Hall also recommended severe measures in "severe cases." For example, Hall suggested the depressant effects of arsenic and saltpeter, while warning against the stimulant effects of cocaine and opium. He also listed bromide, ergot, and lupin as possible pharmacological interventions (Hall, 1904). Hall also discussed possible medical interventions, including clitoridectomy, blistering, sectioning of certain nerves, and the implantation of small medical devices to prevent the act. Hall wrote that circumcision was recommended for the treatment of MAD as it may desensitize the penis to stimulation. He also suggested that pants and undergarments should be loose-fitting with pockets that should be on the side and shallow so not to allow hands near the genitals. Rooms and clothing were recommended not to be too warm and all rooms should always be accessible for adult supervision! Essentially, although Hall was progressive for an academic of his time, he was strongly influenced by the dominant onanist narrative, and a lot of his well-intended advice was either nonsense or made matters worse (Arnett, 2006).

Enter the Early Contra-Onanists

Later in the 20th century, the tide began to change in terms of the medical opinion of masturbation. With the pioneering work of early sex researchers who employed empirical methods, the focus on the topic of masturbation began to shift from medical condemnations to more science-based inquiry. With Kinsey's pioneering publications on the subject in 1948 and 1953, questions about prevalence, frequency, and means of masturbation were being asked and answered for the first time. The famous Kinsey reports, *Sexual Behavior in the Human Male* (Kinsey, Pomeroy, Martin, & Gephard, 1948) and *Sexual Behavior in the Human Female* (Kinsey, Pomeroy, Martin, & Gephard, 1953) proved scientifically what others had hinted at for years: The majority of Americans masturbate!

In other words, these two reports were some of the last nails in the coffin of MAD—at least in the medical community. If almost all males and about two-thirds of women reported masturbating (remember, this was 70 years ago), then where was all the disability and mental illness resulting from all this masturbation? Nowhere! It wasn't happening. This was the "Great Disconnect" that helped disassemble the onanists' insistence that practicing masturbation leads to disease.

Medical dictionaries throughout the first half of the 20th century still referred to masturbation as onanism, using the negative view of the onanist school of thought. Reviewing at-home "medical adviser" books over the past century also reflects the transition of the public view of masturbation. In a review of 16 home-adviser texts, which span the century from 1899 to 1989, the later contra-onanist writers appear to slowly gain dominance in the period after World War II through the 1960s. However, you can still find the term *onanism* in fairly recent (1980s) medical texts and home advisers. Yet the definition of the word has changed over time. The onanists' belief of masturbation as a disease slowly transitioned, as previously noted, to a definition of *coitus interruptus* that is a historically accurate interpretation.

In 21st-century America most people have sufficient sexual health literacy to understand that masturbation does not cause adverse medical consequences (such as reduction in brain size, disability, insanity, and even death) as was commonly believed in 19th-century America. However, masturbation is a topic still very much taboo in Western culture. The modern understanding of masturbation as a normal and healthy sexual activity is far from being universally accepted. For example, many people are not comfortable publicly discussing its practice, especially the enjoyment and benefits of masturbation. Although the contra-onanist school of thought gained prominence, it never fully completely refuted the onanists' message in the American psyche. Parental overreaction and punitive responses still occur commonly ("*You will go to hell for that!*") and teenage suicides are still reported as a result of the guilt over masturbation and religious condemnation. For example, just before presenting the aforementioned paper on MAD at the 2007 SSSS national conference, there was a careful yet sad presentation of a case study involving a young Mormon adolescent who killed himself because of the intense guilt and self-condemnation he experienced due to the belief that he had sinned. His suicide note made his reasons and motivations clear that he succumbed to suicide primarily as a result of his guilt and religious conflict regarding masturbation. Our history of masturbation as disease is part of the unconscious bias (blind spot) that American culture continues to have against pleasure and enjoying our own bodies.

Today, we understand we are sexual beings from the rocking of the cradle to the rolling of the hearse and that masturbation is normal. Masturbation is now often referred to as "self-pleasuring" and considered a healthy part of sexual expression. Modern concerns about masturbation are more likely to be limited to teaching children discretion about the "where and when" of masturbation ("*Yes, it is normal son, but not at the dinner table*"), guilt resulting from the behavior ("*This feels too good not to be bad*"), and excessive masturbation that falls into the range of compulsive sexual behavior ("*I can't seem to stop doing this even when I want it to end*").

SEXOPHRENIA: THE LEGACY OF OUR SEXUAL HERITAGE

In his best-selling book, *America's War on Sex: The Continuing Attack on Law, Lust, and Liberty*, sex educator and therapist Marty Klein (2012) describes American culture as having a schizophrenic relationship with sex. As described in Chapter 3, the authors would agree and would call this relationship *sexophrenic*. Back in the 1990s, I was amused by the possibility that I may have coined a term when I started using the word in publication (Peterson, 1999). A subsequent literature search for the term resulted in some mild disappointment yet further amusement as I found that the term *sexophrenia* had been previously used—as the title of a porn movie!

More satisfying, however, was a recent discovery at one of my favorite events of the year: The Annual Planned Parenthood Book Sale! It is so big it used to occupy a coliseum. The nice lady watching the "collectible" section observed me buying up a bag of old sex manuals, but no doubt noticed my open delight (instead of trying to hide the selected sex books like the regular perverts). She then contrived an ingenious strategy to get rid of me by offering $20 for clearing out the entire "erotica" section, which included several books by notable sex researchers. She made me a deal I couldn't refuse. What a buy!

Inside one of the two large boxes I carried out was the *Lecher's Lexicon*, a sort of sexual dictionary, originally written by J. E. Schmidt in 1967 under the title *Cyclopedic Lexicon of Sex*. I was thrilled to find the term *sexophrenia* listed on page 368, which read like the Grand Old Sigmund wrote it himself. "*Sexophrenia: The state of mind of one whose thoughts are colored or motivated by a conscious or subconscious sex urge.*" This definition implies that a person could experience anxiety while their thoughts are "colored or motivated" by sexual urges.

The use of the term *sexophrenia* in this book is slightly different; it implies not only an avoidance of sex (at times) in the conscious mind but emphasizes the presence of a conflict within. Sexophrenia is a nondiagnostic term that describes a feeling of conflict or anxiety that results from feeling pleasure from a sexual activity on one hand and at the same time feeling uncomfortable because of negative messages learned about that behavior. If this conflict is strong enough, it can cause a person to

1. never engage in a particular sexual behavior,
2. have diminished enjoyment of the sexual behavior,
3. entirely block all enjoyment of the sexual behavior, or
4. sometimes feel a sense of shame and guilt after engaging in the sexual behavior (depending on the degree of conflict).

In short, sexophrenia is feeling a little crazy regarding the topic of sex, especially when it comes to expressing our sexual selves through behavior.

The basic sexophrenic conflict is developed at an early age (one to three years old), so most people do not remember the experiences described in the following paragraphs. As babies, our bodies are entirely sensual and we soon discover the pleasurable feelings associated with touching our genitals (infant masturbation is common, normal, and well documented). As toddlers, we continue to receive pleasure from self-stimulation but also develop another good feeling about our genitals: a sense of pride and mastery when we are toilet trained and accomplish continence. Most children are praised and/or rewarded for becoming continent and joining the rest of society where people do not poop indiscriminately.

However, these two good feelings are short-lived—until the day when little Johnny or Missy comes walking out in front of Mom's bridge party with their hands down their pants (or naked), causing widespread panic in the house! Faces turn red and disapprovals are soon voiced: "*Get your hands out of there—that's dirty—you naughty boy (or girl)!*"

Two-year-old Johnny or Missy may or may not grow up to be a rocket scientist, but even at this tender age they soon understand that something about their genitals upsets others, is somehow different from the rest of their body, and discussing one's sexual curiosity causes others to become noticeably uncomfortable. This awareness is slowly internalized and develops into a sense of mystery and confusion about one's genitals (and sex in general) that is reinforced over many years of living in a family that does not talk about sex (especially in an open and positive way). Before most American children ever hear the word or understand the definition, they are learning and practicing one of the traditional "Great American Taboos," that it is inappropriate to talk about sex.

More than 100 years ago, Freud wrote that when a basic conflict is experienced by an individual to a severe degree, the conflict will manifest as depression and anxiety. Freud used examples such as a married woman having feelings of sexual desire for a man other than her husband and being anxious because of the restraints she places on herself from acting on her sexual desire. The conflict between her desire (from deep within the id) and moral restraints on her behavior (from her superego) create the anxiety that Freud called "hysteria." This was the psychiatric term of the times in a long line of medical diagnoses used to repress sexual expression, especially what men feared most—the natural sexual expression of women. Other examples of pseudo-illnesses include spermatorrhea and sexual neurasthenia (explained later in this chapter).

Few people know that Freud was so sex-negative; he gave up sex at the age of 41, and many of his theories of psychopathology were based upon self-study. Although this may be so, it doesn't mean all of his theories were invalid, even if they are difficult to operationalize and test empirically. However important the contributions Freud made to 20th-century Western civilization, he certainly contributed to the sexophrenic effects within American sexual heritage by characterizing sex so negatively and as the basis for psychopathology.

Sexophrenia and Good-Girl Training

Sexophrenic messages are continually learned by many (if not most) girls as they grow up and are exposed to sexual misinformation and myth. For example, many girls are taught that their genitals are dirty and unsanitary as they mature, as evidenced by direct statements and all the "feminine products" sold to make that part of the female body more acceptable to common sensitivities.

After years of young girls learning negative messages about their genitals, they are also told to "*save that special part of you for marriage when you can share it with the one you love the most.*" That type of double message promotes sexophrenic reactions and obstacles to women's positive self-image. That's why books such as *Read My Lips*: *A Complete Guide to the Vagina and Vulva* (Herbenick & Schick, 2011) are needed to assist women and girls to overcome their negative self-image related to their vulvas in general and vaginas in particular.

Another example of sexophrenic messaging comes from a female veteran who reported receiving a well-intended but totally crazy comment from her mother on the night before her wedding. As a bride-to-be, she was approached by her mother after the traditional dinner before the wedding day and taken aside to have her mother share a little pearl of wisdom woman to woman. The veteran said her mother was clearly uncomfortable with what she was about to say, which made the young bride anxiety-ridden and think she was about to be told something like "You're adopted." The veteran never expected any sex advice as the mother had never spoken a word about sex except to hand her a book about periods when she was 10 years old. The mother's sage advice was, "Now that you will be able to have sex, have the decency not to enjoy it!"

These examples of sexophrenic messaging are straight from the "Good Girl Training Manual" (any edition). Open it up to any page and you will find explicit instructions to young women that good girls should not show too much interest in sex and not express sexual pleasure in any overly enthusiastic way. Otherwise, one may be considered "unladylike" (also known as a bad girl or the many other derogatory names commonly heard). These names reflect social sanctions against females who openly reject the traditional sex-role expectation for women to be Cinderella-like (submissive) and allow only the male to openly initiate sex. This is a direct residual effect of the American historical emphasis on suppressing female sexual expression. What is really confusing to young girls are the media models of adolescent sexuality that emphasize how to be overtly sexy at 12 years old. As a result, girls today have a complicated sexophrenic messages to resolve for a healthy sense of themselves.

Unfortunately, this often results in a kind of "split attitude" about sex for many women, who are conflicted between their good-girl training and their natural interest in sex and pleasure. Fortunately, most young women are able to find ways to overcome this conflict and learn to be comfortable with their sexuality with the support of a caring partner. However, if this conflict is strongly reinforced and becomes rigid, the young girl may feel she has to turn to alcohol or drug use to be sexual (and this, of course, is unfortunate, unnecessary, and dangerous). Three recommended books for helping girls and women resolve this conflict are *Because It Feels Good* (Herbenick, 2009), *Read My Lips* (Herbenick & Schick, 2011), and *The Good Girl's Guide to Bad Girl Sex* by a great sex educator, sex therapist, and former sex surrogate Barbara Keesling (2001).

Sexophrenia and the Teaching of Masculinity to Boys

Boys are not immune from the crazy effects of sexophrenia. Boys are taught that if they want to become a man, they must always be dominant, aggressive, in control, and independent. They are never to ask for help even when hopelessly lost. After all, look at the types of models of ideal masculinity they are given through movies and video games. For baby boomers, they think of the likes of John Wayne, Clint Eastwood, Arnold Schwarzenegger, Bruce Willis, and Denzel Washington. If you are a lot younger, think of Vin Diesel (*Fast & Furious*), Dwayne Johnson (the Rock), Jason Statham (*The Mechanic*), and Chris Hemsworth (*Thor*).

Above all, boys quickly learn not to do anything that possibly could be associated with girls or femininity. Otherwise, a boy is at risk for being called a sissy, pussy, or fag. Such names identify a boy as a target for exploitation and potential violence from other males who wish to demonstrate their dominance and higher level of masculinity. It is an operational model of the proverbial alpha-male pecking order.

Boys who identify themselves as gay face a "double-sexophrenic whammy" to overcome regarding stereotypes of masculinity and heterosexism. They often grow up with a special burden of confusion, fear, and a sense of isolation because they typically have no one to talk to about their experience. Remember Larry King, Matthew Shepard, or any one of the thousands of transgender individuals who have been killed for simply being themselves. There are thousands of young gay men who do remember and want to avoid the same fate. Although violence is always a present danger, this will slowly change as there is increased diversity in media today that includes positive models of mentally healthy and happy gay men (and lesbians as well).

The sexophrenic process for boys includes messaging that they are supposed to be attracted to bad girls (for example, any of a long list of young women who gain celebrity for their bad-girl status) yet they are afraid of literally "not rising to the challenge." The sexophrenic paradox is that boys want to seek out sexually experienced girls but they are also afraid to initiate sex, which might expose their in experience. The traditional expectation of boys is that they are attracted to the bad girls but ultimately want to marry a Madonna-like good girl they can take home to meet Mother. As singer Rick James said, "She's a very kinky girl—the kind you don't take home to Mother."

In addition, boys are socially expected to be the repository of sexual knowledge and be aggressive enough to initiate sex (frequently, of course). How do you accomplish this when you don't know squat? Yet, you'd better have an erection at the drop of a bra or your masculinity is called into question (again). In other words, a boy is expected to grow up to find a virgin to marry and teach her about sexual matters that he has no idea about nor has the skills and permission to ask for guidance about. Yet, he strives to have others to see him as *the Man!*

In our sexophrenic contemporary American culture, it is no wonder that the major social institution attending to women's emotional problems is the mental health system. It is also no wonder that the major social institution attending to men's emotional problems is the prison system. As a society, we are pretty screwed up about this whole masculinity and femininity thing. As a culture, we have started the process of sorting it all out, and we discuss these topics in depth in later chapters. We have reviewed the historical roots of sexophrenia by closely examining one of the most basic and commonly vilified sexual behaviors of all: masturbation. Now let's broaden our scope to the overall influence this history has had on the American psyche and the paradox we find ourselves in related to sexuality.

The Sexophrenic Paradox in the American Psyche

The American experience is one of paradox in the general case as well as the specific case of sexual expression. In the beginning years of American history, the European-descent minority disenfranchised the majority of indigenous peoples. First Nation peoples encountered Europeans who said they came in peace but soon took to a task of subjugation, relocation, and genocide of indigenous tribes. Ironically, early American colonial life was about seeking freedom of the new world (for Europeans), yet they imported slaves to effectively establish an apartheid system that disenfranchised both African and Native peoples. So, the American apartheid was the big "elephant in the room" for a new country based on freedom. It took 200 years and the bloodiest war in American history just to begin to address some of these issues. While fleeing from religious repression, the English Puritans constructed strict codes of conformity related to gender, sexual, and religious practice; placing generations in peril of social sanction for nonconformity. The witch craze of Salem and other colonies was only the most extreme example of repression of nonconformity, directed at forcing women to comply with social expectations of proper femininity and a rigid code of sexual behavior. The scarlet letter and other forms of ostracizing were more common but powerful forms as well. Many parts of American history are not pretty or just but serve to instill the architecture of paradox within the American psyche.

The residual effects of these historical beginnings are monumental and still very much with us today. They are the basis for many of the examples we have examined in this chapter with many names of these residual effects: sexual stereotypes, sexual double standards, sexophrenic messaging, good-girl school, character-deficit socialization of boys, the medicalization of natural sexual interest and function, the outlawing of contraceptive and birth-control practices, the banning of homosexuality, the religious condemnation of sexual identity other than heterosexuality, and our legacy of privilege for sex, race, and class.

Consider this statement: *We are all sexual beings.* What does this simple yet commonly misunderstood statement mean? At the start of the 21st century, sexual health is a topic that is still exceedingly challenging to understand and to achieve. Yet the knowledge and practice of sexual health is absolutely necessary to ensure a positive quality of life. In terms of survival of the species, one could argue sex is the most important, if not essential, aspect of human existence!

Sexual health literacy involves a complex and constantly changing body of knowledge. This is true if you are an individual working on your own personal sexual health, and especially true if you are working on enhancing your sexual health as part of a couple and/or family. Although being sexual is perfectly natural, it is usually not naturally "perfect." Like parenting, it helps the more you know and the more practice you have.

Sexuality is considered one of life's chief paradoxes. A paradox is something that appears contradictory or opposed to common sense, yet is true. As a demonstration, stop all movement right now and be perfectly motionless. Are you motionless? Can you be motionless? Are you still breathing and circulating blood? (Good, keep it up!) Are you traveling in a plane, riding on a train, or rolling down the highway? No? Are you hurtling around Earth's axis and flying around the sun at thousands of miles per second?

Inherent qualities about sexuality do make it challenging to examine, understand, and communicate about sex. This is especially true because of the sexophrenic nature of our American heritage. Yet we are challenged to be comfortable, feel confident, and achieve satisfaction with ourselves as well as with another when we socialize our sexuality.

Another paradoxical aspect of sexuality is that despite its paramount importance in our life, we typically receive very little education about it. Consequently, we stumble our way through relationships and do the best we can with our levels of knowledge and skill. To make matters worse, we not only receive little education but (as noted earlier) society places barriers between us and sources of sex education.

Consider the paradox between sexual information and behavioral practices consistent with sexual health. Having information relevant to improving your sexual health doesn't mean you necessarily make choices in your sexual behavior consistent with the information you know to be true. Look at all the health care professionals (especially nurses) who smoke. Every day they see the adverse effects of smoking (cancer, heart disease, and respiratory disorders) in their patients, yet cannot easily stop smoking themselves.

Sexually speaking, men with problematic sexual behavior (sometimes referred to as sex addicts or having out-of-control sexual behavior) most often know better than to make the choices they do—yet they feel compelled to engage in their compulsive sexual behaviors. Through sexual health clinics, many very intelligent men with advanced degrees and high-profile careers have been assessed and treated for problematic sexual behavior. They cannot seem to stop engaging in behaviors that put them at risk of ruining their health, marriage, or career because they experience a "disconnect" between what they know and what they do. For example, some men continue having anonymous sex with strangers in unfamiliar and often dangerous places until what they fear most happens—getting sent to jail, beaten up, fired from their job, or divorced. Problematic sexual behavior (PSB) is the subject of Chapter 17.

Consider the paradox of another simple statement: *We are all sexual beings from the rocking of the cradle to the rolling of the hearse.* Some people do not want to define themselves as sexual beings. Many do not want to acknowledge their first sexual experiences in childhood, which served as a sexual awakening. Although this statement refers to the "rocking of the cradle," we are actually sexual beings while we are still developing in our mother's womb, based upon prenatal ultrasounds showing male fetuses with erections.

On the other end of the lifespan, many people do not want to recognize the sexual nature of our advanced years as seniors. The general expectation, until recently, has been that when you retire from your work life you also retire from your sex life, somewhere in your 60s. Although it is normal to have sexual thoughts and feelings well into advanced age (actually until we are brain dead), many people do not want to recognize these sexual thoughts and feelings as normal and healthy. Instead, they think ignoring and dismissing them makes it easier to avoid uncomfortable feelings and worries like, "Am I turning into a dirty old lady or man?" Thoughts and feelings about sex are normal. What you do with those thoughts and feelings is another matter altogether. This brings us to the topic of sexual expression.

Consider the paradoxical nature of sexual expression. Our need to express ourselves sexually is driven by an appetite for sexual gratification. This sexual appetite is as natural as your appetite for food. Thank God for the one critical difference between these two appetites: We will not die of starvation if we don't get fed sexually. However, William Masters used to say there were definite physical consequences of not having orgasm, including increased risk of gastrointestinal problems, constipation, prostate problems, vaginismus (a female sexual pain disorder—see the glossary), and increased irritability. While there are those who do not want to be perceived as sexual beings (but still are), many people want to be perceived as sexual beings and are not (at least not by the person to whom they think it matters most).

Here is a short parade of additional sexual paradoxes. Many times, men don't want to have erections, but they do (and at some of the most embarrassing times). Many men want to have erections when they don't (which can be even more embarrassing). Some women want to experience an interest in sex (but they don't). For decades they were raised feeling it wasn't "ladylike" to be very interested or enthusiastic about sex for fear of not being considered a "good girl." Then they sometimes have difficulty "reversing direction" and wanting to have orgasms with a lover or husband. Historically, women have been brought to doctors and therapists by overbearing husbands who basically want them "cured" (defined as getting the women to have a higher interest in sex). These women are often surprised to hear they are normal not to want sex with their controlling and insensitive husbands. In fact, something would be wrong with them if they did want to have sex with these men (unless the wives are masochists who want to enjoy being dominated and humiliated).

Our sexual fantasies, feelings, sensations, and behaviors in the context of relationships are what really get us twisted around. As social creatures, we most often live in relationships that we are ill prepared for and find anxiety-provoking. The constant work at clear communication and having the same expectations is often found to be overwhelming by couples. That's why some marriages actually feel more like work than enjoyment. During courting, we seek out others for emotional comfort and physical intimacy. It is common to be drawn to a particular person who becomes our primary partner and later feel trapped and repelled by him or her over time. With all these challenges, we still keep a priority on establishing and maintaining a primary relationship with that "someone special." This type of balancing act between the needs for intimacy and independence is like a hazing ritual of acceptance into the human tribe. Individuals in harmonious relationships effectively manage this balancing act. Alternatively, a relationship can be a paradoxical source of conflict that can last a lifetime.

The main message here is this: Sexuality, as with life in general, is full of paradox. Yet, despite the risks of relationships in terms of emotional, social, and financial costs, most of us choose to socialize our sex life and live in these things called "primary relationships" (marriages for most of us). We do so because it is partly our biological nature (called pair-bondance) but also because we are socialized to do so and are socially sanctioned if we are not paired with another. Intellectually and emotionally, we live in relationships because we feel it is "worth it" (at least most of the time), despite the (hopefully occasional) hassles of the relationship politics.

Featured Stories of Diverse Perspectives and Experiences

WHAT WOULD JESUS DO? (WWJD): LOIS AND TESS
Written by Richelle Frabotta

It was change of classes and we had 10 minutes to get to Sister Elaine's AP English class. Geneva was feeling poorly. She didn't even have to say because I knew. We were close. I always asked myself, "What would Jesus do?" She rested her head gently on my uniformed skirt lap as my legs jutted out in the hallway. I leaned back on the metal locker and stroked her hair. Whenever she had a headache, this type of comfort helped.

The cold tiled floor was easy to ignore because of the heat I felt between my legs. A curious feeling, but comfortable. She was my best friend in the world. It was okay to feel a deep, abiding love for my bestie. Actually, we both felt better with this loving touch on the hallway floor. Jesus understood. Six minutes until we had to be in English.

While cherishing the moment of connection, my eyes must have closed. I was startled awake as directly in front of my face and hovering over Geneva was Sister Mary Margaret. She looked shocked and disconcerted with her red, contorted wimple-surroundedd face. In a whirlwind of physical activity, Geneva was out of my lap and I was sitting in a hard wooden chair in Mother Katherine Michael's office. A place I had been many times before.

It seems that Geneva in my lap was a bad thing. This "fact" was being told to me in monologue format with no breaths and through closed teeth as I was escorted from the chair to the closet in the corner of Mother Katherine Michael's office. And my father was getting a phone call.

The hard wooden chair I was used to, but the closet was a new place for me to be. It was dark, musty, full of strange, old objects, and the floor was carpeted. I shook my head and waited while Mother Katherine Michael made call after call to reach my father. It seemed he was unavailable to her at all of his numbers. He often said, "The work day is 8 hours solid! No time for outside nonsense, Lois, so don't create any. I'll see you when dinner is served promptly at 6 p.m." I had wondered if he had ever shared this info with Mother Katherine Michael. And then I drifted off to sleep.

Looking back, it was a humiliating ordeal—that business with those nuns at that school. My father retrieved me at 5:30 p.m. from that closet. I had been in there with Mother Katherine Michael coming and going from the office since 9:05 a.m. No food. No water. No bathroom. She expelled me, but then, after a sizable donation from my father, I was allowed to return to school a week later. Geneva and I remained friends as best we could. We navigated the obstacles placed directly and intentionally in our collective path. Eventually, Geneva succumbed to the stress of trying to remain close and I lost who I now consider the first love of my life.

As I sit with Tess, my partner of 47 years, and tell this story to a classroom of undergraduates enrolled in a Later Life Families course, I want them to know: I had no choice but to leave that closet behind.

At 17 years old, armed with a prestigious diploma, a quick wit, and a spirit powered by adventure, I left Devon, Pennsylvania, for Boston, Massachusetts. This was the first of the two best decisions I have made in my 75 years on this planet.

I was desperate to meet other women like me, so I got a job in a bookstore. It was 1959 and I was ready to start breathing. It took a little while, but I found my community. There was no secret handshake, but I did pick up on the lingo and the subtle (or not so subtle for the brave) personal style nuances. Community was heaven and those people were manna. Finding like-minded individuals, both women and men, where I could simply be me was what kept me alive many days, many circumstances.

The second-best decision was saying yes to a double date! It was 1968 and common for us lesbians to date men. When one found one's community, then more dates happened. The men were gay and needed to keep up appearances. We all knew the game: dinner, socializing, kiss on the cheek, and schedule for the next "date." This arrangement was helpful to both parties. Everyone needs to eat, right? And, more importantly, the men needed to have solid reputations.

My buddy and frequent dinner partner, Max, knew that Tess was in town for a librarian conference. He thought we might hit it off, so he called his friend, Michael, and we went to dinner at a classy little Italian restaurant. I had not laughed like that in a decade!

Tess was and is amazing. With the slight raise of the left corner of her mouth, a head tilt to the right, and extra sparkle in her clear, light-green eyes, she lifts my spirits, causes my heart to skip a beat, and moves me into a place of calm.

I've never done "calm." I tend to do high stress, intense focus, and hyper vigilance with my immediate sur-roundings. I typically move through the world in states of extremes: giddiness, joy, and lots of socializing with friends, then to weeks of depression, self-loathing, immobility, and paranoia. My mental health has always placed itself squarely forefront in my world. There's been no denying or hiding my condition from my close friends. Tess has endured the ups and downs with me. She has been always present, kind, and wanting to relieve my pain even when I have been unable to acknowledge or accept her supports.

This is unconditional love. Jesus got behind this concept.

How have Tess and I lasted so long in a culture where we, two unmarried and unrelated women, were not allowed to rent our first apartment without signatures from our fathers? How did we manage to stay together when the medical system denies my love, who is not blood related, visitation with me for months while I healed in the institution? How do we stand in love when marriage, although assumed and expected for me, was not a legal option for us until year 45 of our committed relationship?

The answer to "how" lies in the space that is the community. I came out before Stonewall. I knew the man who created the gay flag. I remember the first pride parade. I need lots of toes and fingers to name all in my personal community who have suffered physical violence at the hands of those who hate.

Honestly, I'm tired. Being visible is tough work. I love that I am visible to Tess.

THE QUEST FOR SEXUAL LITERACY, SEXUAL HEALTH, AND PERSONAL FULFILLMENT

One aim of this book is to provide you with much of what you need to know about sexuality to establish and maintain sexual health, whether you are doing so as an individual or as part of a couple. As already mentioned, what you know doesn't help if you cannot bring it into play for decisions and actions you make about enhancing your sexual health. An outcome of sexual health (and additional aim of this book) is to assist you to become increasingly comfortable being yourself and finding that "more comfortable place" of authenticity as Lois did with Tess—no matter how long it takes.

This book also aims to guide you in building your confidence as a result of practicing what you learn. Part of this process is learning about our sexophrenic past and how the legacy of our sexual heritage can keep us restrained from realizing our sexual health potential. But overall, it mostly comes down to this question: What direct positive changes can you make to your sexual health (and possibly the sexual health of others)?

To bridge the paradox of sexuality and the disconnection between knowledge and behavior, instructions for positive sexual experiences are included later in this book as well as reflected in inspirational stories of people overcoming sexual challenges in their lives. Both are included to motivate you to "put into play" your increased sexual literacy.

The more you learn, the more informed you are and the better your choices. You are invited to keep learning and take the time that is needed to grow in your sexual health. You now have a greater appreciation of historical influences from our sexual heritage, influences that have collectively conspired to keep certain information about sex out of your personal view. Get ready to learn more of what they didn't teach you in school—the advent of sexual science, the discovery of the health benefits of sex, and the many ways to expand your possibilities of self-acceptance and sexual satisfaction.

As a bridge between Chapter 6 and 7, a timeline is provided to identify historically significant events in the development of American democracy and the cultural shift from 19th-century sexosophy to 20th-century sexology. This is not a comprehensive listing to significant events that ultimately affected how history developed between the years 1900 to 2000. Rather, it is a selective listing of events that moved us ahead as a democratic republic drawing from the American women's movement, civil rights movements, LGBTQA history, the push for disability rights, and from general American culture.

REFERENCES

Arnett, J. (2006). G. Stanley Hall's adolescence: Brilliance and nonsense. *History of Psychology 2006, 9* (3), 186–197.

Beaver, D. (2015). *More than just sex: A committed couple's guide to keeping relationships lively, intimate, and gratifying.* San Diego, CA: Cognella Academic Press.

Black, E. (2003, September). The horrifying American roots of Nazi eugenics. History News Network. Retrieved from http://hnn.us/article/1796

Bley, J., & Peterson, F. (2007). Making sexual health a part of your mental health practice. In L. VanderCreek, F. Peterson, & J. Bley (Eds.), *Innovations in clinical practice: Focus of sexual health.* Sarasota, FL: Professional Resources Press.

Brecher, E. (1979). *The sex researcher* (expanded ed.). San Francisco: Specific Press.

Buffem, H., Loving, A., Warren, I., Small, A., Thorndike, W., Smith, J., & Lyman, C. (1905). *The family physician: A twentieth century medica.* Boston: Woodruff.

Cohen, A. (2016). *Imbeciles: The Supreme Court, American eugenics, and the sterilization of Carrie Buck.* New York: Penguin/Random House.

Durant, W., & Durant, A. (1935–1975). *The story of civilization.* New York: Simon & Schuster.

Durant, W. (2001). *Heroes of history: A brief history of civilization from ancient times to the dawn of the modern age.* New York: Simon & Schuster.

Good, B. (1994). *Medicine, rationality, and experience: An anthropological perspective.* Oxford, UK: Cambridge University Press.

Gould, G. (1949). *Gould's pocket pronouncing medical dictionary of the principal words used in medicine and the collateral sciences* (11th ed.). Philadelphia: P. Blakiston's Son & Company.

Hall, G.S. (1904). *Adolescence: Its psychology and its relations to physiology, anthropology, sociology, sex, crime, religion, and education.* New York: Appleton.

Hare, E. (1962). Masturbatory insanity: The history of an idea. *Journal of Mental Science, 108,* 1–25.

Herbenick, D. (2009). *Because it feels good: A woman's guide to sexual pleasure and satisfaction.* New York: Rodale.

Herbenick, D., & Schick, V. (2011). *Read my lips: A complete guide to the vagina and vulva.* New York: Rowman & Littlefield.

Keesling, B. (2001). *The good girl guide to bad girl sex.* New York: M. Evans.

Kellogg, E. (1892). *Science in the kitchen.* Battle Creek, MI: Modern Medicine Publishing.

Kellogg, H. (1888). *The thirty-nine suspicious signs of self-abuse* [Pamphlet]. Battle Creek, MI: Author.

Kinsey, A., Pomeroy, W., & Martin, C. (1948). *Sexual behavior in the human male.* Philadelphia: W.B. Saunders.

Kinsey, A., Pomeroy, W., Martin, C., & Gephard, P. (1953). *Sexual behavior in the human female.* Philadelphia: W.B. Saunders.

Klein, M. (2012). *America's war on sex: The continuing attack on law, lust, and liberty* (2nd ed.). Santa Barbara, CA: Praeger.

Last, C. (2013, February 13). The great (ape) taxonomy debate [Blog]. *Scientific American.*

LeVay, S., Baldwin, J., & Baldwin, J. (2015). *Discovering human sexuality* (3rd ed.). Sunderland, MA: Sinauer Associates.

Money, J. (1985). *The destroying angel: Sex, fitness, and food in the legacy of degeneracy theory, Graham Crackers, Kellogg's Corn Flakes, and American health history.* Amherst, NY: Prometheus.

Money, J. (1986). *Lovemaps: Clinical concepts of sexual/erotic health and pathology, paraphilia, and gender transposition in childhood, adolescence, and maturity.* New York: Irvington.

Money, J. (1998). *Sin, science, and the sex police: Essays on sexology & sexosophy.* Amherst, NY: Prometheus.

Mutrux, G. (Producer), & Condon, B. (Director). (2004). *Kinsey* [Film]. United States: American Zoetrope Myriad Pictures.

Noymer, A., & Garenne, M. (2000). The 1918 influenza epidemic's effects on sex differentials in mortality in the United States. *Population Development Review, 26*(3), 565–581.

Oshinsky, D. (2016). *Bellevue: Three centuries of medicine and mayhem at America's most storied hospital.* New York: Doubleday.

Parker, A. (Executive Producer & Director). (1994). *The Road to Wellville* [Film]. United States: Beacon Communications.

Peterson, F. (1999). Dispelling Sexual Myths. *Weekly Impact,* March. Volume 7, Number 10.

Raj, R., Raj, M., & Peterson, F. (2010). *Joyful, healthy sex: Fundamental education.* Delhi, India: B.R. Publishing.

Robinson, WJ. (1933). *Medical sex dictionary.* New York: Eugenics.

Robinson, WJ. (1934). *Sexual impotence* (19th ed.). New York: Eugenics.

Ryan, C., & Jetha, C. (2010). *Sex at dawn: How we mate, why we stray, and what it means for modern relationships.* New York: HarperCollins.

Schmidt, J. (1984). *Lecher's lexicon: A sizzling erotic dictionary.* New York: Bell.

Schultz, D., & Schultz, S. (2004). *The history of modern psychology.* Belmont, CA: Wadsworth/Thompson Learning.

Shprintzen, A. (2013). *The vegetarian crusade: The rise of an American reform movement, 1817–1921.* Chapel Hill: University of North Carolina Press.

Taylor, T. (1996). *The prehistory of sex: Four million years of human sexual culture.* New York: Bantam.

Tissot, S. (1832). *A treatise on the disorders produced by onanism.* First published in Latin under title: *Tentamen de morbis ex manustupratione*, in *Dissertatio de febribus biliosis* (1758 ed.). New York: Collins & Hannay.

Walling, W. (1904). *Sexology.* Philadelphia: Puritan.

Wright, S., & Peterson, F. (2007). *The life and death of masturbation as a disease: Clinical implications for sex addiction treatment.* Paper presented at the 50th National Conference, Society for the Scientific Study of Sexuality, Indianapolis, Indianapolis.

Yarber, W., & Sayad, B. (2019). *Human sexuality: Diversity in contemporary society* (10th ed.). New York: McGraw-Hill Education.

Significant Events in the American Experiment in Democracy

AND THE CULTURAL SHIFT FROM 19TH-CENTURY SEXOSOPHY TO 20TH-CENTURY SEXOLOGY

The 20th century was one of sweeping, radical changes in the theaters of civil rights, social norms, medical knowledge, sexual understanding, and especially women's roles in society. The turn of the century saw the reelection of President William McKinley, the death of Oscar Wilde, and the births of composer Aaron Copland and novelist Thomas Wolfe. Physicist Max Planck formulated quantum theory, and innovator Georges Méliès applied new technologies to produce the earliest film rendition of *Cinderella*. Every U.S. state government had passed legislation granting married women some control over property and earnings, yet they could not be admitted to or receive credit from most universities. Diagnoses of hysteria and sexual neurasthenia were common to women. The roles of women and men were rigidly cast, and little was understood of gender expression or sexual orientation. Although slavery had been abolished decades earlier, firm segregation laws and a cultural history of racism permeated the fabric of American society. But for all this, change was on the horizon. Over the next 100 years, new technologies, major world events, and shifting political and social ideas would dramatically change the cultural landscape of America. One of the most significant of these changes during the 20th century was the transition from most Americans believing in mythology and folklore about sexuality (sexosophy) to valuing more of a science-based under-standing of sexuality (sexology). The following events are some of the many advances that facilitated this cultural transition from sexosophy to sexology during the 20th century (and the following years since). In historical context, many of these events also represent the initial and dramatic steps forward made by women in their continuing struggle for parity.

The 1900s—the Russian revolution, Norwegian and Cuban independence, and Australia federates into a commonwealth. Seismographs, Geiger counters, and air conditioners.

1901
Germ theory gains acceptance from a growing proportion of the medical community, and antiseptic practices become more commonplace in hospitals. The chance of dying from an infection following surgery in 1865 was 50%; 40 years later, that figure falls below 10%.

Congress establishes Army Nurse Corps and (seven years later) Navy Nurse Corps.

1903
British philosopher Herbert Spencer, originator of the pseudoscience of "Social Darwinism," dies. His ideas, published in a series of 10 books between 1860 and 1897, served as the basis for the American "Manifest Destiny" philosophy and strongly influenced almost every department in American universities.

1904
Although steeped in contemporary moralism, the first American book with the term "sexology" in the title is published by gynecologist William Walling.
G. Stanley Hall (founder of American Psychological Association) publishes *Adolescence*, which includes frank discussion of sexuality. He receives professional sanctions and has to cancel a "sex" lecture series.

Freud publishes *Three Essays on the Theory of Sexuality*.

1905
Helen Bradford Thompson Woolley earns a doctorate degree from the University of Chicago with the first experimental test that challenged the widely accepted "variability hypothesis" (a Darwinian notion that women were biologically inferior to men).

After Harvard refused to grant her a doctorate degree because of her gender, Dr. Mary Calkins is elected the first woman president of the American Psychological Association (later to become president of the American Philosophical Association).

1906
Writer Emma Goldman, an advocate for anarchy, women's suffrage, and gay rights, founds her anarchist journal *Mother Earth*.

Women are still denied opportunity to work after marriage due to the belief that an employed woman, who was also a wife and mother, would cause her husband and children to suffer.

1908
The Ford Motor Company manufactures the first Model T, eventually facilitating America's first sexual revolution (the "Roaring Twenties") by providing private and mobile "beds-on-wheels."

Boston clergyman Elwood Worcester publishes *Religion and Medicine: The Moral Control of Nervous Disorders* and starts the Emmanuel Movement, popularizing "talk therapy" in America.

1909
By invitation of G. Stanley Hall, Freud and Carl Jung tour America, popularizing psychoanalysis and psychological aspects of life in the American psyche.

National Association for the Advancement of Colored People (NAACP) is founded as a result of W.E.B. Du Bois's Niagara Movement.

The 1910s—World War I begins, Russia is embroiled in revolutions, and the Republic of China is established. Cars, zippers, tanks, and Albert Einstein's theory of general relativity.

1913
Congress ratifies the 17th Amendment to mandate direct election of senators by citizens (rather than being chosen by state legislators)

1914

Between 1905 and 1914, about 10.5 million immigrants from southern and eastern Europe enter the United States, diversifying American culture as well as greatly expanding public education. Eugenic beliefs are also on the rise during this time, in response to the influx of minority ethnic groups.

World War I begins with the United States eventually joining. Young American men leave their hometowns to experience the wonders of the world—and the horrors of war.

1916

Margaret Sanger is jailed for opening the first birth-control clinic in America.

Leta Stetter Hollingsworth is granted a doctorate from Columbia University after conducting extensive research debunking the "variable hypothesis." She took the unprecedented step of asserting that social attitudes (rather than biological factors) kept women from becoming fully contributing members of society.

1917

Jeannette Pickering Rankin becomes the first woman elected to the U.S. House of Representatives by the state of Montana (and again in 1940).

During WWI, women serve as nurses and support staff with more than 400 troops killed in action.

The 1920s—Egyptian independence, Prohibition, and the rise of communism and fascism. Television, rockets, and jukeboxes invented.

1920

After decades of political action and protest by the women's suffrage movement, women win the right to vote with the passage of the 19th Amendment.

The Roaring Twenties, encompassing the first American sexual revolution, kicks off. Sheikhs and flappers (sporting straight dresses without waistlines and skirts above the knees) in American cities and on college campuses lead the way.

1921

Progressive reformer Katherine B. Davis publishes *Factors in the Sex Life of Twenty-Two Hundred Women*, one of the first large sex studies.

1923

As a key voice of the women's suffrage movement and after securing passage of the 19th Amendment, Alice Paul works to have the Equal Rights Amendment introduced into Congress, which has yet to be adopted.

1924

The Ford Motor Company produces its 10,000,000th automobile, which literally mobilized America's first sexual revolution.

1925

Alongside advances in condom technology, companies step up their marketing. Sales of condoms skyrocket in this decade.

After more than two centuries of genocide, Native American (First Nations) peoples are uniformly granted U.S. citizenship via the Indian Citizenship Act, passed by Congress.

1927

A New York City ordinance prohibiting women from smoking in public is repealed.

1928

Anthropologist Margaret Mead publishes *Coming of Age in Samoa*, the first of her many books to educate Americans on different patterns of gender behavior. She was a major influence on raising gender consciousness for several decades.

The 1930s – The Great Depression, the Dust Bowl, the New Deal, & World War II begins. Radar, LPs, and color film.

1930

Eleanor Roosevelt transforms the role of the First Lady through her active participation in American politics and assists President Franklin D. Roosevelt in establishing the New Deal (the first federal safety net for the poor and elderly).

In Germany, Magnus Hirschfeld's Institute for Sex Research in Berlin is destroyed by Adolf Hitler's Nazis, prompting the exodus of German intelligentsia and the shift of the center of sexual science to America.

1931	After taking detailed histories of his patients, gynecologist Robert Dickinson (with Laura Beam) publishes *A Thousand Marriages: A Medical Study in Sex Education*, bringing the clitoris into sexual science.
	Frances Perkins becomes the first woman appointed to the U.S. presidential cabinet.
1932	Hattie Caraway becomes the first woman elected to the U.S. Senate (from Arkansas and was reelected in 1938).
1933	Niels Hoyer publishes *Man Into Woman: An Authentic Record of a Change of Sex*, documenting the first-ever identified sex-change operation: that of Lili Elbe (formerly Danish painter Einar Wegener). This first sexual surgery in Germany paved the way for the first American to have sexual surgery two decades later.
1936	Congress amends the Comstock Act, legalizing the distribution of birth-control information, devices, and services.

The 1940s—World War II continues; UN and NATO are founded. The earliest computers, microwaves, and the atom bomb.

1941	Women begin to enjoy greater economic and sexual freedoms as men leave to fight in World War II, a demographic shift that draws women into the workforce. Meanwhile, more than 400,000 women serve in various military positions with 16 killed in action and 88 taken as prisoners of war.
1945	Harvard Medical School begins admitting women for the first time.
1948	President Harry Truman orders the integration of the U.S. Armed Forces.
	Kinsey publishes *Sexual Behavior in the Human Male*, the first large-scale empirical study of American sexual behavior.

The 1950s—the Cold War, Korean War, and Cuban Revolution. Sputnik, solar cells, and polio vaccine.

1950	The Mattachine Society becomes first national gay rights organization (although it serves a primarily social function at first).
1952	Army veteran George Jorgensen becomes the first American to have sexual reassignment surgery, becoming blond bombshell Christine Jorgensen.
1953	Kinsey publishes *Sexual Behavior in the Human Female* as a follow-up to the 1948 publication on males, forever changing America's understanding of female sexuality.
1954	Supreme Court ends racial segregation in public schools after the landmark case *Brown v. Board of Education*.
	Masters and Johnson start a revolutionary research laboratory in St. Louis to study sexual behavior, resulting in the observation and physiological measurement of 10,000 orgasms by about 700 subjects between 1954 and 1966.
1955	Rosa Parks is arrested for refusing to move to the back of the bus, triggering citywide bus boycott in Montgomery, Alabama.
	The word "transsexual" is coined by physician Harry Benjamin.
1957	Psychologist Evelyn Hooker publishes a study showing gay men can be healthy and well-adjusted. Her study would later be cited in the declassification of homosexuality from the *Diagnostic and Statistical Manual of Mental Disorders*.
	Society for the Scientific Study of Sexuality (SSSS) is organized as America's leading professional organization for sex research.

The 1960s—The Vietnam War, Cuban Missile Crisis, and the Kennedy, King, and Malcom X assassinations. Lasers, cassettes, and the moon landing.

1961	The Food and Drug Administration (FDA) approves the first of many versions of oral contraceptive ("the pill"), which has perhaps the single most dramatic effect on sexual behavior of any event in human history.

1962	Helen Gurley Brown publishes frank guide *Sex and the Single Girl.*
1963	Betty Friedan publishes groundbreaking *The Feminine Mystique.*
	Martin Luther King leads the March on Washington for Jobs and Freedom.
	The Great Society was launched by President Lyndon B. Johnson as a set of domestic programs aimed at eliminating poverty and reducing racial injustice.
1964	The Civil Rights Act passes, prohibiting discrimination on the basis of race, color, religion, national origin, or gender.
	Sexuality Information and Education Council of the United States (SIECUS) founded for dissemination of accurate sex information.
1965	The U.S. Supreme Court overturns last state law prohibiting use of contraceptives by married couples.
	Congress passes the Voting Rights Act.
	Masters and Johnson publish *Human Sexual Response,* which becomes a bestseller despite being written for the scientific community.
1966	National Organization of Women founded to promote women's rights, the Equal Rights Amendment, civil rights, and reproductive rights.
	German-born American endocrinologist Harry Benjamin publishes *The Transsexual Phenomenon: A Scientific Report on Transsexualism and Sex Conversion in the Human Male and Female,* and later establishes a professional society for standards of care for transsexual individuals.
	The "Summer of Love" was an ongoing celebration mostly in the San Francisco/Monterey area that highlighted the hippie movement, free speech, opposition to the war, outdoor concerts ("down in Monterey"), and all things counterculture.
1967	Supreme Court overturns state law prohibiting interracial marriages in *Loving v. State of Virginia.* This story was later made into a movie called *Loving.*
	Thurgood Marshall becomes the first African American justice appointed to the Supreme Court.
	American Association of Sex Educators, Counselors, and Therapists (AASECT) founded to create professional standards for a growing number of sexual health educators and clinicians.
	American Indian Movement (AIM) founded as an American Indian advocacy group. Also, Congress passes the Indian Civil Rights Act (ICRA), also called the Indian Bill of Rights for Native Americans.
1968	Congress extends right to vote to 18-year-olds, who, until this time, had been old enough to be drafted and killed in Vietnam, but not to vote.
	Playwright Mart Crowley opens milestone play featuring lives of gay men called *The Boys in the Band,* which is later turned into a main stream cinema movie by the same name (1970).
	Shirley Chisholm, daughter of Caribbean immigrants, becomes first African American woman elected to Congress (New York).

The Stonewall Rebellion at the Stonewall Inn (a bar) in New York City marks advent of modern gay rights movement.

1969 Premier sexologist John Money introduces field of sexual identity, coins many new terms (including gender identity), and, with co-editor Richard Green, publishes ground breaking *Transsexualism and Sex Reassignment.*

Poet Maya Angelou publishes her first of many influential books called *I Know Why the Caged Bird Sings,* igniting a career as a powerful civil rights political activist.

The 1970s—Watergate, the oil crisis, and the energy crisis. *Voyager,* MRIs, and modern computing.

1970 Advent of sex education in public schools and proliferation of sex therapy.

Congress amends the Comstock Act of 1873 by deleting all references to contraception and all prohibitions on mailing advertisements for contraceptives (although the Comstock Act remains in effect today.)

Journalist and political activist Gloria Steinem co-founds the feminist-themed magazine *Ms.*

1972 Parents and Friends of Gays and Lesbians (PFLAG) established, eventually becoming nation's largest LGBTQA support organization with 400 chapters.

Congress passes Title IX, prohibiting sex discrimination in all aspects of education (including sports) that receive federal funding.

Sweden becomes model for United States when they become the first country to allow transsexual individuals the right to legally change their sex status.

1973 Declassification of homosexuality (ego dystonic version) as a mental illness in *Diagnostic and Statistical Manual* (DSM) by American Psychiatric Association (homosexuality was not completely removed from DSM until 1987).

The right to have an abortion is constitutionally protected by the Supreme Court.

1975 Homosexuality legalized in California after passage of Consenting Adult Sex Bill.

Leonard Matlovich becomes first American military service member (USAF) to out himself in protest of existing antigay discrimination.

1976 The Society for Sex Treatment and Research (SSTAR) established.

First women admitted to 4 of the 5 military service academies (West Point, Naval Academy, Coast Guard Academy, and Air Force Academy).

1977 Harvey Milk becomes the first openly gay man to hold public office in the history of California when he is elected to the San Francisco Board of Supervisors.

1979 California becomes first state to classify forced sex by a husband on his wife as rape.

First National Homosexual Rights March on Washington, DC.

The 1980s—The war on drugs, the fall of the Berlin Wall, and the continuation of the Cold War. NES, Atari, and the Macintosh 128K.

1980

The Democratic National Convention becomes the first national party to support gay rights when party leaders insert a new plank into the party platform: "All groups must be protected from discrimination based on race, color, religion, national origin, language, age, sex, or *sexual orientation*."

Sandra Day O'Connor becomes first female justice appointed to Supreme Court.

1981

First case of what would become known as AIDS documented by Centers for Disease Control (CDC).

1982

The Supreme Court rules that single-sex admissions to colleges violate equal protection clause of 14th Amendment (*Mississippi University for Women v. Hogan*).

1985

Leading sexologist Beverly Whipple and coauthors Alice Ladas and John Perry publish *The G Spot: And Other Recent Discoveries About Human Sexuality*.

Gay & Lesbian Alliance Against Defamation (GLAAD) organized to fight for gay rights and accelerate acceptance of the LGBTQA communities.

1986

Oprah Winfrey becomes the first woman to host and own her own national TV talk show (and would later become the first woman billionaire and first woman to start her own TV channel).

1987

For the first time, women earn more master's degrees in the United States than men (women will surpass men for most doctorate degrees in 2005).

Aretha Franklin becomes the first woman inducted into the Rock & Roll Hall of Fame.

1988

Congress passes Civil Rights Restoration Act to preserve and extend civil liberties set out in 1964 Civil Rights Act.

First Sexual Bill of Rights published for people living with disabilities.

Eli Coleman publishes first of several books on sexual health (*Chemical Dependency and Intimacy Dysfunction*), serves as president of several leading sexual health organizations (SSSS, WAS, WPATH, SSTAR), and eventually becomes first endowed academic chair in sexual health.

The 1990s—The Gulf War, formation of the EU, and Rwandan genocide. MP3 players, cell phones, and the World Wide Web.

1990

Congress passes Americans with Disabilities Act to protect and assist the 1 in 5 Americans living with either medical and/or psychological disabilities.

Supreme Court strikes down travel ban barring homosexual foreign nationals from entering the United States.

1993

Intersex Society of North America (ISNA) established.

World Health Organization (WHO) defines sexual health as "a core dimension of being human which includes sex, gender, sexual and gender identity, sexual orientation, eroticism, emotional attachment and love, and reproduction."

Congress passes Family Medical Leave Act, allowing men and women to take time off work to better care for loved ones (e.g., newborns, children, elderly).

1994   Sexual Medicine Society of North America (SMSNM) established.

Don't Ask, Don't Tell (DADT) instituted by Clinton administration as official U.S. policy on military service for gays, bisexuals, and lesbians.

1995   The American Association of People with Disabilities founded.

Supreme Court strikes down Virginia Military Institute's long-standing male-only admission policy (*United States v Virginia*).

1996   Barbara Walters becomes first woman to co-anchor on a major network evening news program.

Supreme Court declares amendment to Colorado state constitution allowing discrimination against gays, lesbians, bisexuals unconstitutional (*Romer v. Evans*).

1997   Comedian Ellen DeGeneres comes out as lesbian. Other openly gay celebrities have their own television shows at this time, starting to become mainstream media.

Madeline Albright becomes first woman to serve as U.S. Secretary of State.

The age of oral medications for sexual enhancement begins with Viagra, changing mainstream media with its sexually oriented ads.

1998   The murders of Matthew Shepard, a gay student at the University of Wyoming, and James Byrd Jr., an African American man in Texas killed by white supremacists, prompts start of wheels turning for federal hate-crime legislation for protection of LGBTQA and racial minorities.

First female fighter pilots fly missions in combat.

1999   Transgender Day of Remembrance founded for those who have lost their lives fighting for rights of transgender people everywhere.

The 2000s—9/11, the war on terror, and Hurricane Katrina. Genome sequencing, social media, and rovers on Mars.

2000   Social critic and writer Gloria Watkins, under the name bell hooks, publishes *Feminism is for Everybody: Passionate Politics* as one of several notable books on the intersectionality of race, gender, and capitalism (including *Ain't I a Woman?* in 1981).

2003   The Supreme Court overturns Texas anti-sodomy statute, stating it (and laws prohibiting same-sex expression) violated the U.S. Constitution.

2004   Massachusetts becomes first state to legalize same-sex marriage (*Lawrence v. Texas*).

2006   The FDA approves Gardasil for prevention of cervical cancer and other HPV-related diseases (including later approval for vaginal and vulvar cancers in 2008).

Nancy Pelosi becomes first woman Speaker of the House.

2007   American actress Candis Cayne, who came out as a woman in 1996, comes to national attention for being the first transgender woman to play a recurring transgender character with a major role on a prime-time television series.

	Barack Obama elected first African American president of the United States.
2008	Ann Dunwoody becomes first woman four-star general in U.S. military history.
	Rachel Maddow becomes first openly gay prime-time anchor to host a major news program in the United States.

	Congress passes the Matthew Shepard and James Byrd Jr. Hate Crimes Prevention Act of 2009.
2009	Sonia Sotomayor becomes first justice of Latinx heritage to serve on the Supreme Court.
	Eric Holder becomes first African American to serve as U.S. Attorney General.
	RuPaul's *Drag Race* cable television show airs on the VH-1 network.

The 2010s—the Arab Spring, political polarization, and Israeli-Palestinian conflict. Quantum computing, the *Rosetta* mission, and virtual reality.

2011	Nikki Haley becomes first female Indian American to become state governor and (later) U.S. Ambassador to the United Nations.
	Don't Ask Don't Tell is repealed.

2012	The FDA approves first rapid home-use HIV test kit that does not require sending a sample to a laboratory for analysis. The FDA also approves first pre-exposure prophylaxis (PrEP) for AIDS as a way for people to prevent getting HIV by taking a pill every day.
	Tammy Duckworth not only elected as one of the first Asian American women to Congress, but is first double-amputee woman elected to Congress (from Illinois), and then later the first disabled woman to be elected to Senate (in 2016), and the first woman to give birth as a senator (in 2018).

2013	The Supreme Court declares the Defense of Marriage Act (DOMA) unconstitutional.

2014	Adm. Michelle Howard is first woman to become a four-star admiral.
	Transgender people gain greater visibility with debut of television series *Transparent*. Actress Laverne Cox makes cover of *Time* issue titled "The Gender Tipping Point." The magazine issue reported that 1.5 million Americans identify as trans.

2015	The Supreme Court legalizes same-sex marriage (*Obergefell v. Hodges*).
	Loretta Lynch becomes first African American woman U.S. Attorney General.
	Caitlyn Jenner, formerly Olympic athlete Bruce Jenner, comes out as transgender and changes her name.

	Hillary Rodham Clinton becomes first woman to win a major party's presidential nomination.
2016	Kellyanne Conway becomes first woman to run a winning presidential campaign.
	President Obama announces Stonewall National Monument, the first national monument to LGBTQA civil rights.

2017

#MeToo, a social media campaign that turned into a social tsunami in the wake of sexual harassment allegations against Hollywood producer Harvey Weinstein, results in the resignation or firing of scores of leading figures in politics, entertainment, private industry, and the federal judiciary.

Virginia elects Danica Roem to House of Delegates, the first openly transgender individual to be elected and seated in a state legislature (defeating a 13-term incumbent who called himself state's "chief homophobe" and introduced the "bathroom bill" into state legislature).

Millions of women (and male supporters) donning pink-knitted "pussy hats" make the 2017 Women's March in Washington, DC, the largest single-day protest in American history and added political push for women to run for political office.

2018

Results of midterm elections sent a record number of women (100+) to an increasingly diverse Congress (Republican and Democratic), including many "political firsts" such as two Native Americans (one openly gay), two of Muslim faith, and one Palestinian American. Many states sent to Congress "first-time" congresswomen including Massachusetts and Connecticut, who sent two black women, while Arizona and Tennessee are getting their first female senators.

CHAPTER SEVEN

America's 20th-Century Journey from Sexosophy to Sexology

Written by Frederick Peterson

INTRODUCTION

America's sexual legacy of the 18th and 19th centuries (detailed in Chapter 6) laid a foundation for how crazy our culture is about sex (not in a good way) as a country coming into the 20th century. This chapter focuses on the key historical changes that occurred in the 20th century that helped illuminate a path of cultural transition to how Americans view sexuality today. A key aspect of this transition has been a shift from believing religion to be the ultimate authority of what is right to believing in science as a competing authority. We are still in that transition, as evidenced by millions of Americans who believe that religion trumps science in every instance, as opposed to seeing science as an alternative and valid point of view.

Religious and spiritual beliefs are very important in many of our lives, yet Americans more often consider factors other than religion when deciding how to behave sexually. For example, most American Catholics would likely agree with this assertion as the majority of Catholic Americans use birth control counter to Roman Catholic dogma. Protestants certainly defy their primary directive to be "fruitful and multiply" by way of the same birth control options. Although both Protestants and Catholics strongly emphasize that sex is to be saved for the sanctity of marriage, plenty of them are single mothers under age 30. The stigma of "shacking up" together 50 years ago has transitioned to premarital cohabitation being a cultural norm. And as the age of marriage keeps increasing, premarital sex has become another new norm (often as a prelude to marriage) despite religious instructions that sex is to be saved for marriage. When it comes to our sex lives, the inconsistencies go on and on.

As reviewed in the first chapters, these are just a few of the contradictions and paradoxes of life that stem from our sexophrenic legacy. How do we make sense of them? It's not easy. Serious explanations are complex and multifactorial. It is easier to note the dramatic differences of today from 50 to 60 years ago. For the most part, these changes reflect a relaxation of strict sexual mores and conventions from the first half of the 20th century (1900–1950). In a way, this chapter is a story of how we have moved from being totally crazy and cruel about sex (circa 1900) to just being moderately neurotic about sex by the year 2000. Although we have made significant progress over the last century, we are also witnessing a backlash in the form of cries for increased control, regulation, and repression of sexual expression.

Even so, Americans receive credit for moving away from the crazy and cruel views of sexuality as a nation (unfortunately, there will likely always be examples of severely crazy and cruel individuals). Consider the following examples from 19th-century America: socially sanctioned slavery, forcing young pregnant girls to give up their babies, involuntary sterilization of disadvantaged people, physical castration and lynching for interracial dating/marriage, forcing treatment on children for the pseudo-disease of masturbation, and diagnosing people as mentally ill simply for loving someone of the same sex. How did we do this? How did we evolve as a nation? The creation of sexual science has been the force propelling America toward a more democratic and humane society over the past century. This chapter is that story.

It's a fascinating story and one not often told. It is not just about sex research geeks who keep coming up with more enlightening study results with the public saying, "Oh, really!" and then changing their opinions and sexual behavior. In some ways, it's just the opposite. World events (such as war) and even local social mores of a university climate have also had significant impact on the world of sexual science. As we look back across the 20th century, we can see the give and take of this dynamic tension, which resulted in decades of liberal and conservative shifts back and forth for the slow but steady progression of sexual science.

At other times, the natural course of biology forces social change, such as the world pandemic of AIDS. Since the disease has first become prevalent, the WHO estimates that more than 70 million people have been infected with HIV and nearly half of them have died (WHO, 2017). The impact of AIDS on the science of sexuality and the sexual practices of Americans is hard to underestimate and will be up to future medical historians to assess. Finally, the changes we have seen over the past century cannot be told without discussion of the many individuals who developed new (and frequently unpopular) perspectives on sexuality.

And that is where we will begin, with a few of those sex-research geeks who went where no geek had gone before. Describing these researchers' work is telling the story of what is referred to as the "*Great Transition*," the period between the domination of sexosophy during the 19th century and the emergence of sexual science in the mid-20th century. Sexosophy, a term coined by medical psychologist John Money, is the philosophy and folklore about sexuality and is often infused with religious moralism. For most Americans, sexology (the scientific study of sex) has slowly superseded sexosophy as the dominant paradigm for understanding sexuality in the 20th century.

It can strongly be argued (from a historical perspective) that each of the first four decades of the 20th century deserves its own individual attention regarding notable events on both the American and world stages. Any history teacher would agree. However, for the purposes of brevity and to maintain a focus on the development of sexual science, the period of 1900–1940 will be treated here as singular. Relatively speaking, not much sexual science occurred during this 40-year period due to the prevailing conservativism and active academic suppression (such as what occurred with G.S. Hall). However, what was happening during the Great Transition was critical for setting the stage of sexual science to evolve.

Also for brevity's sake, the 1940s and 1950s will be described collectively and referred to as the Kinsey years. Masters and Johnson dominated the 1960s and 1970s, a period widely considered the "Golden Age" for sex research. After 1980, America witnessed an increasing medicalization of sex research in response to the advent of the AIDS crisis. As we hop and skip through the past century noting some of the most interesting developments in the new science of sexology, a few associated cultural changes will be mentioned that have influenced how we see sexuality and behave sexually today. Of special note will be the occasion of the most dangerous of all 20th-century phenomena (according to parents everywhere): the birth of rock and roll.

Accordingly, the significance of every important sex study will not be discussed (or even mentioned). To provide a bird's-eye view of the development of sexual science and the significant cultural changes associated, the timetable was provided just before this chapter. To discuss the many important studies in the totality of sexology would require an entire book rather than the summary presented here. We will take the bird's-eye view but swoop down for a closer look from time to time. Those interested in detailed review are referred to *The Sex Researchers* (Brecher, 1979) and *Science in the Bedroom: A History of Sex Research* (Bullough, 1994).

THE GREAT TRANSITION FROM SEXOSOPHY TO SEXOLOGY (PART I):

Antecedents to the American Sexual Revolution

To understand the 20th-century American view of sexuality, we must turn our attention to key thinkers in Europe. This is not surprising, because wealthy 19th-century Americans still saw Europe as the center of culture and studied abroad to earn advanced degrees. As with Tissot's influence from Switzerland on Benjamin Rush during a formative period of American medicine, a group of early European writers on sexuality influenced American leaders of medicine and psychology by planting new seeds in the American sexual psyche in the few decades before World War I. These seeds were not only planted but cultivated by visits from several of these key European scholars.

Many of these brave individuals risked much professionally and were even attacked personally (including physically) for breaking from the dominant medical thought of the 19th century. Many individuals challenged the orthodoxy, but Richard von Krafft-Ebing (1840–1902) and Elizabeth Blackwell (1821–1910) led the first small wave. The most significant names associated with bringing about a change of our view of sexuality (a second and primary wave, if you will) were Sigmund Freud (1856–1939) of Austria, Magnus Hirschfeld (1868–1935) of Germany, and Havelock Ellis (1859–1939) of England. Earning important honorable mentions in this summary are American gynecologist Robert Dickinson (1861–1950), French Princess Marie Bonaparte (1882–1962), German physician Iwan Bloch (1872–1922), German theorist Karl Ulrichs (1825–1895), and American feminist reformer

Margaret Sanger (1879–1966). Collectively, these individuals (and others) led the "Great Transition" period from sexosophy to sexology during the first few decades of the 20th century (Brecher, 1979; Bullough, 1994).

Dr. Richard von Krafft-Ebing, an early Austro-German physician, wrote a seminal work of sexology in 1886, entitled *Psychopathia Sexualis*, which was one of the first attempts by medicine to document and classify sexual variations. Krafft-Ebing collected 238 case studies that featured many examples of sadism, masochism, fetishism, homosexuality, and many other sexual variations (called deviations and perversions at the time). *Psychopathia Sexualis,* which ran through 12 editions, became a widely used and influential reference book for physicians as well as legal professionals. Krafft-Ebing advocated a sympathetic medical approach to treating people with these so-called sexual perversions rather than just putting them to death or locking them up. Hence, he pushed for reform of laws that dealt with sexual criminals. Most importantly, he brought the topic of sexuality into the domain of medicine and stimulated public discourse for decades. Unfortunately, his opinions were rife with the sexual myths of the time, including the notions that masturbation was the root of all sexual evils and any form of recreational sexual activity (all that wasn't intended to make babies) could essentially be considered a sexual perversion. For being the first and so influential (for better or worse), Krafft-Ebing is considered one of the early fathers of sexology (Krafft-Ebing, 1900).

Dr. Elizabeth Blackwell is very unusual as she was born in England but educated in America (the opposite of the usual educational track of the day). She graduated from Geneva Medical College of New York in 1849 and is considered the first woman to fully qualify as a physician (in England as well as the United States). She practiced for 20 years in the United States in a time when there was incredible prejudice against women in general but especially in the profession of medicine. In 1865, she and her sister Emily (also a physician) founded the Women's Medical College of the New York Infirmary. She then returned to England where she became a popular writer on several topics related to sexuality. Her most significant publication was *The Human Element in Sex* (1894), in which she described herself as a Christian physiologist. Like Krafft-Ebing, Dr. Blackwell reflected many of the prejudices and misinformation about sexuality of her time. She was, however, committed to sex education of youth, although it was steeped in Christian moralism and full of caution against the solitary vice of self-abuse. An early feminist, she called men out as morally corrupt and was a crusader against prostitution. Unlike many of her contemporaries, Blackwell concluded that women do have orgasms, although she referred to them as "sexual spasms." Like Krafft-Ebing, she brought sexuality into public discussion and added an important element missing until that time: a female point of view (Brecher, 1979).

THE GREAT TRANSITION FROM SEXOSOPHY TO SEXOLOGY (PART II):

Contributions from Freud, Ellis, and Hirschfeld (1896 to 1939)

What follows now is a brief discussion of the primary voices of the Great Transition—Freud, Ellis, and Hirschfeld. As the best known of the early scholars of sexuality, Freud was discussed briefly in the last chapter. As was noted, although Freud had many limitations to his conceptualization of sexuality, particularly regarding female sexual expression, he was one of the first to tread where most academics dared not go. Freud actually listened to women's experiences and used a careful case-study approach to formulate theories regarding female sexuality. Women experienced problems from a lack of effective birth control, serious risk of death during child bearing, and being diagnosed with hysteria. These were frequent and serious health problems for women a century ago. As mentioned previously, the diagnosis of hysteria represented elusive symptoms, often including sexual thoughts and desires then believed to be pathologic for women.

In his 1896 publication, *Studies of Hysteria* (with his mentor Josef Breuer), Freud introduced the new technique of psychoanalysis and detailed the commonality of most of the women's stories. He called this commonality "premature exposure," euphemistically referring to the sexual misuse of girls. Today, we would refer to this as childhood sexual abuse. Although Breuer argued for more neurophysiologic causes of hysteria, Freud was one of the first to give the sexual misuse of children a name and suggested it was problematic in terms of generating symptoms of hysteria later in life. Additionally remarkable, Breuer proposed that the condition of hysteria could be treated without medical or pharmacological intervention, but rather talk therapy (and Freud adopted Breuer's method of catharsis—a key component of psychoanalysis). Even more, this is one of the earliest scholarly assertions (one of a few in 19th-century Europe) that took a step closer to men having to accept responsibility for the sexual abuse perpetrated upon females, particularly girls.

Okay, this sounds good so far—like Freud is an advocate for women—but check out what happened next. The publication of *Studies of Hysteria* was received with skepticism by Freud's peers. The famous Krafft-Ebing, then-president of the Viennese Society of Psychiatry and Neurology, called Freud's theory a "scientific fairy tale." Freud, angry, called his critics "asses [who] could go to hell" (Schultz & Schultz, 2004). What Freud did next changed the course of history for Western civilization for the next 70 years.

The following year, Freud introduced what has been referred to as the childhood seduction theory. In doing so, he dramatically modified his conclusions by asserting that the stories of his female hysteric patients were actually fantasized accounts and not true memories of childhood experiences. With this seduction theory, Freud preserved his basic assertion that sex is the root cause of neurosis and also made his theory much more acceptable to his peers. After all, if Freud called his female patient reports "fantasies" instead of childhood sexual abuse, then men were off the hook by not being implicated as perpetrators of sexual misuse of their daughters (Masson, 1984).

At the same time, Freud systematically invalidated the voices of women who were survivors of sexual abuse and the topic of childhood sexual abuse would not seriously surface again in academic and scientific circles until the 1970s. In 1909, Freud visited Clark University in Massachusetts upon invitation of its then president, G. Stanley Hall (the previously mentioned founder of the American Psychological Association). Freud was received warmly as a major influence on American thinking; many of his key terms in psychoanalysis became integrated into the everyday language (Freudian slip, ego, pleasure principle, etc.) and even became parlor games of the day. Two years later, the American Psychiatric Association was founded and American psychoanalysis as a medical specialty treatment was off and running.

Although Freud made original and important contributions to understanding the inner workings of the human mind, it is also common opinion that much of his psychoanalytic theories were based on his own personal psychopathology (Schultz & Schultz, 2004). One example is his negative view of sexuality and female sexuality in particular. After all, he is the originator of the phrase, "anatomy is destiny" (often associated with the belief in female inferiority and the penis as the basis of women's envy of men). At age 41, Freud declared to his wife Martha that he was done with sex as he had transcended such a primitive need, even though he is believed to blame his wife for ending their sex life. He is reported to say, "Sexual excitement is of no more use to a person like me" (Freud, 1954). He then proceeded to have an affair with his wife's sister. Freud's theory of neurosis was actually a theory of his own neurotic symptoms, having self-diagnosed sexual neurasthenia that could be caused by masturbation, coitus interruptus, or sexual abstinence (Krull, 1986).

At about the time Freud was rocketing to celebrity stardom of the day, a more humble English physician was writing and speaking out for a more positive view of sexuality and especially a much more positive view of both women's sexuality and homosexuality (Freud's perspectives have been interpreted as sexophobic, homophobic, and misogynist). Havelock Ellis was way ahead of his time and his perspective was not as popularly accepted as Freud's. Although his name may not be familiar to many, his six-volume series called *Studies in the Psychology of Sex* (1897–1910) became an illuminating source that guided physicians, psychologists, and sexologists for decades (Brecher, 1979).

Ellis advocated for the view of sexuality as a positive and pleasurable aspect of life, one even to be celebrated rather than feared. Anticipating the conclusions of Kinsey 50 years later, Ellis argued that many sexual behaviors previously labeled as deviant and abnormal are actually normal. Ellis convincingly drew his conclusions from his own observations as well as studies in anthropology, animal behavior, and history. In this way, Ellis helped counterbalance the severely sex-negative views of Krafft-Ebing, whose work unfortunately became the basis of many legal codes regarding sexual behavior and was influential in the early classification of mental illnesses.

Ellis was one of the early contra-onanists arguing that there was no evidence that masturbation leads to mental or physical disorders. Anticipating the conclusions of research 100 years later (and presented in Chapter 8), Ellis even went way out on a limb by describing masturbation having a positive function of relieving tension! This was unheard of in medical circles of the time because of the widely held notion of masturbation as disease and to speak out against the sex-negative paradigm invited professional repercussions. He also documented that women have sexual desire no less intense than men and women's sexual interests are positive rather than something to be pathologized with a medical diagnosis (Bullough, 1994).

Another critically important figure of the "Great Transition" to sexual science was the great sex researcher Magnus Hirschfeld (a contemporary of Freud and Ellis). As Ellis was the leading reformer in England, Hirschfeld became the leading crusader in Germany, with many groundbreaking achievements. For example, he established the first Institute of Sexual Science with more than 20,000 volumes (1919), edited the first *Journal of Sexology* (1908), wrote and acted in the first gay-rights film (*Different from the Others*, 1919), and was the first to advocate for acceptance of people we today call transgendered individuals. Hirschfeld was in the epicenter of Europe being the leader of sexology for the first 30 years of the 20th century (Wolff, 1986).

Hirschfeld was Jewish, gay, and the first big-time advocate for human sexual rights, especially for gay, lesbian, and transgender people. He organized a grassroots political movement to change German laws that discriminated against those who engaged in same-sex activities as well as cross-dressing. He collected signatures of support from the likes of Albert Einstein, Hermann Hesse, and Leo Tolstoy. In an act of gay bashing, Hirschfeld was beaten in the street and left for dead because of his advocacy of gay rights (he suffered a fractured skull). Many of his contributions to sexology have been neglected (several leading college textbooks on sexuality barely even mention his name) until recent renewed interest in his work. The film *The Einstein of Sex* documented the incredible life and times of this early sexologist (Praunhein, 1999).

Europe was the center for the development of sexology, and other German scholars deserve brief note. The physician Iwan Bloch was the first to propose the field of sexology in his 1907 book, *The Sexual Life of Our Time*. Bloch proposed that sexology be an interdisciplinary field; medicine or any other discipline could not adequately maintain it alone. Bloch was also famous for his research on venereal diseases, which helped establish sexually transmitted diseases as one of the key areas of the field of sexual health (Brecher, 1979).

Along with Hirschfeld and Bloch, Karl Ulrichs deserves special note as being at the epicenter of German (and European) sexology. He began the first theoretical study of homosexuality (with publications as early as 1864) and was an outspoken advocate to end state prosecution of homosexual practices. The term "homosexual" first originated as a neutral legal term, not associated with "perversion" until the medical model was applied to it. Because of his work as an attorney, writer, and advocate, Ulrichs can be thought of as the "grandfather of the gay liberation" (Bullough, 1994).

The center of sexual sciences shifted from Germany to America because of one individual named Adolf Hitler and the rise of the Nazi Party. Only three months after coming into power in 1933, the Nazis organized an attack on the Institute for Sexual Science while Hirschfeld was lecturing in America. All works of Jewish authors, the majority of the library of the institute, and other works considered "un-German" were burned in the street. Freud was quoted as saying, "What progress we are making. In the Middle Ages, they would have burnt me. Nowadays, they are content burning my books" (Schultz & Schultz, 2004).

Sadly and ironically, Freud was wrong. If they could have, the Nazis would have burnt Freud to ashes as they did the staff of the institute and many of the clients who came to its clinic for clinical assistance (the Nazis confiscated the clinic's client list). While 6 million Jews were the primary target and victims of the Holocaust, the Nazis killed another 5 million non-Jews who were individuals who were identified as LGBTQA, physically or mentally disabled, Roma (gypsies), Poles, Soviets, and other Slavic heritage; non-Christian religion followers, and members of competing political parties (Altman, 2003). With significant financial and political assistance from Princess Marie Bonaparte, Freud fled Vienna to London (after his daughter Anna was briefly arrested and jailed). Hirschfeld was heartbroken about his institute and the fates of those involved with it. However, he was fortunate to be out of Germany at the time of the attack and never returned. He died in 1935 while living in Italy in exile. Havelock Ellis died quietly four years later. Freud also died in 1939, but by his choice at the hands of his own physician, who had agreed to assist Freud to die (via euthanasia) when

Freud's oral cancer became too painful (even with his liberal use of cocaine) and essentially too much for him to bear (Brecher, 1979).

Freud, Hirschfeld, and others among the German (and European) intelligentsia immigrated to escape Nazis persecution, many coming to the United States (including those involved in sexology as well as all the sciences). For example, the famous gynecologist Hans Lehfeldt came to New York and later helped establish America's premier sex research organization, the Society for the Scientific Study of Sexuality (SSSS) (Bullough, 1994).

THE GREAT TRANSITION FROM SEXOSOPHY TO SEXOLOGY (PART III):

Contributions from Davis, Dickinson, and Bonaparte (1900 to 1939)

During the first few decades after 1900, few scientific studies were published in America. Three exceptions are of note. One was by Katherine Davis, who surveyed 2,200 women regarding their sexual lives and published the results in a book appropriately entitled *Factors in the Sex Life of Twenty-Two Hundred Women* (1929). American gynecologist Robert Dickinson also published several books on the topics of birth control (1927), an illustrated medical manual for control of conception (1931), and on sexual adjustment (1932). His best-known work (written with Laura Beam) was a study of more than a thousand case studies in a text called *One Thousand Marriages* (Dickinson & Beam, 1932). He kept excellent clinical records on most of his patients; upon retirement, he gave them to a young biology professor at Indiana University. Thereby Dickinson became a major influence on (and adviser to) the later work of Alfred Kinsey (Brecher, 1969).

The third honorable mention goes to the remarkable Princess Marie Bonaparte, the great-grand-niece of Napoleon and wife of Prince George of Greece. As if these aspects of her celebrity were not enough, she was also the first female researcher to take physiological measures regarding female sexuality. Princess Marie got out her ruler and measured the distance between the clitoris and the opening of the vagina (entroitus) on 243 women. She found a direct relationship between the anatomical distance and the likelihood of orgasms reported by these women: The shorter the distance between the clitoris and vaginal opening, the easier it was to climax and the more frequently the women reported having orgasms (Roach, 2008). After reaching this conclusion, she then had her own physician *move her clitoris closer to her vaginal opening!* (Baker-Benfield, 1975). Now THAT is a researcher who believes in her own conclusions.

This research (and surgery) by Princess Marie anticipated the "love surgery" practiced in the 1980s, which realigned the clitoris closer to the vaginal opening. Some women swore by this surgery and thought it greatly improved their sexual satisfaction. That was all fine and good until some obstetricians or gynecologists (OB/GYNS) started doing the procedure without written consent of patients, including one particular physician in Dayton, Ohio. After a while, the nurses in the operating room started asking, "Does he have her permission to do that?" The subsequent class-action suit by a number of his patients resulted in the physician not only losing his Ohio license to practice medicine but ultimately contributing to the closing of the medical center where he practiced. Unfortunately, it also closed down my first research program, which was being conducted at the labor and delivery department of the same hospital. This research investigated biosocial aspects of the transition into parenthood and offered couples a new type of childbirth education to help them deliver their baby (called the Family-Centered Perinatal Education class, described in the next chapter).

THE GREAT TRANSITION FROM SEXOSOPHY TO SEXOLOGY (PART IV):

Sanger, the First Sexual Revolution, World War II, and the Pill (1920s to 1950s)

Aside from World War I, the really big social developments during this period involved the women's suffrage movement, the great migration of Europeans and others into America, and, of course, the Great Depression. Women's suffrage in this country is typically considered to have been formally organized in 1848 at Seneca Falls, New York. After 72 years of continuous struggle after that date, women (that is, only white American women) were granted the right to vote with passage of the 19th Amendment to the Constitution in 1920. If interested, you may enjoy an excellent film depicting these events in the 2004 release named *Iron Jawed Angels* (Bigwood, 2004).

However, a huge battlefront was over control of women's bodies and the right for women to have information about (and receive) birth-control services. Birth control was a new term coined by feminist reformer and early sex educator Margaret Sanger. In 1910, she began publishing material promoting a woman's right to birth control, which violated obscenity laws of the time. Threatened with imprisonment, she fled the country and lived in England, where she worked with (and had an affair with) Havelock Ellis. She later returned to America and opened the first birth-control clinic in the United States in 1916. The opening of this clinic resulted in her arrest for illegal distribution of information about contraception (a violation of the Comstock Law of 1873). Sanger spent 30 days in jail, but it was a huge publicity victory for the fledgling birth-control movement. The subsequent trial and her appeal contributed greatly to the popular acceptance of birth control (even as birth control options were back then—the pill was decades away from development).

In 1921, Sanger formed the American Birth Control League, which later evolved into Planned Parenthood Federation of America. A tireless activist, she worked on reforming laws that were barriers to free distribution of birth-control information and services. Much later, Sanger was instrumental in promoting the development of oral birth control by recruiting Gregory Pincus, a research scientist in human reproduction. Sanger found funding for his development of Enovid, the first oral contraceptive for women, which was approved by the U.S. Food and Drug Administration (FDA) in 1960 (Gordon, 2002). Five years later, Sanger witnessed another (and her last) milestone in the birth-control movement that she had established—the Supreme Court decision of *Griswold v. Connecticut*. This decision overruled an old Comstock law in Connecticut that prohibited any person from using "any drug, medicinal article or instrument for the purpose of preventing conception." Hence, the U.S. Supreme Court decided (in *Griswold v. Connecticut*) that married couples could legally make choices about using medical birth control based on the constitutional right to marital privacy regarding sex (Stone, 2017). Sanger died in an Arizona nursing home the following year (1966). Nearly five decades and two generations later, we often forget how recent these struggles were and how many people sacrificed to make them happen.

A review of the first 40 years of the 20th century demonstrates contractions and loosening of social conventions regarding women's sexual expression. During World War I, there was a "release of sexual restraints" among military personnel serving abroad as well as women back home (Hirschfeld, 1937). Fewer men were available for heterosexual women, who were compelled to be more sexually aggressive to compete for partners. Perhaps women in close emotional friendships were more likely to explore same-sex relations as well. World War I is believed to have fueled a sense of increased social and economic freedom for women. Liberal attitudes expanded during the Roaring Twenties, when women were afforded greater sexual freedoms. The fashions of the day also reflected an increased sense of freedom with a new progressive model of womanhood. This was reflected in the emergence of the flapper, a woman who took liberties to break the feminine conventions of the day. Flappers sported shorter hair ("bobs") and dressed in lanky "straight and flat" styles that did not emphasize breasts or curves. Designer Coco Chanel founded her iconic fashion company as the use of Victorian-age corsets declined, dress necklines plunged, and dress hemlines kept getting higher. Sexual attitudes became more relaxed in this new Jazz Age, and corresponding changes were reflected in popular culture, especially fashion, dance, literature, and the movies. Zelda Sayre was the wife of F. Scott Fitzgerald and embodied the new feminine spirit. Fitzgerald referred to her as "America's first flapper." Louise Brooks was a leading lady in the silent movies and popularized the short bob hairstyle for women. Many flappers were noted for their smoking, drinking, and cursing in public as well as enjoying casual sex.

Young men referred to as sheiks were the male companions of flappers, proud to wear the latest-fashion condoms that had started to show up in men's public bathrooms in American cities and on college campuses. Sheiks slicked their hair back, wore bow ties, and either fedoras or straw hats. But the most notable signs of success for sheiks were their oversized raccoon coats and their big black cars. The advent of mass-produced automobiles cannot be underestimated as a factor creating greater sexual opportunities, whether it was the back seat or the drive to a country pasture. Of course, the Ford Motor Company helped out as much as it could by producing their ten-millionth automobile by 1924 and literally *mobilized* America's first sexual revolution. In the movies, actor Rudolph Valentino epitomized sheiks, and then was followed by the young Bob Hope.

However, these increased liberties were short-lived as the Great Depression had an overall negative effect on the condition of American women. Although women felt more sexually permissive during the 1920s, many returned to more austere and restrictive conventions after the 1929 Crash. While Eleanor Roosevelt may have tried to champion women's rights during the Depression, there were fewer jobs, more financial desperation, and more women struggled to care for and feed their children. This dilemma was further complicated by the shortage of effective birth control. In short, shelter and survival trumped sex. Essentially, women's needs took another step back behind the needs of everyone else. Ms. Roosevelt did work with her husband on the New Deal, trying to improve working conditions and increase social welfare programs. However, World War II is generally credited with ending the economic despair of the Depression, and that is when women entered the work world as a large labor force and reclaimed greater freedoms. Flappers as well as American women in general would not see a return to increased sexual liberties for another decade until the fateful event in December 1941 that drew the United States into the war.

Prior to Pearl Harbor, Franklin Roosevelt's New Deal of social reforms are believed to be partly in response to the increasingly desperate economic conditions of the American people but also partly in response to political upheavals occurring around the globe. The Bolshevik revolution in Russia and the murder of the czar and his family shocked the world. The long fight to end child labor, create safe working conditions, and fair pay for the 40-hour workweek was a century-long struggle. Many in the women's rights movement, such as Sanger and Mother Jones, were very involved in the struggle for workers' rights because of the exploitation of women and children in the workforce.

The fight for workers' rights has a long history in America such as Chicago's Haymarket Massacre in 1886 that helped win the fight for an eight-hour workday. After the success of worker political parties in other countries during and after World War I, America's ruling class feared a home-grown working-class revolution. Their fears intensified after deadly battles across the country such as the Paint Creek-Cabin Creek strikes in West Virginia (1912–1913), the Ludlow Massacre in Colorado (1914), the steelworker strikes (1919), and many other labor revolts that led to hundreds of deaths and thousands of suspected Communists being deported. Most Americans are not aware of the amazing history of the "Mine Wars" that occurred throughout Appalachia but especially with the miners in the mountains of southern West Virginia. Native mountaineers, African American migrants, and European immigrants were all involved in a protracted struggle for workers' rights. Decades of violence, strikes, assassinations, and marches accompanied their attempts to form unions and culminated in the Battle of Blair Mountain in 1921, which was the largest armed insurrection since the Civil War, involving 5,000 armed miners marching through West Virginia. The miners' strikes against worker exploitation raised important questions about what freedom and democracy meant in America and set the stage for the burgeoning middle-class decades later ("The Miner Wars" on *The American Experience*, 2016).

These struggles for worker rights led to progressive concessions in the formation of the New Deal. It also planted the seeds of the Red Scare via the rise of J. Edgar Hoover's reign over the Federal Bureau of Investigation (FBI) and more civil liberty infringements demonstrated by Senator Joseph McCarthy's witch hunt for Communists in the government as well as the private sector. These changes in America's political climate would make it difficult to propose sex research, find funding for such research, and even keep one's job! Early sex researchers such as Vern Bullough and Alfred Kinsey were accused of being Communists. The FBI had a file on Bullough, which he later obtained and read (Bullough, 1994).

THE KINSEY YEARS (1940 TO 1956)

If you have not seen the movie *Kinsey* (Mutrux, 2004) and you are a fan of not-often-told American history, it is highly recommended that you watch this entertaining and educational film. The movie may have taken artistic license in a few places in regard to historical accuracy, but it is an overall fascinating story of Kinsey's life and career. At a 2007 SSSS conference, Kinsey's daughters were on a panel presentation and described the movie as entertaining. The research institute that bears their father's name at the University of Indiana became the mecca for the scientific study of sex worldwide after the burning of Hirschfeld's institute in Berlin. One thing that neither Kinsey's daughters nor the movie addressed in detail was the accusation that Kinsey was a Communist sympathizer as an attempt to discredit his scientific work.

As previously mentioned, medical historian Ed Brecher observed in his book *The Sex Researchers* (1979) that three publications challenged and permanently changed the American view of sexuality. Kinsey and his associates produced two of these groundbreaking works: *Sexual Behavior of the Human Male* (1948) and *Sexual Behavior of the Human Female* (1953). The third publication was *Human Sexual Response* by Masters and Johnson in 1966.

In short, the Kinsey Institute for Sex Research at Indiana University became the mecca of sexology because of three primary reasons: Accidental timing, a protective university environment committed to academic freedom, and the one-track obsessive-compulsiveness of an incredible scientific mind. The timing factor is simply that Kinsey's major work (published in 1948 and 1953) filled an empirical gap between Freud/Ellis/Hirschfeld (they died in the late 1930s) and the work of Masters and Johnson that was done secretly during the 1950s and 1960s but not published until 1966.

The academic protection that Kinsey enjoyed was provided by Indiana University President Herman Wells, which allowed Kinsey to continue his groundbreaking (and extremely controversial) research despite the enormous outcry of public dismay after the publication of *Sexual Behavior of the Human Male* (Kinsey, Pomeroy, & Martin, 1948). This study was based on face-to-face interviews with more than 12,000 men regarding every aspect of their sexual lives. The results were startling. Nearly 4 in 10 men admitted to having affairs, 37% of men admitted to having at least one homosexual-oriented experience after puberty to the point of orgasm, and more than 90% admitted to masturbating as an adult. Although this was shocking to many, it also built the first large empirical sample of adult Americans who said they engaged in masturbation when such behavior was still considered the disease of onanism or self-abuse by many physicians (and the public in general).

One main conclusion of the Kinsey report was that no statistical relationship existed between masturbation and any disease or disability (Kinsey, Pomeroy, & Martin, 1948). In other words, if almost 9 of 10 men said they masturbated, where was all the disease and disability? Kinsey provided long-anticipated empirical support to refute the notion of onanism. The crack in the monolith began to widen. Also evident from Kinsey's work was the great diversity of sexual expression found in this large sample of Americans and the lack of statistical relationship between homosexual activity and any disease or disability. These research findings, along with those from the study of female sexuality, contributed to the major social changes seen decades later, such as the declassification of homosexuality as a mental illness (1973) and the normalization of masturbation as a nonharmful, even positive sexual activity.

The controversy over the 1948 report on male sexuality turned out to be a small molehill compared with the media storm and public condemnation received by the female report in 1953. As a result, the governor of Indiana reportedly called Indiana University President Wells and demanded that Kinsey be fired that same day. Stanchly defending academic freedom as a critical element of university environment, Wells symbolically saluted the governor's demand by raising his middle digit.

Whereas 90% of men admitted to masturbation, 62% of women admitted to doing the same. For women, Kinsey concluded that masturbation was a much more reliable source of orgasm than intercourse and that masturbation also seemed to facilitate a woman's ability to reach orgasm during intercourse. Although the men reported a rate of 37% for same-sex-related experiences to the point of orgasm, women reported the same at a rate of 13% (although 28% reported same-sex experiences that did not involve orgasm) (Kinsey, Pomeroy, Martin, & Geppard, 1953).

For both women and men, one of the most important results of Kinsey's research was the breaking of the taboo of silence regarding sex. Because Americans had a new opportunity to discuss sex, especially the results of large-scale empirical studies, they were more likely to free themselves from the stigma of discussing sexuality. People were less likely to see themselves (as well as others) as perverts and deviants when they were simply people living within a context of incredible diversity across human sexual expression. As a biologist, Kinsey helped us see the world in terms of continuums, not dichotomies; differences between people are a matter of degree, rendering discrete categories (like "homosexuality") less meaningful and less condemning. These concepts led to the famous Kinsey seven-point continuum of sexual orientation (from complete heterosexuality on one end to complete homosexuality on the other). The reconceptualization of sexual orientation as a continuum rather than a dichotomy is now being repeated regarding nonbinary expressions of gender and sexual identity. This is the crux of the gender revolution we find our culture in the midst of today (and discussed in detail in Chapter 11).

Since Kinsey's death in 1956, the Kinsey Institute has continued as a mecca for research and scholarship for all interested in advancing our understanding of this basic component of our existence as humans. I am thankful to the former institute director, Dr. John Bancroft (who personally shared his training model for students interested in clinical sexology) and for the many summer institutes I was able to attend and listen to the leading thinkers in the field of sexual research. They shared their insights with the rest of the world through the Kinsey Institute—people like Kinsey's research associate Paul Gebhard, pioneer sexologist John Money, anthropologist Gilbert Herdt, and a host of other leading researchers. The country and indeed the world is fortunate for this center of research and education that is still today nurturing new generations of leaders in the field of sexual health.

THE MASTERS AND JOHNSON YEARS: THE GOLDEN YEARS OF SEX RESEARCH (1954 TO 1980)

First, an anecdote. From time to time, I find myself in very fortunate circumstances. During my preparation to be a psychologist and sex therapist, I was able to be trained and supervised by Dr. Ron Fox (past-president of the American Psychological Association) as well as Dr. Judith Seifer (past-president of the American Association of Sex Educators, Counselors, & Therapists). In 1993, Uncle Sam sent me on a new adventure. The Department of Veterans Affairs (VA) approved a request to take a sabbatical for academic year 1993–1994 and sent me off to study sex with the pioneer sex researcher William Masters.

In the spring of 1994, there was a buzz around the Masters and Johnson Institute in St. Louis (the Institute). There was talk about producing a documentary film on the life and times of pioneer sex researchers William Masters and Virginia Johnson. In anticipation of using historical materials to produce such a film, Dr. Masters excused me from my duties as clinical fellow and directed me to complete an all-out search to find some of these archived documents. Most prized of all, Doc Masters wanted to find a research film produced three decades earlier, which highlighted the sex physiology research conducted at the Institute from 1954 to 1966. The practical problem at hand was nobody at the Institute had any idea where this film or other archives were located.

The Institute had long moved off the campus of Washington University after notoriety of its sex research program gained national attention. The Institute had moved several times and (in 1994) was located at the Arsenal, a historical site in St. Louis near an Italian neighborhood known as the Hill. I was assigned the task of combing through decades of reel-to-reel recordings, training materials, draft manuscripts, and other usual-and-customary equipment needed in your typical sex research laboratory. Doc was particularly interested finding the famous artificial coition equipment, which simulated sexual intercourse for women by providing a seat with an attached joy stick controlling the speed and depth of a dildo's penetration of the vagina.

What Doc wanted was the equipment that facilitated the world's discovery of how female lubrication actually occurs. You see, Masters and Johnson attached a video camera to the bottom of the dildo, which was made out of clear glass to allow filming of the changes to the inner lining of the vagina during the stages of sexual excitement. For the first time ever, scientists had direct proof of how droplets of vaginal lubrication form, a process named transduation. After millennia of evolution, a key step in *Homo sapiens* sexuality was better understood in terms of the facilitation of conception. As a gynecologist, Doc wanted to include the video of this discovery in the documentary and maybe hoped it would count for consideration of a Nobel Prize in medicine.

No such luck. I later learned that this equipment had been disassembled by clinic staff years earlier (also reported later by Roach, 2008). However, I did find Doc's prized film of the sexual response cycle during female masturbation in the sex laboratory. Before returning to the Institute, I had to get the film converted onto VHS video format (remember, it was the 1990s). I knew this film would have great value to teaching medical students and others about basic sex physiology as well as the history of sexology. I literally had one of those experiences of the devil (in me) speaking in one ear and an angel making the counterargument in the other. "Go ahead! Make a copy for yourself. It is in the name of medical education and many will benefit!" "Don't you dare! You don't have permission! Besides, Doc will give you a copy." In one of those times when you know you just have to do the right thing, I made only one VHS copy of the film and returned with it to the Institute.

Doc was thrilled with the news, and it was the first and only time I saw his austere expression break into a partial smile. Doc immediately arranged for a review of the film with the clinic staff. The grainy white-and-black images showed a female subject masturbating while a narrator explained the physiologic changes being witnessed in her body in very clinical terms, such as the appearance of the sex rash on her upper chest. It was really remarkable watching Doc view this film, which he may not have seen in decades. I made the mistake of asking, "Who is the narrator?" Wow, what a reaction from Doc! Any favor the young steward had gained by finding the film instantly evaporated as Doc curtly explained that HE was the narrator! I had failed to connect the narrator's voice to Doc's voice (as it was on a crude recording and nearly 40 years later). Nearly 25 years after this experience, I still do not own a copy of this Masters and Johnson research film.

However, I did ask. Doc sternly glared and dismissed the question with the comment, "This film is way too raw for the public." At that moment, I realized how far Doc was out of touch with the changed sensibilities of American adults. It was 40 years later and American adults were desensitized to nudity and sexual activity on film, especially students who sign up for college courses on human sexuality.

Perhaps he was also still sensitive to all the intense criticism and personal attacks he endured when *Human Sexual Response* was published (Masters & Johnson, 1966). My initial conversations with Doc when I arrived at the Institute led me to think so. I had asked Doc for his reaction to medical historian Ed Brecher's biography of Doc's life and description of his work. Doc responded that he could not say as he never read it! When I asked Doc why he would not read a biography written of him, Doc explained that he decided never to read anything written about him after the intensely negative public reaction to *Human Sexual Response* in 1966. He added that despite a public outcry in hate letters to the Institute and letters to the editorial page in hometown papers across the country, Americans were *privately* reading the text (which read as dryly as a NASA manual) and bookstores could not keep it on the shelves.

What made some people so incensed? Doc and Virginia Johnson were the first to study human sexuality scientifically and publish their studies for general public consumption. They studied sexual responsiveness of people like other scientists had studied the nervous, digestive, or cardiovascular systems. They were not actually the first to conduct scientific studies of sex physiology, but they did so in a large-scale way while employing empirical methods as other scientists did, including direct observation and measurement of physiological sex reactions of the body. And what really irritated many was that they did so without addressing the question of "love."

This was really too much for some Americans to tolerate without voicing condemnation of Masters and Johnson for breaking the great taboo of not only *talking* about sex, but doing it scientifically without reference to love or marriage. The great American silence on sexuality was broken by Kinsey getting an inside description of what behaviors go on in the bedroom. Masters and Johnson provided a detailed account of what people do with their bodies under the sheets! This was such a monumentally significant approach because it not only provided an accurate picture of sex physiology but also laid the foundation for assisting couples who are experiencing "trouble in the bedroom" by getting sex therapy.

Between 1954 and 1966, the research team at the Institute studied nearly 700 individuals (including 276 married couples) and created a model of human sexual responsiveness based on the physical details of more than 10,000 orgasms, all observed under laboratory conditions. If you could not have an orgasm through masturbation and intercourse while being observed, you were eliminated as a participant. As a research subject, not only did you have to "do it" naked while being watched (and filmed), but you may also at times have to be "wired up" for heart rate, respiration, galvanic skin response, and so on (Masters & Johnson, 1966). That may seem an obvious bias in subject recruitment that would skew research results. However, Masters and Johnson said "poppycock."

They were not measuring attitudes or other sociological aspects of sexuality. They wanted to focus on and measure only directly observable sexual responses of the body. They believed that the body responds in a uniform way sexually, regardless of psychological or social attributes (just as everyone has a heart that works pretty much the same way, as long as they are healthy).

So what are some of the highlights of their research? Here are just a few of the surprising results (surprising at least back in 1966):

1. Male and female sexual responses were similar by going through what is described as a four-stage sexual response cycle: excitement, plateau, orgasm, and resolution. This model of stages has subsequently been revised but remains essentially true to the core description provided by Masters and Johnson.

2. Although men and women go through the same stages, some patterns are more common for men and some more common for women. For example, men move more rapidly through the stages and have a longer resolution stage (young men are more commonly "rabbit style," with quick ejaculations, and take longer than women to "bounce back" with additional erections after orgasm). Women, on an average, move more slowly through the stages (a definite advantage) and are less consistent in experiencing orgasms, yet have a much greater capacity for multiple orgasms.

3. Despite what men would like to believe, women do not need a penis inside the vagina to experience orgasm. Most women achieve orgasm primarily through clitoral stimulation, whether it is provided directly or indirectly (as it is through intercourse).

4. Despite what Freud believed, orgasm by direct clitoral stimulation (as with masturbation) and orgasm through intercourse were physiologically similar for women. This permanently discounted Freud's sexist notion of the "inferior and immature" orgasm by clitoral masturbation as compared with what Freud considered "authentic and mature" orgasms by intercourse.

5. Women have a wider range of means of sexual stimulation than men. Under laboratory conditions, women were able to orgasm by many more types of genital stimulation alone and some were able to orgasm by breast stimulation alone.

6. Masters and Johnson scientifically documented the process of transudation (also referred to as vaginal sweating), in which beads of lubrication form on the vaginal lining.

As mentioned earlier (and unlike Kinsey), the sex physiology research of Masters and Johnson not only led to the first fundamental understanding of how our body works sexually, but also served as a basis for treating couples who experience "trouble in the bedroom." Their publication of *Human Sexual Inadequacy* (Masters & Johnson, 1970) provided guidelines to a therapeutic approach to resolving sexual dysfunction (a term they coined), creating an entirely new professional field: sex therapy. This cognitive-behavioral approach was extensively researched at the Institute with hundreds of couples because Masters and Johnson treated sexual dysfunction as a problem of the couple, not the individual. Chapter 9 provides a good example of this approach by describing a young Latinx couple overcoming the challenges of an unconsummated seven-year marriage.

Results of the research were remarkable; treatment of what they called premature (rapid) ejaculation demonstrated an effectiveness rate of more than 95%. Their behavioral treatment approach has been modified and improved, yet today still serves as the foundation of current sex therapies for rapid ejaculation. If couples had past success with sexual intercourse, the behavioral treatment for erectile dysfunction (ED) was proven to be about 75% effective (Masters & Johnson, 1970). Their behavioral treatment has slightly better efficacy for treating men with ED than taking oral sex medications today (such as Viagra, which has 70% efficacy). Most people are not aware that medications for erectile dysfunction help only about two-thirds of men who try them.

Masters and Johnson on Sex and Human Loving (1986) is recommended reading for those who wish to have a more comprehensive understanding of their work. This publication (co-authored with long-time collaborator Robert Kolodny) was written for the general public, so it does not use the dry scientific style of earlier texts. Also very entertaining (as well as educational from a historical perspective) is Thomas Maier's *The Masters of Sex: The Life and Times of William Masters and Virginia Johnson* (2009).

About 2007, I received a call from Mr. Maier, who introduced himself as an author writing a book on Masters and Johnson. He said he knew that I was the last clinical fellow trained by Masters and asked if there were any stories of the last years of the Institute's operations. There were a few I could share so I sent them to Maier. Time went by and this call was forgotten. In 2009, a former student called up and said, "I've been reading this book on Masters and Johnson, and your name is mentioned. I was wondering if the Fred Peterson they mention is actually you?" "I don't know—I haven't seen the book," I responded. So the student sent it to me and I discovered that Mr. Maier had included some of my stories as well as credited me for them. As enjoyable as the movie *Kinsey* was, I remember thinking *Kinsey* would pale in comparison when Hollywood makes a big-screen version of *Masters of Sex*. Low and behold, in 2013 SHOWTIME took a step toward this by bringing a serialized movie version of the book to the small screen (appropriately called *The Masters of Sex*).

AMERICA'S SEXUAL MAKEOVER: CULTURAL NOTES ON THE 1950S AND 1960S

America in the 1950s represented an amazing stew of social and economic forces that overflowed into overt social reform movements. The major ingredients for America's sexual makeover, resulting in the sexual liberation of the 1960s/1970s, were the wide-reaching effects of World War II, the culmination of the civil rights movement, the second wave of the women's liberation movement, the birth of the modern gay rights movement, the birth of rock and roll, and, of course, the Vietnam War.

World War II is considered one of the most important and fundamental drivers of social change over the past 70 years. Because of all the disruption caused by the war, most Americans wanted a return to normalcy, and there was a strong emphasis on conformity. The conservative tide was rising with the start of the Cold War and so was Senator Joseph McCarthy, who gave his first "Red Scare" speech in 1950. However, American women had joined the workforce in droves to help the war effort and the genie was not easily going back into the "pregnant and barefoot" bottle despite men's best efforts. Women were making economic and sexual gains, albeit by 1950 conventions. Although having to encounter unbridled sexism (as described in the TV series *Mad Men*), women were trying their best to hold on to positions from the cafeteria line to the secretary pool and from missionary to female superior.

World War II was followed by unprecedented economic prosperity for large swaths of the American population. The GI Bill gave millions of veterans an educational ticket into the burgeoning middle class. In 10 years from 1950 to 1960, the number of rolling bed-on-wheels (car) ownership jumped from 49 million to 73 million. Yet much of America's wealth, for the very first time in history, was held by American youth, either by their working or getting it doled out to them by parents. In 1956, it is estimated that the 13 million teenagers in America had $7 billion of disposable income to spend on youth culture—which meant, of course, more cars, more sex, and rock-and-roll records. However, this cultural shift was just starting to percolate by the mid-1950s and primarily benefited middle-class white kids.

Meanwhile, something was cooking on the back burner, about which most white Americans had no idea (mostly because it was way outside their sensibilities). After World War II, the topic of race relations cannot be underestimated as a cauldron of social change. Nobody better understood the hypocrisy of American race relations than war veterans who were of minority status. Native American, African American, Asian American, Latinx American, and other minority veterans were fighting for the freedom of Europeans and Asians, while Japanese Americans were being put in internment camps, blacks were being lynched, and Native Americans continued to be disenfranchised as they had been for the preceding three centuries. Understandably, after fighting for the freedom of others, it was pretty damn difficult to return to a second-class-citizen status in 1950s America.

These veterans were definitely not looking to return to a state of prewar normalcy but rather became more involved with the rise of the civil rights and worker rights movements, led by W. E. B. Du Bois, Dorothy Height, Wallace "Mad Bear" Anderson, Martin Luther King, Cesar Chavez, as well as many others. The Civil Rights Act of 1964 would have never happened as it did without *Brown v. Board of Education* in 1954 (Stone, 2017) and President Dwight Eisenhower enforcing the U.S. Supreme Court decision by sending the troops into Little Rock, Arkansas, three years later.

What about the men and women staying in the military life? President Harry Truman racially integrated the U.S. military by Presidential Order 9981 in 1948, but only in 1954 was the last all-black unit disbanded. In the civilian world, it took a 1967 Supreme Court decision to make interracial marriage fully legal in America (Stone, 2017).

The percolation of influences from World War II spread throughout popular culture, and patriotism was high during the 1950s. Before Elvis Presley joined the Army in 1958, the "Man in Black," Airman Johnny Cash, was the Man in Blue for the U.S. Air Force, where he taught himself guitar and later sang antiwar songs in the 1960s. Veterans Jack Kerouac (of *On the Road* fame) and Allen Ginsberg (of Beat poetry fame) teamed up with William S. Burroughs (of *The Naked Lunch* fame) to serve as the core inspiration for the rise of the Beat Generation and set up the broader counterculture movement of the 1960s.

"Race music" crossed over and became rhythm and blues, but along the way became parent to the birth of rock and roll. In 1952, about 10,000 teenagers joined together in a Cleveland hockey arena for the very first rock concert, an event dubbed the Moondog Coronation Ball (so named by disc jockey Moondog Alan Freed who is also credited for coining the term "rock and roll"). The show was stopped by police after the first act because the kids got "too aggressive," which began the association of rock music with juvenile delinquency. Elvis, Chuck Berry, Little Richard, Bo Diddley, and Cash started replacing Pat Boone and Andy Williams in the record stores. Dick Dale innovated guitar licks that would later define what is called "surf music" of the 1960s (think of the soundtrack to *Pulp Fiction*).

For the first time ever, sex was openly one of the main themes of youth culture and seen as dangerous by the establishment. James Dean and Marilyn Monroe became the personification of the newly unleashed sexuality. The 1950s' main themes of conformity, consumerism, and gratitude were openly challenged and rejected. *The BlackBoard Jungle* (1954) played at drive-in theaters, boasting the very first number-one rock and roll hit—"Rock Around the Clock" by Bill Haley and the Comets. *West Side Story* played on Broadway (1957) and addressed race relations in a tempered fashion suitable for white middle-class sensibilities. If the 1950s represented conformity, consumerism, and gratitude, then the 1960s were an attempt by American youth to replace it all with individuality, ecology, and questioning all authority.

As Elvis had replaced Pat Boone, Elvis was gradually eclipsed by the likes of the Beatles, Rolling Stones, and the rest of the rock-and-roll bands associated with the British Invasion. However, Bob Dylan gave voice to the angst of youth and led the questioning of authority. He also showed the way for an American transition from folk music to rock and roll when he plugged his guitar into an amp at the 1965 Newport Folk Festival. The new call for change was strongly reflected in books such as Harper Lee's *To Kill a Mockingbird* (1960), Rachel Carson's *Silent Spring* (1962), Betty Friedan's *The Feminine Mystique* (1963), and Nena and George O'Neill's *Open Marriage* (1972). Movies such as *The Graduate* (1967), *Easy Rider* (1969), and *Bob & Carol & Ted & Alice* (1969) expressed new attitudes toward sexuality and nonconformity. Of course, the iconic images of the 1960s, sex, drugs, and rock and roll, early on were from the Summer of Love (1967) followed by the Woodstock music festival (1969).

There were no more blatant ways to question authority and tradition than burning your draft card, burning your bra, or sticking it to the man by turning on and tuning out. This new attitude was dominant in the new musical genre of rock and roll, thus becoming the soundtrack to both the 1960s and the Vietnam War. Youth of today are shocked to learn that their contemporaries 50 years ago could be drafted to kill and die in a war, yet were unable to vote as American citizens. Many who previously had felt powerless soon started to believe they didn't have to stand for it anymore in the atmosphere of the 1960s.

Regarding military service, the kids with traditional values swam with the current and eagerly volunteered to serve. They felt they were doing the right thing, and they served their country. Many kids didn't think too much about it—it was just the thing to do, so they signed up thinking they were going to be drafted anyway. Kids who were swimming cross-current sent letters to their draft boards for conscientious objector status, requesting alternative service in the Peace Corps, or just headed north to Canada.

The path each kid took made tremendous differences in family relations for generations. In today's contemporary world, it is hard to understand how families could be split apart for generations after an argument at the dinner table about Vietnam. For the most part, people today support military personnel regardless of how stupid they consider a war's politics. That is not the way it was during the Vietnam War. Today it is hard to understand how a large part of society could not support individuals who found themselves in military uniform and in harm's way. But the social upheaval of the 1960s and 1970s made everything more difficult.

There was a lot of heartache, and a lot of healing has taken place. It has been the good fortune of many Americans to witness some of this healing during the past few decades. This healing is especially visible to staff who serve those who serve our country at the VA. Although this healing is good, there is a lot more needed. While service members are to be honored for their sacrifices, war should not be glorified. One thing that has many Americans worried for themselves (and especially for their grandchildren) is the new and dangerous cultural norm of perpetual war.

THE 1970S: THE COMMERCIALIZATION AND PROFESSIONALIZATION OF SEX THERAPY

In the world of sexology, the 1950s represented a passing of one generation to another. Kinsey died in 1956, primarily of exhaustion. Masters started the sex physiology laboratory in 1954. He met Johnson a few years later and they conducted research together through this laboratory until 1966. Some sex research was going on outside St. Louis during the 1950s and 1960s, but things really started happening in the 1970s.

Many significant contributions to the science of sex happened during this decade. They are too numerous to discuss in the detail they deserve, but I will briefly mention a few here. Once Masters and Johnson published *Human Sexual Response* (1967) and *Human Sexual Inadequacy* (1970), other sex researchers attempted to replicate their findings (with limited success) but made their own contributions. Researchers such as Helen Singer Kaplan, John Bancroft, Julia Heiman, Joseph LoPiccolo, Lonnie Barbach, Harold Lief, Gerald Weeks, and Bernie Zilbergeld expanded and improved research and treatment approaches to human sexuality.

For example, Heiman and LoPiccolo developed an empirically based approach to help women become more comfortable and skilled with arousal and climax. In 1976, they published a do-it-yourself program entitled *Becoming Orgasmic: A Sexual and Personal Growth Program for Women,* which was very effective in providing guidance to women who wished to gradually and systematically achieve orgasm with or without a partner. Barbach was well known for group approaches she innovated to assist women gain confidence about their bodies' capacity for sexual pleasure. The *Becoming Orgasmic* program is still commonly used, and the treatment techniques developed by Barbach continue to be prescribed by therapists today. Being impossible to include all the additional researchers and practitioners who made important contributions, I would be remiss not to mention some of the others whom I have had the benefit of learning from directly, including John Money, Beverly Whipple, Jack Annon, Gene Abel, Barry McCarthy, Larry Kurdek, and Judy Seifer.

The new profession of sex therapy exploded with this golden age of sexual research within the context of the seventies, opening up new opportunities that did not exist a mere decade earlier. A confluence of five historical significant factors fueled the development of the new fields of sexology and sex therapy (Bley & Peterson, 2007):

1. The innovation of the "talking cure" (psychotherapy) by clergy and popularized by Freud (as well as others) culminated in the establishment of the psychoanalysis movement within American medicine.

2. The gradual reaction against the orthodoxy of psychoanalysis inspired the development of behavioralism within American psychology and promoted the application of behavioral counseling techniques to sexual problems.

3. The rise of empirical methods in the study of human sexuality resulted in the establishment of sexual science in America. The work of Kinsey, Masters, and Johnson are seen as the pivotal shift between American sexosophy and sexology. This new emphasis on sexual science ultimately contributed to numerous medical advances, including the discovery of oral contraceptives (the pill) and eventually led to the development of oral sexual stimulants (the first being Viagra).

4. The counterculture movement of the 1950s bloomed into America's second sexual revolution of the 1960s and 1970s, facilitating a relaxation of social conventions regarding sex. This resulted in women questioning attempts to repress their sexual expression, allowed greater access to sources of sexual literacy, and created a consumer demand for sexual health information and services.

5. The social conservatism of academia and professional societies within medicine and psychology prevented any one discipline from "claiming ownership" of the study of sexuality, thus forcing the field of sexual health to be interdisciplinary and include broad perspectives of human sexuality from many fields.

THE 1980S AND 1990S—THE MEDICALIZATION OF SEX AND THE EMERGENCE OF THE FIELD OF SEXUAL HEALTH

Since the human immunodeficiency virus (HIV) made its presence known in 1981, things have never been the same on the stage of American sexuality. After the expansion of liberal attitudes and loosening of inhibitions during the 1960s and 1970s, AIDS was the single most important factor in changing Americans' sexuality and introducing the concept of "safe sex" as household words. In the beginning of the epidemic, people did not live long after their initial diagnosis, on average about two years. The anxiety about contracting AIDS caused a contraction of sexual behavior as well as fearful reactions throughout many aspects of life. For the first few years of the epidemic, no one knew exactly how HIV was passed from one person to another. Fear gripped the nation; people started staying home and attendance at bars, baths, and discos declined. At many hospitals, doctors refused to treat HIV-positive patients and food workers refused to serve meals to these same patients. Children believed to be HIV-positive were refused entrance to school and subject to violence.

Government response to the crisis was slow but accelerated by vocal AIDS activist groups (such as ACT UP). The first drug (AZT) showing it could slow the progression of the disease was not approved by the FDA until 1987. To make matters worse, the FDA also restricted other drugs from use to treat AIDS (as described in the 2013 movie *The Dallas Buyers Club*). By 1989, more than 100,000 Americans were diagnosed with AIDS. Fortunately, medical advances during the following 20 years now enable Americans to live with HIV as a chronic illness for decades after their initial diagnosis. Globally, however, there is not the same level of access to care, and nearly 35 million people have died from AIDS-related causes worldwide (mostly due to *heterosexual* transmission).

Featured Stories of Diverse Perspectives and Experiences

GRIDLOCKED—ROB AND KENNETH
Written by Richelle Frabotta

We love Corgis. They are the most perfect dogs. I always appreciated how they attended and made sure other dogs and people were grouped up. Herding is an intrinsic instinct in Corgis. I think I have that instinct as well.

I met my wife on Christmas Eve. We both served the homeless turkey dinner with all of the trimmings at our local shelter. We were 12 years old the first time we saw each other. We were 20 years old the last time. We grew up together, me and Sandy.

Sandy was a nice girl who matured into a nice lady. She was unassuming, loyal, and wanted to be married with kids, a three-bedroom house with a white picket fence. Sounded good to me, but then again, I had no other script. We hung out when we could, mostly seeing each other at our church youth group once a week. She seemed to get me. We often would be found reading together in the back room or swinging on the church playground. We didn't have much need for the other kids.

It was a no brainer that we'd get married. We tied the knot on January 1, 1978. It was a nice ceremony. Sandy chose our colors: beige and cream. Our families were in attendance and politely applauded after we said our vows. Honestly, it just seemed like business as usual in the judge's chambers.

"To love and cherish in sickness and in health, rich or for poor, all the days of our lives until death do us part." I had every intention of keeping this vow.

I met Kenneth at the same homeless shelter. He was a breath of fresh air in that place! He was handsome in his bright green polo shirt, chatty, and cared very much about the welfare of others. I admired how he interacted with the residents. He was so comfortable even though he had not much in common with the folks. Kenneth, I learned later, had a masters' degree in economics, was a city planner, and loved Corgis. He had a strong church background, too, and his drive to help others was admirable. He was all about social justice and owned every color of polo shirt made. I respected his manner and outlook and loved his style!

It was odd, but I found myself thinking about Kenneth first thing in the morning, last thing at night, and many times in between. I wasn't too concerned until my wife, Sandy, pointed out that I was always mentioning Kenneth. I'm sure that was terribly uncomfortable for her. It wasn't intentional, really. When I thought about Kenneth, I saw vivid color and forgot to breathe. When I interacted with Sandy, I saw beige and cream. Breathing was normal.

There's nothing wrong with beige and cream—but the rainbow was much more intriguing.

Eventually, 137 days after I met Kenneth for the first time, I understood. Hit me like a ton of bricks: I was in love with him. It took me another 43 days to tell my wife. True to form, Sandy was nice. She was sad, but nice. We got a dissolution 63 days later in the office down the hallway from where we married. There was no polite clapping, only sniffling and nose wiping. I was sad, too, but also terribly excited about my future.

Kenneth and I talked every day. It seemed that he felt the same infatuation with me! Who'd have thought it? It was 1981 and it was like my eyes opened for the very first time. I'll spare you the details, but colors were definitely brighter.

Kenneth and I moved in together 142 days after my 21st birthday. I was really alive and I think for the first time. There was no beige or cream. Our house was filled with laughter, music, fat Corgis, and great conversation. So many friends in for dinners and out for social events. Kenneth introduced me to a culture that I had no idea existed.

We frequented a bar where only men went. Community was instant. Everyone was welcome. There were queens, bears, leather men, chicken hawks, lounge lizards, vampires, tinkerbelles, and eyeball queens. We had our challenges, but basically, we were one big gay family. No one needed to employ the hanky code. If you wanted to fool around with someone, you just spoke up. We were adult men, after all, and most of us knew our power and place in our community. We were vested in the co-creation of a safe, kind, loving environment where no one needed to posture or prove anything.

My diagnosis came early 1983: Gay-related immunodeficiency disease (GRID), which soon after I learned the term became AIDS. My love party was over. Even though Kenneth was amazingly supportive, we weren't quite sure what we were dealing with. I just couldn't get well. I stayed sick a lot. The Corgis and I herded ourselves into a corner of the living room and watched out the window as the colors started to fade.

Although Kenneth and I never could legally say, "in sickness and in health," he evidently lived by it. He never left my side or my corner. We were a family. For the next decade, he was vigilant in getting me the latest news, the best doctors, and a plethora of treatment options. I tried every single one of them. My day involved pills, orange juice, more pills, bouts of diarrhea, milk, and more pills. A new meaning to the word cocktail. Occasionally, I took a medicine that increased my appetite. I craved chocolate cake. Somehow chocolate cake was always in the fridge and always in my belly when I wanted it.

My Kenneth took great care of me. We lived as best we could with my health ups and downs for the next 18 years. When I died, Kenneth kept on fighting the good fight. To this day, he is a tireless advocate for HIV+ folks, a caring friend to those who have lost loved ones, and runs a Corgi rescue on the side. He is a recognized pillar of strength in the gay community. He was awarded the key to the city for his vision and execution of rehabbing one of the most blighted and crime ridden areas. That neighborhood used to be known as the "gay ghetto."

Kenneth made sure that there were Corgis etched in my tombstone. And he drops a chocolate cake off once a week. The world may have faded, but my love for him remains a vivid technicolor rainbow.

Numerous and significant events have occurred in America's response to the AIDS crisis since the time of Rob and Kenneth. Some of the initial effects of the crisis were wide spread fear, increased consciousness about the risk of HIV transmission, and the medical search for effective treatments. Not surprisingly, an entire multibillion-dollar industry has developed around the testing, monitoring, and treatment of individuals living with HIV/AIDS. The explosion of medical research and treatments that unfolded for this sexually transmitted infection also promoted an atmosphere of greater medical research (and funding opportunities) on other sexual health concerns, such as sexual dysfunction among men and women.

For example, research for the development of the new class of drugs called PDE-5 inhibitors (such as Viagra) has been facilitated over the past three decades by medicine's increased focus on sexual health. PDE-5 inhibitors can enhance sexual responsiveness by providing pharmacologic support for firmer and longer-lasting erections. People generally know PDE-5 inhibitors as Viagra, Levitra, and

Cialis; however, several others are being developed. Similar medications are being developed for enhancing women's sexual responsiveness. Although the success of the PDE-5 inhibitors has been nothing short of phenomenal, we are likely to see the development of additional sexual medicines in the near future. When an effective medication is found to enhance sexual desire (as opposed to sexual function), it will make the entire hubbub over Viagra seem like a molehill.

By the late 1990s, the landscape for sex therapy had changed dramatically from just 10 years earlier. Besides the development of PDE-5 inhibitors, the use of vasodilators to increase blood supply to the penis had become common. These vasodilators, such as papaverine and prostaglandin E1, were once touted as the cure for impotence because they caused rigid erections independent of sexual desire. These medical interventions, including advances in hormonal and surgical treatments, helped expand the behaviorally focused sex therapy field of the 1960s into the new field of sexual health with many dimensions of medical research/practice and resulting in the new body of sexual science.

The professional field of sexual health is complex, and many different health care disciplines are involved in conducting research that contributes to sexual science. It is a bit difficult to paint an accurate picture of the practice of sexual health to any audience, professional or lay. However, Table 7.1 may help clarify the relationships between different areas of sexual health practice as well as the "big picture." As silly as it sounds, I will attempt to describe the field of sexual health using the image of a three-layer cake. However, due to the need for brevity, some dimensions of the field of sexual health have not (and will not) be discussed beyond the mere mention you are about to receive (such as any detailed discussion of fertility).

The field of sexual health (in the United States) can be described as a three-layer cake with the top layer of the cake having three sections of red, white, and blue icing. The red section is comprised of various professionals involved in the prevention of sexually transmitted infections, especially HIV. The white section is comprised of the millions of medical and counseling professionals involved in fertility services, who are committed to assisting want-to-be-parents become a family. Finally, the blue section represents the millions of health care professionals involved in sexology. Okay, that is the description of the top layer of the cake.

The middle layer is also divided into three sections of red, white, and blue icing, all representing the three major areas of sexology: sex research, sex education, and clinical sexology. The red section, sex research, is often divided into focus areas (e.g., at-risk sexual behaviors or women's sexual desire) or specific populations studied (e.g., adolescents, postmenopausal women). The blue section represents the multiple subtypes of sex educators, including K–12 specialists in schools, specialists working with individuals who live with physical and mental disabilities, and those who teach sexuality courses at college. The third section of cake, the blue one, represents a complex collection of specialists in clinical sexology (described next).

The bottom layer of the cake is also divided into three sections—again, red, white, and blue. This layer represents clinical sexology, which is further divided into areas of sexual surgery, sexual medicine, and sex counseling/therapy. Sexual surgery, the red section, involves urologists, gynecologists, and plastic/cosmetic specialists who do everything from sexual reassignment surgery to breast implantation/reduction to vulva cosmetics. The white section represents sexual medicine specialists who are primary-care physicians, endocrinologists, and psychiatrists involved in treatments as diverse as treating ED with PDE-5 inhibitors, prescribing hormonal supplements, to managing psychotropic medications. Finally, the blue section represents counselors and therapists who specialize in assessing and treating patients concerning the emotional, relational, and spiritual aspects of their sexual lives (especially if they are complicated by sexual trauma or compulsivity).

Much has happened during the 20th century to change how Americans view sexuality. We started 100 years ago with the crazy and cruel notion that masturbation and being gay was not only immoral but diseases requiring treatment to "cure." We believed in eugenics and that certain "undesirable" people should be subject to forced sterilization. We believed we should have laws preventing certain people from marrying each other because of their race or gender. We have gone from the first book on sexology in 1904 to sexology being a complex web of millions of medical and health care professionals just described to you as a giant cake.

TABLE 7.1 **The Interdisciplinary Profession of Sexual Health (by Specialty)**

HIV/STD Prevention	Fertility Services	Sexology
Sex Research	Sex Education	Clinical Sexology
Sexual Surgery	Sexual Medicine	Sex Therapy

A FINAL NOTE TO OUR REVIEW OF THE 20TH-CENTURY JOURNEY TO SEXOLOGY

Although we have come a long way, it is important to remember we have a long way to go. As previously mentioned and well worth repeating, the premier researcher in female sexuality, Dr. Beverly Whipple, makes the point that there is much more we do not know than what we do (at least about women's experience of sexuality). Although our journey led us to a discussion of the medicalization of sex during the 1980s and 1990s, it is important to make note of the cautions regarding this aspect of our progress. Medical and pharmacological research on sexual problems is very important, yet may have a tendency to oversimplify sexual difficulties.

Genital function often becomes the focus of the research rather than whether individuals feel that their sexual concerns are understood, addressed, and satisfactorily resolved. In other words, a man can be helped with his concerns about ED and learn how to have consistent erections suitable for intercourse. A woman with lack of sexual desire can find her libido and get plenty of vaginal lubrication for intercourse. That doesn't mean that they are going to be happy with the treatment outcomes. Yes, each client may be able to learn how to overcome a particular concern yet still unsatisfied with their relationship outcome.

They still may feel their partner is not interested in them, or they may feel like a failure as a sexual partner, or they may feel as depressed as they ever have. The point is, sexual function is only part of the equation. What is most important is a significant and meaningful connection between people, whether or not they have full and unencumbered sexual function. A pill may be helpful but is sometimes not the complete answer to a person's concerns.

In addition to this caution, attention is needed to increased understanding of sexual diversity and keeping the gains we have made in our progress toward a "more perfect" democracy. As previously noted in this chapter, we have seen decades of liberalism and conservatism swinging back and forth for periods of more or less progression of sexual science. Many believe we are still experiencing a cultural backlash against the progressive advances. For example, when the AIDS crisis unfolded in the 1980s, it was the perfect excuse for religious conservatives to declare that our country had gone too far astray and AIDS was God's retribution on what they saw as unchecked immorality. This explanation of the AIDS epidemic is, of course, nonsense. AIDS is simply a terribly devastating virus that took the lives of children as well as adults, straight as well as gay.

One of the most important voices of civil liberty regarding sexual expression is author and sex therapist Dr. Marty Klein. He asserts there is a comprehensive and well-coordinated attack on sexual expression in his 2012 book, *America's War on Sex: The Attack on Law, Lust, and Liberty*. This is a must-read for anybody who wants to stay informed about how to protect our country from steering away from civil liberties. Dr. Klein asks us to pay attention to how sex education, sex entertainment, sexual health care, and many forms of sexual expression are being regulated, defunded, and repressed. He declares, "America has a love-hate relationship with sexuality, or if you will, a schizophrenic relationship with sexuality." Of course for the authors, Dr. Klein's statement directly relates to the notion of sexophrenia and our American history of sexual repression, especially for women but also repression of many sexual behaviors associated with health, which are discussed in the next chapter. As the timeline at the beginning of the chapter highlighted, we have made steps toward greater freedom, especially greater freedom of sexual expression. Nearly 20 years into the 21st century, we still need to be vigilant about sexophrenia and not losing civil liberties. In this next chapter, the health benefits of some of these historically "repressed behaviors" are explored.

REFERENCES

Altman, L. (2003). *The forgotten victims of the Holocaust*. Berkeley Heights, NJ: Enslow.

Barker-Benfield, B. (1975). Sexual surgery in late-nineteenth-century America. *International Journal of Health Services*, 5(2), 279–298.

Bigwood, J. (Executive Producer), & Garnier, K. (Director). (2004). *Iron Jawed Angels* [Film]. New York: HBO Films.

Blackwell, E. (1894). *The human element in sex*. London, UK: Churchill.

Brecher, E. (1979). *The sex researchers* (expanded ed.). San Francisco: Specific Press.

Bullough, V. (1994). *Science in the bedroom: A history of sex research*. New York: Basic Books.

Davis, K. (1929). *Factors in the Sex Life of Twenty-Two Hundred Women*. New York: Harper.

Dickinson, R., & Beam, L. (1932). *A thousand marriages*. Baltimore: Williams & Wilkins.

Freud, S. (1954). The *origins of psychoanalysis: Letters to Wilhelm Fliess, drafts, and notes (1887–1902)*. New York: Basic Books.

Gordon, L. (2002). *The moral property of women: A history of birth control politics in America*. Champaign-Urbana: University of Illinois Press.

Hirschfeld, M. (1937). *Sexual history of the World War: From reports collected by the Institute for Sexual Science*. New York: Falstaff.

Kinsey, A., Pomeroy, W., & Martin, C. (1948). *Sexual behavior in the human male*. Philadelphia: W.B. Saunders.

Kinsey, A., Pomeroy, W., Martin, C., & Gephard, P. (1953). *Sexual behavior in the human female*. Philadelphia: W.B. Saunders.

Krafft-Ebing, R. (1900). *Psychopathia sexualis* (English trans. 1886). New York: Physicians and Surgeons.

Krull, M. (1986). *Freud and his father*. New York: Norton.

Maier, T. (2009). *The masters of sex: The life and times of William Masters and Virginia Johnson*. New York: Basic Books.

Masson, J. (1984). *The assault on truth: Freud's suppression of the seduction theory*. New York: Farrar, Straus and Giroux.

Masters, W., & Johnson, V. (1966). *Human sexual response.* Boston: Little, Brown.

Masters, W., & Johnson, V. (1970). *Human sexual inadequacy.* Boston: Little, Brown.

Masters, W., Johnson, V., & Kolodny, R. (1986). *Masters and Johnson on sex and human loving.* Boston: Little, Brown.

Mutrux, G. (Producer), & Condon, B. (Director). (2004). *Kinsey* [Film]. United States: American Zoetrope Myriad Pictures.

Praunheim, R. (Producer & Director). (1999). *The Einstein of Sex* [Film]. Berlin, Germany: Praunheim Production Company.

Public Broadcasting System. (2016). *The American Experience: The Miner Wars.* Retrieved from http://www.pbs.org/wgbh/americanexperience/films/theminewars/

Roach, M. (2008). *Bonk: The curious coupling of science and sex.* New York: Norton.

Schultz, D., & Schultz, S. (2004). *The history of modern psychology.* Belmont, CA: Wadsworth/Thompson Learning.

Stone, G. (2017). *Sex and the Constitution.* New York: Liveright.

Wolff, C. (1986). Magnus Hirschfeld: A portrait of a pioneer in sexology. London, UK: Quartet Books.

World Health Organization (WHO). (2017). Global Health Observatory (GHO) Data for HIV/AIDS. Retrieved from http://www.who.int/gho/hiv/en/

CHAPTER EIGHT

Health Benefits from Sexual Expression

Written by Frederick Peterson

INTRODUCTION

Harry was a researcher known as the dope and booze professor (teaching psychopharmacology) at Wright State University in Dayton, Ohio, back in the 1980s. When Harry was an undergraduate at Florida State University, he knew a student (Margaret, a pseudonym) who suffered from migraine headaches, which interfered with her studies, especially cramming for exams. A physiology major preparing for medical school, Margaret started to experiment with physical ways to moderate her pain. She tried all kinds of ideas but found that consistently masturbating tended to lessen the intensity of her migraines and shortened their duration. She decided to extend her hypothesis testing into the realm of intercourse and approached Harry with a proposition he could not refuse.

Margaret started having intercourse with Harry several times a week as a preventative measure for pain. She observed that not only could she lessen the intensity and duration of her migraines, but they began to occur less frequently. She also believed that she was having some sort of physiological response that had additional benefit from vaginal containment of Harry (via intercourse) over her own clitoral-focused masturbation. While Harry was happy to oblige at first, after several months he started to feel burdened by her sexual demands on him and his time. Harry said he needed to stop being her "walking dildo" to have more time for his own studies. Margaret and Harry had little emotional attachment, so they were both okay with his disengagement. She quickly found other willing students and continued her sexual self-treatment.

Although Harry's story does not prove sex cures migraines (or even lessens their intensity, duration, or frequency) and his story may even sound a bit perverted to some readers, it is related to a long history of folklore involving use of sexual behavior to relieve many forms of human suffering. Only in the past few decades has science caught up with the folklore. Yet there have been many case studies of the *sexual healing* that Marvin Gaye sang about, and during which many babies have been conceived during the background enjoyment of this getting-down Motown hit. Over the past several decades, a body of research specific to "sexual healing" has slowly developed.

For example, an empirical investigation of 83 women who suffered from migraines was reported in 2001; at least half the women included in this study reported that masturbation brought some degree of pain relief (Evans & Couch, 2001). Although relief from migraines via masturbation appears to be less reliable and less effective than medications, the pain-relieving effects from orgasms are more rapid and less expensive than prescriptions. Many chronic-pain patients would prefer not to take another medication but to use a strategy "immediately at hand" and under their control. Other clients prefer a combined approach; sexual stimulation can sometimes make a difference in using a smaller dosage of an analgesic medication.

A disclaimer and clarification in this introduction is in order: In presenting stories and empirical evidence supporting the assertion that your sexual expression generally benefits your overall health, all referenced sexual activity is assumed to be consensual, safe, protected from sexually transmitted infections, and relatively stress-free. That *excludes* any sexual activity that is coerced or involves risk of violence or transmission of sexually transmitted infections (STIs). Sex-research studies in which health benefits of sex are demonstrated do so within the context of a sexual relationship that is consensual, safe, and stress-relieving rather than stress-inducing.

It is also important to note that although sex may be good for you, improving your physical and psychological health is not necessarily the best reason to have sex. Many media reports have sensationalized (and in some cases exaggerated) the health benefits of sexual activity. Dr. Debbie Herbenick of the Center for Sexual Health Promotion and the Kinsey Institute (at Indiana University) makes this point in her book *Because It Feels Good* (2009). Although she states she is pleased there is more public information on the positive aspects of sexuality (including health aspects), she also describes her frustration with media reports that have implied "men and women should have more sex more often—if not to save their relationships, then to save (or improve) their health" (Herbenick, 2009).

Herbenick adds that trying to have more sex can increase your stress and that the best reason to have sex is because it feels good! The last thing you want in a relationship is having sex feel like work, for that is when couples start avoiding intimacy with each other. Her book title is very sound advice: Remember to have sex primarily because it feels good. This book and her next one (*Read My Lips: A Complete Guide to the Vagina and Vulva*, written with colleague Vanessa Schick) are excellent reads. As noted in the preface of their book, *Read My Lips* is highly recommended for "anyone who has a vulva, loves someone with a vulva, has come from a vagina, or is just plain curious about these parts" (Herbenick & Schick, 2011). *Vulva la difference!*

On the topic of not overstating the possible health benefits of sex, two additional points are noteworthy. First, when the research is relatively weak and only suggestive, it shall be said so. When it is more robust and a finding has been replicated by independent investigators, that will be apparent as well. As outlined in the last chapter, the field of sexual science has a history of suppression, and today it is still difficult to find funding. Consequently, most of the studies cited are within the past 20 to 30 years. Take-home message: The science reviewed here is important, but nowhere near the maturity level of the traditional hard sciences. Please note that although the science of sex is important to understand, do so with the caution not to set unrealistic expectations for yourself. For example, several studies suggest a certain number of orgasms per week as sufficient to create a particular health benefit (like lower risk of prostate infection or breast cancer). Do not get anxious or worried that you are doomed to prostatitis or cancer because you do not meet the "minimum requirement" by averaging only one or two or zero orgasms per week or per month. The sexual science research is "not there yet" in terms of being so definitive, unlike the established heart benefits of a daily low dosage of aspirin. The information in this book is not intended to create another form of performance anxiety related to not having enough orgasmic outlet! The second take-home message: It's good to try out new things, but above all, be yourself!

This chapter will explore the science and folklore regarding the relationship between many forms of sexual expression and different health benefits. Now that we have (very) lightly touched on sexual benefits to migraines, we will explore other forms of pain management through sexual means. This will lead us into a discussion weaving through how orgasms increase the chances of conception, can help with getting an expectant mother ready to go to the hospital, and assist in recovery postpartum. We will even discuss a taboo subject of orgasms incidental to breast-feeding—healthy and positive orgasms. Besides babies, we focus on baby boomers and older folks—especially how sexual expression can help protect them from heart attack and stroke. Frequent sex in older age is now being seen as contributing to quality of life as well as possibly increasing longevity.

The authors of this text are not going to say you can screw yourself into old age, but it probably won't hurt if you want to try. Here again, most of this research involves studies that do not demonstrate the certainty of cause-effect relationships. For example, the relationship between sexual activity and longevity. Are you more likely to live longer because you remain sexually active longer, or are you sexually active longer because you are one of the more healthy and sexy senior citizens around? Probably both are true to some degree. The longer you live and stay sexually active, the more health benefits you are likely to experience. In turn, the healthier you are, the more sexually active you are likely to remain (your basic yin and yang).

One last important caveat: Whether or not you are one of those folks who says, "That's the way I want to go" or "I want to die in the saddle," be forewarned. As just mentioned, more sex can mean more stress. If you have a history of cardiovascular disease (CVD), you may be increasing your risk for heart attack (or stroke) if you engage in strenuous sex that is beyond your cardiovascular stress tolerance. Make sure your sex is fun, feels good, and more stress-relieving than stress-inducing. In other words, don't retire from sex just because you have a medical condition, but you may be best advised to refrain from having sex while hanging from the chandelier or sexually competing for orgasms like it is an Olympic sport. As usual and customary, it's a good idea to get medical clearance from your cardiologist if you are at risk for stroke or CVD.

THE RELATIONSHIP BETWEEN SEXUAL EXPRESSION AND HEALTH—STORIES FROM DOC

As previously noted, the work of William Masters and Virginia Johnson provided a scientific foundation for today's understanding of basic sexual functioning that was never studied empirically until the mid-1950s. Doc Masters used to talk about the similarity between the body's hunger for food and the body's hunger for sex. Most Americans have probably never heard of such a comparison and learned that the purpose of sex was procreation. All other expressions of sex were secondary (or to be avoided) because of the perceived negative consequences (including adverse health effects reviewed in the last chapter). So when Doc asked what clinic staff knew about the health benefits from sexual activity, many of us had to plead ignorance beyond the happiness couples experience from making babies and becoming a family. We just scratched our heads while he shook his and gave his steely stare.

Although most of us knew about wet dreams, we never thought of them as an expression of the body's need for sexual outlet. In his own "Doc-speak," Doc described the first nocturnal emission as *"an activation event for puberty's new reproductive readiness."* But then, why do some teenage boys continue to experience wet dreams through adolescence and into adulthood? This is the body's way of saying there is a need for ongoing sexual outlet through orgasm. If some men are not having regular orgasms through regular masturbation or sex with others, then the body will create its own opportunities. This is true for females as well; it is just not as pronounced and noticeable as with males.

Doc spoke from his observations from decades of basic sex physiology research (1954–1966) and decades of clinical treatment (1960s through 1990s). He was convinced that men who commit themselves to long-term abstinence of all sexual activity (such as some monks and priests) are vulnerable to the ill-health effects from lack of orgasm. Specifically, he declared these men are subject to greater risk for prostate problems (such as infection, called prostatitis), gastrointestinal (GI) problems (such as constipation), and emotional problems (such as irritability). Doc said women who are in the same boat (abstinent from sex with others or themselves) or those who have just never masturbated (often due to a severely sexophrenic upbringing) experience similar effects. He believed these women are subject to the same GI problems but are just as likely to be depressed or irritable. Instead of prostatitis and benign prostate hyperplasia, Doc believed women face greater risks of endometriosis and vaginismus.

Mind you, these are all inferences Doc drew from his five decades of sex research and treatment programs. When asked about empirical support for his conclusions, he gruffly brushed questions aside and said, "That research can't be done." Fatigue in his voice was noted whenever he was asked to explain the importance of sexual expression, providing the same insights hundreds of times over to audiences, let alone clinical fellows at his own institute. Doc was in his final years at his Institute during the early 1990s and he was a bit tired, even though he stayed active writing and presenting. For example, he presented at the National Institutes of Health (NIH) for their first National Consensus Conference on a sexual health topic. He also helped investigate child sex slavery, witnessing children (including American youth) being sold on an action block in Morocco only 25 years ago (1994). Yet he seemed not to fully realize that the average American expects scientific support for such assertions as "your appetite for sex is similar to your appetite for food" and wearied from repeating himself.

He would have likely been pleased with the research over the past 30 years that has supported his notions about sex and health. For example, in a 1997 Canadian study, authors found that celibacy among gay, bisexual, and straight men was correlated with higher scores on measures of depression and risk for suicide (Bagley & Tremblay, 1997). This was especially true for celibate men who self-identified as homosexual. However, were the scores higher for gay men in the sample because they were celibate or because they were gay but did not necessarily have a positive gay identity? Were there other factors that could account for the gay men having higher scores for depression, such as discrimination?

A CASE FOR CELIBACY

Before conquering a full chapter on the health benefits of sexual expression, let us pause to question the good doctor's assertions that celibacy is bad for your health (at least in the three aspects noted above—more GI problems, more irritability, and higher risk for prostatitis for men). With respect for all his considerable knowledge and insight, there are always two sides to an argument, and he would likely have agreed—that is what science is all about. Someone has an observation, an idea, and publishes their conclusion only to expect others to make counter–and/or alternative explanations. So it is here with the question of celibacy. Besides, the authors believe that many healthy people have at least short-term periods of no sexual activity that last from several weeks to several years. Therefore, what are the benefits of celibacy?

When it comes to human sexuality there are plenty of sexual health decisions to make. Some of those decisions are when to become sexually active, what type of sexual activity to engage in, to use or not use contraception, to have or not have kids, and so on. One of those decisions is the conscious choice to be celibate (or abstain from sexual activity) and not just because it is a "default" position when you are not dating or in a long-term relationship. Yarber and Sayad (2019) explain how celibacy implies the avoidance of all forms of sexual activity and often implies the religious commitment to not marry or to maintain a nonsexual life. The term *abstinence* is sometimes interchanged with celibacy, but they are different. Abstinence is the absence of genital contact that could lead to pregnancy. Therefore, one can decide to abstain from intercourse, but still decide to engage in some type of sexual activities (abstinence). However, if you choose to be celibate, you swear off all sexual activity!

Hyde and DeLamater (2014) describe how there are few published studies on people who choose to live celibate lives (usually unmarried and abstaining from sexual activity). However, there are many documented sexual health benefits from living a celibate lifestyle such as

1. never worrying about contracting an STI (except through the unlikely means of blood transfusions, your mother passing an STI to you when you were an infant, or getting bit by a Zika-virus-carrying mosquito),
2. having no risk of experiencing an unwanted pregnancy,

3. never having to decide to be in a relationship because of a pregnancy,
4. never having to decide about an abortion because of an unwanted pregnancy,
5. no worry about bringing more children into an already overpopulated planet,
6. not having to worry about making moral decisions about sexual behaviors,
7. never experiencing anxiety because of any lack of sexual competency,
8. gaining self-confidence because of making good health decisions,
9. experiencing less emotional attachment because of sexual activity,
10. eliminating the risk of problematic compulsive sexual behaviors,
11. appreciating oneself as something other than a sexual object,
12. experiencing oneself as being worthy of being in a relationship that does not place an obligation on sexually pleasuring another person,
13. understanding that love is not limited to romantic sexual relationships,
14. experiencing less stress from the absence of personal politics involved in establishing and maintaining sexual relationships (via dating or marriage),
15. having more freedom of choice without consideration of others' wishes,
16. having potential for a less expensive life (without partners or children),
17. having potential for more productive attention to one's work, and
18. having a simpler, less complicated life.

Wow, that might sound like a strong argument for celibacy. The point is that there are benefits and advantages to celibacy and those who choose to be celibate (either short term or long term) should be respected, not necessarily pitied or assumed they can't attract a partner. Nonsense! They may really know what they are doing!

So, back to the question of health benefits of celibacy. Twenty years later, the authors have to agree with Doc Masters that the research has not been done and believe that it is not known if the benefits of celibacy outweigh the potential risks of celibacy that Doc observed. The authors also believe that there is overwhelming evidence that human beings are social creatures with physical and psychological needs that are mostly met through coupling-up with your sweetie (albeit inconsistently and with costs). And that is what the rest of this chapter is about! As you will see, subsequent studies have supported the assertion that sexual activity, especially when it results in orgasm, provides certain health benefits, including some protection for prostatitis for men and endometriosis for women.

TECHNICAL TIME-OUT: WHAT EXACTLY IS AN ORGASM?

This is a frequently asked question and very relevant to any discussion of health benefits of sex (especially the one we are about to begin). As mentioned in Chapter 2, it is important to describe your own experience of sexual satisfaction and define for yourself what an orgasm is before being overly influenced by the ideas and experiences of others. If you skipped that part, here is a reminder to take some time out to reflect on how exactly *you* would describe what constitutes being happy sexually and whether that involves an orgasm. As you may have already noted (despite cultural expectations and demands), all sexual behavior does not need to result in orgasm to be pleasurable and worth the effort. If your experience does include orgasm (not necessarily every time, of course), what makes it pleasurable for you? How do you know when you have had an orgasm? How do you know when your partner has an orgasm? Would you recommend orgasms to others? To answer these questions, the female, male, and transgender points of view will be considered followed by scientific definitions of orgasm.

Let's first check with the "person on the street" point of view and ask: "What is an orgasm?" to a woman who is comfortable with her sexuality and discussing such questions. So here is an answer from an N = 1 study of the woman's point of view: "Once reached, this pleasurable intoxicating experience may start in my head, then reach my vagina, causing a dizzying pleasurable release of hormones that may last seconds to minutes. This then results in an energizing relaxation that strengthens my bond with my partner and makes the day disappear. We also share with each other something that is a very special and addictive feeling." Okay, that's pretty good—very poetic.

Now let's get the guys' point of view. Most men would give a more precise definition along the lines of an orgasm as "a feeling of loading and exploding." Yes, this is oversimplifying things (even for men). Sometimes men will describe the male orgasm by referring to it to as the process of ejaculation. Of course, I am poking a bit of fun here at the stereotype of men as less insightful and less emotionally oriented than women. Many men do experience orgasm (and ejaculation) as more than "getting their rocks off" and as a means of significant emotional connection with their partners, an incredible sense of wanting to love and be loved.

If you get men to open up and talk about it, they relate to an experience of feeling high or "love drunk" (on the neurotransmitter oxytocin) and during high sexual intensity saying things like, "I want to love you forever," "I want to be with you forever," or "I want to fuck you forever!" Men who are "under the influence" of that oxytocin highball notice how their partners seem to grow wings and glow. And thank heaven it works both ways!

Let's check another point of view, one from a person who has personally experienced both male orgasm and female orgasm. Among the many transgender individuals the authors interviewed for this book, there was an opportunity to hear unique descriptions of orgasm, which happens to be one of the most popular questions university students debate in class: "Who has better orgasms—men or women?" To share an opinion on answering this question, an individual shared her honest and personal description of orgasm below, both as man and as woman.

An Age-Old Question

"As a fully-fledged woman since my gender reassignment, one of those questions I am sometimes asked is 'who has better orgasms, males or females?' There are bodies of scientific literature comparing many aspects of female to male sexuality. However, with all the research scientists have done, they can't really answer this question because the scientific data tells only one side of the equation. The other is the human side. I have known both men and women who don't like sex and that strongly suggests to me that there are scientifically immeasurable elements involved in our experience of sexuality. They needed something they couldn't quite create: A person, actually a male person to have sex with a peculiar woman and then have that man transformed into a woman with fully developed secondary female characteristics with full feeling and responsive breasts (not nipple numbing implants), naturally hormone-enhanced sensitivity of key parts of the body (including the inside of thighs, inner arms, and back of the neck) and of course a fully functional vagina.

In a naturally occurring experiment (when against all the probabilities of the cosmic tumblers falling into one place), interesting factors all came together with me and a very special lover to answer the age-old question at hand. You just have to have firsthand experience to really answer this question. I don't know it for a fact, but I expect my lover and I are one of the few (if not only) couples recorded through this writing to be able to answer this age-old question. As a male, the sex experience is awesome! It begins as a twitch in your groin when you first get a sense of the attraction between you and your sex partner to be. It continues as your sense of smell and touch seems to heighten. When you finally touch and kiss your partner, your sex organ begins to engorge, and your heart begins to beat faster. You begin to perspire and your pheromones begin to emanate from your body. An uncontrollable physical response begins to take over and this is where an internal and external battle begins. As a male who wants to delay gratification, I begin to try to keep control of the uncontrollable—your clothes come off, the warmth of your body seeks hers and your penis gets rock hard. When she's wet, her vagina smoothly accepts your male member and you can feel her pulsating and undulating vaginal muscles begin to try to pull you further into her. At this point you are trying to stay in control of your orgasm, trying to prolong the experience as long as possible for both your pleasure and hers. The strain actually becomes the most pleasurable pain imaginable just before you climax, a strip of sweat breaks along the entire length of your spine and runs down the crack of your ass. Then no matter how much self-control you have, the sensation becomes so painfully pleasurable that your body stiffens, and you explode into her completely exhausting yourself. Collapsing into her arms, you are completely spent. She then wants to talk? OMG! That's an incredible experience, no doubt about it.

"As a woman first realizes that she's about to engage in sexual intercourse, it's a visceral response to pheromones, most often male pheromones but female pheromones if you're a lesbian (as is my case). In that moment, the body begins to warm and it becomes more sensitive to touch. The lips begin to slightly enlarge as blood begins to come to the surface and they also become more sensitive to touch. The kiss itself (especially the first one) becomes a critical part of the sex act. This act excites the rest of the secondary characteristics, with the breasts enlarging, nipples becoming hard, and the vagina extends. Each tongue tweak and finger pinch excites the entire body. If your partner has any knowledge (and self-control) to begin to lick and nibble, you now have a fully engaged body. From the back of your neck to the inside of your thighs, you become more and more sensitive. Your enlightened partner may lightly stroke the inside of the arms (just above and to the inside of the elbow) causing your vagina to become wetter and start to undulate. Then with the first flick of the tongue or touch of a finger or penis (as the case may be) the vagina starts to accept and draw in the sexual stimulating counterpart. Gripping and releasing and gripping even tighter. Just as with the male response, there begins a pleasurable and painful pressure that starts to build and slowly grows to a crescendo that explodes and vibrates the whole body. You instinctively grab your partner in something of a death grip (this is not true; the French word for orgasm is *orgasme* actually means 'little death'). You arch your back while holding on as you do not want him or her to disengage. If you squeeze your legs together and move your hips just right, then you can feel the beginning of another orgasm. As long as you can keep friction applied to your clitoris, your orgasm can leave you completely physically and emotionally satisfied. Having had both experiences, I can happily report we women have it all over males in the orgasm department."

Now that is a description of orgasm you probably have not heard lately! Yet, most important for our purposes here, is the understanding of orgasm from a scientific point of view. Many descriptions in the literature range from vague references of psychological fireworks of pleasure to incredibly technical descriptions that are like reading an assembly manual. The comprehensive scientific definitions of orgasm about to be presented here are taken from *The Science of Orgasm* by Komisaruk, Beyer-Flores, and Whipple (2006). Most sex educators and therapists consider this one of the best books on the science of sex since the original works of Kinsey, Masters, and Johnson. *The Science of Orgasm* devotes an entire chapter to the different definitions of the word *orgasm,* and here are three definitions of love's climax from some of the "Godfathers of Sexology":

- "The expulsive discharge of neuromuscular tensions at the peak of sexual response." (Kinsey, Pomeroy, Martin, & Gebhard, 1953)
- "A brief episode of physical release from the vasocongestion and myotonic increment developed in response to sexual stimuli." (Masters & Johnson, 1966)
- "The zenith of sexuoerotic experience that men and women characterize subjectively as voluptuous rapture or ecstasy. It occurs simultaneous in the brain/mind and the pelvic genitalia. Irrespective of the locus of onset, the occurrence of orgasm is contingent upon reciprocal intercommunication between neural networks in the brain, above, and the pelvic genitalia below. ..." (Money, Wainwright, & Hingsburger, 1991)

Based on students' reactions, many of you likely find appealing the words "voluptuous rapture or ecstasy" in this last definition. This rapture or ecstasy is what most people can relate to rather than all the technical descriptions of physiological changes. Let's move on to the research on health effects.

THE RELATIONSHIP BETWEEN SEXUAL EXPRESSION AND HEALTH—THE RESEARCH

If you are not into research and you are tempted to skip this section, at least read this paragraph! The bottom line is that there is much evidence to support the assertion that sex can have many health benefits, which include reduction in stress, lowered blood pressure, and stronger immunity— all resulting in improved cardiovascular health with reduced risk of heart attack. Orgasm is also believed to relieve pain, reduce a man's risk for prostate cancer, and help you sleep better. Psychologically, good sex (with orgasm) can boost your self-esteem, strengthen your sense of well-being, and improve a couple's intimacy and relationship satisfaction. In a nutshell—there is strong evidence in the medical and psychological literature regarding the empirically proven benefits of sex!

Next, we note a few more studies regarding the use of sexual behavior to manage pain and then describe health benefits in several areas ranging from orgasm increasing chances of conception and going full term with a pregnancy to increasing your protection from heart attack and cancer. A series of laboratory studies in the 1980s (several by Whipple and Komisaruk, reported in Komisaruk, Beyer-Flores, & Whipple, 2006) demonstrated that pain alleviation does result from masturbation. Specifically, these studies demonstrated that female subjects found vaginal stimulation (including pleasurable touch to the clitoris) increased the threshold of pain detection and tolerance. Said simply, women found masturbation to have a measurable pain-relieving effect under laboratory conditions. In a survey study with 1,900 American women, nearly 1 in 10 reported recently using masturbation to find relief from the pain of menstrual cramps (Ellison, 2000). Because of the increased level of endorphins and corticosteroids resulting from orgasm, sexual arousal has also been found to help relieve pain from arthritis, migraines, and neurological conditions that cause muscles to spasm— including pain relief among patients with paralysis and multiple sclerosis (reported in Komisaruk, Beyer-Flores, & Whipple, 2006).

The rest of this review will be divided between physical and psychological benefits, even though this is an artificial division as the physical influences the mental and vice versa. Take the experience of pain from spastic or cramping muscles—is that physical or psychological? It is both. However, for organizing a simpler approach to this review, we will look at physical benefits first, then psychological. The physical benefits are divided into the research showing that sex helps everybody's cardiovascular health, the health benefits for women, and finally, the health benefits for men.

General Health Benefits of Sexual Expression to Men and Women: Cardiovascular Health

Besides pain relief, sexual expression involving arousal and orgasm appears to lower the risk of heart attack, stroke, and diabetes. This effect, of course, may increase the longevity of sexually active adults. Empirical studies on the cardiovascular benefits resulting from sex go back at least the mid-1970s when Abramov found a positive correlation between a history of heart attack and sexual dissatisfaction (defined as a lack of enjoyment of intercourse and/or inability to achieve orgasm). What stood out about this study was its focus on the connection between *women's* cardiovascular health and sexual frigidity (a term no longer used in medicine because it is as inaccurate as it is pejorative). Essentially, the findings of this study suggest that the less a woman enjoys sex and the fewer orgasms she experiences, the more likely she is to have a history of heart attack (Abramov, 1976).

Of course, this was a simple correlational study without follow-up. A longitudinal study with a 10-year follow-up in South Wales (this one involving 918 men) found that men having frequent orgasms (defined as at least two per week in this study) had 50% less mortality than men who had less than one orgasm per month. This is a big difference, both in frequency of orgasm and cardiovascular risk. Said conversely, men having orgasm less than once per month had double the rates for heart attacks as those men who reported a high frequency of intercourse—defined as at least two orgasms per week (Smith, Frankel, & Yarnell; 1997).

In a smaller American study (252 racially diverse people, both men and women) but with a much longer follow-up (25 years), researchers in North Carolina found the frequency of intercourse was a significant predictor of greater longevity for men, but not women. Although current frequency of intercourse was not an overall significant predictor of longer life for women, those females who did report a past history of enjoying sexual intercourse did tend to live longer (Palmore, 1982). The results of this study make me wonder about the average differences in orgasm between men and women through intercourse (the average being less consistent for women as a means of experiencing orgasm). Instead of asking for current and past frequency of intercourse, questions specific to frequency of orgasm may have produced additional interesting results.

A similar study (but with a shorter, five-year follow-up) with similar results was conducted in Sweden. This study was clever in design as it surveyed only 70-year-old men and women (166 men and 226 women) and then checked back to see who reached their 75th birthday and who did not (Persson, 1981). Researchers found that the older the men continued to have sex, the more likely they were to live to age 75. As with the Palmore's North Carolina study, this was true for men only. The authors found no association between women's mortality and sexual intercourse. In terms of women's chances of reaching 75, it did not seem to matter at what age they reported having stopped intercourse. Again, would there be additional results of interest if the participants were asked at what age they stopped having orgasms instead of intercourse?

An interesting line of research studies has been conducted on the relationship between heart health, orgasm, and levels of neurotransmitters such as dopamine, norepinephrine, oxytocin, and vasopressin. Higher levels of these neurotransmitters are released during orgasm and are associated with the subjective feelings of pleasure, euphoria, exhilaration, and bonding. Besides release of higher levels of endorphins, increased levels of corticosteroids and the hormone dehydroepiandrosterone (DHEA) have been measured immediately after orgasm. DHEA is a precursor to the development of testosterone, and both are associated with reports of higher sexual interest for men as well as women. What is less known is that there appears to be a relationship between risk reduction of heart attack and increased levels of DHEA and testosterone. Testosterone is believed to help reduce the risk for heart attack and reduce residual harm to the heart muscles if a heart attack does happen (Booth et al., 1999; Forari et al., 2002). This refers to naturally occurring testosterone levels in men. However, men are also typically warned by their physician that when starting a testosterone replacement treatment they are at slightly higher risk for prostate cancer and possibly increase blood pressure, which in turn can increase risk for stroke or heart attack.

General Health Benefits of Sexual Expression to Women

When it comes to the health benefits of sex specific to women, we will briefly mention six areas of research: breast cancer, endometriosis, regularity of menstrual cycles, female fertility (conception), pregnancy/obstetrics, and menopause. Breast cancer research related to female sexuality is not a strong area to discuss because the studies are few and include small numbers of women. Authors have suggested that the sexual arousal and orgasm of women results in increased release of oxytocin and DHEA, which in turn are associated with a protective effect against breast cancer (Murrell, 1995). There is also a "fetal androgen theory," based on the idea that the hormones experienced during pregnancy (and possibly exposure to sperm) strengthen the immune response and also have a protective effect against cancer (Rossing et al., 1996).

In an interesting review article sponsored by Planned Parenthood Federation of America (2007), this study examined the relationship between sex and breast cancer among French women. A 1989 case-control investigation studied women diagnosed with cancer and matched them with women without cancer in a control group. The authors found a higher risk of breast cancer among the women who reported that they did not have a sexual partner or rarely had intercourse (Lê, 1989). Like the studies discussed regarding the relationship between sex and heart disease, this study is also correlational and does not show any direct causal relationship between sex and protection from breast cancer.

Regarding endometriosis, a much larger study (with more than 2,000 American women) examined the relationship between the frequency of sexual orgasm and the likelihood of being diagnosed with this disorder. Endometriosis is the abnormal growth of endometrial cells outside of the uterus, which results in bleeding, pain, and other complications. Conversely, the women who reported they had engaged in sexual behavior "often or sometimes" during menstruation were significantly less likely to be given the diagnosis. The authors concluded that sexual activity and orgasm during menstruation has a potentially protective effect against endometriosis (Meaddough et al., 2002).

Research regarding the relationship between sex and menstruation, fertility, and obstetrics is much more robust, with many studies involving thousands of women drawing the same conclusions: Women with more frequent sexual activity have more regular menstrual cycles, have a higher likelihood of conception, and are more likely to maintain the pregnancy full term. According to a white paper entitled *The Health Benefits of Sexual Expression* (Planned Parenthood Federation of America, 2007), several studies between 1975 and the early 1990s demonstrated that a regular schedule of sex throughout the month is associated with a more regular menstrual cycle. It is important to note that if a woman wants to have this benefit, she needs to have sexual activity at least once per week during her nonmenstruating weeks (Burleson, Trevathan, & Todd, 1991). This "regulating effect" of sex on menstruation cycles has been observed in straight women as well as lesbians. A study of same-sex activity and the length of menstrual cycles demonstrated stronger menstrual regularity for lesbian women who had sex at least three times per week when compared with women who were abstinent or had sex only occasionally (Cutler, 1991).

Obviously, having a more regular menstrual cycle can aid in a woman's planning for conception and pregnancy. Dr. John Bancroft, the former director of the Kinsey Institute at Indiana University, found that chances were good (80%) for a woman with a regular cycle to conceive within six months if she had sex four times a week. Her chances dropped to only 17% if she had sex less than once per week (Bancroft, 1987). If considering sex frequency only during the woman's "fertility window" (the five-day period before ovulation), a typical woman has a 40% chance of conceiving if she has sex daily during that five-day period. Her chances drop to 17% if she has sex (penile-vaginal, of course) only once during her fertility window (Wilcox, Weinberg, & Baird, 1995).

The occurrence and timing of a woman's orgasm is also an important consideration. Even though it is not required for conception, the female orgasm is highly recommended for increasing the likelihood of conception. Let me repeat that: *female orgasm facilitates conception*. Women who wish to conceive are encouraged to develop the ability to orgasm and enjoy the pleasures of sex rather than getting caught up in the desire-killing pressure of conceiving and experiencing sex like a job (one that you don't like). In addition, it is recommended that women have an orgasm soon after the man's intravaginal ejaculation. Women who have orgasms after the male's ejaculation retain more sperm for conceiving than women who did not have orgasm or women who had orgasm before the male ejaculated. This is important because retention of sperm after female orgasm is associated with increased rates of fertility (Singh et al., 1998).

As an aside, Doc Masters routinely received referrals from across the country of couples who were experiencing difficulty conceiving and their gynecologists saw no medical reason explaining why the women were not pregnant. Couples would travel to the Masters and Johnson Institute to get "talked into pregnancy" through his counsel. Essentially, here is what he would tell them. First, stop screwing like rabbits! Slow down the frequency of intercourse to no more than once every other day to maximize sperm potency. He advised having intercourse two to three times during the woman's five-day fertility window. This is different from the traditional medical advice of "as often as possible," which just exhausts and stresses the couple. Second, he advised the woman to vaginally contain her partner to the deepest point she could manage at the time of his ejaculation. He believed the rear-entry position most often provided this deep penetration, but it was up to the woman to decide.

Doc then instructed the woman to have an orgasm as soon as possible after the man's ejaculation. She was to do so while she was lying on her back with her buttocks elevated by a pillow. He told the couple that this elevation was very important, as her orgasm would then better facilitate the movement of the sperm through the reproductive system (especially aiding sperm travel through her cervix and uterus). His last instruction was for her to remain in this position with her butt elevated for at least 20 minutes. Basically, Doc's instructions were designed to help sperm get planted deeply, get catapulted along their way via the happy dance of the uterus, and then assisted by gravity through elevation. For an outrageous demonstration of this "enhanced process" for conception, check out the Dude's only sex scene in the 1998 cult film *The Big Lebowski*.

Now back to the research! It is not surprising that regular frequency of sex does aid a woman's chances of conception, but what many find surprising is that regular frequency of sex during pregnancy also helps a mother to maintain the pregnancy full term. This is important because many people think sexual intercourse during pregnancy will hurt the fetus and increase the risk of miscarriage. In 1999, German researcher Dr. Kirsten von Sydow conducted a thorough meta-analysis of 59 studies of sex during pregnancy, published in English and German between 1950 and 1996. This comprehensive review resulted in the conclusion that if there are no medical contraindications (such as in a high-risk pregnancy), sexual activity (including intercourse) during a normal pregnancy does not harm the fetus (Von Sydow, 1999). Additional studies show that sexual activity continued through the pregnancy may protect the mother and fetus from early delivery. In an interesting study published in the *Journal of Reproductive Medicine,* more than 1,800 pregnant women were interviewed thrice about their sexual practices (including a postpartum follow-up interview). The investigators concluded that the women who reported sexual activity during the previous two weeks were more likely to have their pregnancy go full term than women who reported they had not had sexual intercourse within the same period (Reamey, White, & Daniel, 1982).

Interestingly, this conclusion was true whether or not the women reported that they had experienced orgasm! This suggests that continued sexual activity (with or without orgasm) late into the third trimester can provide some protection against preterm delivery (Sayle, 2001). One caveat: Avoid confusion between these research findings and the long-standing practice of using intercourse to stimulate labor in the mother with a full-term pregnancy. When young couples are anxious and keep coming to the labor and delivery department (or emergency room) because they think "it is time," a nurse or doctor often takes the couple aside and advises them to return home, have a nice glass of wine, and make love before returning for their third, fourth, or fifth visit.

Regarding women's aging, there have been many studies over several decades on menopause's effects upon the female sexual experience. The excellent review of 40 years of research on this topic supported that old adage "use it or lose it" (Planned Parenthood Federation of America, 2007). Vaginal atrophy (shrinking and thinning of vaginal tissues) and increased problems with vaginal dryness (lack of lubrication during sex) appear to be the most common physical effects of aging experienced by women in these studies. This is partly due to the decreased hormonal support to these tissues, but the good news is women can choose to continue being sexually active and slow down this effect. Additional good news is that women can minimize vaginal atrophy during menopause even without a sexual partner (through masturbation). Women are also more likely to experience adequate vaginal lubrication with continued and regular sexual activity as they age (Masters and Johnson, 1966; Leiblum et al., 1983; Van Lunsen and Lann, 2004).

General Health Benefits of Sexual Expression to Men

While at the VA, one of my jobs was the Health Behavior Coordinator with the Health Promotion and Disease Prevention Program. We had a health and wellness event called "Walk with the Doc," in which veterans enjoyed a walk while asking questions about health in general. A recent conversation went something like this:

Vet: Hey Doc, I heard something about sex being a good thing for the prostate. Is that true? If so, how much is enough and can you write me a prescription for it?

Doc: Well, if you want to avoid infection of the prostate (prostatitis), then at least two to three ejaculations per week should help. But it looks like regular sex with ejaculation also helps prevent prostate cancer. The kicker is you have to "pump up the volume" for getting off to four or five times per week!

Vet: Holy crap, Doc—you're killing me! I guess my days are numbered. How do you expect me to talk the wife into five times a week?

Doc: Believe me, I don't. Wives are only willing to do so much. And don't put this off on the missus. Take the bull by the horn if you need to! It's all in your hands!

Vet: You're a friggin' pervert—you know that?

Doc: Yeah, that's what my friends tell me. It's when my kids say it that it surprises me.

Vet: Well, the old man had it (prostate cancer) and so did my uncle. So I think it's pretty much in the cards for me.

Doc: Not necessarily. Family history is very important but far from a death sentence. There are things you can do to help lower your chances of getting it—like being out here for exercise, having regular ejaculations, and keeping your testosterone in normal range.

Vet: You make it sound easy. You giving me one of your health promotion pitches?

Doc: Sorry about that. Guess it's like most things, easier said than done. The older we get, the higher our chances to get prostate problems. And if we live long enough, chances are pretty fair that we'll both get prostate cancer. The good news is something else will probably kill us off before our prostate does.

Vet: Man, is that what you call good news? Anyone ever tell you that you're a real downer?

Doc: As a matter of fact, yes. A good friend named Art Aaronson. I really miss that guy. He was my running buddy, before he died of prostate cancer.

Here is the research background on this conversation. An excellent prospective study published in 2004 (with long-term follow-up) suggested that the higher a man's ejaculation frequency, the lower his likelihood for getting prostate cancer. In addition, more than 21 ejaculations per month was associated with not only decreased risk for getting cancer, but also the cancer not spreading beyond the prostate if you did get it (Leitzmann, 2004).

Researchers speculate that frequent ejaculations "flush out" potential carcinogens in the prostate or the stress relief of the ejaculation has protective effects against cancerous cell division. The authors of a 2003 Australian study concluded that men who report a history of least four ejaculations per week (before age 50) were one-third less likely to develop prostate cancer than men with less frequent ejaculations (Giles et al., 2003).

Here are a couple more notes for the guys: Some research suggests sex (on a regular basis) can help your sperm quality and help decrease your risk for erectile dysfunction. Sperm can actually be affected by the frequency of ejaculation. After only five days of no ejaculation, the quality of men's sperm is adversely affected. Sperm motility (forward movement) and morphology (structural quality) are both decreased. Conversely, increased ejaculations have been demonstrated to increase the sperm count in the man's ejaculate (Tur-Kaspa et al., 1994). As mentioned earlier, the "use it or lose it" adage tends to be supported by the main body of research on sexual function. Having sex regularly (or at least having frequent erections with or without orgasm), increases blood flow into the penis and elevates oxygen saturation. This helps keep the small microvascular system healthy inside the penis, including the erectile tissue (Zippe et al., 2001).

Think about it: What is the first thing you do when a kid runs up to you and asks you to blow up a balloon? If you are like me, you probably S-T-R-E-T-C-H the balloon out to make it easier to blow air into it. The same is true for a man who does not have frequent erections—it's more difficult to get blood into the penis because the microvascular system in the penis has lost much of its elasticity!

Some men literally cannot remember the last time they had an erection, because it has been so long since they lost the elasticity of their erectile tissue. Some of these men do not want to use medications and have actually regained part of their erectile ability by using a VCD (vacuum constriction device, or "penis pump") to rehabilitate the vascular circulatory system inside the penis. Dr. Jeffrey Albaugh, author of *Reclaiming Sex & Intimacy After Prostate Cancer*, has spent a career researching men's sexual adjustment after having prostate surgery. His work has demonstrated that sex and intimacy need not be lost following surgery for prostate cancer. He developed a sexual rehabilitation program that uses VCD treatment, among other options, to restore erectile response to the degree it can be, which often can be enough to resume sexual intercourse (Albaugh, 2012).

Sometimes what erectile ability men can regain is sufficient for having intercourse, and sometimes it is not. The point is that it is a good idea for men to keep blood flowing in this part of their body. Feeling left out, ladies? Yes, you too can "pump up the volume" in your erectile tissues with the use of a female-styled pump designed to create a vacuum and increase the amount of blood in the clitoris. The FDA-approved device is one of several treatment options for women who have female sexual dysfunction to the degree that it causes significant distress.

General Health Benefits of Sexual Expression: Psychological Well-Being of Men and Women

After discussion of benefits regarding serious health concerns such as heart attacks and cancer, reviewing potential benefits that are psychological and contribute to your "well-being" might sound like the "lighter side" of sex and health. The truth for many people is that quality of life is just as important as, and in many cases more important than, physical health and longevity. This is certainly true for the many Americans who kill themselves every day (like Leelah in Chapter 1 or Pat in Chapter 2); very few of them face a terminal illness or unbearable physical pain. They died because they had no hope that their life could be better, and they wanted to stop the pain—a psychological, not physical, pain in most cases.

The benefits of sexual expression can, in many cases, include improvements in psychiatric conditions such as depression (especially decreasing loneliness and suicidal thoughts). Over the past three decades of work as psychologists, the first two authors have seen that people who feel shame about themselves (regardless of the source) are much more prone to self-criticism and don't accept themselves as human beings of worth. This is especially true, at least for part of their lives, when it comes to the unfortunate shame people experience related to sexual trauma or by shaming regarding LGBTQA orientations. This is not a profound conclusion; it is easily observed, if you look closely enough at your circle of family, friends, or acquaintances. People who do not deem themselves acceptable have great difficulty deeming themselves worthy of being accepted by others and, especially, loved by others. This is true even if they are told and shown they are loved! Individuals with strongly negative views of themselves and their own sexuality will just think, "Sure, you say that, but if you only knew how despicable or shameful I am, there is no way you would love me!" These individuals sometimes feel desperate about keeping their shame a "secret," whether it is being abused, being "the wrong sex," being an "abomination to God," or whatever they had to do to survive as a kid, as a hostage, or as a soldier in a war zone.

It is important to note that, in these cases, sexual expression can also have very damaging effects on people's psychological states, even if the sexual activity is freely chosen (not rape or other coerced or manipulated sexual activity). A common example is a young girl or woman who chooses to have sex, not because she really wants to, but because she believes sex is her only value or only way to maintain a relationship.

The bottom line: Shame and nonacceptance of one's sexual self is a recipe for depression. Conversely, the support and encouragement of individuals over time to accept themselves, and whatever "shortcomings" they perceive themselves to have, is a pathway to health. Sexual expression of individuals with others can be a tremendously transformative experience when that sexual expression is driven by a positive model of sexuality and a recognition of the sexual rights of all people (defined in later chapters). Being vulnerable with another who is caring of you and accepting of whatever perceived "shortcomings" you may think you have is a healing experience. When this process of positive sexual expression occurs and is positively reciprocated, it is a powerful antidote for depression. Moreover, there is a strong association between sex and positive affect, which can be lasting and predictive of both partners' relationship satisfaction. It is important to know that affection and sex promotes a sense of well-being and has long-term relational benefits (Debrot, Meuwly, Muise, Impett, & Schoebi, 2017).

A small study of 30 elderly people found that masturbation was associated with a decreased risk for depression (Catania & White, 1982). In a more recent study of people living with disabilities, 77 adults with amputations were interviewed and measured for sexual satisfaction, pain, and quality of life. Except for level of pain, the highest correlation to quality of life was the factor of sexual expression/satisfaction. However, the researchers also found that the degree to which the amputation interfered with an individual's sexual activity was even a stronger predictor of depression than the pain associated with the amputation (Walters & Williamson, 1998).

In a much larger American study (sample of 3,500 adults), personal happiness was associated with the frequency of sexual activity and orgasm (Laumann et al., 1994). Said differently, the more sex these people said they had, the more happy (less depressed) they said they were as well. A similar conclusion was found in an international study of men from four different cultures, in which the researchers concluded that low sexual activity and satisfaction was closely associated with higher levels of depression (Nicolosi, 2004). A similar study in the Netherlands focused on the sexual activity and use of medications among psychiatric patients. The author found that having more frequent sexual intercourse was associated with a lower need for psychiatric medication (Stiefelhagen, 1994).

Let's talk about that lovely little neurotransmitter again, oxytocin (otherwise known as the "love hormone"). Besides being associated with lower levels of depression (who can be sad when having good sex?), higher levels of oxytocin may also be related to lowered stress, greater intimacy, and higher self-esteem. Sexual activity has long been associated with stress reduction, most likely because of the surge in oxytocin resulting from orgasm (Charnetski & Brennan, 2001). Because this neurotransmitter stimulates feelings of warmth and relaxation, it is difficult to keep feeling tense and anxious after orgasm (Weeks, 2002). In the previously cited study where 1 in 10 women said they masturbated to relieve pain, Ellison (2000) also found that 39% of the 2,600 women surveyed stated that they masturbated to relax. Increased levels of oxytocin are also associated with feelings of affection, intimacy, and closeness (Weeks, 2002).

Simply said, oxytocin can often serve as the glue within relationships and assists in the development of that "lovely-dovey" feeling so many people seek. In fact, some would say that oxytocin-driven sexual expression is not only the glue that holds us together as couples, it may also serve as the glue that holds us together as a family (as with the "love of child," especially during the bonding of breastfeeding). Because the sexual expression of desire is a key ingredient of pair-bonding that creates "the couple experience," it can be reasonably argued that sexual expression is essential to the basic family unit as well as all kinship systems, culture formation, and society itself (Fisher et al., 2002).

Feature Story

THE HEALTH EFFECTS OF BREASTFEEDING AND AN AMERICAN PUBLIC HEALTH CRISIS

[Qualifiers and Trigger Warning: The following discussion of breastfeeding may be upsetting to some.]

Yes, breastfeeding is the most natural, nurturing, and healthy thing a mother can do for her baby. *Yes*, breastfeeding can involve sensuous feelings although mothers do not nurse their children for sensuous enjoyment. In fact, these feelings may be exactly why some mothers choose *not* to nurse. *Yes*, honest and intelligent people may disagree (and the publisher could get some letters about this), but please hear this argument out. *Yes*, acknowledging the fact that the wholesome act of breastfeeding can also be accompanied by sensual pleasure may confuse some; but not addressing these feelings sometimes associated with breastfeeding creates even more problems (as you will see if you read on).

This feature story is included here to support mothers and their babies, not to criticize moms as is commonly done in public discourse about breastfeeding (especially when mothers breastfeed their babies in public, as celebrities occasionally do, causing a "controversial" media storm). Let it also be noted some mothers cannot breastfeed for medical reasons and that some mothers just don't want to breastfeed, and that is their right.

None of the authors are lactation consultants or experts on the subject. However, this subject is included as an important topic of health because I am a husband and father of five (including daughters) as well as a health psychologist and public-health educator concerned for a woman's right to breastfeed her baby should she choose to do so. The authors' concerns stem from the fact that women across the country are frequently asked to leave public places when they breastfeed their babies. Nursing mothers have frequently made the news after being asked to leave public swimming pools, coffee shops, restaurants, health clubs, museums (including the Smithsonian), and even in the ultimate retail capital of women's breasts—Victoria's Secret.

More commonly, nursing mothers are asked to relocate their breastfeeding activity to public restrooms—where, of course, everybody would love to eat their lunch. In November 2011, Target store employees approached a mother who was nursing in the women's clothing department. They threatened that if she did not leave, they would call the cops and she would get a ticket. This family-unfriendly event inspired an inspirational response nationwide when numerous media sources reported a virtual "breastfeeding revolt" in which nursing mothers from across the country staged a "nurse-in" protest at more than 100 Target stores in 35 states (Jonsson, 2011).

During the 1990s, this kind of thing was happening regularly in Ohio. After a nursing mother was asked to relocate her baby to a disgusting public restroom in a local Walmart, a local paper asked me to write a cover story on "feeding-phobia" to explain why Americans are so weirded-out by breastfeeding (Peterson, 2000). The article was called, "Why are Americans so weird about breastfeeding?" The observations that follow are partly based on that cover story, but more on my experience as a sex educator and as a perinatal educator. What do I mean when I say perinatal educator? Someone who provides education and support to those who are planning to have a baby, those actively engaged in childbirth, and those in the postpartum adjustment period.

A brief explanation: I taught the "Fathers & Babies" class at Miami Valley Hospital in Dayton, Ohio, for nearly 20 years (Peterson, 1989, 1990). It was an absolute blast and very satisfying to see how many fathers are so invested in the optimal development of their babies. The fathers and babies class covered topics from changing diapers to infant CPR, including the father's role in supporting the mother breastfeeding the child (keep reading for "Breastfeeding for Dads 101"). Many of the fathers packed their wives' expressed milk to feed the baby during the two-hour class. As fun as the class was, I had an even better time co-teaching the Family-Centered Perinatal Education (FCPC) class, which was a combined prenatal childbirth education class and a postpartum parenting support class (Peterson et al., 1986, 1987, 1991). Breastfeeding was an important educational part (and practice) within this FCPC class.

Prenatally, the FCPC class would guide young couples through a confusing and stressful transition in their lives. The class prepared the expectant couple for the big event at the hospital and instructed them on developing a birthing plan, sex during pregnancy, decisions on circumcision, and assertiveness training for communicating with hospital personnel. After a three-week "birthing break," parents would return postpartum to introduce their baby as a new member of the class. This could allow them to share their birthing stories, provide important training on infant care, and continue social support that developed between couples prenatally. For five weeks postpartum, we would talk about all the important stuff, like the nuances of newborn care, baby massage, infant stimulation, resuming sexual relations, screening for depression, going back to work issues, and, of course, breastfeeding. This class was very appreciated by young couples transiting into their new stage of family life (for further details, see Peterson et al., 1987, 1993). Now that we have covered a little background, please consider the following story.

Breastfeeding Support: A mother had her first baby and when the new bambino was handed to her in the hospital, she started getting the newborn to take her nipple and latch on to learn how to suckle properly. This first lactation experience went well and when she came home, she continued to breastfeed with the support of her husband. There she could relax with privacy and without the stress of the hospital surroundings. It was then she first experienced pleasurable feelings during the breastfeeding of the child. Concerned about these feelings, she wanted to talk to me about them. She thought that these sensuous physical feelings were related to her uterus shrinking and getting back in shape, because that was exactly how it felt. She also described feeling like she was "stretched out and sore." After all, she had just performed the equivalent of passing a small pumpkin through her cervix and vagina. To some degree, she was expecting this because of her reading on the subject.

As she spoke to me about these experiences, I shared my belief that it was all part of a healthy readjustment of her uterus, vulva, and associated girlie parts. Her uterus was contracting during breast stimulation and causing pleasurable feelings that she sometimes described as mild orgasms and sometimes as not-so-comfortable cramping. She talked about the release of oxytocin and the intense emotional bond she felt during breastfeeding—so intense it was the first time she ever knew she would gladly sacrifice her life for another person. This well-read young mother also felt that the release of oxytocin, prolactin, and vasopressin helped minimize the "baby blues" and prevented a more severe reaction of postpartum depression. Fortunately, she had no problems with that.

Although the young mother had read about the benefits of breastfeeding, she did not know these types of sensuous feelings can occur with some nursing mothers. She knew she was not doing anything wrong and was actually doing something very right. I shared with her a great quote from a childbirth and lactation colleague of mine at the time, Donna Walls. Donna used to pose a great question to expectant moms-to-be. First, she asked the parents-to-be to imagine a pill that could be given a child that was free and available, had no adverse side effects, would boost your baby's immune system, prevent many childhood diseases, protect against allergies, maybe make the baby smarter, and give mom several health benefits. The question: Would you choose not to give your child the pill with all those advantages? I told my friend I didn't think Donna ever had a mother-to-be say she would not choose giving her baby the pill. The same was true for my friend every time she nursed her child. She was giving her child all those advantages and, at the same time, was losing her "baby fat" and realigning her uterus and pelvic floor muscles faster, as well as reducing her risk of breast cancer.

She was having what she considered mild orgasms simply from the stimulation of her breasts during feeding. While she knew this was normal, she still felt a little uncomfortable about it, even though all she felt was an intense motherly love for her baby. She wondered how could she feel anything but motherly love for her baby—completely healthy and nonsexual—and still have these orgasms occurring at the same time? We talked about the hormone oxytocin being released during breastfeeding and how it plays a role in her experience as it mediates uterine contraction as well as mother-child attachment. As previously noted, oxytocin is also released during orgasm, pair-bonding is increased, the letdown of milk is facilitated, and around it goes. In addition, prolactin is released at higher levels during breastfeeding, which facilitates a calming effect and pulls nutrients from the mother's blood for the baby. Although this was far from a complete explanation, it did seem to help her feel better and normalize her experience.

Fortunately, she did not feel conflicted enough to stop breastfeeding as she also knew breastfeeding was the healthiest thing she could do for the baby and herself. Unfortunately, many women are not as comfortable with their bodies, especially when they see their breasts only as sexual organs. Too many mothers feel uncomfortable to the point where they either do not even try breastfeeding or they stop after a short period because of the pleasurable (and/or sometimes painful) feelings associated with it.

Medicine has known for at least 50 years that some nursing mothers have sensual pleasure, even to the degree of orgasm. Sometimes these pleasurable feelings are accompanied by guilt or other forms of discomfort during the act of nursing. In 1966, Masters and Johnson reported that they studied the sexual experiences of women who became pregnant, delivered their baby, and nursed for at least two months. These women were a subset in a larger group of subjects (over a 12-year period) participating in their sex physiology research program. Two dozen of the nursing mothers "admittedly were stimulated sexually by the suckling process"; three of them reported experiencing orgasm. Interestingly, the authors reported that "there was a heavy overlay of guilt expressed by six of the twenty-four women" (Masters & Johnson, 1966, p. 162). Unfortunately, researchers and childbirth educators fail to get this information distributed for public consumption because it is such a taboo subject, leading to further generations of young mothers feeling uncomfortable, even to the point of choosing to stop breastfeeding their babies.

New parents are not usually prepared to deal with the naked sexuality of infants and children, even to the degree of not acknowledging that babies do have sexual responses. That's right: babies are easily observed having sexual responses to breastfeeding. For example, baby boys will routinely have erections while suckling the breast, will rhythmically move their hands and feet while feeding, and then experience a total body relaxation characteristic of a release of sexual tension (Kinsey et al., 1948; Nichols & Humenick, 1988). And, of course, this is all perfectly natural and normal. Many parents will attest to this fact simply through observing their own children, from their baby stimulating its own little genitals to their toddlers humping whatever they can hump—including Mommy's leg sometimes.

This behavior continues well into childhood, until kids are old enough to understand our society's sexophrenic messages and choose to engage in sexual behavior privately where they are at less risk of embarrassment and/or punishment. In the *Journal of Pediatrics*, William Friedrich and his associates at the Mayo Clinic published useful empirical evidence of the normative sexual expression of children, including toddlers and preschoolers two to five years old. By interviewing large numbers of mothers, the authors investigated the sexual behaviors of 834 children (from 2 to 12 years old). More than 40% of mothers of the two- to five-year-old children reported that their kids touched the mother's breasts and 4–5% reported that their kids put their mouths on the mothers' breasts. One of four of these same mothers reported that their kids touched their own genitals in public, and this percentage dramatically increased at home. For mothers of these same children, two to five years old, about half reported their kids touching their own genitals at home (Friedrich, Fisher, Broughton, Houston, & Shafran, 1998).

This is partly why the sexual behavior of children and the sensuous nature of breastfeeding need to be acknowledged, even when nursing is a nurturing act. While this nurturing is going on, the mother can sometimes have pleasurable feelings and so can baby. The only thing wrong with that is not to acknowledge that these feelings occur and are normal. If this phenomenon is denied or pathologized, we will continue to have mothers feel uncomfortable about it, therefore choosing not to nurse from the start or discontinue breastfeeding soon after they start.

THE MAGNITUDE OF THE PROBLEM

Statistics from the American Academy of Pediatrics (AAP) indicate just how many mothers feel inhibited and choose not to breastfeed. Approximately three-quarters of new moms opt to initiate nursing (which isn't bad), but that number drops to about 20% by the end of the critical six-month period when babies are recommended to exclusively have breast milk (American Academy of Pediatrics, 2012). The CDC recently estimated that if American mothers breastfeed their babies, as the AAP recommends, approximately 1,000 babies would be saved every year (would not die of various causes) and $13 billion in health care would be saved (American Academy of Pediatrics, 2012). One study found a 36% reduction in sudden infant death syndrome (SIDS) associated with breastfed babies (Ip, Chung, & Raman, 2007).

Two key statistics make this public health crisis staggering. The first is the recommendation by both the AAP and the WHO that babies should feed ONLY from the breast for the first six months. Less than 1 in 5 American mothers (17%) follow that recommendation (and over half of American babies in this sample were introduced to formula before the child was one week old). The second recommendation is that breastfeeding should continue one to two years, depending on which authority you consider (AAP says one year and WHO says two years). Only a mere 5% of American mothers are breastfeeding when their babies have their first birthday (American Academy of Pediatrics, 2012).

These startling statistics are not an indictment of American mothers. Rather, they are an indictment of the American health care system, corporate marketing in America, and the families (mostly fathers) who do not support the mother's interest in breastfeeding her child. Millions of American women *do want* to breastfeed, but often experience a systemic lack of support for nursing. Some mothers experience overwhelming resistance or even hostility. Reasons for this lack of support and resistance are multifactorial and complex. However, as a man who has co-taught family-centered perinatal classes and father-baby classes, I strongly believe that America's sexophrenic relationship with sexuality is partially to blame for this public health crisis. Please note that this crisis is not even identified as a health problem by most Americans. Sexophrenic-related factors that serve as obstacles to breastfeeding are on individual, couple, family, and societal levels.

The obstacles to breastfeeding overlap and affect each other. Already mentioned is the discomfort many women feel about their own bodies and their lack of confidence about successfully breastfeeding. More systemically, this discomfort and lack of confidence can be related to women's lack of positive role models, the lack of positive (public) media images of breastfeeding mothers, lack of comprehensive sexuality education as children (as opposed to sex education focused just on abstinence), lack of partner support, lack of family support (mothers and mothers-in-law), lack of organizational support in the workplace for breastfeeding mothers to express, and the extensive marketing of the bottle-fed culture, including the preponderance of baby bottles appearing in children's books, which defines bottle feeding as the healthy middle-class norm.

Millions of working mothers are employed in the health care field, and many thousands of them may be breastfeeding a baby during any given month. You might think that health care employers such as hospitals might be supportive of their female staff who want to work and continue to breastfeed their child. For this to happen, however, the employer needs to have a designated lactation room that is clean and private where the mother can express her milk and safely refrigerate it until she returns to her baby at the end of her workday. Most of the dozen hospitals and health care systems I have worked in, including federal health care environments, did not have lactation rooms. Only a minority of hospitals have such support for their breastfeeding mother/employees. That is most likely why the Patient Protection and Affordable Care Act (PPACA) directed employers (with more than 50 employees) to have lactation rooms available for working mothers to express, refrigerate, and store their breast milk (see Section 4207 of PPACA). Time will tell if these protections and supports for nursing mothers will survive efforts to abolish or revise this law.

When it comes to sexually related obstacles to breastfeeding, let's not forget the unfortunate women who have been sexually molested or raped (estimated to be one in three or four girls, depending on which study you read). Sexual trauma can contribute to discomfort with one's body, especially sexual feelings being perceived as positive. Unresolved issues of sexual trauma can be triggered from sensuous feelings and remind young mothers of the abuse they suffered. This can be an insurmountable obstacle to breastfeeding for some moms. Unfortunately, many more young women have been abused than there are competent mental health therapists available to assist resolving residual effects of sexual trauma. However, mothers seeking support to resolve trauma issues (or assistance on any sexual health topic) can find the closest certified sex counselor or therapist by visiting the website for the American Association of Sexuality Educators, Counselors and Therapists (AASECT).

While we are talking about abuse, and as incredible as it may seem, mothers who do follow the AAP recommendations of breastfeeding for the entire first year (and especially the longer two-year WHO recommendation) are sometimes ignorantly accused by others of abuse by keeping the child on the breast too long. Mothers are often peppered with questions like "When are you going to give the baby real food?" and comments like "You can't keep them a baby forever." Although these comments may be well intended at times, they can have an overall effect of shaming and discouraging mothers from continuing to breastfeed.

Underlying all of these factors is the outright sexist assumption that women are supposed to "just know" how to care for babies and children by their constitution—that is, by having ovaries. The assumption of an existing, inherent, ovary-based knowledge also can make it especially difficult for young mothers relating to breastfeeding. New mothers are expected to naturally know how to breastfeed, how often to breastfeed, and the duration of breastfeeding through the child's infancy (the first 12 months). This is unfair to young new mothers who are sometimes overwhelmed, especially if they are first-time moms. This is where perinatal education and support can be most needed.

Of course, the reverse stereotype is of the well-meaning yet bumbling dad who might drop the baby on its head. One day when eighteen fathers and their babies showed up for the fathers and babies class, at least six moms were camped outside the door ready to intercede if necessary. Most of the time, it was just a matter of new dads needing some education and support of their own, including addressing some old-fashioned stereotypes. American culture does not expect Dad to support Mom by asking her to express her milk and sharing the responsibility of feeding the baby. Dad's support for Mama can happen via Big Daddy actually getting up in the night and warming up a bottle of Mama's best stock to feed baby and allow Mom to get some rest, have private time, or get out of the house with her friends. Once breast milk is expressed by the mother, can you imagine some fathers caring for their infant and assisting their busy working wives by managing the inventory? Some dads are put in charge of managing the inventory by having sterilized supplies available, labeling the ounces expressed, dating the inventory, rotating stock, and taking the breast milk out of the freezer to plan for the next day. It's a family thing, and it happens.

To the credit of some new dads, they intend to support Mom by feeding the baby with formula instead of breast milk. They most often do not know that "the breast is best" as far as baby food goes. However, I have also talked to many fathers-to-be and new dads who unknowingly become obstacles to successful breastfeeding because of sexist attitudes about their partner's breasts. These attitudes are reflected by statements like "those are mine" and "I don't want to share my wife's boobs with anybody." That's why I always gave expectant fathers a talk called "Breastfeeding for Dads 101" in the Family-Centered Childbirth Education classes and the Dads and Baby classes (Peterson, 2000). These talks included three simple "do's and don'ts."

Breastfeeding for Dads 101

The "Number One Do" is to be there—no excuses. Breastfeeding success means supporting your partner and taking full advantage of the Family Medical Leave Act to be at the birth and be at home (at least one month is recommended). The "Second Do" is defending your partner's right to breastfeed the baby or to express wherever and whenever needed. Infants feed "on-demand" for optimal growth, so this really means whenever and wherever needed, including buses, airplanes, and department stores. The "Third Do" is to encourage Mom by telling her she is making the most incredible contribution to the health of the baby by breastfeeding. As noted earlier, that includes her protecting the baby from a long list of childhood illnesses. Plus, it is important for dads to know that breastfeeding helps get Mom back in shape because the average mother secretes an amazing number of calories (an average of 500 calories per day, the rough equivalent of running five miles).

The three "Don'ts" that fathers should always be instructed about all have to do with—yes, you guessed it—sex. First, dads are counseled not to ask, "Can't you turn those things off?" when she is letting down (has milk coming out of her nipples). This is one of those things the mom has no control over, and she can be embarrassed about "leaking," especially during sex. Just make sure you always have a towel or cloth diaper handy. Second, don't "belly up to the bar" by licking or suckling your partner's free breast when the baby is on the other. This may screw with her mind as she usually has to throw a switch inside her head between the nurturing function and the sexual function of her breasts. Generally speaking, don't complicate things! Her feeding you and the baby at the same time may overload the system and delay the resurrection of your sex life. Just because we learned that some women can enjoy the pleasure of breastfeeding and their body just reacts naturally, this is NOT an invitation!

Speaking of your sex life—this is the third and final "Don't"—don't get upset when it takes six weeks or so to resume your sex life! It may even be longer if there was a C-section or episiotomy (cutting of perineum tissue to allow easier exit for the baby). The hormones involved in breastfeeding can inhibit sexual desire yet help return the girl parts to sexual responsiveness. Time is needed to heal! Besides, it might take a miracle to find the energy to have sex in the first few weeks postpartum. So guys, you need to get a grip on yourselves—literally.

CONCLUSION

Thank you for considering these perspectives and stories on breastfeeding that are admittedly pretty unusual in content. It is only fair to answer the question many of you may have been wondering—"*Was this guy breastfed?*" I think I was, but regardless, I admit to an above-average interest in breasts. They are A-OK with me. But the bigger interest is the health promotion of babies and their mothers. However, one concern remains that needs to be addressed before this chapter ends.

The concern is if you think the authors pulled together a bunch of random research studies to make a point that is not widely accepted—the point that sexual expression is good for your health and well-being. After all, this could be our best effort at pushing an agenda about "sex being a good thing," assisted by a loose association of sex researchers over the past 70 years who have had only one goal: Making America sex-positive! So, just in case. ...

In the last chapter, there was a review of a few of the "Health Adviser" books circa 1900. It is amazing to read how we have made some progress from the time American medicine believed sex was best when generally avoided in all forms except for procreation (and only during marriage and using the missionary position)! Today we have our own versions of these prestigious medical advisers. They have names like the *Mayo Clinic Family Health Book* (Litin, 2009), the *Merck Manual of Health & Aging* (Beers, 2006), and the *Johns Hopkins Medical Guide to Health After 50* (Margolis,

2002). Let's take a brief look at what these leaders of American medicine have to say on the subject of sexual expression as compared with what was printed 100 years ago.

How times have changed! A century ago, these popular texts on health were full of dire warnings for parents to watch for the ill effects of onanism in their children (the dreaded disease of masturbation discussed in the last chapter). Today, the *Mayo Clinic Family Health Book* advises parents that masturbation "provides a way for teenagers to release sexual tension, give themselves pleasure, savor sexual fantasies, and even curb impulses to engage in inappropriate sexual activity with others" (Litin, 2009). The Mayo Clinic text even addresses sexual orientation, advising parents to "stress that if your teenager is gay, lesbian or bisexual, you won't reject him or her." Way to go, Mayo!

The *Merck Manual of Health & Aging* has a section on the primary strategies for preventing the top three causes of death for people over age 65 (heart disease, cancer, and stroke) as well as all the other causes of premature disability and death. Listed prominently at number five under the ten "Tools for Prevention" is the recommendation that "safe sex practices remain important during later adulthood." The authors remind seniors to use a "latex condom every time they have sex," and especially if they have "more than one sex partner" (Beers, 2006). A tip of the hat to the editors at Merck for helping break down the taboos and stereotypes of senior sexuality.

The *Johns Hopkins Medical Guide to Health After 50* includes a terrific section on increasing your likelihood for extended longevity. In what they describe as "the Johns Hopkins Prescription," the ingredients for healthy aging and extended longevity are exercise, a healthy diet, maintaining a healthy weight, not smoking, avoiding excessive alcohol, avoiding excessive sun exposure, reducing stress, and challenging your mind. The details under the "Reduce Stress" section include information similar to what we covered in this chapter: "Studies show that positive social interaction, including sexual activity for those who desire it, lower the levels of stress hormones in the blood, help preserve cognitive function, and prevent depression" (Margolis, 2002). My compliments to the good folks at Johns Hopkins for stating that sexuality is a contributor to one's overall health. This is something rarely seen in general medicine health texts as little as 20 years ago. As the contents of Chapter 3 demonstrated (remember the "Big Wheel of Health?"): Sexuality contributes to general health and your overall health contributes to your sexual satisfaction!

A final salute goes to the Mayo Clinic just because of the *total coolness* of what they say about sexual fantasy and because it is so perfectly related to upcoming chapters that are on sexual identity (Chapter 11) and sexual expression (Chapter 12). The *Mayo Clinic Family Health Book* actually has a section on "Teenage Sexuality" and the role that sexual fantasy plays as part of normal and healthy sexual development during adolescence. So check this out: "It is normal to have sexual fantasies. Sexual fantasies may even be useful in the development of a teen's sexual identity because they allow exploration of sexual situations that would be inappropriate for the teen to act out" (p. 217).

This represents some sound advice to parents in terms of permission given to their kids to explore their body guilt free and with positivity! So are you ready for inspiring stories of real-life experiences of people finding sexual heath? The next two success stories testify to the value of sexual literacy, sexual authenticity, and satisfaction in life as well as illustrate examples of people finding their way around significant obstacles to find peace of mind. Chapter 9 is about a young beautiful Latinx couple who want to have children but find themselves in a seven-year unconsummated marriage. Chapter 10 concludes Section II with a remarkable story of gender transformation from troubled supermasculinity to an authentic femininity.

REFERENCES

Abramov, L. (1976). Sexual life and sexual frigidity among women developing acute myocardial infarction. *Psychosomatic Medicine, 38*, 418–425.

Albaugh, J. (2012). Reclaiming sex & intimacy after prostate cancer. Pitman, NJ: Anthony J. Jannetti.

American Academy of Pediatrics (AAP). (2012, March). Policy Statement: Breastfeeding and the use of human milk. *Pediatrics*, 129 (3), 827–841.

Bagley, C., & Tremblay, P. (1997). Suicidal behaviors in homosexual and bisexual males. *Journal of Crisis Intervention and Suicide Prevention, 18*(1).

Bancroft, J. (1987). Hormones, sexuality and fertility in women. *Journal of Zoology, 213.*

Beers, M. (2006). *Merck manual of health & aging.* New York: Ballantine.

Booth, A., Johnson, D., & Granger, D. (1999). Testosterone and men's depression: The role of social behavior. *Journal of Health and Social Behavior, 40*(2).

Burleson, M.H., Trevathan, W.R., & Todd, M. (2007). In the mood for love or vice versa? Exploring the relations among sexual activity, physical affection, affect, and stress in the daily lives of mid-aged women. *Archives of Sexual Behavior, 36,* 357–368.

Catania, J., & White, W. (1982). Sexuality in an aged sample: Cognitive determinants of masturbation. *Archives of Sexual Behavior, 11*(3).

Charnetski, C., & Brennan, F. (2001). *Feeling good is good for you: How pleasure can boost your immune system and lengthen your life.* Emmaus, PA: Rodale Press.

Cutler, W.B. (1991). *Love cycles: The science of intimacy.* New York: Villard.

Debrot, A., Meuwly, N., Muise, A., Impett, E., & Schoebi, D. (2017, January). More than just sex: Affection mediates the association between sexual activity and well-being. *Personality and Social Psychology Bulletin.*

Ellison, C. (2000). *Women's sexualities: Generations of women share intimate secrets of sexual self-acceptance.* Oakland, CA: New Harbinger.

Evans, R.W., & Couch, R. (2001). Orgasm and migraine. *Headache: Journal of Head and Face Pain, 111*(6), 512–514.

Fisher, H., Aron, A., Mashek, D., Li, H., & Brown, L. (2002). Defining the brain systems of lust, romantic attraction, and attachment. *Archives of Sexual Behavior, 31*(5).

Forari, R., Zoppi, A., Preti, P., Rinaldi, A., Marasi, G., Vanasia, A., & Mugellini, A. (2002). Sexual activity and plasma testosterone levels in hypertensive males. *American Journal of Hypertension, 15*(3).

Friedrich, W., Fisher, J., Broughton, D., Houston, M., & Shafran, C. (1998). Normative sexual behavior in children: A contemporary sample. *Pediatrics* April 1998, 101 (4) e9. DOI: 10.1542/peds.101.4.e9

Giles, G., Severi, G., English, D., & McCredie, M. (2003). Sexual factors and prostate cancer. *British Journal of Urology, 92*(3).

Herbenick, D. (2009). *Because it feels good: A woman's guide to sexual pleasure and satisfaction.* New York: Rodale.

Herbenick, D., & Schick, V. (2011). *Read my lips: A complete guide to the vagina and vulva.* New York: Rowman & Littlefield.

Hyde, J.S., & DeLamater, J.D. (2014). *Understanding human sexuality* (12th ed.). New York: McGraw-Hill.

Ip, S., Chung, M., & Raman, G. (2007). *Tufts-New England Medical Center Evidence-based Practice Center: Breastfeeding and maternal and infant health outcomes in developed countries.* Evidence Report on Technology Assessment (Full Report): 153.

Jonsson, P. (2011, December 29). Breastfeeding moms protest at Target stores, but US public is real mark. *Christian Science Monitor.* Retrieved from www.csmonitor.com/USA/Society/2011/1229/Breastfeeding-moms

Kinsey, A., Pomeroy, W., & Martin, C. (1948). *Sexual behavior in the human male.* Philadelphia: W.B. Saunders.

Kinsey, A., Pomeroy, W., Martin, C., & Gephard, P. (1953). *Sexual behavior in the human female.* Philadelphia: W.B. Saunders.

Komisaruk, B., Beyer-Flores, C., & Whipple, B. (2006). *The science of orgasm.* Baltimore: Johns Hopkins University Press.

Laumann, E., Gagnon, J., Michael, R., & Michaels, S. (1994). *The social organization of sexuality: Sexual practice in the United States.* Chicago: University of Chicago.

Lê, M.G. (1989). Characteristics of reproductive life and risk of breast cancer in a case-control study of young nulliparous women. *Journal of Clinical Epidemiology, 42*(12).

Leiblum, S., Bachmann, G., Kemmann, E., Colburn, D., & Swartzman, L. (1983). Vaginal atrophy in the postmenopausal woman: The importance of sexual activity and hormones. *JAMA, 249*(16).

Leitzmann, M., Willett, W., & Giovannucci, E. (2004). Ejaculation frequency and subsequent risk of prostate cancer. *Journal of the American Medical Association, 291*(13).

Litin, S. (2009). *Mayo Clinic family health book.* Des Moines, IA: Time Inc. Home Entertainment.

Margolis, S. (2002). *Johns Hopkins medical guide to health after 50.* Redding, CT: Medletter Associates.

Masters, W., & Johnson, V. (1966). *Human sexual response.* Boston: Little, Brown.

Meaddough, E., Olive, D., Gallup, P., & Kliman, H. (2002). Sexual activity, orgasm and tampon use are associated with a decreased risk for endometriosis. *Gynecologic and Obstetric Investigation, 53.*

Money, J., Wainwright, G., & Hingsburger, D. (1991). *The breathless orgasm*. Buffalo, NY: Prometheus.

Murrell, T.G.C. (1995). The potential for oxytocin (OT) to prevent breast cancer: A hypothesis. *Breast Cancer Research and Treatment, 35*.

Nichols, F., & Humenick, S. (1988). *Childbirth education: Practice, research, and theory*. Philadelphia: W.B. Saunders.

Nicolosi, A., Moreira, E., Villa, M., & Glasser, D. (2004). A population study of the association between sexual function, sexual satisfaction and depressive symptoms in men. *Journal of Affective Disorders, 82*.

Palmore, E. (1983). Predictors of the longevity difference: A 25-year follow-up. *Gerontologist, 22*(6).

Patient Protection and Affordable Care Act. H.R. Res. 3590, 111th Cong. (2009). Retrieved from https://www.govtrack.us/congress/bills/111/hr3590

Persson, G. (1981). Five-year mortality in a 70-year-old urban population in relation to psychiatric diagnosis, personality, sexuality and early parental death. *Acta Psychiatrica Scandinavca, 64*(3).

Peterson, F. (1989). *Promoting fathering and greater father interaction with infants via the father & baby class*. Paper presented at the meeting of the Annual Men's Studies Conference, National Organization of Changing Men, Pittsburgh, Pennsylvania.

Peterson, F. (1990). *Promoting fathering via family centered childbirth education*. Paper presented at the Annual Convention of the American Psychological Association, Boston.

Peterson, F. (2000). "Why are Americans so weird about breastfeeding?" *Weekly Impact, 8*(10).

Peterson, F., Peterson, K., Redman, E., Nicholls, C., & Blasenak, B. (1986). *Transition into parenthood: A pilot project of the expectant couple's enrichment class*. Paper presented at the American Psychological Association Annual Convention, Washington, DC.

Peterson, F., Peterson, K., Redman, E., Nicholls, C., & Blasenak, B. (1991). *Family centered childbirth education*. Paper presented at the Annual Convention of the American Society for Psychoprophylaxis in Obstetrics, Atlanta, Georgia.

Peterson, K., & Peterson, F. (1993). Family centered perinatal education. In F. Nichols (Ed.), *Clinical issues in perinatal and women's health nursing*. Philadelphia: J.B. Lippincott.

Peterson, K., Peterson, F., Redman, E., Nicholls, C., & Blasenak, B. (1987). Strike while the iron is hot: Combining childbirth education, parenting training, and social support. *International Journal of Childbirth Education, 2*(2).

Planned Parenthood Federation of America. (2007). The White Paper: The health benefits of sexual expression. New York: Planned Parenthood Federation of America in Cooperation with the Society for the Scientific Study of Sexuality.

Reamy, K., White, S.E., & Daniel, W.C. (1982). Sexuality and pregnancy: A prospective study. *Journal of Reproductive Medicine, 27*(6).

Rossing, M., Standford J., Weiss, N., & Daling R. (1996). Indices of exposure to fetal and sperm antigens in relation to the occurrence of breast cancer. *Epidemiology, 7*(3).

Sayle, A. (2001). Sexual activity during late pregnancy and risk of preterm delivery. *Obstetrics and Gynecology, 97*(2).

Singh, D., Meyer, W., Zambarano, R., & Hurlbert, D. (1998). Frequency and timing of coital orgasm in women desirous of becoming pregnant. *Archives of Sexual Behavior, 27*(1).

Smith, G., Frankel, S., & Yarnell, J. (1997). Sex and death: Are they related? Findings from the Caerphilly cohort study. *British Medical Journal, 315*:1641.

Stiefelhagen, S. (1994). De social erotische dienstverlening. In *Seks, lang zo gek nogniet. Symposium over seksualiteit en relaties in de psychiatrie*. Rutgers Stichting, Eindhoven, Netherlands. [The Social-Erotic Services. Presentation in the Symposium on Sexuality, Relationships and Psychiatry, Rutgers Foundation, Eindhoven.]

Tur-Kaspa, I., Maor, Y., Levran, D., Yonish, M., Mashiach, S., & Dor, J. (1994). How often should infertile men have intercourse to achieve conception? *Fertility and Sterility, 62*(2).

Van Lunsen, R., & Laan, E. (2004). Genital vascular responsiveness and sexual feelings in midlife women: Psychophysiologic, brain, and genital imaging studies. *Menopause, 11*(6 Pt 2).

Von Sydow, Kirsten. (1999). Sexuality during pregnancy and after childbirth: A metacontent analysis of 59 studies. *Journal of Psychosomatic Research, 47*(1).

Walters, A., & Williamson, G. (1998). Sexual satisfaction predicts quality of life: A study of adult amputees. *Sexuality and Disability, 16*(2).

Weeks, D. (2002). Sex for the mature adult: Health, self-esteem and countering ageist stereotypes. *Sexual and Relationship Therapy, 17*(3).

Wilcox, A., Weinberg, C., & Baird, D. (1995). Timing of sexual intercourse in relation to ovulation: Effects on the probability of conception, survival of the pregnancy, and sex of the baby. *New England Journal of Medicine, 333*(23).

Yarber, W., & Sayad, B. (2019). *Human sexuality: Diversity in contemporary society* (10th ed.). New York: McGraw-Hill Education.

Zippe, C., Kedia, A., Kedia, K., Nelson, D., & Agarwal, A. (2001). Management of erectile dysfunction following radical prostatectomy. *Current Urology Reports, 2*(6), 4.

CHAPTER NINE

Joe and Marie:

A STORY OF UNCONSUMMATED MARRIAGE AND TRAINING WITH THE MASTER AT THE MASTERS AND JOHNSON INSTITUTE

Written by Frederick Peterson

t was October 1993, and I had not been at the Masters and Johnson Institute (the Institute) but a few weeks, so I was still getting to know my way around. It was still six years before Viagra made its big splash, so the Institute was the premier site for treatment of all things sexual that did not work well. My duties as a clinical fellow were split between three primary activities. First and foremost, was staying on Dr. Masters's good side. He was known to have a bit of a temper. Secondly I was a primary therapist to several clients in the residential program (mostly with people who had horrific histories of abuse and neglect). This was stuff that scared the hell out of me. Finally, I served as an outpatient therapist for couples (who flew in from all over the world for treatment of their sexual dysfunctions) and also conducted research on different topics such as memories of childhood sexual trauma and the process of recall after a period of amnesia.

It was a full plate, even for an energetic young man who was eager to please his famous supervisor. While wary of staying in Dr. Masters's favor, I was extremely grateful for what seemed to be a most unlikely long-shot scenario—namely the U.S. government paying me to go to St. Louis and study sex with the pioneer sex researcher William Masters, MD (aka "Doc"). This sounded pretty crazy and I knew it but jumped at the chance. I could hardly believe I got approvals from my chief of staff, hospital CEO, and the suits in Washington—but that's what happened. It must have been a pretty busy paperwork day and a lot of "just sign this."

This is a story you won't see if you read the book or watch the series called *Masters of Sex*. It is a story of a Midwest kid going to "the big show" at the Institute—THE world's mecca for clinical training related to all things sexual. Specifically, this chapter describes an informative story focused on a beautiful woman and her quest to have children. She was half of a beautiful Latinx couple who were married but never had intercourse. I don't mean they complained of "we never have sex" in terms of frequency (otherwise meaning "rarely"). I mean they had NEVER experienced sexual intercourse in their lives, with each other or anyone else. The reason they had flown in from Florida to seek treatment with Dr. Masters is that they had been married seven years and their parents were saying, "What is up with you two? We want to see some *nietos* (grandbabies)!" That is why the grandparents actually paid for Maria and Joe's treatment at the Institute.

This pair of 20-somethings were no dummies about sex (or otherwise). Maria and Joe (pseudonyms) were young, beautiful, and intelligent. They had met in high school and both had college degrees. At the time of the consultation, she was working as an airline stewardess and he was a stevedore on the docks of Miami. With her sun-soaked brown skin, Maria looked like she could melt metal simply by walking by. Joe also looked stunningly attractive like he should have his shirt off and be put on the cover of a women's modern romance novel.

They knew how to do it, they just never succeeded. To say this young couple never had intercourse is not to suggest that they never had sex. They actually had plenty of sex! They were very much in love and very attracted to each other. Consequently, they reported that they enjoyed sex frequently with each other through manual and oral pleasuring. They loved bringing each other to climax and were quite good at it. With most couples who have all this going for them, it is just a matter of time (and not long) before they work out the practical and physical details of vaginal containment of a penis. However, Maria and Joe had some, let's say, serious complications.

First of all, Joe suffered from a diagnosis of primary erectile dysfunction (ED). This means that he had never been able to get an erection, keep the erection, and use it to complete intercourse (ever, with anybody). Yeah—that's right—what about him enjoying all that other sex with manual and oral pleasuring? Why didn't he just get it up and get it on when he was feeling all those good vibes? You might wonder, "Sounds like Joe could get erections, so was it that hard to stay hard while Maria put him inside her?" Short answer: Yes!

When in college, Joe tried his best to get inside Maria but failed at his first attempt. He reported that he was sort of drunk and went soft shortly after his attempt to penetrate her. Joe became very embarrassed and so anxious about losing his erection, the anxiety would override any good feelings from his penis and all of a sudden—gone! This anxiety (called performance anxiety) became routine and as soon as he wondered if he was going to lose his erection again (like last time)—it was already half-way gone. Joe had no history of abuse and had normal physical function until it came time to penetrate Maria. This soon became an ingrained pattern and a significant obstacle to him being able to complete intercourse. Unfortunately, his ED was not the only obstacle!

Maria was not free from her own challenges that interfered with her desire for her husband and her own pleasure. She had her own diagnosis contributing to the prevention of intercourse: vaginismus. Vagin-*what*? It is a sexual disorder where the outer third of the vagina involuntarily contracts so much that it prevents any entrance of foreign objects, whether that object is a penis, finger, or even a small tampon. The key word is "involuntary" because Maria could be feeling relaxed, feeling sexual desire, and say to Joe, "Come on big boy—let's see what you got!" But then her vagina would also say, "No, no, no; see all you want but that thing IS NOT coming in here!" Maria did not have any history of abuse as well, but, as mentioned, she had very strong social training that nothing was to pass her vaginal opening. So, even if Joe could get it up and keep it up, he had no place to go with it other than some fun outercourse. The couple never considered anal sex and rejected the mere thought of it, which was fine because the severe contractions "down-there" would also prevent any entry into the out-door! (It is important to note here anal eroticism is normal and commonly practiced—about one-fourth of adult Americans say they have done it).

Interestingly, Maria had never heard of vaginismus! She came from a very devout Catholic family who emigrated from Colombia when she was a girl. Maria described herself as coming from "healthy stock" and rarely "doctored" (sought medical service) for anything. Her family never talked about sex and she was given a brief pamphlet and some maxi pads when she started having her period. As far as the rest of her adolescence went, she was on her own. All she knew was to never get too friendly with the boys, especially any she really liked. The reason was that if a boy ever did try to touch her, Maria's brothers, cousins, uncles, father, and grandfather would seriously and permanently dissuade him. For the young men of Colombia, Maria was the reason masturbation was invented.

The couple flew to St. Louis for consultation and to meet with the treatment team on Monday morning. The team was Doc, me, and a female co-therapist named Donna. Donna was a local nurse turned social worker also at the Institute for advanced training in human sexuality. This was an approach to treatment Doc insisted upon; having male and female therapy teams (modeled upon him and Virginia Johnson) and having several professional disciplines represented in the room. Among the three of us, patients had the advantage of perspectives from medicine, psychology, nursing, social work, and education in the same consultation room.

Doc usually reviewed medical records and referral information on new patients but did not have much to share on this new couple. Therefore, the secretary brought Maria and Joe in for the initial orientation that essentially gave patients the plan for the next two weeks (if it took that long). They were told there were three important things to accomplish every day. First, Maria and Joe would meet every morning with the treatment team. After the daily treatment session, Maria and Joe would return to their hotel and practice touching exercises done in the privacy of their hotel room. The third and final daily assignment was to go out in the evening and enjoy St. Louis together, as if they were on their honeymoon again. What Maria and Joe didn't know was that they were actually going to be able to enjoy sex on this honeymoon like they wished they had the first time.

After the first meeting, Doc (a licensed obstetrician/gynecologist) performed a pelvic exam on Maria, her first EVER. Because her vaginal contractions were so extreme, it was too uncomfortable and painful to get a speculum inside of her. This confirmed the diagnosis of vaginismus. Later, and as part of the initial assessment, Donna and I conducted thorough sexual development histories with Maria and Joe. This is how it went: I interviewed Joe, and Donna interviewed Maria. Once the first interview was done (about an hour later), we switched and repeated the interviews. Although this might seem like a repetitive waste of time on the surface, it often revealed additional and valuable information regarding each individual's history and sexual function. People are often more comfortable with (and therefore prefer talking to) a particular interviewer (man or woman) about the details of their personal sex life. Hence, valuable information is gleaned from each and we got a little one-on-one time with each.

The first behavioral prescription for Maria and Joe was to have lunch and return to their hotel to engage in some sensual touching exercises called sensate focus. These exercises are to help couples relax and become more focused on sensual pleasure with each other rather than being sexual and overly focused on the traditional erogenous zones (breast, buttocks, and genitals). The first and most important rule for them using these exercises was that they both had to agree that they would NOT try to have intercourse. They were also forbidden to have an orgasm or to pressure the other to have an orgasm. In other words, there must be an agreement to put a ban on attempting all forms of intercourse and orgasm during the course of therapy.

This had several benefits, including removing any pressure of "performance." This was particularly important to Joe as he then didn't have to worry about whether or not he was going to get an erection (because they become irrelevant in the treatment situation). Additionally, touching areas of the body not considered traditional "erogenous zones" helped expand their awareness and enjoyment of the sensual aspects of the whole person. Finally, there is a "therapeutic double-bind" created with the therapist's insistence that they do not attempt to have intercourse and orgasm. The idea of having penile-vaginal intercourse shifted from a source of frustration and worry to a more erotic experience similar to when Maria and Joe were new to each other. Both being Catholic, the idea of sexual intercourse became the "forbidden fruit" again.

Every day for a week the couple met with us and discussed their touching experiences. They were peppered with questions such as: What did you notice the most about touching your partner? What did you notice about skin texture, hair patterns, temperature, sensitivity, and so on? What parts of the body do you think your partner enjoyed having touched the most? Why? What parts of the body did you enjoy touching the most? Why? The sessions were "tweaked" from day to day to add to the sensual pleasure experience. Different elements were slowly introduced such as massage oil, music, silk, feathers, and so forth. Five days passed until we were sure they had the practice down cold and were feeling good about their sensual touching skills.

Strategically, Doc then made a critical decision. He sent the couple back to Miami to complete an essential treatment component in the comfort of their own home. Doc explained to the couple that they had contracted for two weeks of treatment and they were going to get two weeks of treatment. However, Maria (and therefore the treatment team) did not know she had vaginismus before coming to St. Louis. She needed to complete a treatment program for her vaginismus as a prerequisite to the later stages of treatment for Joe's ED. The couple could stay in St. Louis for the treatment, but that would put pressure on Maria to "get fixed" quickly, and we were not sure how long the treatment of the vaginismus would take. Plus, they weren't independently wealthy and had jobs waiting on them.

Maria and Joe said they understood and were accepting of the notion that the vaginismus was an unknown factor that complicated their situation. They agreed to the "at-home treatment" of the vaginismus and then would later return to St. Louis for the final resolution of the ED. Fortunately, the at-home treatment was pretty easy and did not need daily support. They were given a set of plastic dilators for use at home for the muscular reconditioning of Maria's vagina. This was a set of six dilators starting with the smallest about the size of a skinny pinky finger and going up to the size of a man's full erection. Also, of good fortune, this occurred before airport security got so intrusive and they didn't have to worry about a security officer waving the vaginal dilators around while asking, "What the hell are these?"

The home treatment went very well and Maria studiously progressed through the entire set of dilators in six weeks. Her job was simply to use a special belt that covered her vulva and kept the dilator from squeezing out of her. While she slept, these dilators would gradually expand, loosen, and recondition the muscles inside her vagina. It was my job to call Maria every week, provide support, give encouragement, and respond to any questions.

After six weeks, the couple returned to St. Louis and resumed the sensate focus program to resolve Joe's performance anxiety and ED. The couple didn't miss a beat, in part because they were doing the sensate focus touch at home on a weekly basis. Now that they returned to the final stages of treatment, they jumped right back into the daily exercises and were moving at an accelerated pace. This was a fascinating process to watch unfold—as things went just as Doc predicted.

With the pressure off to get erections, Joe learned how to get out of his head and stay focused on the sensual feelings in his body. As the week progressed, so did the couple moving through the advanced stages of treatment. Maria and Joe were now enjoying touch with the entire body. Joe was having consistent and strong erections, while Maria was given special instructions for providing touch to Joe from above him while she straddled his waist (with her knees to each side of Joe). She spent two sessions providing touch that included "teasing" his penis with her vulva. On Sunday, she was given instructions (apart from Joe) to take his erect penis and slip him into her vagina whenever she felt ready for her first vaginal-containment of her husband. This she did successfully, and, in the end, seven years of unconsummated marriage ended joyously after seven days of sensual pleasuring.

On a follow-up phone conference six months after their last stay in St. Louis, Maria reported that she and Joe had been having intercourse on a regular basis and she just found out she was pregnant! She was elated! What an amazing thing to see—the transformation of this couple into a new family, including the ecstatic grandparents.

A cool part of sex therapy is that you always have Mother Nature working for you. No wonder sex therapists like their job, especially when it comes to clients like Marie and Joe! I thought the news of Marie's pregnancy would be enough to bring a smile to Doc Masters, but no such luck. He momentarily stared blankly at me with no expression at all and said, "Of course, what else did you expect?"

CHAPTER TEN

The Dee Rockwood Story:

FROM HYPERMASCULINE SUPER-ATHLETE TO THE GRANDMA IN THE CHURCH PEW NEXT TO YOU

Written by Frederick Peterson and Dee Rockwood

E very once in a while you come across a person whose experiences seem bigger than life. This is an account of such a person and is included in this book to help you understand the origins of what is experienced by some transgender individuals as their greatest challenge of a lifetime—the challenge of coming to terms with who and what we are as human beings. In some ways, we all have this challenge of discovery no matter who we are. Cisgender individuals just have a more familiar template to follow than the path you are about to read.

For 20 years (starting in the 1980s), I routinely took my university classes on field trips to see the drag shows at the premier gay bar in the tristate area called "1470 West." The purpose of the trip was to have students face their own homophobia and wonder about who was going to see them there. Students always had a great time on these trips and the experience helped them break down stereotypes they had about gay and lesbian people. It was on such an occasion that a student named Michelle came up to me and said, "You have to meet this person over at the bar." So I did. That was the beginning of a friendship now in its fourth decade and one that has included this individual developing into one of the best educators and coaches on the topic of transsexualism. Due to the limits of what can be said in a single chapter, this is only part of her story but still conveys some of the struggle, losses, and victories in overcoming her personal challenges, especially how she came to terms with who and what she is as a person. Of special note, some of the pronouns in the early part of the story are masculine and they change later. Also, there are details of this story many may find hard to believe yet as is often the case, truth is stranger than fiction.

This story begins in the early 1950s with a small child lost in a world of confusion. For any three-year old, people known as Mommy and Daddy are the whole world. Confusion began with memories of a small child being told that he was a "bad boy." It might be hard to imagine a three-year-old as a "bad" person, but John Dee Rockwood III (aka "Rocky") had an affinity for hiding in his mother's closet. In this small private world, he loved smelling the lingering perfumes, feeling the silky fabrics, and enjoying the feminine aura of a woman's intimate private space. In the middle of one such adventure, his father discovered him. The discovery of his son's affinity for female attire caused this traditional 1950s father to go ballistic. He started yelling, threatening, and name-calling. His angry words and loud gestures dominate little Rocky's memory of being found that day. That experience left him frightened and confused as a child. Rocky discovered that what he felt and expressed openly seemed to draw negative attention. Creating drama seemed to be his life. But being a bright child, he learned (over time) to be very careful not to get caught again.

He heard from other kids in the neighborhood that kindergarten was a wonderful place, almost magical, where he would learn many exciting things. So when the first day of school finally arrived, he was happy to find out that it lived up to expectations. He found new friends and new opportunities to express himself. At school, he found there were two groups of people. One played tag, pushed and shoved, and were fascinated by cars. The other group played dolls, houses, jacks, and jump rope. Little Rocky attempted to join the group that looked the most fun to him. The drama, the confusion, and the feeling of being bad all came back in an instant. The teachers said that little boys don't play with dolls and, just like his father, they called him names.

Fortunately, Rocky was bright and there happened to be a library next door to his home. By the time he was five, he had learned to read from the librarian who read stories every Saturday and Sunday. Because he was able to read, write, and understand some math, Rocky was promoted to first grade after only a few months. However, that created more problems as he was already smaller than the other kids in kindergarten and now he was a lot smaller than the other first graders and had a year less experience interacting with other children. He started to develop a bit of a chip on his shoulder in trying to cope with all of the confusion. He barely got through the school year.

One of Rocky's salvations as a child was summertime, where he enjoyed his grandfather's farm in West Virginia, which was on the edge of a Native American reservation. This reservation was started when his great-grandfather married a Cherokee Indian and gave 50 acres to the U.S. government, which then declared it to be a reservation for the Cherokee people. Rocky's summers were full of camping, eating in the big Cherokee lodge, fishing, hunting, riding horses, and playing with the Native American kids. The children played in a very physical way. Their games always involved a great deal of running, jumping, and combat. Even the girls were big on wrestling. Learning all those skills gave Rocky new ways to cope back at school.

When the bullies in school started to tease and push him around, he was ready for war Cherokee style, even though he was many inches shorter and pounds lighter. Rocky found that fighting was punished, usually with paddling and/or time-out, the later involving sitting in the cloak closet. After only a few weeks of this behavior, something had to change. The teacher discovered that he was ahead of the other kids academically so dealing with his boredom was an additional problem. Second grade was even worse because he felt like a misfit because of his small size, younger age, and being somewhat effeminate. There were more playground fights, grades stated to slip, and there was a lot more closet time. Rocky was really glad when second grade was over. While visiting the reservation that summer, one of the tribe's elders (and shaman) would take him on walks. He told Rocky of the ancients and "the people of Two Spirits." The old wise man schooled Rocky in special healing powers and the elder's connection to the shadow world. At age seven, Rocky did not understand mysticism, but he knew that the shaman had seen something in him as a boy that Rocky really didn't want anyone to see.

The following year his father, who was a mortician, was working in a funeral home in a small southeastern town on the Ohio River. He had started developing a drinking problem and slowly became abusive as a father and husband. Rocky's mother believed that the stress of the job and the people in the funeral business were the source of the problem. His father agreed and believed a change in jobs and location would curb and solve the problem. So Rocky experienced his first big move. A family friend helped the father get a job in the steel mill north of Cincinnati. Rocky thought getting away from the boys in his school would help him as well.

Well, there is a line in an old cult classic movie *Adventures of Buckaroo Banzai* that says "NO MATTER WHERE YOU GO, THERE YOU ARE!" which means, "You bring who you are with you and if you are the problem, then the problem comes with you." In Rocky's case, the problems were that he was younger, smaller, and acted funny (seen as effeminate), and none of those changed with a new location. His hopes for something better were soon dashed. Moving to a less affluent "redneck" neighborhood actually made matters worse. The same was true with Rocky's father, as his drinking and abuse behaviors also got worse. He began to drink up the rent money and the domestic violence became a part of family life. Going to the store with his dad meant spending several hours at a local bar. While his dad was getting drunk, Rocky learned to hustle pool and play poker, even as a boy. He saw bar fights and experienced the seedy side of life. No money meant that the family moved around almost every year (sometimes more than once a year). Being the new kid once or twice a year made it even tougher. He felt like he never quite got his feet on the ground, never quite got his balance, and never ever got a real chance to make a friend. Though bright, he still really hadn't figured out exactly what it was that he was doing that was causing all the drama.

When Rocky started at his new school, his problems had grown too big, occurred too frequently, and became too obvious to ignore. Grades plummeted and fights escalated as he didn't wait to be picked on anymore. As soon as any boy just looked like he was going to say something, the fight was on. If someone called Rocky a "sissy" or "homo," then that someone got their ass kicked. Poor grades and fighting led to neuropsychological testing for brain tumors or any physical abnormalities that would explain why this feminine little boy was such an aggressive troublemaker. What they discovered was a very bright, hyperactive, unhappy child from a dysfunctional home. Child evaluations back then did not consider the possibility of gender confusion, and it would be decades before gender dysphoria was officially used in psychiatric nomenclature.

1950s American families (especially a dysfunctional family of Appalachian background) would seldom acknowledge any kind of mental disability. It was decided that Rocky be placed in advanced classes and put in some kind of sports to deal with the extra energy. After a short time experimenting with Little League and intramural basketball (with terrible results), a membership at the YMCA revealed an aptitude for tennis, gymnastics, boxing, diving, swimming, and almost any individual sport. An opinion soon developed that he had a girl's graceful coordination with a boy's physique, resulting in natural athletic ability.

The YMCA had just started a boxing class and Rocky soon was winning junior boxing matches and scored the highest in the physical fitness tests. Rocky came to the attention of the judo coach,

Young Nam Chung, who requested that Rocky join the judo club. The combination of more challenging classes with fewer antagonistic boys (most advanced classes were populated by girls) and judo classes dramatically helped Rocky's situation. His grades went up, fights stopped, and everything appeared to be on track. Although these improvements were welcome, they didn't help Rocky get to the root of the real problem. By nearly nine years of age, he knew he didn't want to be a boy anymore.

Just before his birthday in 1959, something magical happened in America: Barbie was born. Rocky was under the marketing spell targeting every little girl and promptly asked his mom for a Barbie for this birthday. He was told, "Boys don't ask for dolls." He immediately retorted, "Then I don't want to be a boy anymore," which both confused and scared his mother. Her answer was to ignore the problem. She scolded Rocky and gave him a cap gun for his ninth birthday. He became aware that he wasn't ever going to be recognized as the person he was—a she. For the first time in his life, this young boy realized that he was always going to feel like a misfit and be seen as "wrong" if he pursued something that did not exist in 1950s America—being accepted as a girl. He realized that the teasing and the tormenting were never going to stop and so he decided to give in to what seemed to be the inevitable.

From the moment of that epiphany, he set out to become "superboy." Rocky was determined to become "the Rock." He started working out, practicing and competing at everything. It was like something out of the *Karate Kid* or Sylvester Stallone's *Rocky* movies decades later. By sixth grade, he was a straight "A" student and had achieved every school athletic record available. Remember the judo instructor Young Nam Chung who got Rocky to join the judo team? Rocky loved judo. By sixth grade, he won his age division and the physical demands of judo made the elementary school sports a breeze.

All this was just a warm-up for junior high school, where he got involved in wrestling, track, and the Boy Scouts. As his martial arts skills progressed, he became the protector of the weaker kids. Bullies learned very quickly to stay clear of "the Rock." This hero complex sent him down some interesting but very dangerous paths as a way of searching for more ways to make the feelings go away or at least bury them deep enough to be okay. The feeling he strived to bury was that he was living a lie. The fear that someone would see who, and more importantly, what, he really was underneath was a constant companion. His prayers were never answered. Prayers that somehow some sort of accident, or maybe some kind of magic would occur and "he" would wake up a "she." His secret anguish continued on a nightly basis.

When Rocky turned 14 in 1964, it was a very cool year to be a teenager in America. The British were invading again (this time with the Beatles and the Stones), the "hippies" charged up the peace movement, young people were tuning in and turning on with LSD and grass, and, of course, Elvis made a big comeback. The year 1964 was a big year for Rocky as well. He lost his virginity at 14 to a 36-year-old mother of one of his best friends. She was the choir director at church and the Sunday school teacher. Like some boys do, he did not see this as childhood sexual abuse but rather a welcomed early entry into manhood (after all, he was on the super-boy track of hypermasculinity). For the record, whether it was welcomed or not, the young Rocky was sexually exploited by a woman for her own needs.

Most important to Rocky, he soon learned a term that he would eventually come to hate. In 1951, a U.S. Army veteran by the name of George Jorgensen started a series of sex-reassignment surgeries, becoming the first American to complete such surgery and later became a blond bombshell actress and entertainer known as Christine Jorgensen. Much later, she published a personal autobiography (1967) about her life and coined the term "transsexual." A lightning bolt hit Rocky as he read the book and learned this new magical term. It just about stopped his heart because without one moment of doubt, he then knew what was "wrong" with him. The curse now had a name. As important as the book was to Rocky, the one flaw he saw was that no matter how many times he read it—there were no clear directions how to correct this "birth defect" called transsexualism. Jorgensen's experience still seemed like an abstraction and something well beyond the possibilities of a poor boy from Appalachia.

About that same time, Rocky also found religion in the form of a small Presbyterian church not far from where he lived. His thinking was that God had placed him in this living hell and maybe it was a test like with the biblical Job, a test to make him stronger. Thinking that if he studied hard enough, prayed hard enough, believed hard enough, then God would lift this awful curse and cure him as he had the blind and the lepers. So he became an active church member, president of the youth fellowship, Sunday school teacher, usher, and a member of the choir. When he was 16 years old, his pastor sponsored Rocky into the Cumberland Presbyterian Seminary during the summer. He began what was his calling: to become a pastor.

However, it all proved to be too much with the karate, women he was dating, after-school job at a drug store, high school, and college classes. The conflict of how he felt versus the things he was learning in Bible studies was all too much. Just before the end of the school year, Rocky just ran out of steam, ran away, and wound up on a cattle ranch in Virginia. He spent that spring and summer of 1965 working harder than he had thought people were able to work—pitching hay, feeding livestock, and mucking horse stalls. Rocky also got to ride what had became his new best friend, a cow pony named Scout who brought him out to fix fences, work cows, and even do some rodeo.

Eventually, Rocky figured out that the owner of the ranch was trying to work him so hard that he would want to go back home and return to school. And it worked. After six months, he came to another breaking point: castrating steers. Castrating the steers was the breaking point because castration was sort of what Rocky had been dreaming of happening to him his whole life. The irony was too painful, and Rocky decided that he had to hit the reset button. He had to return home, redo some of the classes that he had missed and catch up on seminary studies. Once back at home, Rocky caught up pretty quickly. He also had proven himself to be a wild spirit and independent thinker. At age 16, Rocky got his black belt in tae kwan do. During karate competitions, he gained the attention of the United States Karate Team, and he started competing on a national level. He now spent weekends traveling on a bus while trying to put his torment as far back in his mind as he could. As noted, he was able to fill his life with as much activity as he could. Yet, in his few moments of silence before drifting off to sleep, Rocky was aware that he carried the burden of that awful term echoing in his head: "transsexual."

When Rocky returned to high school and church, he also returned to a world where the comfort zone of anonymity was gone, including returning to old enemies and the pressures of living up to an image he had created. When he became a member of the U.S. Karate Team, the pressures haunted him daily. He walked back into the role of the "Rock" and it started all over again. Having several girlfriends was all for one reason—so no one would or could see his secret. Dating, like the rest of his life, become a supreme paradox. He was a scared 5'6", 120-pound little girl hiding out in a macho buff body, trying to hide who and what he really was. He was dreaming a girl's dream while wanting to become a girl and acting like the proverbial bad boy. He was a motorcycle riding loner, with a bad reputation for fighting and yet going to church every week. I'm wondering if younger people today would know who Fonzie was. Yet Rocky was still crying out in the dark for some kind of miracle. He discovered another paradox along his journey, this time a very intimate one. Rocky discovered that he had to play a sort of mental game to achieve an erection, make sex satisfying, and even reach an orgasm. Rocky exercised a "sexual gymnastics" in his mind. He imagined that what was happening to his partner was actually happening to him. Although managing these mental gymnastics made sex functional, it was another experience of pretending to be someone else.

Little did he know that it would take decades before sexual science learned that it is common for transsexual or transgender people to perform such sexual gymnastics in their minds. All Rocky knew was that no amount of praying, working out, or other diversions (including sex) could ever let him be free of his torment even for a moment. Rocky was always aware that he was living a lie without any signs of how he personally could find a way out. Despite Christine Jorgensen's example from New York City, the "Rock" was so busy and so deep into American adolescence and living up to expectations, he could not find a way to explore Jorgensen's path at that time. As a teenager in the 1960s, he certainly did not have the resources, support, and opportunities that youth today have available.

The year 1969 was one of the most monumental times in American history. Man landed on the moon, antiwar protesters marched on Washington, and a whole lot more. Rocky had become an associate pastor of his church for his seminary internship during his senior year. But for graduation, he made a trip to a little town in upstate New York to an outdoor concert that turned out to be the symbol of the 1960s. Woodstock exploded onto the American consciousness with drugs, alcohol, sex, and bra burning (Rocky just wished he had one to wear). All of these things were at odds with Rocky's sensibilities, and yet he was at a turning point. For nearly a year, he was a pastor trying to figure out what it was he was supposed to be teaching because what he was taught in seminary, what he was asked to preach, and what Rocky saw in the real world were all very different things. It became very obvious that he wasn't nearly old or experienced enough to figure this all out, especially with his internal struggles not getting any better. God had not cured him as God had cured the blind or the lepers. Rocky believed that he was well liked in his church but felt little satisfaction because he had no relief from his personal demons and no ability to help anyone else with theirs. A change in plans was in order.

Rocky decided to apply to the University of Cincinnati (UC) and got accepted to the engineering program pursuing a mechanical engineering degree. Most of the required seminary classes (Bachelor of Arts in Theology from the seminary) transferred to UC. Rocky moved to Cincinnati with the help of scholarships paying for most of his school costs, but he still needed money to live on. So he picked up a part-time job with a small security firm becoming an after-hours mall cop. Unbeknownst to

Rocky, this move to UC and part-time jobs would lead to a series of fortunate events. He was also teaching a college karate class for a few bucks, hustling pool, and playing poker, to make ends meet.

While teaching one of the evening college karate classes, a small Asian man observed the class. Rocky planned to speak to him after class but suddenly noticed the quiet observer had vanished, much as he had appeared from nowhere. A few weeks later the small Chinese man reappeared and watched the class for a few minutes before going into the office of the do-jo (karate studio) to talk to the supervisor. Michael was UC's karate club supervisor and he came out after class to ask Rocky into the office. This is where Rocky met Master Lu Lee Chang for the first time. It turned out that Master Chang was looking for students to learn Wing-Chun Whu Shu Kung Fu. Master Chang said that Rocky showed "potential" and Rocky responded like he had just been called a sissy. They decided to go back out into the do-jo for a little "interview." Rocky thought Master Chang looked like he had just fallen off a charm bracelet, so he reached for the little man planning to take him down gently. What happened next took Rocky years to learn to do. It was to be the most humiliating ass-kicking experience Rocky ever received. Each of Rocky's attacks were repelled with what seemed to be less and less effort by Master Chang. Every kick was dodged or blocked. Every punch was countered and ended with Rocky picking himself up off the floor.

Rocky was a multiple black-belt holder in several different styles of martial arts, not to mention having a lot of street experience. Yet he got his ass handed to him by this old man. Although the experience was humiliating, it was also illuminating. There is this Chinese proverb that says, "You can't take any more water if your glass is already full." Rocky at this point was a member of the U.S. Karate Team and at first wondered what could he learn from an old man teaching a hokey martial art like "kung-fu." Yet, he was covered in bruises, sore, tired, and pretty beaten up. Rocky's glass was now empty. He needed to learn the secretsof how this had happened.

With a greater sense of humility, Rocky began to study with the little old man, who turned out to be one of the Buddhist priests exiled with the Dalai Lama back in the 1950s. Master Chang had gone to California after leaving China and then to Cincinnati, where he started the Golden Dragon Restaurant. After a couple of years, Master Chang started to look for a group of 10 students to pass on the teachings, the philosophies, and the skills of life. That is why the little Chinese man appeared in Rocky's karate class. Rocky turned out to be an apt student, soaking up more than just the martial arts of "fighting skills." What he found most important were the spiritual strengths, the healing arts, acupressure massage and therapies, and energy transference and control through meditation. Rocky also showed a tremendous curiosity about Tao Shaolin Buddhism.

Rocky found Master Chang's intuitive powers to be awe inspiring and beyond rational scientific explanation, such as ascertaining information about a person with just a touch to their skin. Rocky believed it was possible that Master Chang knew everything about Rocky, perhaps even Rocky's deepest secret. Maybe Master Chang figured he could help in the only way he knew how. Master Chang taught Rocky the secrets of chi—kung fu (the internal master of the spirit), which better equipped him to manage his demons. All Rocky knew was that Master Lu Lee Chang became his closest friend and the single most important influence in his survival—physically, emotionally, and spiritually.

After a couple of years of training with Master Chang and while still working as a mall cop, a common occurrence in malls set off a life-changing chain of events. Rocky stopped a shoplifter from getting away by stepping in front of the thief. The perpetrator took a swing at Rocky trying to get away and with a simple move, a very surprised shoplifter found himself on the ground cuffed and arrested in a heartbeat. Rocky was turning 21, and due to this arrest, his mall boss wanted to promote him so Rocky could receive a pay raise. To do this, his boss had to sponsor Rocky into the police academy to become a reserve officer and be licensed to carry a weapon. While at the academy, there was a series of rapes and beatings happening in a nearby college town. The town police force and college security were unable to get a lead, so they decided to put someone undercover. The undercover agent was to act as a student going to classes, local bars, and make themselves a target. However, the small town did not have viable undercover candidates, so they went to the police academy to find a recruit. They were looking for a young female officer able to blend in and appear as another coed at the college.

Rocky was in this particular cadet class and saw that it had very few viable female trainees. They were either too old, too tall, or not physically trained well enough to be safe undercover. Rocky had the right physical stature being only 5'6" and 120 pounds. The class instructors did not view him as good police officer material. So in an attempt to push Rocky out of the program, they chose him to demonstrate an attack scenario by grabbing "the Rock" from behind in a marine-style head lock. What happened next was really funny, unless you were the unsuspecting hand-to-hand combat trainer. Rocky dropped the instructor with an arm-bar submission hold and pinned the sergeant on the mat. This turn of events more than convinced the instructors about the small but very agile, well-trained recruit. When the college town's chief of police asked for a possible undercover candidate, the police academy instructors recommended that the petite, effeminate, blonde, blue-eyed Rocky be the cadet that could pull it off. But, of course, Rocky would have to wear a dress and wig, paint the fingernails, wear the pumps, the whole works. Though Rocky protested heavily, he secretly thought he had received a gift straight from heaven. But when they showed pictures of beaten and raped victims, he was in it for more than the chance to get a new wardrobe.

In short order, Rocky was on his way to the university as a target for the rapist. As expected, there were a few days of prepping with wig, makeup, clothes, walking, talking, and a really extreme makeover before planting him in the college as a coed nursing student. He never missed a chance to complain about the circumstances, but Rocky was secretly loving every minute of it. Except for having his own vagina, just about every late-night dream had come true. Living, working, socializing every day as a woman was amazing, but it did have an alternate purpose, the capturing of a brutal rapist. So along with going to class, there was going to the local pubs, the library, using back-way short cuts, unlighted parking spaces, and every public space a rapist might look for targets. About six weeks later, the set-up decoy worked. The rapist made his move by grabbing Rocky from behind some bushes on a path between campus buildings. Police officers were only 100 yards away and Rocky was wired although he didn't need backup. Rocky let loose 12 years of very intense martial arts training, back-street bar fighting, schoolyard brawls, and a very angry childhood on a very bad man. The rapist was very glad that the beating only lasted for the 30 or so seconds it took officers to run the distance of a football field.

The law enforcement world is a close-knit operation and a big bust is a big deal. Sometimes a single bust can make a career. The hero-complexed and sexually confused Rocky was looking for anything but a law enforcement career, but he had made big news in the police community. After graduation from the police academy, he went back to finish engineering school, but he was soon contacted by the Ohio State Drug Task Force, who wanted him to continue his undercover work by sometimes posing as a high-school student or sometimes as a dropout looking for a drug score. So Rocky gained a reputation as an effective undercover agent that eventually led to training positions with not-to-be-named government agencies and some really crazy undercover work for them.

After graduating from UC but before starting an engineering career, Master Chang wanted Rocky to finish his kung fu training at the highest level possible. So Master Chang arranged for Rocky to travel to a Tibetan Buddhist temple on top of a mountain in China. His goals were to strengthen his mind and body, increase his fighting skills, and enhance his Chi Kung (spiritual strength). After nearly 10 months, the monks sent Rocky back with the title of priest. Some of the experiences Rocky had in China are straight out of martial arts movies. You'll have to read her book to get the details of the temple experience as well as the G-man undercover work, wrestling bears, doing stuntman work in movies, starring on the show *That's Incredible!* and sparring with Master Bruce Lee. The title of the written-but-yet-to-be-published book is "Life, Liberty, and the Pursuit of Happiness A Story of a Transsexual."

But let me not leave you hanging and finish this chapter out with more of this transgender journey. After returning to the states, Rocky worked his way back onto the U.S. Karate Team and competed in the 1974 Pan American Games, where he won two bronze medals for forms and fighting. But the more he accelerated his masculine victories, the more intensely he struggled to hide his secret. However, after his work as an undercover cop, Rocky started to cross-dress more on off-duty occasions.

Rocky became torn with another conflict further complicating his life, one called falling in love. Rocky fell in love with one of his best female students, Debbie. He loved this girl, they moved in together, and he eventually confided to her about his/her identity confusion. After a few months, Rocky decided that this was a bad idea and started to leave. However, Rocky learned Debbie was pregnant and nine months later they had a beautiful baby girl. The couple got married and enjoyed the new family blessings of happiness and prosperity. Rocky also thought that his new family responsibility would create the ultimate diversion from his demons and a chance for normalcy.

But Rocky's demons were ever present, and his internal life as a woman was ever present as well. The longer the marriage endured, the more his wife resented the other woman (Rocky's feminine identity). Life was complicated, and their relationship became less stable and less tolerable. Still meeting hypermasculine expectations of being the Rock, he continued to fight the compulsion of cross-dressing while trying to be a dad. Ironically, being a dad facilitated his feeling more like a mother toward their two children. Yet the fighting continued and escalated to the point where Rocky started to leave his wife again. As before, there was another pregnancy and another daughter. Rocky's maternal feelings tied his/her staying as a united family despite the seriousness of the parental conflict. Ultimately, Rocky's black-belt wife became more upset and violent, putting a couple police officers in the hospital. Even with all of Rocky's internal issues, he won custody after a contentious divorce and spent many years raising his daughters in conjunction with their mother.

Several years later, a second American publication came out on the topic of transsexualism, this time regarding the story of Renée Richards (Second Serve, 1983). Richards was another veteran (Navy this time) who completed sexual reassignment surgery like Jorgensen. Richards played professional tennis and won important legal cases to play as a woman. Although Richards also used what Rocky considered to be an awful term (transsexual), Rocky could completely relate to Richards's story, so the seeds were planted again. There were no existing clinical practice guidelines as to how to get this surgery accomplished back then, but Rocky was now aware of two women who made their escape from a very familiar torment. He started to be determined to eventually follow their path, but there still did not exist a clear map of how to get there. However, this determination focused on surviving the worst and most intense pressure Rocky ever experienced, one that could end his life.

This was the point where the duality of a double life came to a pinnacle and Rocky could no longer continue the gender charade. The weight of role-playing the "Rock" became so heavy with higher and higher expectations (of television appearances, world records, bronze medals, etc.). Although these expectations were rocketing sky-high, so was the anguish of a secret life spiking upward. He arrived at a point where his lack of authenticity became so potent that it served as a psychological braking system on his life. Sooner or later, every person who is hiding a significant part of themselves eventually develops major depression and hits a breaking point. At nearly 40 years old, Rocky hit his. This resulted in Rocky standing in front of a judge (for the third time) and explaining that if the judge did not legally change his sex to female, he would walk out of the courthouse and step in front of the next oncoming bus. Fortunately, the judge finally believed him and declared John Dee Rockwood III a woman under the law. This facilitated the change of name to Dee Arianne Rockwood and a host of other changes of record that Dee documents in her book but will not be enumerated here. Also fortunately, this series of events led to her emotional salvation, lifted her depression, and brought her back from the edge of destruction.

A few years later (late 1980s) is when this chapter started with my university class visiting the drag show and my meeting with this person named Dee Rockwood. By then, she was living full time as a woman, working as a personal trainer, a Chinese medicine practitioner, and as a doorwoman/bartender/bouncer at a local gay bar. She had suffered loses through trans-discrimination by not being able to work in her chosen field of engineering and had to discontinue one of the largest and most successful martial arts practices in Ohio. She was using her marital arts for fund-raising to support AIDS research and guest-speaking in university human sexuality courses all across Southern Ohio and Kentucky.

By 1995, Dee had done all the research and preparatory work to have the gender reassignment surgery, including discussion with the particular surgeon in St. Louis who would perform the surgery. All she had left to do was to find a way to finance the procedure. One Sunday as a mild-mannered woman sitting in her church pew, Dee prayed for a sign from God to show her if she was following the right path. The next week she received notification that she had just had her MasterCard credit line extended to $12,000. The fees from the surgery were $11,999. Away she went to St. Louis for the one thing she prayed for since being a little boy—a miracle to happen to change her to a girl. Throughout her life she continued to pray, and now she was able to get what she always wanted—a surgical correction to a "birth defect!" That is what many transsexual individuals consider their condition, being born in the wrong body as a birth defect.

Since I had completed a postdoctoral fellowship in St. Louis with the Masters and Johnson Institute, I looked forward to reasons to return to the city and offered Dee some company for her big day in St. Louis. The Masters and Johnson connection allowed me to be in the operating room with Dee so I was one of the last people she saw while still a physical male a physical male and the first she saw as a physical female. I sat right next to the surgeon while he did his magic and we traded stories of Doc Masters. He did what was considered to be the "Cadillac" version of the surgery that removes the interior tissue from the penis, preserves the penile skin to serve as the new vaginal lining, and inverts the skin up into a vaginal cavity while attaching the end tissue to a piece of extracted sigmoid colon that makes it a naturally self-lubricating vagina—pretty fancy-schmancy.

After Dee left the recovery room, I presented her a cupcake with a candle in it to represent her new birthday. With it was a card that had a little girl and little boy toddlers on the cover. The little girl is pulling on the front of the boy's pants and looking down to see what she could see. On the inside of the card was written, "Aren't you glad you don't have one of those anymore?"

Today, Dee Rockwood lives a lot quieter life than the notoriety of her early years as a hypermasculine superman. She has a sense of authenticity that brings her a peace of mind that is priceless. It is a peace that helps sooth the losses she has experienced for being her true self, despite objections from society at times. Dee lives a life of leisure on a houseboat floating on the Ohio River, performs weddings as an ordained minister, teaches Tai Chi and kung fu karate classes, provides transgender coaching, scuba dives as much as she can, and does her best to stay in touch with friends and family.

She was inducted into the U.S. Karate Hall of Fame and received a Lifetime Achievement Award for her 60 years of competing and teaching karate. At age 69, she is still competing and recently sparred with a young man from Chinatown in Chicago to earn her 6th-degree black belt in karate. You can watch her breaking cement blocks on Facebook, including a specialty technique called the Dim Mak (which means "shadow or poison hand"). She might be the only person who is not a Chinese Shaolin monk able to perform this amazing transfer of Chi. What's next for the Grand Master? She would like to compete in the World Games and plans to test for her 7th-degree black belt on her 70th birthday.

LET'S BLOW YOUR SEXUAL MIND!

The book's third section (Chapters 11 to 15) is really its heart because these chapters represent the deepest aspects of our collective sexuality as a species: addressing the core issues of what we feel about our sexual identity and how we experience our sexual expression. At the same time, the first three chapters in this section are the most cerebral aspects of any content of the book—designed to blow your mind!

In Chapter 11 we will explore the topic of sexual identity in a whole new way that discusses three aspects of our sexual selves within a new definition of sexual identity. These three aspects (sex orientation, sexual orientation, and sex-role orientation) are combined in a new three-dimensional model called the Sexual Identity Cube (i-Cube). The different combinations of how sexual identity is manifested through the i-Cube blows so far past the traditional ideas of the gender binary that you will never think of sexual identity the same way again.

In a similar manner, Chapter 12 follows the same approach by discussing three major aspects by which we express our sexuality. These three aspects (sexual fantasies, sexual behaviors, and biosocial mediators) make up another three-dimensional model called the Sexual Expression Cube (e-Cube). Both the i-Cube and e-Cube describe the "mathematics of sex" by which there are thousands of varieties of sexual identity and a virtually limitless number of sexual expressions demonstrated across our species.

As if two new three-dimensional cube models of sexual identity and sexual expression are not enough to challenge traditional thinking on the subject, a four-dimensional model called the Sexual Hypercube (h-Cube, or tesseract) is introduced in Chapter 13. The reciprocal and dynamic relationship between sexual identity and sexual expression is described employing the h-Cube as a four-dimensional explanation of three-dimensional human sexuality in a two-dimensional book.

These three chapters are the most abstract and theoretical (and most amazing) content of the book and are followed by two remarkable Success Stories about two couples. Chapter 14 is the story of Gage and Devin, who also inspire and instruct all of us regarding the incredible fluidity of gender. Once you read this chapter, you are likely to believe one of the main assertions of the authors—that sexual identity is not static but rather changes across the lifespan for most people. The story of Gage and Devin just demonstrates a greater than usual degree of gender fluidity. In Chapter 15, Jane and Eddie both inspire and instruct us on the challenges of when our past trauma can sneak up on us and interfere with present-day functioning. Both stories are real-life testimonies to the resiliency of the human spirit.

CHAPTER ELEVEN

Considering Sexual Identity

Written by Frederick Peterson

INTRODUCTION

To a great extent, the following discussion of sexual identity is the most challenging part of this book, yet it is incomplete without the following two chapters on sexual expression (Chapter 12) and the gender-bending, binary-exploding Sexual Hypercube model from the fourth dimension (Chapter 13). This chapter (Chapter 11) explores a few questions you have likely not entertained lately, questions like: What is your identity? What is your sexuality? What is your sexual identity? Are existing definitions of sex and sexual identity adequate? Finally, what is the point of asking these questions, and what does it have to do with your sexual health?

You will see that exploring these questions will lead to three assertions. First, based on review of the literature, a new definition of sexual identity is needed. Second, a new definition of sexual identity is offered and illustrated by a three-dimensional model called the "Sexual Identity Cube." Finally, the advantages of considering different perspectives about sexual identity include the assertion that sexual identity is not static but a fundamental human experience that changes over the lifespan.

This chapter comes with a most complicated yet interesting warning, as it may be the most complicated, yet interesting, part of this book. A necessary endeavor of this chapter is close examination of some very common terms such as sex, sexuality, and identity. We hear these words frequently, but we seldom pause to think about what they precisely mean. While generally avoiding jargon (psychobabble, if you prefer), finer distinctions need to be made in this chapter between different definitions of these terms, and a few of the concepts discussed may be new to some readers. Those of you who liked school may really enjoy this chapter; patience is requested from the rest of you. If that doesn't turn you off and you keep reading (as nerdy as it sounds), you may have some fun with words and their meanings! Some of this stuff you will not believe!

WHAT IS SEXUALITY?

Most of us often think of "sex," but we seldom ponder "sexuality." People generally refer to sex as one of two things. Most often they use the term to refer to sexual intercourse. Sex also means a biological designation of being male or female. The initial chapters of this book focused on your self-assessment as a sexual person and hopefully stimulated your thinking toward an expanded consideration of sex into sexuality and, better yet, sexual health. We have defined sex and sexual health, but what exactly is sexuality?

Not sure? Don't feel bad as many books written about sexuality (and some that even have the term in the title) do not explicitly define the term. Up until a few years ago, some sexuality texts had a glossary and the term *sex* may be included, but not *sexuality* (Strong, DeVault, Sayad, & Yarber, 2005; Lips, 2005; Hyde & DeLamater, 2011).

Some authors who do define sexuality use all-encompassing descriptions of everything sexual about a person. McAnulty and Burnette (2003) define sexuality as "*the sensations, emotions, and cognitions that are associated with physical sexual arousal and that usually give rise to sexual desire and/or behavior.*" Similarly, LeVay and Valente (2003) define the term as "*the feelings, behaviors, and identities associated with sex.*" Greenberg, Bruess, and Conklin (2007) define human sexuality as "*part of the total personality and involving the interrelationship of biological, psychological, and sociocultural dimensions.*"

These authors are well-respected authorities on the topic of sexuality, and their definitions vary considerably. Notice that the first one (McAnulty & Burnette, 2003) is focused solely on the individual whereas the last one (Greenberg, Bruess, & Conklin, 2007) mentions both individual and societal dimensions. The second definition (LeVay & Valente, 2003) is the only one to refer to sexuality being associated to identity. That does not mean any of these authors are wrong, but because sexual science is relatively new, researchers are still working toward a consensus about many topics of sexuality, ranging from a basic definition of what sexuality means to more esoteric topics such as the G-spot, female ejaculation, and the mechanisms of orgasm. As mentioned in Chapter 1, there is much more we do not know about sexuality than we definitively do know.

If we check *Webster's*, the old 12-pound copy of their international dictionary, it has 61 different variations of terms related to sex. This does not include some of the newer sexual terms (like sexting or sex addiction) and, of course, does not include terms beginning with "sex." The entry for the term *sexuality* is surprisingly one of the shortest, even though four meanings are listed. Let us have a brief and playful closer look at what *Webster's* has to offer to this discussion (Webster, 1986).

The most succinct definition is the first meaning: "*the condition of having sex*"—how very strictly reductionistic. The second is even more off-putting: "*the condition of having reproductive functions dictated by the union of male and female*" —how very technical, very heterosexist, and very much defining sex for reproductive purposes only. The third—"*the expression of the sexual instinct*"—is a bit better, but leaves me wondering, what is the sexual instinct? Finally, although the fourth meaning sounds technical, it still attempts to address the complexity of sexuality: "*the condition, potential, or state of readiness of the organism with regard to sexual activity*"—I can live with that. We are all organisms. The good lexicographers at *Webster's* describe sexuality across all the animal and plant kingdoms, not just relative to humans. In this context, they do a pretty damn good job.

We could consult many other good sources (such as the Kinsey Institute, the World Health Organization (WHO), and the American Association of Sex, Educators, Counselors, and Therapists— AASECT), but let's not belabor the point any further. Instead, let's go to the people believed to be *the* authoritative source on all matters of human sexuality in America: the Sexuality Information and Education Council of the United States (SIECUS). It is their job to keep up with the latest research publications on sexuality and offer the best opinions available on sexual health topics as a valuable information service to the public.

SIECUS defines human sexuality comprehensively (brace yourself): "*as encompassing the sexual knowledge, beliefs, attitudes, values, and behaviors of individuals. Its various dimensions include the anatomy, physiology and biochemistry of the sexual response system; identity, orientation, roles and personality; and thoughts, feelings and relationships. The expression of sexuality is influenced by ethical, spiritual, cultural and moral concerns*" (2001). Wow! That is 20 different sexual dimensions of being a human mentioned in one definition! This comprehensive definition is similar to the WHO's definition of sexual health that we considered earlier.

The point of this little academic review is that it is necessary to understand the many aspects of the broader concept of sexuality before we start poking around the notion of sexual identity (the focused topic of this chapter). If we do not have consensus on the basic definition of sexuality, we can also expect varied opinions on the definition of sexual identity.

The original title of this chapter was "Reconsidering Sexual Identity," but it turns out that "Considering Sexual Identity" is a more appropriate title because the literature is so varied in opinion that there is really no accepted single concept to reconsider and argue against. At this point in the development of the field of sexuality, all thoughtful perspectives on the subject of sexuality, especially those developed from a multidisciplinary perspective, can contribute to better understanding of this most basic element of human existence. That is the nature of the evolution of scientific advancement. Varied individual opinions are explored, models are developed, hypotheses are tested, results are discussed and debated, and gradually consensus is developed. A dominant perspective (paradigm) emerges over time and represents a widely accepted (not necessarily unanimous) collective hunch of what reality is, at least until counterarguments and evidence force reconsideration and modification of accepted definitions to better describe the new collective hunch of reality.

WHAT IS SEXUAL IDENTITY?
RESULTS OF A REVIEW OF COLLEGE TEXTBOOKS

As mentioned, wide variation would be expected when we turn attention to the more specific topic of sexual identity. However, college textbooks on any topic are generally considered reflections on the most recent research and accepted reality in any particular field. Respecting the esteemed authors of college textbooks, there was curiosity regarding just how much variation was present in the way sexual identity is conceptualized and described. A sex educator/counselor colleague of mine (named Skip Carter) and I reviewed textbooks to get a good estimate of the degree of variation. Both of us have taught university courses on sexuality, are familiar with most of the college textbooks on the subject, and have struggled with which definitions of sexual identity to teach (as well as the nature of the relationship between sexual identity and overall sexuality).

We reviewed three dozen respected sources of information on sexuality seeking a definition of sexual identity. This set of sources included 27 textbooks on sexuality and gender that could be used as a primary or secondary text within a college course. We found that college textbooks on sexuality and gender did vary greatly in their definitions of the term *sexual identity*, if they listed one at all. Similar to the previous section's discussion of the term *sexuality*, the first distinction found was between those textbooks that did and did not define sexual identity.

Considering only the textbooks, the majority (18 out of 27, or 66 %) did not include sexual identity in the index and did not provide a definition of sexual identity in the body of the text. Nine texts (9 out of 27, or 33 %) had definitions of sexual identity (Peterson & Carter, 2010). On the one hand, this finding astounded us as society looks to college textbooks as authoritative sources on any given topic. Surprisingly, the majority of the textbooks did not define what we considered a core concept of sexuality (sexual identity). On the other hand, this is the state of the field as the scientific study of sexuality is a little more than a century old and has been terribly hindered by social stigma, academic snobbery, and elusive research funding.

As expected, those textbooks providing definitions had significant variation. Variation among the definitions was measured in two ways: how many components of the definition were included and the specific nature of the definition's components. Besides the definitions found in textbooks, there will also be definitions discussed by noted authors and leaders of the field (such as Coleman, Diamond, Levine, Hammock, and Bem) who are not necessarily authors of college textbooks. This gave a total of 15 definitions included in this review with varying numbers of components, including either two-dimensional, three-dimensional, or four-dimensional definitions.

Two-Dimensional Definitions

The texts defining sexual identity as two components basically use biological sex and sexual orientation as the two dimensions. These texts essentially state that sexual identity is synonymous with "sexual orientation." Examples include Yarber, Sayad, and Strong (2010, "*One's self-label or self-identification as a heterosexual, homosexual or bisexual person*") and Aulette, Wittner, and Blakely (2009, "*The terms sexual identity or sexual orientation refer to how people identify or classify themselves sexually*"). While using a limited definition of sexual identity, both these publications are excellent general sexuality textbooks that have been widely used in university classrooms (including courses taught by Skip Carter and myself). Also to the credit of Yarber & Sayad, they updated their definition in their most recent (10th) edition: Sexuality is one's self-label or self-identification as a heterosexual or LGBTQA person (2019).

Although credit is deserved for these texts having a definition, two-dimensional definitions are inadequate because sexual identity is a more encompassing concept than sexual orientation. Sexual identity is not the same as sexual orientation, as sexual identity is a much broader concept. Said differently, two-dimensional definitions do not capture the diversity of how people identify themselves sexually. This is true of contemporary American culture and even more so regarding the greater diversity of cultures around the world.

Three-Dimensional Definitions

These were the most common type (representing half of the definitions found) and varied in what factors comprised the third dimension. The first two dimensions already discussed are included in all of the three-dimensional definitions (such as being a straight woman or gay man = biological sex orientation and sexual orientation). Virtually all the definitions of sexual identity use the components of basic sex identification (sex orientation) and sexual attraction (sexual orientation) as the base to build upon if they expand beyond these two primary components. Regarding the nature of the third component, the additional dimension referenced by several authors included factors such as an "*inner sense of oneself,*" "*specific sexual preferences,*" "*group affiliation,*" "*self-labeling,*" or "*sex (gender) role.*" The most popular third factor referenced was sex (gender) role.

Four-Dimensional Definitions

Two interesting definitions with four components were reviewed. The first is by McCammon, Knox, and Schacht (2004); the second, by Coleman (2004), will be discussed in the next section. McCammon et al. describe sexual identity as "*factors including one's biological sex, gender identity, gender role, and sexual orientation.*" Gender identity is incorporated into the "gender orientation" component of several of the three-dimensional definitions (including the Sexual Identity Cube, discussed later in this chapter). Now let us expand our consideration of sexual identity beyond college textbooks, including Coleman's definition and other leading voices.

OTHER IMPORTANT VOICES CONSIDERED REGARDING SEXUAL IDENTITY

A few authors included in this review were not known for writing college textbooks on sexuality but need to be noted for their thoughtful scholarship on the subject. First and foremost is Dr. Eli Coleman of the Program in Human Sexuality at the University of Minnesota Medical School and past president of several important organizations for the scientific study of sexuality, including the World Association for Sexology. Dr. Coleman has taken a lead on expanding and understanding the definitions of various forms of sexual identity, sexual compulsivity, and sexual health for several decades. He sees sexual identity as comprised of four basic components: *chromosomal sex/natal sex, gender identity, social sex-role,* and *sexual orientation*. If the first two components are combined into one (chromosomal sex/natal sex and gender identity), then his definition is consistent with the three most common dimensions previously discussed (the three-dimensional model). As explained later, Coleman's first two components are combined into one (referred to as sex orientation) in the three-dimensional model of the Sexual Identity Cube.

Dr. Stephen Levine, at the Case Western University School of Medicine, has been a steady and reasoned voice in care of patients with sexual health concerns as well as the training of health care professionals. Levine sees all sexual behavior (of any variety), as being constructed of four basic elements: biological, individual psychological, interpersonal, and cultural (Levine, 2007). Broadening scope, he divides a person's sex life into three components: *sexual identity, sexual function,* and *sexual satisfaction.* He further subdivides sexual identity into gender identity, sexual orientation, and sexual intention. Sexual orientation is what you might expect (gay, straight, bi), but he defines gender identity as *"the sense of the self as masculine or feminine"* (not male or female). His third component of sexual intentions is interesting as he defines the concept as *"what a person wants to do to his or her partner during sexual behavior and what the person wants to have done to him or her by the partner."* Levine's notion of sexual intentions appears to address the issue of unusual (atypical) intentions expressed in a person's struggles with either gender identity, unusual types of sexual practices (such as fetishes, voyeurism, exhibitionism, and other paraphilia), and, according to Levine, even homosexuality when patients are struggling to balance their homoerotic interests and participate in a traditional family life. While contributing a more nuanced definition, this conceptualization of both sexuality and sexual identity reflects a more traditional psychiatric perspective.

Dr. Lisa Diamond, Professor of Psychology and Women's Studies at the University of Utah, has been a strong voice of new insights into female sexuality and challenging the notion of rigid and lifelong sexual orientations (with what she calls "sexual fluidity"—a topic discussed in more detail in the next chapter). Diamond has defined sexual identity as a *"culturally organized conception of the self, usually 'lesbian/gay,' 'bisexual,' or 'heterosexual.'"* She introduces a new lexicon for people to describe themselves, preferring to use such terms as other-sex sexuality (for heterosexuality), same-sex sexuality (for homosexuality), and nonexclusive sexuality (instead of bisexuality). Diamond goes on to make distinctions between sexual identity and sexual orientation and argues for a more sophisticated understanding of sexual identity. Her 10-year longitudinal data from studying adolescent girls turning into young women has shed light onto women's greater flexibility in their sexual expression in relationships (as compared with men). We will return to her work in the next chapter, which is focused on sexual expression (Diamond, 2008).

Dr. Anil Aggrawal is another author of note and represents an international perspective, being from New Delhi and having a background in forensic medicine. He defines sexual identity three-dimensionally, made up of what he calls gender identity, sexual orientation, and gender role (Aggrawal, 2009). This is essentially the same definition (with slightly different wording) seen in several of the American textbooks and very similar to the Sexual Identity Cube model. Finally, we must check in with our friends at SIECUS again and briefly mention two other scholars. If you consult with SIECUS for their meaning of sexual identity, you find a succinct three-dimensional definition: *"An inner-sense of oneself as a sexual being, including how one identifies in terms of gender and sexual orientation"* (SIECUS, 2001).

The final two scholars noted here are Phillip Hammack and Daryl Bem. Both of these important voices have contributed a balanced perspective from an overall life-course human development framework and both argue for an integrative view between the disparate opinions that attempt to explain all matters sexual by either biological essentialist models or by completely social constructionist models. Specifically related to our topic at hand, Hammack sees both biological factors (genes, hormones, and sexual desire) interacting with psychosocial factors (culture, history, personal development) to form sexual identity, which he clearly states is distinct from what we commonly refer to as sexual orientation (Hammack & Cohler, 2009). Bem has contributed a theory of how we direct our biologically based sexual interest toward others through a process he calls the "Exotic-Becomes-Erotic" (EBE) model of sexual attraction. This model is innovative, integrative, and attempts to explain the development of both heterosexuality and homosexuality by the same (EBE) process (Bem, 1996).

DEFINITIONS OF THE THREE BASIC COMPONENTS OF SEXUAL IDENTITY

Here is where the gender-bender mind-twist is about to start. Half the authors included in this review use three basic dimensions in their definitions of sexual identity. Therefore, it would be helpful to define these three primary components: sex orientation (sex-designated status such as male, female, transgender); sexual orientation (such as gay, straight, etc.); and sex-role orientation (such as feminine, masculine, etc.). The following definitions may not make much sense until you read the sections with the headings that start with "*How Are You so Sure That You Are . . .*" (which follow these definitions).

Sex Orientation (Designated Male/Female Spectrum Sex Status)

A person's fundamental status on a male-to-female continuum, which is composed of eight factors, both biological and psychosocial. Sex orientation is a person's most fundamental status of being human and is most often designated as male (having testicular or masculinized tissue present), female (having ovarian or feminized tissue present), or some combination of male-female sex traits referred to as transgender. People are typically considered transgender in one of two ways. Intersex transgender individuals have some combination of testicular (or masculinized) tissue and ovarian (or feminized) tissue present. The second type of transgender individuals are referred to as psychosocial transgender (not being intersex but having a psychological gender identity different from their socially assigned sex designation). Hence, there are four flexible types of sex orientation: male, female, intersex transgender, and psychosocial transgender individuals. These types of sex orientation status are referred to as flexible because, while they remain constant for the majority of people, they do change for a minority of individuals. It is important to note that the term *sex* has been primarily used in the literature to refer to biological characteristics of a person to assign him or her to the status of male or female. However, "sex" is not that simple; as you will see, your sex status is mostly biological but also has psychological and social dimensions.

Sexual Orientation (Sexual Attraction Pattern)

This is a quality within you that determines to whom your sexual, affectionate, and/or love interests are directed. There are four types of sexual orientation: gay, bi, straight, and asexual, but for the purposes of simplicity in this chapter, we are going to primarily use the first three types and respectfully set aside the topic of asexuality for the time being. The word *orientation* has been challenged, and some authors choose to use different terms to describe a person's attraction to others, such as sexual attraction pattern, sexual desire, sexual pathways, sexual lifeways, and so on. The word *orientation* implies a static and inflexible trait that is inconsistent with many people's experience. However, because sexual orientation is the term understood by most people, it is used in this book acknowledging some debate about its use and the understanding that "orientation" is a malleable characteristic that can change over time. As this book later argues, sexual orientation as well as sex orientation and sex-role orientation are all subject to change and do for many people.

Sex-Role Orientation (Gender Role)

This refers to your personal response to role expectations that society associates with your sex, and is manifest in your gender-role attitude and gender-role behavior. There are four basic types of sex-role orientation: traditionally masculine, traditionally feminine, androgynous, and undifferentiated. Again, for the purposes of simplicity in this chapter, we are going to primarily use the first three types, and set aside the topic of undifferentiated sex role for the time being.

Sex orientation, sexual orientation, and sex-role orientation are the basic three components of sexual identity. It is necessary to make these terms clear before getting into the intersection of these concepts. Each of these three concepts can be a bit confusing themselves but will get more complex when we combine them in new ways. But before we do that, let us move to a deeper understanding of your sex, sexual, and sex-role orientations. To do so, there are three key questions for you: How are you so sure of your sex? How are you so sure of being gay, bi, or straight? How are you so sure of being masculine, feminine or androgynous? These questions can be considered irrelevant, provocative, silly, or even insulting. However, the explanations that follow reveal new details of what we take for granted; much like the fish not thinking much of the water that surrounds them.

BASIC SEX ORIENTATION: HOW ARE YOU SO SURE YOU ARE A MAN OR WOMAN?

In what ways do you identify your sex status as a male, female, or transgender individual (whether intersexed or psychosocially transgender)? Did you know there are at least five biological and three psychosocial variables to comprehensively classify your sex status? Most of the eight factors can be reasonably determined by you just by thinking about them. Also, most of them can be determined by a good developmental history, but a few factors always require physical examination by sexual health specialists. For example, one variable that always requires technical assessment is your chromosomal make-up.

The five biological variables include your chromosomes, prenatal hormone exposure, external genitalia, internal reproductive organs, and pubescent hormone development. Obviously, each of these factors has had a specific effect on your sexual development. But there are also three psychosocial variables, which include the sex you were medically assigned at birth (as designated on a birth certificate), the sex you were raised as in your family (this does not always match the sex assigned at birth), and the sex you believe you are (referred to as your gender identity), which may or may not match any of the other dimensions.

Hence, the "simple" question of your basic sex orientation (sex status) does not seem as simple as we once thought. These eight dimensions of sex designation have been written about for decades, but they did not get put together into such nuanced relationships until the 1980s. The degree of complexity continues to increase when we focus on the significant variability within just one of the eight levels of biological sex status: chromosomal sex variations. Are you ready for this?

Traditionally, to have the status of "female," individuals have any of the following sex chromosomes (genotypes): XX (most typical female), XO (Turner syndrome—one X chromosome missing), XXX, or XXXX (see Table 11.1). In addition, individuals considered female can even have a XY sex chromosome combination (typically resulting in masculine development) if they have something called AIS—androgen insensitivity syndrome. Yes, that is right—XY chromosomal "males" can develop as women with a transgender orientation (whether they know of their chromosomal status or not). Individuals with AIS have an XY combination but did not experience the typical effects from the presence of prenatal androgens that flowed over the fetus and typically masculinize the developing sexual organs.

However, XY individuals with AIS (either partial or complete) may either have missing androgen receptors or ones that do not work well. Therefore, the fetus develops as a female anatomically, except they do not have a functional reproductive system. People with AIS can have happy and productive lives, such as Dr. Katie Baratz Dalke, who is a practicing psychiatrist. When she was young, she thought she was a typical girl until she was six years old and doubled over in pain. Her parents first thought she had a hernia but her pain was actually caused by a descending testicle. She grew up as a beautiful woman, got married, adopted children and is an advocate for the civil rights of children born with variations of their sexual anatomy. The good doctor has also been an important health educator on the topic of AIS and been a board member of Advocates of Informed Choice, which works for empowering youth with intersex conditions and raising the visibility of intersex individuals (LeVay, Baldwin, & Baldwin, 2015).

Now let's talk of male chromosomal variations.

Traditionally, to have the status of "male," a person can have any of the following sex chromosomes (genotypes): XY (most typical male), XXY (Klinefelter's syndrome), XYY, XYYY, or other variations that include a Y sex chromosome (see Table 11.1 again). Similar to what was just described above, there are exceptions to the usual male sexual development as a fetus. There are XX chromosomal females that have a condition called CAH—congenital adrenal hyperplasia, which results in masculinization of fetal gonadal tissue. What happens during fetal growth is that the adrenal glands secrete an excessively large amount of androgens during the later stages of development. This results in a baby being born with either an enlarged clitoris (partial CAH) or penis structure if they experienced very significant masculinization (complete CAH).

Before we leave the area of females with gender variations, let's not forget the XY males who have developed a female gender identity. These chromosomal male individuals are also considered female and are classified as psychosocial transgender individuals. Many of these individuals pursue and complete sexual reassignment surgery, and many do not. They are sometimes referred to as male-to-female (M2F) transsexuals or trans women and do not have any (known) variation of sex chromosomes so are not included on the following table of chromosomal variations (Table 11.1).

TABLE 11.1 **Sex Chromosome Variations**

Female Genotype	Syndrome	Prevalence	Male Genotype	Syndrome	Prevalence
XX	Sex-typical		XY	Sex-typical	
XO	Turner	1:2000	XXY or XXXY	Klinefelter's	1:500
XXX or XXXX	Triple-X	1:1000	XYY	Jacobs	1:1500
XX/XXX	Mosaic	Unknown	XY/XXY	Mosaic	Unknown

As with the XY women with female gender identity, let's not forgot the XX chromosomal females who develop male sexual identities. As with their gender counterparts, these individuals are considered to be male socially, but are classified as psychosocial transgender individuals. Many of these individuals pursue and complete sexual reassignment surgery, and many do not. They are sometimes referred to as female-to-male (F2M) transsexuals or trans men and do not have any identifiable variations with their sexual development. These variations occur naturally and regularly among all human births. When you add up their total estimated frequencies for atypical chromosomal variations in sexual development, it approximates a bit under 2% of all live births. Table 11.2 below represents estimated frequencies of selected sexual development variations (chromosomal and hormonal) within every 100 births (from Fausto-Sterling, 2000).

This discussion is not intended to turn you into a specialist in pediatric genetics but rather to drive home the point that there is a lot more to the "simple" assignment of sex status for many people—and we have talked only about chromosomal and hormonal variations. Those two variations add up to nearly 2 in 100 people in the general population. But let me not get ahead of myself; here is a relevant story about the complexity of gender in a world that likes to categorize people into one of two boxes—male or female.

TABLE 11.2 **Frequencies of Most Common Hormonal Chromosomal Variations in Sexual Development (estimated frequencies per every 100 live births)**

XO	(Turner syndrome)	0.03690
XXY	(Klinefelter's syndrome)	0.09220
XY	(Androgen insensitivity syndrome—AIS full)	0.00760
XY	(Androgen insensitivity syndrome—AIS partial)	0.00076
XX	(Congenital adrenal hyperplasia—classic CAH)	0.00779
XX	(Congenital adrenal hyperplasia—late-onset CAH)	1.50000
XX	Vaginal agenesis (females born without a vagina)	0.01690
	True hermaphroditism (both ovaries and testicles)	0.00120
	Idiopathic hermaphroditism	0.00090
	Non-XX or non-XY (except for Turner's and Klinefelter's)	0.06390
	Estimation of Frequency for All Causes	1.72815

Once there was a little girl who was assigned a female status at birth and raised as a girl by her family. She was considered feminine and grew up to be an attractive woman with a traditional bell-shaped figure (sizable breasts with a narrow waist and broader hips). She was athletic, had the strength of a woman, and did well in competition. So well, in fact, that during the 1980s she was Spain's best female hurdler, won international competitions, and planned to go to the Olympics. However, Maria Patiño of Spain was disqualified for participation in the female competition even though she always thought of herself as a woman. The problem the world-level athletic associations had with this hurdler was that, unbeknownst to her, she had a Y chromosome. She eventually was successful in overturning her disqualification and led a high-profile campaign to change the way the Olympics conducted testing for determining sex. There is actually a long list of such examples in athletics. Another notable and recent example is the case of the South African sprinter Caster Semenya, silver medal winner in the 2012 Olympics.

THE MATHEMATICS OF HUMAN SEXUAL DIVERSITY (PART I)

What is wrong with a world with more than two sexes, or at least a world accepting of people who were born with sexual variations? If the Olympics are relaxing their scrutiny and concern about boxing people into gender categories, why can't the rest of the world? Are we ready for more than two sexes? Ready or not, nature will dictate variation among us. How much variation? Let's consider the estimated numbers of all the possible combinations of this thing called sex orientation. Table 11.3 represents the numbers of categories involved in defining a person's basic "sex," followed by an estimation of variations within each category:

TABLE 11.3 **Sexual Development Variables Separated into Biological (5) and Psychosocial (3) Categories**

Biological	**Psychosocial**
Chromosomal	*Gender identity*
(10 variables as described on Table 11.2)	(3 variables: male, female, variant)
Hormonal – both prenatal and pubescent	*Sex assigned at birth*
(2 × 3 = 6 variables)	(2 variables: assigned male or female on birth certificate, mostly for social and administrative reasons more so than medical reasons)
• Prenatal (in utero) hormonal exposure (masculine, feminine, or variant development) • Pubescent hormonal exposure (masculine, feminine, or variant development)	
Anatomical – both internal and external	*Sex raised as*
(2 × 3 = 6 variables)	(3 variables: masculine, feminine, or variant social development involving a child being raised as male and female at different periods of socialization)
• Internal reproductive system (masculine, feminine, or variant development) • External reproductive organs (masculine, feminine, or variant development)	

Let's take a breather. Table 11.3 shows many possible variations of the eight basic factors we started with (the five biological and the three psychosocial) that people typically use to decide their sex status. For the purposes of calculating an estimate of all possible variations of these eight factors, we are going to use the following numbers of different categories for each factor (although these numbers can be subject to different methods of calculation):

1. chromosomal variations = 10 (based on variations on Table 11.2)
2. possible prenatal hormonal variations = 3 (based on male/female/variants)
3. possible pubescent hormonal variations = 3 (based on male/female/variants)
4. possible anatomical internal variations = 3 (based on male/female/variants)
5. possible anatomical external variations = 3 (based on male/female/variants)
6. possible gender identity variations = 3 (based on male/female/variants)
7. possible sex assigned at birth variations = 2 (either assigned male/female)
8. possible sex raised as variations = 3 (child raised as male/female/or combination)

TABLE 11.4 **Estimated Permutations of Typical and Variant Sexual Development**

Chromosomal	10
Hormonal (Prenatal)	x3
	30
Hormonal (Pubescent)	x3
	90
Anatomical (Internal)	x3
	270
Anatomical (External)	x3
	810
Gender Identity	x3
	2,430
Sex Assigned at Birth	x3
	4,860
Sex Raised As	x3
Estimated Permutations	14,580

Okay, now all we have to do is multiply! Table 11.4 does this for us, calculating all possible permutations (for those of you who are not math geeks, permutations are similar to combinations or groups, but you can think of them as specific lists of variables because the order of the factors on the list really matters, much like the order of a gene sequence— you can't just reorder the sequence of genes and have the same genetic code and function).

This estimated number of permutations represents well over 10,000 possible combinations in the "human gender mosaic" (and there are additional "sex chromosomal categories" that could be counted beyond the ten chromosomal variations included in Table 11.1). This estimate of mathematical possibilities for factors we use to designate sex are not necessarily all expressed in nature, but the fact is that *we do not know* to what extent they are. Certainly, the accuracy of these estimated numbers can be rightly argued by honest men and women. However, the point is this: whether there are 10, 100, 1,000, or 10,000 possible permutations of variables we use for basic sex designation, designating one's "sex" is not as simple as we once believed and certainly is not a dichotomous either/or male or female thing. Therefore, the range of *what we conceive as "normal" can be greatly expanded* (BOOM!—that's the sound of the binary system exploding). The world in this way is not changing—this diversity has always naturally occurred and now we are just beginning to understand life in greater detail. While we have always experienced natural variations as part of the evolutionary process, society strongly promotes conformity and discourages individual variation to gender expression, so individual variations have historically been sanctioned and/or hidden in the proverbial closet. In addition, today's greater public visibility of transgender people is attributed to higher levels of social acceptance and expanded coverage for transgender health care (Yarber & Sayad, 2019).

As a consequence, a conceptual revolution is occurring in our thinking about the complexity of this fundamental aspect of being human. As we did in the mid-20th century regarding how we viewed sexual orientation, we have now moved toward viewing our designation of a person's sex on more of a *continuum* (or, if you prefer, a "human gender mosaic"). This was proposed nearly 50 years ago by a Dr. Harry Benjamin and modeled on Alfred Kinsey's continuum for heterosexuality-homosexuality (more on this shortly).

Considering such a continuum of the many facets of sex orientation (sex designation), some among our family and friends likely do not have all the five biological and three psychosocial factors pointing in the same direction. That is to say, the eight sex factors described above are discordant for some people. The term "gender-variant" is sometimes used to describe these individuals. I prefer to simply call them transgender people and consider them part of the beautiful diversity of the human race. Of course, as a general guideline, it is best to ask what way people identify themselves and what terms they prefer you to use to describe them. Regardless of how we see people or what labels we use to describe them, how a person self-identifies and labels is most important. This is true of sex orientation, sexual orientation, and sex-role orientation. Keep in mind, this self-perception thing is tricky business (because of our built-in blind spot, which is also discussed in detail later in Chapter 20), and how we see ourselves can (and often does) change over time.

There are no solid numbers to accurately estimate the incidence of transgender individuals in the general population (although some published estimates are noted below). This is a moving target because of the inconsistent definitions we have as well as not having standardized reporting systems. We have already estimated that almost 2% of people have chromosomal and/or hormonal variations. As previously noted, these possible variations of sex orientation occur naturally and with regularity. For every 100 people you pass on the sidewalk, a couple of them are transgender individuals whether they identify themselves that way or not (considering some do not know they possess chromosomal, hormonal, or internal anatomical variations).

So, who do you know among your family, friends, or coworkers who are transgender? Do you accept the fact that you may know a transgender person and not know they are transgender? Sometimes you just don't know and sometimes you might. It is commonplace (even in the more conservative Midwest) to meet transgender people as cashiers, librarians, booksellers, and all types of professions. According to a recent study based on adults who self-identify as transgender, there are about 1.5 million such Americans (Flores, Herman, Gates, & Brown, 2016). But for reasons explained in Chapter 20, this number very likely represents a significant underestimation of the size of transgender America.

BASIC SEXUAL ORIENTATION:
HOW ARE YOU SO SURE YOU ARE GAY, BI, OR STRAIGHT?

Sexual orientation is the quality within you that determines who your sexual, affectional, and/or love interests are directed toward and with whom you may choose to have sexual relations. Sexual orientation can be defined in many ways; no one definition is universally accepted. Most scholars understand that sexual orientation is much more complex than the traditional consideration of *"with whom one chooses to have sexual relations."* Sexual orientation often (but not necessarily) has components of intense affection and/or love associated with sexual interest. A more common text-book definition is *"the pattern of sexual and emotional attraction based on the gender of one's partner"* (Hyde & DeLamater, 2011). The American Psychological Association defines sexual orientation as *"an enduring emotional, romantic, sexual, and/or affectionate attraction to individuals of a particular gender."* Of course, this can include both males, females, or individuals of different transgender variations.

How we think of sexual orientation today mostly stems from the groundbreaking work of Alfred Kinsey (1948, 1953). The three types of sexual orientation that are generally accepted are represented on the famous Kinsey Scale continuum (see Figure 11.1). These three types of sexual orientation are heterosexuality, bisexuality, and homosexuality. Varying degrees and types of bisexuality are represented by categories 1–5.

This continuum represents the most common model of how we think of the relationship between heterosexuality and homosexuality in 21st-century American culture. However, there are still many people in this country (particularly members of conservative religious groups) who do not accept the Kinsey scale as factual, good science, and certainly not the dominant paradigm. Acknowledging anthropological studies of many same-sex practices around the world (at least where scholars are allowed to conduct such studies), there is a strong rejection of a normalized view of homosexuality outside America and Europe. Indeed, homosexual behavior is still criminalized and reason for publicly sanctioned discrimination and persecution in many places around the world.

However, another way of constructing the concept is to view sexual orientation not on a continuum, but rather as a 2×2 matrix. On one dimension is the variable of attraction to males (low or high). On the second dimension is attraction to females (low or high). This creates four quadrants within this 2×2 matrix of sexual

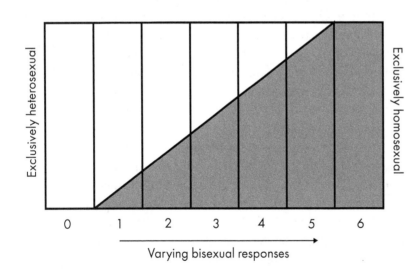

FIGURE 11.1 The Kinsey Scale of Heterosexuality-Homosexuality

orientation when crossing one axis of high attraction to women with low attraction to women and the high attraction to men with low attraction to men (see Table 11.5).

Depending on the sex status of the person in question, two of the four quadrants of this 2×2 matrix represent heterosexuality or homosexuality. The first is a category representing high attraction to men and low attraction to women (lower left quadrant). The second is a category of high attraction to women and low attraction to men (upper right quadrant). However, there are two more quadrants for sexual orientation. The third category is "high attraction to both men and women" is the upper left quadrant and can be considered bisexuality. The fourth category (one not represented on the Kinsey Scale) is "low or no attraction to both men and women" (lower right quadrant) and can be considered asexuality.

Although there is not yet consensus that asexuality is a truly separate orientation or a lack of an orientation (Brotto & Yule, 2017), asexuality is defined as an individual having very low or no sexual interest in others as sexual partners. This is a definition supported by those who self-identify as asexual individuals. Considering the great diversity of human sexual behavior (as well as across the rest of the animal kingdom), it certainly makes sense that there are people who experience little to no sexual interest as there are those who report high interest in sex. An important point in this discussion is that asexual individuals typically have had little to no interest in sex as long as they can remember. Additionally, asexual people do not have an absence of sexual interest because of the effects of medical conditions, related medication side effects, depression, or a history of sexual abuse. Rather, they will likely say, "This is how I always have been."

TABLE 11.5 **Two-by-Two Matrix of Sexual Attraction**

	High Attraction to Males	**Low Attraction to Males**
High Attraction to Females	**Bisexual attraction**	You are **straight** if a man You are **lesbian** if a woman
Low Attraction to Females	You are **gay** if a man You are **straight** if a woman	**Asexuality** (Low/no attraction to either)

How do asexual people differ from bisexual and pansexual individuals? Generally, bisexual individuals often report higher levels of sexual interest as well as a preference toward either males or females as sexual partners. Individuals identifying as pansexual are defined as those who are interested in and open to intimate relations with others regardless of gender (Yarber & Sayad, 2019), inclusive of others who see themselves as queer and/or transgender.

Asexual individuals, on the other hand, not only have little or no interest in sex but also have little or no preference for males or females as a sexual partner. Asexual individuals may abstain from sex or they may have sex at times; but they typically do so for reasons other than sexual desire and/or sexual attraction. For example, they may report that they have sex for reasons such as wanting to be in a relationship for companionship, having children, or simply pleasing a partner. Asexuality a bit abstract to you? Please read on, as you are about to meet the likes of May.

Featured Stories of Diverse Perspectives and Experiences

YOU FEEL ME?—MAY AND JUNE
Written by Richelle Frabotta

I feel nothing. I've tried. I know I'm supposed to, but it just doesn't work. Ok, I'm not exactly telling the truth. I feel some things.

I feel the presence of God when I'm staring at the peaks of the Ouachita Mountains dominating the southeast sky. I feel grave concern about how the presidential election concluded and what my future, my siblings' futures looks like. I feel the need to take my 13-year-old Pomeranian to the vet when he insists on eating electric cords. I feel hunger and am highly attracted to Burger King Whopper Juniors with cheese. Actually, I may have a problem with that last feeling.

When my peers were all like, "Oooooo and ahhhhhhh" over cute brown-skin boys, or wide-eyed light skin girls, well I wasn't. I just kept my nose in my book. When they shared pieces and parts of their sexual exploits, I was like "uh huh" and remained eyebrows deep into chapter 4.

It never occurred to me that wearing a boys' shirt or smelling his neck was supposed to be a sexy thing. Who knew touching boobs was a turn-on? Not only did I learn these types of interesting, nonhygienic tidbits from my peers, but I also learned from books. Specifically, romance novels. They were my source of "all things sexy." And porn. I learn a lot from porn.

When I met June, she was roping cattle with her brothers on a dusty Oklahoma afternoon. Dry doesn't begin to describe it. I was with my Mom delivering water and feed on our weekly route. I know why June came over to me: She wanted a bottle of water. But I'll never understand why she wanted to stay around after she drank it. That was 23 years ago.

I remember the first time she told me that she had a crush on me. We were fixing the fence that the cattle had torn down. I had just set the post deeper into the ground and was holding it while June was pulling the barb wire. She snagged her flannel shirt and blood started staining the area of the tear. I grabbed my bandanna out of my back pocket and tied it securely around the wound. She said that it stung. And then she leaned over and kissed me. On. The. Lips.

To say I was surprised is an understatement. I was flabbergasted. Flummoxed. Dumbfounded. I walked away to retrieve the floating diagonal brace. Picked it up and positioned it on the 18"x2"x6" treated lumber. I waited for June to pick up the hammer and shank nails to secure it. She wasn't moving. She had a look on her face—a look I finally comprehended after seeing it several times over the years.

"Ummmm, did you want to secure this fence?"

Silence.

"Does your injury hurt too bad to hammer the nails in . . . ?"

Silence with a raised left eyebrow. And then, in the quietest of voices, "I just kissed you."

"Yes, yes you did. Come on and let's get this fence finished up."

"Don't you feel it, too? Did I call this wrong?"

"Feel what? Your lips were soft and sweaty. I have a salty taste in my mouth now." And then it was my turn to raise an eyebrow and cock my head.

"I have a crush on you. I really wanted to kiss you. I thought you would want to kiss me back."

"Ohhhhhhhhhh!" as I remembered a couple of pornos. "I am cool with the kiss. Thanks. I'm not sure what to do next. But I do know we're losing daylight and this fence has got to get tight."

June has been beyond patient with me. I know that I love her. We have navigated my lack of desire for emotional, romantic connection together for our entire committed relationship. I recognize that her devotion to me, to us, is essential to loving me. I return that devotion. And it is June who must initiate intimacy. I simply never think about it.

In our intimate moments, when I listen attentively to her stories anticipating belly laughs until we both hold our stomachs, I know we belong together. In our intimate moments when I see the raised left eyebrow, the stare, and realize that I need to learn this moment, I know we belong together. In our intimate moments when her lips start at my neck, move down my sternum, over my belly, landing on my pudenda, I remember not to laugh out loud when it tickles. I recognize that this feels good to her. I want her to feel good. I know we belong together.

We ride hard together. I love her like I love rodeo season. We've made it around the cloverleaf with one stirrup in the dirt because I am surefooted and because she has the spirit to endure the intensity of a fast and scary ride. June is my connection to feelings that I don't have.

She is my dusty cowgirl who rode up on a horse and didn't unlock my passion, but instead: she gave me her heart. I listen to those George Strait love songs. I continue to read romance novels. I will hold tight her heart because it is as precious as the view of the Ouachita Mountains and as sustaining as Whopper Juniors with cheese.

The new sexual health paradigm includes an expanding range of normalcy, and the preceding description of an asexual woman (such as May in her relationship with June) is not pathologized but accepted as another variation in the beautiful diversity of human sexuality. The descriptions for the four different types of sexual orientation (reflected in Table 11.5) reflect dramatic changes in how we conceptualize what is normal in our society and the variations of sexual orientation across individuals. If you are old enough, you may remember that only 50 years ago, the consensus in medicine was that all variations of sexual expression other than heterosexuality constituted pathological mental illness and resulted from an individual's choice of "lifestyle." The critical shift in perception occurred toward a significant expansion in what is considered "normal range" sexual expression. This shift in cultural perspective contributed to the declassification of homosexuality as a mental illness in 1973 and promoted greater self-acceptance among individuals who might otherwise criticize, reject, or even loathe themselves.

This reconceptualization has been accompanied by a shift away from the view of sexual expression simply as a moral "choice of lifestyle" and reflects a movement toward a view of sexual attraction being more biologically determined. However, some fascinating research over the past few decades supports a view that at least some aspects of sexual expression are socially constructed. Excellent examples of this view are the anthropological studies by Gilbert Herdt of the Sambian male rites of passage, where boys experience several years of same-sex sexual behavioral training to learn to be a man through ingestion of semen (from older boys and men). They are reported to then enter adulthood as heterosexual men who select a wife and raise a family (Herdt, 2005).

Sophisticated biosocial theories of the development of sexual attraction (such as Daryl Bem's "Erotic Becomes Exotic" theory) have replaced old (and artificial) "nature versus nurture" explanations.

Bem combines well-researched traits such as child temperament and play preference (representing "nature") with factors such as the influence of social peer groups and who a child sees as different or the "exotic other". The exotic other becomes erotized during pubescent hormonal exposure (the exotic becomes erotic) resulting in either a heterosexual or homosexual orientation, depending on the sex designation of both the child and the eroticized other (Bem, 1996). Bisexuality could be conceptualized to be a variation of this biosocial process. The matter of what used to be called a "lifestyle choice" is now understood to apply more to healthy and responsible sexual behavior, not sexual orientation. Research continues to develop and test new theories of sexual orientation, but the dramatic "societal rethink" of this basic component of sexuality in only a few decades is nothing short of revolutionary.

BASIC SEX-ROLE ORIENTATION: HOW ARE YOU SO SURE THAT YOU ARE AS MASCULINE AND FEMININE AS YOU BELIEVE?

As mentioned earlier in this chapter, sex-role orientation refers to your personal response to gender role expectations that culture places upon members of a particular gender. Your response is expressed in your sex-role attitude and sex-role behavior. What are gender-role attitude and gender-role behavior?

Sex-Role Attitude

Sex-role attitude is your set of beliefs about personality traits and activities that you closely associate with males and females. Some authors describe gender roles as gender scripts or gender expectations. For example, traditional gender-role attitudes involve such stereotyped beliefs in America that men are supposed to be more independent and need to be in control. Traditional stereotypes of women are that they are more submissive, passive, and nurturing. These stereotypes perpetuate many societal ills, from relationship conflict to domestic violence, yet they are ever-present social influences (Bem, 1981a).

Sex-Role Behavior

Sex-role behavior is defined as specific acts or activities in which you engage according to your beliefs about your gender (based on your sex-role attitude). Hence, boys and men may choose (even though they may be unaware of making a choice) to act more aggressively and engage in socially sanctioned activities such as football. Girls and women may choose (even though they may be unaware of making a choice) to act more nurturing and engage in socially sanctioned activities such as selecting nursing as a career, as opposed to engineering (Bem, 1981a).

Let's go back to the definition of sex-role orientation (gender role). It is a combination of your personal attitudinal response to sex-role expectations (which go along with your sex status) and is expressed in your sex-role behavior. The key phrase is personal response, or how people choose (consciously at times, but mostly unconsciously) whether to accept or reject the cultural expectation for them to "swim with the current" and act in a socially sanctioned or expected manner. The boy footballer and female nurse are examples of "swimming with the current" via confluence with cultural expectations in America and would be considered a more traditional response to society's expectations. It is important to note that masculinity and femininity are not polar opposites on the same continuum. Masculinity and femininity are separate concepts on separate continuums, and they both exist within the same individual. For example, a particular person may have both a high degree of masculine traits and a high degree of feminine traits. This is what we refer to as androgyny (Carroll, 2016).

Androgyny is characterized by flexibility in one's response to sex-role expectations through the development of a combination of skills (what researchers call instrumental and expressive traits). The skills and traits we build are influenced by individual differences, historical situations, and our stage of the life cycle. Expressive traits are traditionally associated with females in many cultures, traits such as greater comfort showing affection and demonstrating nurturing behaviors. Instrumental traits are traditionally associated with males in many cultures, traits such as being more inclined to be analytical and more aggressive. This sounds like straight sex stereotyping, but remember, we are talking about very large and general trends on a societal level.

It is important to recognize that sexual orientation and sex-role orientation are independent of each other. What this means is that being gay or straight has little to do with being masculine or feminine. For example, stereotypes of gay men as effeminate florists or lesbians as motorcycle mamas are common. In reality, and in recognition of the great diversity of human experience, some gay men and lesbians do fit these stereotypes. However, the vast majority do not. Of course, the opposite of general sexual stereotyping may be true as well, such as the macho quarterback who identifies himself as gay.

Similar to the matrix involved with our discussion of sexual orientation, Dr. Sandra Lipsitz Bem introduced a 2×2 matrix several decades ago to use as a teaching tool about sex-role orientation (Bem, 1981b). It is created by intersecting the two variables of masculinity (low or high) and femininity (low or high). The left side of the matrix represents high masculinity, while the right side represents low masculinity. It is the same for femininity but "up and down" because femininity is on the side axis. Therefore, high femininity is on the top half of the matrix, whereas low femininity is represented on the lower half of the matrix. Hence, this matrix, results in four quadrants that represent four different sex-role orientations, and here is an important point: each quadrant may represent a man or a woman!

The four quadrants or types of sex-role orientation (gender role) based on this 2×2 matrix are as follows:

1. Traditional masculinity (high masculinity, low femininity).

TABLE 11.6 **Two-by-Two Matrix of Sex-Role Orientation (Gender Role) based on the work of Sandra Bem**

	High Traits of Masculinity	**Low Traits of Masculinity**
High Traits of Femininity	Androgyny	Traditional femininity
Low Traits of Femininity	Traditional masculinity	Undifferentiated

    a. Examples could include a macho cowboy or a woman who mostly displays traditional masculine traits.

2. Traditional femininity (low masculinity, high femininity).

    a. Examples could include effeminate men (gay or straight) or a lipstick lesbian. (A lipstick lesbian is a slang term for one who is feminine in manner or appearance, breaking any stereotype of female homosexuality being associated with masculine traits.)

3. Androgyny (high masculinity, high femininity).

    a. Examples could include metrosexual men or assertive female executives.

4. Undifferentiated (low masculinity, low femininity)

    a. Examples could include men and women who are not easy at first to identify as male or female, and their appearance may be unintentional ("that's just the way I am") or intentionally attempting to generate a confusing presentation of gender (sometimes as a statement of protest against the standard heterosexual standard or against the "well-behaved" gay and lesbian middle-class assimilation).

The category of "undifferentiated" is uncommon, and individuals who identify with this sex-role orientation are not well understood. As we did with "asexual" individuals, this type of sex-role orientation is being respectfully acknowledged, but detailed discussion of it is being set aside for the purposes of the brevity of this chapter. The last example (4.a. above) of individuals who intentionally seek to create unique gender appearances sometimes self-identify as part of queer culture and deserve more discussion than they receive in this chapter.

NOW BACK TO THE CENTRAL QUESTION OF SEXUAL IDENTITY

So, Do You Know What Your Sexual Identity Is?

Even more basic, what exactly is identity? Using the big old *Webster's International Dictionary* again, *identity* is defined as the "*limit approached by increasing similarity*" and the "*sameness of all that constitutes the objective reality of a thing.*" Wow—that's cool. However, the most suitable meaning for our purposes is "*unity and persistence of personality.*" Wow again—how we fit together and have persistence over time is what we call our identity.

To consider the subject of sexual identity, we also need to touch on Erik Erikson's stages of psychosocial development. Let us consider how Erikson conceived of the process by which we form our identity, which begins early in childhood but really blossoms in adolescence (ages 12 to 18). Teenagers often go through a crisis of who they are going to be as grown-ups. Erickson saw the central dynamics of this stage of identity formation involving a basic conflict between "identity vs. role confusion" (Kail & Cavanaugh, 2004). The developmental task for teens is to build a sense of self and personal identity (and to do that through exploration of social relationships). A central question about Erikson's theory on identity formation is "how is an adolescent realistically able to develop a sense of personal identity without developing a sexual identity as part of that overall identity as a person?" (Erikson, 1968).

Most kids do not wake up in the morning wondering if today is the day they figure out their identity in general and their sexual identity in particular. If they can think beyond breakfast, they might worry about how they are going to do their homework before they get to school or at least before they get to class. Any "big-picture thinking" is usually forced on them by an exceptional teacher who might engage the class in a stimulating discussion of "who are we?" as girls and boys, as sons and daughters, as Americans, or even human beings.

Identity has many aspects that each of us collectively call "me." Consider the roles of our ethnic, racial, and cultural backgrounds in the development of our overall identity. Many folks have identities closely tied to their religious training and beliefs. What we do for work and eventually as a career plays a significant part in how we respond to the question *"Who are you?"* When introducing themselves to a new person, few people start off their answer with "I am a lesbian" or "I am a heterosexual." The point is that your sexual identity is a part of your overall identity. Yet, for most people, sexual identity is much more a fundamental element of our identity than, say, what we do to pay the bills. However, the opposite may be true as well. For some people, being a mother or a soldier or a writer is all-consuming of their attention and energy on a day-to-day basis, much more so than being a sexual person.

That's why people are sometimes surprised to hear sexperts say "sex is not the most important thing in the world," yet at the same time, and quite paradoxically, it is very important. The evolutionists would say it is the most important element in life because perpetuation of the species is involved. If you don't think sex is so important, ask yourself the following questions. If you are gay, how would your life be different if you were straight? If you are straight, how would your world be different if you were gay? How about if you were another gender?

A NEW DEFINITION OF SEXUAL IDENTITY AND THE SEXUAL IDENTITY CUBE

Based on the discussion presented in this chapter of all the significant variations across the many definitions of sexual identity, here are several conclusions:

1. If you are going to write a book, a journal article, or even present a lecture about sexuality, it would be good to define terms like sexuality and sexual identity.
2. Sexuality is a core experience of being human and can be generally considered all things about you as a sexual being. The formal definition of sexuality used in this chapter is from SIECUS: *"Sexuality encompasses the sexual knowledge, beliefs, attitudes, values, and behaviors of individuals. Its various dimensions include the anatomy, physiology and biochemistry of the sexual response system; identity, orientation, roles and personality; and thoughts, feelings and relationships. The expression of sexuality is influenced by ethical, spiritual, cultural and moral concerns."* This is an excellent definition; my only suggestion is that it should include a reference to sexuality being a lifetime experience.
3. Sexuality can be broadly divided into your sexual identity and your sexual expression.

4. Sexual identity is not the same as sexual orientation, as sexual identity is a much broader term that encompasses sexual orientation. Sexual identity is part of one's overall identity as a person. SIECUS defines sexual identity as "*an inner-sense of oneself as a sexual being, including how one identifies in terms of gender and sexual orientation*."

5. Based on reviewing three dozen sources authored by leading authorities on human sexuality, there is a lack of consensus across these experts' attempts to define sexual identity. A new definition is needed; one that reflects the central elements most authors use yet reflects the great diversity of the human sexual experience.

The following definition of sexual identity is offered as a potential step toward the ultimate goal of developing a consensus of what sexual identity is (with further revisions expected). This definition is primarily based upon

1. The three most commonly used components for definitions found in the review of sexuality and gender textbooks;
2. sex-role orientation (gender role) being the most commonly used "additional dimension" used in three- and four-dimensional definitions; and
3. the integration of key principles of leading scholars on the topic.

Sexual Identity—A New Definition

> *Sexual identity is the sense of who one is as a sexual being and is a fundamental human experience comprised of a person's sex orientation, sexual orientation, and sex-role orientation.* Sexual Identity is a central part of a person's sexuality and changes over the lifespan of an individual. The behavioral expression of sexual identity is different from the identity itself, encompasses a great diversity of expression transculturally, and is based on one's personal development of eroticism that is mediated by culturally and biologically based factors.

The italicized (first) sentence above is the core definition of sexual identity, while all three sentences make up the full definition. This definition captures many key points made in the literature on sexual identity as well as the discussion presented in this chapter. As a visual representation of this definition, the Sexual Identity Cube (i-Cube for short) is presented as a conceptual teaching tool. The i-Cube was originally developed to expand existing models beyond the limits of biological sex status and sexual orientation. This expansion is needed to more accurately reflect the complexity of sexuality in contemporary culture. However, the original version of the i-Cube was oversimplified (Peterson, 2007), and this revised version is expanded to be more inclusive, which is one of the goals of the i-Cube as a conceptual and teaching tool.

This new definition of sexual identity (and the i-Cube; see Figure 11.2) is intended to more accurately describe the tremendous diversity of sexual identities among people that is well documented across the literature of anthropology, medicine, psychology, and sociology. This i-Cube model is designed to promote greater self-acceptance as well as acceptance of individual differences among us as people. Differences (in and by themselves) are often, especially historically, seen as a bad thing. Differences are actually a good thing, whether you are talking about sexual differences, different opinions, or biodiversity. As an evolving human culture, it is in our best interests to stop pathologizing variations in sexual identity and expression simply because they diverge from a cultural norm (Bley & Peterson, 2007). Oversimplified definitions of sexual identity limit the range of "what is normal" and therefore can limit a person's capacity for developing a positive self-worth. Consequently, they may contribute to some individuals concluding that they (as a person) do not fit the current definitions of healthy sexual identity and result in unnecessary self-perceptions of being different and abnormal.

The i-Cube is a pictorial reflection of what we have discussed in this chapter, only in the visual form of a 4×4×4 polygon. The i-Cube represents all four types of sex orientation (male, intersex transgender, psychosocial transgender, and female), all four types of sexual orientation (attracted to neither men nor women, attracted to both men and women, attracted to women, attracted to men), and all four types of sex-role orientation (traditional masculine, androgynous, traditional feminine, and undifferentiated).

This i-Cube has 64 "vector areas" representing many different sexual identities that range from common identities like traditionally feminine heterosexual women and traditionally masculine heterosexual men (think Barbie and Ken) to vector areas like the effeminate gay man and androgynous bisexual woman. The sexual identity of our aforementioned Olympian (Maria Patiño) is represented in the i-Cube by the vector area for androgynous heterosexual intersex transgender women. Before discussing "Joe, Cody, and Pam" on the illustration, let me make some very important points about how to interpret what you see in the i-Cube (because what you *believe* you see can be very misleading).

Point 1

The directional *arrows* are much more important than what appears to be the smaller subunits of the i-Cube. The arrows represent a *continuum* or spectrum of characteristics as opposed to discrete categories within sex orientation, sexual orientation, and sex-role orientation. So, pay more attention to the continuum arrows as they are the most important visually.

Point 2

The smaller subunits within the i-Cube should be thought of as areas around a vector that represent the intersection of the three factors of sex orientation, sexual orientation, and sex-role orientation.

Point 3

Although our brain wants to see lines and squares as having firm boundaries between one side of a line and the other side (or the inside of a square and the outside), please inform your brain that all the lines of the i-Cube are diffuse and permeable. Think of the lines as being made of concentrated lines of fog as opposed to any solid boundary. Although the "lines" may be misleading, it is visually necessary to have the lines for teaching purposes to visually locate the vector area that is being discussed, such as Joe, Cody, and Pam.

Point 4

As mentioned, the "lines" within the i-Cube are permeable and do not represent discrete categorical states of sexual being, therefore representing the flexible nature of sexual identity and the possibility of change of self-identified sexual identity over time.

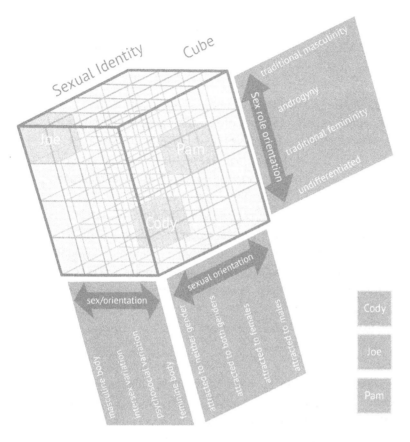

FIGURE 11.2 The Sexual Identity Cube (Illustrated by Max Fleishman)

Point 5

Said differently, people can "move around" the i-Cube from one stage of life to another, changing aspects of their sexual identity as they go (whether that is change in their sex orientation, sexual orientation, and/or sex-role orientation). As will be later argued, *most people do change* at least one of these three dimensions during their lifetime (most often sex-role orientation). Sometimes these changes are voluntary choices and sometimes they are not.

Back to Joe, Pam, and Cody (in that order). What does the vector area identified for Joe represent? Joe is in the upper-left corner of the i-Cube and represents an individual who identifies as a male with a masculinized body, displays traditional masculinity, and who is not attracted to either men or women (asexual). Get it?

The vector area directly behind Joe represents an individual who is a traditionally masculine man such as Joe but who happens to be bisexual. Pam represents a bit more common sexual identity than Cody. Pam identifies herself as an androgynous woman who is attracted to women. BOOM— that's how the i-Cube works.

Let's try Cody (this is an example of where the lines are very helpful for locating the vector area). If you follow the lines, Cody would be identified as an intersex transgender individual who is attracted to females and has an undifferentiated sex-role orientation. Depending on how Cody identifies as male/female/trans, he/she/they (using the singular "they") might also identify as a straight guy or identify herself as a lesbian. To be even more gender-nuanced, they may also identify their sexual orientation as something different (bi?) if they self-identify their sex orientation as *neither or both male and/or female*. Is your gender-bender brain spinning yet? Yes, please don't be discouraged. This can get complicated, but so is the nature of human sexual diversity. You'll get it.

Joe, Pam, and Cody are intended to help you get the basic idea of identifying different sexual identities with the i-Cube. While illustrative of how these three individuals identify themselves at a particular point in their life span, it is important to remember Point 5 on the previous page: that people can "move around" within the i-Cube across time by experiencing changes in their sex, sexual, or sex-role orientations. So, let's use some additional examples to reflect this movement.

Chapter 5 introduced you to Alex, the Navy Seal, who (to the outside world) appeared to be a traditionally masculine, heterosexual male. However, through a completed gender reassignment surgery, Alex became an androgynous lesbian woman deeply in love with her wife. Chapter 10 introduced you to Dee Rockwood, who was also raised as a traditionally masculine (hypermasculinized) heterosexual boy. However, Dee discovered that she was not a "regular boy" at all, as she prayed every night to wake up a girl. She also discovered that she had an extra "X" chromosome, making her start in life as an intersex transgender individual (she prefers the term "transsexual") and transitioning to an androgynous lesbian woman. Finally, Chapter 14 will introduce you to Gage, one of the best examples to "mobility" and gender fluidity you will ever meet. Gage's movement within the Sexual Identity Cube includes several vectors, including times in his life when he was:

a. A traditionally feminine, heterosexual girl (including birthing a son);
b. More of a masculine lesbian woman;
c. Transitioning to a traditionally masculine man in a heterosexual relationship;
d. Meeting and falling in love as a transman living life as part of a gay couple.

This may be an unusual way to explain the i-Cube, but the point is this: we need a very large tepee to allow all human beings to feel like they belong to the tribe. To promote health and acceptance of your children and their children, we want to avoid teenagers feeing like they don't belong if they don't identify with the historically defined, socially sanctioned models of normalcy (traditionally masculine heterosexual men and traditionally feminine heterosexual women). If our children reject these traditional models and have few other socially sanctioned choices to which to relate, they are at increased risk for isolation, confusion, and possibly mental health problems. Many youths today do reject the limited models offered them and therefore seek their own definition and style of expression, often assimilating with other alternative youth to become a "member of their own tribe" and sometimes doing so at great personal risk.

Although the i-Cube represents an expanded consideration of factors contributing to the formation of sexual identity, the new definition allows for consideration of important intersecting factors, which not only shape an individual's sense of sexual identity but partly determine the nature of their sexual expression. These cultural factors include, but are not limited to, such variables as ethnicity and racial identity, religious and nationality affiliations, historical context, disability status, age, personal sexual developmental factors, and familial factors. Many of these variables can come into play simultaneously. This is called "intersectionality" and refers to the accumulative influences on an individual as a result of identification with multiple cultural groups, especially those considered sexual minorities. For example, "African American women veterans who come from families that have been part of rural Appalachia for generations (referred to as Afrilachians) are more at risk for depression and other health care disparities (such as hypertension, diabetes, and obesity)" than white male heterosexual veterans (Cohen, Peterson, Bottoms, Resch, Burgess, & Richards, 2013).

Considering the interactive and intersecting nature of both sexual identity and expression, the number of permutations regarding cultural factors serving as influencing variables is virtually endless. Now THAT is the essence of human diversity! This interaction between sexual identity and expression is the focus of Chapter 13, and there the Sexual Hypercube will be introduced to visually represent this interaction.

What Is the Point?

This is a fair question about this whole matter of considering different points of view related to sexual identity. There are several responses to this question as to why this chapter's discussion is necessary. First of all, one goal of this model is to more accurately understand sexuality based on emerging research findings and to stimulate further research questions. This may lead us a bit closer to consensus on the use of the term *sexual identity*. As noted in the first section of this chapter, we are far from that. The process of exploring and discussing the concept and personal meanings of sexual identity is a value-added aspect of personal growth for anyone as well as it stimulates the possibility of advancing sexual science.

Better understanding the complexity of human sexuality helps us sort out commonly confused differences between sexual identity and sexual orientation as well as the differences between sexual identity and sexual expression. This chapter focused on your identity as a sexual being. As mentioned, this is different from your orientation and how you choose to sexually express yourself behaviorally (the focus of the next chapter). The authors' hopes are that we gain greater clarity for understanding two key points regarding the incredible complexity of human sexuality. The first is that the Sexual Identity Cube (i-Cube) has the potential to bring a greater inner peace, increased self-understanding, and self-acceptance. Promoting greater self-understanding and self-acceptance of sexual identity minimizes internal conflict and negative self-image. So, on an individual basis, an expanded perspective of the full range of sexual identity may lead to less unnecessary stress (cultural press, as some authors define it) and more personal satisfaction. The second key point is about interpersonal relations. The definition offered in this chapter and in the i-Cube are intended to promote greater tolerance of others as well as oneself. This can lessen the incidence of fear, prejudice, and violence toward those we *perceive* as different from us.

THE KICKER FOR THE SEXUAL IDENTITY CUBE: THE MATHEMATICS OF SEXUAL DIVERSITY (PART II)

Now before we talk about the expression of sexual identity (in the next chapter), let's make one last attempt to blow your mind about the Sexual Identity Cube (i-Cube). Remember Table 11.4? It describes the estimated combinations of typical and variant paths of sex orientation (the designation of sex) using the eight dimensions of sex designation (which were separated into "Biological" (5) and "Psychosocial" (3) categories). Blowing up the idea of binary gender, the eight categories were estimated to total more than 14,500 different possible permutations of sex orientation (sex designations)! If you thought this set of mathematics was ridiculous, just wait until you get a load of what is coming next!

Here is the rest of the story on the i-Cube. Remember, the i-Cube is a three-dimensional model of sexual identity composed of sex orientation, sexual orientation, and sex-role orientation. The estimated calculation of 14,500+ permutations represent only the variations of one of the three dimensions of the i-Cube: *sex orientation*. Now let's include the other two dimensions. Considering the i-Cube continuum of *sexual orientation* (asexual, bisexual, gay, and straight), the mathematics play out to generate more than 58,000 permutations (14,580 x 4 = 58,320). Now let's calculate *sex-role orientation* into the mix. These are another four dimensions of the continuum of sex role orientation: androgynous, feminine, masculine, and undifferentiated. Considering these four additional variables, the mathematics generate more than *233,000 different possible sexual identity variations* (58,320 × 4 = 233,280).

Wow—is that crazy or what? Is human sexual identity really that complicated? The authors assert that we (as a people) historically oversimplify sex and gender to make it easier to understand and deal with, using sexual and gender stereotypes to construct a perception of the interpersonal world that would not be as overwhelming (or possibly personally threatening).

Could the i-Cube be making things a lot more complicated than needed? Let's hold on a minute and consider any other way the mathematics of sexual diversity could be calculated using the i-Cube model. There is a more conservative method of calculating sexual diversity and it has to do with how one considers the chromosomal variations within the dimension of sex orientation. In the above set of calculations, the value used for the chromosomal variations was the number 10 because it was based on Table 11.2 (the estimated frequencies of sexual development variations published by Fasto-Sterling in 2000). There could be an argument for using the value of 3 instead of 10 if one wanted to simplify the calculation by combining all 10 chromosomal variations into only 3 categories: typical male development, typical female development, and "all variations." If the calculations are made with the value of 3 instead of 10 for chromosomal variations, then the overall estimate of possible sex orientation variations is significantly reduced. Using the more conservative number (of 3 instead of 10), the estimate of sex orientation (sex designation) permutations is lowered from 14,580 to 4,374 as Table 11.7 illustrates.

Carrying forward, now consider the i-Cube categories of *sexual orientation* (asexual, bisexual, gay, and straight), and the mathematics play out to generate 17,496 permutations (instead of 58,320). Again, now calculating *sex-role orientation* into the gender mosaic mix, the four dimensions of sex-role orientation (androgynous, feminine, masculine, and undifferentiated) generate more than 69,984 different possible sexual identity variations (instead of 233,280). Hence, *the range of estimates*

TABLE 11.7 **Minimal Estimated Permutations of Typical and Variant Sexual Development**

Chromosomal 3	3
Hormonal (prenatal)	x3
	9
Hormonal (pubescent)	x3
	27
Anatomical (internal)	x3
	81
Anatomical (external)	x3
	243
Gender identity	x3
	729
Sex assigned at birth	x2
	1,458
Sex raised as	x3
Estimated permutations	4,374

(employing both minimal and expanded calculation methods) is that there is between nearly 70,000 and more than 233,000 permutations to sexual identity using the three-dimensional definition supported by the extant literature (Table 11.8).

TABLE 11.8 **Mathematics of Sexual Diversity: Comparison of Limited & Expanded Approaches to Empirical Estimates of Sexual Identities**

	Sex Orientation (8 dimensions with 3 or 10 as genetic variable)	**Sexual Orientation** (across four dimensions)	**Sex-Role Orientation** (across four dimensions)	**Estimated Permutations for Sexual Identities**
Limited Approach (genetic variable =3)	4,374 (Table 11.7)	(X4) = 17,496	(X4) = 69,984	69,984
Expanded Approach (genetic variable =10)	14,580 (Table 11.2 & Table 11.4)	(X4) = 58,320	(X4) = 233,280	233,280

If one considers the incredible complexity of the human genome, the numerous naturally occurring chromosomal-hormonal variations of sexual development, the psychosocial and cultural aspects of the construction of sex and gender, and the interactive dynamics between our environment and the natural predisposition with which we are born: why would anybody be surprised that YES, the finer details of the science of sex and gender are that complex.

A key point not yet made is that although there is the potential for great diversity of sexual identity among people, we do not have any idea of the frequency of the most common types of sexual identities. More on this in the last chapter. One other note before this chapter closes. Whether the real amount of variation within sexual identity approximates the nearly 70,000 estimate or is more expansive (233,000), readers should know that these mathematical estimates are the result of my consultation with a doctorate-level biostatistician at the Heritage College of Osteopathic Medicine, Ohio University (Heh, 2017). The resulting consultation report from the biostatistician is in Appendix B.

Good golly, Miss Molly! (and don't assume Molly identifies as a woman) — that is a lot of different types of sex and gender variation! She/he/they can be about anything they can imagine themselves to be. And Molly is all natural, all healthy, and fits under the big tent of human sexual diversity. Whichever way you want to look at it or whatever way you want to calculate, sexual identity is a lot more complex than we have traditionally conceptualized. *Now* let's talk about sexual expression.

REFERENCES

Aggrawal, A. (2009). *Forensic and medico-legal aspects of sexual crimes and unusual sexual practices*. Boca Raton, FL: CRC Press.

Aulette, J.R., Wittner, J.G., & Blakely, K. (2009). *Gendered worlds*. New York: Oxford University Press.

Bem, D. (1996). Exotic becomes erotic: A developmental theory of sexual orientation. *Psychological Review, 103*.

Bem, S. (1981a). Gender schema theory: A cognitive account of sex typing source. *Psychological Review, 88*, 354.

Bem, S. (1981b). The BSRI and gender schema theory: A reply to Spence and Helmreich. *Psychological Review, 88*, 369–371.

Benjamin, H. (1966). *The transsexual phenomenon*. New York: Julian Press.

Bley, J., & Peterson, F. (2007). Making sexual health a part of your mental health practice. Found in L. VanderCreek, F. Peterson, & J. Bley (Eds.), *Innovations in clinical practice: Focus of sexual health*. Sarasota, FL: Professional Resources Press.

Brutto, L., & Yule, M. (2017). Asexuality: Sexual orientation, paraphilia, sexual dysfunction, or none of the above? *Archives of Sexual Behavior, 46*(3), 619–627.

Carroll, J. (2016). *Sexuality now: Embracing diversity* (5th ed.). Boston: Cengage Learning.

Cohen, J., Peterson, F., Bottoms, J., Resch, W., Burgess, B., & Richards, M., (2013). *Healthcare in 21st century Appalachia: The arranged marriage of cultural competency training and relationship-based care approaches*. Paper presented at the Southwestern Social Science Association Annual Conference, New Orleans, Louisiana.

Coleman, E. (2004) *Bisexuality: Challenging our understanding of human sexuality and sexual orientation*. In E.E. Shelp (Ed.), *Sexuality and Medicine* (Vol. 1, pp. 225–242). New York: Reidel.

Coleman, E. (2011). Assessment and treatment of impulsive and compulsive sexual behavior. In M. Grant & J. Potenza (Eds.), *Oxford handbook of impulse control disorders*. New York: Oxford University Press.

Diamond, L. (2008) *Sexual fluidity: Understanding women's love and desire*. Cambridge, MA: Harvard University Press.

Erikson, E. (1968). *Youth: Identity and crisis*. New York: Norton.

Fausto-Sterling, A. (2000). *Sexing the body: Gender politics and the construction of sexuality*. New York: Basic Books.

Flores, A., Herman, J., Gates, G., & Brown, T. (2016). *How many adults identify as transgender in the United States?* Los Angeles: Williams Institute, UCLA.

Greenberg, J., Bruess, C., & Conklin, S. (2007). *Exploring the dimensions of human sexuality*. Burlington, MA: Jones and Bartlett Learning.

Hammack, P., & Cohler, B. (2009). *The story of sexual identity: Narrative perspectives on the gay and lesbian life course*. Cambridge, UK: Oxford University Press.

Heh, V. (2017). Statistical Consultation Report (Appendix A). Athens: Ohio University.

Herdt, G. (2005). *The Sambia: Ritual, sexuality, and change in Papua New Guinea*. New York: Wadsworth.

Hyde, J., & DeLamater, J. (2011). *Understanding human sexuality*. New York: McGraw-Hill.

Kail, R., & Cavanaugh, J. (2004). *Human development: A life-span view* (3rd ed.). Belmont, CA: Wadsworth/Thompson.

Kinsey, A., Pomeroy, W., & Martin, C. (1948). *Sexual behavior in the human male*. Philadelphia: W.B. Saunders.

Kinsey, A., Pomeroy, W., Martin, C., & Gephard, P. (1953). *Sexual behavior in the human female*. Philadelphia: W.B. Saunders.

LeVay, S., Baldwin, J., & Baldwin, J. (2015). *Discovering human sexuality* (3rd ed.). Sunderland, MA: Sinauer Associates.

LeVay, S., & Valente, S. (2003). *Human sexuality*. New York: W.H. Freeman.

Levine, S. (2007). *Demystifying love: Plain talk for the mental health professional*. New York: Routledge.

Lips, H. (2005). *Sex and gender*. New York: McGraw-Hill.

McAnulty, R., & Burnette, M. (2003). *Exploring human sexuality: Making healthy decisions*. Boston: Pearson Education.

McCammon, S., Knox, D., & Schacht, C. (2004). *Choices in sexuality*. Cincinnati, OH: Atomic Dog.

Merriam-Webster. (1986). *Webster's third new international dictionary of the English language*. Springfield, MA: Author.

Peterson, F. (2007). *The complexity of sexual diversity: Sexual identity cube and self-awareness exercise*. In L. VanderCreek, F. Peterson, & J. Bley (Eds.), *Innovations in clinical practice: Focus on sexual health*. Sarasota, FL: Professional Resource Press.

Peterson, F., & Carter, R. (2010). *Re-defining Sexual Identity and Introduction to the Sexual Health and Wellness Satisfaction Scale* (unpublished manuscript). Paper presented to the Annual Conference of the Ohio Psychological Association, Columbus, Ohio.

Sexuality Information & Education Council for the United States (SIECUS). (2001). SIECUS Report, Vol. 30–31. Charlottesville, VA: Author.

Strong, B., Yarber, W., DeVault, C., & Sayad, B. (2005). *Human sexuality: Diversity in contemporary America*. New York: McGraw-Hill.

Yarber, W., Sayad, B., & Strong, B. (2010). *Human sexuality: Diversity in contemporary America* (7th ed.). New York: McGraw-Hill.

Yarber, W., & Sayad, B. (2019). *Human sexuality: Diversity in contemporary society* (10th ed.). New York: McGraw-Hill Education.

FIGURE CREDIT

Fig. 11.1: A. C. Kinsey, W. P. Pmeroy, C. E. Marttin, "The Kinsey Scale of Heterosexuality-Homosexuality," *Sexual Behavior in the Human Male*. Copyright © 1948 by Indiana University Press. Reprinted with permission.

CHAPTER TWELVE

Sexual Expression

Written by Frederick Peterson

INTRODUCTION

Like the last chapter, this one explores a few central questions: What is sexual expression? What is the relationship between sexual identity and sexual expression? What are the primary forms of sexual expression? Why is the question regarding "Is it nature versus nurture" the wrong question? What are the most common themes among sexual fantasies and how are they directed by this thing called a "lovemap?" What are the types of sexual behaviors that result in orgasm, both through sex with yourself and sex with others? What are the biological and social factors that modify our sexual expression?

Also like the last chapter, exploring these questions will lead to several assertions, such as there is little consensus regarding a definition of sexual expression, let alone what constitutes healthy sexual expression. In the absence of consensus, the best scholarly opinions are brought to the forefront for your consideration. A second point is that there is a reciprocal relationship between sexual identity and sexual expression, with mutual influences going both ways. Third (and similar to the Sexual Identity Cube model in Chapter 11), three major dimensions guide sexual expression and comprise a model referred to as the Sexual Expression Cube (e-Cube). The three dimensions, later discussed in detail, are sexual fantasies, sexual behaviors (that result in orgasm), and bioculturally bound modifying factors.

WHAT IS SEXUAL EXPRESSION?

Let's go back to a previous chapter's definition: Sexual identity is the sense of "who one is" as a sexual being based on one's sex orientation, sexual orientation, and sex-role orientation. The behavioral expression of one's sexual identity is different from identity itself and is conceptually organized by culturally defined factors and one's personal development of eroticism.

This definition of sexual identity not only references sexual expression but also begins to define sexual expression. The purpose is to emphasize the distinction between the two concepts. Of course, this description is not sufficient as a full definition unto itself. However, finding a definition for sexual expression is even more challenging than defining sexual identity, in part because sexual expression is an even more general notion than sexual identity. It is easier for most authors to define more specific concepts such as sexual desire, sexual intercourse, or masturbation.

If you go to commonly used dictionaries (such as *Merriam-Webster*, *Oxford*, *the Free Online Dictionary*), you will not find an entry for sexual expression. Interestingly, you will find that dozens of definitions of different types of sexual expression use the phrase "sexual expression" within their definitions but give no specific definition of sexual expression itself. Just for fun, if you go to Wikipedia, you will find that it does not have an entry for sexual expression either, but it does define a specific type of sexual expression called a Masturbate-a-thon, which is an event where participants masturbate to raise money for charity and to dispel shame or taboo still associated with self-pleasuring. Of course, the same authors who have written college textbooks (from Chapter 11) were reviewed again for further understanding of sexual expression. Of all the textbooks with a glossary, no definition of sexual expression was found. In reviewing the subject index of these textbooks, only two contained a specific reference to sexual expression.

It is interesting to note that most all of the textbooks on sexuality literally are full of descriptions of sexual expression but do not enumerate the basic building blocks of the concept. Of all the textbooks on sexuality, only two have chapters with titles using the term sexual expression. The first one (Strong, DeVault, Sayad, & Yarber, 2005 up through the latest 10th edition by Yarber & Sayad, 2019) has a chapter simply entitled "Sexual Expression" describing theories of sexual attraction, different types of relationships, sexual desire, sexual fantasies, and masturbation. The second textbook, *Sexuality Now: Embracing Diversity*, (Carroll, 2007) has two chapters using the term in chapter titles: "Sexual Expression: Arousal and Response" and "Varieties of Sexual Expression". Interestingly, this author includes physiological arousal and responses under the umbrella of sexual expression along with the many types of sexual behaviors (like masturbation, different types of common sexual activity with others, unusual sexual practices with others, and safer sex behaviors). Carroll also addresses how our sexual expression changes as we age.

If you remember our definition of sexuality, only two of the meanings were really useful for our purposes: "The expression of the sexual instinct" and "the condition, potential, or state of readiness of the organism in regard to sexual activity." The term *expression* can describe anything related to symbolism (one thing representing something else) as in artistic expression, musical expression, and sexual expression.

The phrase "condition, potential, or state of readiness" is also all-encompassing when it comes to sexual activity and certainly includes not only the more obvious activities such as sexual behaviors, but also the less visible activities such as dreams, fantasies, and physiological responses.

Essentially, sexual expression is the manifestation of your sexual self through your sexual thoughts, sexual feelings, and sexual behaviors; all of which are significantly mediated by bioculturally bound modifiers. These modifiers include factors that influence (and can even completely inhibit) the overt expression of sexual identity. Some of the primary examples of these factors are your religious beliefs, the legal-political system you live within, disability status, ethnicity, and race.

Sexual expression has as its foundation your physical substructure and your sexual identity but is also interactive with both of them. Said differently, forget all those traditional and artificial divisions between biology and psychology, between behavior and hormones, and between nature and nurture. As noted, your "sex" has been historically defined as your biology (chromosomes, gonads, and hormones), but this view is limited and could be better described as one's "biological sex." And as described in the last chapter, put your biological sex together with these three psychosocial dimensions (sex assigned at birth, sex raised as, and gender identity) and you have your sex orientation. This is your real sex designation, and it is a more inclusive perspective of people's experience of being male, female, or transgender. It is much more demonstrative of the biopsychosocial approach that has been emerging as the dominant paradigm in the scientific study of sexuality.

NATURE VERSUS NURTURE? (THE WRONG QUESTION)

The influences in our lives that govern our sexual expression simply are not easily divided into strict categories of internal or external, cultural or physiological, or nature or nurture. Relative to sexual expression, "nature and nurture" are often equated with "internal and external." It can be argued that sexual fantasies and dreams are "internal" sexual activity (sexual behavior) as opposed to external behaviors that can be more easily observed and measured. Although dream activity can be measured and analyzed objectively (via sleep studies measuring rapid eye movement), the content is subjectively experienced. Both dreams and sexual fantasies can be considered "activities" and in a sense a behavior. However, we have less choice about dreams as behavior in terms of initiation, content, and termination of the activity. Fantasies are more under our control as we can willfully generate them as people often do during daydreaming and masturbation.

But what about your increased heartbeat, respiration, and pupil dilation when you meet someone you find sexually attractive? These are sexual arousal responses that are not under your control but yet occur. They happen even if you don't want them to and even if you try to think your way out of your attraction. Are these "expressions of the sexual instinct" or "the condition, potential, or state of readiness" for sexual activity? The authors believe they are. In addition, they also defy any artificial division of nature or nurture because the physiological attraction you experience (increased heartbeat, respiration, and pupil dilation) is absolutely influenced by culturally defined notions of beauty.

Consider the difference between Western and Eastern culturally defined images of masculine strength. Take the sumo wrestler of Japan for instance; the physicality of masculine strength is triangular with a wide, low base and narrowing as one moves up toward the apex of the head. In Western culture, it is the opposite. Masculine strength has been traditionally and closely associated with an inverted triangle of broad strong shoulders and narrowing as one looks down to smaller hips and a tiny tush.

Culture and biology have many interactive influences upon each other; some we are just understanding with the passing of time and development of further science. American culture during the early 20th century dictated that proper care of infants included a sterile environment and limited physical touch (beyond basic feeding and changing). The mild-to-moderate effects of this cultural "nurture" factor (or lack of it) led to stunted physical and intellectual growth for many children.

Children with the most severe effects of touch deprivation died from a medical condition called "failure to thrive" syndrome. Most Americans would be surprised to learn that only 100 years ago, it was not unusual for orphanages to have one-fourth to one-third of their smallest children die before their third birthday (Blum, 2002).

Through today's MRI technology, we now understand how neglect and abuse result in specific changes to a child's brain growth. The different brain growth patterns in turn can result in behavioral changes that often make the child even more vulnerable to neglect and abuse. As we are learning more of the complexity of human beings, we understand that there really is no nature verses nurture—only nature and nurture as one commingled force of growth stimulus.

So as we consider different models of sexual identity and sexual expression, please remember that the Sexual Identity Cube is comprised of biological, psychological, and cultural factors. As mentioned, even something as simple as your sex is also defined by this combination of factors. And so it is with sexual expression. One of the most common examples of this is the relationship between low testosterone levels and frequency of sexual activity. Low testosterone levels for both men and women typically result in a lower interest in sex and, consequently, less initiation of sexual behaviors. Conversely, the more frequently a man has sexual relations, the more testosterone he produces.

While we have examined the interactive influences between biological and cultural factors, an overarching relationship allows mutual influences to occur and is responsible for our continued sexual development across the lifespan. This is the relationship between your sexual identity and your sexual expression. Obviously, part of your sexual identity (either as a straight guy or lesbian) will influence whom your sexual behavior is directed toward. That is an example of how sexual identity influences sexual expression. Influences can move in the reverse direction as well, as we will see later in this chapter.

A BRIEF NOTE ON NORMALCY

Before getting into the nuances of the many varieties of sexual expression, two questions need to be addressed as the leading concern for most people: "Am I normal?" and "What is unhealthy?" What some folks consider unhealthy is actually believed to be healthy for many others. There is a very wide range of sexual activity that is considered normal when sexual researchers employ the five dimensions of considering sexual behavior—the biological, psychosocial, behavioral, clinical, and cultural measures. Some sexual behaviors are considered atypical in terms of being statistically infrequent but do not really cause problems for people or their sexual partners. Examples of these types of behavior are people who want their earlobe gently sucked to the point of orgasm (eargasm) or rub their thighs together rhythmically to the point of orgasm (cricket orgasm). Both of these behaviors could be considered unusual but do not hurt anyone and can even be seen as exceptionally skilled sexual behavior. Now consider these behaviors as part of the sexual repertoire of individuals living with a severe physical disability, like quadriplegia or cerebral palsy. Exceptional indeed.

Consider these behaviors as part of how people draw a line in their mind between what they believe is and is not normal. It is not as simple as we may think. It is a distinction that is often arbitrary and subjective based on many factors, including religious values, prevailing cultural norms, and one's level of sexual literacy of sexual practices of other people within a culture as well as sexual practices in other cultures. When the authors are asked by students or clients "Am I normal?" they usually give one or more of the three following responses:

1. Put the concern within the context of five dimensions of understanding sexuality and see what conclusions can be drawn. Again, these five dimensions are biological, psychological, behavioral, clinical, and statistical aspects of the sexual activity. How do these considerations change the question?

2. When a person is involved with sexual variations such as sadomasochism, sometimes it comes down to ensuring it is a consensual sexual exchange and whether there is tissue damage. If two adults freely engage in some bondage or sadomasochism and no one is seriously injured, that's up to them. Two commonly used bottom lines are: Sex has to be consensual and not involve serious bleeding.

3. Look at the consequences of the behavior and ask if the typical person would feel it is worth the costs (consequences) of the behavior. As a popular pop psychology guru (Dr. Phil) famously asks, "So, how's that working for you?" Considerations of consequences include, but may not be limited to: relational, emotional, financial, spiritual, vocational, health, and legal consequences.

For example, a young 20-something couple came to the clinic regarding his apparent "impotency." The fellow could not get an erection (first time ever) after a hard night of drinking. On the subsequent evening, he was not able to get it up again (most likely due to excessive worry this time—called performance anxiety). The couple was getting married in a couple of months and wanted to correct this problem before getting hitched. They were told to go home, not to have sex for three days, not to drink the third day (alcohol interferes with erectile ability), and try it again. They called the clinic after a week to report everything was fine again because they were "back to acting like rabbits." Let's apply the three guidelines to this scenario.

Their situation was understandable on a biological basis as his difficulty was due in part to heavy alcohol use (to be expected). From a psychosocial perspective, his anxiety regarding his failure to get erections for the first time with his girlfriend and subsequent worry during the second attempt also contributed to his dreaded surprise (but no real surprise as anxiety can override high attraction and erectile response anytime). Behaviorally, this is a very common experience for men: he was perhaps too young to know this and maybe expected that he could defy the laws of physics. Clinically, he certainly did not meet any diagnostic criteria and culturally he was very typical of young men (and many young women) who believe a man should always have an erection at the drop of a bra or boxer shorts.

An analysis of the consequences of his drinking could (one hopes) lead him to stay within recommended limits of alcohol use and avoid unnecessary frustration (such as the argument they had, his thinking that he was impotent, and her thinking she wasn't attractive enough to him). Finally, there were two consenting adults (only the penis was not) and no one was getting seriously hurt. Conclusion: This scenario and the couple's concerns were very normal (they just didn't know it). They may not have considered their experience as healthy, but his certainly was not a case of erection dysfunction as they feared.

LOVEMAPS, PARAPHILIAS, AND SEXUAL EXPRESSION

The three dimensions of the Sexual Expression Cube are sexual fantasies, sexual behaviors (that lead to arousal or orgasm), and bioculturally bound modifying factors. For reasons explained below, the first two factors (fantasies and behaviors) are described as "ideoerotic." This does not mean we get turned on by idiots nor does it mean that we turn into idiots when we get turned on (although some of us may think back to when this latter meaning may have applied). Ideoerotic attraction and expression means each person has an individual pattern of what really gets their sexual motor running.

The term *ideoerotic* comes from the concept of lovemaps developed by the late John Money, the noted medical psychologist at Johns Hopkins University. Money defined a lovemap as follows:

> A developmental representation or template synchronously in the mind and in the brain depicting the idealized lover, the idealized love affair, and the idealized program of sexuoerotic activity projected in imagery or actually engaged in with that lover. (Money, 1994)

Money described lovemaps as the filter through which we see our sexual world, and one that dictates our sexual interests and behaviors. The development of our lovemap is directed by pre-natal hormonal exposure and coded environmentally through sensual input to the brain via the senses, especially by tactile sensation through the skin and augmented by smell, taste, sight, and sounds. Money's notion of lovemaps is thought of as a cognitive and emotional guide for erotic interests that is developed at an early age and directs sexual behaviors in relationships later in adolescence and adulthood. Lovemaps can develop into heterosexual, homosexual, bisexual, asexual, or a paraphilic pattern. Although Money's ideas are helpful to accurately describe certain aspects of human sexuality, there is much we do not know about the specific neuropathic mechanisms by which lovemaps develop.

A paraphilia is an unusual form of sexual activity considered to be "alongside" (para) or outside the usual expression of love (philia) (American Psychiatric Association, 2013). Some paraphilias are private and may not cause distress to the paraphilic individual or a partner. An example is a man who sometimes cross-dresses with women's lingerie for sexual pleasure and spicing up his sex life with his wife but does so with his wife's knowledge and input as to what lingerie to buy (cross-dressing can also be done for fun, entertainment, or parody, not necessarily as a paraphilia). Some paraphilias are considered a crime, a mental illness, or both (such as when a person acts out a paraphilic disorder by victimizing a child).

People with paraphilic lovemaps tend to have fantasies and behaviors that are long-standing, compulsive in nature, and distressing to the individual (and their partners as well). One's lovemap usually serves as a guide to sexual enjoyment but does not prevent one from deciding to engage in other forms of sexual activity (via trying something new through sexual experimentation). However, a minority of people have a paraphilic lovemap that requires the compulsive use of unusual imagery or behavior (to the exclusion of all other forms of sexual gratification).

THE SEXUAL EXPRESSION CUBE: FANTASY, BEHAVIOR, AND MEDIATORS

Similar to the Sexual Identity Cube visually representing the three primary components of the definition of sexual identity, the three primary dimensions of sexual expression are represented by a 3-D Sexual Expression Cube (e-Cube). These three primary dimensions are sexual fantasies, sexual behaviors (that may or may not result in orgasm), and bioculturally bound mediating factors. The illustration of the e-Cube (Figure 12.1) is represented as a bit "wavy" compared with the i-Cube because sexual expression is less defined than sexual identity. As noted in the opening pages of this chapter, the literature on sexual expression reflects this fact, although there seems to be an endless variety of specific sexual fantasies or behaviors that have been the focus of countless authors.

This apparent paradox (less definition with endless description) also contributes to the reason the e-Cube appears "wavy." As will be discussed shortly, fantasies and behaviors (the latter to a lesser extent) leading to sexual arousal or orgasm cannot be easily enumerated precisely because of the extraordinary diversity of sexual expression among human beings. Therefore, the examples of sexual fantasies and behaviors listed in the e-Cube are representative of a larger set of fantasies and behaviors that people experience. The same is true for mediating factors of sexual expression.

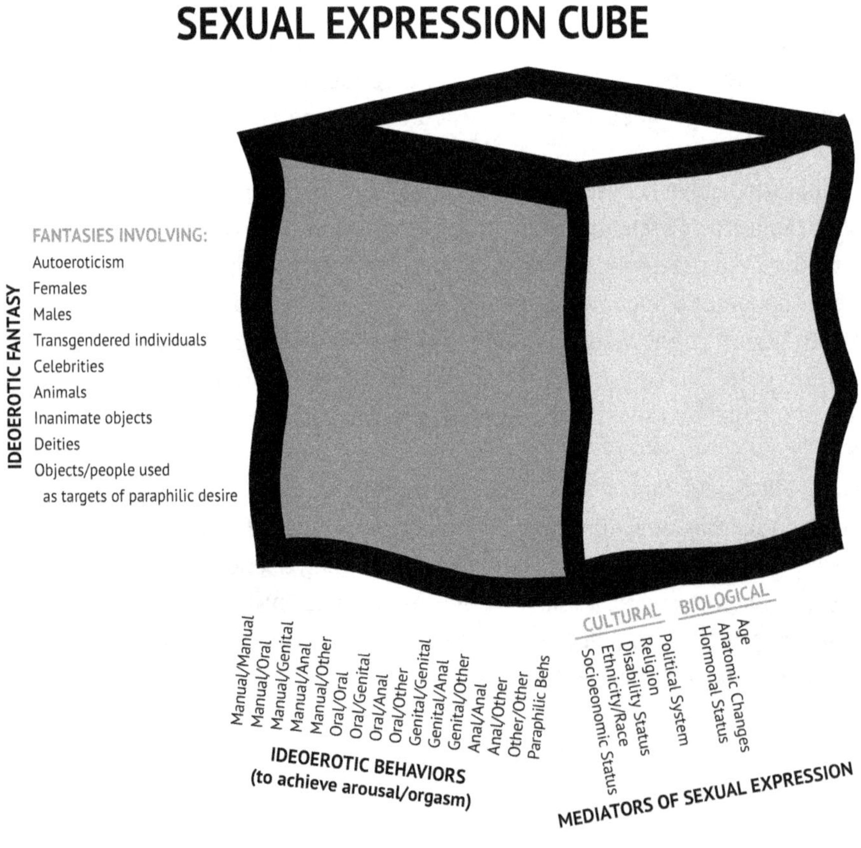

FIGURE 12.1 The Sexual Expression Cube. (Illustrated by Max Fleishman)

Sexual Expression: Fantasy

Sexual fantasy is defined as imagined sexual experiences while you are awake (as opposed to erotic dreams). A person's fantasies can be from an unlimited number of sources of erotic inspiration. If you can imagine it, someone somewhere likely takes erotic pleasure in the fantasized imagery of it (ranging from terrible pain and humiliation to corpses as sexual partners to eating animals alive or being eaten alive by an animal). Some fantasies are intentional and purposively created for sexual gratification, whereas others seem more "automatic" and repetitive. Both the variety and degree of intentional creation of sexual fantasies are heavily influenced by a person's individual lovemap.

The exact number of possible sexual fantasies can never be counted as evidenced by the endless supply and variety of erotica published every year. However, one can identify some categories of ideoerotic fantasies (resulting in a person experiencing arousal or orgasm) that are more popular than other varieties. Autoerotic fantasies are those enjoyed by people who fantasize about themselves, in part (like focusing upon their breasts) or whole (like making love to themselves). Others fantasize about the "generic male or female" (whole or part) or specialized types of individuals such as celebrities, transgender partners, or the newest hottie at the office. Others prefer to imagine themselves having sexual relations with (or having relations enhanced by) nature, deities, or mythological creatures and entities. Each one of these categories might be considered within a normal range of sexual fantasy and might have literally thousands of variations.

Paraphilic fantasy is also a world unto itself and can be divided generally into coercive and noncoercive. Descriptions of paraphilic imagery and behavior are beyond the scope of this chapter so only some of the most popular types will be mentioned. People with paraphilic lovemaps fantasize about animals (zoophilia), inanimate objects (fetish), individuals of a certain age (such as enduring sexual interest in prepubescent children), interactions with others involving domination and submission (sadomasochism, or S&M), bondage and pain (B&D), contact with body waste (coprophilia and urophilia), sexual contact with a corpse (necrophilia), making obscene phone calls (scatologia), exposing oneself (exhibitionism), secretively watching others undress or have sex (voyeurism), kissing or fondling a sleeping person (somnophilia), touching or rubbing up against a nonconsenting person (frotteurism), and sexual excitement from compulsive cross-dressing. These are just the most common paraphilic fantasies and there are many more varieties specific to ideoerotic paraphilic lovemaps (American Psychiatric Association, 2013; Money, 1986).

A general observation of individuals who disclose a capacity to enjoy sexual fantasies is that they are generally more sex-positive and able to share a greater capacity to explore and share sexual pleasure. Most people do report that they enjoy sexual fantasy and it is a value-added aspect of their sexual life. There are many positive benefits to sexual fantasy, and it is a necessary step for women to learn when they come to the clinic with reports of not being able to become sexually aroused and/or climax. Research shows that people who place positive value on their sexual fantasies are more sexually assertive, regarding both the initiation of sex as well as the refusal of unwanted sex, than people who are negative about sexual fantasy (Santos-Iglesias, Sierra, & Vallejo-Medina, 2013). Men engage in fantasy more than women, but women have more frequent fantasies around the time of their ovulation (Dawson, Suschinsky, & Lalumière, 2012). Clinically, the only concerns masturbation sometimes cause is if an individual has guilt about experiencing pleasure, a person masturbates excessively (especially with pornography) to the reduction of interaction with a partner, or the small minority of men who become sexually compulsive with erotic fantasy to the point it becomes problematic with their behavior.

Of course, individuals can just fantasize about objects of desire or they can also choose to express their interests behaviorally. Most any type of fantasy (paraphilic or nonparaphilic) can be acted out in behavior but certainly does not need to be acted out in every instance. For many reasons, people fantasize about sexual activity they never would act out in real life. That is one of the many functions of fantasy—to have sexual pleasure without explicit sexual behavior. Of course, very often the only explicit behavior that does accompany sexual fantasy is masturbation, as explained in the next section on ideoerotic behaviors.

Remember the *Mayo Clinic Family Health Book's* section on "Teenage Sexuality" (Chapter 8)? This is the exact point they were making when they stated: "It is normal to have sexual fantasies. Sexual fantasies may even be useful in the development of a teen's sexual identity because they allow exploration of sexual situations that would be inappropriate for the teen to act out" (Litin, 2009).

William Masters and Virginia Johnson studied the importance of fantasies as part of healthy sexual expression. Besides the function (just noted above) of a "safe alternative" to behavioral acting out with another person, Masters and Johnson enumerated several functions that sexual fantasy serves (Masters, Johnson, & Kolodny, 1995). The functions that fantasy serves include, but are not limited to:

1. inducing sexual arousal as an initial boost to get things underway;
2. enhancing arousal to help achieve orgasm during sexual relations;
3. allowing privacy that affords creativity without accountability;
4. improving our sexual self-image by fantasizing desired attributes;
5. reminiscing the joy of positive sexual experiences in the past when the partner is not available;
6. releasing anxiety/guilt by serving as psychological "safety valves"; and
7. allowing opportunity for controlled rehearsal in preparation of how to act in a future sexual encounter.

Sexual Expression: Ideoerotic Behaviors

Ideoerotic behaviors are what we do during sexual activities that lead to orgasm. They are certainly more limited than the endless varieties of fantasy, yet there are scores (perhaps hundreds) of behavioral variations that result in orgasm and fall under numerous categories. As with fantasy, ideoerotic behaviors are also guided by Money's concept of lovemaps. One could argue that sexual fantasies can be included within a broad range of sexual behaviors and, if so, then sexual behaviors would need to be divided between external overt behaviors (such as intercourse) and internal "unobservable" behaviors (such as thinking of a sexual fantasy). In this chapter, fantasy is separated from behavior (into two categories) for teaching purposes of the Sexual Expression Cube and making the overall idea of sexual expression easier to communicate.

Ideoerotic behaviors can be either solo (with yourself) or social (with others) as well as either nonparaphilic or paraphilic behaviors. They can also be relatively commonplace or can be relatively rare. The

TABLE 12.1 **Examples of Common and Uncommon Sexual Behaviors with Self and Others**

	Nonparaphilic	**Paraphilic**
Common sexual acts with self	Masturbation	Shoe fetish
Uncommon sexual acts with self	Cricket orgasm	Autoerotic asphixiphilia
Common sexual acts with others	Intercourse	Voyeurism
Uncommon sexual acts with others	Eargasms	Lust murdering

TABLE 12.2 **Forms of Self-Pleasuring**

	Manual	**Oral**	**Genital**	**Anal**	**Other**
Manual Pleasuring (by hand)	Self-hand massage/ touch				
Oral Pleasuring (by lips/tongue/teeth)	Touching lips, sucking fingers, licking, kissing, orbiting hand	Kissing, licking, and biting own lips			
Genital Pleasuring (by vulva, penis, or scrotum)	Solo genital masturbation	Self-fellatio, self-cunnilingus	Indirect rubbing of genitals (humping)		
Anal Pleasuring (by anus, buttocks, perineum)	Solo anal masturbation, anal eroticism, prostate massage				
Other Forms of Pleasuring (by breasts, ears, neck, legs, feet, hair, etc.)	Self-seductive touch, sex toy use, breast stimulation	Licking/biting own breasts, feet, hair, etc.; sex toy use; use of fruit	Sex toy use (dildos, vibrators, etc.); vaginal containment of animals and objects	Sex toy use (dildos, vibrators, etc.); rectal containment of animals and objects	Thigh contractions (cricket orgasms)

2×4 matrix of these groupings generates four broad types of sexual behaviors as described in Table 12.1.

Common Sexual Behaviors with Yourself and Others

Common sexual behaviors with yourself include both direct and indirect stimulation of parts of your body that turn you on. Most of the time that involves touching the penis for men and the clitoris for women (but far from always). Women are believed to have a greater number of ways to arouse themselves to orgasm than men. However, many variations to stimulating body parts other than the genitals are common. Examples include touching your breasts, rubbing earlobes, stroking hair, and sensually stimulating your anus or perineum.

Just as common are indirect touching of the genital and anal areas with sexual aids of many different styles, including handheld (sometimes hand-mounted) vibrators for the clitoris or penis, vibrating and non-vibrating dildos for vaginal or anal insertion, vaginal and anal dilators, anal beads, and don't forget some common household items such as fruit (like a banana), vegetables (like a cucumber), or candles. People commonly smell body odors and/or taste body parts or fluids for arousal and orgasm.

Of course, there are the tried-and-true methods of rubbing the genitals against an object (humping), which may be more common to girls and women for masturbation but is also employed by boys and men. Humping is exceedingly common with preschoolers as a form of self-soothing and is often carried through childhood (and even adulthood) to cope with tension and/or emotional distress. Many types of sexual behavior displayed by children are fairly common (as described in Chapter 8 by the Mayo Clinic study) and cannot necessarily be considered as evidence that child abuse has occurred. Table 12.2 delineates many, not all, of the many variations of sexual self-pleasuring.

The category that usually raises most eyebrows is the oral-genital self-pleasuring behavior. Many people do not believe that this is possible, so additional explanation is needed here. A man who can essentially give himself his own "blow job" is very rare, but you can see how this is possible given a man with a high degree of flexibility combined with an unusually long penis. A woman who is physically able to contort her body into a position by which she can orally stimulate her own genitals is extraordinarily rare and harder to believe possible. However, there is some evidence to believe both these types of self-pleasuring are possible. The Internet continues to surprise and

TABLE 12.3 **Common Sexual Behaviors with Others**

	Manual	**Oral**	**Genital**	**Anal**	**Other**
Manual Pleasuring (by hand)	Mutual petting, hand-holding				
Oral Pleasuring (by lips/tongue/teeth)	Touching lips, sucking fingers, kissing, licking or biting hand	Kissing, licking and biting (mouth to mouth)			
Genital Pleasuring (by vulva, penis, scrotum)	Genital masturbation (single or mutual); G-spot stimulation; ball play	Fellatio, cunnilingus, oral ball play	Penile-vaginal intercourse, vulva-vulva intercourse (tribadism-humping), sword fighting		
Anal Pleasuring (by anus, buttocks, perineum)	Anal masturbation, anal eroticism, prostate massage	Analingus (rimming)	Anal/penile intercourse, interbuttock intercourse*; anal/clitoral intercourse**		
Other Forms of Pleasuring (by breasts, ears, neck, legs, feet, hair, etc.)	Seductive touch, sensuous massage; sex toy use; breast stimulation	Licking/biting any part of body; breast stimulation; earlobe sucking (eargasms)	Use of knee, thigh, or other body part to stimulate genitals; sex toy use (dildos, vibrators, etc.); Interfemoral*** or interbreast**** intercourse	Use of other body parts to stimulate anus; sex toy use (dildos, vibrators, etc.)	All forms of breast stimulation, thigh contractions (cricket orgasms)

*"hot dog in the bun" without penetration of anus

**with a very large erect clitoris

***by penis (or very large erect clitoris) between the thighs

****by penis (or very large erect clitoris) between the breasts

shock viewers related to things people will video themselves doing for the planet to watch. Any good skeptic would also acknowledge the possibility of trick photography and the imagery of self-oral-genital contact being faked. At the same time, the likelihood exists of rare individuals in our sexually diverse world that do possess such abilities.

Alfred Kinsey and his associates documented the phenomenon of "self-fellation" more than 70 years ago. While acknowledging "Self-fellation is an anatomic impossibility for most human males," Kinsey was aware as a biologist that "it is a common form of masturbation among rhesus monkeys, the macaque, mandrill, chimpanzees, and other primates." "It has taken special interviewing techniques to get adults to admit to such experiences, but a considerable portion of the population does record attempts at self-fellation, at least in early adolescence. Only two to three males in a thousand are able to achieve the objective." This estimate was based on a sample of 12,214 American men completing in-depth interviews that required several hours, including one 31-year-old man who depended on self-fellation as his chief masturbatory technique for most of his life (Kinsey, Pomeroy, & Martin, 1948).

Common Sexual Behaviors with Others

Common sexual behaviors with others (Table 12.3) include many forms of pleasuring that many people do not consider "sex." Sexual pleasuring behaviors that you might think of as minor foreplay may actually be a very important (if not essential) aspect of another person's formula for sexual satisfaction and orgasm. For many people, these behaviors are *the* most important aspects of sexual satisfaction as opposed to sexual intercourse. These behaviors include simple things like holding hands, touching your partner's lips, stroking their hair, sensual massage, or sucking a finger! (Remember when holding hands was such a big deal?)

Usually when we think of sex with others, we immediately go to intercourse—what many believe to be the Holy Grail of Sex! There is a reason for this: Heterosexual Americans of all ethnic groups overwhelmingly prefer vaginal intercourse over all other forms of sexual pleasuring. Rumor has it that the Patron Saint of Procreation smiles every time penis meets vagina. Yet America's top preferences for the most appealing sexual relations also include giving/receiving oral sex and watching your partner undress.

Exceedingly popular as well are practices such as masturbating your partner, mutual masturbation, and use of sexual toys and aids. Less frequent but common forms of interpersonal sexual touch include anal eroticism, rubbing vulvas together (tribadism), rubbing boobs together (titty mashing), interfemoral intercourse (penis between the legs), inter-breast intercourse ("titty fucking"), and inter-buttock intercourse (humping).

Uncommon Paraphilic Sexual Behaviors with the Self and Others

Uncommon paraphilic sexual behaviors with the self are a bit more complicated. Let's recall that paraphilias are unusual sexual behaviors often practiced by a person who may experience distress and compulsion about the activity. The official definition of paraphilia is a mental disorder that is characterized by recurrent, intense, sexually arousing fantasies, urges, or behaviors (lasting at least six months) that involve objects or animals, the suffering or humiliation of oneself or a partner, or children or other nonconsenting individuals. Examples of uncommon paraphilic sexual behavior during masturbation include a person who requires either just the fantasy and/or the actual act of the paraphilic object, imagined lover, or activity. This may involve fantasies of (or actual activity) involving pain, fantasies of handling or wearing certain materials (such as lingerie or rubber), or fantasies of certain types of imagined sexual partners, such as a dead person (necrophilia).

Literally, any type of paraphilia can manifest during masturbation through use of fantasy. This includes the many types of paraphilias that are not listed in the official *Diagnostic and Statistical Manual of Mental Disorders* (DSM), which is considered an authoritative guide to mental illnesses published by the American Psychiatric Association (2013). Another type of solitary paraphilic sexual behavior, which is relatively deadly, can be called autoerotic asphyxia. This practice involves (partial) self-strangulation during masturbation in an effort to restrict oxygen supply to the brain to increase the intensity of the climax experience. The self-strangulation is accomplished by a number of mechanical methods (very often using ropes, chains, or cords for partial suspension or hanging) and involves great risk of losing consciousness during the act of masturbation. Estimates of approximately several hundred to about one thousand American youth die this way every year. But adults can die by this manner of asphyxia as well, as it has been reported the actor David Carradine (of *Kung Fu* fame) is thought to have died this way when his body was found hanging naked in a hotel with a rope around his neck and genitals (LeVay, Baldwin, & Baldwin, 2015). The accuracy of these estimates is difficult to determine because of the varied accuracy of the reported cause of death. The cause of death may intentionally (or unintentionally) be ruled a suicide because of the greater stigma to the family of autoerotic asphyxia. What is more taboo than suicide? Suicide by (solo) sex.

Uncommon paraphilic sexual behaviors with others can overlap with the same activities one can do alone. The practice of restricting oxygen supply to the brain during sex can also occur between partners. Obviously, this practice is not recommended and great caution is advised if you partake. You could die, and the other person could be charged with your murder, or the other person dies and you go to jail! These are pretty heavy stakes for a few moments of feeling good. More typical of uncommon paraphilic sexual behaviors between partners is the fairly widespread (worldwide) practice of domination and submission (D/S) and its most common form of bondage and discipline (B&D).

It is important to note that, as with cross-dressing, many couples engage in D/S or B&D activities as a lifestyle or to playfully spice up their sex lives (think pink furry handcuffs). These couples are not necessarily people with a paraphilia. It is the individual who has a strong and enduring preference for this type of sexual expression and has to do it compulsively (at least in fantasy if not in behavior) who is paraphilic.

An extremely damaging paraphilic behavior involving another person is pedophilic disorder because the object of this paraphilia is prepubescent children. It is considered so damaging because of the negative long-term effects on the victims and because of how common it is, with an estimated 1 of 4 females and 1 of 10 males reporting that they had been sexually molested by age 18 (American Psychiatric Association, 2013). Dr. Gene Abel of Emory University, one of the leading authorities on this subject, estimates that men with this one paraphilia (pedophilia) may account for up to a staggering 95% of child molestations (Abel, Wiegel, & Osborn, 2007). Hence, it is particularly important to understand this type of sexual expression, improve current practice of assessment and identification, and innovate better treatment approaches toward a goal of increased prevention of childhood sexual abuse.

Of course, the most dangerous and destructive type of paraphilic behavior involving others is the lust-murderer who serially kills people, in part for sexual gratification. Gary Ridgway, also known as the Green River serial killer, is such an example of this paraphilia. Over a period of 16 years, he killed 48 young women and girls in the Seattle area, mostly by strangling them during sexual encounters. Most of the victims were sex workers and Ridgway was under the delusion he was performing a community service and believed he could kill as many prostitutes as he wanted without getting caught. He avoided the death penalty by agreeing to give police information about the location of the victims' bodies. Fortunately, this type of paraphilia is rare (LeVay, Baldwin, & Baldwin, 2015).

MEDIATORS OF SEXUAL EXPRESSION: BIOCULTURALLY BOUND FACTORS

The expression of our sexual selves is not only directed by our sexual identity and guided by our ideoerotic pattern of pleasure-seeking, but it is also mediated by many factors that are primarily cultural influences yet include some biological factors. It is important to note that both culture and biology are major influences in sexual expression and the formation of sexual identity. Many people think of "identity" as something more internal within us, more biological, and unchanging over time. Many people also think of "expression" as an external experience, demonstrated only in overt behaviors, and completely influenced by culture. As noted previously and to be expanded upon in the next chapter, the hypercube model of sexuality challenges both these notions.

As there are biological and cultural influences upon both identity and expression, they also go back and forth mediating each other. As a component of sexual identity, sex-role orientation is primarily (but not entirely) a cultural phenomenon that is a reflection of the sexual scripts created in a particular society and learned by boys and girls to which they conform. As a component of sexual expression, biological factors such as menopause or other changes to one's physical body (like a mastectomy) can also influence women's sexual expression.

Culturally Bound Mediators of Sexual Expression

Culturally bound mediators of sexual expression are some of the more familiar social influences we think of when considering culture. These cultural factors include, but are not limited to, such things as how society interprets your age, ethnicity and racial identity, religious beliefs, nationality affiliations, linguistic preferences, disability status, socioeconomic status, your particular family history, and your personal sexual developmental history. Age may seem like an unlikely cultural factor as it certainly is a biological process. But it is the culture that produces the general views about how to define someone called a "child" or a "senior." The culture also defines how we treat these members of society and if we give them special protections (from sexual exploitation), restrict their activity (like preventing their own private access to birth control), or give them a discount at the movies or burger joint.

Like sexual fantasies, several of these cultural factors have so many variations that they are too numerous to list if that would even be possible. Disability status literally involves thousands of different types of disease and illness, but they could be enumerated on a finite list (a very long finite list). Nationality and religious affiliations may be in the same boat. What about ethnicity and race? Have the anthropologists ever created an all-inclusive list of types of people? Basic listings have been compiled of the major types of ethnic and racial groupings, but no all-inclusive listing has been achieved or probably ever will. But never say never—as the human genome project may eventually demonstrate.

Also, many of the cultural mediating factors in the e-Cube (such as religion, ethnic, and racial identification) strongly influence your vulnerability to learning and using sexual stereotypes as well as your ability to correct the same stereotypes depending on your family's openness or avoidance to discuss sexuality. To enhance your sexual health literacy, it is necessary to be aware of sexual stereotypes that we may have learned growing up and replace them with accurate, unbiased information from sexual science (Peterson & Peterson, 2007). Some stereotypic assumptions about other people (as well as ourselves) are often hidden from our own awareness in a part of our psyche called the "blind spot" (which is a topic explored at length in Chapter 20).

Let's talk about intersectionality again—the perspective of multiple considerations at the same time in which many different factors can exert influences on our behavior at any given time. With intersectionality, we can understand that we express our sexuality depending on many cross-cutting and simultaneous influences on our behavior. Let's take Joe, for example, a 70-something black gay man. So, what do we have here in our description so far: age, race, sex orientation, and sexual orientation. Just counting these four factors, in what ways would Joe likely be expressing his sexuality? Think about it for a minute. How would these factors influence both sexual identity and sexual expression, as well as influence one another? Would these factors possibly influence how Joe would be in or out of the closet, be married or single, have children or not, live alone or with another person, be in an exclusive relationship or date multiple people? Going beyond those basic four factors, consider the differences in sexual expression if Joe lives in downtown Chicago or Ohio Appalachia, if he is poor or rich, and if he is Muslim or atheist? (Okay, okay—we are just about to retire Joe.)

Biological Mediators of Sexual Expression

Biological mediators of sexual expression include several health factors such as your hormonal status, having a chronic illness, having dramatic changes to your physicality, and, of course, your age. If you consider being a 71-year old Joe for another few moments—your sexual expression might change remarkably if you were actually 20 years old or 20 months old. Yes, babies have sexual expression—although they don't know it yet.

Of course, age also influences hormone levels, as we produce different levels of hormones at different ages until our production levels out as adults before starting a gradual decline in middle age. These changes affect men and women differently. Lowered levels of hormones (especially estrogens) are more dramatic for women as they go through menopause, which can make it more challenging to maintain a general sense of sexual well-being, harder to maintain the thickness and elasticity of the vaginal lining, and more difficult to get and maintain vaginal lubrication. Menopause also means a decrease in the production of hormones for women, and this lowered level can typically be associated with some decline in sexual interest and decreased participation in sexual activity.

Men's decline in testosterone is usually much more gradual than that experienced by women. This is most likely due to the continued production of testosterone by the testes that do not go through such a dramatic shutdown as happens with ovaries. Lower testosterone levels as we age are associated with less interest in sex and how we feel in (and about) our bodies. These changes often include reduced sensitivity of the genitals and nipples, overall reduction in your ability to experience physical arousal, diminished energy levels, gaining weight, and decreased body hair and muscle mass. Those are some serious biological influences on how we see ourselves and how we feel about expressing our sexuality.

Notice we are talking about the effects of aging here, not illness and disability. Do you know some individuals who rarely get sick and others who seem to get sick often? Some folks have more difficulty managing stress and/or have a constitution that is more vulnerable to frequent illness (not disability). Sexuality can be adversely impacted by these biological influences because nothing can make you feel less sexy than feeling crappy. Of course, illnesses can eventually develop into a significant disability. Regarding disability, influences upon sexuality vary tremendously depending on if you were born with the condition (congenital disability) or developed it later in life (acquired disability). The younger you are when you are affected by a disability (loss of sight, hearing, or body part), the more impact it has on your developing sexual identity and expression. However, there is also greater possibility and likelihood for adaptation and finding paths to positive sexual identity, expression, and satisfaction.

Biological mediators are not limited to the effects of aging or changing hormone levels. Mastectomy was mentioned earlier and while often secondary to breast cancer, there are other causes. The same is true for orchiectomies (removal of one or more of the testicles). It is very unfortunate when a woman loses a breast (say by cancer) or a man loses one of his testicles. Yet, this type of loss affects a person in a different way than losing an arm, foot, or sensory organ would because it may have a strongly negative influence on one's sexual expression. Such effects may include greater isolation secondary to inhibiting one's sense of confidence regarding being with others. Strong and supportive relationships can buffer us from the adverse effects of serious injury or changes in our body image. Although loss of a breast or testicle always has a serious impact on a person, people with positive and supportive partners can experience these events more often as a life transition rather than a life crisis.

THE SEXUAL TIPPING POINT

Discussion of sexual expression would be incomplete without including explanation of the sexual tipping point (STP) model, which is an amazingly sophisticated description of how individuals decide to either initiate or suppress their own sexual behavior. The STP model serves as an individual example of sexual expression that complements the general model presented in the Sexual Expression Cube (e-Cube). This model enumerates and details the specific mechanisms (both intrapersonal and interpersonal) that result in the sexual behaviors represented in the e-Cube. The e-Cube emphasizes the diversity of sexual fantasy and behaviors that humans demonstrate. The STP model is more descriptive of the specific means by which sexual expression is accomplished. In addition, the STP model includes much overlap with the biocultural mediators of sexual expression, which are referred to as biosocial-cultural factors that can either promote sexual expression (accepting an invitation to an orgy) or suppress sexual expression (living in a political system that criminalizes same-sex expression). Therefore, the combination of the identity and expression cubes (represented by the hypercube model and emphasizing the diversity of human sexuality) are complemented by the STP model that represents what is happening on an individual basis. Each model alone is based on the leading sexual science research of the past several decades and together represents the most comprehensive explanation of human sexual diversity and interaction.

The STP model was developed over the past four decades beginning with the pioneer sexologist Helen Kaplan and her first book, *The New Sex Therapy* (Kaplan, 1974). Kaplan was a contemporary of William Masters and Virginia Johnson and, as a psychoanalytic psychiatrist, had a different perspective from Masters's point of view as an obstetrician, gynecologist, and reproductive researcher. Kaplan modified Masters and Johnson's two-week pioneering residential program, and her book became the standard text for many students across several disciplines. As a result, it had a national impact on where and how people were treated for sexual problems for several decades.

Kaplan was known for expanding the role that sexual desire (motivation) plays in sexual inter-action—something thought lacking in the more physiological four-stage model of Masters and Johnson. Kaplan expanded their model by emphasizing multilevel causality in sex therapy and popularized her "Kaplan model" by collaboration with many of her students, who later became leaders in the field of clinical sex therapy (Perelman, 2014). In her final book (1995), she describes a psychosomatic (mind-body) dual-control model of sexual motivation emphasizing "inhibition/excitation" processes that is the heart of the STP model. She acknowledged borrowing from the work of Kupferman (1991), who wrote, "All examples of physiological motivational control seem to involve dual effects—inhibitory and excitatory—which function together to adjust the system" (p. 751). Similar to the dual sets of inhibiting and stimulating mechanisms that regulate body temperature, Kaplan (and her collaborators) applied this perspective to the TSP model in a sort of force-field analysis with the "let's get it on" factors on one side and "I'd rather not" factors on the other. These factors can actually be the same factors (such as testosterone), but differing levels of the hormone with sufficient or high levels promoting a "let's get it on" state of mind and insufficient (low) levels effecting the "I'd rather not" inhibiting influence.

The "let's get it on" mechanisms involved in the initiation of sexual behavior include both phys-iological and psychological factors. Physiological factors include adequate testosterone levels, use of aphrodisiac drugs, physical/genital stimulation (of sufficient duration and intensity), whereas psychological factors include positive attraction to a potential sexual partner, high erotic (seductive) stimulation, fantasy, feeling of being in love, and welcomed courtship rituals.

The "I'd rather not" suppressant factors also have both physiological and psychological factors (as explained above) and are many of the same variables but with inadequate levels or a negative valence. These suppressant factors include hormone disorders (such as hypogonadism), negative sexual side effects from medications (or other substance use), and the physiological aspects of mood disorders (such as clinical depression). The "I'd rather not" suppressant factors of a psychosocial nature include not having sufficient attraction to a potential sexual partner, negative fantasies about the potential sexual encounter, negative emotions such as fear or anger, and not being able to relax (too much anxiety) to respond.

In the STP model, all these inhibitory and exciting factors get weighed against each other simultaneously in the hypothalamic and limbic sex-regulating centers of the brain resulting in one of three outcomes: (1) excitation state of being and sexual readiness (let's get it on); (2) an inhibited state of sexual unreadiness (or resistance—"I'd rather not"); or (3) a neutral state of approximate sexual equilibrium. In the most recent versions of the STP model, these three outcomes are represented by Hot (on), Not (off), or Neutral terms of getting your sexual motor running. Of course, this is all going on within the individual in terms of their level of sexual motivation to pursue or avoid sexual engagement. In a sense, the STP model indicates the likelihood of the sexual encounter (or solo activity) actually occurring based on one individual's experience as well as considering some external factors. There are many more external factors involved that may come into play, such as if the person is aroused by sexual fantasy but restricted by lack of access to his object of sexual desire (such as being alone in a prison cell).

In the impressive further development of the STP model since Kaplan was directly involved (she died in 1995), Perelman and other researchers have included consideration of "all factors, known and unknown" which may have a bearing on "the mix" within the hypothalamic and limbic sex-regulating centers mentioned above and the resulting outcomes of sexual readiness, inhibition, or neutrality. Perelman's evolution of the STP model provides a valuable guideline for clinicians who wrestle with considerations of all the intrapersonal and interpersonal variables of their clients' sexual function/dysfunction. Perelman (rightfully so) considers the STP model as the characteristic threshold for an expression of a given sexual response in any given set of circumstances. Besides illustrating normal sexual balance, the STP concept is particularly useful for modeling treatment when things are not going so well and can be used to explain the benefits and risks of treatment options for those with sexual disorders. Teaching the STP model to the patient and partner can reduce despair and anger, while providing hope through a simple explanation of how the problem's causes can be diagnosed, parsed, and "fixed" (Perelman, 2006, 2009).

Aside from its clinical utility assisting those with sexual health concerns, the graphics of the STP model have evolved to very sophisticated visuals that have contributed to popularizing the model over the past 20 years. Perelman reports that in 2013, the STP trademark registration was assigned to the MAP Education & Research Fund, Inc., so that STP resources could be distributed worldwide for free. Today's more sophisticated and nuanced figures feature "building blocks" that can be used to assemble unique representations of any given individual's STP at a particular moment in time. Key STP images as well as fully narrated video descriptions of the STP model may be found on YouTube and Vimeo channels. You are encouraged to pursue any curiosity regarding the STP model and learn more about this important model by visiting the following resources (https://www.youtube.com/watch?v=1HUCTf_g78g and www.mapedfund.org/history/) or reading noted references by Michael Perelman at the end of this chapter.

AS THIS CHAPTER CONCLUDES

Remember Joe? He's still waiting to retire, but let's give him some fun on the way out by considering the application of intersectionality once more as well as the STP model. This will allow him (and us) to consider the infinite—always a blast (Joe loves learning about the cosmos). Remember, Joe's description included factors from both the Sexual Identity Cube (sex orientation of being designated as a man and sexual orientation of being attracted to men) as well as the Sexual Expression Cube (age and ethnicity/racial identification). Consider the three major dimensions of sexual identity and the three major dimensions of sexual expression. With the considerations that we know and the considerations we do not know, do we really know Joe beyond stereotyped images and beliefs that come to mind? Do we know the most important questions to consider to really know Joe and appreciate him as a unique human sexual being? We already asked a few questions earlier when we introduced Joe but still may be wondering:

- Is Joe in or out of the closet?
- Is he single or married, and to whom?
- Does Joe have children or not?
- Does he live alone or with another person—man, woman, or both?
- Is Joe in an exclusive relationship or does he date multiple people?
- Does he live in downtown Chicago or Ohio Appalachia?
- Is he wealthy, middle class, working class, or poor?

Now consider that each of the basic factors contained within the STP model as well as the i-Cube and e-Cube are all interactive, and the number of possible interactions regarding how Joe expresses his sexual self is greatly expanded. There are now a few additional questions that arise that could help us get to know Joe better:

- What are Joe's inhibiting and excitatory influences (per the STP model) such as his level of bioavailable free testosterone?
- What is the outcome of these factors' interaction (readiness, resistance, or neutrality for initiating sex)?
- How does Joe self-identify his sex orientation—is it different from male?
- How does Joe self-identify his sexual orientation—is it different from "gay?"
- How does Joe self-identify his sex-role orientation?
- Is Joe influenced by religious beliefs?
- Is there any conflict between Joe's spirituality and sexuality?
- What kind of sexual fantasy does Joe actively enjoy?
- How does Joe identify his ethnicity and race status?
- Does Joe have a light, medium, or dark complexion?
- What medical conditions does Joe get treated for by his health care system (which happens to be the VA)?

- How does his amputation for combat injuries in Vietnam influence his sexual self-image?
- Does Joe use any sex-enhancement medications (such as Viagra) or aphrodisiac drugs intended to intensify his sexual experience?
- Does Joe have any adverse sexual side effects from any medications he is prescribed or recreational drugs he may use?
- Is Joe able to enjoy what he considers highly erotic stimulation and fantasy?

The list of questions goes on and on in terms of how to help oneself really appreciate the unique individual that people call Joe (as opposed to relying on stereotypes and assumptions). You see, Joe is a real man with real losses and dreams and people who love him. Most of the time, people see Joe and don't think too much about him. They just pass him on the street or in the hospital hallways and barely notice him except for his effort to be visible and simply be acknowledged by others.

Folks don't know he was terribly misused as a child and grew up with so much chaos that he never learned to read and write past a sixth-grade level but joined the Army to serve his country. Most folks, even some of his family, don't know that he earned a Purple Heart from injuries carrying two fellow soldiers out of a firefight. He doesn't like to talk about that. Most folks don't know he came back from Vietnam and started his own business to raise a family and at the same time hide his illiteracy. Most folks don't know how he truly loved a woman who was the mother of his children for decades before he lost her to cancer. Most folks don't know that to Joe's surprise (and everybody else in his family), in time he fell in love again.

Mostly people see an old African American man shuffling past them, looking them in the eye, and tipping his head with a smile. Thanks Joe, you've done well! You have served your country and had a full life. You have also led us to the Sexual Hypercube—the subject of the infamous Chapter 13! You can finally enjoy your retirement watching all the science shows you want about the universe and fourth dimension while tipping your hat in appreciation of your favorite astronomer, Carl Sagan.

REFERENCES

Abel, G., Wiegel, M., & Osborn, C. (2007). Pedophilia and other paraphilia. In L. VanderCreek, F. Peterson, & J. Bley (Eds.), *Innovations in clinical practice: Focus on sexual health.* Sarasota, FL: Professional Resource Press.

American Psychiatric Association [APA]. (2013). *Diagnostic and statistical manual of mental disorders* (5th ed.). Arlington, VA: American Psychiatric Publishing.

Blum, D. (2002). *Love at Goon Park: Harry Harlow and the science of affection.* New York: Perseus.

Carroll, J. (2007). *Sexuality now: Embracing diversity* (2nd ed.). Belmont, CA: Thomson Wadsworth.

Dawson, S., Suschinsky, K., & Lalumière, M. (2012). Sexual fantasies and viewing time across the menstrual cycle: A dairy study. *Archives of Sexual Behavior, 41,* 173–183.

Diamond, L. (2008). *Sexual fluidity: Understanding women's love and desire.* Cambridge, MA: Harvard University Press.

Kaplan, H. (1974). *The new sexual health.* New York: Brunner/Mazel.

Kinsey, A., Pomeroy, W., & Martin, C. (1948). *Sexual behavior in the human male.* Philadelphia: W.B. Saunders.

Kupferman, I. (1991). Hypothalamus and limbic system motivation. In E.R. Kandel, J.H. Schwartz, & T.M. Jessell (Eds.), *Principle of neural science* (3rd ed.). New York: Elsevier.

LeVay, S., Baldwin, J., & Baldwin, J. (2015). *Discovering human sexuality* (3rd ed.). Sunderland, MA: Sinauer Associates.

Litin, S. (2009). *Mayo Clinic family health book.* Des Moines, IA: Time Home Entertainment.

Masters, W., Johnson, V., & Kolodny, R. (1995). *Human sexuality* (5th ed.). New York: Harper-Collins.

Money, J. (1986). *Lovemaps: Clinical concepts of sexual/erotic health and pathology, paraphilia, and gender transposition in childhood, adolescence, and maturity.* New York: Irvington.

Money, J. (1994). *Reinterpreting the unspeakable.* New York: Continuum.

Perelman, M. (2006). The sexual tipping point: A model to conceptualize etiology, diagnosis and combination treatment of female and male sexual dysfunction. *Journal of Sexual Medicine*, 3 (Suppl. 1), 52.

Perelman, M. (2009). The sexual tipping point: A mind/body model for sexual medicine. *Journal of Sexual Medicine, 6*(3), 629–632.

Perelman, M. (2014). The history of sexual medicine. In APA History of Sexuality and Psychology, Vol. II: Contextual Approaches (pp. 137–179). Washington, DC: American Psychological Association.

Peterson, F., & Peterson, C. (2007). A healthcare professional's guide to contemporary sexual myths. In L. VanderCreek, F. Peterson, & J. Bley (Eds.), *Innovations in clinical practice: Focus on sexual health.* Sarasota, FL: Professional Resource Press.

Santos-Iglesias, P., Sierra, J.C., & Vallejo-Medina, P. (2013). Predictors of sexual assertiveness: The role of sexual desire, arousal, attitudes, and partner abuse. *Archives of Sexual Behavior, 42*, 1043–1052.

Strong, B., DeVault, S., Sayad, B., & Yarber, W. (2005). *Human sexuality: Diversity in contemporary America* (5th ed.). Boston: McGraw-Hill.

Yarber, W., & Sayad, B. (2019). *Human sexuality: Diversity in contemporary society* (10th ed.). New York: McGraw-Hill Education.

CHAPTER THIRTEEN

Sex and the Fourth Dimension:

THE SEXUAL HYPERCUBE

Written by Frederick Peterson

INTRODUCTION

If we combine the three-dimensional Sexual Identity Cube (i-Cube) with the three-dimensional Sexual Expression Cube (e-Cube), then you have a model of sexual interaction describing much of human sexuality! This world of sexual possibilities is captured within a model called the "Sexual Hypercube" (hypercube, or h-Cube), illustrating an incredible mutually influencing relationship between sexual identity and sexual expression. The Sexual Hypercube is a theoretical model that accounts for the amazing diversity of human sexuality and, as argued in this chapter, helps explain why and how we humans change our sexual identity and expression from one stage of life to another.

As you read this chapter, please consider a key question: Will any significant relationships in your life dissolve to nothingness over time without expanding your knowledge about the Sexual Hypercube? Probably not. If you are confident you understand how your sexual identity and expression influence each other, and you know (and practice) your sexual rights—then you probably don't need to read this chapter. However, it may be hard to resist—who doesn't want to know what a Sexual Hypercube is and be able to talk about it at your next party! Maybe it will be the next great thing in pick-up lines: *Didn't I see you last weekend at the hypercube?* (it does sound like a swinging dance club). Alternatively, maybe coming off as the sexual science nerd might work with the girls at the science club social.

It's fair if you have concluded by now that the authors are either wannabe mad scientists or clinicians with a far different perspective on this whole sexuality thing. You could be correct on each count. After all, a hypercube model borrowed from the fourth dimension does sound a bit nutty. Valid criticisms could be: Can't you just explain human sexuality in the same three dimensions that we live in? How do you expect to explain a four-dimensional concept within a three-dimensional world, especially in two-dimensional representation (print)?

Before getting into the details of the Sexual Hypercube, let's make a few clarifications. We are first and foremost clinicians and teachers in the field of sexual health and sex education who sit and listen to people's sexual stories for a living. We are not by any means mathematicians, research scientists, or Rhodes scholars. Fortunately, you don't need to be a clinician to understand human sexuality from the different perspectives presented in this chapter. Secondly, there will not be any attempts to teach everything there is about hypercubes as this is a book about sex, not geometric modeling. The hypercube as a model is employed for its ability to visually represent concepts and relationships that have been discussed in the last two chapters. There will be no attempt to explain the connectivity of every human sexual possibility. That will be left to academic scholars whose dissertations compete for the Stephen Hawking of Sexuality Award. Therefore, with all due respect (and apologies) to my colleagues in the math and physics departments, the rules of applied mathematics have little bearing on the forthcoming explanation of the hypercube, just as the ordinary laws of physics do not apply either (at least in a three-dimensional world).

Having said that, there is a little background on this thing called "the fourth dimension" that is both interesting and helpful to our discussion of using a hypercube as a model for sexuality. Back to the question: *Can't you just explain human sexuality in the same three dimensions that we live in? Why a hypercube as the model?* It just comes down to this: There may be sexual science scholars who have the knowledge and/or creativity to know and/or imagine an excellent three-dimensional model of how sexual identity and sexual expression relate to each other. We are not three of them. The closest three-dimensional model is the concept of organic symbiosis, but it has its own limitations, which illustrates an earlier point that is worth repeating again. The sexual hypercube model presented in this book is certainly not the only general model of human sexuality.

However, as we shall see, there are some advantages of moving to higher dimensions to gain additional perspective and understanding complex phenomena. Take combat of yesteryear, for example. Say you are in the midst of a bloody battlefield wielding your sword or ax. Perhaps you have your closest friend with you back-to-back, a man you would (and may) die to defend. While he covers what is behind you, all you can see is the next enemy running toward you with a spear or saber and all you have are seconds to kill or be killed. You are doing your best to survive the battle; you really do not have much idea of what else is going on beyond your immediate proximity. And so, one of the first rules developed regarding war was to win the higher ground (when available).

In a sense, the higher ground provides a shift in perspective from a relatively two-dimensional "flat" fighting space for the individual to a more three-dimensional perspective the general has who is safely sitting on his horse on the hilltop. The elevation of perspective gives distinct advantage to allow movement of troops for a decisive win or make retreat to fight another day. Even though we may not be able to travel to the fourth dimension physically (at least in the foreseeable future), borrowing concepts from higher dimensions can (and often does in math and physics) provide additional and valuable perspectives to explain the phenomena that we do see in our three-dimensional world.

THE FOURTH DIMENSION, HYPERSPACE, AND THE SEXUAL HYPERCUBE

Some Interesting Background

The idea of a fourth dimension has been around for over a century and, for purposes of discussion here, does not refer to the notion of time being the fourth dimension. In our three-dimensional world (beyond length, width, and height), height refers to how *high or low* we consider the third dimension, which is *vertical*. When looking for an address of a friend, we typically think of a two-dimensional grid by which we can find a location (a map is a representation of this two-dimensional grid). But what if the friend you are seeking does not live on a farm but lives in a condo on the 35th floor of a skyscraper. Then we need to operate in a three-dimensional concept of the world. Of course, we need not only physical coordinates to locate our friend but *temporal* coordinates as well. We need to be in the same physical space as well as the same temporal space to enjoy lunch with our friend. In some ways, this all seems so commonsense. But until the beginning of the 20th century (1905, to be precise), time and space were scientifically considered separate entities.

The notion of time as the fourth dimension was most notably employed by Albert Einstein to link time and space together within his model of the space-time continuum. His theory of special relativity and discovery of the mathematical equation ($E = MC^2$) to explain the space-time continuum is widely considered the most important scientific advancement of the 20th century. However, time is not what we are talking about here. When using the term *fourth dimension* in the title of this chapter, we are referring to a spatial concept that our three-dimensional brains have great difficulty visualizing. Yes, Einstein forever integrated space and time together scientifically. Hence, some consider time the fourth dimension and any additional spatial dimension the fifth dimension. But for the purposes of this chapter, when you read *fourth dimension*—reference is being made to the fourth spatial dimension.

Can you imagine the mind of a person who was the first to come up with the idea that there are additional visual and geometric dimensions beyond what our perception allows? This was the mind of Charles Hinton, a British mathematician and science-fiction writer who came to the United States to teach mathematics and later worked at the U.S. Naval Observatory. Like Einstein, Hinton was a mathematician who also worked at the patent office. He was an eccentric and fascinating character who was jailed at one time for bigamy and, while teaching mathematics at Princeton University, invented the first pitching machine for the college baseball team. Hinton is credited for coining the term *tesseract* as another name for a hypercube in his book *A New Era of Thought* (1888).

It is fascinating when something old becomes forgotten in popular culture and then resurfaces again to enjoy another period of popularity. This is actually the case with the concept of the fourth dimension. After Hinton's publication, many authors started to jump on the "fourth-dimensional bandwagon" and the topic began to be a matter of general speculation and discussion at social gatherings for a 30-year period between 1890 and around World War I. People exchanged ideas about the fourth dimension possibly being the location of heaven, angels, demons, extraterrestrials, and so on.

One century later, the fourth dimension is popular again. Haven't heard anyone talking about it lately? Try doing an Internet search for scientific articles and books about the fourth dimension. You will find Michio Kaku, who is a leading theoretical physicist based at the City College of New York and has written much to popularize the concept of the fourth dimension in recent years. In his book *Hyperspace* (1994), he explains the history of the late-19th-century popular fascination with the fourth dimension, claiming it was very influential in literature and the arts. In literature and especially science fiction, Kaku cites the significant impact the fourth dimension had on author H.G. Wells. In the arts, the fourth dimension had significant impact on expressionism and cubism, including Pablo Picasso and Salvador Dali.

Admittedly, hypercubes and higher dimensions are not typically part of common public discourse these days (at least not since the popularity of the 1960s singing group, the Fifth Dimension). I was on my way to give a lecture at an institute of technology awhile back and I had dinner with one of my daughters the night before. She is an amazing elementary school teacher with an advanced degree dedicated to public school Montessori education but was not familiar with the fourth dimension. After she inquired about the next day's address and hearing my explanation, she responded with some constructive feedback by saying, "That sounds really interesting, Dad. I am sure you will be a hit but maybe you ought to reconsider including that last part." I asked, "What last part—the hypercube and the fourth dimension?" "Right!" she said. "I wouldn't want them to disregard all the good information you are sharing by hearing about that higher dimensional stuff and think you're a kook! I responded, "Wow—that is very helpful! Remember my audience—they are at an institute of technology. Let's do an experiment. Do you know any friends who are mathematicians or physicists?" I asked. She did and agreed to ask the husband of her girlfriend about the fourth dimension (the husband was getting his doctorate in physics). A few days later, I called her up and asked what the physicist had to say. She laughed and responded, "He said, 'fourth dimension? Boring! We are already working on the eleventh!'"

THE SEXUAL HYPERCUBE MODEL

The Sexual Hypercube (h-Cube) is a four-dimensional conceptual model of human sexuality that combines the three-dimensional Sexual Identity Cube (i-Cube) with the three-dimensional Sexual Expression Cube (e-Cube) to describe the reciprocal influences between the two and provide a foundation for understanding the wide-ranging diversity inherent in human sexuality. A hypercube is one type of many geometrical models in the fourth dimension and can theoretically exist in other higher dimensions as well. So far, what we have discussed regarding "cubes" is a Sexual Identity Cube (i-Cube) and a Sexual Expression Cube (e-Cube). As you will see, the hypercube of the fourth dimension is a model that puts these two cubes in relationship to each other in a very dynamic and animated way.

At its core, the h-Cube is a teaching tool; its utility is as an aid to communication about sexuality in general and sexual health in particular. As previously noted, there is much to discover in understanding basic concepts of human sexuality. The h-Cube is one model that defines these basic concepts, describes their relationship to each other, and in doing so, gives a snapshot of the "big picture" representing the complexity of sexuality. Based on discussions with students, the h-Cube is relatively easy for most people to grasp (after all, we are not talking about the Higgs Boson of particle physics).

However, the h-Cube model is a bit different from what most of us have been exposed to because it is a four-dimensional model and we live in a three-dimensional world. As a result of its unfamiliarity, it may seem a bit mind-blowing the first time you see a hypercube in action. However, the potential benefit of applying such a model to sexuality is that it can help those struggling to understand their sexuality find where they fit in the world, assist them in becoming more accepting of themselves, and feel more comfortable with their sexuality as well as the sexuality of others. As noted, the h-Cube is simply one model (among others) to help us figure out this whole sex thing. Enough clarification; let's get into the details.

The h-Cube we are going to focus on is a four-dimensional model (analog) of the regular three-dimensional cube. To better understand the whole four-dimensional aspect of this, please consider the following relationship. *The hypercube is to a regular cube as a regular cube is to the square.* In a sense, a square (in two dimensions of length and width) can simply be expanded or "folded out" into a cube of three dimensions (length, width, and height). In turn, the three-dimensional cube can be expanded (folded out) to a four-dimensional hypercube (length, width, height, and kata—the last term is described below).

If we were an animal that perceived the world only in two dimensions (say, like the protozoa), then we would only consider moving left, right, diagonally, forward, or backward. If we could consider it though, we (as protozoa) would never think, "Hey everybody, let's go up there!" Living in a world in which we see three dimensions, humans have similar difficulty thinking about additional dimensions in which to see the world. For example, few people have ever heard of the word *kata* used as a spatial dimension or direction and would not understand instructions to "move kata" like most people would understand instructions to "duck" or "come up here." Kata and anana are names of two additional directions in the fourth dimension (also described by Hinton in *A New Era of Thought*).

Hypercubes can theoretically exist in many dimensions, and some astrophysicists believe the cosmos needs at least four spatial dimensions to be described accurately. Some cosmologists (especially those who subscribe to string theory) believe there must be more than three dimensions; otherwise their mathematical equations of the universe do not work. Four-dimensional hypercubes are referred to by several names; probably the most common is *tesseract*. Essentially, the four-dimensional hypercube is an equal-sided cube within another equal-sided cube that has correlating and parallel lines (as in Figure 13.1). Notice that each corner (or vertex) of the outer cube is connected to the corresponding corner of the inner cube. To the three-dimensional human brain, this type of illustration causes an optical illusion of shifting perspectives.

The purpose of this brief technical description of the hypercube is to build an analog model of how the components of the sexual identity and expression cubes relate to one another. An analog model represents data by means of one or more physical properties and can express any value along a continuous scale (much like the positions of hands on a clock are considered an analog representation of time). Time is a continuous scale that can be divided by many different units of measurement, such as 3,600 seconds in an hour or by the convention of 12 numbers around the face of a traditional

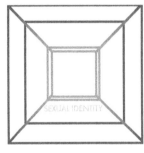

SEXUAL EXPRESSION

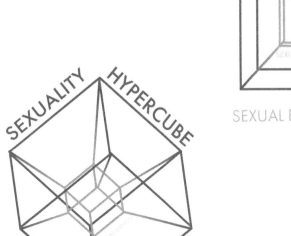

FIGURE 13.1 The Sexual Hypercube (Illustrated by Max Fleishman)

clock representing 12 units of 5 minutes, each equaling an hour. These two units of analog measurement (3,600 seconds and one hour) are considered equal in quantity of time.

This point is particularly important relative to the sexual cubes. The Sexual Identity Cube appears to be divided into 4×4×4 line segments limited to four sections. These divisions are artificial, as each dimension can be organized on a continuum, with points on the continuum designating four or a million units of measurement (just like the analog of the clock measuring an hour by 3,600 seconds or by one movement of the hour hand). So, the "four" designations of sex orientation (male, female, transgender intersex, or transgender psychosocial) could alternatively be measured by one thousand points ranging from a completely masculinized body to a completely feminized body.

The same can be said for the Sexual Expression Cube (e-Cube); it's all how you divide it up. Let's use another brief example: your pinky finger. If you bend it, you see it divides into three sections between the base knuckle (this first large knuckle closest to the palm of your hand) and the tip of the digit. So, you could say these sections represent three different parts of your finger. You could also count the number of skin cells in a straight line between your base knuckle and the tip of your pinky. This second form of measurement renders thousands of points along a continuum. Both measurements are accurate, and they represent the same length of space.

Where the expression cube looks like a fuzzy cube, consider it as the same dimensions as the identity cube. Consider the lengths of corresponding and parallel line segments in the expression cube and the identity cube to be equal. For example, the line in the identity cube representing sex orientation (divided into four segments) would be considered the same dimensions of the line in the Sexual Expression Cube representing sexual fantasy, even if the latter line segment may have thousands of points representing different varieties of sexual fantasy.

Therefore, there are three important considerations to remember in understanding the Sexual Hypercube (Figure 13.1). First, as just described, any given line in either the identity cube or the expression cube can be measured differently but represents equal dimensions. The line can be measured using few divisions (four segments, as with sex orientation) or thousands of divisions (as with sexual fantasy), yet are equal. This is the concept of measuring the pinky by sections of the finger or number of skin cells.

Second, each line in both the identity cube and expression cube can expand or contract depending on a multitude of factors. Staying with the anatomical metaphor, you can extend your pinky finger or pull its tip back to touch the base of the finger. When your pinky is fully extended, it is about three times the length as when it is contracted. Perhaps better anatomical symbols would be erectile tissue, such as erectile bodies found within the clitoris and penis.

Third, this is the wild thing. Are you ready for the wild thing? The wild thing is that the hypercube moves! Imagine turning a flip book of the h-Cube and watching it create a simulation of perpetual movement. As the h-Cube moves, the smaller inner cube of the hypercube (identity) expands outward and envelops the once-larger outer cube (expression). Now the inner cube of identity becomes the outer, and the former outer cube (expression) becomes the smaller one in the center of the hypercube! Then the process continues with constant reversals. The movement represents how the h-Cube is dynamic, interactive, and synergistic.

Beside a flip-book simulation taking up the next 30 pages, another engaging way to demonstrate the reciprocal nature of the h-Cube (that is also beyond the present publishing possibilities) is to imagine the scene from *Star Wars* when the Rebel leaders assemble in their War Room around a rotating hologram to plan an attack against the Death Star. Someday, I hope to have a similar hologram of the Sexual Hypercube to rotate and peer inside to explain to students the many sexual identities contained within. Until then, the next best option is to view a sophisticated simulation of hypercube movement by googling any of the readily available "animated hypercube" videos on the Internet. It is a very cool visual experience of your 3-D brain viewing a representation from the fourth dimension. *That* is the wild thing!

APPLICATION OF THE SEXUAL HYPERCUBE MODEL

The detailed explanations of terms and concepts discussed in this book so far were all necessary to get to this point: How the h-Cube works! Conceptually, the dynamic interactive nature of the movement of the h-Cube reflects how the elements of the i-Cube and the e-Cube influence each other. For practical application of the inter-workings of the h-Cube, we will examine the sexual development process during two stages of life, adolescence/young adulthood and later life.

The Sexual Hypercube Feedback Loop in Adolescence/Young Adulthood

One of the two major tasks of adolescence is establishing a sexual identity, which usually (but not always) involves initiating sexual experiences with others (expression). The other major developmental task is establishing autonomy and independence from parents. For the fortunate few, forming a sexual identity and establishing sexual activity seems to be completely programmed, is accomplished without any conscious planning, and takes as much effort as breathing. For the rest of us, adolescence is a struggle with major insecurities and paralyzing confusion over what the whole sex thing is about. Most adolescents essentially fumble their way through this stage of life trying to preserve any shred of dignity. Alas, many of us did well simply not to succumb to our private anxieties (or the sheer terror) of being the gangly awkward creatures we were.

Therefore, the key processes involved in adolescent sexual development are sexual maturation (involving physical changes of puberty), psychological processing of changes to the body (involving emotional responses to physical changes), sexual experimentation (involving masturbation and often sexual behaviors with others), and self-identification (involving the beginnings of self-attribution and self-labeling). The process of sexual identity development is complex (as reflected in the many influencing factors of the i-Cube) and can occur over the course of one or two decades. Sexual identity results from the biological, psychological, and social variables (discussed in Chapter 11) but is strongly influenced by the other two key processes of adolescent sexual development: self-exploration and sexual experimentation.

Self-exploration is confusing regarding the sexual metamorphosis of our bodies and, of course, also occurs over a long course of time. The process of sexual experimentation and expression with others can be confusing because of the process of trial-and-error. The key point here is that the feedback loop between our sexual identity and our sexual expression is a core and essential part of the developmental growth process. Of course, our developing sexual identity has strong and direct influence on how we express ourselves sexually and to whom. However, the way we see ourselves sexually (identity) is also determined, at least in part, by our self-exploration and the sexual experiences we have with others (expression).

Let's use a person's identification as being lesbian or gay, for example (as a reminder, this is not a person's full sexual identity, just a pattern of sexual attraction). In retrospect, many individuals who identify as lesbian or gay knew from a very early age that they were not attracted heterosexually. Many closeted themselves for protection and self-preservation (depending on the environment). Other individuals took years to develop a self-awareness of being lesbian or gay (bisexual as well) and slowly came to the conclusion through different sexual experiences.

In her book *Sexual Fluidity: Understanding Women's Love and Desire*, Diamond describes the greater fluidity of female sexuality when she found that 1 of 4 young women she studied (over a period of 10 years) spent some time in same-sex relationships. She described popular terms to capture these developmental explorations, such as "heteroflexibility," "has-bian," and "LUG" (lesbian until graduation) (Diamond, 2008). Sometimes after periods of same-sex experimentation, individuals settle into long-term heterosexual patterns. One way to understand these phenomena is to consider them a reflection of a feedback loop process with interactive influences between sexual identity and sexual expression.

The lack of sexual expression (both solo and socially) can essentially disable the feedback loop during the developmental stages of youth and slow down the movement of the Sexual Hypercube. Consequently, the delay (especially absence) of sexual expression handicaps the development of a confident sense of sexual identity and may make achieving sexual satisfaction more challenging (especially interpersonally). As seen in the sexual health clinic, individuals with the least amount of experience with masturbation (and especially a complete lack of it) tend to have the most difficulty achieving personal sexual satisfaction in relationships. It is very common for women with problems of sexual desire, arousal, and climax with their partner to report that they seldom or never masturbate. This scenario most often represents a lack of effective feedback looping within the dimensions of sexual expression, and on occasion reflects a lack of feedback looping between identity and expression as well.

The following story shows another pathway for the development of sexual identity. Brett's feedback loop for development of his sexual identity appears to have been set very early. He is clear of his identity by an early age and the feedback loop between identity and expression just seemed to reinforce his sexual identity, straight through adolescence into his 50s. This is the story of a loud and proud, self-proclaimed sissy-boy.

Featured Stories of Diverse Perspectives and Experiences

NOW YOU SEE ME AND I RUN—BRETT AND ROLAND
Written by Richelle Frabotta

I remember the very first time someone called me a sissy boy. I was 5 years old and wearing my mother's lipstick, Peachy Pink, in a 'not-so-stay-in-the-lines kinda' way. I love that color. My Mom shared with me a decade later that she thought the Fuchsia Gloss went better with my skin tone and my purple sparkly sequined knee-high zipper boots. I love those boots.

As a matter of record, I still have a pair of those boots. As my feet grew, I'd get a new pair in my bigger size. My parents thought it a good idea that I not wear them to church or the grocery store or to my friends' birthday parties, but I vehemently disagreed. My older brother told me that if I wore the boots, I should be prepared to run in them. I didn't understand. March in them, twirl, high kick?? Sure, yes, can do! But no need to run in them.

Let me be clear: I *am* a sissy boy. I was at age 5 and I am at age 55. No apologies. It seems that running has never been my way.

When my purple boots and I wanted to strut around outside of the safety of home, my brother would make it an issue. He'd do his best to dissuade me; punch me in the arm, even. Really hard. I'd burst into tears, drop to the floor, and remain traumatized in a heap until my Mother put me back together with hugs, kisses, promises of a new lipstick, and unconditional love. I never ran. My brother walked away, shaking his head and muttering under his breath every time, for years.

We'd go 'round and 'round verbally until it ended up in fisticuffs. I seemed to know exactly what to say that would infuriate him. My words were weapons. I could never understand why he seemed to enjoy hurting me so. Bloody lips, black eyes, bruised knuckles were his comfort zone it seemed. Neither of us ever ran and I think, ultimately, he respected me for it.

One day, it happened. I stopped using words and caught him in the chin with a left hook that left him dazed and shaking his head. I thought he was going to kill me. I was so scared I forgot to drop to the ground and cry. I just stood there. He got his wits about him quickly and let loose with the biggest whoop and "hellllllllyeahhhh" I'd ever heard. He grabbed me by both shoulders and I stiffened like a board. He brought me into his chest; into the biggest hug I've ever had to this day. He clapped me on the back with enthusiasm and started saying the best and most affirming statements.

We were definitely having a moment, but I was clueless. Once I got air back in my lungs, I gently spoke up and inquired as to his major mood shift. He explained it to me:

"Brett, my favorite brother (I was his only brother), I've been so hard on you because I know you don't run. You have to learn how to hit back. You just did that, brother!!"

"I don't want to hit back. My knuckles are turning red and hurt already. This sucks."

"Brett, someday when you're walking—the way that you walk—down a strange street in a big city, somebody is going to beat you up. You've got to butch it up! I don't want you to die."

"But I'm not going to change. You've known me all these years and I haven't changed yet. No one is going to cage who I am!"

Clearly, my brother and I had a contentious relationship until that moment when I finally understood what he was trying to accomplish. I loved him for caring about me . . . even though our fights did not feel like "caring." He really was trying to help me navigate a world where sissy boys like me are often targets. My big brother was my tormentor and my protector.

He left home at 18 to join the Marines. I won't lie: I was both elated and devastated that he left. Being 5 years younger, 87 pounds lighter and 2.5 inches shorter, even in my purple sparkly sequined knee-high zipper boots, I was never quite his match.

My brother served 1,892 days when he was shot and killed in the line of duty at 23 years old. He died protecting others and advancing freedom. He is my hero.

You know who else loves my purple sparkly sequined knee-high zipper boots? My husband. He has never once made fun of me or told me where I could not wear them. He's an awesome man in both size and spirit and I still can't believe he's mine for the last 35 years.

Roland and I met when the moon was full and my heart was empty. I had just been released from a brief stay in the hospital. It seems every other year since my brother's death, I just need to emotionally disconnect, fall apart even. The grief I carry is heavy. Roland lifts me up so that I don't have to shoulder my sadness alone.

The anniversary of my brother's death continues to be painful even after so many years have passed. To have Roland, who cherishes me and loves me for how I swish through this world, is a gift beyond measure.

The Sexual Hypercube Feedback Loop in Later Adulthood

Another reflection of feedback looping between identity and expression is the process of the changes to sexual identity and expression over the course of the lifespan, especially culminating in changes during later adulthood. For some, a variant version of the process described in Diamond's work with young women also occurs at the other end of the developmental process with older men and women. When we are young, we are much more cognizant of traditional sex-role expectations and generally more compliant (sex-typed) in our behavior. It is common for people to do so because they believe it is necessary for the purposes of courting and mate selection. After several decades of "swimming with the current" of the more traditional sex-role orientation, men and women essentially become more relaxed and less concerned about meeting sex-role expectations. In a sense, they give themselves the gift of being more authentic. This change was described in the last chapter as related to Carl Jung's theory of sex-role convergence (Jung, 1960).

This process is a gradual and, for the most part, unconscious shift in the Sexual Identity Cube for some individuals, moving from the more traditional sex-role behavior (whether masculine or feminine) to more of an androgynous expression of the self. The mechanisms by which this shift occurs are biological (hormonal shift), psychosocial (changing priorities), and behavioral ("forget that macho shit"). They can be described as the long-term workings of feedback looping between the Sexual Identity and Sexual Expression Cubes within the hypercube across the lifespan.

The intent of the hypercube model is to provide an alternative means of understanding the complex and confusing world of sexuality; to promote greater opportunities for individual self-acceptance and "finding oneself" within a model of diverse sexual experiences; and finally, to facilitate movement toward higher levels of sexual health on individual, family, and community levels. The hypercube model is based on a multidisciplinary perspective (biological, psychosocial, behavioral, clinical, and cultural dimensions) that is interwoven into the human experience of sexuality. It is not meant to be an all-encompassing model for explanation of all things sexual, but rather another tool for those attempting to help themselves (or others) answer questions about sexuality or overcome challenges to personal sexual health.

WHAT EVIDENCE IS THERE THAT SEXUAL IDENTITY AND EXPRESSION CHANGE?

To help one think about more complex ways to conceive sexual identity and expression, examples are offered here of many types of change that occur across the lifespan. There is evidence, in both animal and human models, that creatures small and large make transitions in their sexual status. Using the three-dimensional model of identity, changes in *sex orientation, sexual orientation,* and *sex-role orientation* among people are presented. But first, let us examine a few animal models as a reminder of how biological sex can change naturally in the wild.

ANIMAL MODELS OF CHANGES IN BIOLOGICAL SEX AND EXPRESSION

There are actually hundreds of examples of species that change their sex status, especially if one looks at insects and fish. Only a few of the more celebrated examples of dramatic sex transitions are presented in this section. Interestingly, animals can make changes to their sex status on a "species-specific" basis (the individual member changes from female to male) or on a "species-wide" basis (such as when a species has "eliminated" an entire sex status category). The question is: If fish can do it, can people?

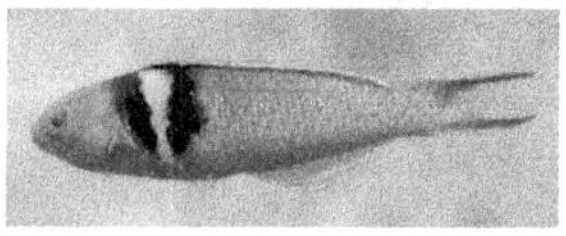

The Blue-Headed Wrasse (*Thalassoma bifasciatum*)

These fish live in harems of 10 to 12 females jealously guarded by a single male. If the male is killed (by another fish) or removed from the group

FIGURE 13.2 Blue-headed Wrasse

(say by a researcher), the largest female (and she alone) literally changes into a male in terms of appearance and behavior. "He" now runs the harem and, in time (about two weeks) starts to fertilize the eggs of females with sperm this "new male" is now able to produce (Piper, 2007; Schärer & Vizoso, 2003).

FIGURE 13.3 Green Spoonworm

The Greenspoon Worm (Bonellia veridis)

This marine worm lives on the sea floor (10 to 100 meters deep) and is sexually undifferentiated until its larval stage. Then, the larvae move to the top of their little mud pile. The females then use a long proboscis (arm-like nose) to sweep the sea floor for other larvae. If a larva is not touched by the proboscis, then the female remains female. If a larva is touched by the hormones on the proboscis, then it develops into a male. The new male worm remains small in size and crawls inside the body of the larger female, where it spends the rest of its life supplying sperm to the female (from inside her). So, the sex of a green spoonworm is thus determined by external, environmental factors (the presence or absence of bonellin), not by internal, genetic factors (Berec, Schembri, & Boukal, 2005).

FIGURE 13.4 Desert Grassland Whiptail Lizard

The Desert Grassland Whiptail Lizard (Aspidoscelis uniparens)

One of the most well-known examples of animals making a "species-wide" change in sex status is the sex-free reproduction of the whiptail lizard, which has managed to find a way to eliminate the male version of itself. Females simply lay eggs that hatch only daughters via a cloning process. Although there are scores of examples of animals that reproduce asexually (especially insects and fish), until recently the whiptail lizard was the most complex animal to do so in the wild (Harmon, 2010).

FIGURE 13.5 Transcaucasian Mole Vole

The Transcaucasian Mole Vole (Ellobius lutescens)

In 1995, researchers discovered that the males of this mammal species do not have a Y chromosome or have even an SRY gene (sex-determining region). In fact, it is believed that all mole voles (both males and females) have a single X chromosome, making for an XO sex chromosome set. They are born, live, have babies, and die—all without the disadvantages of a Y chromosome (Starr, 2008). This rodent species found a way to activate the masculinization of its males by activating a "gene relay" a couple of stages down the line from SRY gene—thereby saving the species from the need to carry a Y chromosome and providing protection from all the inherited generic flaws that come with it. Hence, the mole vole is the only mammal known to have successfully escaped the inevitability of a Y-chromosome-driven extinction (Starr, 2008).

You might think these animal models are interesting but don't have much relevance to us. But according to Oxford University's top geneticist, Bryan Sykes, the human race is also vulnerable to Y-chromosome-driven extinction that eventually will lead to a future of *humans without men*. However, in his book *Adam's Curse*, Sykes explains that a human race without men will not bring an end to the human species—that is, if we can go the way of the mole vole. Because of Y-chromosome decay in humans and the resulting decline in male fertility (0.1% decline each generation), it will take about 5,000 generations before "XY men" become extinct (Sykes, 2003). Holy cow! If you consider a generation to be 20 to 25 years, that's only 100,000 to 125,000 years from now! (Somebody better start working on a plan here!)

Other scholars don't believe male extinction will take that long because there has been a dramatic decline in male fertility measured over the 50-year span from 1940 to 1990. Ryan and Jetha (authors of the *Sex at Dawn*) note that the decline has been measured in both sperm concentration and total sperm count. Average sperm concentration declined approximately 42% from 1940 to 1990 (from 113×10^6/mL to 66×10^6/mL), and the average total sperm count declined approximately 42% during the same period from about 480 million sperm per ejaculate to about 280 million sperm per ejaculate (Ryan & Jetha, 2010).

What is going on here, and what reasons are there for the Y-chromosome deterioration and the decline in male fertility? The speculations are many and their exploration is fascinating yet beyond the focus of this chapter. Fortunately, women have always served as the cradle of civilization in human history and women's creativity may assist future men to continue their existence in a new form of masculinized "XX men or XO men," if, that is, women choose to still have us around by then (guys, I wouldn't count on it based on how things are at present).

HUMAN MODELS OF MOVEMENT ACROSS THE SEXUAL HYPERCUBE

Human beings also experience sexual transitions across the lifespan, which most frequently and dramatically involve changes in sexual expression. Changes also regularly occur in sexual identity and on a regular basis with many (but not all) people. Of course, animals are not believed to be influenced by the same kind of culture as humans and are not pressed upon by cultural scripts as we are. Again, if we use the three-dimensional model of the Sexual Identity Cube, we can examine changes in sexual identity as they occur within sex orientation, sexual orientation, and sex-role orientation.

Movement Across the Sexual Identity Cube: Sex Orientation

The examples of changes in sex orientation are divided into those that are voluntary and those that are not, because that is how these changes are experienced by people (see Table 13.1). Let's discuss the voluntary changes first. Adult sex reassignment surgeries started in the late 1920s in Europe upon the request of the patients (voluntary). The first recorded sex change was that of a Danish painter named

Einar Wegener, who believed he developed a feminine personality named Lili Elbe and requested surgical reassignment (Hoyer, 1933). This story is the basis of the movie *The Danish Girl* (Chasin, Israel, Morgan, Reisman, & Hooper, 2015). Today, accounts of these procedures are fairly commonplace, such as the several featured stories in this text (and other sources) of remarkable transgender individuals.

Culturally sanctioned gender transitions involve cultures that allow space in their society for individuals to change sex designation from male to female (or vice versa). This category of voluntary transition is considered a "cultural" change of sex status and usually does not involve surgical change to anatomy. Transculturally, the most commonly known examples include the Hijra of India and the Two-Spirited of North America; the latter have been documented in many Native American tribes (LeVay, Baldwin, & Baldwin, 2015; Masters, Johnson, & Kolodny, 1995; Yarber, Sayad, & Strong, 2010). In many communities across America (as well as most large international cities), one can find individuals living as an alternative sex (alternative to their sex designated at birth) as a permanent lifestyle (with or without hormonal or surgical intervention). These examples are all considered voluntary transitions in sex orientation.

Examples of involuntary transition are when some of the same surgical procedures just described with adults are performed on children and babies who cannot make their own health care decisions. Similarly, people with genetic and hormonal variations (including XX males, XY females) are considered to have involuntary transitions because they also did not make a choice about their sex orientation. Injections of embryonic SRY (sex-determining region on the Y chromosome) are currently performed on animals only and so cannot be used for evidence of human transition of sex orientation at this time. If they are ever performed with human fetuses, then they would, of course, also be considered involuntary.

TABLE 13.1 Voluntary-Involuntary Changes in Human Sex Orientation

Voluntary	Involuntary
Adult sex reassignment surgery	Infant/child sex reassignment surgery
Culturally sanctioned gender transition (two-spirited)	Genetic/hormonal variations (XX males, XY females)
Adult hormonal sex transition (nonsurgical)	Embryonic SRY injection (animal models currently)

TABLE 13.2 Voluntary-Involuntary Changes in Human Sexual Orientation Status

Voluntary	Involuntary
Studies of "sexual fluidity" among women	Childhood cultural scripting (studies of Sambian boys)
Celebrity cases (Anne Heche, Julie Cypher)	Case studies of partners to M2F trans women (like Alex's wife in Chapter 5)
Clinical case studies	

Movement Across the Sexual Identity Cube: Sexual Orientation

Changes in sex orientation are more dramatic and rare compared with changes in sexual orientation. Like sex orientation, examples of changes in sexual orientation are also divided into those that are voluntary and those that are not (see Table 13.2). Again, let's discuss the voluntary changes first. As mentioned earlier, Diamond described what she calls "greater sexual fluidity" when she studied young women who had spent some time in both heterosexual and same-sex relationships. Her data suggest that some women experiment with lesbian relationships before settling into a heterosexual pattern. A key question is if periods of demonstrated sexual fluidity do or do not represent actual changes in what we consider sexual orientation. It is complicated, and the jury is still out, but certainly it is an important line of research. Students and clients of the authors report that they, and many people they know, not only experiment with same-sex relations as adolescents (which is not considered unusual) but also go back and forth "switching teams" (sometimes several times) over the course of adulthood.

Not as many studies support similar sexual flexibility among males. Yet, there are volumes of reports regarding men being sexual with other men before, during, and after heterosexual relationships. It appears that there is less visibility regarding sexual fluidity among men, in part because of the higher social stigma associated with man-to-man sex than with lesbian relationships. In fact, many men do not consider their sexual contact with other men as "relationships," such as those associated with the colloquial phrase "down-low."

This disparity of social acceptance between gay and lesbian relationships also plays out in the world of celebrity. High-profile couples such as Ellen Degeneres and Anne Heche (who were together for nearly four years) garnered much attention when their relationship ended and when Heche then had a child with Coleman Laffoon during their five-year marriage. Throughout history, there are many more celebrity examples of women taking female partners in long-term relationships and then entering into heterosexual marriages. There are not as many corresponding celebrity examples of men transitioning from long-term gay relationships to heterosexual marriages. Historically, married men who identified as gay or bisexual were more likely to keep same-sex relations out of the public view (such as actor Rock Hudson).

However, it is not uncommon for men who have been married to women and then divorced to have long-term gay relationships (including marriages, more recently). These types of relationships do not come out of clinical files but are easily found in most LGBTQA communities. Whether gay or lesbian, these individuals are often considered to be finally accepting their "true" orientation of sexual attraction. However, this assumption is challenged when they later "switch teams" again and take up heterosexual partners. This raises the question of "serial bisexuality" as well. Of course, many relationships of similar nature can be drawn from clinical cases when questions and stress increase significantly to a point where mental health consultation is sought. I believe this latter scenario is the exception, as most people with questions about their sexual orientation never seek counsel from health care professionals for a multitude of reasons (the least of which are that many health care professionals do not feel comfortable or competent in addressing the sexual health concerns of their patients).

When discussed by university students, the particular matter of involuntary changes of sexual orientation is typically considered even more controversial than voluntary changes. This may be related to the fact that involuntary changes sometimes involve children in particular and that the topic of cultural relativity is almost always a decidedly controversial area within academics. Case in point is the cultural scripting ritual of Sambian boys (Herdt, 2005). As described in Chapter 11, these prepubescent boys leave their family hut, join a male-only communal hut, and engage in several years of sexual maturing by means of ingesting the semen of older boys. This is not a voluntary choice; it would be nearly impossible for these boys to refuse this developmental process that is culturally defined as the essential path to manhood and eventually the ability to select a bride and raise a family. It could be also argued that this form of sexual development does not necessarily involve a change of sexual orientation.

Similarly (and finally), the matter of sexual orientation of partners of post-op transsexual or transgender individuals may also not be considered any kind of change of sexual orientation. However, many partners do have significant concerns not only about the changes occurring with their trans spouses but also what these changes mean in terms of their own sexual orientation "category." For example, if you are a woman who married a man who later becomes a woman, does that make you a lesbian? The common refrain is, "I didn't sign up for this." Some spouses don't see it like that and some do. The point is, besides the stress related to the change of their trans spouse's sex orientation, they are often stressed about their own sexual status. Alex's wife (Chapter 5) was a wonderful example of a supportive spouse who did not allow questions of "categories" to interfere with a loving and successful relationship. Of course, if there is any type of categorical change in the sexual orientation status of the spouse, it could be considered a "definitional change" with the partner as opposed to an actual anatomical change with the transsexual or transgender individual.

Of course, none of this applies if both you and your spouse are transsexual and essentially switch roles as husband and wife. While exceedingly rare, this does happen (as evidenced by the story of Devin and Gage in the next chapter). I once co-presented at psychiatry grand rounds with such an individual. He is a trans man psychiatrist who used to be the female in his marriage. His present wife used to be the male husband in the same marriage. Although very rare, the Internet draws these stories together from around the world under the rubric "double sex change couples." A web search will render multiple such couples, including an article entitled, "Seven Unique Double Sex Change Couples" (Murano, 2013).

Movement Across the Sexual Identity Cube: Sex-Role Orientation

Although changes in sex orientation are the least frequent (followed in frequency by changes in sexual orientation), the changes that occur in sex-role orientation are very common. One could argue that they are unavoidable for a majority of people. Although changes in the previous two categories (sex and sexual orientations) are fairly distinguishable, the distinction regarding changes in sex-role orientation is much more blurred. For example, if people choose to make voluntary changes about anything in their lives, there is an inherent assumption that they are conscious of their options and conscious of deciding to make the change. Involuntary changes may be made with or without conscious awareness. The Sambian boys are old enough, certainly, to be aware of what happens to them, but they are also not conscious of the overall cultural process that strongly directs their sexual development rituals. It is exceedingly unlikely that any Sambian boy is going to forsake the cultural press upon him and say, "That's okay—I'll just skip this whole ritual thing about becoming a man."

The same is true of Jung's sex-role convergence theory. If you are old enough, you probably know people who seem to have significantly "mellowed out" over the course of several decades. Some of these individuals are cognizant of the changes they have made and others are not. Did they mellow out as a result of reflection and conscious choice, gradual changes in metabolism and hormonal levels, or social expectations of how older folks should behave? The answer is probably "yes" as the underlying process is multicausal and, as previously mentioned, a result of the interactive feedback looping within the Sexual Hypercube.

Hence, the distinction between voluntary and involuntary is not as important related to changes in sex-role orientation. Regarding Table 13.3, personal observations of the authors (anecdotal evidence) and Jung's sex-role convergence theory have been briefly discussed. At the same time, there are examples of changes that more reflect a voluntary status. Two will be mentioned here. The first is evidence from clinical case studies involving individuals who identify themselves as female-to-male (F2M) trans men. Simply stated, these cases involve individuals who are planning to, or who have already accomplished, sexual reassignment surgery (SRS) and they seek consultation in terms of how to appear to others as more masculine. They voluntarily undergo SRS (which changes their sex orientation) and they voluntary seek counsel in an effort to masculinize themselves (to change their sex-role orientation). Of course, the same is true for male-to-female (M2F) trans women who seek counsel on feminizing their appearance and behavior. Both types of consultation are provided through many sexual health and gender clinics as well as many transgender-oriented support groups.

TABLE 13.3 **Voluntary-Involuntary Changes in Human Sex-Role Orientation Status**

Voluntary	Involuntary
Clinical case studies (F2M trans men)	C. Jung's theory of sex-role convergence
Personal observations	Change in sex-role reference group

WHAT GUIDELINES GOVERN CHANGES IN SEXUAL IDENTITY AND EXPRESSION?

1. Sexual identity (along with sexual expression) does change over time and cannot always be considered a constant fixed trait of development for many people.
2. These changes in status appear to occur by choice in some instances (voluntary) and, in other instances, without choice or even the awareness of the individual (involuntary). These transitions in sexual status appear to occur by various means but include three broad types:
    a. Physical (direct physical transitions in an individual involving genetic, anatomical, hormonal, or surgical change).
    b. Cultural (direct transition in an individual involving sexual scripting and, in many cases, socially sanctioned changes).
    c. Definitional (indirect transition based on relationship to another person, such as a partner's specific change of status).
3. Changes in sexual status are commonly believed to be based on an artificially separated set of influences involving apparent "biological"" aspects of sexuality ("nature") and the apparent environmental aspects of sexuality ("nurture"); when in reality both types of factors influence each other in mutually reciprocal ways, facilitating continuous development and changes throughout the lifespan.

4. Within the model of the Sexual Hypercube, these changes can be seen as resulting from a multitude of causal factors related to interactive influences between the Sexual Identity Cube and the Sexual Expression Cube.

What Other Guidelines Might Emerge, and What Is the Point?

It is difficult to project what other trends will emerge that guide changes in the development of sexual identity and expression. If the Sexual Hypercube serves as a model of human sexuality, then the few principles listed in this exploratory discussion will be corrected, amended, or expanded upon. What are the benefits of considering different points of view about sexual identity and expression reflected by the Sexual Hypercube model?

1. To more accurately understand sexuality through a general model based upon existing research findings and to stimulate further research questions, which may lead to more of a consensus on the use of the term "sexual identity." As noted in Chapter 11, we are far from a consensus.

2. To have a broader perception of the complexity and diversity of human sexuality in modern culture, including the difference between sexual identity and sexual expression. This book focuses on the complexity of a person's identity as a sexual being. This is different from how individuals have a predisposition to, and/or choice to, manifest their sexual identity in terms of behavioral expression.

3. To assert an empirical basis for considering sexual identity to be of a flexible (fluid) nature for many individuals over the course of their lifetime (a normalizing effect) and not a fixed trait as has been traditionally assumed.

4. To promote greater self-acceptance of one's sexual identity and thereby minimize negative sexual self-image. On an individual basis, an expanded perspective of the full range of sexual identity and its correlated sexual expression may lead to a greater sense of self-worth and personal satisfaction.

5. To use the model as a conceptual learning tool to promote greater tolerance of others as well as lessen the incidence of prejudice and violence toward those who appear different from ourselves.

Now, let's turn our attention from theoretical models of human sexuality to the real-world lives of people trying to do what most people want to do. They want to have a sense of health, self-worth and purpose, and have healthy relationships. The next chapter features two individuals named Gage and Devin who demonstrate the fluidity of gender and sexuality while trying to seek health and authenticity. Of one thing the authors are fairly sure: You are unlikely to have ever known a more fluid couple as next described. In Chapter 15, Jane and Eddie inspire and instruct us on the challenges of when our past trauma can sneak up and interfere with present-day functioning. Therefore, this chapter, while important in illuminating paths to healing, comes with trigger warnings. Both stories are real-life testimonies to the resiliency of the human spirit.

REFERENCES

Berec, L., Schembri, P., & Boukal, D. (2005). Sex determination in *Bonellia viridis* (Echiura: Bonelliidea): Population dynamics and evolution. *Oikos Journal: Synthesizing Ecology, 108* (3), 473–484.

Chasin, L., Israel, U., Morgan, K., Reisman, L. (Producers), & Hooper, T. (Director). (2015). *The Danish Girl* [Film]. United States: Focus Feature Films.

Diamond, L. (2008). *Sexual fluidity: Understanding women's love and desire*. Cambridge, MA: Harvard University Press.

Harmon, K. (2010). No sex needed: All-female lizard species cross their chromosomes to make babies. *Scientific American*. Retrieved from https://www.scientificamerican.com/article/asexual-lizards/

Herdt, G. (2005). *The Sambia: Ritual, sexuality, and change in Papua New Guinea*. Belmont, CA: Wadsworth.

Hinton, C. (1888). *A new era of thought*. London, UK: Swan Sonnenschein.

Hoyer, N. (1933). *Man into woman: An authentic record of a change of sex*. New York: E.P. Dutton.

Jung, C. (1960). The stages of life. In G. Adler, M. Fordham, & H. Reads (Eds.), *The collected works of C. G. Jung: Vol. 8. The structure and dynamics of the psyche*. London, UK: Routledge.

Kaku, M. (1994). *Hyperspace: A scientific odyssey through parallel universes, time warps and the tenth dimension*. Oxford, UK: Oxford University Press.

LeVay, S., Baldwin, J., & Baldwin, J. (2015). *Discovering human sexuality* (3rd ed.). Sunderland, MA: Sinauer Associates.

Masters, W., Johnson, V., & Kolodny, R. (1995). *Human sexuality* (5th ed.). New York: HarperCollins.

Murano, G. (2013). Seven unique double sex change couples. Retrieved from www.oddee.com/item_98756.aspx

Piper, R. (2007). *Extraordinary animals: An encyclopedia of curious and unusual animals*. Westport, CT: Greenwood Press.

Ryan, C., & Jetha, C. (2010). *Sex at dawn*. New York: HarperCollins.

Schärer, L., & Vizoso, D.B. (2003). Earlier sex change in infected individuals of the protogynous reef fish *Thalassoma bifasciatum*. *Behavioral Ecology and Sociobiology, 55* (2), 137–143.

Starr, B. (2008). Why no Y? Gender-bending Transcaucasian Mole Voles. Retrieved from https://ww2.kqed.org/quest/.../why-no-y-gender-bending-transcaucasian-mole-voles/

Sykes, B. (2003). *Adam's curse: A story of sex, genetics, and the extinction of men*. Oxford, UK: Oxford University Press.

Yarber, W., & Sayad, B. (2019). *Human sexuality: Diversity in contemporary society* (10th ed.). New York: McGraw-Hill.

FIGURE CREDITS

Fig. 13.2: Tibor Marcinek, "The Blue-Headed Wrasse," https://commons.wikimedia.org/wiki/File:Blue-headed_wrasse_det.jpg. Copyright in the Public Domain.

Fig. 13.3: Copyright © Sylvain Ledoyen (CC BY-SA 3.0) at https://commons.wikimedia.org/wiki/File:Bon%C3%A9lie_(Bonellia_viridis)_PC301461.JPG.

Fig. 13.4: Copyright © Brent Myers (CC by 2.0) at https://commons.wikimedia.org/wiki/File:Desert_Grassland_Whiptail_Lizard_(7959635438).jpg.

Fig. 13.5: Copyright © Mikhail Kolesnikov and Marina Korobchenko (GNU General Public License) at https://commons.wikimedia.org/wiki/File:Ellobius_talpinus.jpg. A copy of the license can be found here: https://www.gnu.org/copyleft/gpl-3.0.html

CHAPTER FOURTEEN

The Gage and Devin Story

Written by Frederick Peterson

INTRODUCTION

"I love you too," Devin says into his smartphone as he responds to another pageant contestant in between bites of food. It is the first night of a long week of pageants and he and Gage are really too busy to meet with me. But like Gage says, "We have to eat." So there we are, the three of us at the Siam Pad Thai restaurant, trying to eat dinner, simultaneously conduct an interview, and the two of them taking calls from people freaking out because of hotel room changes, substituting judges, and problems with videographing divas during the first night's evening-wear competition. Gage looks right at me with a wry smile and adds, "It isn't pageant week if something isn't f'ed-up."

"Holy wow! This is amazing yum-yum. What is this called again?" I declared. "It's called Thai tea," Devin explains. It was sweet, cool, and delicious. And very needed for anyone like me who can't even eat food with a #1 rating on the 1 to 4 spicy range. A video message comes in from another contestant who is just wanting to send his love and inform Devin that he has arrived in Dayton for the pageant. "This is a crazy business," Gage says with animation. One of their staff then calls talking about last-minute changes to the gifts and awards they get for the judges and staff. Gage explains they have seven judges, four officials, two contestant liaisons, and one all-purpose runner-utility man.

The reason all these people are needed and that the pageant lasts all week is that 70 individuals from across the country qualified to compete. Each of them participated in an evening-wear competition, talent competition, and interview. Some came to compete in the Miss USofA Diva pageant, some for the Mister USofA MI (Male Illusionist) pageant, and the rest for the USofA MI Classic pageant. Gage explained that the "MI Classic" competition is for the more senior contestants that have been around awhile (33 years or older). "Like me," he says. Gage has been competing and transitioning for well over a decade. Having served as a mentor to many contestants, he humbly accepts an unofficial title of the "Godfather of Drag." "For the record," he adds, "all the contestants have to be assigned as a female at birth (perceived as baby girls), so they identify as either women or trans-men. They compete *with* each other as opposed to against each other. It's a Brotherhood."

Sitting within this whirlwind of food, conversation, and video calls, I wondered how these two remarkable individuals got to where they are. Among the many stories of fluid expressions of sex and gender (not only in this book but anywhere), there are only a few that cover such a wide spectrum of gender experience within one person as the story you are about to read. It begins with two young girls and ends with two men named Devin and Gage who are nationally known performers and national pageant producers in the world of male impersonators. Gage has been on his journey of transition a bit longer and sees himself as more at the masculine end of the traditional gender continuum. Devin sees himself as more gender fluid and just being himself, Devin. They were gracious enough to share their stories in an effort to help promote understanding of people who are gender nonconforming, gender fluid, and otherwise considered transgender individuals. Awesome!

This chapter continues with Gage's story (as he is older and been transitioning longer), then Devin's story, and how the two found each other to live and love each other in one of the most unique sets of lives described in this book. To keep it easier to follow these stories (gender-wise) and use their preferred pronouns—all personal references used will be masculine, regardless of how Gage and Devin have been viewed by society in the past. In addition, this short chapter is a very brief description of a long and detailed history that is fascinating and beyond the scope of this chapter.

GAGE'S STORY

Gage was born as a female in Jacksonville, Florida, with a family that was full of military men—father, uncles, and grandfather. In other words, there was a lot of masculine energy while Gage grew up as a girl and he always remembered wanting to join the military. During his childhood, he went back and forth in terms of gender-conforming. At times, he followed the socially sanctioned norms as a little girl and played typical activities as a girl. In eighth grade, though, there was a small rebellion. Gage decided to cut off all his hair to get negative attention. He liked the negative reactions of being thought of as a boy, but then later decided to grow it long again and conform to female expectations once the bullying got worse. As a teenager, he eventually felt compelled by social convention and dated boys.

Through typical sexual exploration, Gage eventually got pregnant and birthed a son at age 17. He and the father lived together as teenage parents for approximately two years but could not make it as a family. As a teenager, Gage was not ready for parenthood or marriage, and the parents never wed. Gage lost custody because he was living as a lesbian, had cut his hair short again, and was living with a Jamaican girlfriend in Virginia. The father was living in a traditonal Southern small town in Florida. Gage even married a good friend of his (a man) in an attempt to avoid losing custody of his son (he was also planning to join the service and it was a problem being a single parent in the military). Although he loved his son, a court order eventually gave custody of the boy to the father when his son was about five years old. The marriage between Gage and his friend was for practical purposes and ended a year after they wed.

Gage continued to struggle with women's roles and particularly his role in a society that limits women's participation. Gage felt very similar to a popular tune sung by Gwen Stefani (of the group No Doubt) which says, "*Don't you think I know exactly where I stand, this world is forcing me to hold your hand . . . Cause I'm just a girl, I'd rather not be.*"

However, Gage was strong, brave, and wanted to break social expectations of women, so he joined the military. This was something that was still uncommon in the 1990s. He always knew something was "out of sync" with how he saw himself—already living as a lesbian but knowing there was more in terms of his growing identity as a male. He joined the U.S. Army (1996–1999) and was assigned to a detail of mortuary affairs, which was quite traumatic in terms of dealing with death, serving as a technician assistant during autopsies, and getting bodies back to their families for burial. Not only did Gage feel compelled to serve his country for four years in the U.S. Army but, remarkably, he then joined the U.S. Navy!

Although Gage felt more comfortable in nonconventional situations, he was not happy as he still had sexist expectations placed on him as an active-duty woman. The problem was that he was seen as a woman, and he did not feel like a woman, did not want to be a woman, and wanted to correct the problem of wrong anatomy. Gage started to play with his gender during his Navy service, spending a year getting more masculine. He was the first of female Navy personnel to serve as a line coach on a firing range helping sailors to improve their firearm skills. However, the stresses of his job in the Army (which gave him PTSD) in combination with the stress of gender dysphoria resulted in a medical discharge for Gage. Although Gage loved military life, it did stress him out at times, such as his job of working with dead bodies and assisting with autopsies. His three years of service in the U.S. Navy ended in 2003.

Finished with the military? No way! Almost unbelievably, Gage could not let go of military life even after a medical discharge! He could not resist the opportunity of joining the U.S. Army Reserve and serving as a military police (MP) officer. It was then when he started to bind his breasts down and did all the required physical training (PT) to the male standards. After two more years of service, Gage finally ended his military career (in 2005) after figuring out what next he wanted to do.

After his final military year, Gage wanted to start gender-specific transition treatment. Although he felt like a man, he was still a bit unsure of social reaction to his commitment to fully transition until a key event occurred that propelled him further on his gender-transition journey. While he was surrounded by a very strong military family, Gage's experience of family support for sexual reassignment was patchy and less than enthusiastic. One day while Gage was at a family gathering, his man-among-men grandfather took him aside and in front of all to hear told Gage that he loved him and whatever Gage wanted to do with his life, his grandfather would support him. It was this show of strength and love between them that helped Gage feel he had all he needed to move forward with his plan. He knew if his grandfather threw his support behind him, then many others would as well or at least try. And those who would not, Gage knew he would have to leave behind.

After leaving the military, Gage really started to ramp up his gender transition by exploring the world of drag kings, where women dress as males and usually impersonate famous male singers (like Elvis). New to the world of male illusionists, Gage met many new friends and found creative expression extremely rewarding. It was freedom to be himself, and Gage thrived. Gage excelled at his performances and developed a highly celebrated performance impersonating country music star Tim McGraw. He soon started to tour nationally winning many titles, appearing regularly on television, and being covered in numerous publications (visit his website for details).

Yet Gage still struggled with his gender and eventually came to the conclusion that he was a transgender man. Gage began hormonal transition and he began to exhibit secondary male characteristics, with his voice changing to a more masculine tone, increased facial hair, a more muscular body, and had a double mastectomy and a hysterectomy. Gage's goal was to successfully transition to male, and after completing the necessary legal paperwork, Gage had his social security card, driver's license designation, passport, and legal name all changed.

ENTER DEVIN

In 2005, Gage met Devin Dame—another male illusionist at a drag king pageant. Gage became a mentor to Devin for performance and they become dear friends as well as co-performers. They were friends for about three years till eventually they found themselves in a romantic relationship. As their relationship progressed, they became lovers and began to live together. Gage's role as mentor in male illusionist performance transitioned to become Devin's husband. Gage was then legally recognized as a man and then asked Devin to marry him. This was before same-sex partners were legally allowed to marry, but it didn't matter because Gage was a man in what was seen as a heterosexual relationship.

Gage and Devin became man and wife and enjoyed a marriage as a heterosexual couple. So, the transformation of Gage (as perceived by the world) included being a heterosexual mother, then transitioning to a lesbian woman, and then transitioning to a man in a heterosexual relationship with Devin. Let's pause again for a moment to appreciate the sexual fluidity going on here. Using different terms, let's take stock of the transitions with this individual named Gage. At his first transition, he changed from a heterosexual wife and mother to lesbian woman and then transitioned to become a heterosexual husband.

Let's introduce Devin's background, which includes being born in a small town of Woodsfield, Ohio, but later being raised in Middletown, Ohio. He comes from a good family with positive support for him as a young girl. He was active in sports and describes his childhood in very positive terms. Devin knew early on in his childhood that he was attracted to other girls and identified early as being lesbian. He did date guys for a short while as a teenager, but he came out to others as a lesbian at age 18. For the most part, Devin sees his family as supportive of his gender-nonconforming behavior, gender fluidity, and transitioning to male more recently.

As he always considered himself gender nonconforming, Devin always wanted to join the military. At age 20, he joined the U.S. Army and was first assigned to duty in heavy construction but later transferred to operations when our country was under attack on 9-11. He had to keep track of several hundred soldiers at all times, knowing exactly where they were and what they could do for the defense of our country. Devin was injured during his service in the Army and medically discharged in 2003. After separation from the service, Devin started working in the family business. His confidence was greatly increased when he underwent significant breast reduction surgery in

2012. Recently, Devin had a cancer scare and had a full double mastectomy, which is protective of his health but also consistent with his moving further forward toward masculinity.

In retrospect, Devin considers his drag king/male illusionist experience as a catalyst influence moving him more toward male identity, but he always saw himself as gender divergent. Devin has been with Gage for eight years, and they have been married about half that time. Devin was seen as the woman in the beginning of the relationship, but not anymore. As sexually fluid as this story reflects, it does not end here. Devin continues to transition to male, thus making Gage and Devin a homosexual couple as two gay men. Said differently, as Devin fully transitions hormonally to male status, the couple will have been on a journey that started as a lesbian couple, then changed to a heterosexual couple, and is now changing to a couple of gay men who love each other.

Gage and Devin are now advocates and activists in gender/trans equality, run a transgender support group, and have become LGBTQA community leaders in the greater Dayton area as well as being known nationally. They lead a transgender support group in Dayton and have sponsored similar groups in other states. The mission of Gage and Devin's groups are to raise awareness, provide education, and act as an outlet for transgender, nonconforming-gender identity individuals, and their allies. Through their work, they also provide safe meeting places, social functions, newsletters, and referrals to LGBTQA-friendly professionals.

Their story is very unusual to say the least but perfectly demonstrates the fluidity of sexual identity and the diversity of human sexual expression. By physical appearances as male or female at birth, society tries to keep us in designated boxes with absolute binary labels. It is a common function of the human brain to generalize and oversimplify a very complex world. As human beings, we do this to struggle to understand a very complex world but, in the process, confuse ourselves by missing many important nuances of gender variations, which are natural and frequently occurring. *Yet, it is the resiliency of the human spirit and need to live authentically with a personal sense of freedom which fuels the unlimited diversity of human sexual expression.*

Today, society's traditional gender expectations can no longer keep an individual's inner identity from emerging. An individual's mind, heart, and soul need authentic expression for balance and happiness. Each of us, transgender and cisgender, can strive to become more authentic and comfortable with expressing our true selves. Gage and Devin are exceptional examples of this process.

BACK TO THE PAGEANTS

Three national pageants were produced by Gatlyn Dame Group in Dayton, Ohio, during March 5–12, 2017. I went downtown to check out Gage and Devin's handiwork. It was about midnight Saturday evening at Club Masque, and the place was packed. The stage was lit up with an amazing digital backdrop accompanied by an equally dazzling light show and sound system. Several folks, including Devin and Gage, walked around wearing red and white college-style letterman jackets with "MI" on the front like they were wearing their school's initials. A skinny, handsome, and half-naked waiter came up to me and offered refreshment with a tray of shots. I passed on the booze but appreciated the tattoo displayed prominently across his chest: *Live life with courage and conquer death.* Right behind him strutted a 300-pound, seven-and-one-half-foot-tall drag queen (including her pumps and bouffant style wig). Of course, drag shows of both the king and queen varieties bring out the best of us with fun, interestingly diverse crowds!

The divas and male illusionists were competing with each other for the crowns of Miss USofA Diva 2017, Mister USofA MI 2017, and Mister USofA MI Classic 2017. The coveted jewel crowns for the top competitors were being shown off on a red satin cloth above an elevated part of the bar. The contestants performed their hearts out for the judges, and the audience was very appreciative of the diverse styles of performances from the Beyoncé impersonator and way-big-boy cowboy to the duets and the dance ensemble composed of the male illusionist and several backup singer/dancers. Apologies to country singer Luke Bryan, but I will never think of his song "Country Girl (Shake It for Me)" the same after the MI version was performed that Saturday night. To see lists of the participants and pictures of the crown winners, please check out www.MisterUSofAMI.org and www.MissUSofADIVA.org.

Regarding the boy that Gage had many years ago, both Gage and Devin have a positive relationship with him. Several years back, a young man contacted Gage over social media asking, "Do I know you?" Gage responded, "You should, I'm your mother." That was when Gage's son was 14 years old. Over a period of reconnecting, the son came to live with Devin and Gage for about three years. During that time, he earned a degree from a community college and the two got to know each other again as son and parent. The young man then returned to Florida, is gainfully employed, and is happy living with his girlfriend.

Besides managing drag king/male illusionist pageants across the country, Devin and Gage stay busy being spokespersons for the LGBTQA communities, conducting LGBTQA-affirming groups, and educating medical students and other health care professionals. When they are not serving as advocates or running competitions, they enjoy their lives together in Dayton with their seven dogs, five cats, a turtle, and a bearded dragon!

CHAPTER FIFTEEN

The Story of Jane and Eddie Finding a Way Through the Pain

Written by Frederick Peterson

[Authors' Note: Some details of this story have been changed to protect identity and privacy for this couple, yet the story remains consistent with their experience, which they gave permission to reproduce here as a teaching example of triumph and recovery.]

INTRODUCTION

She came in looking small, frail, and trepidatious. Although I asked her on the phone to bring her husband, Eddie, she looked like she was glad she did not have to arrive alone. She also told me that she was from out west, so we met in an office overlooking downtown Yellow Springs. The village is a small bastion of California culture in an otherwise conservative Midwest, a place I thought might be welcoming to her. She was able to look me in the eye and articulate herself clearly but spoke with a note of desperation, reflecting the long and difficult road they had been on to arrive in my office.

It took several sessions to understand the different layers of what she sought, including how to help her husband with his confusion as to how to be with her as his wife, be supportive, and to love her without triggering her into panic whenever he initiated any type of physical contact. He was clearly a smart fellow, with advanced degrees and obvious intellect. However, his professional confidence stood in contrast to the hesitation and tension he felt as he described his experience as "walking on eggshells" around her at home. They both appeared to be caught within a classic approach-avoidance dilemma of showing his love and interest in her while not overwhelming her from the smallest signs of affection. She was afraid of his affection although she desperately wanted it. She was anxiety stricken deciding to respond to his hug or caress as she worried he might think this would be seen as a green light for sex. Therefore, they did what most couples do—they practiced a dance of avoidance with grace and skill. Jane and Eddie, like many young couples, had fallen into an unfamiliar space of anxiety and uncertainty within their relationship. They said that they truly loved each other, got along well, and had not had sex for more than a year.

You see, when Jane and Eddie met and courted, they fell deeply in love and their incredible chemistry overruled all. What Eddie didn't know, because Jane did not either, was that there was a very scary presence lurking in the shadows yet to make its existence known. Neither one realized it, but when they shared sexual intimacy, Jane went on autopilot and dissociated herself psychologically from the sexual encounter. While she was able to engage her husband sexually and even orgasm at times, she unfortunately was consumed with a deep sense of shame after climax. While this shame was her only clue to the presence in the dark, she was always acutely aware of pain.

SEXUAL PAIN

Jane experienced serious irritation of her vulva, particularly around her labia, whenever she had contact to this area of her body. It caused her so much discomfort Jane never wore pants simply due to the discomfort generated from the pressure of the cloth upon her skin. When she attempted to have intercourse, she reported severe and intense pain in her genitals, especially around the opening of her vagina (the introitus). I asked her to see a sexual medicine colleague of mine for a specialty assessment of dyspareunia (what physicians call sexual pain). At this consultation, she was diagnosed with vestibularitis, which is an infection of the tissue around the vaginal opening. This was not a surprise. What was a surprise was her diagnosis of vaginismus, which was also a source of her pain in addition to the uncomfortable tenderness she felt from the infected tissue.

Vaginismus is a type of sexual pain resulting from the involuntary contraction of the outer third of the vagina, even when a woman consciously has decided to have intercourse and even if she desires the sexual intercourse. In effect, her vagina says "NOTHING is coming in here—no way, no how!" If a woman's vaginismus is severe enough, she would not even be able to use a tampon. This condition is sometimes the primary reason for unconsummated marriages (as described in Chapter 9). Fortunately, Jane's case was not that severe but severe enough to cause significant pain. In turn, this pain created her own approach-avoidance dilemma. Through her fear of the pain—she increased her own muscular tension and thus increased her level of pain. It was both a process of classical conditioning and a negative reinforcement so that she would tense her pelvic muscles at just the thought of sex!

Thus far, Jane's story has been a bit complicated with the sexual pain (from both vestibulitis and vaginismus), a lack of sexual desire (and even aversion to it), and the marital tension they experienced in their short marriage (they had been together about three years). The complexity of these concerns, however, was fairly manageable with the help of sex therapy and sexual medicine. However, Jane had additional challenges when the lurking stranger made his presence known. You see, her pain is understandable based on her infected tissue and vaginal tension. But her shame after having a climax was mysterious and confusing. Mysterious, that is, until Jane was teaching one day and a small child surprised her by placing his hand up her dress.

THE DARK PRESENCE CLOAKED BY THE PSYCHOBIOLOGY OF TRAUMA

At that moment, Jane was flooded with memories, sensation, and imagery all associated with being molested as a child. Suddenly, in response to the touch from this innocent child, she was paralyzed with an experience of reliving her abuse at the hands of an older male perpetrator. As a seven-year-old, Jane had dissociated her childhood trauma and broke the trauma experience into separate aspects according to her senses and cognitive processing. Instead of becoming an integrated memory like most memories that we have when we think about an event in our past, Jane's audio, visual, tactile, taste, olfactory, and narrative aspects of her childhood abuse were separated and encoded on a sensory-motor level in her body. Because these different dimensions of the abuse were segregated (as a survival mechanism of childhood), Jane did not have what most people would consider a typical memory of her abuse experience and therefore was not conscious of these events.

Full discussion of all the factors involved in how and when Jane became consciously aware of her childhood abuse are beyond the scope of this brief story. If you are interested in detailed descriptions, readers are referred to the writings of Bessel van der Kolk and particularly on the psychobiology of the brain as a result of trauma. Without trying to turn you into neuroscientists, a brief oversimplified explanation follows here focused on two key parts of the brain and how their function changes during memory processing when trauma occurs. The two key parts of the memory-making process involve the amygdala and the hippocampal structure.

The amygdala is considered the "meaning-making" organ in the brain because it strongly influences how our nonconscious mind (mental activity outside our conscious awareness) determines how our memory operates under certain conditions and what we remember. Usually, the amygdala is giving a signal indicating "this stuff is not very important, so let's forget about it." The information is not processed to be sent to long-term memory, so we actually do forget about it in a matter of hours or days. However, when there is important information being processed—especially if it has emotional significance, then the amygdala sends a signal for the information to be processed through the hippocampal structure that provides a "bundling function." This bundling of information puts together different aspects of our experience into what we consider a typical memory with a beginning, middle, and end (like a first kiss, first crush, or first sexual experience). The bundling function of the hippocampal structure not only organizes the narrative story of the memory but attaches the sensory-related aspects of the experience (such as accompanying visuals and auditory input) as well as emotional components (such as love, pleasure, or pain). These are what we refer to as explicit memories and are typically within our ability to recall at will.

What Van der Kolk and others assert is that traumatic experiences can often radically alter the memory process so that the information bypasses the bundling function of the hippocampal structure and separate aspects of a trauma experience (which usually come together into a typical explicit memory) stay separated. Because the amygdala is giving a signal of strongest possible distress during a trauma event, the different aspects of the event are retained separately on a sensory-motor level without the usual narrative story being sent to long-term memory. This is what is referred to as implicit memory and is not as available to voluntary recall.

It is important to note that most people who were sexually molested do remember that they were abused but at the same time, many do not remember many aspects of their trauma experience (especially the worst parts of it). However, when childhood sexual trauma occurs that is more extensive in terms of duration, intensity, and physical pain, then the need for dissociation to survive is greater. When these factors are present (in the most severe cases), dissociation is almost always a long-term effect of the trauma.

This was the case for Jane. When she came to understand how trauma effects memory, the sense of shame that accompanied her sexual arousal (and especially orgasm) suddenly made sense to her. For many survivors like Jane, the process of dissociation and recalling takes a lot of time, from being abused originally (Point A), to developing an amnesic response (Point B), to first suspecting you might have been abused (Point C), to finally becoming sure that you do have an abuse history by remembering some important parts of the experience (Point D). Sometimes, the cloak of dissociation causes childhood traumas to remain in the shadows of consciousness for many decades before being reclaimed into an individual's personal narrative (moving from Point A to Point D). In Jane's case, she reported that she started having "strange symptoms" around 1999 but did not reach certainty and start psychological treatment regarding her sexual abuse until 2005.

In a 1994 study conducted with 55 women being treated for post-traumatic stress disorder (PTSD) secondary to childhood sexual trauma at the Masters and Johnson Institute, the longest time between Point A (age of child abuse) and Point D (being sure of being abused after a period of amnesia) was 42 years. However, once the survivor starts to suspect he or she has an abuse history, then the process goes much faster. The average length of time was four years for women to cognitively move from her first suspicions of abuse (Point C) to believing that her abuse was real without any doubt (Point D). These results, along with the full report, were presented at the national conventions of the International Society of Traumatic Stress Studies (Peterson & Roe, 1994) as well as the American Psychological Association (Peterson & Roe, 1995).

There were several specific consequences of this self-revelation that created a consistent and unfortunate pattern of Jane's abuse history jumping up from the past and interfering with her ability to be present during sex (without dissociation). First and foremost, this innate ability to dissociate as a long-held survival mechanism helped her get through childhood and adolescence without killing herself. A second consequence of her dissociating was not being able to turn it off and on, so she was not able to be present with Eddie to really enjoy pleasure and intimacy with him. Subsequently, she was unable to experience authentic pleasure free from any guilt and shame associated with arousal and orgasm.

In a sense, the only way she was able to orgasm was to mentally think of herself as a different person (the "bad girl") who did shameful things (in Jane's perspective) but was able to climax. The psychological connection between her past abuse and her present sexual function needed to be severed. This separation would be necessary for Jane to enjoy sex without shame. However, another level of complexity was added to Jane's search for health. This complexity also made more difficult the assessment and treatment of the sexual pain issues, as Jane was very fearful of physical examination and especially the touch involved with the physical therapy needed to treat her vaginismus (even when it was Jane touching herself).

THE HEALING PROCESS

Working with Jane was quite amazing and very rewarding. However, it was sometimes difficult to see her in so much pain and frustration, slipping into anxiety and self-doubt so deeply. In the beginning of treatment, Jane was often caught up in a sense of pressure and tension she felt regarding demands on her to have sex with her husband. While Eddie may have wished to resume sexual relations with his wife, he and I privately talked about the effects of trauma and the importance of patience and grace being exercised during the treatment process. Jane slowly came to see how she created guilt and pressure on herself by not accepting Eddie's commitment not to be demanding. Even though there was no possible way for Eddie to truly understand what she had been through, he accepted her, came to see therapy as an investment in his marriage, and was very supportive to Jane.

While it took significant time for Jane to become fully aware of her abuse memories, it also took significant time to work through her trauma history to break the connection from past to present. In a sense, this process is akin to a survivor doing a jigsaw puzzle but completely in the mind. When we usually work on jigsaw puzzles, where do we start? We start with the edges or border pieces because we recognize them and they are easier to identify in terms of seeing which piece fits with another piece. As previously mentioned, most survivors are aware of some details of their trauma, which represent the outer edge of the puzzle.

As survivors work through the therapy process of building safety, remembering and mourning, and reconciling their past, each detail remembered comes into greater clarity in terms of the shape and how it fits into the neighboring piece—which defines another detail of the trauma experience. Ironically, it really doesn't matter if a survivor remembers all the details of the trauma experience (and metaphorically completes the center of the jigsaw puzzle). In fact, they rarely do. What is most important is that they remember enough to understand enough of the abuse. With appropriate safety and therapeutic guidance, survivors can build a personal narrative that transforms them as a person in a healing way.

Jane was very active in exploring many different pathways to healing her sexual injuries. She practiced yoga religiously and found greater confidence in her body. She engaged in body work through Rolfing, a therapeutic form of massage involving intensive manipulation of the muscular fascia and internal organs to relieve physical and emotional tension. To treat her vaginismus, she participated in specialized physical therapy to help her learn to relax her pelvic floor muscles, used biofeedback techniques to enhance her own relaxation response, and utilized a set of graduated dilators that were used to recondition (loosen up) her vaginal muscles. This she did at her own pace and only with a sufficient level of personal sense of safety, which she learned to create for herself.

By emphasizing her sense of safety, including use of imagery to create a personal safe place as a sanctuary from any threat of harm, she was able to gain a mastery over her fear and transform her abuse experience to something less scary and more manageable. In a sense, the frightening presence that had been lurking in the shadows of her psyche was brought out into the light of her self-healing process. The trauma made her feel like a small powerless child. Her paths to finding trauma resolution were all self-empowering, each expanding her confidence and giving her courage to enter new doorways. Additional readings reinforced her growth, including Judith Herman's *Trauma and Recovery* (1992) and Tara Brach's *Radical Acceptance: Embracing Your Life with the Heart of a Buddha* (2003). Throughout this whole process, Eddie expressed patience, did his best to under-stand, and stayed involved with Jane instead of just saying "go get fixed and don't let it take long." When questions arose and doubts about where they were to go next, supportive individual and couple counseling served as a healing balm for the relationship.

During the course of the treatment, Jane's mother died and Jane grieved this loss. Jane served as a major support to her mother while the mother went through her cancer treatment and eventual hospice care. Sessions became less frequent, more focused on Jane entering a new stage of life, and less often involving Eddie. There was more discussion of spiritual matters and her purpose in life. When their marriage was talked about, it centered on enhancing other aspects of their relationship, not just "fixing their sex life." They began having sex on a regular basis because of her new positive expectations for wanting to be physically intimate with her husband, rather than just seeing sex as something to engage in because of Eddie's expectations.

REFLECTIONS ON JANE'S PATH TO HEALTH

When asked to reflect back on the tremendous transformations she achieved, what first occurred to Jane was that she was not depressed and anxious anymore. She expressed how her view of sex-uality had totally changed from something to dread and experience shame over to see as another positive means of connection with Eddie and source of satisfaction in the marriage. Jane no longer saw herself as being a victim who was afraid of everything in life. She now embraced an identity of a woman who is confident, self-accepting, and grounded. As opposed to the former sense of her sexual abuse being in the driver's seat, Jane feels she is in control over how past events affect her life (including her sex life). This includes moving past how she used to be paralyzed with fear and pain during sex to a place where she learned what makes her body feel comfortable and even enjoy the sensual pleasure she shared with Eddie.

Jane wanted to live what she felt was a normal life, not one defined and consumed by her abuse history. This didn't mean she never felt down, anxious, or frustrated with her husband. It doesn't mean she never thought of the abuse again. It meant that when she does thinks of it, she does so less often, with less intense emotional upset, and without getting distracted from what she wants to accomplish any given day. To a great extent, this was exactly the self-transformational change Jane sought when she first came to therapy. She was not able to articulate this transformation in words but was able in time to trust herself and the therapeutic process to allow the transformation to happen.

About five years after treatment ended, I was delighted to hear her familiar voice on my phone messages. Jane had called for a consultation concerning a family member who was struggling with issues of abuse and she just wanted to talk over the matter. We set a time to meet and I looked forward to hearing an update about how her life evolved after treatment. When she arrived at the clinic, she looked radiant with positive energy and was equally beautiful. It seemed as if I was seeing her with new eyes because she looked so physically different from how I remembered her. She smiled with a confidence that showed an honest authenticity, as if to humbly say, "I really like myself and you probably will too."

Jane described how her and Eddie were getting along well and enjoying life together. They had joyful, healthy sex on a regular basis like they never would have imagined at the start of treatment. She had started a business and was successful enough to expand it recently. I told her about the book and she graciously gave permission to have her story shared. This is Jane and Eddie's journey together. One filled with love for one another, commitment to each other, trust in the healing process, and true resiliency of the human spirit.

REFERENCES

Brach, T. (2003). *Radical acceptance: Embracing your life with the heart of a Buddha.* New York: Bantam.

Herman, J. (1992). *Trauma and recovery: The aftermath of violence from domestic abuse to political terror.* New York: Basic Books.

Peterson, F., & Roe, K. (1994). *Repressed memories of childhood sexual abuse: A preliminary report.* Paper presented at the Annual Conference of the International Society for Traumatic Stress Studies, Chicago.

Peterson, F., & Roe, K. (1995). *Recalling childhood sexual abuse: Suspicions and "being sure."* Paper presented at the Annual Convention of the American Psychological Association, New York.

Van der Kolk, B. (2014). *The body keeps the score: Brain, mind, and body in the healing of trauma.* New York: Random House.

PUTTING YOUR SEXUAL MIND INTO PLAY

The final section of this book has some information that is inbtended to acknowledge that sex can be used to hurt others and to hurt oneself, but also to look at how people can heal from those injuries. Our emphasis so far has been helping you understand your sexual-self, focus on the negative and positive messages you grew up with about sex; understand the benefits of healthy sex; expand your knowledge of the various types of sexual expression; and hopefully have a positive impact on your acceptance of the amazing similarities and differences we share in our human sexuality.

In Chapter 16 we will explore the painful topic of sexual victimization by looking at the history of the laws governing rape and the biases in our culture toward the victims. You will read a very detailed account of a victim's response to having been raped and her disappointment in the judicial response. You will also learn about the various diagnoses and treatments used by mental health professionals to help sexual assault survivors recover. Chapter 17 looks at problematic sexual behaviors and those behaviors that can lead to causing some people to become compulsive in their practice of various sexual activities. This chapter also illustrates approaches to treatment, especially the intensive outpatient treatment program of the first author.

Chapter 18 is an incredible story that chronicles the successful "self-reclamation" of one woman's spirit and documents her journey to sexual health. Chapter 19 presents treatment approaches related to difficulties with attraction, why humans mate, and other fun facts. It also has some exercises that you may choose to do to enhance your sexual communication, sexual fantasies, sexual self-image, and sexual pleasure. Chapter 20 is a fascinating look inside the human psyche, utilizing a conceptual learning tool called the Johari Window. The last chapter is also an invitation to keep on growing and learning about sexuality in terms of self-knowledge, understanding, and acceptance.

CHAPTER SIXTEEN

When Sex Hurts

Written by Jill Bley

INTRODUCTION

This book is focused on sexual health because we (the authors) are firm believers in, and are crusaders for, educating children, adolescents, and adults about human sexuality. We want everyone to learn about the amazing ways that sexuality can and does enhance a person's life. However, we must, unfortunately, acknowledge, understand, and attempt to help people when sex has been hurtful.

We have talked a lot in this book about the ways in which people have been hurt by the negative, sexophrenic messages of our culture. In this chapter, I, the second author, will address the horrible damage that sexual abuse does to a person's sexual, emotional, psychological, and spiritual self. I have been involved for many years in the issue of sexual abuse. In 1972 I was part of a small group of women who started a rape crisis center, in Cincinnati, Ohio. When we began the center, there was little research available about the issue of sexual abuse. Therefore, we had to train ourselves. We traveled to another Rape Crisis Center in Omaha, Nebraska, to see what they were doing. Then we went to the University of Alabama where a woman, Annette Brodsky, who was interested in the issue, was teaching students about what she was learning.

When we came back to Cincinnati we began the enormous task of changing the attitudes of local health care professionals, police officers, and especially prosecutors. Specifically, these professionals included:

1. the hospital staff that treated victims and gathered evidence for the police;
2. the police department, whose job should be to help victims and to make reports in a manner that will aid the prosecutor when an arrest is made; and
3. the prosecutor's office, whose job is to prosecute the alleged assailant. This all took lots of blood, sweat, and tears. We had to do a lot of educating, cajoling, and intimidating.

We also had to go to our state capitol and lobby the legislature (along with many other women) to change the rape laws in Ohio. During this concerted effort that lasted (for our center) approximately 10 years, we were finally successful at getting the system to begin to respond appropriately to victims.

I was working as the Counseling and Training Coordinator at the Center and decided that I wanted to do more. I was accepted to the graduate program at the University of Cincinnati where I studied clinical psychology. My master's thesis and my dissertation were both on the topic of jury attitudes toward rape victims. After I received my PhD, I started a private practice with a specialty in sexuality issues that includes sexual abuse. I also taught sex therapy to graduate students and made sure that the course included a lot of information about sexual abuse and treatment. During my career as a clinical psychologist, I have treated hundreds of sexual abuse survivors.

Before beginning the part of this chapter that will address the psychological aftermath of sexual abuse and treatment issues, I will cover some of the history of attitudes toward sexual abuse as demonstrated by the laws governing rape. Then, one of the most powerfully described cases of sexual assault and its prosecution will be discussed using the survivor's own words in the Stanford University case involving a varsity athlete, Brock Turner. An amazing letter follows in an unprecedented response to this Stanford survivor written by none other than a sitting vice president of the United States. Then I will review some of the statistics related specifically to sexual assaults on campus.

The chapter continues with a brief review of how a diagnosis developed to describe a clinical condition that has become common use in mainstream American culture: post-traumatic stress disorder (PTSD). Not only is PTSD described, but effective evidence-based treatments are explained to inform survivors and anyone interested in understanding the harm done to survivors and the hope of recovery. Finally, the chapter concludes with important guidelines regarding the promotion of a consent culture (as opposed to our tradition of a rape culture) and sexual assault prevention.

HISTORY OF LAWS GOVERNING RAPE

It has taken a very long time for humans to recognize how prevalent sexual abuse has been in almost every society in the world, and even longer for us to acknowledge how severe the damage has been, or to acknowledge that sexual abuse is a crime and should be punished. In 1975 Susan Brownmiller wrote *Against Our Will: Men, Women and Rape*. In it, she outlines the history of rape laws beginning with the Code of Hammurabi, who was the sixth king of Babylon. This ancient code of law dates back to about 1754 BC. It describes the type of offense and the penalty that must be imposed. If a married woman was raped, the law required that she share the blame equally with the rapist. No matter what the circumstances of the crime, it was labeled "adultery," and both were bound and thrown into the river.

The ancient Hebrews were influenced by Hammurabi's code but they were more specific regarding who the victim was and where the offense occurred. They also substituted drowning with stoning to death (Brownmiller, 1975). The Hebrew elders decided that if a woman was raped in the city limits, both victim and attacker were stoned to death, reasoning that someone would surely have heard her cries for help if it was really a rape. Therefore, because no one did hear her cry for help, she must have been complicit. If the attack happened in the fields, where it was assumed no one might hear her screams for help, and she was a married woman, the attacker had to make restitution to her spouse and the spouse could decide her fate, which was usually to put her out. If the female in the field was not married, the rapist had to pay her father the bridal price or dowry of 50 silver shekels and the attacker had to marry her. If the victim was betrothed to someone, then the rapist was stoned to death and the victim was not punished. However, she often experienced the same fate as the married woman who was raped in the fields. Notice that all of these laws assume that the woman is "owned" by a man and that men are never raped.

Brownmiller continues to trace the rape laws from biblical times up until 1975 and ends with English law, upon which American law is based. Prestigious men of the bar such as English Lord Chief Justice Sir Matthew Hale (1609–1676), English jurist and judge Sir William Blackstone (1723–1780), and U.S. jurist and expert in the law of evidence John Henry Wigmore (1863–1943) warned against the female victim and worried about her motivations and reputation. These jurists were cited and quoted frequently in case comments and law journal articles whenever a case was being made for preserving rape laws that require corroboration and nonconsent (Bley, 1978).

Preservation within the law of a need to establish nonconsent to prove rape sets that crime apart from other forcible assaults as can be seen from this quote from a 1969 decision by the United States Court of Appeals for the District of Columbia:

> A man who handles a lady vigorously and with some force (against her will) is plainly guilty of an assault—of an indecent assault. But he does not have an intent to commit rape if his actions are taken in the hope or expectation of thereby awakening desire, and with the further intention of desisting if his approach does not arouse desire or lead to acquiescence but rather encounters continued resistance. When a defendant intends to use the kind of "force" that is enough in his mind to test the existence or persistence of complainant's true intentions, but not enough to achieve sexual intercourse if she "really" rejects him, there is no intention to commit rape.

Because of the laws requiring corroboration and proof of nonconsent, it has been rationalized that the rules of evidence should permit introduction of the sex history of the victim. This belief was articulated in an article titled "Complainant Credibility in Sexual Offense Cases: A Survey of Character Testimony and Psychiatric Experts":

> Whether character evidence is presented as general reputation, personal opinion, or specific acts, it is admissible because the complainant's past conduct is considered relevant in an evidentiary sense to the issue of consent to a particular act committed. The underlying presumption of relevance is that an unchaste complainant is more likely to have consented to a sex act than to have been coerced. Theoretically, this presumption leads to an inference that the complainant has falsified his or her accusation of forcible assault. (*Journal of Criminal Law & Criminology*, 1973)

In recent years, due to the influence of the feminist movement, there has been a nationwide campaign aimed at changing each state's rape laws so as to keep information concerning the victim's sex life from being introduced as evidence in rape cases (Bley, 1978). As you may note all of these quotes are from the 1960s and 1970s. At this point, 2018, all of the states have changed their laws, making the process of reporting and prosecuting somewhat easier on the victim. The problem is that many victims are so traumatized by the crime that they do not want to report, let alone go through a trial and have to deal with the attacker in court. However, even with the changes in the law concerning the evidence that may and may not be admitted, the courts at times still render opinions and judgments that cause many women to continue to believe that they are better off "just forgetting" about it than to try to report and prosecute.

Part of the reason for their reluctance is that even though the laws have changed, the attitudes of many people in this country have not changed. In fact, in 2012, Todd Akin, a member of the U.S. House of Representatives and a candidate for the U.S. Senate, said "If it's a *legitimate rape*, [emphasis added] the female body has ways to try to shut that whole thing down." He was echoing a position that a physician, John Willke, stated when he started the Right to Life Movement in Greater Cincinnati and the state of Ohio. Dr. Willke said that he believed that the stress of rape caused the female body to inhibit conception. He stated, "Rape can radically upset (a woman's) possibility of ovulation, fertilization, implantation and even nurturing a pregnancy." He did concede that pregnancy following rape was "possible" but rare (*Cincinnati Enquirer*, 2012).

David Grimes, an obstetrician and gynecologist, who was chief of the abortion surveillance branch at the Centers for Disease Control and Prevention, criticized Willke: "To suggest this doesn't happen is cruel, cruel, cruel. Rape is an ugly and common occurrence" (*Cincinnati Enquirer*, 2012). Also in 2012, another candidate for the U.S. Senate, Richard Mourdock, said, "Even when life begins with that horrible situation of rape, that is something that *God intended to happen [emphasis added]*." Rick Santorum, who was a senator and presidential candidate, said, "The right approach is to accept this horribly created, in the sense of rape, but nevertheless . . . a gift of human life, and *accept what God is giving to you [emphasis added]*." Ron Paul, a member of the U.S. House of Representatives and presidential candidate, said, "If it's an *honest rape [emphasis added]*, that individual should go immediately to the emergency room. I would give them a shot of estrogen." Future Speaker of the House Paul Ryan (he became Speaker of the House in 2015), along with 250 other members of the U.S. House of Representatives, voted on May 4, 2011, to prohibit federal funding of abortions except in the instances of "an act of *forcible rape [emphasis added]*, or, if a minor, an act of incest" (H.R. 3, 112th Cong.). That house bill was then sent to the Senate. The Senate did not pass the bill. And then the most egregious statement of all was made by Texas gubernatorial candidate Clayton Williams in 1990 when speaking about rape, "*If it's inevitable, just relax and enjoy it [emphasis added]*."

These attitudes have set the stage for the judiciary to ignore the severity of the crime of rape and the consequences to the victim and focus their concern on the consequences to the perpetrator. We have seen this judicial attitude time and time again in this country and around the world. The effects of those attitudes are poignantly stated in this letter that a student at Stanford University, who was the victim of a vicious rapist (charged with three counts of sexual assault), read aloud to her attacker after he was convicted of the charges and then given an incredibly light sentence by the judge. The perpetrator was also a Stanford student and an athlete.

[Authors' Note: The following narrative contains a very explicit description of a horrible sexual assault. Reading it may be very difficult for many people, especially if you or someone you know has been a victim of sexual assault. You may feel triggered and retraumatized. Even if you are

not a victim and do not know anyone who is a victim, this brave woman's account of her ordeal may bring tears to your eyes, as happens to me every time I read it.]

The Survivor's Letter Read to the Rapist in Court After He Was Sentenced to Only Six Months in County Jail and Probation[1]

Your Honor, if it is all right, for the majority of this statement I would like to address the defendant directly.

You don't know me, but you've been inside me, and that's why we're here today.

On January 17th, 2015, it was a quiet Saturday night at home. My dad made some dinner and I sat at the table with my younger sister who was visiting for the weekend. I was working full time and it was approaching my bed time. I planned to stay at home by myself, watch some TV and read, while she went to a party with her friends. Then, I decided it was my only night with her, I had nothing better to do, so why not, there's a dumb party ten minutes from my house, I would go, dance like a fool, and embarrass my younger sister. On the way there, I joked that undergrad guys would have braces. My sister teased me for wearing a beige cardigan to a frat party like a librarian. I called myself "big mama," because I knew I'd be the oldest one there. I made silly faces, let my guard down, and drank liquor too fast not factoring in that my tolerance had significantly lowered since college.

The next thing I remember I was in a gurney in a hallway. I had dried blood and bandages on the backs of my hands and elbow. I thought maybe I had fallen and was in an admin office on campus. I was very calm and wondering where my sister was. A deputy explained I had been assaulted. I still remained calm, assured he was speaking to the wrong person. I knew no one at this party. When I was finally allowed to use the restroom, I pulled down the hospital pants they had given me, went to pull down my underwear, and felt nothing. I still remember the feeling of my hands touching my skin and grabbing nothing. I looked down and there was nothing. The thin piece of fabric, the only thing between my vagina and anything else, was missing and everything inside me was silenced. I still don't have words for that feeling. In order to keep breathing, I thought maybe the policemen used scissors to cut them off for evidence.

Then, I felt pine needles scratching the back of my neck and started pulling them out of my hair. I thought maybe, the pine needles had fallen from a tree onto my head. My brain was talking my gut into not collapsing. Because my gut was saying, help me, help me.

I shuffled from room to room with a blanket wrapped around me, pine needles trailing behind me, I left a little pile in every room I sat in. I was asked to sign papers that said "Rape Victim" and I thought something has really happened. My clothes were confiscated and I stood naked while the nurses held a ruler to various abrasions on my body and photographed them. The three of us worked to comb the pine needles out of my hair, six hands to fill one paper bag. To calm me down, they said it's just the flora and fauna, flora and fauna. I had multiple swabs inserted into my vagina and anus, needles for shots, pills, had a Nikon pointed right into my

---

1   Emily Doe, "Stanford Victim Letter," https://www.sccgov.org/sites/da/newsroom/newsreleases/Documents/B-Turner%20 VIS.pdf. Copyright in the Public Domain.

spread legs. I had long, pointed beaks inside me and had my vagina smeared with cold, blue paint to check for abrasions.

After a few hours of this, they let me shower. I stood there examining my body beneath the stream of water and decided, I don't want my body anymore. I was terrified of it, I didn't know what had been in it, if it had been contaminated, who had touched it. I wanted to take off my body like a jacket and leave it at the hospital with everything else.

On that morning, all that I was told was that I had been found behind a dumpster, potentially penetrated by a stranger, and that I should get retested for HIV because results don't always show up immediately. But for now, I should go home and get back to my normal life. Imagine stepping back into the world with only that information. They gave me huge hugs and I walked out of the hospital into the parking lot wearing the new sweatshirt and sweatpants they provided me, as they had only allowed me to keep my necklace and shoes.

My sister picked me up, face wet from tears and contorted in anguish. Instinctively and immediately, I wanted to take away her pain. I smiled at her, I told her to look at me, I'm right here, I'm okay, everything's okay, I'm right here. My hair is washed and clean, they gave me the strangest shampoo, calm down, and look at me. Look at these funny new sweatpants and sweat-shirt, I look like a P.E. teacher, let's go home, let's eat something. She did not know that beneath my sweatsuit, I had scratches and bandages on my skin, my vagina was sore and had become a strange, dark color from all the prodding, my underwear was missing, and I felt too empty to continue to speak. That I was also afraid, that I was also devastated. That day we drove home and for hours in silence my younger sister held me.

My boyfriend did not know what happened, but called that day and said, "I was really worried about you last night, you scared me, did you make it home okay?" I was horrified. That's when I learned I had called him that night in my blackout, left an incomprehensible voicemail, that we had also spoken on the phone, but I was slurring so heavily he was scared for me, that he repeatedly told me to go find [my sister]. Again, he asked me, "What happened last night? Did you make it home okay?" I said yes, and hung up to cry.

I was not ready to tell my boyfriend or parents that actually, I may have been raped behind a dumpster, but I don't know by who or when or how. If I told them, I would see the fear on their faces, and mine would multiply by tenfold, so instead I pretended the whole thing wasn't real.

I tried to push it out of my mind, but it was so heavy I didn't talk, I didn't eat, I didn't sleep, I didn't interact with anyone. After work, I would drive to a secluded place to scream. I didn't talk, I didn't eat, I didn't sleep, I didn't interact with anyone, and I became isolated from the ones I loved most. For over a week after the incident, I didn't get any calls or updates about that night or what happened to me. The only symbol that proved that it hadn't just been a bad dream, was the sweatshirt from the hospital in my drawer.

One day, I was at work, scrolling through the news on my phone, and came across an article. In it, I read and learned for the first time about how I was found unconscious, with my hair disheveled, long necklace wrapped around my neck, bra pulled out of my dress, dress pulled off over my shoulders and pulled up above my waist, that I was butt naked all the way down to my boots, legs spread apart, and had been penetrated by a foreign object by someone I did not recognize. This was how I learned what happened to me, sitting at my desk reading the news at work. I learned what happened to me the same time everyone else in the world learned what happened to me. That's when the pine needles in my hair made sense, they didn't fall from a tree. He had taken off my underwear, his fingers had been inside of me. I don't even know this person. I still don't know this person. When I read about me like this, I said, this can't be me, this can't be me. I could not digest or accept any of this information. I could not imagine my family having to read about this online. I kept reading. In the next paragraph, I read something that I will never forgive; I read that according to him, I liked it. I liked it. Again, I do not have words for these feelings.

It's like if you were to read an article where a car was hit, and found dented, in a ditch. But maybe the car enjoyed being hit. Maybe the other car didn't mean to hit it, just bump it up a little bit. Cars get in accidents all the time, people aren't always paying attention, can we really say who's at fault.

And then, at the bottom of the article, after I learned about the graphic details of my own sexual assault, the article listed his swimming times. She was found breathing, unresponsive with her underwear six inches away from her bare stomach curled in [a] fetal position. By the way, he's really good at swimming. Throw in my mile time if that's what we're doing. I'm good at cooking, put that in there, I think the end is where you list your extracurriculars to cancel out all the sickening things that've happened.

The night the news came out I sat my parents down and told them that I had been assaulted, to not look at the news because it's upsetting, just know that I'm okay, I'm right here, and I'm okay. But halfway through telling them, my mom had to hold me because I could no longer stand up.

The night after it happened, he said he didn't know my name, said he wouldn't be able to identify my face in a lineup, didn't mention any dialogue between us, no words, only dancing and kissing. Dancing is a cute term— was it snapping fingers and twirling dancing, or just bodies grinding up against each other in a crowded room? I wonder if kissing was just faces sloppily pressed up against each other? When the detective asked if he had planned on taking me back to his dorm, he said no. When the detective asked how we ended up behind the dumpster, he said he didn't know. He admitted to kissing other girls at that party, one of whom was my own sister who pushed him away. He admitted to wanting to hook up with someone. I was the wounded antelope of the herd, completely alone and vulnerable, physically unable to fend for myself, and he chose me. Sometimes I think, if I hadn't gone, then this never would've happened. But then I realized, it would have happened, just to somebody else. You were about to enter four years of access to drunk girls and parties, and if this is the foot you started off on, then it is right you did not continue. The night after it happened, he said he thought I liked it because I rubbed his back. A back rub.

Never mentioned me voicing consent, never mentioned us even speaking, a back rub. One more time, in public news, I learned that my ass and vagina were completely exposed outside, my breasts had been groped, fingers had been jabbed inside me along with pine needles and debris, my bare skin and head had been rubbing against the ground behind a dumpster, while an erect freshman was humping my half naked, unconscious body. But I don't remember, so how do I prove I didn't like it.

I thought there's no way this is going to trial; there were witnesses, there was dirt in my body, he ran but was caught. He's going to settle, formally apologize, and we will both move on. Instead, I was told he hired a powerful attorney, expert witnesses, private investigators who were going to try and find details about my personal life to use against me, find loopholes in my story to invalidate me and my sister, in order to show that this sexual assault was in fact a misunderstanding. That he was going to go to any length to convince the world he had simply been confused.

I was not only told that I was assaulted, I was told that because I couldn't remember, I technically could not prove it was unwanted. And that distorted me, damaged me, almost broke me. It is the saddest type of confusion to be told I was assaulted and nearly raped, blatantly out in the open, but we don't know if it counts as assault yet. I had to fight for an entire year to make it clear that there was something wrong with this situation.

When I was told to be prepared in case we didn't win, I said, I can't prepare for that. He was guilty the minute I woke up. No one can talk me out of the hurt he caused me. Worst of all, I was warned, because he now knows you don't remember, he is going to get to write the script. He can say whatever he wants and no one can contest it. I had no power, I had no voice, I was defenseless. My memory loss would be used against me. My testimony was weak, was incomplete, and I was made to believe that perhaps, I am not enough to win this. His attorney constantly reminded the jury, the only one we can believe is Brock, because she doesn't remember. That helplessness was traumatizing.

Instead of taking time to heal, I was taking time to recall the night in excruciating detail, in order to prepare for the attorney's questions that would be invasive, aggressive, and designed to steer me off course, to contradict myself, my sister, phrased in ways to manipulate my answers. Instead of his attorney saying, Did you notice any abrasions? He said, You didn't notice any abrasions, right? This was a game of strategy, as if I could be tricked out of my own worth. The sexual assault had been so clear, but instead, here I was at the trial, answering questions like:

How old are you? How much do you weigh? What did you eat that day? Well what did you have for dinner? Who made dinner? Did you drink with dinner? No, not even water? When did you drink? How much did you drink? What container did you drink out of? Who gave you the drink? How much do you usually drink? Who dropped you off at this party? At what time? But where exactly? What were you wearing? Why were you going to this party? What'd you do when you got there? Are you sure you did that? But what time did you do that? What does this text mean? Who were you texting? When did you urinate? Where did you urinate? With whom did you urinate outside? Was your phone on silent when your sister called? Do you remember silencing it? Really because on page 53 I'd like to point out that you said it was set to ring. Did you drink in college? You said you were a party animal? How many times did you black out? Did you party at frats? Are you serious with your boyfriend? Are you sexually active with him? When did you start dating? Would you ever cheat? Do you have a history of cheating? What do you mean when you said you wanted to reward him? Do you remember what time you woke up? Were you wearing your cardigan? What color was your cardigan? Do you remember any more from that night? No? Okay, well, we'll let Brock fill it in.

I was pummeled with narrowed, pointed questions that dissected my personal life, love life, past life, family life, inane questions, accumulating trivial details to try and find an excuse for this guy who had me half naked before even bothering to ask for my name. After a physical assault, I was assaulted with questions designed to attack me, to say see, her facts don't line up, she's out of her mind, she's practically an alcoholic, she probably wanted to hook up, he's like an athlete right, they were both drunk, whatever, the hospital stuff she remembers is after the fact, why take it into account, Brock has a lot at stake so he's having a really hard time right now.

And then it came time for him to testify and I learned what it meant to be re-victimized. I want to remind you, the night after it happened he said he never planned to take me back to his dorm. He said he didn't know why we were behind a dumpster. He got up to leave because he wasn't feeling well when he was suddenly chased and attacked. Then he learned I could not remember.

So one year later, as predicted, a new dialogue emerged. Brock had a strange new story, almost sounded like a poorly written young adult novel with kissing and dancing and hand holding and lovingly tumbling onto the ground, and most importantly in this new story, there was suddenly consent. One year after the incident, he remembered, oh yeah, by the way she actually said yes, to everything, so.

He said he had asked if I wanted to dance. Apparently I said yes. He'd asked if I wanted to go to his dorm, I said yes. Then he asked if he could finger me and I said yes. Most guys don't ask, can I finger you? Usually there's a natural progression of things, unfolding consensually, not a Q and A. But apparently I granted full permission. He's in the clear. Even in his story, I only said a total of three words, yes yes yes, before he had me half naked on the ground. Future reference, if you are confused about whether a girl can consent, see if she can speak an entire sentence. You couldn't even do that. Just one coherent string of words. Where was the confusion? This is common sense, human decency.

According to him, the only reason we were on the ground was because I fell down. Note: if a girl falls down help her get back up. If she is too drunk to even walk and falls down, do not mount her, hump her, take off her underwear, and insert your hand inside her vagina. If a girl falls down help her up. If she is wearing a cardigan over her dress don't take it off so that you can touch her breasts. Maybe she is cold, maybe that's why she wore the cardigan.

Next in the story, two Swedes on bicycles approached you and you ran. When they tackled you why didn't you say, "Stop! Everything's okay, go ask her, she's right over there, she'll tell you." I mean you had just asked for my consent, right? I was awake, right? When the policeman arrived and interviewed the evil Swede who tackled you, he was crying so hard he couldn't speak because of what he'd seen.

Your attorney has repeatedly pointed out, well we don't know exactly when she became unconscious. And you're right, maybe I was still fluttering my eyes and wasn't completely limp yet. That was never the point. I was too drunk to speak English, too drunk to consent way before I was on the ground. I should have never been touched in the first place. Brock stated, "At no time did I see that she was not responding. If at any time I thought she was not responding, I would have stopped immediately." Here's the thing, if your plan was to stop only when I became unresponsive, then you still do not understand. You didn't even stop when I was unconscious anyway! Someone else stopped you. Two guys on bikes noticed I wasn't moving in the dark and had to tackle you. How did you not notice while on top of me?

You said, you would have stopped and gotten help. You say that, but I want you to explain how you would've helped me, step by step, walk me through this. I want to know, if those evil Swedes had not found me, how the night would have played out. I am asking you: Would you have pulled my underwear back on over my boots? Untangled the necklace wrapped around my neck? Closed my legs, covered me? Pick the pine needles from my hair? Asked if the abrasions on my neck and bottom hurt? Would you then go find a friend and say, Will you help me get her somewhere warm and soft? I don't sleep when I think about the way it could have gone if the two guys had never come. What would have happened to me? That's what you'll never have a good answer for, that's what you can't explain even after a year.

On top of all this, he claimed that I orgasmed after one minute of digital penetration. The nurse said there had been abrasions, lacerations, and dirt in my genitalia. Was that before or after I came?

To sit under oath and inform all of us, that yes I wanted it, yes I permitted it, and that you are the true victim attacked by Swedes for reasons unknown to you is appalling, is demented, is selfish, is damaging. It is enough to be suffering. It is another thing to have someone ruthlessly working to diminish the gravity of validity of this suffering.

My family had to see pictures of my head strapped to a gurney full of pine needles, of my body in the dirt with my eyes closed, hair messed up, limbs bent, and dress hiked up. And even after that, my family had to listen to your attorney say the pictures were after the fact, we can dismiss them. To say, yes her nurse confirmed there was redness and abrasions inside her, significant trauma to her genitalia, but that's what happens when you finger someone, and he's already admitted to that. To listen to your attorney attempt to paint a picture of me, the face of girls gone wild, as if somehow that would make it so that I had this coming for me. To listen to him say I sounded drunk on the phone because I'm silly and that's my goofy way of speaking. To point out that in the voicemail, I said I would reward my boyfriend and we all know what I was thinking. I assure you my rewards program is non-transferable, especially to any nameless man that approaches me.

He has done irreversible damage to me and my family during the trial and we have sat silently, listening to him shape the evening. But in the end, his unsupported statements and his attorney's twisted logic fooled no one. The truth won, the truth spoke for itself.

You are guilty. Twelve jurors convicted you guilty of three felony counts beyond reasonable doubt, that's twelve votes per count, thirty six yeses confirming guilt, that's one hundred percent, unanimous guilt. And I thought finally it is over, finally he will own up to what he did, truly apologize, we will both move on and get better. Then I read your statement.

If you are hoping that one of my organs will implode from anger and I will die, I'm almost there. You are very close. This is not a story of another drunk college hookup with poor decision making. Assault is not an accident. Somehow, you still don't get it. Somehow, you still sound confused. I will now read portions of the defendant's statement and respond to them.

You said, being drunk I just couldn't make the best decisions and neither could she.

Alcohol is not an excuse. Is it a factor? Yes. But alcohol was not the one who stripped me, fingered me, had my head dragging against the ground, with me almost fully naked. Having too much to drink was an amateur mistake that I admit to, but it is not criminal. Everyone in this room has had a night where they have regretted drinking too much, or knows someone close to them who has had a night where they have regretted drinking too much. Regretting drinking is not the same as regretting sexual assault. We were both drunk, the difference is I did not take off your pants and underwear, touch you inappropriately, and run away. That's the difference.

You said, If I wanted to get to know her, I should have asked for her number, rather than asking her to go back to my room.

I'm not mad because you didn't ask for my number. Even if you did know me, I would not want to be in this situation. My own boyfriend knows me, but if he asked to finger me behind a dumpster, I would slap him. No girl wants to be in this situation. Nobody. I don't care if you know their phone number or not.

You said, I stupidly thought it was okay for me to do what everyone around me was doing, which was drinking. I was wrong.

Again, you were not wrong for drinking. Everyone around you was not sexually assaulting me. You were wrong for doing what nobody else was doing, which was pushing your erect dick in your pants against my naked, defenseless body concealed in a dark area, where partygoers could no longer see or protect me, and my own sister could not find me. Sipping fireball is not your crime. Peeling off and discarding my underwear like a candy wrapper to insert your finger into my body, is where you went wrong. Why am I still explaining this?

You said, during the trial I didn't want to victimize her at all. That was just my attorney and his way of approaching the case.

Your attorney is not your scapegoat, he represents you. Did your attorney say some incredulously infuriating, degrading things? Absolutely. He said you had an erection, because it was cold.

You said, you are in the process of establishing a program for high school and college students in which you speak about your experience to "speak out against the college campus drinking culture and the sexual promiscuity that goes along with that."

Campus drinking culture. That's what we're speaking out against? You think that's what I've spent the past year fighting for? Not awareness about campus sexual assault, or rape, or learning to recognize consent. Campus drinking culture. Down with Jack Daniels. Down with Skyy Vodka. If you want to talk to people about drinking go to an AA meeting. You realize, having a drinking problem is different than drinking and then forcefully trying to have sex with someone? Show men how to respect women, not how to drink less.

Drinking culture and the sexual promiscuity that goes along with that. Goes along with that, like a side effect, like fries on the side of your order. Where does promiscuity even come into play? I don't see headlines that read, Brock Turner, Guilty of drinking too much and the sexual promiscuity that goes along with that. Campus Sexual Assault. There's your first powerpoint slide. Rest assured, if you fail to fix the topic of your talk, I will follow you to every school you go to and give a follow up presentation.

Lastly you said, I want to show people that one night of drinking can ruin a life.

A life, one life, yours, you forgot about mine. Let me rephrase for you, I want to show people that one night of drinking can ruin two lives. You and me. You are the cause, I am the effect. You have dragged me through this hell with you, dipped me back into that night again and again. You knocked down both our towers, I collapsed at the same time you did. If you think I was spared, came out unscathed, that today I ride off into sunset, while you suffer the greatest blow, you are mistaken. Nobody wins. We have all been devastated, we have all been trying to find some meaning in all of this suffering. Your damage was concrete; stripped of titles, degrees, enrollment. My damage was internal, unseen, I carry it with me. You took away my worth, my privacy, my energy, my time, my safety, my intimacy, my confidence, my own voice, until today.

See one thing we have in common is that we were both unable to get up in the morning. I am no stranger to suffering. You made me a victim. In newspapers my name was "unconscious intoxicated woman," ten syllables, and nothing more than that. For a while, I believed that that was all I was. I had to force myself to relearn my real name, my identity. To relearn that this is not all that I am. That I am not just a drunk victim at a frat party found behind a dumpster, while you are the All American swimmer at a top university, innocent until proven guilty, with so much at stake. I am a human being who has been irreversibly hurt, my life was put on hold for over a year, waiting to figure out if I was worth something.

My independence, natural joy, gentleness, and steady lifestyle I had been enjoying became distorted beyond recognition. I became closed off, angry, self-deprecating, tired, irritable, empty. The isolation at times was unbearable. You cannot give me back the life I had before that night either. While you worry about your shattered reputation, I refrigerated spoons every night so when I woke up, and my eyes were puffy from crying, I would hold the spoons to my eyes to lessen the swelling so that I could see. I showed up an hour late to work every morning, excused myself to cry in the stairwells, I can tell you all the best places in that building to cry where no one can hear you. The pain became so bad that I had to explain the private details to my boss to let her know why I was leaving. I needed time because continuing day to day was not possible. I used my savings to go as far away as I could possibly be. I did not return to work full time as I knew I'd have to take weeks off in the future for the hearing and trial, that were constantly being rescheduled. My life was put on hold for over a year, my structure had collapsed.

I can't sleep alone at night without having a light on, like a five year old, because I have nightmares of being touched where I cannot wake up, I did this thing where I waited until the sun came up and I felt safe enough to sleep. For three months, I went to bed at six o'clock in the morning.

I used to pride myself on my independence, now I am afraid to go on walks in the evening, to attend social events with drinking among friends where I should be comfortable being. I have become a little barnacle always needing to be at someone's side, to have my boyfriend standing next to me, sleeping beside me, protecting me. It is embarrassing how feeble I feel, how timidly I move through life, always guarded, ready to defend myself, ready to be angry.

You have no idea how hard I have worked to rebuild parts of me that are still weak. It took me eight months to even talk about what happened. I could no longer connect with friends, with everyone around me. I would scream at my boyfriend, my own family whenever they brought this up. You never let me forget what happened to me. At the end of the hearing, the trial, I was too tired to speak. I would leave drained, silent. I would go home turn off my phone and for days I would not speak. You bought me a ticket to a planet where I lived by myself. Every time a new article came out, I lived with the paranoia that my entire hometown would find out and know me as the girl who got assaulted. I didn't want anyone's pity and am still learning to accept victim as part of my identity. You made my own hometown an uncomfortable place to be.

You cannot give me back my sleepless nights. The way I have broken down sobbing uncontrollably if I'm watching a movie and a woman is harmed, to say it lightly, this experience has expanded my empathy for other victims. I have lost weight from stress, when people would comment I told them I've been running a lot lately. There are times I did not want to be touched. I have to relearn that I am not fragile, I am capable, I am wholesome, not just livid and weak.

When I see my younger sister hurting, when she is unable to keep up in school, when she is deprived of joy, when she is not sleeping, when she is crying so hard on the phone she is barely breathing, telling me over and over again she is sorry for leaving me alone that night, sorry sorry sorry, when she feels more guilt than you, then I do not forgive you. That night I had called her to try and find her, but you found me first. Your attorney's closing statement began, "[Her sister] said she was fine and who knows her better than her sister." You tried to use my own sister against me? Your points of attack were so weak, so low, it was almost embarrassing. You do not touch her.

You should have never done this to me. Secondly, you should have never made me fight so long to tell you, you should have never done this to me. But here we are. The damage is done, no one can undo it. And now we both have a choice. We can let this destroy us, I can remain angry and hurt and you can be in denial, or we can face it head on, I accept the pain, you accept the punishment, and we move on.

Your life is not over, you have decades of years ahead to rewrite your story. The world is huge, it is so much bigger than Palo Alto and Stanford, and you will make a space for yourself in it where you can be useful and happy. But right now, you do not get to shrug your shoulders and be confused anymore. You do not get to pretend that there were no red flags. You have been convicted of violating me, intentionally, forcibly, sexually, with malicious intent, and all you can admit to is consuming alcohol. Do not talk about the sad way your life was upturned because alcohol made you do bad things. Figure out how to take responsibility for your own conduct.

Now to address the sentencing. When I read the probation officer's report, I was in disbelief, consumed by anger which eventually quieted down to profound sadness. My statements have been slimmed down to distortion and taken out of context. I fought hard during this trial and will not have the outcome minimized by a probation officer who attempted to evaluate my current state and my wishes in a fifteen minute conversation, the majority of which was spent answering questions I had about the legal system. The context is also important. Brock had yet to issue a statement, and I had not read his remarks.

My life has been on hold for over a year, a year of anger, anguish and uncertainty, until a jury of my peers rendered a judgment that validated the injustices I had endured. Had Brock admitted guilt and remorse and offered to settle early on, I would have considered a lighter sentence, respecting his honesty, grateful to be able to move our lives forward. Instead he took the risk of going to trial, added insult to injury and forced me to relive the hurt as details about my personal life and sexual assault were brutally dissected before the public. He pushed me and my family through a year of inexplicable, unnecessary suffering, and should face the consequences of challenging his crime, of putting my pain into question, of making us wait so long for justice.

I told the probation officer I do not want Brock to rot away in prison. I did not say he does not deserve to be behind bars. The probation officer's recommendation of a year or less in county jail is a soft timeout, a mockery of the seriousness of his assaults, an insult to me and all women. It gives the message that a stranger can be inside you without proper consent and he will receive less than what has been defined as the minimum sentence. Probation should be denied. I also told the probation officer that what I truly wanted was for Brock to get it, to understand and admit to his wrongdoing.

Unfortunately, after reading the defendant's report, I am severely disappointed and feel that he has failed to exhibit sincere remorse or responsibility for his conduct. I fully respected his right to a trial, but even after twelve jurors unanimously convicted him guilty of three felonies, all he has admitted to doing is ingesting alcohol. Someone who cannot take full accountability for his actions does not deserve a mitigating sentence. It is deeply offensive that he would try and dilute rape with a suggestion of "promiscuity." By definition rape is the absence of promiscuity, rape is the absence of consent, and it perturbs me deeply that he can't even see that distinction.

The probation officer factored in that the defendant is youthful and has no prior convictions. In my opinion, he is old enough to know what he did was wrong. When you are eighteen in this country you can go to war. When you are nineteen, you are old enough to pay the consequences for attempting to rape someone. He is young, but he is old enough to know better.

As this is a first offence I can see where leniency would beckon. On the other hand, as a society, we cannot forgive everyone's first sexual assault or digital rape. It doesn't make sense. The seriousness of rape has to be communicated clearly, we should not create a culture that suggests we learn that rape is wrong through trial and error. The consequences of sexual assault needs to be severe enough that people feel enough fear to exercise good judgment even if they are drunk, severe enough to be preventative.

The probation officer weighed the fact that he has surrendered a hard earned swimming scholarship. How fast Brock swims does not lessen the severity of what happened to me, and should not lessen the severity of his punishment. If a first time offender from an underprivileged background was accused of three felonies and displayed no accountability for his actions other than drinking, what would his sentence be? The fact that Brock was an athlete at a private university should not be seen as an entitlement to leniency, but as an opportunity to send a message that sexual assault is against the law regardless of social class.

The Probation Officer has stated that this case, when compared to other crimes of similar nature, may be considered less serious due to the defendant's level of intoxication. It felt serious. That's all I'm going to say.

What has he done to demonstrate that he deserves a break? He has only apologized for drinking and has yet to define what he did to me as sexual assault, he has re-victimized me continually, relentlessly. He has been found guilty of three serious felonies and it is time for him to accept the consequences of his actions. He will not be quietly excused.

He is a lifetime sex registrant. That doesn't expire. Just like what he did to me doesn't expire, doesn't just go away after a set number of years. It stays with me, it's part of my identity, it has forever changed the way I carry myself, the way I live the rest of my life.

To conclude, I want to say thank you. To everyone from the intern who made me oatmeal when I woke up at the hospital that morning, to the deputy who waited beside me, to the nurses who calmed me, to the detective who listened to me and never judged me, to my advocates who stood unwaveringly beside me, to my therapist who taught me to find courage in vulnerability, to my boss for being kind and understanding, to my incredible parents who teach me how to turn pain into strength, to my grandma who snuck chocolate into the courtroom throughout this to give to me, my friends who remind me how to be happy, to my boyfriend who is patient and loving, to my unconquerable sister who is the other half of my heart, to Alaleh, my idol, who fought tirelessly and never doubted me. Thank you to everyone involved in the trial for their time and attention. Thank you to girls across the nation that wrote cards to my DA to give to me, so many strangers who cared for me.

Most importantly, thank you to the two men who saved me, who I have yet to meet. I sleep with two bicycles that I drew taped above my bed to remind myself there are heroes in this story. That we are looking out for one another. To have known all of these people, to have felt their protection and love, is something I will never forget.

And finally, to girls everywhere, I am with you. On nights when you feel alone, I am with you. When people doubt you or dismiss you, I am with you. I fought every day for you. So never stop fighting, I believe you. As the author Anne Lamott once wrote, "Lighthouses don't go running all over an island looking for boats to save; they just stand there shining." Although I can't save every boat, I hope that by speaking today, you absorbed a small amount of light, a small knowing that you can't be silenced, a small satisfaction that justice was served, a small assurance that we are getting somewhere, and a big, big knowing that you are important, unquestionably, you are untouchable, you are beautiful, you are to be valued, respected, undeniably, every minute of every day, you are powerful and nobody can take that away from you. To girls everywhere, I am with you. Thank you

After reading the powerful statement written by this courageous victim, when it went viral on the Internet, Vice President Joe Biden, who was the sitting vice president at the time, wrote an open letter to her (Biden, 2016). Vice President Biden was very concerned about the issue of violence toward women. In 1994 he wrote the Violence Against Women Act. He has been a strong advocate to spread awareness about campus sexual assault. Here is the letter he wrote to her:

An Open Letter to a Courageous Young Woman[2]

I do not know your name—but your words are forever seared on my soul. Words that should be required reading for men and women of all ages. Words that I wish with all of my heart you never had to write.

---

2   Joseph Biden, "An Open Letter to a Courageous Young Woman." Copyright in the Public Domain.

I am in awe of your courage for speaking out—for so clearly naming the wrongs that were done to you and so passionately asserting your equal claim to human dignity.

And I am filled with furious anger—both that this happened to you and that our culture is still so broken that you were ever put in the position of defending your own worth.

It must have been wrenching—to relive what he did to you all over again. But you did it anyway, in the hope that your strength might prevent this crime from happening to someone else. Your bravery is breathtaking.

You are a warrior—with a solid steel spine. I do not know your name—but I know that a lot of people failed you that terrible January night and in the months that followed.

Anyone at that party who saw that you were incapacitated yet looked the other way and did not offer assistance. Anyone who dismissed what happened to you as "just another crazy night." Anyone who asked "what did you expect would happen when you drank that much?" or thought you must have brought it on yourself.

You were failed by a culture on our college campuses where one in five women is sexually assaulted—year after year after year. A culture that promotes passivity. That encourages young men and women on campuses to simply turn a blind eye.

The statistics on college sexual assault haven't gone down in the past two decades. It's obscene, and it's a failure that lies at all our feet.

And you were failed by anyone who dared to question this one clear and simple truth: Sex without consent is rape. Period. It is a crime. I do not know your name—but thanks to you, I know that heroes ride bicycles.

Those two men who saw what was happening to you—who took it upon themselves to step in—they did what they instinctually knew to be right. They did not say "It's none of my business."

They did not worry about the social or safety implications of intervening, or about what their peers might think. Those two men epitomize what it means to be a responsible bystander.

To do otherwise—to see an assault about to take place and do nothing to intervene—makes you part of the problem. Like I tell college students all over this country—it's on us. All of us.

We all have a responsibility to stop the scourge of violence against women once and for all. I do not know your name—but I see your unconquerable spirit.

I see the limitless potential of an incredibly talented young woman—full of possibility. I see the shoulders on which our dreams for the future rest.

I see you. You will never be defined by what the defendant's father callously termed "20 minutes of action." His son will be.

I join your global chorus of supporters, because we can never say enough to survivors: I believe you. It is not your fault. What you endured is never, never, never, NEVER a woman's fault.

And while the justice system has spoken in your particular case, the nation is not satisfied. And that is why we will continue to speak out. We will speak to change the culture on our college campuses—a culture that continues to ask the wrong questions: What were you wearing?

Why were you there? What did you say? How much did you drink? Instead of asking: Why did he think he had license to rape?

We will speak out against those who seek to engage in plausible deniability. Those who know that this is happening, but don't want to get involved. Who believe that this ugly crime is "complicated."

We will speak of you—you who remain anonymous not only to protect your identity, but because you so eloquently represent "every woman." We will make lighthouses of ourselves, as you did—and shine.

Your story has already changed lives. You have helped change the culture. You have shaken untold thousands out of the torpor and indifference towards sexual violence that allows this problem to continue.

Your words will help people you have never met and never will. You have given them the strength they need to fight. And so, I believe, you will save lives.

I do not know your name—but I will never forget you. The millions who have been touched by your story will never forget you.

And if everyone who shared your letter on social media, or who had a private conversation in their own homes with their daughters and sons, draws upon the passion, the outrage, and the commitment they feel right now the next time there is a choice between intervening and walking away—then I believe you will have helped to change the world for the better.

There is an addendum to this case that illustrates how difficult it is for a victim to feel that the criminal justice system in our country is truly "just." It turned out that the assailant in this case, Brock Turner, served only three months of his measly six-month sentence. When released, he only had to serve three years of probation (when he could have been sentenced to over a decade in prison). Turner believes that his conviction was wrong and unjust, so he appealed his convictions to try to clear his record. He was convicted of digitally penetrating an intoxicated and unconscious person and one count of assault with intent to commit rape. His argument was that even though two bicyclists saw him thrusting on top of the victim, who was half naked, he was only trying to have "outercourse" with her. His lawyers (pathetically) argued that he was practicing a version of "safe sex" and that since he did not penetrate her with his penis (only his finger), it was not really a rape of an unconscious woman. Part of his lawyers' ridiculous "outercourse only" argument was that the intoxicated Turner would have never attempted to have intercourse with the victim if Turner had not been stopped by the cyclists (and then tried to run away).

One of the appellate justices hearing the case was reported as saying, "I absolutely don't understand what you are talking about." However, it did turn out to be correct that Turner, according to California law, could not be convicted of rape because the rape law was specifically confined to sexual intercourse. In the end, justice was partially served as the appellate court did not accept the "outercourse only" argument. The appellate court did not set aside his convictions and Brock Turner will always have a record for sexual assault, have to serve three years of probation, and will always have to register as a sex offender (Furmin, 2016). Further, this case brought some important changes to the laws about sexual assault in California. The loophole in the law (about rape only being penile-vaginal intercourse) was closed in 2016 so that the crime of rape now includes digital or oral penetration. Another positive outcome of this case was the public attention focused on the influences that gender, race, and class privilege played in the sentencing of Brock Turner. The public outrage about the outrageously lenient six-month sentence (only half served) was so great that the citizens of Santa Clara County were able to unseat the judge who sentenced Brock Turner by voting to recall him from the bench by 60% of the vote. Looks like the Vice-President was right in his letter to Emily Doe: "... you will have helped to change the world for the better."

At the time of the Stanford rape, 2015, it was reported that there had been 30 known reported sex offenses on the Stanford campus that year. That means that there may have been two times that number since many sexual assaults go unreported. One study estimated that for every 1,000 college women, 35 incidents of rape occur each academic year; off-campus rape (66.3%) is more common than on-campus rape (33.7%); less than 5% of completed or attempted rapes were reported to law enforcement; however, 66% did tell another person, usually a friend (Fisher et al., 2000).

In another study, 18% of the sample experienced attempted or completed rape since entering college. Most of the victims were incapacitated by alcohol or drugs, and the perpetrator was someone they knew (Krebs et al., 2007). Yet another study showed that 1 in 20 (4.7%) women reporting rape in college were raped in the first seven months of the academic year. Nearly 72% of those rapes happened while the victims were so intoxicated that they could not consent. The researchers also found that students living in sorority houses were about three times more likely to be sexually assaulted than students living in dorms. They also found that women from colleges with medium-to-high binge drinking rates had a 1.5% higher risk of being raped than colleges with low binge rates (Mohler-Kuo et al., 2004).

In 2016, an online study of United States university students found that more than 50% of male athletes admitted to "sexually coercing a woman in a manner that meets the legal definition of rape" (Young et al., 2016). That is a mind-blowing statistic! One hypothesis that could be drawn from that data is that the "rape culture" in our country is strongest among men who play sports. Another hypothesis might be that athletes have learned that the universities in our country are more concerned about protecting their athletic programs than they are about protecting their students from sexual assault.

In fact, those hypotheses have been found to be true and so troubling that in 2014 President Barack Obama created the White House Task Force to Protect Students from Sexual Assault (McGovern & Murray, 2016). This comprehensive study reviewed the literature on "a hegemonic masculine culture of sports with an emphasis on violence and misogyny." They cite studies that show "When these violent ideals are present in social spaces that also treat women as exploitable and create a sense of privilege for athletes, they contribute to a rape-prone culture among college athletes (Martin, 2016; Sanday, 1996).

We have all read countless stories in the press about universities covering up cases of sexual abuse to protect their athletic programs. Lombardi (2009) reported on December 1, 2009, that she found a "culture of secrecy" surrounding sexual assault cases on university campuses across the United States.

Given the overwhelming number of sexual assault victims in this country, it is likely that almost everyone who is reading this book has either been sexually assaulted, knows someone who has been sexually assaulted, or is currently a friend or family member of someone who has been sexually assaulted, but the friend or family member has not told you about their victimization, so you are unaware that you know someone who has been sexually assaulted. Therefore, it is important that you learn what the psychological, emotional, and behavioral aftermath of sexual assault looks like so that you can develop as much empathy and understanding for them as possible.

DEVELOPMENT OF THE DIAGNOSIS OF PTSD IN THE TREATMENT OF RAPE VICTIMS

Knowing about the laws that have governed sexual abuse until about 40 years ago will hopefully help you understand why it has taken so long for us to really investigate and learn how to provide effective treatment for survivors. Because victims were unlikely to come forward to report the crime, they were also not likely to talk about how the crime affected them. Therefore, there was very little discussion of the issue of sexual abuse in the psychological or psychiatric literature. Many mental health professionals relied on the beliefs that Sigmund Freud espoused about the topic. He did not do any controlled studies on the prevalence of sexual abuse in the population or on the credibility of those who spoke to him about it, or what type of symptoms were common among survivors.

But wait, that last statement is only half true. Freud did know something about the symptoms that many of his patients who reported that they were sexually abused were trying to cope with. He labeled those women "hysterical" because many of them had very similar symptoms. At first, he believed their accounts of sexual abuse and that the sexual abuse was the cause of the "hysterical" symptoms. His psychiatrist colleagues had heard similar stories from their patients but dismissed the stories as lies and fantasies. In April 1896, Freud presented a paper titled, "The Etiology of Hysteria" to the Society for Psychiatry and Neurobiology in which he presented his belief that sexual abuse was the cause of hysterical symptoms (Freud, 1896). His colleagues gave his speech a very cold reception. After that experience Freud changed his mind and decided that his patients' stories of sexual abuse were indeed fantasies as opposed to actual accounts of childhood sexual abuse. In fact, he came to believe that these stories of abuse were actually related to a woman's unconscious desire for a penis.

Freud believed that the clitoris was an inferior sexual organ that led girls to be very envious of their father's penis. It also caused them to be unable to develop into strong, independent people with high moral standards. He believed that the ability to do so belonged only to men because they possessed a penis and ergo had no penis envy. However, he believed, as crazy as it may sound today, that if a woman were able to give birth to a penis (meaning a male baby), then their uterus would calm down and they would be less hysterical. In addition, these women were thought to be more willing to accept their inferior, dependent position in the world (Freud, 1927). By devising this theory about the consequences of not having a penis, he made it almost impossible for anyone who wanted to have a career in mental health to be able to help a woman who reported that she was a victim of sexual abuse. According to psychoanalytic theory (in original form), the treatment for such a woman would be for the diagnosis of hysteria. Her reports of sexual abuse memories would be ignored.

The feminists of the 1970s did much to help liberate women from the horrors of Freud's sexist theories. The movement enabled many women to speak out about their sexual abuse. It also gave many researchers the opportunity to begin studying the effects of sexual abuse on the survivors. The effort to study the incidence of this abuse in the population led to recognizing how widespread it was in female populations (about 1 in 4) and in male populations as well (about 1 in 6) before age 18 (Finkelhor et al., 1990). More recently, the FBI National Press Office released the 2015 Uniform Crime Reporting Program (UCR) on September 26, 2016. The report included a statement about an important change made by the FBI in how rape was defined. It stated the following:

Prior to 2013, the FBI's UCR Program collected rape data in the Summary Reporting System under the category "forcible rape." In 2013, the program removed the term "forcible" from the title and revised the definition. The legacy UCR definition of rape is "The carnal knowledge of a female forcibly and against her will." The revised UCR definition of rape is "Penetration, no matter how slight, of the vagina or anus with any body part or object, or oral penetration by a sex organ of another person, without the consent of the victim."

Of the 18,439 city, county, university and college, state, tribal, and federal agencies eligible to participate in the UCR Program, 16,643 submitted data in 2015. A high-level summary of the statistics submitted, as well as estimates for those agencies that did not report, follows:

- In 2015, there were an estimated 1,197,704 violent crimes. Murder and non-negligent man-slaughter increased 10.8% when compared with estimates from 2014.
- Rape and aggravated assault increased 6.3% and 4.6%, respectively, whereas robbery increased 1.4%.

It is reasonable to hypothesize that the increase noted in the reporting of rape may have been due to the very significant change in how rape was defined during the more recent reporting periods (i.e., eliminating the word "forcible" and allowing that it happens to any person, not just females). However, no matter how hard reporting agencies work to learn what the prevalence of rape is, we probably never will know how many women and men are raped each year. What we do know is that those who do come forward asking mental health professionals for help are plagued with a variety of serious, debilitating symptoms.

When rape crisis centers began to open around the country in the early 1970s, there was not much known about the sequelae of rape or how to help the victims. So researchers began to study the victims. They learned that rape victims were likely to suffer from a number of behavioral, psychological, and physical symptoms and reactions that may last a very long time. They labeled the cluster of symptoms rape trauma syndrome (RTS) (Burgess & Holmstrom, 1974). They observed that RTS progressed in stages. The *Acute Stage* begins right after the victim is able to grasp what has happened to her. It is a time of intense emotions with psychological, physical, and behavioral changes. To cope with the intensity of these emotions, the victim will begin to appear to others as if she is okay. This is the *Underground Stage*. She tries very hard during this stage to go back to her pre-rape life. However, she is never able to go back to what was her life. She then enters the

Reorganization Stage, which is a time when she learns how to adjust to her new life as a survivor of rape (Burgess & Holmstrom, 1979).

At the same time that rape researchers were struggling to understand the sequelae of rape, other researchers were trying to come to terms with the trauma they were observing in the men returning from the Vietnam War. They were seeing large numbers of Vietnam veterans in VA hospitals who were presenting with symptoms similar, but in many cases, more severe than they had seen in veterans of previous wars who had been labeled "shell shocked." The researchers were observing that men who had been discharged years prior were showing more severe symptoms than they had seen at the time they were discharged. Over time they came to realize that all of the veterans they were treating had symptoms that manifested in clusters that were labeled intrusive symptoms, avoidant symptoms, and arousal symptoms. The men with these symptoms all were describing traumatic war events that they were trying desperately to forget. But the horrible feelings were very easily "triggered" by something as benign as the sound of a helicopter overhead or the backfire of a car or truck, no matter how hard they tried to forget the war trauma and move on with their lives.

In the mid-1970s, these clusters of symptoms were given a name: post-traumatic stress disorder (PTSD). Early in 1978, the term was used in a working group, the Committee of Reactive Disorders that recommended that PTSD be formally recognized in the third edition of the *Diagnostic and Statistical Manual* (DSM-3) published by the American Psychiatric Association in 1980 (Saigh & Brenner, 1999). At first there was some controversy in the mental health field as to whether or not that diagnosis should be reserved for war trauma or if other traumas could cause such serious and often long-term symptoms. The end result of the discussions about PTSD was that a traumatic event was seen as a catastrophic stressor that was "outside the range of usual human experience" (DSM-4). Therefore, PTSD is unique among mental health diagnoses because it is the only one that requires a "stressor criterion" (exposure to an event that is considered traumatic) to make the diagnosis.

SYMPTOMS RELATED TO PTSD (DSM-4)[3]

1. The person has been exposed to a trauma that was an actual or a threatened death, caused serious injury or was a violent sexual attack. The traumatic event could have been either directly experienced or the person witnessed a trauma to another person, or they found out that a close family member or friend experienced a traumatic event. The person could also have been someone whose role is to be a first responder who is frequently exposed to traumatic events

2. The intrusive symptoms can be flashbacks of the traumatic event, distressing dreams or nightmares of the event or extreme reactions to things in their environment that remind them of the event. The reactions can be caused by psychological or physical "triggers" or cues.

3. The avoidant symptoms are efforts on the part of the person to keep from thinking about, remembering or feeling what they experienced. They may accomplish this by avoiding people, places, activities, or anything else that reminds them of the trauma.

---

3   Judith Herman, from *Trauma and Recovery: The Aftermath of Violence—from Domestic Abuse to Political Terror*, p. 121. Copyright © 1997 by Perseus Books Group. Reprinted with permission.

4. The symptoms related to negative alterations in cognitions and mood are the inability to remember important parts of the event, negative beliefs or expectations about self and others, distorted beliefs about the meaning of the event leading to self-blame, remaining in a state of negative emotions, lack of interest in many aspects of life, feeling apart and detached from people, and struggling to experience any positive emotions.

5. The arousal symptoms may include anger, irritability, and self-defeating, even destructive, behaviors. The person may become hyperalert and develop a serious startle response. Many have problems concentrating and learning new things. Sleep disturbances are extremely common.

You might wonder why placing a mental health diagnosis on a person is important. There are certainly many good reasons not to "label" anyone with such a diagnosis: for example, sometimes the labels can cause a person to be rejected for life insurance, or a vindictive spouse may try to use it against their ex in a custody battle, and so on. However, clients and their families want to know the name of the disorder causing so much havoc in their lives. In addition, those of us who provide mental health services need to know what we are treating to be effective and actually help our patients. People who suffered with the symptoms of PTSD but have been misdiagnosed as having bipolar disorder, borderline personality disorder, dependent personality disorder, etc., were usually treated with drugs, and/or (especially in the case of a personality disorder) were dismissed due to the fact that many health care practitioners believe that a person with a personality disorder cannot be helped.

Fortunately, some evidence-based treatments have been developed that are effective in the treatment of PTSD. Many researchers have been studying the effects of trauma on the mind and body for a number of years. The research indicates that treatments that include asking the survivor to Recall, Revisit, and Resolve the memory of the event (3 Rs) are the most effective modalities for treatment.

Recall

The therapist asks the survivor to remember the details of the traumatic event and tell the story. As the person remembers and relates the details of the traumatic event, the therapist notes what pieces of the story elicit the most emotion. The therapist keeps in mind that there will probably be parts of the story that the survivor may not remember at this time.

Revisit

The therapist asks the survivor to try to recall the event while applying a "desensitization" technique. There are various techniques that a therapist might use to help the survivor achieve the most vivid revisiting of the trauma possible. Those that this author has used are progressive relaxation, which allows the survivor to be calmer and more relaxed before beginning to revisit the memory (Bernstein & Borkovec, 1973). Hypnosis also enables the survivor to go into a deep state of trance that enhances their ability to relax and provides heightened focus on the memories of the event (Hammond, 1990). Eye movement desensitization reprocessing (EMDR) is another evidence-based therapy that allows the desensitization to the memory to happen within a shorter period of time without the intense and prolonged anxiety that may accompany the other methods of desensitization (Shapiro, 1989). During the process of revisiting, the therapist makes sure that the aspects of the traumatic event that have elicited the most emotion receive a sufficient amount of attention and focus to facilitate trauma resolution.

Resolve

During this phase of the treatment the therapist pays attention to what beliefs about the event and the self may need to be corrected. For example, common self-beliefs that are problematic are "It is my fault that I was raped because I was wearing a short skirt"; or "No one will ever want to marry me because I am not a virgin anymore"; or "If I weren't so stupid, this would never have happened to me."

The work is successful when the survivor reports that she is no longer plagued by unwanted, intrusive memories, dreams, emotions, reactions, or beliefs about self that are related to the traumatic event. There is, of course, a caveat to this statement of "cure." As the survivor goes through life there may be times that there will be a need to return to therapy or otherwise deal with something new in her life that may be bringing up some parts of the trauma again. Many times when a survivor marries, she may find that she is avoiding sexual encounters with her spouse and not understanding why. Often the avoidance is because of the feeling after marriage that sex is now "obligatory." Feeling obligated may cause her to feel angry or trapped. She may need to revisit the rape trauma again to deal with that part of the experience of being forced against her will to submit.

Another time in a survivor's life that may require more therapy is when the survivor has a child and the child is now the age that she was when she (the mother) was raped. The survivor's fears for her child's safety may cause her to become very emotional when the child is not under her control. Again revisiting that part of the trauma that "triggered" those fears will probably help the survivor to be able to handle her fears.

EMDR

- In 1989 Francine Shapiro published the results of a study she had conducted using a new technique that she had discovered and developed. In that study she called the technique EMD.
- She discovered that during a single session of EMD during which the generation of rhythmic, multi-saccadic eye movements while the subjects concentrated on a traumatic memory successfully desensitized the subjects' traumatic memories and dramatically altered their cognitive assessments of the situation, effects that were maintained through the three-month follow-up check. This therapeutic benefit was accompanied by behavioral shifts that included the alleviation of the subjects' primary presenting complaints related to rape, molestation, and combat.
- Shapiro believed that the movement of the eyes in an awake state enabled the brain to replicate the process that occurs in the brain during REM (dream) sleep. There are data that suggest that if a person is deprived of REM sleep for one week they will develop symptoms similar to psychosis. If allowed to sleep normally and REM activity resumes, the person will

return to normal functioning. Therefore, she concluded that REM sleep is the main function of the brain that keeps us "sane."

- In this 1989 article, Shapiro describes the EMD procedure:

Clients are requested to follow with their eyes the therapist's finger, which is moved very rapidly from side to side 10–20 times as a means of eliciting from them rhythmic, bilateral saccadic eye movements, while they simultaneously visualize the traumatic event and internally repeat the associated irrational cognition or negative self-statement. Preliminary testing suggested that the procedure had the capacity to:

1. desensitize a highly traumatic memory within a short period of time (one session) without intense and prolonged anxiety;
2. produce a cognitive restructuring of the verbalized self-statement or assessment;
3. along with a redefined visual representation; and
4. cause congruent and substantial behavioral shifts.

[Authors' Note: Further research has indicated that the "curative" function that REM sleep provides is a result of the fact that both hemispheres of the brain are activated during REM; that is the reason that the eyes move back and forth. Therefore, providing a rhythmic bilateral auditory stimulation to the ears or a pulsing tactile sensation to shoulders, hands, etc., provides the same result as eye movement (Siegel, 2002; Van der Kolk, 2002).]

DIAGNOSIS OF DISSOCIATIVE IDENTITY DISORDER (DID) ADAPTED FROM DSM-4

But now we need to consider the victims of prolonged sexual trauma. As noted above, when rape crisis centers were starting around the United States in the 1970s, we barely knew anything about the incidence of incest and other forms of prolonged sexual abuse. In the 1980s that issue entered the social conscience. We began to hear more and more stories from our patients of prolonged abuse especially during childhood, and again, thanks to the feminist movement, we believed them. We also had a lot of data about the psychological aftermath of the abuse. The symptomatology of prolonged sexual abuse or any other kind of prolonged abuse is much more complex. There are some major differences in the presentation (symptoms) and the treatment of a single event of sexual abuse and sexual abuse perpetrated by one (or more) perpetrator who has control over a person for a number of years.

Most parents of young children want to protect their children from harm. Due to society's heightened awareness of the prevalence of sexual abuse, children are routinely told to be careful around strangers (stranger danger). They stress to their children that they should not take gifts from strangers, get into a car with strangers, leave school with a stranger who tells them that their parent sent them to pick them up, that no one can touch their "private parts," and so forth. All of this is excellent advice and if heeded may prevent harm. The part that most parents do not talk to their children about is what to do if Uncle Frank or their best friend's father or the babysitter harms them.

Unfortunately, the most likely person to sexually abuse a child or adolescent is someone known to the child or adolescent. Recent data points to 96% of perpetrators being known to their victim (National Center for Victims of Crime, 2008). Only 4% were strangers. Often the person who perpetrates has continued and prolonged access to the child. When this happens the resulting trauma sequela is severe and complex. A seminal book, about prolonged trauma, was *Trauma and Recovery: The Aftermath of Violence—from Domestic Abuse to Political Terror* (Herman, 1992). In this very important book, Judith Herman explains what she calls "complex PTSD." She believes that when a person is exposed to prolonged trauma, especially when it is perpetrated by another human who has control over them, the symptoms of PTSD are not enough to describe the very intense and extreme symptoms survivors experience. In her earlier work, Herman describes those symptoms and suggests some methods of treatment.

SYMPTOMS OF COMPLEX POST-TRAUMATIC STRESS DISORDER (PTSD)

History of subjection to totalitarian control, including childhood physical or sexual abuse.

1. Alterations in affect regulation
   a. persistent dysphoria
   b. chronic suicidal preoccupation
   c. self-injury
   d. explosive or extremely inhibited anger (may alternate)
   e. compulsive or extremely inhibited sexuality (may alternate)
2. Alterations in consciousness, including
   a. amnesia or hypermnesia for traumatic events
   b. transient dissociative episodes
   c. depersonalization/derealization
   d. reliving experiences, either in the form of intrusive PTSD symptoms or in the form of ruminative preoccupation
3. Alterations in self-perception, including
   a. sense of helplessness or paralysis of initiative
   b. shame, guilt, and self-blame
   c. sense of defilement or stigma
   d. sense of complete difference from others (may include sense of specialness, utter aloneness, belief no other person can understand, or nonhuman identity)
4. Alterations in perception of perpetrator, including
   a. preoccupation with relationship with perpetrator (includes preoccupation with revenge)
   b. unrealistic attribution of total power to perpetrator (caution: victim's assessment of power realities may be more realistic than clinician's)

5. Alterations in relations with others, including
    a. isolation and withdrawal
    b. disruption in intimate relationships
    c. repeated search for rescuer (may alternate with isolation and withdrawal)
    d. persistent distrust
    e. repeated failures of self-protection
6. Alterations in systems of meaning, including
    a. loss of sustaining faith
    b. sense of hopelessness and despair

The loss of memory of the abuse is a symptom that can become complete amnesia for the trauma. During the 1980s and 1990s, therapists were reporting that they were seeing more and more examples of loss of traumatic memories among their patients. The therapists were becoming more aware of the symptoms of sexual abuse and were more inclined to help patients with amnesia for the traumatic event retrieve those memories. This change in awareness and treatment caused a sensational controversy among clinicians and researchers that received a lot of attention in the press. Were therapists planting memories that were not real in the minds of vulnerable patients and causing them to believe that a relative or family friend abused them? It became known as the "false memory" controversy. The controversy was so intense that some therapists were frightened to suggest to a patient that their symptoms may be the result of trauma, even though therapists knew that a number of the patients they treated who had symptoms of trauma had repressed the memory of the trauma.

The "false memory" controversy was fueled by an ardent denier of repressed memory, Elizabeth Loftus. She believed that there was no such thing as repressed memory because during her work in the laboratory she showed students videos of horrible, traumatic events and then asked them to recall and describe what they had seen. She observed that no matter how traumatic the images were, the students did not forget or "repress" what they had seen. She also found that even though they had not forgotten the traumatic event, their recollections were not always accurate. She decided that her laboratory data showed that traumatic events in real life were just as likely not to be repressed (Loftus, 1994).

The controversy ended when a graduate student, Linda Williams, did her dissertation on the topic of repressed memory. Williams decided to do a real-life study of the aftermath of trauma. Her research involved getting contact information for 129 women who presented in the emergency room (ER) *(as children)* with substantiated sexual abuse trauma in 1973 to 1975. She contacted the victims about 17 years after they had been seen in the hospital ER. She asked them about the abuse. Eighty of the women she spoke with reported that they recalled the abuse. Of those who recalled the abuse, 16% had forgotten it at some time in the past. Those with a history of forgetting the abuse were younger than the other victims at the time of the abuse and were less likely to have received support from their mothers (Williams, 1995). There have been other studies that support the fact that abuse survivors do repress memories or parts of memories of abuse (Briere & Conte, 1993; Van der Kolk, 1994).

Herman and others continued to research and publish their findings about the complexity of the symptoms of prolonged sexual abuse and the treatment methods used to alleviate those symptoms.

When the 1994 version of the *Diagnostic and Statistical Manual* (DSM-4) was published, the diagnosis of dissociative identity disorder (DID) was included. This diagnosis has replaced the concept of a complex PTSD (which was never a diagnosis that was accepted for publication in the DSM).

DSM-5 DIAGNOSIS OF DISSOCIATIVE IDENTITY DISORDER (DID)

1. The person has two or more personalities that have been identified either by oneself or observed by others. There is a serious disruption in how they identify themselves. There are alterations in their behavior, emotions, memory, perception, the way they think and speak.
2. There are major gaps in the memory of events, important information about oneself, and/or traumatic events.
3. The person has clinically significant distress or serious difficulty in social, work, or other important areas of their life.
4. The problems with the personality are not because of an accepted cultural or religious practice.
5. There is no indication that the observed changes in the personality are related to substance abuse.

Prolonged sexual abuse such as incest, sexual slavery, and domestic abuse (which often includes sexual abuse) causes in the victim a disruption of identity that can produce more than one personality. In the past, mental health providers believed that dissociative identity disorder was very rare. Now we know that it is much more common and can easily be misdiagnosed if the therapist doesn't identify the cause of the symptoms they are seeing.

The diagnosis of DID means that during the abusive events the victim has been able to develop a way to survive the overwhelming emotions and physical pain by psychologically removing herself from the reality of the trauma. She is able to preserve her psyche by blocking it out.

Many victims describe their experience during the abuse from a perspective that is outside of their body. For example, "When I remember him getting in my bed and starting to touch my vagina, I am seeing me laying on the bed and him on top of me. I'm not in my body when I remember it."

Part of the treatment during the revisiting stage is to help the victim return to her body so that she can associate her visual memory of the abuse with her emotional and tactile memory of it. It is a scary process for the victim. Therefore, sufficient safety skills are required. The payoff for being able to actually revisit and relive the trauma is that the memory no longer has the same intense hold on her psyche. In the case of disruption of identity that is severe enough to create separate parts (personalities or ego states), the process of association is critical to being able to help the victim "integrate" the dissociated parts back into her psyche to form a whole person.

You might wonder why I have taken time and space to talk about the diagnosis of PTSD, complex PTSD, and DID. The answer is because it is very important that you understand that the person who has been diagnosed with these syndromes is not inherently a "sick" person. They have, through no fault of their own nor due to their genetic makeup, developed the symptoms, problems, and issues. Essentially, survivors experience normal reactions to extraordinarily abnormal personal events. Many years of therapy have been wasted and many patients have suffered needlessly even after going to therapy because they did not receive the correct diagnosis that then resulted in receiving ineffective treatments.

Understanding that traumatic events produce a predictable set of symptoms has revolutionized the clinical practice of most mental health professionals. Once there was an understanding that the symptoms were the result of exposure to a traumatic event, many researchers began to develop treatment techniques that could help the person "resolve" the traumatic memory of the event. As discussed previously, that research has led to many treatment options that address the emotional, psychological, and physical symptoms.

Another reason is to help you understand how sexual abuse affects the victim. As the letter written by the Stanford University student illustrates, the damage to the victim is life changing. When another person penetrates the boundaries of someone's body against the will of that person, they set in motion a lifelong struggle on the part of the victim to find peace and healing. The symptoms are intense, deeply rooted, long-lasting, and severe. The symptoms are manifested in every area of the victim's life and in every part of her mind, body, soul, and spirit. As one researcher puts it, "The body keeps the score," and "The body does not lie" (Van der Kolk, 1994).

SEXUAL ASSAULT PREVENTION

During the news coverage of the outrageous sexual assault and the trial of the perpetrator in the Stanford University case, I read a letter that a father had written to the *New York Times* that stated that after reading about this case he was reluctant to send his daughters to college. His reaction is, unfortunately, what many well-meaning fathers might think is the right thing to do to protect their daughters from rape. As I read it, my thought was, "No, we should be concerned about sending our sons to college because our daughters would be safer if our sons were not there to rape them."

I have been on committees the purpose of which was to figure out how to stop rapes on campus. The ideas that were floated around the table seemed to always be about how to limit the activity of females on the campus to keep them safe. The problem is that we cannot and should not protect women by limiting their behavior because that is what we have always done. For far too long, people have believed that what the victim was doing or not doing is the reason she was sexually assaulted. The real truth is that sexual assault happens because there are people who live among us *who want to and will rape*, period! Some are serial rapists. Some are perpetrators of incest and/ or abuse of nonfamily children. Some are people (usually males) who become part of the "rape culture" that exists in certain settings. Protecting people from being victimized by perpetrators of sexual assault depends on what type of perpetrator we are targeting.

As mentioned earlier in this chapter, in 2014 President Obama created the White House Task Force to Protect Students from Sexual Assault (McGovern & Murray, 2016). This comprehensive study reviewed the literature on:

> "a hegemonic masculine culture of sports with an emphasis on violence and misogyny" and then devised a questionnaire titled, "Sexual Consent Perceptions-Male Students" which included 18 items. The results indicated that male athletes were more likely to misperceive consent than male non-athletes. Female athletes were more likely to misperceive consent than female non-athletes. (McGovern & Murray, 2016)

McGovern and Murray made the following recommendations based on their findings:

- Need for more programs presented by sexual assault victims and/or offenders.
- Programs involving peer-to-peer discussions led by counselors or other experts would be particularly effective for female athletes.
- A variety of delivery modes is most effective, particularly for male athletes.
- Use the "team" construct to effect positive change.
- Programs need to be reinforced throughout the college athlete's career.

Another major report, "Addressing Sexual and Relationship Violence on College and University Campuses" (2016), was published by the American College Health Association (ACHA). The report presented guidelines "to building a comprehensive program" using a public health framework and an "ecological approach," which includes prevention strategies, risk reduction strategies, and response to sexual and relationship violence. The guidelines recommended for prevention are the following:

- Allocate specific resources of time and money to prevention as a priority.
- Use thoughtful and innovative prevention efforts in the absence of evidence-based strategies.
- Coordinate prevention-related messaging throughout campus, starting with a common language, including definitions of types of sexual and relationship violence, consent, etc.
- Recognize that prevention programming is ongoing, multidose, and comprehensive.
- Address the significant, nuanced relationship between alcohol and other drugs and sexual violence.
- Support efforts toward providing an environment of physical and emotional safety.
- Educate event hosts and security on creating social environments that promote sexual and interpersonal respect.
- Include active bystander strategies as part of training for faculty, staff, and students.
- Include positive concepts of healthy relationships.
- Help students develop communication skills and practices specific to consent. (ACHA, 2016)

A Note About the Work of This Task Force

The White House Task Force to Protect Students from Sexual Assault (McGovern & Murray, 2016) that was mentioned earlier in this chapter not only established guidelines for prevention of sexual abuse on campuses, President Obama's administration also set guidelines for dealing with reported cases of sexual assault on college campus. The Obama guidelines suggested that the universities weigh the "preponderance of evidence" in determining the guilt or innocence of the accused.

In 2017, President Donald Trump appointed Betsy DeVos as the Secretary of Education and told her to change President Obama's directive so that the universities should weigh whether or not the evidence against the accused is "clear and convincing."

President Obama's guidelines were interpreted to mean that the evidence needed to show that there was a crime had to be 51% or more. The new guidelines seem to indicate that the evidence needed to show that there was a crime should be close to 100%. Setting the standard that high for a crime that is usually a "she said, he said" (no witnesses) situation, will probably lead to an extremely low rate of assigning guilt to an accused perpetrator and make the burden of proof so heavy that many more victims will not report the crime (https://www.theodysseyonline.com/title-ix-rescinded).

PREVENTION OF CHILDHOOD SEXUAL ABUSE

Prevention of child sexual abuse is a problem that has plagued society for many years. In one year alone about 1 in 12 children are sexually abused (Finkelhor et al., 2005); overall, 6.1% of all children surveyed had been sexually victimized in the past year and nearly 1 in 10 (9.8%) over their lifetimes (Finkelhor et al., 2009), and about 1 in 3 girls and 1 in 7 boys will be sexually abused before the age of 17 (Briere & Elliott, 2003).

Strategies for prevention are aimed at parents (some of whom, unfortunately, may be the perpetrator) and concerned community members. They are the following:

- Develop positive, open communication with children.
- Model and teach about healthy relationships. Help children to create and express boundaries about being touched.
- Teach children about healthy sexual development.
- Teach children that secrets about touching and being touched are not safe secrets to keep.
- Help children to identify adults they trust whom they can confide in.
- Monitor children's Internet use. Talk to them about the dangers of Internet predators.
- If a child or adolescent exhibits inappropriate sexual behavior, talk with a professional to assess the need for help. (National Sexual Violence Resource Center, 2011)

Sexual predators such as serial rapists are the scariest type of sexual abusers. However, they are also the rarest type. When a community must deal with the presence of a sexual predator, the public should be aware of, and cooperative in following, whatever safety precautions the local law enforcement agency recommends.

It is extremely unfortunate that a book like this, which is intended to provide information that can help men and women learn more about the joys of exploring their sexual selves, must include a chapter about the horrible reality of how frequently sexual abuse occurs in our culture and the devastating effect it has on the victims. So it is important to remind everyone to stay safe, but also to enjoy all of the wonderful, exciting, beautiful experiences healthy sexuality can bring to life.

SUMMARY OF STATISTICS IN STUDIES ON SEXUAL ABUSE

Incidence of Sexual Abuse During Childhood

- All children: 1 in 4 females and 1 in 6 males (Finkelhor et al., 1990).
- Before age 17: 1 in 3 girls and 1 in 7 boys (Briere & Elliott, 2003).
- In one year alone: 1 in 12 children (Finkelhor et al., 2005).
- In one year alone: 6.1% of all children and nearly 1 in 10 over their lifetime (Finkelhor et al., 2009).

- Of all perpetrators, 96% are known to the victim and often have prolonged access and only 4% are unknown to the victim (National Center for Victims of Crimes, 2008).

Incidence of Sexual Abuse on College Campuses

- For every 1,000 college women, 35 incidents each academic year (Fisher et al., 2000):
- 63.3% happen off campus and 33.7% happen on campus.
- Less than 5% are reported.
- 66% tell another person.
- Of a sample of 20 women, 4.7% reported rape happening in the first seven months of the academic year; 72% of those raped were so intoxicated they could not give consent or refuse (Mohler-Kuo et al., 2004).
- Students in sorority houses were three times more likely to be sexually assaulted than dorm students.
- Women in medium-to-high "binge" colleges were 1.5% at a higher risk of rape than in low "binge" colleges.
- Of a sample of women, 18% experienced an attempted or completed rape (Krebs et al., 2007).
- Most were incapacitated by alcohol or drugs and knew the perpetrator.
- In U.S. universities, 50% of male athletes admitted to "sexually coercing" a woman in a manner that meets the legal definition of rape (Young et al., 2016).

REFERENCES

American College Health Association. (2016). *Addressing sexual and relationship violence on college and university campuses.* Hanover, MD: Author.

American Psychiatric Association. (1980, 1994, 2013). *Diagnostic and statistical manual of mental disorders.* Washington, DC: American Psychiatric Publishing.

Bernstein, D., & Borkovec, T. (1973). Progressive relaxation training: A manual for the helping professions. Champaign, IL: Research Press.

Biden, J. (2016, June 9). An open letter to a courageous young woman.

Bley, J. (1978). *Effects of Knowledge of Sex History in Sexual and Non-Sexual Assault Cases and Related Attitudes* (Master Thesis). Division of Graduate Studies, University of Cincinnati, OH.

Bley, J. (1980). *Effects of prior sex history and physical resistance evidence on verdicts of individuals and simulated juries in rape trials* (Doctoral dissertation). Division of Graduate Studies, University of Cincinnati, OH.

Briere, J., & Conte, J. (1993). Self-reported amnesia for abuse in adults molested as children. *Journal of Traumatic Stress, 6,* 21–31.

Briere, J., & Elliott, D. (2003). Prevalence and psychological sequelae of self-reported childhood physical and sexual abuse in general population. *Child Abuse and Neglect, 27,* 1205–1222.

Brownmiller, S. (1975). *Against our will: Men, women and rape.* New York: Ballantine.

Burgess, A., & Holstrum, L. (1979). *Rape crisis and recovery.* New York: R. J. Brady.

Burgess, A., & Holstrum, L. (1994). *Rape: Victims of crisis.* New York: R. J. Brady.

Cincinnati Enquirer. (Aug. 25, 2012). "Legitimate Rape" rarely causes pregnancy. A1 & A12.

Complainant Credibility in Sexual Offense Cases: A survey of character testimony and psychiatric experts. (1973). *Journal of Criminal Law & Criminology.* Boston, Williams & Wilkins Co., for Northwestern University Law School, *64,* 67–76.

Federal Bureau of Investigation (FBI). (2016). *Uniform Crime Report.* Washington, DC: Author.

Finkelhor, D., Hotaling, G., Lewis, I., & Smith, C. (1990). Child sexual abuse in a national survey of adult men and women: Prevalence characteristics and risk factors. *Child Abuse and Neglect.* (14) 1, 19–28.

Finkelhor, D., Ormrod, R., Turner, H., & Hamby, S. (2005). The victimization of children and youth: A comprehensive, national survey. *Child Maltreatment, 10,* 5–25.

Finkelhor, D., Turner, H., Ormrod, R., Hamby, S., & Kracke, K. (2009). Children's exposure to violence: A Comprehensive National Survey (NCJ 227744). Washington, DC: U.S. Department of Justice, Office of Justice Programs.

Fisher, B., Cullen, F., & Turner, M. (2000). *The sexual victimization of college women*. Washington, DC: National Institute of Justice, Bureau of Justice Statistics.

Freud, S. (1896). *The etiology of hysteria*. Paper presented to the Society for Psychiatry and Neurology.

Freud, S. (1927). The psychological consequences of the anatomical distinction between the sexes (Trans. J. Strachey). *International Journal of Psycho-Analysis, 8*(2), 133–142.

Frumin, A. (2016). Brock Turner registers as a sex offender in Ohio. (U.S. News. Posted September 6, 2016). https://www.nbcnews.com/news/us-news/brock-turner-registers-sex-offender-ohio-n643376

Hammond, C. (Ed.). (1990). *Handbook of hypnotic suggestions and metaphors*. New York: Norton.

Herman, J. (1992). *Trauma and recovery: The aftermath of violence—from domestic abuse to political terror*. New York: Basic Books.

H.R. 3-112th Congress: No Taxpayer Funding for Abortion Act. www.GovTrack us. 2011. May 4, 2018. https://www.govtrack.us/congressbills/112/hr3

Krebs, C., Linquist, C., Warner, T., Fisher, B., & Martin, S. (2006). The Campus Sexual Assault (CSA) Study. Washington, DC: National Institute of Justice.

Loftus, E., & Ketcham, K. (1994). *The myth of repressed memory: False memories and allegations of sexual abuse*. New York: St. Martin's Press.

Lombardi, K. (2009). Sexual Assault on Campus Shrouded in Secrecy: High Rates of Rape, Closed Hearings and Confusing Laws. Center for Public Integrity. www.publicintegrity.org/2009/12/01/9047/sexual-assault-campus-shrouded-secrecy

Martin, P. (2016). The rape prone culture of academic contexts: Fraternities and athletics. *Gender and Society, 30*(1), 30–43.

McGovern, J., & Murray, P. (2016). *Consent communication: What does it mean for student athletes?* Paper presented at the NCAA National Conference, San Antonio, TX.

Mohler-Kuo, M., Dowdall, G., Koss, M., & Wechsler, H. (2004). Correlates of rape while intoxicated in a national sample of college women. *Journal of Studies on Alcoholism, 65*(1), 37–45.

Mourdock, R. (2012). *Rape, Pregnancy and God's Plan*. www.politico.com/story/2012/10/mourdock-rape-pregnancy-and-gods-plan-082795

National Center for Victims of Crime (NCVC). (2008). *Child sexual abuse*. June 2–4, Portland, Oregon.

National Sexual Violence Resource Center (NSVRC). (2011). *Child sexual abuse prevention*. Enola, PA: Author.

Paul, R. (2012). If it's an Honest Rape, Women Should go to the Emergency Room. www.crooksandliars.com/heather/ron-paul-if-its-an-honest-rape-women-should-g

Saigh, P., & Bremner, J. (Eds.). (1999). *Posttraumatic Stress Disorder: A comprehensive text*. Boston: Allyn & Bacon.

Sanday, P. (1996). Rape prone versus rape-free campus cultures. *Violence Against Women, 2*(2), 191–208.

Santorum, P. (2012). *Rape and Pregnancy*. www.theguardian.com/commentisfree/believe/2012/jan/25/rick-santorum-rape-pregnancy

Shapiro, F. (1989). Efficacy of the eye movement desensitization procedure in the treatment of traumatic memories. *Journal of Traumatic Stress, 2*, 199–223.

Shapiro, F. (Ed.). (2002). *EMDR as an integrative psychotherapy approach: Experts of diverse orientations explore the paradigm prism*. Washington, DC: American Psychological Association.

Siegel, DJ. (2002). The developing mind and the resolution of trauma: Some ideas about information processing and an interpersonal neurobiology of psychotherapy. In *EMDR As An Integrative Psychotherapy Approach*. Shapiro, F. (Ed). Washington, DC: American Psychological Association, 85–121.

Thomas, J. (December 3, 2009). Report: Universities try to cover up rapes. *USA Today*, first published in the *Indianapolis Star*.

Van der Kolk, B. (1994). The body keeps the score: Memory and the evolving psychobiology of PTS. *Harvard Review of Psychiatry, 1*(5), 253–265.

Van der Kolk, B. (2002). Beyond the Talking Cure: Somatic Experience and Subcortical Imprints in the Treatment of Trauma. In *EMDR As An Integrative Psychotherapy Approach*. F. Shapiro, (Ed). Washington, DC: American Psychological Association, 57–83.

Williams, C. (1990). Texas Candidate's Comment About Rape Causes a Furor, New York. https://www.nytimes.com/1990/03/26/us/texas-candidate-s-comment-about-rape-causes-a-furor.html

Williams, L.M. (1995). Recovered memories of abuse in women with documented child sexual victimization history. *Journal of Traumatic Stress, 8*(4), 649–673.

Young, B., Desmarais, S., Baldwin, J., & Chandler, R. (2016). Sexual coercion practices among undergraduate male recreational athletes, intercollegiate athletes and non-athletes. *Journal of Violence Against Women, 23*(7).

CHAPTER SEVENTEEN

When You Hurt Others and Yourself:

PROBLEMATIC SEXUAL BEHAVIOR

Written by Frederick Peterson

INTRODUCTION

This chapter focuses on many different aspects of people who hurt others by their sexual behavior and how they can change their ways to stop hurting others as well as making themselves the better people they wish to become. Whereas the last chapter explored pathways to healing and recovery for victims of sexual trauma, this chapter "swims upstream" in a sense to examine the ways individuals with problematic sexual behavior (PSB) can change that behavior. The chapter mainly focuses on a wide range of sexual behaviors, including those commonly referred to as compulsive sexual behavior or sex addiction–like behavior. PSB encompasses most of the types of behaviors that are typically treated in a sexual health clinic, including, but not limited to, relational conflict resulting from use of pornography, having sexual affairs, and using sex workers (prostitution).

Most often, PSBs are legal but can have devastating consequences such as the end of a marriage, breakup of a family, and sometimes loss of employment. The chapter also addresses PSB that is not legal and can result in imprisonment. For whatever category of PSB an individual is doing to hurt others (as well as him- or herself), a general process of recovery is described in this chapter to assist that individual to understand what needs to happen to stop hurting others and become a healthy person. Inherent in this statement is that one cannot achieve health while habitually hurting others, especially by sexual means.

For simplicity and clarity of the chapter, the language most often used to describe the person with PSB will be male pronouns. Today, it is well understood that women can have PSB that habitually causes hurt and pain for partners, children, and others. The authors have worked with many men who have been sexually victimized by females. For those men who have been sexually abused and who have become sex abusers (victim to victimizer), treatment is not effective unless issues regarding their own victim status are resolved. Although women can be perpetrators of sex crimes, it is also true that the majority of PSBs are engaged in by men. Another important note about gender is that people hurt by PSB and sex offenses are not all female but male and transgender as well. Men and women, girls and boys, and people who identify by other descriptors are victimized by PSB.

WHAT ARE PROBLEMATIC SEXUAL BEHAVIORS?

As noted above, PSB encompasses many varied behaviors. Too much interest in sex and the resulting sexual behavior toward others can cause serious problems and long-lasting adverse effects for others and the individuals themselves (Abel, Wiegel, & Osborn, 2007; LeVay & Baldwin, 2015). Per the National Intimate Partner and Sexual Violence Survey conducted by the Centers for Disease Control and Prevention, LGBTQA individuals are believed to be at additional risk for these adverse effects (CDC, 2014). When it comes to sex, there is a very wide range of behaviors that can be considered normal and desirable under some circumstances, whereas others consider the same acts as undesirable, unhealthy, or even criminal.

Some of the most typical PSBs are listed below and represent reasons which people routinely want consultation with mental health, human resource, or legal professionals. The examples of PSB listed in this chapter are problems with which the authors frequently discuss with clients.

- Sexual harassment, either the "quid pro quo" type (for example, "You have sex with me or kiss your job goodbye") or the hostile environment type (pornographic magazines on desk or sexually suggestive posters on walls). Sexual harassment involves one person making unwanted sexual advances (or other intimidating sexual behavior) toward another, usually, but not always, in a workplace. A long history of inappropriate treatment of women in their place of employment has resulted in the #MeToo social media campaign, which has turned into a social tsunami in the wake of sexual harassment allegations and resulted in the resignation or firing of scores of leading figures in politics, entertainment, private industry, and the federal judiciary.

- Masturbation (also called sexual self-pleasuring) is widely practiced and considered a healthy behavior by most health professionals. But when used excessively, it can raise complaints resulting in a person believing that their sexual partner has started to use masturbation to the point where it significantly diminishes the couple's sex life or even is used as a substitution for relational sex.

- Pornography use (also called erotica or sexually explicit material) refers to depictions of people or behaviors intended to be sexually arousing and is closely related to complaints of solo masturbation when it has adverse effects on relational sex. However, it also can have additional concerns of a partner feeling like they cannot compete with Photoshopped models in the porn as well as issues of sexual objectification of women (although there is pornography made by women for women). Obviously, pornography is extremely common in our increasingly technology-based culture and in the opinion of the authors has unfortunately overtaken school-based education and parental instruction as the most common form of sex education in America. There is much concern regarding the addictive-like features of pornography that will be discussed later in this chapter.

- Marital affairs (also traditionally called infidelity or cheating) are also very common and a frequent reason for divorce, especially when they occur in a serial way. Although some couples seek additional-partner alternatives for marital satisfaction, either single monogamy or serial monogamy is generally considered the cultural norm, and all else is stigmatized with social sanctions. About one-quarter of married men and just under one-fifth of married women admit in large national surveys (Laumann, Gagnon, Michael, & Michaels, 1994; Mark, Janssen, & Milhausen, 2011) to having affairs, and the actual incidence is generally thought to be higher.

- Cyber-sexing (via Twitter/SnapChat/PM/DM/GrindR/WhatsApp/web-cams/ad nauseam) is any web-based communication that you can send sexually explicit images and communication. These forms of technology facilitate new forms of sexual "e-affairs" that cause major relationship conflict when discovered. They are very popular forms of sexual expression because of the accessibility, the affordability, and the perceived anonymity people believe they have (Cooper, 2002). Occasionally, catfishing is also a problem behavior, which is when a person reels another person into an emotional and sexual (online) relationship that is based on deception.

- Miscellaneous sexual acting-out, which includes a collection of sexual behaviors such as visiting massage parlors (usually with sexual contact), employing sex workers (in-person prostitutes), frequenting strip clubs or adult XXX book stores (with or without sexual contact), and sex tourism (visiting abroad expressly for sexual purposes) without their partner's knowledge.

- There is an additional set of sexual behaviors that can cause significant distress with others that are related to paraphilias, some legal and some not. Obviously, illegal paraphilic behavior can be very harmful to others (as well as the individual), but these will be discussed in a special section later in the chapter.

So, when do these sexual behaviors become problematic? Some sexual behaviors are *always* problematic, such as sexual harassment and sexual assault. However, sometimes it depends on the context and circumstance of the individual as well as the perspective of others who are involved. As mentioned earlier, masturbation is a normal healthy behavior whether it is solo activity or shared between couples. Is masturbating once, twice, or five times a day healthy? How about 10? Use of porn can seem to have an addictive quality, yet erotic videos and films can be enjoyed by couples as an enhancement experience to be shared. Affairs can devastate marriages and families, yet some polyamorous couples like to have an additional lover or bring another couple into their relationship to explore and expand their sexual lives. The question is—where do we draw the line between healthy and problematic?

Many therapists get concerned if their clients report masturbation more than once a day. Some researchers in the past such as Kafka (1997) suggested that anyone who has more than six orgasms per week (over six months) should be suspected of having a sex addiction/compulsivity. REALLY? Some couples with a joyful, healthy sex life share (together) six orgasms per week on a routine basis (some do not). Yet many healthy women can have six or more orgasms per evening or even during a one-hour sexual encounter. In addition, there are some women (and some men) wanting to know where to sign up to learn how to have multiple orgasms.

WHAT OTHER NAMES DO PSBs GO BY, AND WHY DO MEN ENGAGE IN THEM?

Historically, we can look back to times when too much interest in sex was described by many medical terms that pathologized people's (especially women's) natural interest in sex. Most generally, women have been moralistically considered to engage in "promiscuity" when they are thought to be surpassing community standards for interest in sex and especially their number of sexual partners. Some authors (such as Marty Klein in his 2011 book *America's War on Sex*) argue that the recent focus on "excessive interest" in sex and the resulting behavior is just the latest form of modern pathologizing of sexual expression.

What has been considered excessive interest in sex has also been referred to by many names, including (alphabetically) compulsive sexual behavior, Don Juanism, erotomania, high-frequency sexual behavior, hypersexuality, hypersexual disorder, hyperphilia, hysteria, impulsive/compulsive sexual behavior, lust disorder, nymphomania, out-of-control-behavior, paraphilia-related disorder, problematic sexual behavior, promiscuity, satyriasis, sex addiction, sexual compulsivity, and sexual disorder NOS (not-otherwise-specified). This is far from an exclusive, all-encompassing list of terms used to describe excessive intertest in sex.

When it came to men expressing "too much" interest in sex or sexual behavior, then terms such as satyriasis or Don Juanism or womanizer have been traditionally employed. More recently, terms used in the mental health fields have included hypersexual disorder, sexual disorder NOS (not-otherwise-specified), paraphilia-related disorder, compulsive sexual behavior, or impulsive/compulsive sexual behavior (American Psychiatric Association, 2013; Coleman, 2011). The DSM actually does not have a diagnosis of sex addiction because there is not enough scientific support for sex addiction to be considered an addiction in the medical definition of other addictions, such as opiate addiction (American Psychiatric Association, 2013).

However, while the American Psychiatric Association has not yet recognized PSB or "sex addiction-like behaviors" as a recognized mental health disorder, the world leaders of all-things-mental-health have. Authors of the International Classification of Diseases (published by the World Health Organization) have included such a diagnosis in their most recent draft of ICD-11 (planned to be implemented internationally by 2025). According to the ICD, Compulsive Sexual Behavior Disorder (CSBD) is a diagnosis characterized by a persistent pattern of failure to control intense repetitive sexual impulses resulting in compulsive sexual behavior. CSBD is also associated with numerous unsuccessful efforts to reduce a repetitive sexual behavior and a continuation of the behavior, despite adverse consequences or deriving little or no satisfaction from it.

While some advocates of the diagnosis of CSBD hailed its inclusion in ICD-11, other reasonable voices warn us that it is very important to address the widespread over-use of the term "sex addiction" that has been inappropriately employed to describe everything from healthy masturbation to relationship conflict resulting in old-fashion marital affairs (Ley, 2018). "Sex addiction" has been used to stigmatize undesired behavior of individuals because their spouses, ministers, or therapists have declared that individual a sex addict. Looks like the new diagnosis (CSBD) will be listed under impulse control disorders (instead of the section for addictions) and comes with several qualifiers, such as disallowing self-identification as a sufficient basis for a diagnosis of CSBD. Also, the sexual behaviors in question cannot be pathologized with a diagnosis of CSBD simply because of moral reasons (such as breaking the rules of a church or religion) nor because it exceeds some perceived normalcy for frequency of sexual activity (such as more than one orgasm per day). The position of the American Association of Sex Educators, Counselors & Therapists (AASECT) is that "linking problems related to sexual urges, thoughts or behaviors to a porn/sexual addiction process cannot be advanced by AASECT as a standard of practice for sexuality education delivery, counseling or therapy" (AASECT, 2016). I adhere to this position and work with men to understand the important points debated in the research. However, when men are so inclined, I also endorse them using twelve-step approaches to supplement their therapy. They sometimes find the fellowship helpful for the wisdom shared and not feeling so alone. The psychological treatment of PSB and the self-help groups can, and do, support the same goals of individual health and relationship repair.

At the same time, the most commonly used term in the general public has been sex addiction, primarily because of the similarity some PSBs have with alcoholism in terms of the PSBs being repeated behaviors that are self-destructive, yet the individual does not seem to be able to stop doing the PSBs, even when the person says they wish to and even in the face of increasingly adverse consequences. The term "out-of-control sexual behavior" (OCSB) has become employed frequently to describe repeated patterns of sexual behavior that causes such adverse consequences (Braun-Harvey & Vigorito, 2016). In their recent book, Braun-Harvey & Vigorito outline a balanced and positive approach to assisting clients with these concerns.

For simplicity and ease of reference, the all-encompassing descriptor "Problematic Sexual Behavior" (PSB) is preferred by the authors. If it is a sexual behavior that causes problems (adverse consequences) for an individual or a couple, then it is a PSB. In addition, most sexual behaviors are "out-of-control" in limited situations (especially when there is a perception of no transparency and accountability) and are actually "within-control" most other times. The term PSB also avoids the matter of frequency as with "high-frequency sexual behavior" (Sugrue, 2007) because sexual behavior often is a problem of "too often". But how often is "too often?" If a man engages in a particular sexual behavior just once a year but it threatens to end his marriage and ruin his career, is that behavior "out-of-control" or "too often?" Not sure, but it certainly is problematic if it wrecks the marriage or career.

Other authors who have labeled PSB as a sex addiction (Carnes, 2001; Delmonico & Griffin, 2014; Weiss, 2013) draw on comparisons to physical addictions such as the intense and repeated cravings for sex (that people have until they complete the desired sexual act) like people's craving for drugs. The endless exposés in the media regarding "celebrity sex addicts" have propelled the popularization of sex addiction in the public consciousness, with golfer Tiger Woods and actor Charlie Sheen being well-known examples. Another important similarity between the idea of sex addiction and drug addiction is the activation of the same pleasure centers of the midbrain, particularly the amygdala (which helps regulate emotions) and the nucleus accumbens (which controls the release of dopamine, a feel-good neurotransmitter). Besides the neurobiology of having the feel-good chemical experience in the brain, the strong effects of operant conditioning cannot be underestimated as a reinforcement of sex-seeking behavior. It is essentially the pleasure principle of "if it feels good, do it" in operation, which Freud described as a primary function of the id (Schultz & Schultz, 2004).

The cyclical nature of the repeated sexual behavior also resembles the repeated cycle of drug dependence in that both have a particular sequential pattern of behavior. The four-stage cycle of sex-addiction behavior described by Pat Carnes (Carnes, 2001; LeVay, Baldwin, & Baldwin, 2015) is

1. the craving for sex (often a particular type of sexual exchange);
2. a ritualized search for sexual outlet;
3. doing the problematic sexual behavior; and
4. guilt/despair/shame after the sexual behavior.

The resulting guilt, despair, and shame experienced by the individual serves as a source of angst and unrest. These feelings create a state of physiological disequilibrium that contributes to the next craving for sex and temporary relief (therefore propelling the cycle of addiction behavior). The impulse to engage in the PSB is intensified, and the ability to exercise control over the PSB is diminished when an individual is suffering from clinical comorbidities (such as anxiety and depression), is emotionally isolated and not able to reach out for help (the latter being a long-standing and forbidden no-no of traditional masculinity), or made vulnerable to relapse by (one or more) being hungry, angry, lonely, or tired (the old HALT reminder from our friends in AA). This four-stage cycle of sex addiction is consistent with the writings of Dr. Dennis Sugrue (sexual health authority and past president of the American Association of Sex Educators, Counselors, and Therapists) who attributes sexual acting out (PSB) to multiple causal factors and uses the term "high-frequency sexual behavior" (Sugrue, 2007).

Sugrue (2007) published a useful classification of high-frequency sexual behavior (what we are calling PSB in this chapter) that can aid in our understanding of when sexual behaviors become problematic. He classifies high-frequency sexual behavior into five categories: healthy, neurotic, characterological, organic, or addictive/compulsive. For brevity, all five types will not be described, but two will be compared for our purposes here: healthy sexual expression and sex addiction/compulsivity. He describes people with healthy sexuality as having a positive value on the pleasure of sexual contact. He believes this indicates normal brain function. They have significant control over their sexual behavior, they do not exploit others with their sex or put themselves at significant risk, and they do not have an underlying psychological agenda motivating their sexual behavior.

In contrast, people with compulsive behaviors have limited value and appreciation for the pleasure involved in the sexual behavior (often not involving orgasm). They may have normal brain function, or it may be mildly impaired (such as having a biological profile similar to those with obsessive-compulsive disorder). They seem to have limited control over the behavior (like the relationship alcoholics have to drinking). They do exploit others and put themselves at high risk for adverse consequences, and they do seem to have an underlying psychological agenda, such as stress reduction, emotional regulation, or recapitulation of past trauma (Sugrue, 2007).

According to Sugrue, there are four factors that have to be present for a sexual behavior to be considered sex compulsivity. These factors are:

1. a high frequency of sexual behavior and/or sexual preoccupation;
2. inability to maintain control over the behavior or preoccupation;
3. a high risk for negative consequences for oneself or others; and
4. the behavior and lack of control are not attributable to an identifiable organic condition (such as traumatic brain injury or delayed developmental disorders).

Certainly, intelligent people can disagree with this point of view, but the authors find Sugrue's classification and definition very useful in terms of assisting clients seeking assistance in sorting out the confusion, anger, and curiosity about what can be done to help their marriage and family. Another useful contribution by this author is his take on relapse prevention and his brief guideline for establishing an effective relapse prevention plan that is shared later in the chapter.

ADDITIONAL APPROACHES TO DETERMINING IF SEXUAL BEHAVIORS ARE PROBLEMATIC OR NOT

Back to the question: Where do we draw the line between healthy and problematic? Beyond Sugrue's insights, there are several practical approaches involved in answering this question. Remember our discussion of what is normal in Chapter 12 on sexual expression? First, we put the concern within the context of five dimensions of understanding sexuality and see what conclusions can be drawn. We consider biological, psychological, behavioral, clinical, and statistical aspects of the sexual activity. Then we ask how these considerations change our perspective if the activity is a problem and if it is something that we can deal with, have to change, or it has got to go!

Second, when a person is involved with sexual variations such as sadomasochism, sometimes it comes down to ensuring it is a consensual sexual exchange and whether there is tissue damage. If two adults freely engage in some bondage or sadomasochism and no one is seriously injured, that's up to them. Two commonly used bottom lines are: Sex must be consensual and not involve serious bleeding. If these two conditions are not met, then it must change or it has got to go!

Third, we look at the consequences of the behavior and ask if the typical person would feel it is worth the costs (consequences) of the behavior. Considerations of consequences include, but may not be limited to: relational, emotional, financial, spiritual, vocational, health, and legal consequences.

Let's take another look at the consequences approach as it applies to PSB. The following review represents real examples of consequences to clients of the authors:

- Emotional—shame, remorse, embarrassment, and humiliation guilt for offenders. Sense of betrayal, confusion, anger, shame, embarrassment, and humiliation for partners, children, and other family members. The most severe emotional consequences include extreme anxiety or depression requiring hospitalization to avoid suicide.

- Relational—marital discord, separation from spouse and children, divorce, isolation from family and friends who turn against the offender, loss of reputation, and sometimes relocation to start their life over.
- Health—sexually transmitted infections for offenders (and spouses), stress responses, exhaustion from sleep deprivation, lowered immune response, and being beat up during encounters for anonymous sex.
- Financial—costs of porn, sex workers, therapy, health care, and attorneys.
- Spiritual—dissonance or misalignment between spiritual/religious beliefs and sexual practices, resulting in self-perception as unforgiven, freaks of nature, or condemned.
- Vocational—tardiness from use of online porn or sexual harassment behavior, loss of license for violation of professional boundaries, loss of job from on-the-job use of porn.
- Legal—prosecution and/or imprisonment for solicitation of prostitution, gross sexual imposition, sexual assault, exhibitionism, voyeurism, or possession of child pornography.

Across these seven levels of consequences, any individual or couple may assess each level as low, moderate, or high in terms of the severity of how they are impacted by the PSB. Most often, the emotional and relational consequences are the most severe and difficult to manage in the short term. The vocational and legal are often the most difficult to deal with long term, it is not always easy to determine. As a general guideline, if there are at least two of the seven levels of consequence at a high level of adverse impact, then the behavior is considered PSB. However, only one domain of severe consequences (such as something that lands you in prison) can qualify as a PSB. Remember the unfortunate story of the physician who took her life in Chapter 2? The dominant consequence for her was spiritual, in that her sense of being unforgiven was the key facilitator in her suicide.

THE RECOVERY PROCESS

When there is recognition that a PSB is causing problems in a relationship, couples sometimes choose to seek professional consultation and may engage in treatment with the hope of correcting the PSB. The recovery process from the effects of PSB takes many paths for many people depending on their particular circumstances. These details are as varied as the types of sexual behaviors that compel people to seek professional help. A key factor is if the partner to the individual wishes to stay in the relationship or not. There is no strict right or wrong in terms of making this decision as each person must make their own choices. However, there are a few guidelines that are helpful to consider, including the history of the relationship, amount of emotional investment one has in the other person, and what the desired outcomes are for each individual. If the partner chooses to stay in the relationship (at least to see if there are signs of improvement in the short term), then this is a key factor in the recovery of the man who has been sexually acting out.

The partner's decision to stay, whether they stay long-term or not, usually provides motivation for change as the man often wants to do what he can to preserve the marriage and keep his family intact. If the partner immediately decides the relationship is over, it is a whole other story, and the man often continues a path of self-destruction until he hits rock bottom in a pick-up bar, hospital, jail, or morgue. When there is an alignment of factors that allows the recovery process to occur, it may often occur in fits and starts with relapse an expected part of the path to health. Of course, this requires hope, commitment, and determination of the individual with PSB to continue to pursue higher levels of health. If they haven't hit bottom or paid enough in significant damages to their life (as well as others), then they are likely to continue to sexually act out. They may possibly completely wreck their lives (and others) and even may get to a point of wanting to end it all.

It takes even more hope, patience, and grace for the partners of men sexually acting out and who choose to preserve their relationship with these men. Wives and partners find themselves in states of shock, betrayal, and with a whirlwind of intense emotions when they discover the secret PSB life of husbands and boyfriends. There is often not a lot of support available to these partners. Even when partners seek out support, they are sometimes confronted with judgments, misinformation, and advice they don't want to hear—such as "he will never change and the only rational thing to do is to divorce him immediately." This may be true for men who refuse to acknowledge they have a problem and who continue to engage in the PSB.

However, many men engaged in PSB do change for the better and to tell distraught partners that there is no hope of change is a disservice. At the same time, they should expect their husband/boyfriend to create accountability and transparency. These are requirements for the man who wants to do all he can to preserve his marriage. Every partner of a man who is sexually acting out needs to be able to receive several disclosures that can help facilitate a decision to stay and heal the relationship.

- The most important disclosure is an explanation of why and how the PSB happened.
- The explanation should be delivered in a way that is acceptable to the partner (no blaming).
- Inherent in the explanation are reasons why the partner would possibly believe they will not experience pain and anguish repeatedly if they decide to stay in the relationship.

Sometimes typical counseling that is available in the community is sufficient to resolve matters using some of the guidelines mentioned above (and below in the following section). However, many times an intensive outpatient treatment approach is needed, especially when the PSBs have proven to be a repeated cycle of being caught, submitting to counseling, and the man then goes back to the PSB. The intensive outpatient treatment approach is made up of at least four of the following six components, which include the following:

- A sexual health and mental health evaluation that involves input from the partner, review of the history of the relationship and PSB, psychological screenings for anxiety and depression, more in-depth personality testing, and separately solicited desired outcomes.
- Individual counseling for the man with PSB that emphasizes the explanation to the partner (mentioned above) and effective planning/execution of relapse prevention skills.
- Participation in a professionally led men's sexual health group that facilitates accountability and support among men learning the skills to live a mission-guided, healthier life.
- Marital (or relationship) counseling with an emphasis on communication training, making amends, reestablishing trust, and healing the relationship.

- Individual or group counseling for partners of the men with PSB to support their healing and decision making.
- Optional yet recommended participation in a community-based group such as Sex Addicts Anonymous (SAA), Sex & Love Addicts Anonymous (SLAA), Celebrate Recovery (CR), or a similar support group that the man with PSB can attend any given day he chooses.

THE STORY OF KARL: A DEMONSTRATION OF MEN WITH PSB

Karl came into the clinic in a crisis period of his marriage and career. He was married to a beautiful wife whom he loved named Eve, had a young family he adored, and was a well-respected academic, having written several books on the criminal justice system. Karl was a man in his late 40s with many blessings yet was unhappy in his life and had started drinking more over the past couple years. He was tall, athletically built, and a man few men would want to cross.

Although he could be an imposing figure, he sat in the consultation office slumped over in what appeared to be the personification of shame. He held his head hanging down in his hands, eyes to the floor, and barely able to speak. After a few moments, Karl spoke just above a whisper and explained that his life had spiraled out of control. Earlier that week, Eve found a text on her phone that invited her to meet Karl for a sexual rendezvous that was intended for someone else. She told Karl to move out of the house, their children cried for days, and his boss was sending him for a fitness of duty examination due to a discovery that some of his sexual acting out occurred either at work or when he was supposed to be there.

He told a story of a life falling apart characteristic of men caught up in repeating cycles of PSB spinning further out of control. He explained his getting lost and being adrift in life, moving away from the people and things he always held most dear in his heart. There was an overwhelming sense of powerlessness and confusion mixed with guilt and embarrassment. Here sat an intelligent, well-respected man in his field who for the life of him couldn't figure out how he got to be sitting in a shrink's office and, more importantly, how to get out of the corner into which he painted himself. Karl's story covered a decade of slow-growing cancer in his marital relationship. His marriage started out with high ideals as both he and Eve were strong in their religious faith and were virgins when they married. As is often the case, he reported the first five years together as the best period of the marriage with a sense of blessings as a new family, approaching life as an adventure together, and starting a new family and career. Over the course of their next 10 years, he experienced a diminishing closeness with Eve as his best friend, less sexual intimacy, and getting bored with the routine of his life, despite his love for his wife and children.

He soon started watching online pornography and masturbating, as a rationalization in his mind for the lessening amount of sex he was having with Eve. Increased masturbation is a common strategy used by an individual who has a partner who is less interested in sex. However, Karl started using masturbation as a substitute for relational sex with Eve, and the couple began increasingly to avoid sex over time, creating a low-sex/no-sex marriage. As the pornography and masturbation became increasingly problematic, their communication stopped and Karl's secret activity facilitated the construction of a double life. Eve once caught him viewing his pornography and insisted on marital counseling, to which Karl acquiesced. As a result, things appeared to improve temporarily, but Karl had only made external changes to appease her and stay in the marriage. He did not acknowledge or make internal changes regarding his emotionally restricted life, talk about his growing sense of depression, or acknowledge his increased drinking. No meaningful internal changes occurred with his emotional state, self-perception, or sense of purpose and mission in life.

This was where Karl failed himself, Eve, and his family. Part of his shame was that he knew it. He had a responsibility and accountability that he could not bring himself to face. He had already built what is called the "addiction bubble," in which an individual loses rational thought and creates a denial system that serves as an illusion by which Karl began thinking that he could engage in a double life without consequences to his marriage, family, or himself. So, after a year, the couple had lost any benefit from the marital counseling and regressed back into a pattern of emotional/sexual avoidance. Karl started again with his double life of PSB but this time graduated to more serious forms of PSB, including starting an affair with one of his graduate students. Within another year, he was going to neighboring cities to hire prostitutes, having anonymous sexual encounters using social media, and taking "business trips" with a high-class escort that he convinced himself was his mistress. The day before Eve ever received Karl's erroneous text, she had more than just suspicion that he was cheating on her already. Even though they had sex very infrequently, she had become symptomatic and was diagnosed by her physician with herpes. Karl was Eve's only sexual partner (ever) and she knew what a diagnosis of herpes meant. She was incredibly conflicted by her love for this man and the anger and betrayal she felt toward him. Karl was full of shame that his life, in his words, had fallen so deep into "hedonistic debauchery."

Meanwhile, Eve was in the waiting room on my request, apparently there just to make sure she had an opportunity to help me assist her husband by understanding him through her eyes. Eve got to talk alone without her husband present (he was asked to wait in another room). She was a beautiful young woman a few years Karl's junior. Her eyes were red and tearful—full of pain, betrayal, and anguish. Although it had been a few days since the discovery of her husband's second life, she still had an aura of being shell-shocked. Eve made it clear that her being there was not to be seen as "standing by her man" and that she had given herself a gift of not pressuring herself to make any immediate decision about the marriage. She was explicit regarding the possibility that she may not choose to continue the relationship.

Her immediate input from the start was both appreciated and critical to the treatment outcome for Karl, if not the couple. By being there, she provided invaluable input as to the extent of the problem and what consequences were a result of his PSB. She also informed herself by asking questions about what this intensive outpatient treatment for PSB was about and how it was different from the counseling they had previously tried. In addition, she was invited to call or text any information about her husband's behavior that she thought may be relevant to his treatment.

During the course of meeting with this couple, it was the first time any therapist in the clinic had ever had to physically step between a husband and wife. Why? Because Eve could not control her anger and was physically waling on Karl around the head and shoulders. She was told that her feelings were valid and understandable yet she would have to refrain from violence. She was told that Karl would be the primary focus of treatment, but as long as the marriage had a potential for being preserved—their relationship would be the second client in the treatment room. Eve agreed that she needed her own source of support to help her sort out her feelings and come to a decision regarding the marriage. Therefore, she agreed to receive her own short-term individual counseling to help her deal with her anger, impulses of violence, and being triggered into rabbit holes of despair. If and when Eve ever decided that she wanted to work on healing the relationship between her and Karl, then marital counseling would be initiated.

Karl was almost at rock bottom. His marriage was likely over, he was separated from his children, and he might not be found fit for duty by his academic dean. Even if he did not lose his job, his reputation was seriously damaged. Although Karl had developed himself professionally through his writing as an authority and consultant to the criminal justice system, his specific area of expertise was the investigation and prosecution of sex crimes. Beyond getting himself healthy and saving his marriage (for real this time), Karl was very concerned about his children. He was worried about whether or not the children could understand what was going on and the changes related to his living separately. For a short while, he did not see his children at all and then started to see them only with another supervising responsible adult present.

The reason for this was that Eve was blindsided by the discovery of his double life and was really questioning how well she knew Karl. Basically, she wondered that if she did not know about all the many PSBs for such a long time—what else does she not know about her husband? She started to question if the children were safe from harm when they were in his care. Specialty assessments were then employed to determine if Karl demonstrated any evidence of sexual interest in children. These tests were negative (showing an absence of sexual interest in children). This was reassuring to Eve, and the couple worked out a visitation schedule by which Karl could maintain a significant and emotionally meaningful connection with the children.

Karl's crisis stabilized for the time being because he now had some hope that Eve was not immediately moving to end the marriage as well as reestablishing contact with his children. He saw grace in her taking a "wait-and-see" approach to her decision making. Karl obsessed about how he had brought himself to a place that was so distant from where he wanted to be. He kept thinking about how his life was not perfect, but so much better a few years ago when his marriage, family, and career were intact. What had his life come to? Now, he felt like a pathetic, lonely man in a dumpy apartment wanting to masturbate to porn or call up hookers. Karl saw himself as a poisonous influence in his family's life and seriously thought that they would be better off without him. He felt that he had no one to call who would want to talk to him or cared if he lived or died. In fact, he convinced himself there were many people who wished that he would kill himself. Karl was a man without any sense of worth.

Through a combination of individual and group therapy, Karl was given guidance to reflect on his internal life and sort out the factors that brought him to such a miserable place in his life. Through his emotional exploration, he gained insight into the factors that helped put him on his path of self-destruction. During the course of treatment, Karl developed a sense of safety and supportive structure to explore long-standing issues that he had traditionally ignored and pushed to the edge of his consciousness. He came to understand that these factors were not excuses at all for his sexual acting out but were factors in the development and maintenance of his cycles of PSB. For Karl, his individual mix of contributing factors included:

- feelings of abandonment related to his mother leaving him as a child;
- sexual molestation as a boy by a female babysitter and her boyfriend;
- developing unanswered questions about his sexual orientation;
- seeing sexual relations as a means of reinforcing his heterosexuality;
- having doubts about being masculine enough and a good enough lover;
- self-beliefs about needing to be in control and nonemotional as a man;
- having an undiagnosed case of severe clinical depression;
- drinking excessively and experiencing disinhibition of behavior;
- guilt from previous sexual indiscretions that were unknown to his wife; and
- not having the communication skills to resolve marital resentments (due to alexithymia—not having the awareness of affect and/or ability to express feelings).

Feeling he was condemned by God for being an abomination, Karl also joined the Men's Sexual Health Group, which brings together men who struggle with their demons and search for personal growth and healthy relationships. As unlikely as it seems, the men's group starts out as a collection of strangers who slowly create a safe space to speak honestly about their sexual compulsions without fear of judgment or attack, admit their shortcomings and disappointments in themselves, and face the hurt they have caused others. Once men reach both a sense of safety and honesty, they have an opportunity to begin healing themselves, making amends, and rebuilding relationships. Karl was rather a traditional guy and very hesitant to join in the mix of conversation, so he sat and listened for several weeks.

He found that for some men, it is sometimes too late when they find their way to the group. He learned that those men had to deal with too much anger, suspicion, and hopelessness. They faced the fact that whatever life still remained in the relationship had been damaged beyond resuscitation. Karl heard stories of men with partners in their marriage or business who had already passed their point of no return. The group could only help those men find a way to make the unbearable a bit more bearable: to find ways to manage the loneliness, guilt, and pain of personal ruin so they could get past the point of wanting to die and could start to build a new life.

Karl also witnessed other men who had begun the process of recovery. He hoped to replicate a similar salvation of his own marriage and career. Some men may be slow to lay down the burden of secrecy and begin rebuilding trust with their partners (as well as with themselves). Karl witnessed men starting to make authentic changes within themselves, not just for window dressing in the marriage. Fortunately, he found most men lucky enough to come into the group while there was still time for healing to take hold. Like Karl, most of them were also fortunate to have partners willing to suspend any decision to exit the relationship until they could judge for themselves if the man is making genuine changes for the better.

Karl found that the men hold confidential what they hear in group and that this trust with each other is of paramount importance. He discovered that trust was the essence of the safe space that allowed sharing of painful details of their lives. In one group meeting, Karl watched as a man shared some of the details of his personal dilemma, a marriage on the rocks that was in crisis after his wife discovered his inappropriate email communications on his personal laptop with a woman at work. The man (we will call him Roger) started the group off by sharing an anxiety-provoking situation in which a flirtatious relationship with an employee threatened to wreck both his marriage and his career. He was married and anxious to save his marriage, but he also described a history of pornography use and masturbating as a substitute to intimacy with his wife. This rang a bell for Karl. He felt the shame in the man's words, and Karl only wished that he had stopped his self-defeating behavior before escalating to having affairs.

Karl thought Roger looked like a tightly wound metal spring, full of anxiety and barely able to get his words out, especially when Roger also confessed his temptation to continue the emotional affair with his coworker. Another man named Joe encouraged Roger to have a plan ready in case he experienced strong impulses to sexually act out with her. Joe shared a bit about his relapse prevention plan and encouraged Roger by sharing his phone number with him in case he needed to talk. Joe had been in the group longer and proudly shared that he had gone five months without using pornography and was now channeling all his sexual energy toward his wife. Joe also knew he was damn lucky that this level of intimacy was possible after his wife's discovery of his porn use and online flirtations. Usually, there is a long trust-rebuilding process before sexual relations resume.

Karl was learning the process of shoulder-to-shoulder support and was shocked to find men talking this way. As Roger finished the part of his story he wanted to share that night, another group member (Jim) compassionately related his own experiences that the group discussed at length. Jim was very solemn as he started to describe the events that shook him up so much that week when unexpected visitors appeared at work unannounced: his mother and father. Karl tuned in even more when Jim went on to describe to the group an aspect of his history that they did not know. Jim came from a very abusive childhood home where he was subjected to emotional, physical, and sexual abuse. All the men in the room were silent, listening intently as Jim shared his story. The men listened with an intention to share empathy and support. Jim had cut off all contact with his parents because they would never admit to or acknowledge the history of abuse. Jim felt they were not safe for him to be around, nor was it safe for them to be around his children. Jim missed contact with some of his other family but agreed with his wife that their children's safety was of paramount importance. No phone calls or texts were returned when his parents tried to make contact. Jim had a sister who previously did the same thing because she also had been abused and wanted to protect her children. Jim didn't understand his sister's stance at first when she cut off contact with the parents but came to agree with her that their parents could be a risk to the grandchildren due to their mental illness. The parents believed it was Jim's and his sister's obligation to take care of them in their old age. They had no sense of boundaries with Jim or his sister. The parents refused to acknowledge the abuse or to get counseling for themselves.

Karl felt the fear Jim transmitted as it was very real to all. It was the fear men feel that leads them to protect their children and themselves. Jim explained that he told his children to never get in a car with his parents even if they said that Jim had been in an accident and they were going to drive the children to the hospital. Jim said that he was at work standing in front of his lathe machine when he caught somebody out of the corner of his eye standing in the doorway. He turned his head to see his parents there. The first thing to pop into his brain was "How did you get in here?" They answered that they told the guards that it was Jim's birthday and they were here to surprise him. That it was!

Instantly, he felt like a scared little boy, just like he did when he was in his parents' house of abuse. Karl could identify. He never had heard a man talk about his abuse history as a child, let alone how bad it must have been to still have such intense feelings about it as a man. Karl felt his eyes welling up. Jim ended his story by sharing how he diplomatically walked his parents to the door and explained to them that he did not feel safe around them and did not want to have his children around them. He informed them that he would contact them when he felt he wanted to and would only consider doing so after they got counseling. Until then, he said he would not have contact with them. The parents cried and walked away. Then he cried. Jim was praised by the group for setting firm boundaries and effectively managing a very difficult family situation at his work.

Karl felt a bit confused but also knew he did not know the whole story. He was in a state of amazement and began to feel a profound appreciation for where he was. Ricky (another man) initiated a conversation about being at a basketball game and getting anxious about his ex-affair partner being at the same game also. He was worried about his wife's reaction if she saw the ex-affair partner and how she was going to react, so he sat and watched, hoping his wife would not notice. A group member named Maximus jumped into the conversation to supportively confront Ricky as to how he handled the situation. Max did so by sharing his own "oh-shit moment" when he walked in a restaurant to meet his wife and the first thing he saw was his ex-affair partner sitting at the first table by the door.

Max assumed they had not seen each other but did not know. He walked right past the first table (without stopping or speaking), found his wife at the back of the restaurant, and sat next to her. After saying hello, Max told her that so-and-so was there and asked his wife if she wished to go to another place to eat. Max's wife thanked him for telling her and decided to stay and enjoy dinner together instead of running away from the situation. Ricky was stunned by Max's story and shared that he wished that he did the same because Ricky's wife ran into Ricky's ex-affair partner when she went to the concession stand! Tony (another group member) shared a bit of twisted wisdom, speaking from his history of lying about his secret life to his wife. Tony shared that his marriage never started to heal until he decided that it was more important to be honest than be married! This statement struck fear into Karl's heart, but Tony explained that the more he lived "in the light" with honesty, the more healing could happen in his marriage and the more likely he would be able to save not only himself but his family.

Finally, Karl had an opportunity to speak and shared a few details of why he was joining the group. The common joke is "What are you in for?" He shared as much as he was comfortable disclosing because he was the new guy, saying that he wished to do everything he could to make things right with his wife, but there was one thing he dreaded and could not bring himself to do—and that was going to a Sex Addicts Anonymous (SAA) group as part of his recovery program. Karl had heard a couple of the men mention that they attended SAA but explained that he was too ashamed of what he had done to his wife and family. He could not think of how talking about it in a public meeting could help. He was also fearful of being identified by someone that he works with at the university (like a student) or someone who attends the same church. Another man in the group (Carlos) reached out to Karl saying he remembered having the same fears and that Carlos also had a job that was very much in the public eye. Carlos explained that Karl's public embarrassment probably couldn't get worse than what Karl had made it and that confidentiality had never been a problem at the meeting as everyone maintains everyone else's trust. He offered to meet Karl before the Saturday morning meeting and attend the meeting together.

Karl realized he was in the middle of a group of men who were committed to improving their own health as well as the collective health of each other. This, of course, was a key step in improving the health of his marriage and family. He was not sure what was going to happen in additional groups, but his initial apprehension melted away to a positive anticipation to return and learn. He did not know all the how-to of repairing his life and relations with his family. He only felt hope about being in the right place to learn. Karl accepted Carlos's invitation.

KEY COMPONENTS OF THE RECOVERY PROCESS

This section of the chapter highlights useful guideposts on the path to health from sexual compulsivity/sex addiction (PSB) through changes in relationship, understanding, behavior, and spirituality. Although every individual has a specific set of contributing factors to their own PSB and unique details of sexually acting out that must be addressed, there are many common behaviors as well. Hence, there are common strategies employed to begin recovery and travel a path back to health. The idea is not only to achieve abstinence (or sobriety) over the PSB, but to gain new levels of quality of life. Therefore, the individual is less vulnerable to relapse as well as more successful in pursuing the three key things most everybody desires in life: a sense of health and well-being, a sense of purpose and meaning, and healthy relationships with oneself and others.

What follows in this section are the key components of the recovery process a person can use that is a multiple-resource approach to not only breaking the PSB cycle but also getting healthier than they may have ever been. These guidelines are general enough to assist most people in successfully finding their way to health. They are not meant to be a specific checklist where every recommended recovery strategy is marked off. Many people can recover successfully using most of these guidelines. Which set of recommendations works best for which individual is uncertain. Obviously, the more of these guidelines that a person can put into play, the more likely the person will move forward to achieve healthy recovery goals. Before reviewing these guidelines, two important tools are briefly discussed that are very helpful to many individuals: medications and a relapse prevention plan.

Although using short-term medications is an option some people do not choose in their recovery, the use of psychotropic medication is always considered when an individual with PSB is evaluated. Medication is more likely to be recommended when a man:

- has been clinically diagnosed with a mood and/or anxiety disorder;
- has engaged in a long-term, well-established pattern of PSB;
- has experienced very serious consequences to his behavior; and
- has failed other treatment approaches addressing his PSB.

Medications are effective for treating anxiety, depression, and PTSD. These meds assist men to better deal with the chaos they created and have less symptoms. They have fewer symptoms to disadvantage their ability to cope and abstain from their cycle of PSB. Most of the psychotropics employed (especially SSRI drugs) have the additional benefit of suppressing sexual libido and "taking the edge off" to facilitate abstinence. Some people come to understand just how anxious and depressed they are once the meds take effect. Others prefer not to use medications, and that is fine if their levels of symptoms continue to decrease over time.

Effective relapse prevention planning is a fundamental skill for men to develop early on treatment. Otherwise, there is little likelihood of successful crisis stabilization and subsequent recovery. Below, components of an effective relapse prevention plan are offered by Sugrue (2007).

- Sexual behaviors in inner circle (compulsive behaviors I must stop).
- Sexual behaviors in middle circle (dangerous behaviors I must avoid).
- What is at stake if I don't control my behavior?
- What I have to gain by maintaining control of my sexual behavior.
- Ways to take better care of myself.
- Ways to take better care of my relationships.
- Behaviors and situations I must avoid.
- Circumstances that should put me on alert.
- Early signals of pending relapse.
- In case of emergency: my mantra, whom to call, my most effective control techniques, and my first-aid kit.

These components (as well as additional interventions) are integrated within Stage I of the Positive Sexuality Recovery Model (see next section). Beyond the common building blocks of most basic relapse prevention plans, additional value-added components found useful by clients are as follows:

- stepping back and looking at the big picture by defining one's personal mission (sense of purpose) in life;
- organizing a personal mission support team;
- writing out the most likely relapse scenario; and
- establishing a positive reinforcement system for positive changes to facilitate recovery, including a reward system for effective plan execution (replacing unhealthy reinforcement of PSB).

The following three stages of recovery overlap and the length of time an individual spends in each stage varies depending on several factors. It is recommended that individuals take advantage of both mental health counseling (from a professional experienced in assisting clients with PSB) as well as self-help groups (such as SA, SAA, SLAA, CR—see below). It is important for each individual to remember how long their PSB took to develop and that recovery will not occur overnight. It is a process that may take several years. The following guidelines come from several sources but are drawn liberally from Wayne Floyd, an experienced, well-respected psychotherapist practicing in Dayton, Ohio. Mr. Floyd contributed significantly to this section from his *Foundation of Recovery Program* (Floyd, 2017).

THE POSITIVE SEXUALITY RECOVERY MODEL

Stage 1: Crisis Stabilization and Abstinence (3 to 6 Months)

Relationships: Immediate and sustained focus on relationships (versus isolation) is paramount as isolation fuels PSB and relationships promote recovery.

Relationship with oneself

- Acceptance—admitting the problem.
- Recognition that "I can't do this alone" (no trying to "John Wayne" it).

Relationships with others

- Fellowship with others during recovery/Working Step #1.
- Developing personal timeline/Meeting and working with a sponsor.

Understanding

- Understanding the "how" of one's own particular PSB and steps to recovery/the withdrawal process and the cycles of PSB/the basic neuroscience of the drugs in your brain (adrenaline, dopamine, oxytocin).
- Developing an effective relapse prevention plan to break the PSB cycle/Defining personal mission and purpose/Establishing mission support team/Listing emotional and situational triggers/Planning for healthy coping behaviors/Writing out the most likely relapse scenario (for early radar detection)/Establishing a positive reinforcement system for positive changes to facilitate recovery.

Behavior

- With professional consultation (if necessary), make decision regarding appropriate level of care (self-help, standard counseling, intensive-outpatient or residential).
- Finding and working with an attorney (when necessary) to stay out of jail.
- Finding and working with the right counselor (certified sex therapist or professional experienced with PSB).

Spirituality

- Values clarification/Developing a connection to a higher power (when appropriate).

Stage 2: Sobriety Moving into Recovery (6 to 12 Months)

Relationships

Relationship with oneself

- Resolving the basic impulse to self-destruct.
- Commitment to oneself that you are worth saving and deserve to be healthy.

Relationships with others

- Relationship repair and trust building/Staying in fellowship/Deepening your work in therapy.
- Taking inventory of your social support system/Deepening and expanding key relationships.

Understanding

- Gaining clarity regarding your psychological agenda driving your pattern of PSB.
- Reexamining your mission and checking for alignment with daily living.

Behavior

- Learning the skills and developing proficiency at safety and mindfulness/Getting help with any concurrent diagnoses (such as anxiety, depression, etc.).
- Getting your health-house in order (primary care and specialist consultation)/Practicing effective use of mission support team with reinforcement system/Seeking amends and forgiveness, including self-forgiveness for personal shortcomings.

Spirituality

- Practicing acceptance, compassion, and openness (toward others and self).
- Seeking spiritual guidance/Finding your spiritual center.

Stage 3: Recovery as a Long-Term Sustained Change (18 to 24 Months)

Relationships

Relationship with oneself

- Commitment to live an examined and healthy life.

Relationships with others

- Exploring each other's needs and expectations.
- Building long-term relationship satisfaction.

Understanding

- Increasing sexual health literacy/Being more aware of choices to be healthy sexually, physically, emotionally, relationally, and spiritually.
- Addressing developmental gaps/Trauma resolution and healing.

Behavior

- Integrating daily practices of centeredness for recovery (meditation, prayer, yoga, Tai Chi, reading, reaching out to another, therapeutic writing, practicing appreciation, a.m.-p.m. check-ins).
- Striving for better health through exercise, eating wisely and working toward a healthy weight, limiting or eliminating alcohol intake, limiting or eliminating tobacco use, and reducing or eliminating unnecessary stress and health risks.
- Further skill development options such as the Higher Steps/self-parenting/self-hypnosis/dialectical behavior therapy (DBT).

Spirituality

- Whole spiritual practice/Living a spiritually intentional life.
- Further value clarification and appreciation of what is most important to us.

Commitment to Positive Male Sexuality

- Men with positive sexuality will possess most, if not all, of the following 12 characteristics:

    1. Feelings of self-worth as a man (integration of positive male identity).
    2. Sense of self-security with an internal locus of control so a man does not feel like he must prove his masculinity to others.
    3. Commitment to the principles and practices of consensual sex.
    4. Acceptance and appreciation of a positive sexual self-image.
    5. Ability to avoid and/or recover from cyclic patterns of PSB.
    6. Ability to positively practice self-pleasuring in healthy manner.
    7. Communication and intimacy skills to experience emotional closeness.
    8. Openness to continuously learning how to be a better sexual partner based on his partner's sensual/sexual interests and preferences.
    9. Active exercise to be healthy and well via the Big Wheel of Health.
    10. Tolerance and acceptance of others who are different from himself.

11. Understanding that sexuality is another form of communication that serves an overall goal of meaningful and emotional connection.
12. Understanding and practicing the value of lifelong learning regarding the unique aspects of positive sexuality at every stage of life.

ILLEGAL PSBs THAT HURT OTHERS: SEX OFFENSES

So far in this chapter, we have discussed PSBs that are legal for the most part. PSBs that involve different types of sex workers may or may not be illegal. For example, employing prostitutes in America is legal only in Nevada (but only in some counties and only in brothels). Also, sex workers who utilize phone sex or online live video interaction are not necessarily engaged in illegal activity (assuming all parties are consenting adults). Obviously, there are many PSBs that are illegal and are commonly referred to as sex offenses. Some of the most common types of sex-offending behaviors include, but are not limited to, the following PSBs:

- Any sexual contact adults have with minors (considering all age-of-consent laws).
- Any production, possession, or distribution of pornographic images or depictions of sexual activity involving minors.
- Importuning and "traveler" sex offenders (think of the television show *To Catch a Predator*)
- Nonconsensual sex contact between adults that may be considered sexual harassment, rape, sexual assault, or gross sexual imposition.
- Exhibitionism (sexual arousal to the act of displaying genitals to nonconsenting others in public) or violations of public indecency.
- Voyeurism (sexual arousal to the act of viewing unsuspecting others while they are undressing, naked, or engaged in sex) and/or viewing of naked people without their consent.

In this section of the chapter, the assessment and treatment of sex offenders is briefly addressed. It is a specialized area for mental health professionals across several disciplines, including psychology, psychiatry, counselors, and social workers as well as others. A full discussion of the special issues involved in this type of evaluation and counseling is beyond the scope of this chapter let alone this section. However, the topic is included here because it includes the most serious types of PSB and it is important to make several points that are not necessarily well understood (or accepted) in the general population as well as the mental health and law enforcement communities.

As mentioned earlier in this book, the terms *pedophilia* and *child molestation* represent related, but separate, phenomena. Said differently, the men engaged in these activities are separate but overlapping populations (Abel, Wiegel, & Osborn, 2007; Camilleri & Quinsey, 2008). The pedophilic individual will express sexual interest in young children (usually prepubertal or early pubertal children) that is intense and enduring. He may or may not ever actually commit a sex offense by sexually touching a child. Intense sexual interest in prepubertal children (pedophilia) is different from men's sexual interest in teenagers. Adults who have a sexual interest in adolescent, post-pubertal children (who display secondary sex characteristics) are biologically, sociologically, and psychologically common. Of course, it is not normal and is a sex-offending crime for adults to pursue adolescent minors and engage in sex with them.

Child molestation does involve a contact sex offense of a child by an adult, but the sex offender may or may not have a pedophilic disorder. It is important to note the difference because there are an increasing number of prosecutions involving the possession of child pornography, and because it is estimated that the clear majority (perhaps up to 95%) of contact sex offenses against children are committed by men with pedophilic disorder (Abel, Wiegel, & Osborn, 2007). This ability to accurately diagnose pedophilia and differentiate non-pedophilic offenders is also important regarding the type of assessment strategies used in the evaluation of sex offenders and the types of treatment approaches employed.

Regarding assessment considerations, men who have pedophilic interests are very skilled at concealing this interest because of social stigma and fear of prosecution. Individuals accused of child sex offenses typically undergo a standard sex offender evaluation involving psychiatric interview, psychological testing of various self-report measures, and review of his developmental history, including his legal history. Evidence of pedophilic interest during the evaluation can be manifest through his self-disclosure (rare), his documented legal history (more often), or through demonstration of objective measures of his sexual interest (becoming more common). The standard approach to sex offender assessment, while having some important utility, may be inadequate without objective measures of the individual's sexual interest patterns precisely because the individual can do such a good job of hiding his pedophilic interest from the examiner.

At the 2011 National Strategy Conference on Combating Child Pornography, then Attorney General Eric Holder said, "Unfortunately, *we've also seen a historic rise in the distribution of child pornography, in the number of images being shared online, and in the level of violence associated with child exploitation and sexual abuse crimes. Tragically, the only place we've seen a decrease is in the age of victims. This is—quite simply—unacceptable [emphasis added]*." Because of greater emphasis on combating child pornography, there have been increasing numbers of prosecutions. The number of arrests for child pornography in the United States tripled between 2001 and 2010 (Seto, 2013). Hence, there is increased need for comprehensive assessments that include objective measures, particularly because there is also a common notion that all individuals who view child pornography are eventually going to commit a contact sex offense against a child.

Increased attention to battle child abuse is extremely important, and all available law enforcement resources should be directed to saving children being harmed and trafficked (one story of extreme harm follows this chapter with the story of Kala in Chapter 18). Child abuse most often occurs in the home (as with Kala), but with the advent and availability of email, predators can also solicit children online and travel to them for the purposes of committing a sex offense: so-called "travelers" (DeLong, Durkin, & Hundersmarck, 2010). However, the notion that all people who look at child pornography are at high risk for attempting to have sex with children (become a traveler) is just not accurate. Some people look at many different types of online pornographic images and never intend to act in such a way that reflects the content of the pornography (i.e., watching a video of a person having sex with an animal).

Perhaps a better explanation would be people who view online films regarding the Holocaust. Some viewers may be considered individuals who want to learn about genocide and teach their children about it with the hope of never seeing another example of genocide in their lifetime. Some viewers watch it only because it is a high school or college assignment. However, there may be some viewers who watch the film for the purpose of criticism and picking it apart because they are Holocaust deniers. There may even be dangerously deviant viewers who watch the film footage because they enjoy sadistic fantasies of planning the next genocide.

At a law conference of judges and attorneys discussing the topic of judicial sentencing of individuals convicted in child pornography cases, forensic psychiatrist Fred Berlin (who testified in many famous cases, including the Jeffrey Dahmer case) presented on the topic of pedophilia and child pornography. Dr. Berlin shared that the reason for people watching child pornography was all about the *intent of the viewer*. He used an example of people who enjoy being scared by watching horror movies. "Fans of horror movies don't want to be in one," he explained (Berlin, 2015). Knowing the intent of a person for viewing pornography may be important clinically but perhaps more important to the court is what does the intent of viewing mean in terms of an individual's risk for committing a contact sex offense.

Some people view different types of porn out of curiosity, some view child pornography because it is sent to them and they didn't know what it was, some view it because of severe obsessive-compulsive disorder, some view it as a stress response to the objectification of children killed in war, some view it as a means of self-punishment to prove how depraved they are, and some view it because they do find it sexually interesting (clinical cases of DeLong, Peterson, & Associates). After conducting a long-term study of a large group of men who had been convicted of possession of child pornography, leading researcher of sex offender behavior Michael Seto stated (in his 2012 testimony to the U.S. Sentencing Commission) that less than 5% (2.1%) of men arrested for online child pornography went on to commit a contact sex offense against a child. Understanding the difference in risk factors between men arrested for online child pornography and men arrested for actually having sexual contact with children is exceedingly important.

For example, if a man arrested for child pornography possession is evaluated and found to not demonstrate sexual interest in children or be a risk of harm to any child, then he may be granted an alternative sentence that better serves the community as well as his rehabilitation. If that same man can serve a sentence of incarceration during weekends and be allowed to work his regular job during the week, he can then serve his time, still pay his debt to society (including taxes), and continue to support his family. Such judicial judgments in sentencing have been made in appropriate cases that present very low risk of a sexual contact offense (clinical cases of DeLong, Peterson & Associates). Of course, child pornography is illegal expressly because of the abuse children experience in the production of it. It should be illegal, and its use should be prosecuted. But the intent of the viewer's use makes a big difference in terms of the risk for either repeating the crime or committing a contact offense.

If a person does show evidence of pedophilic interest and he is determined to be at risk of harm to others, then treatment is often provided during incarceration, and many of the same treatment guidelines previously outlined in this chapter still apply. The treatment is typically more intense, more frequent, and longer in duration during incarceration. If treatment is on an outpatient basis, probation or parole stipulations exist, and they must be integrated into the treatment program. Community monitoring occurs as well with sex offenders regularly reporting to their probation officer and sometimes wearing electronic ankle monitors.

Per research on public perception of sex crimes, the many law-and-order shows (as well as *CSI* shows) lead the clear majority of the American public (75%) to erroneously believe that almost all sex offenders are hardened criminals who will always be repeat offenders (Levenson, Brannon, Fortney, & Baker, 2007). Public animosity toward men labeled sex offenders (from exhibitionists and peeping-toms to child molesters) and the public skepticism toward the effectiveness of sex offender treatment was well represented within a special issue of TIME (May 21, 2018) that had a cover photo of a man standing in the shadows with the bold caption "Can Bad Men Change?" (Dockterman, 2018).

When an individual is struggling with illegal PSB, there is a general stereotype of all sex offenders as having "high and frightening" recidivism rates, a phrase often cited in court decisions, including the Supreme Court (J. Barna, personal communication, March 20, 2015). The notion of "high and frightening" recidivism rates reflects a common attitude that all sex offenders will commit another sex crime so it's better to keep them in prison. There is certainly a small subset of sex offenders who are resistant to treatment, are violent in nature, and continue to be dangerous to others. These are the hardened criminals who do fit the stereotype. And they are the reason that 20 states have special civil commitment laws (as controversial as they are) that allow judges to keep some sex offenders incarcerated after they have served their sentence, albeit they remain incarcerated in treatment centers with locked doors and razor wire (Mears, 2010).

However, the research clearly supports the view that sex offender treatment is effective, that most sex offenders do change for the better, and that only a minority of sex offenders are reconvicted for sex crimes. Well-known sex-crime researchers Hanson and Morton-Bourgon conducted a large-scale meta-analysis of recidivism rates of adult sex offenders and found a rate of 14% over five to six years. Recidivism rates usually increase the longer the period the sex offender is studied, and when they expanded their period of review to 15 years, the recidivism rates for adult sex offenders are estimated to increase to 24% (Hanson & Morton-Bourgon, 2005).

SUMMARY: FINAL THOUGHTS OF PSB

An intensely interesting aspect of my work is assisting men and couples to recover from PSB and the adverse consequences which follow. Each case is like a mystery to solve by assisting the individual to discover his intent and motivations for engaging in the PSB, get in touch with the pain and confusion he has created, help his family have hope for positive change, and walk a path that leads to what most people want in life—health, a sense of purpose, and meaningful relationships.

Whether the PSB is legal or illegal, much of the process of recovery is the same. There must be a recognition and acceptance that the problematic behavior can no longer be tolerated, and then the process can begin of building relationships to heal. That recognition comes in many forms. Sometimes it is forced upon a person by the law, by their failing health, or by a partner walking out after many requests for change have been ignored. This recognition can lead to connection with others through reaching out for a relationship. Sometimes it does not happen because the individual is paralyzed by fear and an overwhelming dread of having what is secret brought out to the light. It is the fear and anxiety that keeps people trapped in their dilemma and continues to perpetuate the cycle of the PSB. Therefore, isolation and fear fuels PSB (of any type) and connection into a relationship (with self and others) is what promotes recovery and health.

No matter what personal challenges we face, sexual in nature or otherwise, walking a path of health is a balancing act of the right amounts of the right ingredients at the right times. The ingredients are love, peace, faith, and wisdom. All four of these ingredients are the basic building blocks of the three stages of health and recovery reviewed earlier in this chapter. Love encompasses acceptance and compassion for oneself as well as others. Peace involves finding ways to quiet the noise and finding one's center. Faith means hope and the belief in the resiliency of the human spirit. Wisdom knows that each of us, as life itself, are full of paradox and contradiction, yet we can decide to make the right choices to build a life that may be far from perfect but is well worth living.

By the way, Karl found the right amount of the right ingredients in time to save himself and his marriage. He added liberal amounts of three additional and critical elements: promoting a sense of safety, exercising transparency, and making a friend of accountability. He no longer is depressed and having thoughts of self-destruction but instead appreciates his daily life with his wife and children. After sufficient support to Karl's wife and healing of the relationship, a shift occurred from "how could you do this to me" to "how can we move forward together," to make a new normal that is satisfying to both of them. The marital relationship has grown past the hurt and betrayal to a focus on living in the present and sharing enjoyment of each other's company as well as pleasure in touching one another. They have a renewed sense of themselves individually, as a couple, and as a family.

REFERENCES

Abel, G., Wiegel, M., & Osborn, C. (2007). Pedophilia and other paraphilia. In L. VanderCreek, F. Peterson, & J. Bley (Eds.), *Innovations in clinical practice: Focus on sexual health.* Sarasota, FL: Professional Resource Press.

American Association of Sex Educators, Counselors, & Therapists (2016). AASECT Position Statement on Sex Addiction. Chicago: Author.

American Psychiatric Association [APA]. (2013). *Diagnostic and statistical manual of mental disorders* (5th ed.). Arlington, VA: American Psychiatric Publishing.

Barna, J. (2015). Personal communication with James Barna, JD, PhD at Gilvary Symposium (Sentencing on Pornography Cases), School of Law, University of Dayton, Dayton, Ohio (March 20, 2015).

Berlin, F. (2015, March 20). *The paraphilias with an emphasis on pedophilia and viewers of child pornography.* Presentation at the Gilvary Symposium (Sentencing on Pornography Cases), School of Law, University of Dayton, Dayton, Ohio.

Braun-Harvey, D., & Vigorito, M. (2016). Treating out-of-control sexual behaviors—Rethinking sex addiction. New York: Springer.

Camilleri, J., & Quinsey, V. (2008). Pedophilia: Assessment and treatment. In D. Law & W. O'Donohue (Eds.), *Sexual deviance: Theory, assessment, and treatment.* New York: Guilford.

Carnes, P. (2001). *Out of the shadows: Understanding sexual addiction* (3rd ed.). Center City, MN: Hazelden Press.

Centers for Disease Control and Prevention (CDC). (2014). Prevalence and characteristics of sexual violence, stalking, and intimate partner violence victimization: National Intimate Partner and Sexual Violence Survey, United States. Atlanta, GA: Author.

Coleman, E. (2011). Assessment and treatment of impulsive and compulsive sexual behavior. In J. Grant & J. Potenza (Eds.), *Oxford handbook of impulse control disorders.* New York: Oxford University Press.

Cooper, A. (2002). *Sex and the internet. A guidebook for clinicians.* New York: Brunner-Routledge.

Delmonico, D., & Griffin, E. (2014). *Sexual addiction: Assessment, management, and treatment.* New York: Routledge.

DeLong, R., Durkin, K., & Hundersmarck, S. (2010). An exploratory analysis of the cognitive distortions of a sample of men arrested in internet sex stings. *Journal of Sexual Aggression,* Vol. 16, No. 1, pp. 1–12.

Dockterman, E. (2018). Inside sex offender treatment. Time (May 21, 2018).

Floyd, W. (2017). *Foundation of recovery program.* Unpublished manuscript.

Hanson, K., & Morton-Bourgon, K. (2005). The characteristics of persistent sexual offenders: A meta-analysis of recidivism studies. *Journal of Consulting and Clinical Psychology, 73*(6).

Holder, E. (2011). Comments during an address at the National Strategy Conference on Combating Child Exploitation in San Jose, California, May 19, 2011.

Kafka, M. (1997). Hypersexual desire in males: An operational definition and clinical implications for males with paraphilia and paraphilia-related disorders. *Archives of Sexual Behavior, 26*(5), 505–526.

Klein, M. (2011). *America's war on sex: The continuing attack on law, lust, and liberty* (2nd ed.). Santa Barbara, CA: Praeger.

Laumann, E., Gagnon, J., Michael, R., & Michaels, S. (1994). *The social organization of sexuality: Sexual practices in the United States.* Chicago: University of Chicago Press.

LeVay, S., Baldwin, J., & Baldwin, J. (2015). *Discovering human sexuality* (3rd ed.). Sunderland, MA: Sinauer Associates.

Levenson, J., Brannon, Y., Fortney, T., & Baker, J. (2007). Public perceptions about sex offenders and community protection policies. *Analyses of Social Issues and Public Policy, 7*(1).

Ley, D. (2018). Compulsive Sexual Behavior Disorder in ICD-11: What does this mean, for advocacy against sex addiction diagnosis? Psychologytoday.com. Posted Jan 24, 2018. https://www.psychologytoday.com/us/comment/973268

Mark, K., Janssen, E., & Milhausen, R. (2011). Infidelity in heterosexual couples: Demographic, interpersonal, and personality-related predictors of extra-dyadic sex. *Archives of Sexual Behavior.* doi:10.1007/s10508-0111-9771-z

Mears, B. (2010, May 17). Supreme Court: Sex offenders can be held indefinitely. CNN. Retrieved from news.blogs.cnn.com/2010/05/17/supreme-court-says-sex-offenders-can.

Schultz, D., & Schultz, S. (2004). *The history of modern psychology.* Belmont, CA: Wadsworth/Thompson Learning.

Seto, M. (2012). *Child pornography offender characteristics and risk to reoffend.* Testimony to the United States Sentencing Commission (February 6, 2012), Washington, D.C.

Seto, M. (2013). *Assessment and treatment of Internet sex offenders.* Paper presented at the national conference of the Association for the Treatment of Sex Abusers, Chicago.

Sugrue, D. (2007). Sexual addiction/compulsivity—Diagnosis and treatment. In L. VanderCreek, F. Peterson, & J. Bley (Eds.), *Innovations in clinical practice: Focus on sexual health.* Sarasota, FL: Professional Resource Press.

Weiss, R. (2013). *Cruise control: Understanding sex addiction in gay men* (2nd ed.). Carefree, AZ: Gentle Path.

CHAPTER EIGHTEEN

The Mind Is a Tricky Thing, but the Body Never Forgets:

KALA'S STORY

Written by Frederick Peterson

[Authors' Note: Parts of the following story may be disturbing to some readers as it describes a woman's history of child abuse and neglect.]

Do you ever wonder if there is any rhyme or reason to how each of us was born into our particular family, or is it truly based on the complete randomness of the universe? Was it just chance that you may have had sane parents who protected you from harm whereas others are born to crazy folks who exposed their kids to all types of danger or even just sell them to strangers for money or drugs? Why did you end up in America whereas others are born into slavery or to a family who find themselves in the middle of a war zone? Sometimes we give pause to wonder, especially when you meet a person like Kala.

This is another story from my experience at the Masters and Johnson Institute during the 1990s. It was a gray November morning at the Institute when I had a new patient assigned to me who had been screened and accepted into the residential treatment program for sexual trauma at the Institute. The day started with a staff briefing to update us regarding how our clients did with their self-care over the weekend, any news about special programming for the week, and announcements from our clinical team leaders.

After the briefing, the community meeting with both staff and clients was held and served as a "check-in" for clients to express themselves about any pressing needs or concerns. Immediately afterward, all clients participated in a group therapy for nearly two hours and then met with their individual counselor for the next hour. Then it was lunchtime, followed by art therapy, psychodrama therapy, and then a "checkout" group with all clients to make sure they were safe leaving for the day.

I was introduced to Kala that morning. She did not look me in the eye and barely looked up at me to acknowledge my presence. I told her that we would have a chance to get to know each other after the morning group. She was a beautiful African American woman, thin as a rail and not even five feet tall. She just nodded and joined all of us in the group room but didn't really join the group. Although coming to treatment of her own free will, she looked like it was the very last place she wanted to be. Kala pulled her feet up onto the chair, dropped her head down to rest her face on her knees, and didn't say a word. And that's how she spent the first three group meetings.

In our first one-to-one meeting, I was fascinated to learn how Kala came to the Institute. She was in her church choir and became upset regarding having feelings of attraction to her choir director. She would pinch and hit herself as self-punishment because she also reported being attracted to her husband. The conflict of having attraction to both her husband and the choir director created significant conflict and intense guilt within her. Kala was distraught by her father's death two years earlier and her mother's suicide only six months before she came to the Institute. She became increasingly depressed, even to the point of considering her own suicide.

Kala explained that her relationship to her mother was a complicated one, with strong ambivalence between desperately wishing for a seemingly unobtainable acceptance and fearsome loathing from a breathtaking history of intentional neglect. The first few years of her life were remembered as relatively normal. Kala enjoyed her brothers and sisters with parents that seemed to care and protect her. She had a kitty cat who loved her and kept her company at night. Then something very disturbing happened when Kala was about seven years old.

It's hard to know for sure what exactly happened, but something fundamentally shifted inside the psyche of the mother and caused unbelievable changes in Kala's childhood. The best I could piece together from her description was that her mother developed schizophrenia or possibly had long-term effects take hold of her from her own history of trauma. Regardless of the diagnosis put on it, the mother started to perceive Kala as a "bad seed" among her five children. Kala reported that her mother did not see her other children any differently but started to segregate Kala to protect the other children from "contamination."

This might not have had such a profound effect on Kala if her mother's behaviors were not so extreme. The mother, despite the presence of a timid father in the home, started to have Kala live separately in the basement of their small home. Kala told stories of hearing the rest of the family carry on life as normal one floor above her, and of being terrified of nightfall just as any seven-year-old would be anywhere, let alone in a basement of an old house.

She told her story of having a dog collar placed around her neck and having a leash attached to one of the steel posts that supported the first floor. Most of the time, she did not have enough clothes on to stay warm. She slept on a bare mattress on a concrete floor. During the day, she developed an imaginary friend to play and pass her time. She named her Burly. They would play made-up games from Kala's imagination and wonder about what was happening above them. Burly was a creative invention to help a small child survive incredible neglect and abuse. However, she was not the end to Kala's imagination.

When the lights drifted into dusk and then blackness, the only light came from under the cellar door. When Burly would say good-bye, Kala would await another friend who was more of a protector than a playmate. Her name was KB, an extraordinarily fierce protector from everything Kala could be afraid of in a basement alone overnight. In her youthful mind, she believed the bogeyman was real but could only strike her down if he caught her by surprise. As Kala explained her relationship to KB, Kala would rely on her to wake up Kala at any possible threat of harm. KB was her repository of all fearful fantasies a child could imagine. The repository was deep and full by the time Kala's period of segregation ended.

KB would do even more for Kala. It was not yet time for Kala to know the full extent of how KB protected her. For such protection, Kala also did not know the high price she would pay over time. For example, I met Kala as a 29-year-old married woman with four children. At that time, it had been more than two decades since she was able to sleep all night without waking up to nightmares. It had been that long also since Kala felt a real sense of safety and security. For 22 years Kala engaged in obsessive-compulsive behaviors like sleeping with covers over her head and having her blanket completely tucked in under her body much like a cocoon. Obviously, these behaviors presented challenges to the marital relationship and parenting her children (even though she was considered a good mother and wife by those who knew her).

During the course of her six-week treatment program, I thought I saw a glimpse of KB one day. It was during the psychodrama group therapy when Kala was the focus of the treatment. This meant she had to share her childhood history with others, explain her family dynamics, and have other clients play the roles of Kala's family members. Kala explained that she was fed and clothed to go to school, played the role of an ideal student, and then returned home only to be fed and then sent downstairs. She explained that she never spoke of her abuse with anyone, fearing that she would be further punished and that her mother would make good on a promise to "get rid of her." Kala also feared her mother's threat to place one of her sisters in the basement as a replacement for Kala (after Kala "disappeared").

Other clients were astounded by Kala's story and poured empathy toward her. They were even more surprised to learn that her subterranean exile lasted five years from age 7 until age 12. The reason it ended was that Kala started to suffer from failure-to-thrive syndrome and had stopped growing physically. By age 12, she was so behind her peers that she was referred to the nurse. A home visit was conducted by a social worker because the mother refused to attend a meeting at school concerning Kala. During the visit, the other children never reported that Kala slept in the basement (as Kala also never reported) because the siblings feared the mother would enforce her threat to have them join (or replace) Kala.

The social worker noticed a complete lack of concern from the mother toward Kala and seemed to sense there was something amiss but could not exactly identify what it was. It was apparent that the mother reigned supreme as overlord of the home. Kala distinctly remembered the nurse asking about whether there was any extended family that could be of help and perhaps have Kala visit for a while. At this query by the nurse, the mother exclaimed, "Could that happen—could she live somewhere else?" This simple inquiry evidently illuminated a possibility within Kala's mother that shocked her into opting for a socially sanctioned way of getting rid of Kala for good. To Kala, it was an unbelievable opportunity of escaping a torturous cycle that may have ended her young life. For whatever reason that ran through her mother's head, this simple inquiry led to Kala living with her paternal grandparents for the rest of her childhood and possibly saving her life. Kala reported that she slowly bloomed physically and had what she considered a normal adolescence.

Working with Kala during her individual therapy, I learned she strongly felt she did not belong in the treatment program as many other clients suffered from sexual abuse and she considered her experience a matter of neglect (perhaps extreme neglect, yet still not abuse). This appeared important for her to maintain as a belief, so it was not a matter of debate. However, the day she shared all this history with the rest of the clients during psychodrama therapy, something unexplainable occurred that resulted in her bolting from the group therapy room where she was participating in the psychodrama therapy.

Kala ran out of the room and I instantly followed her as the other co-therapist reassured the other clients. As I stepped into the hallway, I saw the back of her lower leg turn the corner into another group room at the end of the hallway. I was relieved that she did not try to flee the Institute but rather retreated to a room where I knew there was no other exit. Yet, as I entered the room I found it completely empty except for the furniture. I was dumbfounded. It appeared that she disappeared into thin air. I walked over to examine a window for signs of escape.

As I did, I found Kala in a fetal position on the floor behind a chair—pulled into a tiny ball of tortured humanity. I cautiously sat next to her on the floor, did not touch her, and just waited for her to open her eyes. Slowly, she started to move her hands along the carpet and feel the fibers like it was a new sensation to her. Her eyes opened, and she glanced around the room with the look of a wounded animal. She appeared scared and confused. I started to speak to her in a soft and reassuring manner that she was safe and protected. When her glance arrived to me, she was physically taken aback several inches, recoiling while remaining in a crouched position near the floor.

"Where am I, who are you?" she whispered. I explained, "You are safe here at the Masters & Johnson Institute, and I am your therapist." Her eyes were dilated and brow furrowed. She started to say something else but leaned her head down to the carpet. She remained motionless for several moments and then raised her head again. Glancing around the room and then staring at me, she loudly said, "What are we doing in here?"

The next day was the Tuesday before Thanksgiving and Kala complained of pelvic pain at the morning check-in group. She secured an appointment with her primary care physician and was examined with negative results. There were no signs of infection or apparent causes of the pain and burning she described. She continued to complain of discomfort for another day but did not mention it again that week. As the pain diminished, so did the concern about her symptoms—at least temporarily.

About three weeks later, Kala complained of pelvic pain and burning. Again, she was examined and again, nothing unusual was observed. However, the art therapist on the treatment team really earned her pay that week by asking Kala to draw what she felt in her lower pelvic area. The art therapy creation she produced was nothing short of stunning. Strange as it sounds, it looked like a stack of pancakes with an inverted burning red candle coming off the bottom—except the pancakes were layers of intestines represented by different colors of blue, purple, red, and brown. The inverted red candle represented the feeling of a burning and bleeding vaginal canal.

This drawing represented a transformational moment for Kala, as more of the historical truth of her "neglect" was added to the personal narrative that she was able to recall concerning those terrible five years. Some experts in post-traumatic stress disorder (PTSD) would say that the associated memories of her abuse were originally separated as a survival mechanism, and now as an adult, Kala was reassociating her experience into an integrated memory of her childhood trauma.

Some would say she was reclaiming repressed memories as a step toward her own recovery. Some would say the ego-state of KB was being retired by Kala, and KB was now surrendering the worst of the trauma to a grown-up Kala who was ready to know. However one describes the process, Kala became certain that she was not only neglected but was subject to her mother inserting objects into her vagina on the occasions of certain holidays.

Of course, Kala was devastated by her own revelation. Later, she described the moment of realization in the following manner. Imagine you are playing cards with some good friends you know and trust. Then one of them lays down the "eleven of hearts" card, to which you exclaim "What the hell is that?" You laugh and think it is a joke but as you look at the faces of the other players, you realize they are looking at you like YOU are the nutty one. The problem is not them, but you. It's like you have been playing cards but have been somehow blind to certain cards. Or, it's like you believed you were sure of the details of your life story and all of a sudden, someone points out a chapter that you never read.

Integrating this information into her personal history was nothing short of changing identity for Kala. She went into a deep depression and was on suicide watch for several days. After intensive individual, group, and art therapy, she seemed to come out of the worst of it. She started interacting with other clients and staff as she had before the self-revelation of sexual trauma. She was fully participating with all aspects of the program and expressing interest in getting home to be with her husband and children. She particularly wanted to attend a special church service on New Year's Eve with her family. After due consideration, the medical director approved her request for an overnight pass.

What the treatment team did not know is that we were being bamboozled. Kala was faking her apparent dramatic improvement the last few days and we were all taken in by the impressive performance. She had special plans, but they were not about going to a church service with her family. What we also did not know is that someone else knew of Kala's motives and that Kala would be served in the most powerful way that the treatment team could never serve her.

Kala arrived at home after being picked up by her family. She lovingly prepared a wonderful dinner and enjoyed her reunion back in her own home. She then assisted her daughter with her hair and dressed all her children in their best Sunday-come-to-meeting outfits. As time for departure to church approached, she explained to her husband that she did not feel well and wanted to go to bed early instead of attending the service. She explained she would wait for their return and look forward to spending the rest of the evening with them.

As soon as her husband got on the road with the kids, Kala sat on the kitchen floor with all the gas burners turned on high and no flame. She waited for the gas to overtake her and relieve her of the torment within. She thought of her beautiful children, how she loved touching them again, and how much better they would be without her. She was acutely aware of two competing forces within her, both with the intention of ending the pain within her. One force was to end the pain through death. The other was a basic instinct to live. But she didn't know how to live with an unbearable pain of being broken, feeling disposable, and unloved.

What Kala explained of her experience next was her way of making the unbearable bearable. She remembers sinking to the floor, feeling the coolness of the linoleum, and her surrounding table and cabinets getting hazy. Out of the confusion of her senses, she slowly became aware of another presence. KB sat next to her, holding her hand, and pleading that she did not want to die. Kala's old friend returned to make one last effort to protect her. Once again, she was together with the one who stood between her and any threat of harm. It was at that moment the balance shifted inside of Kala, and she crawled slowly to the door to kick it open. A neighbor noticed the door ajar, knew the family had left for church and came over to investigate. Kala was admitted to the hospital for two days and then readmitted to the Institute.

From that point on, Kala's recovery was real. She earnestly wanted to reclaim and reconcile her life. As fearful and hurtful as her childhood beginning was, she worked to accept the joy and meaning available to her, and even try to embrace it. The passing of her mother slowly became a metaphor representing Kala passing from a life where her trauma past controlled her, to being in the present and living her life fully, without the old fears and pain. It did not mean she would be free of memories of her childhood. But when she occasionally did have thoughts of her abuse, they would not be as intense, as frequent, and would not engulf her in shame. In short, her recovery did not mean her life was going to be perfect, just infused with a sense of worth and meaning that helped her feel she wanted to live the life she had, one well worth living.

She soon returned to her home in Texas and rejoined a family happy for her return. The last time I saw Kala, it was the end of her outpatient follow-up treatment. Smiling, she brought another drawing with her and handed it to me. It was a picture of her lying in front of her fireplace at home with a glow around her. I recognized the glowing aura from previous drawings, like the one she created showing KB on the kitchen floor with her. In that drawing, the aura enveloped both Kala and KB. In this last drawing, the aura was surrounding Kala as she slept in front of her hearth. She informed me the drawing was created to celebrate the first time she had slept all the way through the night since she was seven years old.

Approximately ten years after I last saw Kala, I received a lovely surprise by way of a package addressed to Sexual Health Clinic of the VA Medical Center. Within were pictures of Kala and her children—all smiling and holding each other close. Her daughter was a younger version of herself, beautiful and looking ready to conquer the world. Another photo was Kala in a clown outfit hugging her son at a Halloween party in his 3rd grade classroom. Their smiles looked identical and their hearts full. Kala looked healthy and bubbling with joy. It was obvious that she was doing much right as a mother and had constructed a rewarding life for herself and her family (a remarkable feat considering her beginnings).

A note was included which stated that she had been having some health issues lately, but she didn't let them get her down. "At least I no longer suffer from the horrendous emotional pain that I did for so many years, the pain that brought me to the weird place I met you. I used to keep journals full of in-depth writings about my pain and complaints...for the past few years I've been keeping journals in which I write about all the things I find joy in each day. Sometimes it's amazing to me that even on some of the most difficult days, there are always blessings."

CHAPTER NINETEEN

Making Sense of All You Have Learned

Written by Jill Bley

THE PLEASURE OF IT ALL

So now what do you do with all that you have learned? How do you take this information and use it to achieve a level of sexual health and satisfaction that will contribute to the happiness and contentment that all of us hope to have in our lives? Clearly, it is not easy to find happiness and contentment if you are not conscious of what you want and why you want it. An interesting article that was published in the August 2007 issue of the *Archives of Sexual Behavior* titled "Why Humans Have Sex" may help you understand another facet of your sexual health (or lack there of). This article reports the results of two studies. In the first study, Meston and Buss asked participants to respond to the following instruction: "*Please list all the reasons you can think of why you, or someone you have known, has engaged in sexual intercourse in the past.*"

The second study was an attempt to uncover which reasons were most popular or most important for the individuals. They listed the 237 reasons given in the first study and asked participants to rate each reason on a 5-point scale. The analysis of their data found four large factors and 13 subfactors:

Large factor	Subfactors
Physical	Stress reduction
	Pleasure
	Physical desirability
	Experience seeking
Goal attainment	Resources
	Social status
	Revenge
	Utilitarian
Emotional	Love

Insecurity

Commitment

Expression

Self-esteem boost

Duty/pressure

Mate guarding

Meston and Buss found that 20 of the most popular 25 reasons for having sex were the same for both men and women. However, the differences between men and women followed the stereotypes about each gender. Men tended to value physical appearance more and women more often longed for an emotional bond (women used the word "love" more often). Here are the top 10 reasons for men and women:

Men

1. I was attracted to the person.
2. It feels good.
3. I wanted to experience physical pleasure.
4. It's fun.
5. I wanted to show my affection to the person.
6. I was sexually aroused and wanted the release.
7. I was horny.
8. I wanted to express my love for the person.
9. I wanted to achieve an orgasm.
10. I wanted to please my partner.

Women

1. I was attracted to the person.
2. I wanted to experience physical pleasure.
3. It feels good.
4. I wanted to show my affection to the person.
5. I wanted to express my love for the person.
6. I was sexually aroused and wanted the release.
7. I was horny.
8. It's fun.
9. I realized I was in love.
10. I was in the "heat of the moment."

Sadly, some of the participants' reasons for having sex are rather dark. Some examples are the following: "I wanted to give someone a sexually transmitted disease," "I wanted to hurt my enemy," "Someone dared me," and "I was slumming." One of the authors of the study said that there were many people who reported that they were profoundly scarred by coercive sex and sex that they called "obligatory." Many reported sexual "regret."

The major drawback of the study is that all of the participants are college students. This study doesn't tell us why older, more mature adults have sex. I suspect that the results would be somewhat different because a much larger percentage of an older population would be in committed relationships. However, studying the reasons for being sexual among college students is useful because it sheds some light on what motivates young adults to mate and ultimately commit to someone in a relationship.

So that leads to the next area of inquiry: what causes humans to commit in a relationship? An anthropologist by the name of Helen Fisher was fascinated by that question. She wrote a book titled *Why We Love: The Nature and Chemistry of Romantic Love* (2004). Notice the title says "romantic love," because there are many different types of love. How we love our children is different from how we love our parents, which is different from how we love our siblings. Romantic love is quite different from all of those. Because it includes a very strong drive to have intimate sexual contact with the loved person.

Fisher worked with a team of scientists. They scanned the brains of people who said they were in love, using MRI technology. She found that specific areas of the brain "light up" with increased blood flow in people who reported that they were madly in love.

She compared the scans of people who were newly and madly obsessed with a strong desire to be with the "loved" object with the scans of drug addicts and found that the scans were identical: that is, a part of the brain that produces a powerful "feel-good" chemical, dopamine, was activated and "sprayed" the brain with the dopamine. So she decided that although the two people called what they felt "love," the feeling was more accurately called "lust." She found that the intense feelings associated with that kind of brain activity were usually sustained for about 10 months. After that, if the couple remained together, the brain activity changed. The scans of couples who remained together beyond 10 months looked similar to the scans of mothers bonding with a child and also showed activity in the part of the brain that was activated by those in the "lust" stage. This period she called "bonding," and can last for about seven years. The scans of couples who had bonded, who were still together after 25 years and reporting that they were content in the relationship and still loved one another very much showed similar activity in the part of the brain that was activated by people in the lust phase. That is the period that is probably more accurately called "love."

These data help to explain what many people have observed and reported about relationships. Some people say that they are no longer in "love" when the lust phase goes away. Those people may never achieve the kind of sexual health that leads to being able to maintain long-term meaningful relationships because when the lust is gone, they are gone. People who can stay connected after the lust is gone but fail to bond with their partner may have many long-term relationships during their lifetime, but not arrive at the stage of feeling contentment and peace that is experienced by couples who successfully bond and then deeply love their partner.

Esther Perel is a sexuality therapist whose book, *Mating in Captivity: Reconciling the Erotic and Domestic* (2006), addresses a problem that everyone who is a sex therapist has encountered many times in their work with clients: low sexual desire. We live so much longer now than previous generations. However, we, as a society, still believe that it is good and wise to maintain the same marriage with the same partner for as long as we live. That means that couples may be together for as long as 60 years. Therefore, keeping desire alive for many years means that couples must learn what turns them on repeatedly from one stage of life to another.

Perel spoke with many couples and asked them when they felt the most desire for each other. The most frequent answers were about seeing the partner be independent; watching the partner be themselves; watching the partner excel at something; and that they were most turned on by their partner when they were apart and then returned (absence does make the heart grow fonder and the dopamine flow). She believes that the need to feel secure conflicts with erotic desire because when one partner displays a lot of neediness, it tends to diminish the other partner's desire. We are the only animals on earth who have an erotic life. We can imagine and fantasize. She believes that using the ability to imagine, to fantasize, and to be playful is also key to maintaining desire in long-term relationships.

The main focus of this book has been on achieving sexual health. A person can certainly achieve a very high level of sexual health without bonding or loving one person. However, because our culture puts a lot of emphasis on coupling, many people do not feel that they have been able to achieve true satisfaction in their lives if they do not have a partner. Being able to maintain a long-term relationship that leads to that "love" stage requires another kind of health that has to do with the ability to maintain intimacy in one's relationship.

Intimacy, in this context, is defined as the ability to maintain intellectual, emotional/spiritual, and sexual closeness in a committed relationship. So there are four components:

1. *Intellectual intimacy* means that the couple can share information and experiences, resolve differences, and enjoy each other's company.
2. *Emotional/spiritual intimacy* means that the couple can share both positive and negative feelings, aspirations, dreams, desires, and innermost secrets.
3. *Sexual intimacy* is the ability to share freely and openly each other's sexuality in all of its dimensions.
4. *Commitment intimacy* means that each person in the relationship strives to make the relationship more important to them than their work, family of origin, friends, and so on.

THE SEXUAL COMMUNICATION EXERCISE

How does one work toward achieving a sexual health that includes these other components of intimacy? Here is where I am going to borrow from a forthcoming book that the first two authors of this book have written together, *The Pleasure Playbook*, to talk about how a couple can work on the sexual component of intimacy.

> [Authors' Note: Please keep in mind as you read the rest of this chapter that we are using male and female couples to illustrate the exercises and discussions. The only reason we are doing that is to make it easier to convey the information because it would become very complicated if we attempted to be explicit with each example as to how to apply the instructions to male/male; female/female; transmale/transmale; transfemale/transfemale; transmale/transfemale;

and so on. At times, we will use the singular form of "they" or "them" to refer to your partner in the exercises described. Therefore, we are going to leave it to you to translate the information to whatever your particular situation happens to be.]

The first two authors of this book have more than 60 years of combined experience as sex therapists. One of the most important things that we have learned is that communication is the number one problem that couples have, especially those who try to live together. Even couples who don't identify communication as a problem often learn during marital/sex therapy that they really aren't as free of obstacles to communication as they thought.

The first issue that usually alerts the therapist that communication is a problem is often presented as, "She never initiates sex. If I didn't ask for it, it would never happen." She responds by saying that she does initiate it sometimes but he doesn't "get it." She will ask for a back rub and "it relaxes me and then when he is done, we usually have sex." In her mind she is initiating sex, but he thinks she is initiating a back rub for herself and he knows that if he accommodates her, he will likely get sex.

So, what's wrong with this way of communicating? Everything! She isn't telling him that she could probably get interested in having sex if he would be willing to help her relax and feel connected to him by giving her a massage. He is likely to get tired of having to give her a massage because it has begun to feel like a lot of work to have sex with her without him having to ask for it, again! Eventually, this lack of good communication will probably cause anger and resentment.

In many cases the problem is that one or both partners is inhibited about asking for and/or showing that they are interested in having sexual pleasure. Some couples simply don't have the words or feel really uncomfortable saying sexual words so they use actions that the other person is supposed to understand as an invitation to have sex.

Here is an exercise that is designed to help couples develop a mutually agreed-upon sexual language. Find some private time of at least one hour with no interruptions from phones, children, pets, and anything else. Get a large piece of paper, such as the kind that children use on an art easel. Decide who will be the one to write everything on the paper.

At the heading of the paper write the anatomically correct name for all of the sexual parts of men and women and various sexual activities. So, across the top of the paper you write BREASTS, NIPPLES, VULVA, VAGINA, INNER AND OUTER LIPS, CLITORIS, LUBRICATION, FEMALE PROSTATE (G-SPOT), ANUS, TESTICLES, SCROTUM, PENIS, FELLATIO, CUNNILINGUS, INTERCOURSE, ANAL SEX, PENETRATION WITH FINGER, ERECTION, ORGASM, PROSTATE.

Then, start with the first word and take turns telling each other all of the words that you know that are used to indicate that part or activity and write the words down under the word you are working on. For example, under BREASTS you might have "knockers," "boobs," "hooters," "headlights," and so on. Under TESTICLES you might have "balls," "family jewels," and "rocks." Be sure to list words that may be "pet" names for body parts that the two of you have used during your relationship. Under INTERCOURSE you might have "get it on," "get laid," "screw," and so on. Continue through all of the words and activities.

When you are finished doing that part of the exercise, each of you takes turns crossing out all the words that you do not want your partner to use when referring to that body part or activity.

Then you circle the words that you prefer. All the words that are not crossed out or circled should be considered optional but not preferable.

If you find that there are no words that you can agree on between you that are comfortable to say and/or to hear, you really have a major sexual communication problem that won't get better if you don't work on it. The way to work on it is to try to explore the emotion that you feel when you try to say some of the words to your partner. Is it the words that are difficult to say, or is it using those words with an intimate partner that makes the word difficult to say?

If it is the words that are the problem, try to identify the origin of your discomfort. For most people who have difficulty speaking about sexual things, the problem started in their childhood. Try to go back in time and remember how your family of origin dealt with sexual topics, especially sexual information. Were you made to feel that sex was something that you just don't talk about? Was your family inappropriately open about sexuality? Did you have some negative experience around sexuality? Exploring the origins of sexual inhibitions often can be very helpful toward overcoming those inhibitions.

When you have finished this exercise make a plan that each of you will take a turn one day in the next week to initiate sex. The rule should be that the initiator has to use words that the two of you have agreed to use to ask for sex and that all through the sexual experience you will use your sexual language to tell your partner what you want them to do. Make an agreement that you will share the initiation of sex for at least six months. Meaning that after one partner initiates sex, there will be no sexual encounters until the other partner initiates it.

Also, make a rule that whenever the two of you have a discussion about anything that has to do with body parts and/or sexual activity, you will use the agreed-upon language. The more often you make yourselves talk about sexual things, the easier your verbal communication about it will flow.

To make sure the ways you communicate about sex are fun (and stay that way), try this exercise in nonverbal communication. Talk about who will go first and plan a date on which each of you will take your turn. When the time for your turn to do this exercise approaches, begin to plan how and what you will do. The goal of the exercise is to nonverbally, but *clearly*, convey your intention to be sexual with your partner. There are a number of ways that you could choose to convey the message.

An example would be to check with your partner to make sure that you both know when you will be home that day. Then the partner whose turn it is to nonverbally communicate arrives early and takes pieces of clothing off one at a time, forming a "trail" to the room where you will be waiting, nude and in a seductive position. When your partner arrives you slowly undress them while touching them teasingly. Everything that you intend to do or that you want your partner to do needs to be nonverbally and *very clearly* conveyed.

> **[Authors' Note: Make sure that you do not attempt to initiate anything that you know your partner would object to doing or have done to them.]**

For instance, if you want to perform oral sex on your partner, you could gently kiss and lick around the breasts and/or nipples, then slowly move to the lower abdomen; using your hand, touch between the thighs as you move your mouth and lips slowly toward the genitals. If your partner is unclear about your intentions or does not want you to do what you are indicating, then they should change position in a way that will keep the intimate moment flowing but gently change the direction.

Another nonverbal way to communicate that you are interested in sex could be to prepare a special setting such as a candle-lit dinner with music. When it is time for dessert, begin to strip seductively as you move to whatever place in the house you have decided to have your sexual encounter. Have that place prepared with candlelight and whatever sex toys or creams or lotions you would like to use.

Whatever nonverbal communication you decide to use to indicate that you are interested in having sex, make sure that you won't be misunderstood. Be obvious and provocative. If you find that you are feeling embarrassed and/or inhibited about being so provocative, see if you can learn the origin of those negative feelings. Often the origin is in childhood or adolescence. Some women and men are inhibited about being provocative because they have a very negative body image. (Ways to feel better about body image issues will be addressed later in this chapter.)

Doing these verbal and nonverbal exercises can not only improve and enhance your sexual relationship, they will help you overcome any shyness or embarrassment that has inhibited your ability to express your sexuality. Generally, women need to learn how to overcome their inhibitions about explicitly asking for sex verbally and nonverbally and become more genitally focused. Men often need to learn how to make sexual encounters more romantic and less genitally focused.

Realtors say that the most important aspect when selling a house is location, location, location. Sex therapists say that the most important aspect of a good sexual relationship is communication, communication, communication. Angelia and Shelly demonstrate this point well ...

A LIFELONG LOVE STORY—ANGELIA AND SHELLY

I didn't know if a Chinese birth certificate could get me into a bar, but I had to try. It was early 1980s and she was 21, in college, head lifeguard at the neighborhood pool where my mom worked the concession stand. She had the tightest abs I'd ever seen. She also had a girlfriend. A pretty one. What was I thinking? How could she ever feel about me the way that I felt about her? When she said she was heading to 1470 West that night, I had to meet her there. I was determined to be seen.

It was the first time I was ever in a bar ... let alone a gay bar! So many dancing, drinking people exchanging glances, making out in the dark places, colored lights bouncing off sweaty touching bodies. The rhythmic pounding of the music: Soft Cell, Culture Club, Whitney Houston, Dead or Alive ... bands with anthems declaring alternative ways to love. Those lyrics spoke to me in a way I had not heard anyone talk out loud in my sheltered Catholic community. That bar was a living, breathing, sensuous creature and I was home.

When I approached her, even though I had nothing but water to drink, I felt drunk. I was loopy, swoony, blurry intoxicated with the dire need to profess my feelings that I had been hiding for two summers. So, I did.

"I think I'm in love you ..." was met with "Awwww, sweetie," a barely perceptible wink and half-grin.

"No, really, you're amazing and I want to be your girlfriend."

"Well I'll tell you what, you tie this cherry stem in a knot with just your tongue, and we'll talk."

"Seriously? No hands, just my mouth? Ok, if I do this, you have to kiss me. Deal?"

She responded with a chuckle—this sound I learned to recognize as confident unease, a combination of "I got this, whatever it is that's about to happen"—and simply replied, "Deal."

"Time me." She twisted her wrist to look at her Swatch, but her eyes never left mine.

Six seconds, that's all it took. She laughed from that nervous place deep inside, through sly smiling lips and wide-open denim blue eyes. My 16-year-old self registered notes of shock, admiration, and skin hunger. I did the task. I tied that cherry stem with just my tongue. When I stuck it out a little bit to offer proof, she moved toward my mouth subtly, gently, and pulled the knot taut with her lips barely touching mine. I was on fire. I had never felt anything like this. Wild. Focused. Desire. And this inappropriate happiness felt so very right.

Then four seconds after that, with the tied stem fully consumed in her mouth: my first kiss that mattered. It was full of inquiry, passion, probing, wonder, and lasted forever on my lips. Time froze. Music kept playing and people were moving around us, but I was on full stop. The stem was in my mouth . . . untied. Our eyes locked in a gaze that I knew would never be repeated with another person. Ever.

And then she was gone. Walked away to the other side of the bar toward her girlfriend.

That was 35 years ago. We've literally had a lifetime to find, mold, deconstruct, and finesse our love. Commitment is not an easy word to define. We've discovered that it's a fluid concept and interpreted different ways at different moments. In truth, we redefined commitment every time we saw each other over the years.

We landed in the same spot about year 20 of our lifelong love story. Jesus, that was 15 years ago! She still has her tiny house about 15 minutes across town. It's good to have another space. It's proven a beneficial investment for her and for us. We currently share my modest 111-year-old home with a woodsy backyard in a typical urban neighborhood where folks look out for each other. Our neighbors like us for the most part. Our four dogs have great lives complete with squirrels who flirt with an early demise, and foliage in which to roll and sunbathe. Our backyard has witnessed tremendous parties with the most authentic people, lots of belly laughs, bawdy stories, creatively contrived plots to end tyranny, grilled deliciousness, and booze.

She's a blue-collar worker who never sits still, loves crossword puzzles, and doesn't take any shit from anybody. I'm an academic with a bent for social justice and teaching difficult topics, a need to read sci-fi fantasy novels, and lead singer in a classic rock band with an uncanny ability to quote applicable lyrics in the worst moments to do such. We've had other lovers, other girlfriends over the years, but have always returned to each other.

Our families love us both. A lot. We're fortunate to understand the power of unconditional love as demonstrated by her parents, my brother, and our different but similar ethnic heritages. Family gatherings are raucous, full of boasts and storytelling, and lots of hugging. Although I wasn't a consistent part of her large Appalachian fam-clan, I've known her siblings since I was an undergrad. And now the 10 nieces and nephews know me. She holds me when I grieve the loss of my Mom. It is a gift to be known by her through the measures of time and life events. And to be known from inside out where our hearts beat our respective truths and our actions speak a language that only we can translate. And sometimes we "translate loudly."

The fights are as passionate as our love of well-prepared food, colorful tattoos, paying off debt, and the yarns we spin about what we'll do when we retire. At a collective age of 105, we can chat all things "free time" we want, but in reality, she'll retire long before I can.

I worry about her body. Working labor in her 5'3" frame for 30 years has wreaked havoc on her joints. Alcohol is a coping mechanism for so long, then you actually have to seek medical supports. We've been going to a few more doctor's appointments lately. I'm happy to go with her because then I know what's going on. I'm quite the mouthy advocate. She, too, has my back. She's held my hand through two radical surgeries (where, during recovery, I was less than a nice person), a horrific car accident that I caused, and my Mom's ugly, too-early death from lung cancer.

Time is weird. I look at her long grey hair that still has streaks of blonde, her tired denim blue eyes still wide open, and her rounded belly and see her at 21 years old when we kissed the first time in that old, nasty bar. She tells me I'm beautiful every morning upon waking when we wake together. When we're not together, she texts me the message. I've grown to believe that I am beautiful because she is just so damn convincing.

Honestly, I don't know what she sees in me, but I trust that she sees it nonetheless. What we have built is solid. It's not unshakeable, but its fortitude is forged in dedication to our truths, an uncanny need to be who we are respectively, and the simple beauty of choosing to breathe together.

She is my home.

SHARING SEXUAL FANTASIES

Angelia and Shelly have shared many sexual fantasies together. Angelia's fantasy of Shelly was the spark to a lifelong love affair. Fantasies are part of the glue, sustenance, and stick-to-itiveness between them. The following section is full of suggestions and guidelines of incorporating fantasy sharing into an erotic relationship. It uses language that reflects a heterosexual couple, but the guidelines are applicable to all varieties of couples who have good communication, are not overly subject to jealousy, and are open to expanding their relationship through the sexual play of fantasy sharing.

After you feel that you and your partner have learned and practiced good communication skills, you can continue to enhance your sexual relationship by sharing your sexual fantasies. There are a lot of reasons why you may not want to share your fantasies. You may feel that sexual fantasies should only be about your partner. You may be afraid that your partner will get jealous and/or angry about any fantasy that isn't about them. You may be afraid that your partner will be judgmental about the fantasies and see them as "weird" or "perverted." You may fear that if you tell what you fantasize about, your partner may expect you to actually play out the fantasy with them. You may find that communication between you and your partner lacks any avenue for sharing the fantasies.

Therefore, it would be a good idea to question yourself about what fears you might have about sharing your fantasies. If you believe that sexual fantasies should only be about your partner, take a minute to consider an important aspect of being able to fantasize. Fantasy enables humans to continue to be interested and motivated to behave as sexual beings. Anticipation of being able to feel the wonderful feelings we experience when we are aroused is the primary reason that a person is motivated to be sexual. If at least one person in a couple isn't thinking about and building up a need to be sexual, the sexual relationship will probably end or be very infrequent.

Earlier in this chapter I referred to research that was conducted by Helen Fisher, who wrote the book *Why We Love: The Nature and Chemistry of Romantic Love*. She used MRI scanning to help her understand what happens in the human brain when people say they are "in love." She learned that people who are in the early stages of a relationship in which they feel as if they are "in love" have MRI brain scans that look like the brain scans of addicts. Therefore, she hypothesized that when a person is in the early stages of a relationship, they are "addicted" to that person. They want to be with them all the time; they feel a longing sensation when they are not with them; and they describe the person in very positive words. She called that period of time the "lust" period and found that the "lust" period only lasts about 10 months, unless the "lust" is for a person that one can either not see very often or who is a partner in an ongoing illicit affair.

She found that after the lust period, humans will either end the relationship or they will enter a new phase of the relationship that is a bonding time. Fisher believes that only after lusting and bonding are successful can a couple be truly "in love."

If we stop to think about what all that means for long-term relationships, we would figure out that keeping the lusty feelings that once were there alive and well requires that we remember (fantasize) about how it was in the earlier days of the relationship. Or we make sure that we devise experiences with our partner to rekindle those feelings, and/or we invent new and exciting fantasies about our partner or about others.

Given that many relationships last 20, 30, 40, 50, or even 60 years, it only makes sense that sexual fantasies should be nurtured and accepted as normal for both partners. One caution, however: never share a sexual fantasy that would be hurtful to your partner, even under the guise of being "honest." Like the warnings before viewing some movies, "Discretion is advised." For example, it isn't wise to share fantasies about the following:

- your partner's sibling;
- your partner's parent;
- an old lover;
- your partner's (teenage or adult) child;
- your partner's best friend; and
- sexual behaviors that you know your partner will never agree to do with you because it will probably be perceived as an attempt to put pressure on them to do it.

Use good judgment when sharing fantasies so that the sharing does not cause the intimate connection to be weakened instead of enhanced.

If jealousy is an issue in your relationship, you need to try to find out why. Has there been actual behavior that has caused jealousy? If so, the cause of the jealousy needs to be addressed before sharing fantasies can be expected to go well. Has this been an issue for the jealous partner in all relationships? If that is the case, the partner with the jealousy problem should try to find out why they are so insecure. Always being jealous in relationships is related to low self-esteem that contributes to insecurity.

If you are worried that your partner will be judgmental about your fantasies, ask yourself if you are predicting this outcome because you plan to actually tell them a fantasy that would evoke jealousy from the majority of people. If that is the case, just don't do it! If you are worried about being judged but you know that the fantasies that you would share are fantasies that the majority of people would find arousing and not offensive, then ask yourself if your fears are justified. Do you have previous experiences with your partner where you have, in fact, been judged? If that is so, you need to try to resolve that issue with your partner before you do these exercises. If you fear that your partner will expect you to actually play out any fantasy that you share, you need to clarify beforehand that you find the fantasy arousing only in the fantasy state, not in reality. If lack of an avenue for communication about sexuality is the problem, go back to the earlier part of this chapter about sexual communication and do the recommended exercises.

Fantasy-Sharing Exercise

When you decide to do this exercise, make the environment safe. Make sure that you will not be interrupted. Also make sure you have enough time to do the exercise and (if you both agree) time to be sexual when you finish sharing your fantasies.

Begin by just telling each other some of your favorite fantasies. Tell each other why you like the fantasy and when you use the fantasy. Then *construct some fantasies together*. Because women generally need to learn to develop sexual fantasies and men generally need to learn to develop romantic fantasies, start with the male partner describing a romantic scene. Then the female partner adds a little sexuality to the romance. Then he continues with a romantic aspect and she adds a sexual part. When you are happy with your fantasy, do another.

Next let him tell a story with a long prelude of romance. She ends the story with explicitly sexual behaviors that are prolonged and detailed. See how many fantasies you can construct together. Rate the fantasies by how much of a turn-on each one is for you.

If any problems come up while you are doing this exercise, talk about what the problem is, what caused it and what you can do to solve it. For example, if one partner gets so embarrassed that they can't continue, try to explore why telling someone with whom you are very intimate about a fantasy is embarrassing to you. Or why hearing or saying certain sexual words is embarrassing to you.

The next step you might choose to do together is to pick one of the romantic/sexual fantasies and *act it out together*. You may have to tweak it a little to apply it to real life. See if you can have fun with it (that is the main idea). You can also decide that each of you will invite the other to act out one of the fantasies that you both liked. However, don't tell your partner which one! Just invite them to go along with you on a "fantasy date" and have fun with it.

Here is an example of a fantasy where the male provides the romantic parts and the female provides the explicit sexual parts. **(If you are not a male/female couple but you need to learn how to share fantasies too, you will need to decide who needs to learn to be more romantic and who needs to learn to be more sexual.)**

Male's part (romantic): He is a man going to his new job. He is introduced on the first day to one of the women with whom he shares office space. He is immediately attracted to her, but he knows that it is not a good idea to mix work with intimate relationships. He tries to ignore his attraction to her, but he finds it difficult to focus on his work whenever she is around. One day he goes to lunch with a few of his coworkers and she is with the group. He manages to sit next to her and to talk with her. He joins this group every day, just so he can be near her in a non-work situation. He can tell from how she looks at him that she probably feels the same.

Whenever he is near her he smiles, tries to engage her in conversation, and pays her a compliment. On the evenings after work when everyone goes out for a drink, he sits by her and listens to what she says. He lets her know that he is listening by commenting on what she says. One Friday evening, after work, she discovers that she left her wallet at the office and can't pay for her drinks. He pays her check and offers to take her home. She accepts. On the way home, he tells her that she is someone that he admires because she seems to care a lot about the same important issues that he does and seems to have a lot of empathy for other people's struggles.

Female's part (sexual): She puts her hand on his thigh while he drives and talks to her. When they arrive at her apartment, she invites him in. She offers him a drink and then sits on the couch beside him. She tells him that she thinks that he is a very caring man and that caring men turn her on. She takes his hand and puts it inside her bra on her breast. She kisses him deeply and rubs her hand on the inside of his thigh.

She asks him to follow her into her bedroom. She slowly takes off her dress. She sits on her bed and offers him one foot so that he can remove her shoe; then the other. She stands and takes his hands to her hips and grasps her pantyhose with his hands. She lets him pull them off. She takes his hand and rubs it on her buttocks then lifts his hands with hers to take off her bra.

She stands looking at him, inviting him to come to her. First, she takes off his jacket, then his tie and shirt. She puts his hand on her breast while she loosens his belt. As she unzips his fly, she starts to slide down to caress his penis in her mouth while holding his hand on her breast.

Male's part (romantic): He gently lifts her up to his mouth and kisses her softly on her lips and then on her face and neck. He takes her hand and touches his face with it. He kisses her hand and sucks on each finger. He tells her that he wants to pleasure her. He gently touches her face, her neck, and her shoulders as he kisses those spots with his lips and his tongue. He tells her that he wants to go slowly and savor every minute of the night with her.

He begins to talk with her and asks her about herself. He wants to know everything about her. He shares who he is. He tries to get to understand who she is, what she aspires to, her deepest desires and passions. He shares with her those things about himself.

Female's part (sexual): She becomes more and more aroused as he talks to her and shares with her and wants to know about her. She feels herself getting so hot that she can't wait any longer. She puts her finger to his lips and says, "No more talk. I want you to fuck me. I want your hand on my breast. I want your finger in my pussy. I want you to put your penis inside of me."

She takes his hand and guides it toward her vagina. She is so wet and so ready to be touched that she comes as soon as his finger penetrates and thrusts only four times. Then she puts her breast in his mouth while she manipulates his penis. Slowly she glides down his chest, sucks gently on his nipples, continues to his stomach, and then puts her lips on the tip of his penis. At the same time, she cups his balls in her hand and gently manipulates them. Then she allows his entire, hard penis to penetrate her mouth. She sucks on his penis and flicks her tongue around the tip and ridge of the head that comes together with the seam that travels up the length of the shaft.

Male's part (romantic): He massages her back and runs his fingers though her hair as she is manipulating his body. He tells her that he has never been with any woman who knows what she wants and goes for it. He loves the way she knows how to please him and isn't shy about doing it. He tells her how sensual her body, mind, and spirit are to him.

Female's part (sexual): She continues to suck his penis until he comes. His penis remains hard and she gets on top of him to put him inside of her. She thrusts and grinds and then moans with satisfaction as she orgasms once, then again.

Male's part (romantic): He puts her next to him and holds her close. He touches her face and tells her how beautiful she is, how much he loved watching her enjoy his penis. He asks if he can spend the night so that they can make love in the morning.

As an exercise, you and your partner can describe what happens in the morning. *Remember: The male's role is romantic and the female's role is sexual.* Because it is now Saturday in the fantasy, you can prolong the exercise by describing what they do for the rest of the weekend. Have fun with as many different variations and endings to this fantasy as you can. Enjoy!

SENSATE FOCUS EXERCISES

Now that you feel comfortable sharing your fantasies with your partner, the exercises described below will help you to feel comfortable freely sharing your body with your partner and freely exploring your partner's body. These exercises have been used by sexuality therapists since they were developed and published by Masters and Johnson in their landmark book *Human Sexual Response* (1966). They were originally designed to help couples overcome sexual dysfunctions related to erection, lubrication and orgasm problems. Therapists have learned over the years that these exercises can also help couples learn to feel more comfort in giving and receiving pleasure.

They are named "sensate focus" because the exercises help the couple learn to focus on the pleasurable sensations one experiences when touched in a sensual manner. They help to greatly reduce and eventually eliminate anxiety that has built up over time as couples struggled to fix their sexual problems or discomforts.

These exercises are here for four purposes. First, to help people who are having certain problems regain their previous level of functioning; second, to give couples who cannot have sexual intercourse (permanently or temporarily) ideas about how they can continue to have a loving sexual relationship without intercourse (through loving touch referred to as "outercourse"); third, to encourage couples to take a break from focusing on intercourse and orgasm as the most important aspect of their sexual relationship and learn how to enjoy one another in a less-genitally focused way; and fourth, to reconnect as a couple by building an emotionally significant and meaningful connection.

The fourth point deserves some special emphasis because when a couple builds an emotionally significant and meaningful connection, they are building the intimacy bond that is crucial for promoting and sustaining the kind of long-term commitment that most couples hope for. True intimacy requires that two people develop closeness by bonding intellectually, emotionally, spiritually and sexually in a committed relationship. These exercises provide an excellent tool for bonding emotionally, spiritually and sexually. When a couple has emotional, spiritual and sexual bonding, the intellectual part and the commitment part are so much more likely to grow and thrive.

Sexual dysfunctions (such as the inability to have orgasm, ejaculating too fast, no lubrication, and erection problems) are most likely to respond well to these exercises. However, the couple must follow the step-by-step instructions from Sensate Focus I through Sensate Focus III. Here are the ground rules that couples should follow if they decide to do the exercises. These ground rules apply to each phase of the exercises. Remember, you need to follow the instructions carefully, step by step, and not be tempted to jump ahead to the next level too soon, if you want to get the full benefit of the experience.

The first and most important rule for using these exercises is that both partners agree that they will not try to have intercourse until they progress through the steps to Sensate Focus III, nor have an orgasm or pressure their partner for orgasm. In other words, there must be an agreement to put a ban on intercourse and orgasm during the time that you are going through the steps together. If either partner finds it really difficult not to have an orgasm for the period of time that they are doing these exercises, that partner should masturbate alone, making sure that they do not put any pressure on their partner to provide the orgasm for them.

You should decide ahead of time who will initiate the request to do the exercise. The best way to arrange this is to agree that whoever asks first will not initiate again until the other initiates. That way, each of you will have the responsibility to ask for sexual pleasuring about 50% of the time. Most couples are used to leaving that responsibility to one or the other partner most of the time. If you share the initiating, you will both have an opportunity to learn how to ask for sex and how to say "yes" or "no." If your response is "no," then the rule should be that the one who says "no" must offer an alternative time and then be ready to do the exercise at the designated time without being reminded.

Before you get started, it is helpful for couples to talk about what kind of sexual language they have. If you have none (i.e., you don't say anything when you want sex), just start to kiss or touch or give some other non-verbal indication; you may find it very helpful to figure out together whether that is okay with both of you or if you would like to be able to ask for a sexual encounter. You could also discuss how to say "no" without the other's feelings being hurt.

The person whose turn it is to initiate the pleasuring exercise is responsible to make sure the room temperature is comfortable enough to be nude without clothes or blankets. That person should also set the "mood," paying attention to the lighting and perhaps soft music. Have lotions, oils or creams available that are at room temperature. Find some fabrics in your home that might feel good if used to touch your partner, (e.g., a piece of fur, a silk scarf, a piece of soft felt). The initiator is also responsible to make sure that both partners have paid adequate attention to hygiene before the encounter. You may both like to start the pleasuring time by showering together. Make sure your breath is pleasing to your partner so that you both feel free to kiss and/or use your mouth to provide touching.

A question that most couples have when they are beginning these pleasuring experiences is, "How much time should we do this?". The answer is not always an easy one. If either partner finds touch to be unpleasant, the couple must take things slowly and allow "de-sensitization" to touch to happen. Avoiding touch never solves the issues related to fear of touch. However, forcing prolonged discomfort won't help either. So it needs to proceed at a pace that allows the person to become comfortable with touch gradually. If there are no issues around touch, the general answer is to make sure that you touch your partner long enough that you have been able to touch the entire body and have given yourself the chance to touch until you feel "lost" in the joy of touching. You are now ready to begin Sensate Focus I.

SENSATE FOCUS I: NON-GENITAL PLEASURING

The Initiator begins to touch the partner all over the body, excluding genitals, breasts, and buttocks. The touch should be like a loving massage, making sure that the pressure is comfortable (not too soft or too hard). The Initiator should be focused on touching the partner for the Initiator's own pleasure, allowing themself to be "lost" in the experience of giving pleasure and touching. The Receiver just relaxes and focuses on the pleasure of receiving loving, sensual touch and allows themself to be "lost" in the sensations of the body. No one talks during the pleasuring except to indicate pleasure or ask the Receiver to turn over or to check out whether or not the touch is comfortable.

The Receiver should enjoy pleasurable touch to both the front and back of the body. The Receiver may talk to indicate if something is uncomfortable and may show the Initiator how to touch in a particular area in order to make the touch more comfortable.

When the Initiator feels that they are ready to stop touching, then the two change places. The Receiver becomes the one who touches and the Initiator receives the pleasuring touch. Remember both should focus on "getting lost" in the sensations of touching and being touched. Repeat these exercises and enjoy Sensate Focus I on several occasions (four to six times is a suggested minimum) before progressing to the next level of exercises.

SENSATE FOCUS II: NON-GENITAL & GENITAL PLEASURING

You are ready to move on to this step only if both partners are enjoying the sensations of "getting lost" in the feelings of pleasure produced by the loving touch they were experiencing while doing Sensate Focus I. The rules and suggestions for Sensate Focus II are the same. Except that this time the genitals and breasts and buttocks are included in the pleasuring touch. However, there should be no more emphasis on the breasts, genitals and buttocks than on the other parts of the body. In other words, the difference between these two exercises is to merely include the breasts and genitals and buttocks in an overall body sensual massage, with the person whose turn it is to initiate the exercise going first and being responsible to set the mood.

If you are doing these exercises to correct a sexual problem, there continues to be a ban on intercourse and orgasms. Do not sabotage your progress by putting pressure on your partner to violate this ban. If you feel you simply must have an orgasm, do it privately by bringing yourself to climax. This privacy keeps your partner from feeling pressure or guilt for not "giving" you the orgasm.

If you are hoping to correct an orgasm problem, this exercise is great for learning to control the timing of orgasm. If the problem is coming too fast, you can learn how to slow down. If the problem is taking too long (or not at all), you can enjoy the teasing and building of sexual tension.

If you are hoping to correct an erection or lubrication problem, pressure to "use" it right away if an erection or lubrication occurs will usually result in success for the moment but will probably not produce the long-term solution you are hoping for. Ridding oneself of "performance anxiety" and/or inhibitions to receiving pleasure will not be overcome if you try to have intercourse as soon as you have an erection or begin to lubricate.

If you are using these exercises as a way to maintain sexual closeness during a period of time when you cannot have intercourse, or to enhance your sexual relationship, there is no ban on orgasm. However, you may want to have an agreement that you will occasionally decide together to have a ban so that you can keep the emphasis and focus on the touch and loving sensations instead of orgasm. If you are using these sensual play exercises to fix a sexual problem, it is really important to return to these exercises at times in order to ensure that "performance anxiety" never intrudes on your sexuality again. If you are using the exercises to enhance your sexual relationship, we suspect you will want to plan to go back to them just to experience the wonderful, loving, sensual feelings you get from them.

SENSATE FOCUS III: INTERCOURSE PLEASURING

You are ready to move on to these exercises only when a.) both partners are enjoying the feelings of "getting lost" in the sensations of being lovingly touched and caressed all over the body, (now including the breasts, genitals, and buttocks) and b.) the partner with the identified sexual problem is feeling comfortable and secure about lubrication or erection, (i.e., they can depend on it and do not feel inhibited or worried about their performance).

The rules about how to initiate are the same. Begin this exercise by doing Sensate Focus II. Do not take turns touching each other now. Sort of "choreograph" a mutual "dance" of loving touch. Then when both partners feel ready, begin to pleasure one another with intercourse, starting out in one position and then gracefully and rhythmically changing to another position. After a while, change positions again. NOTE: vaginal lubrication is not necessarily a sign that a woman is ready for vaginal containment. Therefore, it is important for the female partner to indicate when she is ready. Some ideas for various positions for intercourse will be discussed later in this chapter.

If premature orgasm is the problem, be sure that you do not start this exercise until you are confident in your ability to prolong your pleasure by withholding the ejaculation for an agreed upon time. Achieving this skill is done by using the "Stop-Start" technique for stimulating the penis during masturbation and then using "Stop-Start" during Sensate Focus II pleasuring. The instructions for doing "Stop-Start" can be found in many books that focus on male sexuality. An "oldie but goodie" is *The New Male Sexuality,* by Bernie Zelbergeld (1992).

If inhibited orgasm is the problem, Sensate Focus III, with no pressure at all to produce an orgasm, may help an orgasm to happen. If it does not and you cannot have an orgasm even with masturbation, then you need to give yourself an orgasm with masturbation first and then teach your partner how to touch your genitals to replicate your own touch and then "Bridge" these sensations to intercourse. "Bridging" the orgasm from self-stimulation to partner stimulation requires informing the partner when one is approaching orgasm and then directly involving the partner right before orgasm starts. You only move from one step to the next when you have been able to have orgasm during each step.

INTERCOURSE POSITIONS

Many couples who begin Sensate Focus III (Intercourse Pleasuring) realize that they have a very limited repertoire of positions for intercourse. Most are very familiar with the "male superior" position where the male is facing the female (better known as the "missionary" position). Even though this is the most popular position, it often is not the best position for the female partner to receive as much stimulation of the clitoris and/or G-spot as she may need.

Another "male superior" position is for him to enter her vagina from the rear. She is in a "doggy" pose on her forearms (so that her rear end is elevated higher than the front end) and knees on the bed or floor. This is a great position for her to receive stimulation to the G-spot, so while you are pleasuring with intercourse you will have an opportunity to see if you can experience pleasure from the G-spot. This position also allows for the opportunity for him to stroke and caress her buttocks and/or anus.

There are many "female superior" positions. They are similar to the above except, of course, she is on top. In the superior position the female can guide the penis into her vagina. She can decide how fast or how slow she wants to let the penis enter. She can also decide how fast or slow the in and out movements will be. Being on top also provides an opportunity for her to ask her partner to stroke and caress her clitoris and/or her breast.

She can turn and be in the superior position with her back to him and her legs and feet toward his head. In this position she provides the opportunity to have her partner stroke and caress her buttocks and/or her anus.

The side-by-side position is a face to face position with neither partner "superior". Couples may have to practice a bit and play with positioning in order to make this a comfortable and pleasurable position for both of them. Most couples find that if she opens her legs so that he can put one leg between hers, he can enter her vagina more easily. So, it is really a side-by-side entwined position.

There are many variations on the "male superior" and the "female superior" which can be accomplished by sitting, squatting, standing or kneeling. When experimenting with any position, good support and balance is required. Be sure to check how sturdy the furniture is, if the chandelier will hold your weight, and if you are able to support one another's weight. It can be rather painful to fall with an erect penis inside the vagina.

Remember, the point of Sensate Focus III is to be playful, enjoy and experiment with intercourse together with no pressure for orgasm. Of course, the standard illustrated reference guides are recommended to make the many positions of love-making clear in your mind. The ancient classic of the *Kama Sutra* (the book, not the movie) is the ultimate sex guide from antiquity. More recently, *The Joy of Sex: A Gourmet Guide to Lovemaking* is the American classic illustrated guide to sex (Comfort, 1987). Of course, let's not forget the highly recommended and favorite reference guides of the first author, *Sex for Dummies* (Westheimer, 2007) and *The Complete Idiot's Guide to Amazing Sex* (Locker, 2005).

SEXUAL SELF-IMAGE EXERCISES

As mentioned earlier, one reason that many women (and some men) do not want to have sex is because of very negative feelings and beliefs about their bodies. Because much of our economy is based on consumerism, we are routinely inundated with advertised messages that reinforce the belief, "I am not good enough." Of course, the rest of the message is that by buying the right clothes, right weight-loss pills, or the right cosmetic surgery (the list is virtually endless), we can be happy and more attractive to others. Within this type of environment, it is not surprising that so many people have a negative self-image, including poor sexual self-image.

The purpose of the sexual self-image exercise is to feel better and more confident about your physical body. No matter what shape or level of fitness a person is in, everybody can make themselves feel better or worse emotionally based on what we tell ourselves about our physicality. Many people have a history of criticizing their body in regard to media-based images and standards of beauty. This practice is not only unnecessary but damaging to a person's sense of well-being.

The following exercises are effective strategies you can employ to counter the effects of self-criticism and highlight the positive aspects of your body that is something to appreciate, including the beauty, strength, functionality, softness, and sensitivity of parts of your body often ignored. They are also an opportunity to appreciate the positive aspects of the parts of your body that you may have always cringed about and wished were different. In other words, it's all about how you see yourself and the *messages you tell yourself*.

There is only one way to do these exercises wrong—that is to continue to criticize yourself. NO CRITICISM ALLOWED for the few minutes you are engaged in any of these activities. Even if it is something you always wished was different about you, find something nice to say! Your mission is to identify at least one positive attribute of every part of your body. Not only are you to identify the positive attribute, but you are asked to write down your descriptions for a full list of your body parts, head to toe. If you absolutely no-way-no-how can generate a positive quality or attribute to the body part, leave it blank and go on to the next part. NO CRITICISM.

The list of positive attributes is simply a baseline for your self-image at the time you do it. Your list can then be used to measure your growth over time in self-appreciation and being kind to yourself. If you need to view yourself fully clothed or in your undies, then that's where you are and that's where you start. Be accepting of yourself for where you are. That does not mean that you can't want to lose weight or shape up. Just do it with kindness and appreciation of yourself!

Instructions:

1. Self-Affirmation Sexual Self-Image Exercises.
   a. Use a room that is warm, well lit, and provides privacy.
   b. Commit to no use of criticism for the duration of this exercise.
   c. If you can, get naked in front of a large mirror that shows all or most of your body (when starting out, various degrees of undress are acceptable as well).
   d. Have a pen and paper next to you for recording your responses.
   e. Go from the tip of your crown to the tip of your toes finding positive attributes about every part of your body that is visible to you.

f. Commenting on internal features of our anatomy (like your heart) is acceptable, but the emphasis is on your external features.

g. Record in detail your body features on a list and record to the right the positive attributes. To what level of detail, you wonder? Let's use your head as an example:

    i.   Hair color
    ii.   Hair texture
    iii.   Hair style
    iv.   Hair line
    v.   Hair on the face
    vi.   Eye color
    vii.   Eye shape
    viii.   Eyelashes
    ix.   Eyebrows
    x.   Eye's ability to see
    xi.   Nose size
    xii.   Nose shape
    xiii.   Nose's ability to smell
    xiv.   Ear shape
    xv.   Ear size
    xvi.   Ear color
    xvii.   Ear's ability to hear
    xviii.   Teeth shape
    xix.   Teeth smile
    xx.   Teeth's ability to eat
    xxi.   Lips' color
    xxii.   Lips' shape
    xxiii.   Lips' smile
    xxiv.   Skin complexion
    xxv.   Cheekbones
    xxvi.   Dimples?
    xxvii.   Chin

h. Go down the rest of your body with the same level of detail while recording what you can appreciate and using positive attributes only. If you have the fortitude, *share your list* with someone you can trust to affirm you for the positivity of your self-image. This could be a trusted spouse, lover, or therapist. Security tip—make sure you have your list password protected or in a place no one else will discover. Repeating this exercise at a later date, such as several months or several years, gives you the opportunity to compare your new list of attributes with your first list and measure the growth of your positivity regarding self-acceptance, sexual self-image, and your ability to find self-validation (all very important skills for health and well-being).

Self-Sharing Sexual Self-Image Exercises

Ready to bump up the affirmation? If you have a trusted lover or spouse, repeat this exercise as a couple, and again—*only positive comments are allowed!* Create two lists—you finding the positive aspects of their body and your partner doing the same with you.

Get naked in front of that person and have them go from the tip of your crown to the tip of your toes identifying *only positive aspects of your body.* Doing this exercise as a shared exercise not only challenges you to higher levels of positive self-image but builds trust and greater understanding of what your partner appreciates about your body. Again, it may be the part of you that you dislike the most but now you may be surprised as to what positive qualities your partner comes up with about that very same thing.

Really want to get crazy with the sexual self-image affirmation? If you think the shared self-image experience is challenging with a person you know and trust—what about a room full of strangers? It happens all the time at self-image workshops around the planet. The objective is you being able to stand naked in front of the world and say, "Hello everybody, this is what a human being looks like and I'm pretty darn happy with me." Talk about positive self-image!

This last "global" version of the sexual self-image experience may not be your cup of tea, and that is perfectly allright. That's why there are so many varieties of tea! You are encouraged to complete the single-person version of enhancing your self-image at the very least to take another step forward in your sexual health. What do you have to lose?

In this chapter, we've talked about the many reasons people choose to have sex, ways to maintain erotic excitement in relationships, styles of communicating in general about sex, examples of sharing sexual fantasy, and improving your sexual self-image. The idea of this chapter is to give you some ideas to explore, prompt you to apply what you have learned about sexual health, and enhance your sexual comfort and confidence.

And now, Chapter 20. This last chapter takes you on a trip through the psyche (using a powerful perceptual tool called the Johari Window), explores the implications of the Sexual Hypercube as an engine for the Gender Revolution, and discusses a Sexual Bill of Rights from the World Association of Sexology. And if you think the sexual self-image exercise (global style) was a bit much, wait till you get a load of the Sexual Health Challenge at the end of the last chapter!

REFERENCES

Comfort, A. (1987). The joy of sex: A gourmet guide to lovemaking. New York: Pocket Books.

Fisher, H. (2004). *Why we love: The nature and chemistry of romantic love.* New York: Holt.

Locker, S. (2005). The complete idiot's guide to amazing sex. New York: Alpha Books.

Meston, C., & Buss, D. (2007). Why humans have sex. *Archives of Sexual Behavior, 36,* 417–507.

Perel, E. (2006). *Mating in captivity: Reconciling the erotic and domestic.* New York: HarperCollins.

Peterson, F., & Bley, J. *The pleasure playbook* (unpublished manuscript).

Westheimer, R. (2007). Sex for dummies. Hoboken, NJ.: Wiley Publishing, Inc.

CHAPTER TWENTY

Are There Ever Any Final Thoughts on the Topic of Sex?

Written by Frederick Peterson

INTRODUCTION

Per the chapter title, sexuality is a part of life that is continually changing. Even after all the changes of childhood and adolescence, people are often surprised by the transitions in sexuality they experience from one stage of adulthood to another. There are changes within ourselves, changes with others, and, of course, the "big show" of cultural changes we watch in real life real time. Unlike the alphabet and multiplication, sexuality is something that requires lifelong learning to keep current and sexually literate. Even if you read any of the excellent contemporary sexuality textbooks used in college courses, it may still be a challenge to know how to apply this knowledge to increase your comfort and confidence as a sexual being. That is the whole goal of this book, putting knowledge (from many sources) into play for you to have optimal sexual health. Before introducing new material in this last chapter, let us briefly review (in bullet fashion) a few key points of what the book has covered so far. It won't take long as there are only 15 points to note here.

1. Three questionnaires were introduced to measure your satisfaction regarding how your childhood family experiences influenced your sexual development, the amount and nature of your satisfaction regarding your current sexual life, and the level of satisfaction you have regarding your overall health.
2. Although the questionnaires were not intended to be the only means of measuring your health, we learned that these measurements relate to your sense of satisfaction with yourself and your sense of authenticity—particularly important aspects of your well-being. There are many measures of health referenced, and you were encouraged to explore and utilize them with your health care team.
3. Remember sexophrenia? It is the nonclinical term used for anxiety and conflict regarding sexuality, and it may have residual effects on you without you even knowing (consider it a part of your blind spot, a concept we will cover shortly within the Johari Window).

4. As a culture, we have been through some real craziness regarding sexuality. We have gone from considering many forms of sexuality (especially masturbation and homosexuality) as a disease requiring treatment to today's leading perspective that they are healthy forms of sexual expression.

5. Not only did we track the historical shift leading to the consensus opinion that masturbation and being gay are healthy, we reviewed research studies that strongly suggest many health benefits of sexual expression for men and women (and also threw in a special featured focus on the health benefits of babies at the breast).

6. We spent two chapters (and an extensive timeline) gaining an overview and insights into the interplay of two separate yet closely related historical developments during the 20th century that progressively and irreversibly changed the American experience: The forward movement of women toward a more equitable role in our culture as well as the transformational shift from sexosophy to sexual science over the same period.

7. We learned that there is little consensus on a definition of sexual identity and the role it plays in your sexual health as well as your overall health. A new model of sexual identity was introduced (the i-Cube) with a new definition for not only sexual identity, but also sex orientation (the combination of the five dimensions of biological sex and the three dimensions of psychosocial sex).

8. There is even less agreement regarding what sexual expression is (as crazy as it sounds), even though there is a growing body of evidence demonstrating that it is good for you.

9. We explored the incredible diversity of how people identify themselves in terms of sexual identity (via the many variations of the i-Cube and the intersections of sex orientation, sexual orientation, and sex-role orientation) and how sexual identity can be viewed more accurately as an intersection of these three continuums rather than a limited set of categories that restrict self-identification within a culturally biased and subjectively arbitrary range of "normalcy."

10. We explored the extreme diversity of sexual expression (via the e-Cube), which represents a world so broad and encompassing that general models do not exist, forcing us to speak of sexual expression "piecemeal" (behavior by behavior) and missing the inherent advantages of a general model.

11. Employing both cubes (the i-Cube and e-Cube), the Sexual Hypercube model was introduced as an interactive developmental process (via feedback looping) by which we grow in our sense of who we are as sexual beings and our preferences on everything from whom we prefer to have as partners to how we prefer to sexually behave privately.

12. We learned that the apparent biological aspects of sexuality ("nature") and the apparent environmental aspects of sexuality ("nurture") can and do influence each other in mutually reciprocal ways, which promotes continuous development and changes throughout the lifespan (again, with some changes affecting you without you even knowing).

13. The nature of sexual victimization was described to help illuminate the many pathways to recovery. Specific means and examples of tapping into the resiliency of the human spirit were promoted for rebuilding a healthy and meaningful life.

14. Numerous aspects of problematic sexual behaviors (PSBs) were outlined as another significant source of suffering stemming from individuals engaged in PSB, including an illustration of how men hurt themselves as well as those they love. Guidelines for recovery were included to show how positive change is possible through an intensive outpatient treatment program.

15. Guarding against this book being too abstract and theoretical, many real-life stories were sprinkled throughout the history and science as illustrations of how individuals can put all this sexual health and gender revolution stuff into play on a personal level.

Really, you may have not learned all that much that is new to you because much of this information (with a few exceptions) has been around for decades. These concepts from 70 years of sex research have just been integrated into a new model, and there is still much speculation about how the whole sexuality thing works. It's far from perfect as an explanation of all things sexual about humans yet it is perhaps another step toward an overall model of how we relate to ourselves and others sexually.

So, where does that bring us? The phrase "without even knowing" was used in the third and twelfth bullets above (as well as other places in this book). How can such significant factors about our core sexuality (such as sexophrenic feelings or changes in our sex-role orientation) influence us without even knowing it is happening? Look around your family, friends, and others. How and why do some people seem to change their sexual identity and expression over time while some do not? In the big picture, how do we collectively decide to get along with each other and sexually interact with others? What are the implications for these ideas of the gender revolution and new sexual health? These are all topics addressed in this last chapter of free-flow ideas of the new sexual health.

"WITHOUT YOU EVEN KNOWING" (A TRIP INSIDE THE PSYCHE)

The following is a story of a man named Rick (a pseudonym, story used with permission) for teaching purposes on how some influences make their impact without us knowing that it has already occurred. When Rick was a young man starting his early college career, he had a professor of anthropology that he really liked named Dr. Lang. One day the professor asked Rick, "What are you studying to be?" Rick told him that he was going to be a shrink. Dr. Lang raised his bushy eyebrows, shook his head as if Rick was going to waste his talents, and said, "Okay, Rick. You're a good student and going to do well whichever way you go. If you go into the health sciences, just watch out for the behaviorists."

Rick was bewildered by the sage's comment and soon forgot about it in the hurry of day-to-day details of college life. Not long after, Rick was accepted into a well-respected school that he completed and prepared to do a residency. Six years had passed since Dr. Lang's curious warning to Rick and he had forgotten Dr. Lang's gloomy forecast, even after being exposed to many behaviorally focused professors and researchers, who would promptly ask him to leave their office if Rick wanted to discuss any topic that was not a behavior. The rule Rick learned well was that "if it can't be observed or measured, it can't matter." There were even a few hard-core behaviorist professors who were rumored to find a way to flunk students if a student were to ever mention Freud in anything but a disparaging way. Rick was well schooled in this approach to science and considered himself a card-carrying behaviorist.

Rick married his first wife Amanda before his residency and as with many young couples, the plan was to complete school before having children. Well, you probably know where this story is going next as Rick was informed by his wife that they would be having a baby later in the first year of residency. Rick had just started the program and was happy to be a dad (a very cool thing in his book) but was also worried about how they could make it financially while managing school and the strain on the new marriage. Something funny started to happen later in Amanda's pregnancy. Something that would completely change how Rick viewed himself, others, and the world.

Six months or so into the pregnancy, Amanda started telling Rick that he would "shush" her during the night when she was rolling over or would occasionally cough. Rick didn't believe her and told her it was probably an effect of the increased hormones (ugh!—typical guy). A month or two later, Amanda told him that she made a noise getting up to go to the bathroom and Rick told her to "hush" and then told her to outright "shut-up" later on. He really didn't know what to make of this information except that she was dreaming or that she could maybe talk to her obstetrician to get a scrip to help her sleep better.

About six weeks before their son was born, something happened for which Rick had no way to understand or explain. They were on their last vacation trip before the big day and the total change of lifestyle that accompanies parenthood. They went to the seashore with family friends. After going to bed one night, Rick fell asleep as he usually did. But then, he found himself doing something that he didn't know he was doing. Rick described the experience much like the way some people describe suddenly becoming conscious in the middle of the night and find themselves walking down the sidewalk in their pajamas.

All of a sudden, Rick found himself sitting on the side of the bed, leaning over Amanda with his hand over her mouth. He said it was like he was trying to keep her quiet or stop her from saying something. Rick had no recall of why he had positioned himself physically in the bed to do what he was doing, except *to be doing what he was doing*! The last thing he remembered was falling sleep and then POW—his hands were over Amanda's mouth and her eyes were as big as saucers. She was obviously upset. She could have said, "Do you believe me now?" Instead, she suggested that if Rick wanted to be a shrink, he better go see one. So, he did.

In every graduate program, there are old sages around to occasionally help students work out problems and stay in the program. Rick inquired and was steered to such a fellow, who did the usual shrink thing. He had Rick talk about his childhood. The old professor looked interested when Rick told him how his mother thought there was something wrong with him because he hardly ever talked. Rick's mother had taken him to a doctor when he was two or three years old and expressed her concern. "What does he do when he is thirsty and wants a drink"? the pediatrician asked. "He just tugs on a skirt and points!" his mother responded and went on to explain that Rick had a lot of skirts to tug on with three older sisters. The answer was clear that he really didn't need to talk.

Rick asked, "So, what's this have to do with acting rudely during my sleep?" The old professor explained that Rick was telling a story of an early life that was pretty darn good for the first few years. Then something happened that completely turned Rick's little world upside down. It wasn't Sputnik or Cold War preparation drills for a nuclear attack, it was the arrival of his brother. With a new baby on the scene, Rick experienced a huge shift in attention away from him. He was just not getting his needs met in the fashion to which he had become accustomed. In other words, there was a revolution and the little prince was dethroned!

Rick went on to say that he truly treasures his brother as a grown-up man today. But at first he was not too happy about it, and it took some time getting used to having the little guy around. The shrink Rick was sent to (after his experience of being a sleep bully) calmly explained something called a "parallel process" by which Rick was reexperiencing an emotional reaction based on his early life. A parallel existed between his early distress from losing the attention from caretakers (mother and sisters) and the anticipatory fear of losing the attention of his wife. In reality, Rick was already experiencing the loss of some attention because of the normal and understandable preoccupation with the pregnancy as well as the birth of their son. Ironically, Rick was truly excited about becoming a dad and there was no way, no how, he wanted to acknowledge some petty feeling about not receiving all the attention he wanted from his tired and pregnant wife. However, those petty little feelings were coming out in ways "without him even knowing," at least until he could no longer deny it. This is what blind spots are, and there are simple as well as more complicated versions (such as this story of the sleeping bully).

"WITHOUT YOU EVEN KNOWING" (THE ACADEMIC EXPLANATION)

Ever hear of the Johari Window? It is the experience of the authors that most clients, students, and health care staff have not been exposed to this important perceptional model. The Johari Window is a conceptual tool dating back to 1955 when Americans Joseph Luft and Harry Ingham developed it as a means of promoting greater self-awareness (Luft, 1955). The tool became a staple of the Human Potential Movement of the 1970s and 1980s and is still used with regularity in many different training venues, including leadership and management development programs (Hase, Davies, & Dick, 1999; Handy, 2000). For example, when I served as a Director of Medical Education (Associate Chief of Staff) at a VA hospital, a talented group of faculty (Robert Scherer, Roger Cooper, Gene Buzzone, and Marcia Hockett) served as the brain trust of a year-long development program in which hundreds of health care supervisors and managers were trained in using the Johari Window as a personal learning tool and managerial team-building strategy.

Participants in this management development program used the Johari Window model to increase their awareness of how others viewed them. As a result, several publications and presentations at national venues were made from this research on topics of health care training, gender perceptions in supervision, and management development (Peterson, Cooper, & Scherer, 2000; Cooper, Scherer, & Peterson, 1998; Scherer, Peterson, & Cooper, 1996; Scherer, Canty, Peterson, & Cooper, 1995; Peterson, Scherer, & Cooper, 1991). It is important to include the Johari Window in our discussion of sexual health as it explains how we sometimes are not aware of aspects of our own sexuality.

The Johari Window explains how it can take years for some people to identify themselves as gay when their mother has known (or at least has had strong suspicions) since the kid was five years old. A young man named John is a good example of this. He was intelligent, articulate, and even insightful but was also raised with church teachings that were strongly condemning of homosexuality. His own religious beliefs, and those of his closest friends, were so staunchly antigay that he literally would shake physically in his chair when sexual orientation was discussed at his first consultation. It was like a part of him knew he was gay, but he could not bring himself to be conscious, let alone accepting, of the possibility that he was gay. That is, until he had enough support, permission, and psychological readiness to come for evaluation, where he was not judged but was told outright that he was a worthy and beautiful person (regardless of any sexual orientation consideration). After a few sessions, John's shaking stopped, many questions were answered, and he went about the business of building a strong and positive sexual identity that included being a gay man.

Although it is a dramatic example, John's story is an excellent demonstration of how we can have a blind spot regarding our sexuality. The process of discovering his blind spot is how he came to understand, accept, and eventually celebrate the newly recognized aspect of his sexuality. It is this process of identifying our blind spots and bringing them into conscious awareness that we call insight. This insight is the same process that underlies all personal and professional growth. Having insight serves as a primary path for people making important changes in their lives, whether that is realizing they are an alcoholic, admitting to having PSB, or discovering they are a "chauvinistic sexist pig" (as some male managers learned they were during the management development program mentioned above). But how does one become aware of blind spots when, by definition, they are beyond our awareness? We learn through the mirror others hold up to us, if and when we are ready to look.

Johari Window: The Open Self and the Undisclosed Self

Figure 20.1 illustrates a Johari Window, which is a 2×2 matrix created by intersecting two perceptional dimensions—your self-perception and other people's perception of you. There are things that you know about yourself and things you don't know about yourself. Similarly, there are some things that others know about you and some things other folks do not know about you. The intersection of these two bipolar dimensions creates four quadrants of perceptional possibilities. The first two are straightforward—the open "public domain" quadrant (Cell 1) and the undisclosed "private domain" quadrant (Cell 2) in Figure 20.1. Things that you know about you and others know about you are the "open" self, representing public information (the public arena, or sometimes called the public persona). Cell 2 quadrant represents the "undisclosed" self with information you know about yourself but others do not know about you (sometimes referred to as the private domain).

→ Yours PERCEPTION ↓ Others	Things I Know About Myself	Things I Do Not Know About Myself
Things Others Know About Me	Cell 1 Open/public domain	Cell 3 Blind spot/shadow domain
Things Others Do Not Know About Me	Cell 2 Private/undisclosed domain	Cell 4 The great unknown domain

FIGURE 20.1 The Johari Window

An example is in order. Let's use one from teaching health care staff at a hospital. As part of accreditation requirements, every hospital must demonstrate that their health care employees are both clinically and culturally competent while serving patients. Therefore, staff are trained on how to maintain clinical skills as well as develop cultural competency. When staff come to cultural competency training, they are sometimes surprised to see me (an old white guy) as their instructor on this topic. My general age, race, and biological sex are all public information instantly accessible simply by looking at me (included in the public persona). What the staff do not know (unless I tell them or they learn from another source) is that I have been involved in training and publishing on the topics of cultural diversity and cultural competency for a very long time.

For example, psychiatrist Florence Coleman (who is African American) and I taught a course called Cultural Competency in Clinical Practice for about 10 years at the School of Medicine of Wright State University. In addition, psychologist James Dobbins, Dr. Coleman, and I created a model of cultural competency development called the Pyramid Metaphor (Peterson, Dobbins, Coleman, & Razzouk, 2007). This model of cultural competency was then adapted into a version called the Mountain Model that became the basis for cultural diversity training with staff and residents providing federal health care in Ohio Appalachia (Peterson, Williams, Resch, Thull, & Dennis, 2011; Cohen, Peterson, Bottoms, Resch, Burgess, & Richards, 2013). However, my original introduction to the world of cultural diversity began while working with LGBTQA individuals (Haffey, Peterson, & Glaus, 2007). Most people have no reason to know this history and would not likely assume that I have worked so closely with cultural diversity issues. So, I share some of this information with new audiences who do not know my background to promote disclosure by participants in my classes as well as giving myself a bit more credibility to some students as their instructor. The meta-communication is that cultural diversity is important to everybody, and if this old white guy can work on being culturally competent, anybody can.

Johari Window: The Blind Spot

The last two quadrants of the Johari Window are where things get much more interesting. The third quadrant (Cell 3) is the proverbial blind spot that has been referenced. It is the intersection of what you do not know about yourself and what others do know about you. Examples include that strange sleeping bully and the brave young man coming to a conscious realization of his sexual orientation. A simpler, less complicated example of a blind spot could be useful here. Besides a man having to be told his fly is down or there is food in his mustache, let's use an academic example to illustrate a blind spot. When teaching sexuality at the University of Dayton, a colleague of mine was approached after class by a young student who informed him that she was surprised and disappointed by his use of language in class. At first, he thought she was talking about the explicit terms used in a sex class or his occasional use of profanity. Not at all! The student promptly identified his use of the phrase "rule of thumb" in both PowerPoint slides and the spoken word. He asked her to explain, and she proceeded to teach the teacher.

The young female scholar helped him consider her understanding of the history of that phrase, which she believed to be a linguistic residual of the part of American history when women were considered the property of their husbands. She said the phrase was believed to be derived from a time when husbands were legally allowed to beat their wives as long as they did so with a stick or instrument of discipline that was less than the thickness of the husband's thumb. There is debate as to whether or not this phrase has such sexist etymological roots as there are historical references to support such an association yet there is significant evidence that this specific interpretation cannot be substantiated. The most accepted origin of the phrase 'rule of thumb' is that it developed as an estimate of measure, the thumb being about an inch in width. Whether or not it is true that "rule of thumb" can be directly connected to English law allowing wife-beating, it certainly has such an association in American mythology and has become associated with our strong and undeniable history of suppressing women's rights. To this young woman (and probably several other less assertive students), the use of the phrase "rule of thumb" reflects the inherent, institutionalized sexism in American culture. The preference of the student was the use of a term like "guideline," which does not reflect the same history of patriarchy as "rule of thumb." (This is the same patriarchy that delayed the classification of forced sex of a woman by her husband as rape. California was the first state to criminalize this type of sexual assault in 1979). The young female scholar helped illuminate the professor's blind spot, not just in terms of the historical association of his words but also how he did not have any awareness of student perception that he was either ignorant, careless, or (even worse) sexist with his words. In a figurative sense, the history of American patriarchy was speaking through this professor outside his awareness.

So, he could have stood back all "professor-like" and said, "Girl, you've got a lot of ovaries" before telling her to leave his classroom. He could have listened politely, seen her as a student overstepping her role, and simply dismissed her perception. Or, he could have changed his slides and language to be less off-putting to a section of his students. And that's what he did because that is what he thought was best for the student's classroom learning experience. Regardless of the fact that the class was under the academic umbrella of the Women's and Gender Studies program, he genuinely believed making the change was the right thing to do. Would such a small change in language really make any difference diminishing sexism? He did not know for sure. But in some small way, even if it is hard to measure or define, he switched to the word "guideline" instead of "rule of thumb" because he wanted to feel that the world would be one small iota less sexist for the sake of his daughters, his sons, and all students.

This little experience helped remind him that sexism, just like many of the "-isms," is really not as much about the intent of a behavior but rather the effect that our behaviors have on others. This is the nature of perception and why the Johari Window is an important concept. He certainly was not intending to be sexist and he recognized that intelligent people could earnestly disagree whether or not he was actually acting in a sexist manner (a sexist effect without intention). All that is secondary to him as professor, as his primary concern was that a student took offense at his language for what he believed was a pretty good reason. Even if he didn't believe there was a good reason for her objection, he would still be concerned about a potential barrier to learning for her and other students who may have felt the same way.

At the same time, the professor was a colleague teaching a course in human sexuality. If the student objected to the use of sexual terms (like *dick* or *pussy*), the use of explicit adult sexual health education videos (some students may mistakenly call porn), or the coverage of certain sexual health topics (like rape and abortion), then that student probably signed up for the wrong class. As an educator, the good professor endeavored to remove barriers to learning and enhance the student's classroom learning experience. Yet the full frontal addressing of any sexual matter has to be able to be open for discussion in any university course on sexuality. Whether one is in a classroom or not, he believed that it is constructive for him to know the perception of the others (what they may know about you but you don't), if in fact he is interested in making meaningful connections with students as well as giving himself opportunities to identify his own blind spots.

Johari Window: The Great Unknown

Finally, the last quadrant (Cell 4) is referred to as "the great unknown" that results from the intersection of things you don't know about you and things other people do not know about you. Maybe if you and others don't know about something pertaining to yourself, how would anyone know if it actually exists? And if it does exist, is this even important? Well maybe, maybe not—depending on what "it" is. What if you and your sexual partner don't know that you (or they) have been exposed to HPV or HIV? Most people infected with a sexually transmitted infection (STI) do not know they are until they notice symptoms. In the case of chlamydia, 75% of infected women and 50% of infected men are asymptomatic (LeVay, Baldwin, & Baldwin, 2015).

This quadrant has also been referred to as the unconscious or the nonconscious (the latter for those who do not want to evoke associations with Freud). Cognitive psychologists and cognitive neuroscience researchers of the past 30 years (the folks who prefer the term *nonconscious*) have come to several conclusions about this part of the human mind. While learning occurs at both conscious and nonconscious levels, most cognitive researchers agree that we are influenced by stimuli outside our awareness ("without you even knowing") and that most human mental processing occurs at the nonconscious level (Schultz & Schultz, 2004). Therefore, humans experience perception without awareness (content within the blind spot, or great unknown). Additionally, the nonconscious plays a significant role in problem solving, hypothesis testing, and creativity. Nonconscious processing is believed to be faster, more efficient, and more sophisticated than mental activity at the conscious level (Bornstein & Pittman, 1992; Bornstein & Masling, 1998). Science writer Malcom Gladwell provided a well-written summary of the cognitive research on nonconscious mental process in his popular book, *Blink: The Power of Thinking Without Thinking* (2005).

When cognitive neuroscientists say we only use a small portion of our brain, they are talking about conscious thinking. The nonconscious explains how some people can be their own alarm clock, waking up at any time they wish consistently without fail. At times, the nonconscious can be asked to assist the conscious mind, such as information that is available through hypnosis but not through normal memory recall. A colleague once relayed a story that he had the occasion of running late to give a lecture and was looking around his house for his car keys while carrying his books and lecture notes. Out of frustration, he heard himself say, "Damn it, where are my keys?" He reported that as soon as he uttered those words, he became aware of the sensation of the keys—in his hand under all the teaching materials he was carrying around!

In a related story, a veteran also told a remarkable account of unexplained behavior that likely involved his nonconscious processing. Along with the entire platoon, he shoveled a hole in preparation for an onslaught by the enemy force and, indeed, an intense firefight ensued accompanied by mortar shelling. In the middle of the fight, he was overwhelmed with an impulse to do something that he believed may likely end his life. He experienced an incredibly strong compulsion to get out of his foxhole, which he was taught never to do unless a full retreat was called by his commanding officer. He heard no such call but leaped out of his hole onto his belly and crawled to a creek bed while enemy rounds whizzed by his head. Moments later, a mortar round created a crater where he was bunkered down two minutes before. For some, this event could be strictly coincidence, could be divine intervention, could be due to metaphysical explanations, or could be his sixth sense (like Spiderman's "spidey senses" tingling). Could it also be that his nonconscious processing was sensing data beyond his usual awareness and understanding (the blind spot or great unknown)? No one knows. The veteran doesn't know but he has thought about it for 50 years.

The point of going into so much detail about the Johari Window is to better understand how perception works in general and how blind spots occur in particular, especially about sexuality. A key point is that we all have blind spots. We cannot *not* have them! This understanding is fundamental to how the feedback looping process occurs between sexual identity and sexual expression of the hypercube. Said differently, it is fundamental to how we can change over time and have little awareness (perhaps no idea at all) about how we have changed and how much we have changed. Of course, we *are* aware of many changes through our own observation and insight. This conscious awareness is typically what we base our decisions on. This is good and part of the conscious processing of feedback looping. However, I hope you are now at least open to the possibility of blind spots existing within each individual and how they allow changes in sexual identity or expression without the person being (fully) aware of these changes, especially if they occur slowly over time.

Besides not knowing what is hidden in our own individual blind spots, none of us know what will emerge from the collective Great Unknown—we only know that new discoveries will emerge! Why? Because this is the true nature of science. Even a brief review of the history of science demonstrates a basic cyclic pattern that is replete through time: What was thought to be impossible, magic, or just unacceptable can eventually become possible, established by science, and widely accepted or practiced. Here are just a few reminders from earlier chapters:

- Evolution of the biological understanding of conception out of a history of magical thinking going back to the Greek philosophers.
- The development of sexual science over the past century from an academic tradition that excluded sexual matters as beyond acceptable limits of study.
- The development and gradual acceptance of people with gay and lesbian identities from a history including discrimination and extermination.
- The greater understanding and acceptance of the existence of transgender individuals when the concept did not exist in American culture 100 years ago (except as "two-spirit").
- The evolution of genetics to (first) explain sexual differences between men and women and (now) to help deconstruct the gender binary, explain the great diversity of sexual identity, and celebrate the unlimited variation of human sexual expression.

This list could easily be expanded to go on for pages, but you probably get the point. If you consider examples of scientific discovery that are not directly related to sexuality (radio waves or neutrinos), then the list would be almost endless. However, many technical advances that were never conceived to have anything to do with sexuality eventually have important implications for human sexual behavior, including the vulcanization of rubber (for condoms) and the invention (and mass production) of an affordable bed on wheels (the Model T).

The final points to make about the Johari Window are about its utility for enhancing sexual relationships (which may be another example of technical advances with unexpected sexual implications). The movement of information from one quadrant to another is of particular importance to sexual health as well as overall relationship satisfaction. Here are the most common examples of movement that promote sexual health as well as overall health:

- *The Great Unknown quadrant to the Undisclosed or Open quadrants*: As already mentioned, what you don't know can hurt you. Getting regular health screenings, including those for STIs, is particularly important. Of course, many types of medical screenings are just as important (if not more) for potential discovery, such as a nearly blocked artery.

- *The Blind Spot quadrant to the Undisclosed or Open quadrants*: We understand ourselves better when we have a mirror held up to us. Accurate information from others (especially about aspects of our behavior that are outside our awareness and is delivered in a way that is acceptable) can be of tremendous value for personal growth. The caveat is not to be overly dependent on other people's opinions. It may be valuable to know others' perceptions of you, but how much you care is completely up to you.

- *The Undisclosed/Private quadrant to the Open/Public quadrant*: This is the most frequent type of benefit from increased awareness via movement of information. Couples benefit from sharing their internal emotional life with each other because these disclosures become the building blocks of intimacy. When a sense of closeness exists between a couple, affectionate and sexual sharing increases. On an individual level, a person can disclose information to gain a sense of authenticity, honesty, and live without anxiety of some undisclosed secret being discovered. This is particularly important to individuals with PSB. Learning to live with safety, transparency, and accountability can be valuable for everybody as well as important tools for recovery.

The importance of the movement of information from the Undisclosed/Private quadrant to the Open/Public quadrant deserves additional attention. If the act of sharing information from private to public involves personal information about the self and it is purposely communicated to another person, then it is called *self-disclosure*, a particularly powerful form of interpersonal communication (Adler, Rosenfeld, & Proctor, 2015). Self-disclosure ("I'm feeling blue") is different from sharing other information publicly ("I don't like the color blue") and is the building block for intimacy referred to above. In their book, *Interplay: The Process of Interpersonal Communication*, the authors emphasize the value of the Johari Window as a learning tool and discuss the advantages of relationship building through self-disclosure, which include increasing honesty and depth in a relationship ("Wow, I didn't know you felt that way"); catharsis ("I need to get something off my chest"); self-clarification ("I need to talk a problem out"); self-validation ("I think I did the right thing"); and reciprocity ("inviting self-disclosure from a partner"), as well as other advantages (Adler, Rosenfeld, & Proctor, 2015). The conclusion is that building skills of self-disclosure can have a powerful impact of improving relationships and is particularly important in maintaining a sense of connection and intimacy.

ACROSS THE SEXUAL HYPERCUBE: THE GENDER REVOLUTION AND NEW SEXUAL HEALTH

Many of the most important changes that have happened in the past century have been about women's expanding roles in American culture. To the greatest extent, this book is primarily a reflection of these changes and particularly the increases in sexual health that women have made happen for themselves. As highlighted in the timeline between Chapters 6 and 7, this gender revolution has been going on a very long time but has accelerated its pace in the 20th century, especially during the first sexual revolution in the 1920s and then again in the 1960s/1970s.

Similar improvements in women's cultural status will continue to accelerate during the 21st century, but at an even faster pace. These gained opportunities will go far beyond a female president, and there will likely be three times as much progress occurring three times as fast as they did in the past century. This will result in women leading far more robust roles in American society, including increased acknowledgment of women's (present and past) accomplishments and more equitable sexual relations (less double standards). It is the authors' opinions that this progression is a positive movement closer for many Americans to realize their pursuit of happiness and to live in a more perfect union.

The transgender revolution in America has been unfolding all around us and has been for at least several decades. The very beginnings go back to Europe nearly 90 years ago, but the first American steps started in the 1950s/1960s with physician Harry Benjamin and his groundbreaking work (after all, he coined the word *transsexual*). Army veteran George Jorgensen, who was the first American to have sexual reassignment surgery, and then became the blond bombshell Christine Jorgensen. The 1960s witnessed a relaxation of social conventions and easing of the strict sex-role expectations of the 1950s. Since then, America has watched a parade of celebrities bringing cultural examples of gender bending to an increasing level of mainstream consciousness.

As mentioned earlier, the "big show" of cultural changes related to gender used to be watched on *The Ed Sullivan Show*, and then MTV, then YouTube, then an explosion of technologic streams of information. Of course, rock and roll led the way with early gender-bending rock stars like Little Richard, David Bowie, and Mick Jagger, who blazed paths for later gender-twisting celebrities such as Prince, Annie Lennox, Lenny Kravitz, and Steve Tyler. Movies featuring gender-bending started becoming mainstream with *Some Like It Hot* (1959), *The Rocky Horror Picture Show* (1973), *Hairspray* (1988), *To Wong Foo, Thanks for Everything!* (1995), *The Birdcage* (1996), *The Danish Girl* (2015), and many others. Other examples of gender-challenging media attention came with comedy skits such as "It's Pat" as a regular character on *Saturday Night Live* during the 1990s. Many gender activists used their celebrity to raise public awareness about transgender issues, such as RuPaul, Chaz Bono, and Laverne Cox. In 2015, Laverne Cox spoke at Wright State University in Dayton, Ohio, where she suggested that the future holds the possibility of gender variation becoming the norm. She believes that America will not live up to its ideal of equality and freedom for all until the day when it doesn't really matter what gender you are (Cox, 2015).

Many started writing gender-challenging books that reflect and propel the gender revolution. As one measure of how widespread the transgender revolution has grown within American culture, it is interesting to note that there are far too many activists, authors, and transgender celebrities to detail in this book. This is because the number of "ordinary folks" as well as celebrities who identify as trans (or as an identity other than cisgender) has virtually exploded over the past two decades. However, among the thousands of examples that could be used to demonstrate this point, there are a few individuals who will be noted here for either their books and/or celebrity related to transgender America: Christine Jorgensen, Renée Richards, Kate Bornstein, Nicole Maines, and Caitlyn Jenner.

These five individuals were selected from many others because they represent three stages of transgender evolution in America: The beginning, the middle transition, and current activism. As previously mentioned, Christine Jorgensen will always be remembered for being the first American to undergo sex-reassignment surgery in 1952 and living a celebrated life as described in her 1967 autobiography. After Jorgensen, American ophthalmologist Renée Richards is one of the best-known trans-women of the late 20th century. She contributed another book of the gender revolution, Richards's *Second Serve* (1983), which documented her gender reassignment in 1975 and transition from a highly ranked professional tennis player on the men's circuit to a competitive female player during the 1970s. Jorgensen and Richards are among the "first wave" of Americans who identified as transsexual, before the popular (and more inclusive) use of the term transgender took hold. Bornstein represents a bridge between the early beginnings and current activism and is noted for her writing *Gender Outlaw* (1994) and her memoir *A Queer and Pleasant Danger* (2012). In her autobiographic memoir, she wrote, "I don't call myself a woman and I know I am not a man." She simply is herself, Kate Bornstein.

Maines and Jenner represent more contemporary examples of transgender activism. Pulitzer Prize–winning science journalist Amy Nutt has written a beautiful account of the development of a beautiful young woman by the name of Nicole Maines (*Becoming Nicole: The Transformation of an American Family*, 2016). Nicole was born as one of two male twins, but she always identified as female. She is an amazing young activist who is quoted as saying, "There is an infinite amount of space on the gender spectrum. Being trans doesn't mean that you have to be feminine or masculine." (LeVay, Baldwin, & Baldwin, 2015). Of course, the most well-known gender story of the first two decades of the 21st century was the transitioning of Olympian athlete and reality TV star Bruce Jenner to Caitlyn Marie Jenner. Once known as the "greatest athlete in the world" and for being on the cover of Wheaties cereal boxes, Caitlyn is likely the most famous openly transgender woman in the world. Her transition from Bruce to Caitlyn occurred over many years, but she officially was considered public as Caitlyn during 2015 when she came out during a *20/20* interview with Diane Sawyer, appeared on the cover of *Vanity Fair* magazine, and had a television show focused on her transition called *I Am Cait*.

There is another measure of how widespread the gender revolution has been integrated into contemporary American culture: How common it is now to have trans-people represented on television and in movies as well as to have transgender individuals openly represented in communities across the country. Yes, it is easier to find trans-communities in larger cities, and that pattern is likely due to the greater acceptance/protection for trans-people in urban life. This is in part due to the increasing number of adult Americans who identify as transgender, an estimated 1.5 million (Flores, Herman, Gates, & Brown, 2016). However, the presence of trans-families is becoming more public and integrated into small-town life as well. The well-known activists mentioned above are far outnumbered by thousands of Americans who identify as trans and also consider themselves "regular people."

The everyday faces of transgender individuals in America are not just these well-known celebrities but several of the people described in this book, such as Alex, Zay, Dee, Gage, and Devin. While courageous and having to face significant challenges in their lives (as their stories have shown), these five individuals all live, for the most part, quiet lives in the conservative heartland of the Midwest. They are known as our neighbors, high school kids, veterans who served our country, volunteer drivers at the senior center, insurance agents, and others. That is the remarkable thing about the transgender revolution of the early 21st century: it is not only known for the differences of trans-people but the common everyday similarities with cisgender people.

Of course, there are important differences between those on the front lines of the gender revolution and the general cisgender community, and those differences are the very reasons to have a revolution. Some of these differences are very visible, and some are not. Especially with younger members of different trans-communities, these differences are highly visible and worn with pride. A special edition of *National Geographic* magazine ("The Shifting Landscape of Gender," January 2017) highlighted beautiful young people who represent the incredible gender diversity across the globe as well as within the trans-communities of America. The proliferation of the many varieties of self-identification is astounding as well as a testimony to the courage and fortitude of these youth in defining their own sense of gender. These individuals identified themselves as:

- nonbinary
- queer
- androgynous
- trans woman
- trans man
- trans boy
- bi-gender
- intersex nonbinary
- nonbinary genderqueer
- trans-activist
- cisgender
- agender
- gender fluid
- gender nonconforming and
- gender neutral.

Wow, what diversity! Like Nicole Maines said, "There is an infinite amount of space on the gender spectrum" (LeVay, Baldwin, & Baldwin, 2015). The authors would agree, considering the mathematical calculations for the thousands of different sexual identities within the Sexual Identity Cube as well as the unlimited permutations of the Sexual Expression Cube. The proliferation of terms for variations in self-identification may be seen as a reflection of our growing awareness of the amazingly diverse variations among human beings (as reflected within the Sexual Hypercube).

Science journalist Robin Marantz Henig contributed an excellent article entitled "Rethinking Gender" to the special issue of *National Geographic*, in which the "evolving notions" about gender are explored and which prompt Facebook to offer more than 50 terms to users to describe their gender in their profiles (Henig, 2017). The young people highlighted in this special issue and the thousands like them are the people leading us forward to what gender will mean in the future. Kudos to *National Geographic* for addressing gender issues and documenting such an excellent field report of the gender revolution, including all the "snapshots" of what gender variations look like around the world in 2017.

Another important consideration regarding these terms is that they may simply represent some of the most common varieties of sexual identity and expression being self-identified. In other words, if there are 10,000 permutations of sexual identity and you get a sample of 10,000 random people to identify their sexual identity, you are not going to have 10,000 different terms used for self-identification. Only the most commonly (frequent) occurring types of sexual identity will be represented in any particular sample.

Consider if each person of the N = 10,000 sample would receive hormonal, genetic, anatomic, radiologic (for internal reproductive tissues), and psychologic study. That way, each person can be fully informed as to their actual status among the eight different dimensions used to designate the sex of a person. For example, a few men may be surprised to discover that they have internal ovarian tissue (a designation of intersex) or a genetic variation of having an extra X chromosome (Klinefelter's syndrome).

The Mathematics of Sexual Diversity: Part III

Let's put this notion into play. All the people in the sample would have to be 18 years old or older to apply research-based calculations (see below). Hypothetically, a large majority of the random sample of 10,000 people would identify as cisgender. Based on previous research (Table 11.2 from Fausto-Sterling, 2000), an estimated frequency of 1.7 of 100 live births (0.017) involve infants with genetic variations. Applied to the sample (N = 10,000), approximately 170 people may have some variation of sexual identity based only on these genetic differences. According to the most recent report of the prevalence of adult Americans who identify as transgender (which comes from the Williams Institute of UCLA: Flores, Herman, Gates, & Brown, 2016), the estimated number of transgender American adults has doubled over the past 10 years to a population estimate of 0.6% (0.006). Applied to our sample, that would be 60 people.

Do the individuals with genetic variations (170) overlap with the individuals estimated who identify as transgender (60)? Most likely there would be some overlap, but no one knows how much (if any). Hence, in consideration of genetic variations (via Fausto-Sterling) as well as what would be considered more psychological variations (Flores, Herman, Gates, & Brown, 2016), the estimated subset of our sample of 10,000 adult Americans would be between 110 to 230 people who likely have a genetic and/or psychological basis for having a sexual identity other than cisgender

(0.017 – 0.006 = 0.011, for lower estimate if complete overlap and 0.017 + 0.006 = 0.023, if there is no overlap). In other terms, approximately 100 to 200 adult Americans of the 10,000 sample would likely have a genetic and/or psychological basis for having a sexual identity under the transgender umbrella. However, how many different terms or different ways would be used to describe the variety of sexual identities represented in this subset of 100–200? No one knows, but the authors are sure that each of the individuals in this subset would be able to find themselves within the Sexual Hypercube.

In the big picture, adults make up only about 76% of the U.S. population (or roughly 242,470,820 adult Americans based on 2013 data). Therefore, when the two empirically based population estimates are employed in combination (genetic variations as well as psychological self-identification), an estimate between 2.7 million (2,667,179) and 5.6 million (5,576,828) adult Americans have a genetic or psychological basis for self-identification as transgender individuals. These are simple estimates, and there may be honest disagreements with how they are calculated. However, the authors believe that the number of Americans identifying as transgender in the report by the Williams Institute of UCLA (Flores et al., 2016) are likely an underestimate of the actual number of Americans identifying as transgender. The Williams Institute study did not include teenagers who identify as trans. In addition, younger people more often identify as transgender than older Americans, which indicates that the prevalence rates of transgender are just going to increase (and are daily). As the estimated number of adults who identify as transgender has doubled from 0.3% to 0.6% over the past few years, the authors believe that there will likely be a fourfold increase by 2030 (potentially an estimated increase to an approximate range of 12 to 25 million adult Americans identifying as trans by 2030).

MOVEMENT ACROSS THE SEXUAL HYPERCUBE: CHANGE OF SEXUAL IDENTITY THROUGHOUT THE LIFESPAN

Of the three dimensions of sexual identity, changes in sex-role orientation are far more common than changes in sex orientation (transgender status) and changes with sexual orientation. However, the ways our sex-role orientation change are far from universal, and there are traditional gender-role differences between men and women. For example, there are many notable historical examples of women who live their lives within a traditionally male gender role, but they were always considered women by their communities. They may be called masculine, adventurous, butch, or even witch, but they are clearly considered women. Historical examples include Eleanor Roosevelt, Amelia Earhart, and Joan of Arc. During the Inquisition's prosecution of Joan of Arc, she was condemned to die as a witch and one of the charges leveled against her was not having the traditional long locks common of women but sporting a hair style of a man.

Despite drastic consequences from widespread repression of women, females have been exercising greater expansion of their sex role since the Industrial Revolution, especially during the 20th century. While they have had to fight for all advancements and paid significant costs, women are celebrating the 100th anniversary of their voting rights in 2020. Because of the suffrage movement, the labor demand caused by World War II, and the resurgence of the feminist movement in the 1960s/1970s, women have been able to integrate into the mainstream workforce with a strong presence during the past century. In addition, women have created a significant sector of the business world: women-dominated workforces in particular areas of the economy and women-owned businesses. Along with these changes, a concurrent relaxing of social conventions have occurred that has empowered women to have more socially sanctioned choices, from doing whatever type of work they choose to dressing pretty much any way they wish.

One of my daughters can wear a "Mannequin Pussy" band T-shirt, become an engineer, or get a head-banger tattoo when not one of these three options was socially acceptable a generation ago (the latter is still not acceptable to her father, but he will adjust if it happens). Another of my daughters can be a Montessori teacher and continue to be a teacher if she gets married when she would be disallowed from the teaching world just two to three generations ago (because of the societal expectation that married women should focus on having and raising babies instead of working outside the home). Both of them can wear suits to school or work and look sexy or smartly conservative if they choose. These increased choices are a good thing. Men do not have the same flexibility in attire (except for a few occupational areas) and, in fact, can easily be confused with, or diagnosed with, a mental illness of transvestism (cross-dressing) if they prefer to dress in what is considered women's attire. The point is that there are many restrictions both men and women still have today that are unnecessary. These restrictions are based strictly on gender stereotypes and can promote harm to others (including violence). Fortunately, the past few decades of American history have brought further loosening of the strict sex-role expectations that were thought to be so important in the 1950s.

Going back to the Johari Window briefly, involuntary changes that occur over the lifespan include the phenomena of sex-role convergence (cross-over effect) and changes in reference groups. Carl Jung describes something he called the "cross-over effect" of gender identity, in which certain aspects of personality are suppressed in adolescence and young adulthood but reemerge later in life. Jung believed that women typically suppress what society considers the masculine aspects of their personality and behavior when they are young (boys and young men are believed to do the opposite—suppress their femininity). The famous psychoanalyst proposed that later in life, we slowly develop these long-suppressed aspects of ourselves as an attempt to achieve balance between our masculine and feminine characteristics (more toward a state of androgyny). For example, men often try to emphasize more family, nurturing, and mentoring activities when they get older. Achieving more balance can typically give men and women more confidence and a stronger sense of identity later in life. This phenomenon is also thought to account for how certain older couples seem to act more alike (sometimes even looking more alike) as they grow older together.

When it comes to changes in sex-role orientation, transitions usually occur across several decades (such as the cross-over effect or sex-role convergence described earlier). However, people sometimes make what seem to be more radical changes in much shorter time frames. Men, for example, once they retire and/or have a few of their friends die from heart attacks, sometimes start examining their lives and realizing they may not have as much time remaining as they thought. Many readers may notice this with their own fathers who can become more affectionate in their later years. Older fathers may start freely and routinely hugging and kissing their grandchildren and adult children goodbye when they leave. It may take a little getting used to, but the show of affection is a wonderful gift to enjoy while it is possible.

A remarkable example of this wonderful behavioral change occurred with one of my relatives, Uncle Kenny. He was an old Navy vet from World War II who got shrapnel in his butt when a Japanese plane strafed his vessel. After serving his country, he loved to ride big motorcycles, talked tough, and was generally seen as a "hard-ball-of-steel" kind of guy (even though he had a big heart). He was married to Aunt Betty, who was kind and seemed at times to protect children nearby because she knew they might be a little frightened of Uncle Ken. His change (softening up) was more dramatic than the usual slow process over decades. The catalyst for Uncle Ken's change was an unfortunate loss, a tragedy when one of his sons (Johnny) died in a car accident. Because of the support of Aunt Betty, a caring family, and a support group of parents who lost children, Uncle Kenny did not turn his pain inward but started to share his feelings with his family and friends. This tough old bird who had children staying out of his way was now hugging them and telling them he loved them! The love he passed around also came back to him and helped him with his loss of Johnny.

IMPLICATIONS OF THE SEXUAL HYPERCUBE

The Sexual Hypercube model raises new questions for further consideration. If sexual identity does change for some people (as the authors assert), what percentage of people experience changes, and what types of changes do they experience? Can sexual identity (after adolescence) continue to be considered a constant fixed trait of human development? Not universally. If changes do occur commonly in sexual identity, how many appear to occur by individual (voluntary) choice? How many happen without individual choice or even the awareness of the individual (involuntary)? What types of lifespan transitions in sexual identity and expression can be considered to occur? What transitions are considered to happen in the physical domain (involving genetic, anatomical, hormonal, or surgical change), a cultural domain (direct transition in an individual involving sexual scripting), or definitional domain (transitions based on the relationship you have to another person or tribe)?

This book has essentially been an assertion that some long-held notions of human nature that have been considered "set, stable, and static" need to be reexamined in the light of the sexual science of the past several decades. The weight of evidence is far from conclusive but strong enough to suggest further study and consideration of different ways to conceptualize sexual identity. This is what the Sexual Identity Cube, Sexual Expression Cube, and Sexual Hypercube represent: A design of how the different aspects of sexuality are interrelated within a general model.

What are the implications of this general model? As mentioned, one of the most important implications is the promotion of greater self-acceptance as well as acceptance of differences between people. This is accomplished through the expanded model of sexual identity and expression, with a wider range of normalcy than what we had 50 years ago, even 10 years ago. The growing number of pediatric gender clinics across the country is a measure of these changes. It is a reflection of our culture's emphasis on the opportunity for all Americans to achieve health, including transhealth.

If the pursuit of health is considered a human right in the 21st century, and if health is considered a fundamental right of all people, is sexual health considered a right as well? The authors believe sexual health is a universal right for all people and is another implication for the Sexual Hypercube model. This is not just the view of the authors or an academic argument, but, on a grand scale, it is the position of the World Health Organization (WHO). Although several groups have been working on different forms of sexual rights; the World Association of Sexology (WAS) developed an official *Sexual Bill of Rights*. As you can see, these sexual rights address both sexual identity and sexual expression (WAS, 2014)[1]:

1. The right to equality and non-discrimination
2. The right to life, liberty, and security of the person
3. The right to autonomy and bodily integrity
4. The right to be free from torture and cruel, inhuman, or degrading treatment or punishment
5. The right to be free from all forms of violence and coercion
6. The right to privacy
7. The right to the highest attainable standard of health, including sexual health; with the possibility of pleasurable, satisfying, and safe sexual experiences
8. The right to enjoy the benefits of scientific progress and its application
9. The right to information
10. The right to education and the right to comprehensive sexuality education
11. The right to enter, form, and dissolve marriage and similar types of relationships based on equality and full and free consent
12. The right to decide whether to have children, the number and spacing of children, and to have the information and the means to do so
13. The right to the freedom of thought, opinion, and expression
14. The right to freedom of association and peaceful assembly
15. The right to participation in public and political life
16. The right to access to justice, remedies, and redress

Remember, these rights are endorsed and promoted by the WHO and considered fundamental and universal. They are based on an acceptance of the inherent freedom, dignity, and equality of all human beings. These rights are taken for granted in some locations and out-right rejected in other locations. Where these rights are antithetical to people's personal values (in this country as well as locations around the world), homosexuality is targeted for violence (or still criminalized), female infanticide is common, and/or honor killings of children occur with regularity.

In America, we have our share of children being abused and used as sexual slaves. We have significant challenges in fulfilling the spirit and potential of individual freedom and sexual rights. We have far to go to exercising these rights and integrating them so they are a commonplace experience. For example, we are very handicapped by our conflicting models of sex education in our schools due to fights for political control of local school boards, and the exclusion of sex education in some schools. A national consensus is needed to develop a rational approach to sex education to support the goals of both sides of the culture wars—the reduction of unplanned pregnancies and lowering the rate of abortions. In addition, health professionals of all disciplines need to have sexual health education integrated into their field-specific curriculums. Sexual health research needs to be funded free from political bias and regardless of the changes of which party

---

1 Adapted from "Declaration of Sexual Rights." Copyright © 2014 by World Association for Sexual Health..

is in charge of Congress or the White House. Sexual health goals also need to be integrated into all existing public health programs.

For greater appreciation of the complexity of human sexuality, the authors have made a call for reconsidering the concept of sexual identity and considering it to be of a fluid and flexible nature for many individuals over the course of their lifetime. To do so promotes greater self-acceptance of one's sexual identity, thererby minimizing negative self-image. On an individual basis, an expanded perspective of the full range of sexual identity and its correlated sexual expression may lead to less intrapersonal conflict and more personal satisfaction. On an interpersonal basis, the Sexual Hypercube is intended as a conceptual learning tool to promote greater tolerance of others as well as lessen the incidence of prejudice and violence toward those different from ourselves.

THE END POINT: THE SEXUAL HEALTH CHALLENGE

You have reached the end of this book, but hopefully there is no end point to your lifelong learning! How do you feel now? It is the sincere hope of the authors that you feel reading this book was well worth your time and energy. If you experienced any increase in comfort and confidence about your personal sexuality, then we consider writing this book well worth our efforts.

Here is a bottom-line question: Have you taken the SHAWS a second time? It is the measure of personal satisfaction (Sexual Health and Wellness Satisfaction Scale) that you hopefully completed in Chapter 2. Another copy of the SHAWS appears in Appendix A, and it is there for a second measure to compare to your baseline scores. You are encouraged to examine what ways you have increased your sexual health literacy, your comfort, and your confidence about matters sexual.

If you have areas of low satisfaction reflected by scores of 0 or 3, did they increase a bit on your second completion of the SHAWS? What ways can you really bring up your satisfaction in areas that really matter? High scores are very important in the domain of self-satisfaction, especially self-sexual image, self-love, and sexual identity (sex orientation, sexual orientation, and sex-role orientation). This is a final reminder that sexual health is a continuing learning and developmental process! And the good news is that you not only have already started your journey, you have really propelled yourself down the road to greater sexual health by completing this text.

THE SEXUAL HEALTH CHALLENGE is to keep up the momentum! Remember, you deserve a well-earned reward for completing this book, but the Sexual Health Challenge is a lifelong commitment to learning what you can in order to be the healthiest you can be! Throughout the book, there have been suggestions for continued development to increase your sexual health literacy and how to improve low areas of satisfaction on the SHAWS. Recommendations have been for increasing your self-affirmation, your sense of authenticity, and your personal relationships. Pay particularly close attention to the content of Chapter 19, which is designed to assist you in increasing your personal satisfaction.

The heart of the Sexual Health Challenge is finding ways you can really bring up your satisfaction in areas that really matter. You are encouraged to examine your lowest scores on the SHAWS and see which activities from the following list of suggestions might help you raise your satisfaction in those areas. Here are a few suggestions to consider, which may meet your personal needs to continue your pursuit of higher levels of sexual health:

- Discover one of the coolest sex educators on the web, Laci Green.
- Also discover the Green brothers (no relation to Laci) who have some entertaining and informative YouTube "Crash Courses" on sex and gender.
- Explore SIECUS: Sex Info & Education Council for the Unites States.
- Enjoy the best of the best TED talks on sexual topics.
- Watch the movie *Kinsey*, the film on the first major American sex researcher.
- Visit and/or support the Kinsey Institute at Indiana University.
- Visit the Museum of Sex (MoSex) in New York City.
- Start a local group to promote sexual health education.
- Speaking of sex education, check out the *Masters of Sex* series.
- What about Germany's Hirschfeld? Check out *The Einstein of Sex*.
- Do something with others to promote consent culture.
- Complete the Sexual Self-Image Affirmation (mirror) Exercise.
- Enjoy the best homework/play assignment ever given in a college class—the Sensate Focus sensuous touching exercises (per Chapter 9).
- Try sharing fantasies with your sexual partner (per Chapter 19).
- Consider becoming an LGBTQA ally or join a student-gay alliance.
- Observe the International Transgender Day of Remembrance.
- Start an LGBTQA Committee at work to promote positive visibility.
- Volunteer at your local women's shelter or advocacy group.
- Don't have one? Organize a small dedicated group to start one!
- Start a 5K walk/run or roll for sexual health awareness!
- Attend educational conferences on sexual health topics.
- Attend a Sexual Attitude Re-adjustment (SAR) workshop.
- Invite an author to speak to your book club on a sexual health topic.
- Use the Johari Window to discover and learn about your blind spot.
- Review the Bill of Sexual Rights to ensure you are good on all of them.
- Take a human sexuality course at your local college/university.
- Don't want to get out of your pajamas? Take one of the excellent MOOCs (massive open on-line courses) through edx.com from outstanding faculty, such as Dr. Janice Stewart's course on sex and gender at the University of British Columbia.
- Go all the way—get a college degree in human sexuality!
- Join the American Association of Sex Educators, Counselors, & Therapists.
- Take a self-defense class to develop skills to survive a hate crime.
- Explore or support a gay-affirming church as a guest or member.
- Volunteer and/or support your local gay and lesbian center.
- Support your favorite female or LGBTQA political candidate.
- Got mad lately? How about running for office yourself!

- Attend the annual National Sex Education Conference in New Jersey.
- Join a writers' group to write the story you have inside (of what you learn and love).
- Take matters into your own hands, ladies (DIY) with the *Becoming Orgasmic* program.
- Take matters into your own hands, fellas (DIY) with the *You Can Last Longer* program.
- Or, consider getting into sex therapy to increase your sexual health.
- Go to the max by participating in a couples' intensive weekend!
- Join one of the many organizations devoted to advancing sexual science, promoting sexual health, and protecting the Sexual Bill of Rights such as (with apologies to the many worthy groups inadvertently not listed):
  - American Sexual Health Association
  - American Association of Sexuality Educators, Counselors, and Therapists
  - Association for the Treatment of Sexual Abusers
  - Council for Sex Information and Education of the United States
  - Gay and Lesbian Alliance Against Defamation
  - International Society for the Study of Women's Sexual Health
  - International Society for Sexual Medicine
  - Parents, Families and Friends of Gays and Lesbians
  - Planned Parenthood
  - Professionals United for Sexual Health
  - Society for Sex Therapy and Research
  - Society for the Scientific Study of Sexuality
  - World Association of Sexology

Those are just a few ideas to get you started! The authors encourage you to continue your journey by employing some of the above suggestions and/or finding your own specific paths to greater sexual health. Take inspiration from the many success stories of sexual health in this book: Scott, David and Jill, Maria and Joe, Jane and Eddie, Kala, Karl, and the Courageous Young Woman by whom Vice President Joe Biden was so moved to write his open letter. This Courageous Young Woman is one of two people to whom this book is dedicated.

The authors hope also you took inspiration from the success stories of Alex, Zay, Dee, Gage, and Devin. Their narratives of resiliency and determination to survive hold lessons for us all as to how to overcome hurdles and build a life well worth living. Some of us make it. Some do not. The other individual this book is dedicated to is Leelah Alcorn, who represents the many who do not.

These 12 stories of courage and stick-to-itiveness show real-life road maps to not only sexual health but the pursuit of what most of us really wish for in our dreams: the real relation (the underlying need). Take inspiration, have self-appreciation, and be as healthy as you can aspire to be.

The main message is congratulations for helping yourself move along the continuum of sexual health and be the healthiest individual you can be! It is a big world out there regarding sex and gender. Strive to be happy with yourself most of all. Be productive and work to have healthy relationships. These are the things we all want most in the end. Good luck.

REFERENCES

Adler, R., Rosenfeld, L., & Proctor, R. (2015). *Interplay: The process of interpersonal communication* (13th ed.). New York: Oxford University Press.

Bornstein, K. (1994). *Gender outlaw: On men, women, and the rest of us.* New York: Routledge.

Bornstein, K. (2012). *A queer and pleasant danger: The true story of a nice Jewish boy who joins the Church of Scientology, and leaves twelve years later to become the lovely lady she is today.* Boston: Beacon Press.

Bornstein, R., & Masling, J. (1998). Introduction: The psychoanalytic unconscious. In R. Borstein & J. Masling (Eds.), *Empirical perspectives on the psychoanalytic unconscious.* Washington, DC: American Psychological Association.

Bornstein, R., & Pittman, T. (1992). *Perception without awareness: Cognitive, clinical, and social perspectives.* New York: Putnam.

Cohen, J., Peterson, F., Bottoms, J., Resch, W., Burgess, B., & Richards, M., (2013). *Healthcare in 21st century Appalachia: The arranged marriage of cultural competency training and relationship-based care approaches.* Paper presented at the Southwestern Social Science Association Annual Conference, New Orleans, Louisiana.

Cooper, R., Scherer, R., Peterson, F. (1998). Training organizational assessment and consultation skills. *Psychologist-Manager Journal, 2*(2), 59–66.

Cox, L. (2015). *Address to student body on transgender liberation.* Nutter Center, Wright State University, Dayton, Ohio.

Fausto-Sterling, A. (2000). *Sexing the body: Gender politics and the construction of sexuality.* New York: Basic Books.

Flores, A., Herman, J., Gates, G., & Brown, T. (2016). *How many adults identify as transgender in the United States?* Los Angeles: Williams Institute, University of California, Los Angeles.

Gladwell, M. (2005). *Blink: The power of thinking without thinking.* New York: Back Bay.

Haffey, B., Peterson, F., Bley, J., & Glaus, K. (2007). Addressing sexual health concerns of sexual minority clients. In L. VanderCreek, F. Peterson, & J. Bley (Eds.), *Innovations in clinical practice: Focus on sexual health.* Sarasota, FL: Professional Resource Press.

Handy, C. (2000). *21 Ideas for managers.* San Francisco: Jossey-Bass.

Hase, S., Davies, A., & Dick, B. (1999, September). The Johari Window and the dark side of organizations. *UltiBASE In-Site.* Lismore, Australia: Southern Cross University.

Henig, R. (2017, January). Rethinking gender. Article within special issue on the gender revolution. *National Geographic* magazine. Washington, DC: National Geographic Society.

Jorgensen, C. (1967). *Christine Jorgensen: A Personal Autobiography.* New York: Bantam Books.

LeVay, S., Baldwin, J., & Baldwin, J. (2015). *Discovering human sexuality* (3rd ed.). Sunderland, MA: Sinauer Associates.

Luft, J., & Ingham, H. (1955). *The Johari window, a graphic model of interpersonal awareness.* Proceedings of the Western Training Laboratory in Group Development. Los Angeles: University of California, Los Angeles.

Nutt, A. (2016). *Becoming Nicole: The transformation of an American* family. New York: Random House.

Peterson, F., Cooper, R., & Scherer, R. (1991). *Relationship between perceptions of managerial competence and sex role.* Paper presented at the National Conference of the American Association of Sex Educators, Counselors, and Therapists, Orlando, Florida.

Peterson, F., Cooper, R., & Scherer, R. (2000). Organizations change: Initial results in a health care setting. *Psychological Reports, 86*(2), 608–610.

Peterson, F., Dobbins, J., Coleman, F., & Razzouk, J. (2007). Culturally competent sex therapy. In L. VanderCreek, F. Peterson, & J. Bley (Eds.), *Innovations in clinical practice: Focus on sexual health.* Sarasota, FL: Professional Resource Press.

Peterson, F., Williams, M., Resch, W., Thull, J., & Dennis, R. (2011). *Better Serving Veterans in Ohio Appalachia: Using the Mountain Metaphor to Develop Cultural Competency Among Healthcare Professionals.* Paper presented at the 34th Annual Conference of the Appalachian Studies Association, Richmond, Kentucky.

Scherer, R., Canty, A., Peterson, F., & Cooper, R. (1995). Identification of managerial behavior dimensions in a federal health care agency. *Psychological Reports, 76*(2), 675–679.

Scherer, R., Peterson, F., & Cooper, R. (1996, July/August). Training resources decision matrix. *Training Today.*

Schultz, D., & Schultz, S. (2004). *The history of modern psychology.* Belmont, CA: Wadsworth/Thompson Learning.

World Association of Sexual Health (2014). *The Sexual Bill of Rights.* http://www.worldsexology.org.

FIGURE CREDIT

Fig. 20.1: Source: Stewart Hase, Alan Davies and Bob Dick, "The JoHari Window and The Dark Side of Organizations." UltiBASE, 1999.

Baseline Measure of Satisfaction:

SEXUAL HEALTH AND WELLNESS SATISFACTION (SHAWS)

Read the definition provided to you for each dimension of sexual health. It is provided to help you understand the aspect of your sexuality that you will be rating. Try your best to answer each question regarding your level of satisfaction. For example, even though you may not know something like your hormone level, please rate your satisfaction based upon what you do know ("We'll, I've never had a problem in that area") or your general feeling. Use the following rating scale to answer each question:

        12 = very high level of satisfaction
         9 = high level of satisfaction
         6 = moderate level of satisfaction
         3 = low level of satisfaction
         0 = very low level of satisfaction

DNK means you "do not know" your level of satisfaction (think about it and try not to use this option often). Use NA if you feel the question does "not apply" to you, such as if you are asked to rate your satisfaction with a primary relationship and you don't have one. You can either rate the question on your last relationship with a primary partner or just use DNK (or NA if you prefer).

Sexual Self-Satisfaction

Sexual health literacy (knowledge). Accurate information regarding sexuality that is not biased by prejudices and politics.

____ How satisfied are you with your level of knowledge about human sexuality?

Sexual self-image. How you see your own physical appearance, including attractiveness (based on how you see yourself).

____ How satisfied are you with the sexual attractiveness of your body?

Sense of self-love. A tender feeling of kindness, self-care, and acceptance toward yourself, associated with self-respect and positive feeling.

___ How satisfied are you with your ability to love yourself? (This does not mean masturbation, which is the following question.)

Sexual self-pleasuring (sexual function of desire, arousal, and climax through masturbation). Positive feelings resulting from any physical stimulation that makes you sexually interested and aroused (including, but not requiring, orgasm and not involving another person).

___ How satisfied are you with your ability to experience sexual desire associated with self-pleasure (masturbation)?

___ How satisfied are you with your ability to experience sexual arousal (erections for men and vaginal lubrication for women) associated with self-pleasure (masturbation)?

___ How satisfied are you with your ability to experience sexual climax (orgasm) associated with self-pleasure (masturbation)?

Sexual fantasy. Thinking about sexy things that create or increase sexual feelings (whether or not a person masturbates).

___ How satisfied are you with your ability to enjoy sexual fantasy?

Sexual health service access. Being able to access sexual health services (such as seeing a doctor, getting reproductive services, or getting sex counseling) based on your location and financial status.

___ How satisfied are you in your ability to access sexual health services?

Relational Sexual Satisfaction

Overall relationship satisfaction. Your total satisfaction resulting from all aspects of your relationship with another person (including, but not limited to, emotional, affectionate, sexual, intellectual, financial, spiritual, and safety aspects of your overall relationship).

___ How satisfied are you with the overall relationship with your primary partner? (If you are not in what you consider a "primary relationship" at present, you may respond to this item based on thinking of a particular partner or your last primary relationship. Use NA if it does not apply.)

Overall sexual satisfaction. Your total satisfaction resulting from all SEXUAL aspects of your relationship with another person (including, but not limited to, frequency, duration, climax-consistency, and emotional aspects of your overall sexual relationship).

___ How satisfied are you with the overall SEXUAL relationship with your primary partner? (If you are not in what you consider a "primary relationship" at present, you may respond to this item based on thinking of a particular partner or your last primary relationship. Use NA if it does not apply.)

Sense of love for another. A feeling of affection, tenderness, and connection toward a person, often associated with a feeling of passion and a longing for intimacy with that person.

___ How satisfied are you with your ability to experience love toward another person?

Sexual pleasuring with a partner (sexual function of desire, arousal, and climax with another person): Your ability to experience sexual desire, sexual arousal, and orgasm with a sexual partner.

___ How satisfied are you with your ability to experience sexual desire associated with sexual relations with another person?

___ How satisfied are you with your ability to experience sexual arousal (erections for men and vaginal lubrication for women) associated with sexual relations with another person?

___ How satisfied are you with your ability to experience sexual climax (orgasm) associated with sexual relations with another person?

Social acceptance of sexuality. The average amount of acceptance you feel you receive from people in your social networks regarding your sexuality (including an average of support from family, peers, organizational membership, or community as a whole).

___ How satisfied are you with how your sexuality is accepted within your social network (such as family, peers, and community-at-large).

Sexual-spiritual relationship. The degree of alignment between one's spiritual/religious beliefs and one's sexual practices (whether the sexual behaviors are practiced alone or with another person).

___ How satisfied are you with the relationship between your sexuality and your spiritual/ religious beliefs? (You can use NA if you do not think this item applies).

Medical Sexual Satisfaction

(Special Note: The previous items are based on the general premise that the more you have (like self-acceptance or ability to have orgasms), the higher your satisfaction. With the exception of the question about fertility, the items in this section are the opposite; the less you have usually means the higher your satisfaction—but not always.)

Sexual pain status. Pain primarily experienced by women (although men can be affected as well) during or immediately after sexual activity (especially sexual intercourse).

___ How satisfied are you with your degree of comfort (absence of pain) during or after intercourse?

Sexual injury status. Sexual trauma or abuse that has been forced upon you by one or more perpetrators against your consent.

___ How satisfied are you that all your sexual relations have been with your consent?

Sexually transmitted infections status (sometimes referred to as sexually transmitted diseases). Related to illness caused by a virus, bacteria, or parasite that has a high probability of transmission between people by means of sexual contact.

___ How satisfied are you with your ability to prevent yourself from getting a sexually transmitted infection? (Please answer regardless of whether or not you actually know if you have a sexually transmitted infection.)

Sexual hormone status. Natural substances produced by the body (primarily testosterone and estrogen), which make a person more interested in sex as well as increasing one's fertility, sense of vitality, and overall health and well-being.

___ How satisfied are you with your status of sexual hormones? (Please answer regardless of whether or not you have actually had your hormone levels measured.)

Problematic sexual behavior status (sexual compulsivity/addiction). When individuals report being unable to control their sexual behavior despite increasingly adverse consequences as a result of their "out-of-control" sexual behavior (consequences such as ruining their health, relationships, and careers).

___ How satisfied are you with your ability to prevent yourself from engaging in problematic sexual behaviors (also referred to as "out-of-control" or "sex addiction" behaviors)?

Sexual reproductive status. The natural capacity to conceive and have children as well as the ability to prevent pregnancy (regardless of one's sexual orientation).

___ How satisfied are you with your fertility (your ability to have children and/or keep from having offspring)?

Sexual Identity Satisfaction

Sex orientation. Physical anatomy and/or traits that most often make people see themselves as male, female, or transgender (transgender defined as a combination of both male and female sex designation).

Please list your identified (designated) sex: _____

(Female, male, transgender, or whatever term you prefer)

___ How satisfied are you with your identified sex (being a man, woman, transgender, or alternative term)?

Sexual orientation. An enduring pattern of emotional, romantic, and/or sexual attraction you have toward men, women, both sexes, or neither sex.

Please list your identified sexual orientation: _____

(Asexual, bisexual, gay, lesbian, heterosexual, or whatever term you prefer)

___ How satisfied are you with your sexual orientation (being asexual, bisexual, gay, lesbian, heterosexual, or alternative term)?

Sex-role orientation. A person's self-description as being traditionally masculine, traditionally feminine, androgynous (having high amounts of both masculine and feminine traits), or a preferred alternative term (such as queer or non–gender conforming).

Please list your identified sex-role orientation: _____

(Traditionally feminine, traditionally masculine, androgynous, or whatever term you prefer)

___ How satisfied are you with your sex-role orientation (androgynous, feminine, masculine, or preferred alternative term)?

Domain and Overall Sexual Health Scoring and Summary

Instructions: This page allows you to summarize your ratings and draw conclusions regarding your sexual health satisfaction.

List how you see your sexual identity:

_____

_____

List your areas of high satisfaction (your highest scores). These can be considered the strengths of your sexual health.

_____

_____

List your areas of low satisfaction (your lowest scores). These are likely to be the areas of your greatest concern and focus of expanding your sexual health.

_____

_____

Add up the sum totals for each section above:

Sexual Self-Satisfaction Indicator   _____

Relational Sexual Satisfaction Indicator _____

Medical Sexual Satisfaction Indicator   _____

Sexual Identity Satisfaction Indicator   _____

Overall Sexual Health Indicator _____

MAKING SENSE OF YOUR SHAWS BASELINE SCORES

The preceding summary page is designed to help you have a better understanding of your areas of satisfaction and, as noted, draw conclusions about what your ratings mean. There is wide variation to the guidelines, so remember that exceptions exist for some of the following generalizations.

Scoring is designed to approximate a continuum of 0 to 300, with 300 representing complete (or nearly complete) satisfaction in all areas of sexual health. A score of 300 represents an ideal model of sexual health. For most people, it is unrealistic to assume they should be anywhere close to a score of 300. People who have been diligently working toward enhancing their sexual health are more likely to be within the 240–270 range. This simple 0–300 "continuum design" is based on several factors:

1. There are 25 dimensions of sexual health you have rated 0–12 for satisfaction (equaling a possible range of scores from 0–300).
2. Two items are subdivided into separate sections (questions 4 and 10 about sexual self-pleasuring and sexual pleasuring with a partner) and they are to be scored as three equal dimensions of sexual function.
3. You are to try your best to give an answer for every area of sexual health. If you cannot, then your total score will be artificially lowered and any missing answer must be taken into account during interpretation.
4. If you responded to any item with "DNK" (do not know) or "NA" (not applicable) because you are not in a primary relationship or a sexual relationship, then adjust your score accordingly. For example, if you used NA one time; your total responses are in relationship to a highest possible total of 288, not 300. Hence, you are not penalized (numerically) for not being in a primary relationship.
5. The following interpretation guidelines for scores are similar to what you used in the first chapter with the Self-Assessment of Family Support.

290–300	Come on, stop fooling yourself!
250–289	Very high satisfaction
200–249	High satisfaction
150–199	Moderate satisfaction
075–149	Low satisfaction
000–075	Stop being so hard on yourself!

The listing of your sexual identity traits simply helps you clarify your core sexual identity The listing of your areas of highest and lowest levels of satisfaction have specific purposes as well. Your areas of highest satisfaction are represented by your highest rating (typically a rating of 12). These are the strengths of your sexual health and are important not only in "counterbalancing" your areas of low satisfaction, but possibly in assisting you with strategies to enhance your sexual health satisfaction.

Your areas of lowest satisfaction are represented by your lowest ratings (typically a rating of 0 or 3). These are the areas of your greatest concern and should guide you in focusing your efforts in expanding your sexual health. Pay particular attention to the chapters that focus on increasing your satisfaction in the areas of your lowest ratings.

Statistical Consultation Report

Written by Victor Heh, PhD

May 16, 2017

This consultation was initiated by Dr. Peterson, Department of Specialty Medicine, OU. He requested three key calculations within the two 3-dimensional cubes of the Sexual Identity Cube and the Sexual Expression Cube, which in combination constitute the 4-dimensional Sexual HyperCube Model. Below are the key estimates requested:

1. An empirically based estimate of all possible permutations within the sex orientation component (sex designation) of the sexual identity cube.
2. An empirically based estimate of all possible permutations within the entire three-dimensional sexual identity cube.
3. An empirically based estimate of all possible permutations within the entire three-dimensional sexual expression cube.

A cube (as in data cube) is a multidimensional structure that contains information for analytical purposes and it is used to represent data along some measure of interest. When you slice a cube along the levels of one of the dimensions, you obtain multiple 2-dimensional tables that are equal to the number of levels of the third dimension. Hence, the cube represents multiple identical 2-dimensional tables put together. Therefore, the cube can be 2-dimensional, 3-dimensional, or even higher dimensional.

The dimensions define structure of the cube and represent some attributes of concern such as Biological and Psychosocial factors that may define an individual's sexuality. These attributes also have levels, which in combinations can define [a] number of hierarchical combinations of factor levels possible. The overall size of the data cube is dependent

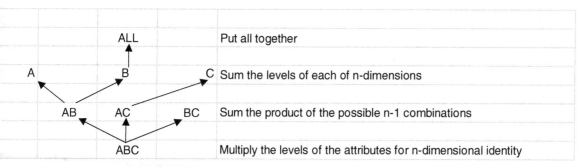

	ALL		Put all together
A	B	C	Sum the levels of each of n-dimensions
AB	AC	BC	Sum the product of the possible n-1 combinations
	ABC		Multiply the levels of the attributes for n-dimensional identity

RE 1: Multi-way array aggregation technique.

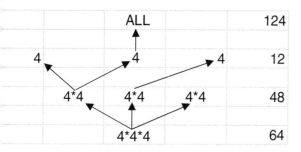

	ALL		124
4	4	4	12
4*4	4*4	4*4	48
	4*4*4		64

URE 2: Computations based on sexual identity cube.

upon the dimensions and the levels of each attribute defining a dimension. The size of the cube increases exponentially with the number of attributes and linearly with the levels [of] those attributes.

Goal of Consultation:

The goal of the empirical computation is to provide an empirically based estimate of the potential number of ways that individuals could identify themselves using [a] combination of factors.

Methodology:

One of the ways to achieve this goal is to use data computation involving multi-way array aggregation of data, Zhao et al. (1997) (Figure 1). This involves [an] array-based bottom-up approach, which uses multi-dimensional chunks for cube computation. The bottom level determines the number of small sub-cube [s] that make up the overall cube based on the number of dimensions and levels. For example, for a 3-dimensional cube with levels A, B and C, the number of combinations of the three attributes is given by A*B*C. What this means is that, a 4 by 4 by 4 (3-dimensions with four levels in each dimension) would produce 64 unique combinations of three attributes as the first-way in multi-way approach. That's not all; it is also possible to have 48 unique combinations of two attributes AB, AC and BC (AB+AC+BC) at the second level of aggregation, and then A+B+C at the third level, and finally putting ALL together as an aggregate. This structure (number of vertices involved in aggregation) is applicable to all data structure with three attributes.

Hence, given n-dimensional cube defined by attributes $A_1, A_2, \ldots A_n$; the number of combinations of n unique attributes is given by $A_1^* A_2^* \ldots \ldots A_n$; and the number of combinations of $n-r$ (where $r=1$ to n) unique attributes is given by the sum of the $_nC_{n-r}$ products (when n-r≥2) defining the $n-r$ attributes at subsequent levels of the multi-way breakdowns. For $n-r=1$, sum the $_nC_{n-r}$ single values.

The three ways plus the aggregate ("ALL" in Figure 1) represents the number of vertices (8) in [a] 3-dimensional cube. The eight vertices represent all the nodes in the multi-way chunks involved in the counting process.

In general, the formula to count r-cells in n-dimensional cube is $_nC_r*2^{n-r}$. This formula produces the number of points or nodes in the counting process and represents 0-cells (vertices) in n-dimensional cube. In addition, n-cells in n-dimensional cube would always produce one n-dimension cube as the bases for splitting the cube into several chunks determined as the multiplicity of all the levels in the attribute. Overall, if we consider number of attributes as dimensions with any number of levels, we are able to break down the counting process into multiple ways determined by the number of attributes and number of nodes as 0-cells in n-dimension cube.

Using the counting strategy described above for combinations or permutations of sex designation based on:

1. Chromosomal (10);
2. Hormonal-prenatal (3);
3. Hormonal-pubescent (3);
4. Anatomical-internal (3);
5. Anatomical-external (3)
6. Sex assigned at birth (2);
7. Sex raised as (3); and
8. Gender identity (3).

We can assume an 8-dimensional cube for the purposes of determining the number of points in the counting process and also proving that there is one 8-dimensional cube to be split into multiples of the levels of the dimensions as the bottom level of the counting process. There would be 255 different vertices involved in the counting process. Therefore, the number of factor unique expressions or identities would be 10*3*3*3*2*3*3 = 14,480. We would then have to count the combinations of 7, 6, 5, 4, 3, 2, 1 levels that would contribute to the overall counting process.

<u>Empirical-based estimate of the different combinations/permutations of complete sexual identity cube</u>

As shown in Figure 2, there are 64 sex orientation, sexual orientation and sex role orientation combinations in the identity cube.

In addition, 48 two combinations of the 3 attributes and 12 different single attributes are possible, giving rise to 124 different ways to identify people based on the identity cube.

Note: Each of the multi-ways represent combinations at that level. If desired, permutations are obtained by multiplying each number by n! before aggregating at the ALL node.

Theoretically, the estimated permutations of sexual expression could be unlimited, however, I do not see it being unlimited based on data cube computation (if categories are bounded)!

Final Conclusions:

A cube is a multidimensional structure that contains information for analytical purposes and it is used to represent data along some measure of interest. The dimensions define [the] structure of the cube and may represent certain attributes of interest. These attributes also have levels, which in combinations represent number of combinations of factor levels possible. The overall size of the cube depends on the dimensions and the levels of each attribute. The size of the cube increases exponentially with the number of attributes and linearly with the levels of those attributes. Hence, given n-dimensional cube defined by attributes $A_1, A_2, \ldots A_n$, where A_n represents the number of levels in attribute n, the number of combinations of n unique attributes is given by $A_1^* A_2^* \ldots \ldots A_n$. $= PA_i$ The number of permutations of n elements is then given by $PA_i^* n!$

Using the counting strategy described above for combinations or permutations of sex designation based on:

1. Chromosomal (10);
2. Hormonal-prenatal (3);
3. Hormonal-pubescent (3)
4. Anatomical-internal (3);
5. Anatomical-external (3)
6. Sex assigned at birth (2);
7. Sex raised as (3); and
8. Gender identity (3),

we can determine the number of 8 combinations of sex orientation as $10^*3^*3^*3^*3^*2^*3^*3 = 14{,}580$. This represents the number of levels in sex designation that can be combined with other attributes in the whole sexual identity cube.

Empirically based estimate of the different combinations/permutations of complete Sexual Identity Cube

Using the counting principle established earlier for combinations or permutations of sex designation (14,580), sexual orientation (4) and sex role orientation (4), we can count $14{,}580^*4^*4 = 233{,}280$ unique three-attribute combinations.

Is it reasonable in science fashion to describe the estimated permutations of the Sexual Expression Cube as unlimited?

Theoretically, the estimated permutations of sexual expression could be unlimited, however, I do not see it being unlimited based on data cube computation (if the categories are bounded)! Victor Heh, PhD.

Biostatistician, Office of Research and Grants
Heritage College of Osteopathic Medicine
Ohio University.

Zhao, Y., Deshpande, P.M., & Naughton, J.F. (1997). An Array-Based Algorithm for Simultaneous Multidimensional Aggregates. *ACM SIGMOID Record*, 26(2), 159–170. Retrieved from http://dl.acm.org/citation.cfm?id=253288

The size of the cube increases exponentially with the number of attributes and linearly with the levels of those attributes (n.d). Retrieved from http://www2.cs.uregina.ca/~dbd/cs831/notes/dcubes/dcubes.html

GLOSSARY

AASECT: American Association of Sexuality Educators, Counselors, and Therapists.

AIDS: Autoimmune Deficiency Syndrome (see HIV/AIDS).

Amygdala: Part of the limbic system consisting of an almond-shaped mass of gray matter in the anterior extremity of the temporal lobe which is associated with emotional regulation and considered important to experiencing pleasure and determining how our memory works.

Analingus: A sexual behavior in which the anus is stimulated by using the mouth and lips (also called "rimming").

Androgen insensitivity syndrome (AIS): A condition in which an individual born with XY sex chromosomes does not have functional androgen receptors so the typical masculinization process does not occur during fetal development, resulting in a female appearance.

Androgyny: Fluidity in male/female sex-role orientation. Traditionally considered a state of an individual having both masculine and feminine characteristics.

Circumcision: Surgical removal of the foreskin of the penis.

Cisgender: An adjective used to describe a person whose gender identity and gender expression align with sex assigned at birth (people who identify with the gender that was assigned to them at birth and a person who is not transgender or gender nonconforming).

Clitorectomy: Surgical removal of the clitoris of the vulva.

Complex PTSD: A diagnosis developed by Judith Herman to help explain symptoms observed in survivors of prolonged abuse. It has since been replaced by the diagnosis of dissociative identity disorder (see DID).

Congenital adrenal hyperplasia (CAH): A condition in which an individual lacks one of the enzymes the adrenal glands use to produce hormones that help regulate metabolism, the immune system, blood pressure, and other essential functions (also resulting in masculinization of XX female fetal tissue).

Contra-onanists: Those opposed to the belief that masturbation causes illnesses.

Cunnilingus: A sexual behavior in which the vulva is stimulated by using the mouth and lips.

DID: Dissociative identity disorder is a diagnostic syndrome that describes the symptoms observed in survivors of prolonged and intense abuse.

Don Juanism: A male expressing what is considered excessive interest in sex.

Dopamine: A neurotransmitter that helps control the brain's reward and pleasure centers as well as helps regulate movement and emotional responses.

Down-Low: A slang that identifies a man (usually African American) who has a heterosexual lifestyle but also has sex with men.

E-Cube (Sexual Expression Cube): Pictorial reflection of three dimensions, including sexual fantasies, sexual behaviors, and bioculturally bound modifying factors.

EMDR: Eye movement desensitization reprocessing, a therapy technique that was developed by Francine Shapiro and used to reduce anxiety, especially anxiety related to trauma.

Erotomania: A condition in which a person expresses what is considered excessive interest in sex.

Estrogen: A hormone that causes the development and maintenance of the characteristics in the body that determine female gender identification.

Eugenics: A 19th-century pseudoscience developed primarily by Francis Galton, who studied methods of controlling which people can procreate.

Family-Centered Perinatal Education (FCPE): A combined prenatal childbirth education and postpartum parent support/education class to facilitate positive outcomes for couples becoming families.

Fellatio: A sexual behavior in which the penis is stimulated by the mouth and lips.

Flapper: Women of the 1920s who took liberties to break the feminine conventions of the day regarding dress, smoking, and sexual behavior.

Gender dysphoria: Feelings of conflict regarding one's sexual identity.

Gender fluid: An identity that does not conform to any defined sex-role or sexual orientation.

Gender nonconforming: A descriptive term for an individual whose gender identity, role, or expression differs from what is normative for their assigned sex in a given culture and historical period.

Genotypes: An individual's chromosomal makeup producing particular characteristics (phenotype).

Germ theory: Modern belief (since 1880s) in medicine that germs cause illness.

Good Health Doctrine: Historical line of beliefs regarding the cause of physical Illness and mental disturbances; emphasizes particular food, exercise, rest, fresh air, and healthy sex (no masturbation and missionary position only) as means of maintaining good health.

HALT: Acronym used in Alcoholics Anonymous as a reminder of one's vulnerability to relapse if a person allows themselves to become too (letters stand for) Hungry, Angry, Lonely, Tired.

Has-bian: A term proposed to describe college-age women who experiment with lesbian sex but later resume a heterosexual pattern.

Hegemony: Social, cultural, or economic influence or authority exerted by a dominant group.

Hermaphroditism: A person with both ovarian and testicular tissue (more often referred to as "intersex").

Heteroflexibility: A term proposed by Lisa Diamond referring to a pattern of sexual behavior predominantly heterosexual yet having periods of same-sex behavior.

Hijra: A member of a community of transvestites primarily found in South Asia.

Hippocampus: A structure of the mid-brain that provides a "bundling function" in which bundling of information puts together different aspects of an experience into what is considered a typical memory with a beginning, middle, and end.

HIV/AIDS: Human Immunodeficiency Virus/Acquired Immune Deficiency Syndrome: A viral infection that today is managed as a chronic illness but if untreated can deplete the immune system, allowing the individual to be vulnerable to additional opportunistic illnesses, which can be fatal.

Homophobia: An irrational fear of lesbian, gay, bisexual, transsexual, queer, and asexual (LGBTQA) individuals that can lead to hatred and violence toward those perceived as LGBTQA.

Humorism: A belief that dominated ancient and medieval times that posited that body fluids need to be in balance or an imbalance or deficiency would cause illness.

Humors: Within the belief system of Hippocratic medicine, body fluids as blood, phlegm, black bile, and yellow bile.

Hyperphilia: A condition characterized by what is considered an excessive interest in sex.

Hysteria: An outdated psychiatric diagnosis with symptoms of conversion of psychic pain to physical symptoms, under-controlled emotional states (including sexual desire), and attention-seeking behaviors.

I-Cube (Sexual Identity Cube): A pictorial reflection of a 4×4×4 polygon representing a model of sexual identity that includes four types of sex orientation, sexual orientation, and gender-role orientation.

Id: A Freudian concept characterized by the Pleasure Principle and aggressive drives (the part of the human psyche that craves and seeks pleasure).

Ideoerotic: A term coined by John Money when he was developing his theory of "lovemaps," referring to the particular erotic interest pattern of each individual.

Implicit memory: When different aspects of an experience are retained separately on a sensory-motor level without the usual narrative story (and hence the memory of the event is not usually available to voluntary recall as explicit memories are).

Intersectionality: Accumulative and interactive influences upon an individual as a result of identification with multiple cultural groups.

Intersex: Variations in gender characteristics caused by chromosomes, gonads, or genitals that sometimes create an ambiguous biological identification of sex determination. Intersex can also refer to having both ovarian and testicular tissue within the same individual.

Introitus: The opening in the vulva to the vagina.

Johari Window: A perceptual model developed as a mechanism of promoting greater self-awareness.

Klinefelter's syndrome: A genetic variation of one or more extra X chromosomes in a male (XXY or XXXY).

Leelah's law: A proposal to Congress (April 2015) to make conversion therapy against the law in the United States (it has become law in a dozen states but has yet to be passed on a federal level).

Lexicography: The art of defining words.

Lovemap: A term coined by John Money and described as the filter through which we see our sexual world, and one that dictates our sexual interests and behavior.

LUG (lesbian until graduation): A term proposed to describe young women who engage in same-sex behavior during college and resume heterosexual dating upon graduation.

MAD: An acronym for Masturbation as Disease.

Masochists: Individuals who enjoy being dominated and/or humiliated sexually.

Mastectomy: Removal of one or both breasts.

Medical massage: A medical treatment for hysteria during the 19th century that involved manual stimulation of female genitals (especially the clitoris) to the point of female orgasm. It has no connection today to modern medical massage, which is a valued (nonsexual) treatment within health care.

Miasma theory: A belief which attributed the cause of illness to chemical agents (vapors) from decaying matter (such as corpses) or sewers.

Misogynist: One who displays behaviors and beliefs of contempt and prejudice toward women.

Misogyny: Contempt and prejudice toward women.

Neurotransmitter: Any substance in the human body that sends chemicals between neurons, e.g., dopamine, norepinephrine, serotonin.

Neutrinos: A neural subatomic particle.

Norepinephrine (NE) or Noradrenalin (NA): A chemical that is a stress hormone and a neurotransmitter.

Nucleus accumbens: A nucleus of the basal ganglia that helps control the release of dopamine, is part of the reward system of the brain, and is involved in experiencing pleasure and addictive behavior.

Onanism: Belief that masturbation causes illness (name originates from reference to Onan in Old Testament).

Onanists: Authors who believed masturbation caused illness (or made vague references to that belief).

Orchiectomy: Removal of one or both testicles.

Orgasm: Muscular contractions in a person that occur when stimulation of the genitals and/or other erogenous areas of the body produce intense muscular tension. The contractions of the muscles and release of tension are associated with pleasurable and euphoric feelings.

OXYTOCIN: A narcotic pain reliever medication.

Pair-bondance: A biological drive to be in a primary relationship.

Paradigm: A model, a pattern, such as a theory or a method.

Paraphilia (now referred to as paraphilic disorder): A condition characterized by persistent and intense atypical sexual arousal patterns that are accompanied by clinically significant distress or impairment (these erotic arousal patterns used to be called sexual deviancy or sexual perversions).

Pedophilia: A type of paraphilia that is characterized by an intense and enduring sexual attraction to a prepubescent child.

Procreational sex: Sex intended to result in babies, so individuals do not try to prevent conception.

Progesterone: A hormone secreted by the corpus luteum to prepare a woman's uterus for pregnancy.

Prostate: An organ that surrounds the urethra at the base of the bladder, controls the release of urine from the bladder, and secretes fluid (alkaline) that is part of the semen emitted during orgasm.

PTSD: Post-traumatic stress disorder is a diagnosis that describes a syndrome of symptoms that may occur when a person is exposed to a traumatic event that personally threatens them, such as rape or violent physical assault.

Pubococcygeal (PC) muscle: A hammock-like muscle that forms the pelvic floor in females.

Rolfing: Therapeutic massage involving intense manipulation of the muscular fascia and internal organs.

SSSS: Society for the Scientific Study of Sexuality.

Sex negative: Teaching, believing, or behaving in a manner that portrays sex as wrong, bad, sinful, or evil.

Sex orientation: Sex-designated status such as male, female, or transgender.

Sexology: The scientific study of sex, which slowly superseded sexosophy as the dominant paradigm.

Sexophobic: Fear of hearing about, seeing, or engaging in sex.

Sexophrenia: (definition by Schmidt, 1967) The state of mind of one whose thoughts are colored or motivated by a conscious or subconscious sex urge. (definition by Peterson, 1999): An avoidance of sex in the conscious mind and the presence of a conflict within a person's psyche about sex. It is a nondiagnostic term to describe a feeling of conflict or anxiety that results from feeling pleasure from a sexual activity and at the same time feeling uncomfortable because of negative messages one has learned about a sexual behavior.

Sexosophy: A term coined by medical psychologist John Money describing the philosophy and folklore of sexuality, often infused with religious moralism.

Sexual expression: The manner in which a person portrays their unique sexuality in behaviors, fantasies, and culturally defined factors.

Sexual Hypercube (h-Cube): A four-dimensional conceptual model of human sexuality that combines the three-dimensional Sexual Identity Cube (i-Cube) with the three-dimensional Sexual Expression Cube (e-Cube) to describe the reciprocal influences between the two and provide a foundation for understanding the wide-ranging diversity inherent in human sexuality.

Sexual identity: The sense of who one is as a sexual being; this is a fundamental human experience comprised of a person's sex orientation (sex-designated status such as male, female, transgender), sexual orientation (such as gay, straight, etc.), and sex-role orientation (such as feminine, masculine, etc.).

Sexual incontinence: An outdated term to describe excessive sexual activity, especially masturbation.

Sexual neurasthenia: An outdated term to describe a condition of general weakness and vague symptoms believed by early American physicians to be caused by masturbation.

Sexual orientation: A component of sexual identity that includes a person's sexual and emotional attraction to another person and the behavior and/or social affiliation that may result from this attraction (Gay, straight, lesbian, bisexual, transgender, etc.).

Sexual Tipping Point (STP): A model of sexual interaction developed by Helen Kaplan and Michael Perelman that describes the specific means by which sexual expression is accomplished by an individual.

Sex-role convergence theory: Jung's belief that as humans age, they "mellow" and modify their stereotypic sex-role attitudes and behaviors (and those changes are usually gradual and unconscious).

Sex-role orientation: An individual's response to society's expectations of their designation as male or female and generally referred to with terms such as *feminine, masculine, androgynous.*

SHAWS: Sexual Health and Wellness Satisfaction.

Sheikh: A term to describe male companions of women flappers during the Roaring Twenties.

SIECUS: Sexuality Information and Education Council of the United States.

Sigmoid colon: The part of the large intestine that is closest to the rectum.

STI/STD: Sexually transmitted infection; also known as sexually transmitted disease.

Stonewall: The term used to refer to the rebellion which occurred at the Stonewall Inn in New York City in 1969 and is generally accepted as the advent of the modern gay rights movement.

Social Darwinism: A theory that humans are subject to the same laws of selection that Darwin thought controlled the evolution of plants and animals.

Spermatorrhea: The name of an outdated medical notion ("disease") of involuntary nocturnal ejaculations.

Testosterone: A hormone that causes the development and maintenance of male sexual characteristics. It is an androgen and is also present in smaller amounts in the female body.

Transgender: An umbrella term used to describe a full range of people who cross or transcend culturally defined categories of gender. The gender identity of transgender people differs to varying degrees from the sex they were assigned at birth.

Transsexual: A descriptive term for individuals who want to change (or have changed) primary and/or secondary sex characteristics via feminizing or masculinizing medical intervention (hormones and/or surgery), accompanied by permanent change in gender role.

Transudation: "Vaginal sweating," in which beads of lubrication form on the vaginal lining during sexual arousal.

Two-spirited: A term sometimes used to describe members of American Indian tribes who are gay, lesbian, or transgender.

Vaginismus: Involuntary contractions of the pubococcygeal muscle that surrounds the vaginal opening, causing pain and/or the partial or full inability to penetrate the vagina.

Vestibularitis: Infection of the tissue around the vaginal opening that usually causes pain during attempts to have intercourse.

WHO: World Health Organization.

WPATH: The World Professional Association for Transgender Health.

REFERENCES

Abel, G., Wiegel, M., & Osborn, C. (2007). Pedophilia and other paraphilia. In L. VanderCreek, F. Peterson, & J. Bley (Eds.), *Innovations in clinical practice: Focus on sexual health*. Sarasota, FL: Professional Resource Press.

Abramov, L. (1976). Sexual life and sexual frigidity among women developing acute myocardial infarction. *Psychosomatic Medicine, 38*, 418–425.

Adler, R., Rosenfeld, L., & Proctor, R. (2015). *Interplay: The process of interpersonal communication* (13th ed.). New York: Oxford University Press.

Aggrawal, A. (2009). *Forensic and medico-legal aspects of sexual crimes and unusual sexual practices*. Boca Raton, FL: CRC Press.

Al-Ghazali, A. (1995). *Breaking the two desires*. Book XXIII of *Revival of the religious sciences*. Cambridge, UK: Islamic Texts Society.

Al-Ghazali, A. (1995). *Disciplining the soul, refining the character, and curing the sickness of the heart*. Book XXII of *Revival of the religious sciences*. Cambridge, UK: Islamic Texts Society.

Albaugh, J. (2012). Reclaiming sex & intimacy after prostate cancer. Pitman, NJ: Anthony J. Jannetti.

Alcorn, L. (2014). Suicide note. Tumblr. Retrieved from www.dailydot.com/news/leelah-alcorn-transgender-tumblr-suicide-note/

Altman, L. (2003). *The forgotten victims of the Holocaust*. Berkeley Heights, NJ: Enslow.

American Academy of Pediatrics (AAP). (2012, March). Policy Statement: Breastfeeding and the use of human milk. *Pediatrics, 129* (3), 827–841.

American Association of Sex Educators, Counselors, & Therapists (2016). AASECT Position Statement on Sex Addiction. Chicago: Author.

American Association of Sex Educators, Counselors, and Therapists. (2016). Standards for certification. Retrieved from www.aasect.org

American College Health Association. (2016). *Addressing sexual and relationship violence on college and university campuses*. Hanover, MD: Author.

American Psychiatric Association. (1980, 1994). *Diagnostic and statistical manual of mental disorders*. Washington, DC: American Psychiatric Publishing.

American Psychiatric Association [APA]. (2013). *Diagnostic and statistical manual of mental disorders* (5th ed.). Arlington, VA: American Psychiatric Publishing.

Aulette, J.R., Wittner, J.G., & Blakely, K. (2009). *Gendered worlds*. New York: Oxford University Press.

Bagley, C., & Tremblay, P. (1997). Suicidal behaviors in homosexual and bisexual males. *Journal of Crisis Intervention and Suicide Prevention, 18*(1).

Bancroft, J. (1987). Hormones, sexuality and fertility in women. *Journal of Zoology, 213*.

Barker-Benfield, B. (1975). Sexual surgery in late-nineteenth-century America. *International Journal of Health Services, 5*(2), 279–298.

Barna, J. (2015). Personal communication with James Barna, JD, PhD at Gilvary Symposium (Sentencing on Pornography Cases), School of Law, University of Dayton, Dayton, Ohio (March 20, 2015).

Beaver, D. (2015). *More than just sex: A committed couple's guide to keeping relationships lively, intimate, and gratifying*. San Diego, CA: Cognella Academic Press.

Beers, M. (2006). *Merck manual of health & aging*. New York: Ballantine.

Bem, D. (1996). Exotic becomes erotic: A developmental theory of sexual orientation. *Psychological Review, 103*.

Bem, S. (1981a). Gender schema theory: A cognitive account of sex typing source. *Psychological Review, 88*, 354.

Bem, S. (1981b). The BSRI and gender schema theory: A reply to Spence and Helmreich. *Psychological Review, 88*, 369–371.

Benjamin, H. (1966). *The transsexual phenomenon*. New York: Julian Press.

Bennett, D. (2016). Banking against Alzheimer's. The scientific American mind. *Scientific American*, July/August, 28–37.

Berlin, F. (2015, March 20). *The paraphilias with an emphasis on pedophilia and viewers of child pornography.* Presentation at the Gilvary Symposium (Sentencing on Pornography Cases), School of Law, University of Dayton, Dayton, Ohio.

Bernstein, D., & Borkovec, T. (1973). Progressive relaxation training: A manual for the helping professions. Champaign, IL: Research Press.

Biden, J. (2016, June 9). An open letter to a courageous young woman.

Bigwood, J. (Executive Producer), & Garnier, K. (Director). (2004). *Iron Jawed Angels* [Film]. New York: HBO Films.

Black, E. (2003, September). The horrifying American roots of Nazi eugenics. History News Network. Retrieved from http://hnn.us/article/1796

Blackwell, E. (1894). *The human element in sex.* London, UK: Churchill.

Bley, J. (1978). *Effects of Knowledge of Sex History in Sexual and Non-Sexual Assault Cases and Related Attitudes* (Master Thesis). Division of Graduate Studies, University of Cincinnati, OH.

Bley, J. (1980). *Effects of prior sex history and physical resistance evidence on verdicts of individuals and simulated juries in rape trials* (Doctoral dissertation). Division of Graduate Studies, University of Cincinnati, OH.

Bley, J., & Peterson, F. (2007). Making sexual health a part of your mental health practice. Found in L. VanderCreek, F. Peterson, & J. Bley (Eds.), *Innovations in clinical practice: Focus of sexual health.* Sarasota, FL: Professional Resources Press.

Blum, D. (2002). *Love at Goon Park: Harry Harlow and the science of affection.* New York: Perseus.

Bockting, W.O. (1999). From construction to context: Gender through the eyes of the transgendered. *Siecus Report, 28*(1), 3–7.

Bombeck, E. (1976). *The grass is always greener over the septic tank.* New York: McGraw-Hill.

Booth, A., Johnson, D., & Granger, D. (1999). Testosterone and men's depression: The role of social behavior. *Journal of Health and Social Behavior, 40*(2).

Bornstein, K. (1994). *Gender outlaw: On men, women, and the rest of us.* New York: Routledge.

Bornstein, K. (2012). *A queer and pleasant danger: The true story of a nice Jewish boy who joins the Church of Scientology, and leaves twelve years later to become the lovely lady she is today.* Boston: Beacon Press.

Bornstein, R., & Masling, J. (1998). Introduction: The psychoanalytic unconscious. In R. Borstein & J. Masling (Eds.), *Empirical perspectives on the psychoanalytic unconscious.* Washington, DC: American Psychological Association.

Bornstein, R., & Pittman, T. (1992). *Perception without awareness: Cognitive, clinical, and social perspectives.* New York: Putnam.

Brach, T. (2003). *Radical acceptance: Embracing your life with the heart of a Buddha.* New York: Bantam.

Brannon, L., Updegraff, J., & Feist, J. (2018). *Health psychology: An introduction to behavior and health* (9th ed.). Boston: Cengage Learning.

Braun-Harvey, D., & Vigorito, M. (2016). Treating out-of-control sexual behaviors—Rethinking sex addiction. New York: Springer.

Brecher, E. (1979). *The sex researcher* (expanded ed.). San Francisco: Specific Press.

Briere, J., & Conte, J. (1993). Self-reported amnesia for abuse in adults molested as children. *Journal of Traumatic Stress, 6,* 21–31.

Briere, J., & Elliott, D. (2003). Prevalence and psychological sequelae of self-reported childhood physical and sexual abuse in general population. *Child Abuse and Neglect, 27,* 1205–1222.

Brownmiller, S. (1975). *Against our will: Men, women and rape.* New York: Ballantine.

Brutto, L., & Yule, M. (2017). Asexuality: Sexual orientation, paraphilia, sexual dysfunction, or none of the above? *Archives of Sexual Behavior, 46*(3), 619–627.

Buffem, H., Loving, A., Warren, I., Small, A., Thorndike, W., Smith, J., & Lyman, C. (1905). *The family physician: A twentieth century medica.* Boston: Woodruff.

Bullough, V. (1994). *Science in the bedroom: A history of sex research.* New York: Basic Books.

Burgess, A., & Holstrum, L. (1979). *Rape crisis and recovery.* New York: R. J. Brady.

Burleson, M.H., Trevathan, W.R., & Todd, M. (2007). In the mood for love or vice versa? Exploring the relations among sexual activity, physical affection, affect, and stress in the daily lives of mid-aged women. *Archives of Sexual Behavior, 36,* 357–368.

Burschka, J., Keune, P., Oy, U., Oschmann, P., & Kuhn, P. (2014). Mindfulness-based interventions in multiple sclerosis: Beneficial effects of tai chi on balance, coordination, fatigue and depression. *BMC Neurology, 14,* 165.

Camilleri, J., & Quinsey, V. (2008). Pedophilia: Assessment and treatment. In D. Law & W. O'Donohue (Eds.), *Sexual deviance: Theory, assessment, and treatment*. New York: Guilford.

Capehart, J. (2015, April 10). Obama comes out against "conversion therapy" to support "Leelah's Law." *Washington Post*. www.washingtonpost.com/blogs/post-partisan/wp/2015/04/10/

Carmody, J., & Baer, R. (2008). How long does a mindfulness-based stress reduction program need to be? A review of class contact hours and effect sizes for psychological distress. Journal of *Clinical Psychology, 65*(6), 627–638.

Carnes, P. (2001). *Out of the shadows: Understanding sexual addiction* (3rd ed.). Center City, MN: Hazelden Press.

Carroll, J. (2007). *Sexuality now: Embracing diversity* (2nd ed.). Belmont, CA: Thomson Wadsworth.

Carroll, J. (2016). *Sexuality now: Embracing diversity* (5th ed.). Boston: Cengage Learning.

Catania, J., & White, W. (1982). Sexuality in an aged sample: Cognitive determinants of masturbation. *Archives of Sexual Behavior, 11*(3).

Centers for Disease Control and Prevention (CDC). (2014). Prevalence and characteristics of sexual violence, stalking, and intimate partner violence victimization: National Intimate Partner and Sexual Violence Survey, United States. Atlanta, GA: Author.

Centers for Disease Control and Prevention. (2016). Website from Division of Nutrition, Physical Activity, and Obesity, National Center for Chronic Disease Prevention and Health Promotion. Retrieved from www.cdc.gov/nccdphp/dnpao/index.html

Charnetski, C., & Brennan, F. (2001). *Feeling good is good for you: How pleasure can boost your immune system and lengthen your life*. Emmaus, PA: Rodale Press.

Cincinnati Enquirer. (Aug. 25, 2012). "Legitimate Rape" rarely causes pregnancy. A1 & A12.

Cohen, A. (2016). *Imbeciles: The Supreme Court, American eugenics, and the sterilization of Carrie Buck*. New York: Penguin/Random House.

Cohen, J., Peterson, F., Bottoms, J., Resch, W., Burgess, B., & Richards, M., (2013). *Healthcare in 21st century Appalachia: The arranged marriage of cultural competency training and relationship-based care approaches*. Paper presented at the Southwestern Social Science Association Annual Conference, New Orleans, Louisiana.

Coleman, E. (2004) *Bisexuality: Challenging our understanding of human sexuality and sexual orientation*. In E.E. Shelp (Ed.), *Sexuality and Medicine* (Vol. 1, pp. 225–242). New York: Reidel.

Coleman, E. (2011). Assessment and treatment of impulsive and compulsive sexual behavior. In M. Grant & J. Potenza (Eds.), *Oxford handbook of impulse control disorders*. New York: Oxford University Press.

Comfort, A. (1987). The joy of sex: A gourmet guide to lovemaking. New York: Pocket Books.

Complainant Credibility in Sexual Offense Cases: A survey of character testimony and psychiatric experts. (1973). *Journal of Criminal Law & Criminology*. Boston, Williams & Wilkins Co., for Northwestern University Law School, *64,* 67–76.

Cooper, A. (2002). *Sex and the internet. A guidebook for clinicians*. New York: Brunner-Routledge.

Cooper, R., Scherer, R., Peterson, F. (1998). Training organizational assessment and consultation skills. *Psychologist-Manager Journal, 2*(2), 59–66.

Cox, L. (2015). *Address to student body on transgender liberation*. Nutter Center, Wright State University, Dayton, Ohio.

Cutler, W.B. (1991). *Love cycles: The science of intimacy*. New York: Villard.

Davis, K. (1929). *Factors in the Sex Life of Twenty-Two Hundred Women*. New York: Harper.

Dawson, S., Suschinsky, K., & Lalumière, M. (2012). Sexual fantasies and viewing time across the menstrual cycle: A dairy study. *Archives of Sexual Behavior, 41,* 173–183.

Debrot, A., Meuwly, N., Muise, A., Impett, E., & Schoebi, D. (2017, January). More than just sex: Affection mediates the association between sexual activity and well-being. *Personality and Social Psychology Bulletin*.

Delmonico, D., & Griffin, E. (2014). *Sexual addiction: Assessment, management, and treatment*. New York: Routledge.

DeLong, R., Durkin, K., & Hundersmarck, S. (2010). An exploratory analysis of the cognitive distortions of a sample of men arrested in internet sex stings. *Journal of Sexual Aggression*, Vol. 16, No. 1, pp. 1–12.

Department of Veterans Affairs (VA). (2013). Core messages from the National Center for Health Promotion and Disease Prevention, Office of Patient Care Services. Durham, NC: Author.

Diamond, L. (2008) *Sexual fluidity: Understanding women's love and desire*. Cambridge, MA: Harvard University Press.

Dickinson, R., & Beam, L. (1932). *A thousand marriages*. Baltimore: Williams & Wilkins.

Dockterman, E. (2018). Inside sex offender treatment. Time (May 21, 2018).

Durant, W. (2001). *Heroes of history: A brief history of civilization from ancient times to the dawn of the modern age.* New York: Simon & Schuster.

Durant, W., & Durant, A. (1935–1975). *The story of civilization.* New York: Simon & Schuster.

Ellison, C. (2000). *Women's sexualities: Generations of women share intimate secrets of sexual self-acceptance.* Oakland, CA: New Harbinger.

Erikson, E. (1968). *Youth: Identity and crisis.* New York: Norton.

Evans, R.W., & Couch, R. (2001). Orgasm and migraine. *Headache: Journal of Head and Face Pain, 111*(6), 512–514.

Fausto-Sterling, A. (2000). *Sexing the body: Gender politics and the construction of sexuality.* New York: Basic Books.

Federal Bureau of Investigation (FBI). (2016). *Uniform Crime Report.* Washington, DC: Author.

Finkelhor, D., Hotaling, G., Lewis, I., & Smith, C. (1990). Child sexual abuse in a national survey of adult men and women: Prevalence characteristics and risk factors. *Child Abuse and Neglect.* (14) 1, 19–28.

Finkelhor, D., Ormrod, R., Turner, H., & Hamby, S. (2005). The victimization of children and youth: A comprehensive, national survey. *Child Maltreatment, 10,* 5–25.

Finkelhor, D., Turner, H., Ormrod, R., Hamby, S., & Kracke, K. (2009). Children's exposure to violence: A Comprehensive National Survey (NCJ 227744). Washington, DC: U.S. Department of Justice, Office of Justice Programs.

Fisher, B., Cullen, F., & Turner, M. (2000). *The sexual victimization of college women.* Washington, DC: National Institute of Justice, Bureau of Justice Statistics.

Fisher, H. (2004). *Why we love: The nature and chemistry of romantic love.* New York: Holt.

Fisher, H., Aron, A., Mashek, D., Li, H., & Brown, L. (2002). Defining the brain systems of lust, romantic attraction, and attachment. *Archives of Sexual Behavior, 31*(5).

Flores, A., Herman, J., Gates, G., & Brown, T. (2016). *How many adults identify as transgender in the United States?* Los Angeles: Williams Institute, University of California, Los Angeles.

Floyd, W. (2017). *Foundation of recovery program.* Unpublished manuscript.

Forari, R., Zoppi, A., Preti, P., Rinaldi, A., Marasi, G., Vanasia, A., & Mugellini, A. (2002). Sexual activity and plasma testosterone levels in hypertensive males. *American Journal of Hypertension, 15*(3).

Freud, S. (1896). *The etiology of hysteria.* Paper presented to the Society for Psychiatry and Neurology.

Freud, S. (1927). The psychological consequences of the anatomical distinction between the sexes (Trans. J. Strachey). *International Journal of Psycho-Analysis, 8*(2), 133–142.

Freud, S. (1954). The *origins of psychoanalysis: Letters to Wilhelm Fliess, drafts, and notes (1887–1902).* New York: Basic Books.

Friedrich, W., Fisher, J., Broughton, D., Houston, M., & Shafran, C. (1998). Normative sexual behavior in children: A contemporary sample. *Pediatrics* April 1998, 101 (4) e9. DOI: 10.1542/peds.101.4.e9

Frumin, A. (2016). Brock Turner registers as a sex offender in Ohio. (U.S. News. Posted September 6, 2016). https://www.nbcnews.com/news/us-news/brock-turner-registers-sex-offender-ohio-n643376

Gander, K. (2014, December 30). Transgender teenager Leelah Alcorn took her life because "parents would not allow her to transition." *Independent.*

Giles, G., Severi, G., English, D., & McCredie, M. (2003). Sexual factors and prostate cancer. *British Journal of Urology, 92*(3).

Gladwell, M. (2005). *Blink: The power of thinking without thinking.* New York: Back Bay.

Good, B. (1994). *Medicine, rationality, and experience: An anthropological perspective.* Oxford, UK: Cambridge University Press.

Gordon, L. (2002). *The moral property of women: A history of birth control politics in America.* Champaign-Urbana: University of Illinois Press.

Gould, G. (1949). *Gould's pocket pronouncing medical dictionary of the principal words used in medicine and the collateral sciences* (11th ed.). Philadelphia: P. Blakiston's Son & Company.

Goyal, M., Singh, S., Sibinga, E., Gould, N., Rowland-Seymour, A., Sharma, R., & Haythornthwaite, J. (2014). Meditation programs for psychological stress and well-being: A systematic review and meta-analysis. *JAMA Internal Medicine, 174*(3), 357–368.

Greenberg, J., Bruess, C., & Conklin, S. (2007). *Exploring the dimensions of human sexuality.* Burlington, MA: Jones and Bartlett Learning.

Grinonneau-Denton, A. (2018). Marriage and Family Therapists' Comfort and Willingness to Discuss Sexual Issues of the Couples They Work With. Dissertation in progress at the University of Akron.

H.R. 3-112th Congress: No Taxpayer Funding for Abortion Act. www.GovTrack us. 2011. May 4, 2018. https://www.govtrack.us/congressbills/112/hr3

Hackett, A. (2016, May 5). Becoming Zay: Growing up trans. *Yellow Springs News*.

Haffey, B., Peterson, F., Bley, J., & Glaus, K. (2007). Addressing sexual health concerns of sexual minority clients. Found in L. VanderCreek, F. Peterson, & J. Bley (Eds.), *Innovations in clinical practice: Focus on sexual health*. Sarasota, FL: Professional Resource Press.

Hall, G.S. (1904). *Adolescence: Its psychology and its relations to physiology, anthropology, sociology, sex, crime, religion, and education*. New York: Appleton.

Hammack, P., & Cohler, B. (2009). *The story of sexual identity: Narrative perspectives on the gay and lesbian life course*. Cambridge, UK: Oxford University Press.

Hammond, C. (Ed.). (1990). *Handbook of hypnotic suggestions and metaphors*. New York: Norton.

Handy, C. (2000). *21 Ideas for managers*. San Francisco: Jossey-Bass.

Hanson, K., & Morton-Bourgon, K. (2005). The characteristics of persistent sexual offenders: A meta-analysis of recidivism studies. *Journal of Consulting and Clinical Psychology, 73*(6).

Hare, E. (1962). Masturbatory insanity: The history of an idea. *Journal of Mental Science, 108*, 1–25.

Hase, S., Davies, A., & Dick, B. (1999, September). The Johari Window and the dark side of organizations. *UltiBASE In-Site*. Lismore, Australia: Southern Cross University.

Heh, V. (2017). Statistical Consultation Report (Appendix A). Athens: Ohio University.

Henig, R. (2017, January). Rethinking gender. Article within special issue on the gender revolution. *National Geographic* magazine. Washington, DC: National Geographic Society.

Herbenick, D. (2009). *Because it feels good: A woman's guide to sexual pleasure and satisfaction*. New York: Rodale.

Herbenick, D., & Schick, V. (2011). *Read my lips: A complete guide to the vagina and vulva*. New York: Rowman & Littlefield.

Herdt, G. (2005). *The Sambia: Ritual, sexuality, and change in Papua New Guinea*. New York: Wadsworth.

Herman, J. (1992). *Trauma and recovery: The aftermath of violence from domestic abuse to political terror*. New York: Basic Books.

Hirschfeld, M. (1937). *Sexual history of the World War: From reports collected by the Institute for Sexual Science*. New York: Falstaff.

Holder, E. (2011). Comments during an address at the National Strategy Conference on Combating Child Exploitation in San Jose, California, May 19, 2011.

Hyde, J., & DeLamater, J. (2011). *Understanding human sexuality*. New York: McGraw-Hill.

Hyde, J.S., & DeLamater, J.D. (2014). *Understanding human sexuality* (12th ed.). New York: McGraw-Hill.

Ip, S., Chung, M., & Raman, G. (2007). *Tufts-New England Medical Center Evidence-based Practice Center: Breastfeeding and maternal and infant health outcomes in developed countries*. Evidence Report on Technology Assessment (Full Report): 153.

Jahnke, R., Larkey, L., Rogers, C., & Etnier, J. (2010). A comprehensive review of health benefits of qigong and tai chi. *American Journal Health Promotion, 24*(6), e1–e25.

Jehl, D. (1994, December 10). Surgeon General forced to resign by White House. *New York Times*.

Jonsson, P. (2011, December 29). Breastfeeding moms protest at Target stores, but US public is real mark. *Christian Science Monitor*. Retrieved from www.csmonitor.com/USA/Society/2011/1229/Breastfeeding-moms

Jorgensen, C. (1967). *Christine Jorgensen: A Personal Autobiography*. New York: Bantam Books.

Jung, C. (1960). The stages of life. In G. Adler, M. Fordham, & H. Read (Eds.), *The collected works of C. J. Jung*: Vol. 8. *The structure and dynamics of the psyche*. London, UK: Routledge & Kegan Paul.

Jung, C. (1971). The relations between the ego and the unconscious. In Campbell, J. (Ed.), *The portable Jung*. New York: Viking Press.

Kafka, M. (1997). Hypersexual desire in males: An operational definition and clinical implications for males with paraphilia and paraphilia-related disorders. *Archives of Sexual Behavior, 26*(5), 505–526.

Kail, R., & Cavanaugh, J. (2004). *Human development: A life-span view* (3rd ed.). Belmont, CA: Wadsworth/Thompson.

Kail, R., & Cavanaugh, J. (2015). *Human development: A life-span view*. New York: Wadsworth.

Kaplan, H. (1974). *The new sexual health*. New York: Brunner/Mazel.

Kavanaugh-Jones, B. (Executive Producer), & Nichols, J. (Director). (2016). *Loving* [Film]. United States: Focused Films.

Keesling, B. (2001). *The good girl guide to bad girl sex*. New York: M. Evans.

Kellogg, E. (1892). *Science in the kitchen*. Battle Creek, MI: Modern Medicine Publishing.

Kellogg, H. (1888). *The thirty-nine suspicious signs of self-abuse* [Pamphlet]. Battle Creek, MI: Author.

Kinsey, A., Pomeroy, W., & Martin, C. (1948). *Sexual behavior in the human male*. Philadelphia: W.B. Saunders.

Kinsey, A., Pomeroy, W., Martin, C., & Gephard, P. (1953). *Sexual behavior in the human female*. Philadelphia: W.B. Saunders.

Klein, M. (2012). *America's war on sex: The continuing attack on law, lust, and liberty* (2nd ed.). Santa Barbara, CA: Praeger.

Komisaruk, B., Beyer-Flores, C., & Whipple, B. (2006). *The science of orgasm*. Baltimore: Johns Hopkins University Press.

Krafft-Ebing, R. (1900). *Psychopathia sexualis* (English trans. 1886). New York: Physicians and Surgeons.

Krantz, D., & McCeney, K. (2002). Effects of psychological and social factors on organic disease: A critical assessment of research on coronary heart disease. *Annual Review of Psychology*, *53*, 341–369.

Krebs, C., Linquist, C., Warner, T., Fisher, B., & Martin, S. (2006). The Campus Sexual Assault (CSA) Study. Washington, DC: National Institute of Justice.

Krisanaprakornkit, T., Krisanaprakornkit, W., Piyavhatkul, N., & Laopaiboon, M. (2006). Meditation therapy for anxiety disorders. Cochrane Database of Systematic Reviews, Cochrane Art. No: CD004998, DOI: 10.1002/14651858. CD004998.pub2.

Krull, M. (1986). *Freud and his father*. New York: Norton.

Kupferman, I. (1991). Hypothalamus and limbic system motivation. In E.R. Kandel, J.H. Schwartz, & T.M. Jessell (Eds.), *Principle of neural science* (3rd ed.). New York: Elsevier.

Larson, E. (1995). Sex, Race, and Science: Eugenics in the Deep South. Baltimore: Johns Hopkins University Press.

Last, C. (2013, February 13). The great (ape) taxonomy debate [Blog]. *Scientific American*.

Laumann, E., Gagnon, J., Michael, R., & Michaels, S. (1994). *The social organization of sexuality: Sexual practice in the United States*. Chicago: University of Chicago.

Lê, M.G. (1989). Characteristics of reproductive life and risk of breast cancer in a case-control study of young nulliparous women. *Journal of Clinical Epidemiology*, *42*(12).

Leiblum, S., Bachmann, G., Kemmann, E., Colburn, D., & Swartzman, L. (1983). Vaginal atrophy in the postmenopausal woman: The importance of sexual activity and hormones. *JAMA*, *249*(16).

Leitzmann, M., Willett, W., & Giovannucci, E. (2004). Ejaculation frequency and subsequent risk of prostate cancer. *Journal of the American Medical Association*, *291*(13).

Leunge, D., Chan, C., Tsang, H., & Jones, A. (2011). Tai chi as an intervention to improve balance and reduce falls in older adults: A systematic and meta-analytic review. *Alternative Therapies in Health and Medicine*, *17*(1), 40–48.

LeVay, S., & Valente, S. (2003). *Human sexuality*. New York: W.H. Freeman.

LeVay, S., Baldwin, J., & Baldwin, J. (2015). *Discovering human sexuality* (3rd ed.). Sunderland, MA: Sinauer Associates.

Levenson, J., Brannon, Y., Fortney, T., & Baker, J. (2007). Public perceptions about sex offenders and community protection policies. *Analyses of Social Issues and Public Policy*, *7*(1).

Levine, S. (2007). *Demystifying love: Plain talk for the mental health professional*. New York: Routledge.

Ley, D. (2018). Compulsive Sexual Behavior Disorder in ICD-11: What does this mean, for advocacy against sex addiction diagnosis? Psychologytoday.com. Posted Jan 24, 2018. https://www.psychologytoday.com/us/comment/973268

Lips, H. (2005). *Sex and gender*. New York: McGraw-Hill.

Litin, S. (2009). *Mayo Clinic family health book*. Des Moines, IA: Time Home Entertainment.

Locker, S. (2005). The complete idiot's guide to amazing sex. New York: Alpha Books.

Loftus, E., & Ketcham, K. (1994). *The myth of repressed memory: False memories and allegations of sexual abuse*. New York: St. Martin's Press.

Lombardi, K. (2009). Sexual Assault on Campus Shrouded in Secrecy: High Rates of Rape, Closed Hearings and Confusing Laws. Center for Public Integrity. www.publicintegrity.org/2009/12/01/9047/sexual-assault-campus-shrouded-secrecy

Luft, J., & Ingham, H. (1955). *The Johari window, a graphic model of interpersonal awareness*. Proceedings of the Western Training Laboratory in Group Development. Los Angeles: University of California, Los Angeles.

Maass, V. (2009). *The Cinderella test: Would you really want the shoe to fit?* Santa Barbara, CA: Praeger.

Maier, T. (2009). *The masters of sex: The life and times of William Masters and Virginia Johnson.* New York: Basic Books.

Margolis, S. (2002). *Johns Hopkins medical guide to health after 50.* Redding, CT: Medletter Associates.

Mark, K., Janssen, E., & Milhausen, R. (2011). Infidelity in heterosexual couples: Demographic, interpersonal, and personality-related predictors of extra-dyadic sex. *Archives of Sexual Behavior.* doi:10.1007/s10508-0111-9771-z

Martin, P. (2016). The rape prone culture of academic contexts: Fraternities and athletics. *Gender and Society, 30*(1), 30–43.

Masson, J. (1984). *The assault on truth: Freud's suppression of the seduction theory.* New York: Farrar, Straus and Giroux.

Masters, W., & Johnson, V. (1966). *Human sexual response.* Boston: Little, Brown.

Masters, W., & Johnson, V., & Kolodny, R. (1986). *Masters and Johnson on sex and human loving.* Boston: Little, Brown.

Masters, W., Johnson, V., & Kolodny, R. (1995). *Human sexuality* (5th ed.). New York: Harper-Collins.

McAnulty, R., & Burnette, M. (2003). *Exploring human sexuality: Making healthy decisions.* Boston: Pearson Education.

McCammon, S., Knox, D., & Schacht, C. (2004). *Choices in sexuality.* Cincinnati, OH: Atomic Dog.

McGovern, J., & Murray, P. (2016). *Consent communication: What does it mean for student athletes?* Paper presented at the NCAA National Conference, San Antonio, TX.

Meaddough, E., Olive, D., Gallup, P., & Kliman, H. (2002). Sexual activity, orgasm and tampon use are associated with a decreased risk for endometriosis. *Gynecologic and Obstetric Investigation, 53.*

Mears, B. (2010, May 17). Supreme Court: Sex offenders can be held indefinitely. CNN. Retrieved from news.blogs.cnn.com/2010/05/17/supreme-court-says-sex-offenders-can.

Merriam-Webster. (1986). *Webster's third new international dictionary of the English language.* Springfield, MA: Author.

Merriam-Webster. (2016). *The Merriam-Webster Dictionary.* Springfield, MA: Author.

Meston, C., & Buss, D. (2007). Why humans have sex. *Archives of Sexual Behavior, 36,* 417–507.

Mohler-Kuo, M., Dowdall, G., Koss, M., & Wechsler, H. (2004). Correlates of rape while intoxicated in a national sample of college women. *Journal of Studies on Alcoholism, 65*(1), 37–45.

Mokdad, A., Marks, J., Stroup, D., & Gerberding, J. (2004). Actual causes of death in the United States, 2000. *Journal of American Medical Association, 291*(10), 1238–1245.

Money, J. (1985). *The destroying angel: Sex, fitness, and food in the legacy of degeneracy theory, Graham Crackers, Kellogg's Corn Flakes, and American health history.* Amherst, NY: Prometheus Books.

Money, J. (1986). *Lovemaps: Clinical concepts of sexual/erotic health and pathology, paraphilia, and gender transposition in childhood, adolescence, and maturity.* New York: Irvington.

Money, J. (1994). *Reinterpreting the unspeakable.* New York: Continuum.

Money, J. (1998). *Sin, science, and the sex police: Essays on sexology & sexosophy.* Amherst, NY: Prometheus.

Money, J., Wainwright, G., & Hingsburger, D. (1991). *The breathless orgasm.* Buffalo, NY: Prometheus.

Mourdock, R. (2012). *Rape, Pregnancy and God's Plan.* www.politico.com/story/2012/10/mourdock-rape-pregnancy-and-gods-plan-082795

Mullen, M. (2010, December 15). Joint Chiefs of Staff testimony to Senate on ending ban on gays in military. 156 Cong. Rec., Pt. 15, 22138.

Murrell, T.G.C. (1995). The potential for oxytocin (OT) to prevent breast cancer: A hypothesis. *Breast Cancer Research and Treatment, 35.*

Murthy, V. (2015, June 25). The Surgeon General's prescription for happiness. TED MED Talk [Video]. Retrieved from www.tedmed.com/talks/show?id=527633

Mutrux, G. (Producer), & Condon, B. (Director). (2004). *Kinsey* [Film]. United States: American Zoetrope Myriad Pictures.

National Center for Victims of Crime (NCVC). (2008). *Child sexual abuse.* June 2–4, Portland, Oregon.

National Sexual Violence Resource Center (NSVRC). (2011). *Child sexual abuse prevention.* Enola, PA: Author.

Nichols, F., & Humenick, S. (1988). *Childbirth education: Practice, research, and theory.* Philadelphia: W.B. Saunders.

Nichols, M. (2000). Therapy with sexual minorities. In S. Leiblum & R. Rosen (Eds.), *The principles and practice of sex therapy* (3rd ed., pp. 335–367). New York: Guilford.

Nicolosi, A., Moreira, E., Villa, M., & Glasser, D. (2004). A population study of the association between sexual function, sexual satisfaction and depressive symptoms in men. *Journal of Affective Disorders, 82.*

Noymer, A., & Garenne, M. (2000). The 1918 influenza epidemic's effects on sex differentials in mortality in the United States. *Population Development Review, 26*(3), 565–581.

Nutt, A. (2016). *Becoming Nicole: The transformation of an American family.* New York: Random House.

Olson, T. (2010, January 8). The conservative case for gay marriage. *Newsweek* https://www.newsweek.com/con-servative-case-gay-marriage-70923

Oshinsky, D. (2016). *Bellevue: Three centuries of medicine and mayhem at America's most storied hospital.* New York: Doubleday.

Palmore, E. (1983). Predictors of the longevity difference: A 25-year follow-up. *Gerontologist, 22*(6).

Parker, A. (Executive Producer & Director). (1994). *The Road to Wellville* [Film]. United States: Beacon Communications.

Patient Protection and Affordable Care Act. H.R. Res. 3590, 111th Cong. (2009). Retrieved from https://www.govtrack.us/congress/bills/111/hr3590

Paul, R. (2012). If it's an Honest Rape, Women Should go to the Emergency Room. www.crooksandliars.com/heather/ron-paul-if-its-an-honest-rape-women-should-g

Perel, E. (2006). *Mating in captivity: Reconciling the erotic and domestic.* New York: HarperCollins.

Perelman, M. (2006). The sexual tipping point: A model to conceptualize etiology, diagnosis and combination treatment of female and male sexual dysfunction. *Journal of Sexual Medicine*, 3 (Suppl. 1), 52.

Perelman, M. (2009). The sexual tipping point: A mind/body model for sexual medicine. *Journal of Sexual Medicine, 6*(3), 629–632.

Perelman, M. (2014). The history of sexual medicine. In APA History of Sexuality and Psychology, Vol. II: Contextual Approaches (pp. 137–179). Washington, DC: American Psychological Association.

Persson, G. (1981). Five-year mortality in a 70-year-old urban population in relation to psychiatric diagnosis, personality, sexuality and early parental death. *Acta Psychiatrica Scandinavca, 64*(3).

Peterson, F. (1989). *Promoting fathering and greater father interaction with infants via the father & baby class.* Paper presented at the meeting of the Annual Men's Studies Conference, National Organization of Changing Men, Pittsburgh, Pennsylvania.

Peterson, F. (1990). *Promoting fathering via family centered childbirth education.* Paper presented at the Annual Convention of the American Psychological Association, Boston.

Peterson, F. (1999). Dispelling Sexual Myths. *Weekly Impact,* March. Volume 7, Number 10.

Peterson, F. (2000). "Why are Americans so weird about breastfeeding?" *Weekly Impact, 8*(10).

Peterson, F. (2007). *The complexity of sexual diversity: Sexual identity cube and self-awareness exercise.* In L. VanderCreek, F. Peterson, & J. Bley (Eds.), *Innovations in clinical practice: Focus on sexual health.* Sarasota, FL: Professional Resource Press.

Peterson, F., & Bley, J. *The pleasure playbook* (unpublished manuscript).

Peterson, F., & Carter, R. (2010). *Re-defining Sexual Identity and Introduction to the Sexual Health and Wellness Satisfaction Scale* (unpublished manuscript). Paper presented to the Annual Conference of the Ohio Psychological Association, Columbus, Ohio.

Peterson, F., Cooper, R., & Scherer, R. (1991). *Relationship between perceptions of managerial competence and sex role.* Paper presented at the National Conference of the American Association of Sex Educators, Counselors, and Therapists, Orlando, Florida.

Peterson, F., Cooper, R., & Scherer, R. (2000). Organizations change: Initial results in a health care setting. *Psychological Reports, 86*(2), 608–610.

Peterson, F., Dobbins, J., Coleman, F., & Razzouk, J. (2007). Culturally competent sex therapy. In L. VanderCreek, F. Peterson, & J. Bley (Eds.), *Innovations in clinical practice: Focus on sexual health.* Sarasota, FL: Professional Resource Press.

Peterson, F., & Peterson, C. (2007). A healthcare professional's guide to contemporary sexual myths. In L. VanderCreek, F. Peterson, & J. Bley (Eds.), *Innovations in clinical practice: Focus on sexual health.* Sarasota, FL: Professional Resource Press.

Peterson, F., Peterson, K., Redman, E., Nicholls, C., & Blasenak, B. (1986). *Transition into parenthood: A pilot project of the expectant couple's enrichment class.* Paper presented at the American Psychological Association Annual Convention, Washington, DC.

Peterson, F., Peterson, K., Redman, E., Nicholls, C., & Blasenak, B. (1991). *Family centered childbirth education.* Paper presented at the Annual Convention of the American Society for Psychoprophylaxis in Obstetrics, Atlanta, Georgia.

Peterson, F., & Roe, K. (1994). *Repressed memories of childhood sexual abuse: A preliminary report.* Paper presented at the Annual Conference of the International Society for Traumatic Stress Studies, Chicago.

Peterson, F., & Roe, K. (1995). *Recalling childhood sexual abuse: Suspicions and "being sure."* Paper presented at the Annual Convention of the American Psychological Association, New York.

Peterson, F., Williams, M., Resch, W., Thull, J., & Dennis, R. (2011). *Better Serving Veterans in Ohio Appalachia: Using the Mountain Metaphor to Develop Cultural Competency Among Healthcare Professionals.* Paper presented at the 34th Annual Conference of the Appalachian Studies Association, Richmond, Kentucky.

Peterson, K., & Peterson, F. (1993). Family centered perinatal education. In F. Nichols (Ed.), *Clinical issues in perinatal and women's health nursing.* Philadelphia: J.B. Lippincott.

Peterson, K., Peterson, F., Redman, E., Nicholls, C., & Blasenak, B. (1987). Strike while the iron is hot: Combining childbirth education, parenting training, and social support. *International Journal of Childbirth Education, 2*(2).

Planned Parenthood Federation of America. (2007). The White Paper: The health benefits of sexual expression. New York: Planned Parenthood Federation of America in Cooperation with the Society for the Scientific Study of Sexuality.

Praunheim, R. (Producer & Director). (1999). *The Einstein of Sex* [Film]. Berlin, Germany: Praunheim Production Company.

Public Broadcasting System. (2016). *The American Experience: The Miner Wars.* Retrieved from http://www.pbs.org/wgbh/americanexperience/films/theminewars/

Raj, R., Raj, M., & Peterson, F. (2010). *Joyful, healthy sex: Fundamental education.* Delhi, India: B.R. Publishing.

Reamy, K., White, S.E., & Daniel, W.C. (1982). Sexuality and pregnancy: A prospective study. *Journal of Reproductive Medicine, 27*(6).

Risen, C. (2007). How to do a sexual health assessment. In L. VanderCreek, F. Peterson, & J. Bley (Eds.), *Innovations in clinical practice: Focus of sexual health.* Sarasota, FL: Professional Resources Press.

Roach, M. (2008). *Bonk: The curious coupling of science and sex.* New York: Norton.

Robinson, W.J. (1933). *Medical sex dictionary.* New York: Eugenics.

Robinson, W.J. (1934). *Sexual impotence* (19th ed.). New York: Eugenics.

Rossing, M., Standford J., Weiss, N., & Daling R. (1996). Indices of exposure to fetal and sperm antigens in relation to the occurrence of breast cancer. *Epidemiology, 7*(3).

Ryan, C., & Jetha, C. (2010). *Sex at dawn: How we mate, why we stray, and what it means for modern relationships.* New York: HarperCollins.

Saigh, P., & Bremner, J. (Eds.). (1999). *Posttraumatic Stress Disorder: A comprehensive text.* Boston: Allyn & Bacon.

Sanday, P. (1996). Rape prone versus rape-free campus cultures. *Violence Against Women, 2*(2), 191–208.

Santorum, P. (2012). *Rape and Pregnancy.* www.theguardian.com/commentisfree/believe/2012/jan/25/rick-santorum-rape-pregnancy

Santos-Iglesias, P., Sierra, J.C., & Vallejo-Medina, P. (2013). Predictors of sexual assertiveness: The role of sexual desire, arousal, attitudes, and partner abuse. *Archives of Sexual Behavior, 42*, 1043–1052.

Satcher, D. (2001). The Surgeon General's call to action to promote sexual health and responsible sexual behavior. Rockville, MD: Office of Surgeon General/Office of Population Affairs.

Sayle, A. (2001). Sexual activity during late pregnancy and risk of preterm delivery. *Obstetrics and Gynecology, 97*(2).

Scherer, R., Canty, A., Peterson, F., & Cooper, R. (1995). Identification of managerial behavior dimensions in a federal health care agency. *Psychological Reports, 76*(2), 675–679.

Scherer, R., Peterson, F., & Cooper, R. (1996, July/August). Training resources decision matrix. *Training Today.*

Schmaltz, H., Southern, D., Ghali, W., Jelinski, S., Parsons, G., King, K., & Maxwell, C. (2007). Living alone, patient sex, and mortality after acute myocardial infarction. *Journal of General Internal Medicine, 22*, 572–578.

Schmidt, J. (1984). *Lecher's lexicon: A sizzling erotic dictionary.* New York: Bell.

Schultz, D., & Schultz, S. (2004). *The history of modern psychology.* Belmont, CA: Wadsworth/Thompson Learning.

Seto, M. (2012). *Child pornography offender characteristics and risk to reoffend.* Testimony to the United States Sentencing Commission (February 6, 2012), Washington, D.C.

Seto, M. (2013). *Assessment and treatment of Internet sex offenders.* Paper presented at the national conference of the Association for the Treatment of Sex Abusers, Chicago.

Setoodeh, R. (2008, July 8). Young, gay, and murdered. *Newsweek* https://www.newsweek.com/young-gay-and-murdered-junior-high-92787

Sexuality Information & Education Council for the United States (SIECUS). (2001). SIECUS Report, Vol. 30–31. Charlottesville, VA: Author.

Shapiro, F. (1989). Efficacy of the eye movement desensitization procedure in the treatment of traumatic memories. *Journal of Traumatic Stress, 2,* 199–223.

Shapiro, F. (Ed.). (2002). *EMDR as an integrative psychotherapy approach: Experts of diverse orientations explore the paradigm prism.* Washington, DC: American Psychological Association.

Shear, M. (2015, April 9). Obama to call for end to conversion therapies for gay and transgender youth. *New York Times.* Retrieved from https://www.nytimes.com/2015/04/09/us/politics/obama-to-call-for-end-to-conversion-therapies-for-gay-and-transgender-youth.html

Shprintzen, A. (2013). *The vegetarian crusade: The rise of an American reform movement, 1817–1921.* Chapel Hill: University of North Carolina Press.

Siegel, D.J. (2002). The developing mind and the resolution of trauma: Some ideas about information processing and an interpersonal neurobiology of psychotherapy. In *EMDR As An Integrative Psychotherapy Approach.* Shapiro, F. (Ed). Washington, DC: American Psychological Association, 85–121.

Singh, D., Meyer, W., Zambarano, R., & Hurlbert, D. (1998). Frequency and timing of coital orgasm in women desirous of becoming pregnant. *Archives of Sexual Behavior, 27*(1).

Smith, G., Frankel, S., & Yarnell, J. (1997). Sex and death: Are they related? Findings from the Caerphilly cohort study. *British Medical Journal, 315*:1641.

Stiefelhagen, S. (1994). De social erotische dienstverlening. In *Seks, lang zo gek nogniet. Symposium over seksualiteit en relaties in de psychiatrie.* Rutgers Stichting, Eindhoven, Netherlands. [The Social-Erotic Services. Presentation in the Symposium on Sexuality, Relationships and Psychiatry, Rutgers Foundation, Eindhoven.]

Stone, G. (2017). *Sex and the Constitution.* New York: Liveright.

Strong, B., DeVault, S., Sayad, B., & Yarber, W. (2005). *Human sexuality: Diversity in contemporary America* (5th ed.). Boston: McGraw-Hill.

Sugrue, D. (2007). Sexual addiction/compulsivity—Diagnosis and treatment. In L. VanderCreek, F. Peterson, & J. Bley (Eds.), *Innovations in clinical practice: Focus on sexual health.* Sarasota, FL: Professional Resource Press.

Taylor, T. (1996). *The prehistory of sex: Four million years of human sexual culture.* New York: Bantam.

Thomas, J. (December 3, 2009). Report: Universities try to cover up rapes. *USA Today,* first published in the *Indianapolis Star.*

Timm, T. (2009). "Do I really have to talk about sex?" Encouraging beginning therapists to integrate sexuality into couples' therapy. *Journal of Couple & Relationship Therapy, 8,* 15–33. doi:10.1080/15332690802626692

Tissot, S. (1832). *A treatise on the disorders produced by onanism.* First published in Latin under title: *Tentamen de morbis ex manustupratione,* in *Dissertatio de febribus biliosis* (1758 ed.). New York: Collins & Hannay.

Tur-Kaspa, I., Maor, Y., Levran, D., Yonish, M., Mashiach, S., & Dor, J. (1994). How often should infertile men have intercourse to achieve conception? *Fertility and Sterility, 62*(2).

Van der Kolk, B. (1994). The body keeps the score: Memory and the evolving psychobiology of PTS. *Harvard Review of Psychiatry, 1*(5), 253–265.

Van der Kolk, B. (2002). Beyond the Talking Cure: Somatic Experience and Subcortical Imprints in the Treatment of Trauma. In *EMDR As An Integrative Psychotherapy Approach.* F. Shapiro, (Ed). Washington, DC: American Psychological Association, 57–83.

Van der Kolk, B. (2014). *The body keeps the score: Brain, mind, and body in the healing of trauma.* New York: Random House.

Van Lunsen, R., & Laan, E. (2004). Genital vascular responsiveness and sexual feelings in midlife women: Psychophysiologic, brain, and genital imaging studies. *Menopause, 11*(6 Pt 2).

Vogel, M. (2015). *Raising Zay* [Film]. Retrieved from www.ciccinnati.com/story/news/2015/02/21/transgender/ Cincinnati.

Von Sydow, Kirsten. (1999). Sexuality during pregnancy and after childbirth: A metacontent analysis of 59 studies. *Journal of Psychosomatic Research, 47*(1).

Wallace, A. (2009, September 14). The rise and fall of the Cincinnati boner king. *Gentleman's Quarterly* https://www.gq.com/story/smilin-bob-enzyte-steve-warshak-male-enhancement

Walling, W. (1904). *Sexology*. Philadelphia: Puritan.

Walters, A., & Williamson, G. (1998). Sexual satisfaction predicts quality of life: A study of adult amputees. *Sexuality and Disability, 16*(2).

Weeks, D. (2002). Sex for the mature adult: Health, self-esteem and countering ageist stereotypes. *Sexual and Relationship Therapy, 17*(3).

Weiss, R. (2013). *Cruise control: Understanding sex addiction in gay men* (2nd ed.). Carefree, AZ: Gentle Path.

Westheimer, R. (2007). Sex for dummies. Hoboken, NJ.: Wiley Publishing, Inc.

Wilcox, A., Weinberg, C., & Baird, D. (1995). Timing of sexual intercourse in relation to ovulation: Effects on the probability of conception, survival of the pregnancy, and sex of the baby. *New England Journal of Medicine, 333*(23).

Williams, C. (1990). Texas Candidate's Comment About Rape Causes a Furor, New York. https://www.nytimes.com/1990/03/26/us/texas-candidate-s-comment-about-rape-causes-a-furor.html

Williams, L.M. (1995). Recovered memories of abuse in women with documented child sexual victimization history. *Journal of Traumatic Stress,* 8(4), 649–673.

Wolff, C. (1986). Magnus Hirschfeld: A portrait of a pioneer in sexology. London, UK: Quartet Books.

World Association of Sexual Health (2014). *The Sexual Bill of Rights*. http://www.worldsexology.org.

World Health Organization (WHO). (2004). *Progress in reproductive health research—A new focus for WHO*. (Pamphlet No. 67). Geneva, Switzerland: Author.

World Health Organization. (2006). *Sexual and reproductive health: Defining sexual health*. Geneva, Switzerland: Author.

World Health Organization (WHO). (2017). Global Health Observatory (GHO) Data for HIV/AIDS. Retrieved from http://www.who.int/gho/hiv/en/

WPATH. (2012). *Standards of care for the health of transsexual, transgender, and gender-nonconforming people* (7th ed.). Retrieved from www.wpath.org

Wright, S., & Peterson, F. (2007). *The life and death of masturbation as a disease: Clinical implications for sex addiction treatment*. Paper presented at the 50th National Conference, Society for the Scientific Study of Sexuality, Indianapolis, Indianapolis.

Yarber, W., & Sayad, B. (2019). *Human sexuality: Diversity in contemporary society* (10th ed.). New York: McGraw-Hill Education.

Yarber, W., Sayad, B., & Strong, B. (2010). *Human sexuality: Diversity in contemporary America* (7th ed.). New York: McGraw-Hill.

Young, B., Desmarais, S., Baldwin, J., & Chandler, R. (2016). Sexual coercion practices among undergraduate male recreational athletes, intercollegiate athletes and non-athletes. *Journal of Violence Against Women, 23*(7).

Zippe, C., Kedia, A., Kedia, K., Nelson, D., & Agarwal, A. (2001). Management of erectile dysfunction following radical prostatectomy. *Current Urology Reports, 2*(6), 4.

INDEX

A

Abel, G., 140, 234, 310, 329
Abramov, L., 157
Aggrawal, A., 198
AIDS: Autoimmune Deficiency Syndrome. *See* HIV/AIDS
Albaugh, J., 163
Alcorn, L., 7–9, 47–49, 382
Al-Ghazali, A., 43
Altman, L., 127
American Academy of Pediatrics, 168
American Association of Sexuality Educators, Counselors, and Therapists, 169, 382
American College Health Association, 305
American Indian Movement, 115
American Psychiatric Association, 42, 116, 125, 229, 234, 297, 312
American Psychological Association, 97, 112, 125, 271
Amygdala, 270, 313
Analingus, 232
Androgen insensitivity syndrome, 201–202
Androgyny, 32, 211–212, 377
Appalachia, 131, 182, 217, 236, 348, 367
Arnett, J., 98
Aulette, J., 196

B

Bagley, C., 152
Bancroft, J., 133, 140, 159
Barker-Benfield, B., 128
Barna, J., 332
Beaver, D., 92
Beers, M., 171–172
Bem, D., 198, 209
Bem, S., 211
Benjamin, H., 77, 83, 114–115, 205, 372
Bennett, D., 64
Berec, L., 254
Bernstein, D., 298
Biden, J., 291, 382
Bigwood, J., 129
Bingham, L., xvii
Black, E., 251
Blackwell, E., 123–124
Bley, J., xvii, xviii, 6, 77, 277, 341

Blind Spots, 26, 365–366, 369, 370
Blue-Headed Wrasse, 253
Blum, D., 225
Bockting, W., 78
Bombeck, I., 43
Booth, A., 158
Bornstein, K., 373
Bornstein, R., 373
Brach, T., 272
Breastfeeding, 150, 165–171
Brecher, E., 123–124, 127, 132, 135
Briere, J., 302, 306
Brown, H., 24, 205, 373, 375
Brownmiller, S., 278
Brown v. Board of Education, 114, 138
Buffem, H., 98
Bullough, V., 131
Burgess, A., 296
Burleson, M., 159
Buzzone, E., 365

C

Calkins, M., 112
Camilleri, J., 329
Capehart, J., 9
Carnes, P., 313
Carroll, J., 223
Carter, R., 196
Catania, J., 164
Centers for Disease Control, 117, 280, 310
Charnetski, C., 164
Chasin, L., 256
Cinderella, 6, 23–24, 102
Circumcision, 97–98, 166
Cisgender, 180, 266, 373–375
Cohen, A., 93
Cohen, J., 217, 367
Coleman, E., 117
Coleman, F., 367
Comstock Act, 114, 116
Congenital adrenal hyperplasia, 201–202
Conversion therapy, 7, 9
Cooper, A., 311
Cooper, R., 365
Cox, L., 119, 372
Craig, D., 69
Crawford, Z., 49

Cunniligus, 345
Cutler, W., 159

D

Dalke, K., 201
Davis, K., 128
Dawson, S., 229
Debrot, A., 164
Defense of Marriage Act, 5, 119
DeGeneres, E., 118, 257
Delmonico, D., 313
DeLong, R., 330
Department of Veterans Affairs, 65, 133
Diamond, L., 198
Dickinson, R., 114, 123, 128
Dissociative identity disorder, 300, 303–304
Dobbins, J., 367
Don't ask don't tell, 119
Dopamine, 314, 326, 343
Du Bois, W., 112, 138
Durant, W., 88

E

Ellis, H., 123, 126–127, 129
Ellison, C., 157, 164
Encyclopedia Britannica, 88
Entroitus, 128
Erickson, E., 212
Erotomania, 312
Estrogen, 82, 236, 280, 387
Eugenics, 93, 145
Evans, R., 118
Eye movement desensitization reprocessing
    (EMDR), 82, 298

F

Family-Centered Perinatal Education (FCPE), 129,
    166
Fausto-Sterling, A., 202, 375
Featured stories of diverse perspectives
    and experiences, 142, 208, 251
Fellatio, 232
Finkelhor, D., 306
First Nation People, 103
Fisher, B., 168, 294, 350
Fisher, H., 343, 350
Flappers, 113, 130–131, 399
Fleishman, M., 216, 228, 248
Flexman Clinic, xvii
Flexman, J., xvii

Flieshman, M., xvii
Flores, A., 205, 373, 375
Floyd, W., 326
Forari, R., 158
Ford Motor Company, 112, 130
Fox, R., xvii, 68, 133
Frabotta, R., xvii, 24, 106, 142, 208, 251
Freud, S., 123, 295
Friedan, B., 115, 139

G

Gander, K., 8
Gender dysphoria, 77–81, 83, 264
Gender fluidity, 192, 217, 265
Genotypes, 201
Germ theory, 90, 112
Giles, G., 162
Gladwell, M., 369
Goldman, E., 112
Good, B., 90
Good Health Doctrine, 90, 92–93
Gordon, L., 129
Gould, G., 94
Greenberg, B., 194
Green, L., 107, 268
Greenspoon Worm, 254
Grinonneau-Denton, A., 32

H

Hall, G., 97–98, 112, 117, 123, 125, 190
HALT, 314
Hammack, P., 198
Hammond, C., 298
Handy, C., 365
Hanson, K., 332
Hare, E., 94
Harmon, K., 254
Has-bian, 250
Hase, S., 365
Health care disparities, 217
Heh, V., 220, 390, 393
Henig, R., 375
Herbenick, D., 101–102, 149
Herdt, G., 133, 209, 257
Herman, J., 132, 205, 272, 301–303, 373, 375
Hermaphroditism, 202
Heteroflexibility, 250
Hijra, 256
Hinton, C., 245, 247
Hippocampal, 270
Hirschfeld, M., 113, 123, 126–128, 130, 132, 381

HIV/AIDS (Human Immunodeficiency Virus/Acquired Immune Deficiency Syndrome), 143
Hockett, M., 365
Holder, E., 119, 330
Hollingsworth, L., 113
Homophobia, 180
Hooker, E., 114
Hooper, Hoyer, N., 256
Humorism, 90
Humors, 90, 94
Hyde, J., 152, 194, 206
Hyperphilia, 312
Hysteria, 95, 101, 111, 125, 295, 312

I

Implicit memory, 270
Intersectionality, 118, 217, 236, 240
Intersex, 117, 199, 201, 215–217, 248, 374, 375
Ip, S., 168

J

Jehl, D., 51
Jenner, C., 119, 373
Johari Window, 276, 360–361, 365–371, 377, 381
Johnson, V., 102, 114–115, 123, 132–137, 140–141, 151, 156, 160–161, 167, 175, 177, 190, 230, 238, 256, 271, 335, 338
Joint Chief of Staff testimony to Senate, 26
Jorgensen, C., 114, 184–185, 189, 372–373
Jung, C., 44–45, 112, 252, 258–259, 377

K

Kafka, M., 311
Kail, R., 44, 212
Kaku, M., 246
Kaplan, H., 140, 238–239
Kavanaugh-Jones, B., 64
Kay, J., xvii
Keesling, B., 102
Kellogg, A., 95, 97
Kellogg, H., 94
King, L., 23, 26, 102, 114–115, 138, 208
Kinsey, A., 29, 89–90, 96, 98, 114, 123, 126, 128, 131–133, 135–137, 140–141, 149, 156, 159, 167, 195, 205–207, 233, 381
Klein, M., 99, 146, 312
Klinefelter's syndrome, 201–202, 375
Komisaruk, B., 10, 156–157
Kraft-Ebing, R., 123–126

Krebs, C., 294, 307
Kupferman, I., 238

L

Last, C., 52, 125, 222, 224, 252, 276, 309, 360, 363
Laumann, E., 164, 311
Leelah's Law, 9
Leiblum, S., 161
Leitzmann, M., 162
Lê, M., 159
LeVay, S., 6, 33, 97, 194, 201, 234–235, 256, 310, 314, 369, 373–374
Levenson, J., 331
Levine, S., 196–198
Lips, H., 101–102, 149, 194, 208, 359
Litin, S., 172, 230
Loftus, E., 302
Lovemap, 222, 227, 229–230
Loving v. Virginia, 5
Low sexual literacy, 2, 6, 21–23, 26
Luft, J., 365
LUG (lesbian until graduation), 250

M

Maass, V., 24–25
Maier, T., 137
Maines, N., 373–374
Marantz, R., 375
Margolis, S., 171–172
Mark, K., 311
Martin, P., 98, 115, 132–133, 138, 156, 233, 294
Masson, J., 125
Mastectomy, 237
Masters in Sex, 137
Masters, W., xvii, 105, 114–115, 123, 132–137, 140–141, 151, 153, 156, 160–161, 167, 175–176, 179, 190, 230, 238, 256, 271, 335, 338, 381
Masturbation as disease (MAD), 93, 99, 126
Mathematics of Sexual Diversity, 218, 375
Matlovich, L., 116
Mayo Clinic, 69, 168, 171–172, 230, 232
McAnulty, R., 194
McCammon, S., 197
McGovern, J., 294, 304–305
Meaddough, E., 159
Merriam-Webster, 20, 42, 223
Meston, C., 341–342
Miasma theory, 90
Miner's war, 131
Misogyny, 294, 304
Mohler-Kuo, M., 294, 307

Mokdad, A., 54
Mole vole, 254–255
Money, J., 6, 90–92, 116, 122, 133, 140, 156, 227, 229–230
Mother Jones, 131
Mullen, M., 26
Murano, G., 258
Murrell, T., 158
Murthy, V., 63–64
Mutrux, G., 89, 131

N

National Center for Victims of Crime, 301
National Sexual Violence Resource Center, 306
Neurotransmitter, 154, 158, 164, 314
Nichols, A., 167
Nichols, F., 84
Nichols, M., 84
Nicolosi, A., 164
Norepinephrine, 158
Noymer, A., 90
Nucleus accumbins, 314
Nutt, A., 373

O

Olson, T., 26
Onanism, 92–94, 96, 98–99
Onanists, 95, 98
One Pulse Foundation, 25
Orchiectomy, 237
Orgasm, 153, 156
Oshinsky, D., 90
Oxytocin, 154, 158, 164–167, 326

P

Pair-bondance, 106
Paraphilia, 198, 227, 233–235
Parents and Friends of Lesbians and Gays, 116
Parker, A., 95
Patiño, M., 203, 215
Pedophili, 329–331
Perel, E., 343–344
Perelman, M., 238–239
Perkins, F., 114
Persson, G., 158
Peterson, C., 236
Peterson, F., 5, 31, 51, 67, 87, 121, 148, 175, 180, 193, 222, 243, 262, 268, 309, 331–333, 335, 361, 365, 367
Peterson, K., 166

Piper, R., 254
Planned Parenthood Federation, 129, 158–159, 161
Post-traumatic stress disorder (PTSD, 55, 78, 81, 271, 278, 297, 301, 338
Praunheim, R., 127
Procreational sex, 91, 93
Prostate, 163
Pulse Nightclub, 25

R

Raj, R., 96
Reamy, K., 160
Redman, E. (Scott), 4
Richards, R., 189, 217, 367, 373
Roach, M., 128, 134
Robinson, W., 87, 94, 97–98
Rockwood, D., 47, 180, 189–190, 217
Rolfing, 272
Rossing, M., 158
Ryan, C., 6–7, 87–88, 255, 280

S

Saigh, P., 297
Sanday, P., 294
Sanger, M., 113, 124, 129–131
Santos-Iglesias, P., 229
Satcher, D., 51
Sayle, A., 160
Schärer, L., 254
Scherer, R., 365
Schmidt, J., 94, 100
Schultz, D., 92, 97, 125–127, 314, 369
Scientific American, 64
Seifer, J., xvii, 133, 140
Self-Assessment for Family Support, 27
Self-Assessment for Satisfaction for Overall Health & Well-Being, 57–58
Self-Assessment for Sexual Health and Wellness Satisfaction (SHAWS), 2, 27, 194
Semenya, C., 203
Seto, M., 330–331
Setoodeh, R., 26
Sex negative, 6, 18, 27, 86, 92, 101, 126
Sexology, 2, 86–87, 111, 121, 123–124, 126, 128–129, 145, 156, 197, 360, 379, 382
Sexophrenia, 99–102
Sex orientation, 32, 37, 191, 197, 199–200, 203, 205, 214–216, 218–219, 222, 224, 236, 240, 248, 253, 255–256, 258, 387
Sexosophy, 86–87, 111, 121–124, 128–129

Sex-role orientation, 32, 37, 44, 60, 191, 199–200, 205, 210–212, 214–216, 235, 240, 362–363, 376–377, 380, 387–388
Sexual expression, 164, 224
Sexual Expression Cube (e-Cube), 2, 192, 222, 227–228, 230, 237, 240, 243, 246, 248, 260, 375, 378, 390, 393
Sexual Health and Wellness Satisfaction (SHAWS), 32, 380, 384
Sexual Hypercube (h-Cube), 2, 192–193, 218, 241, 243–246, 248–250, 252, 255, 259–260, 360, 362, 372, 375–376, 378–380
Sexual identity, 32, 40, 196, 214–215, 222, 250, 259
Sexual Identity Cube (i-Cube), 2, 39, 191, 193, 197–198, 213–214, 216–218, 222, 225, 228, 240, 243, 246, 248, 253, 255–256, 258, 260, 374, 378, 390, 393
Sexual incontinence, 94
Sexuality Information & Education Council for the United States, 115, 195
sexual neurasthenia, 92, 94, 101, 111, 126
Sexual orientation, 37, 198, 206, 387
Sexual tipping point, 237
Shapiro, F., 299–300
Shear, M., 9
Sheik, 113, 130
Shprintzen, A., 94
Singh, D., 160
Social Darwinism, 112
Society for the Scientific Study of Sexuality, 93, 114, 128, 382
Spack, N., 48
Spencer, H., 112
Spermatorhea, 101
Sprankle, E., 18
Stanford University sexual assault survivor, 278, 280, 304
Starr, B., 254–255
Stiefelhagen, S., 164
Stone, G., 5, 26, 130, 138
Stonewall Rebellion, 116
Strong, B., 194, 196, 223, 237, 256
Sugrue, D., 313–314, 325
Sykes, B., 255

T

Taylor, T., 88
Temporary able-bodied, 70
Testosterone, 45, 158
Thomas, J., 3, 5, 111, 137
Tissot, S., 94–95, 123

Transgender, 49, 77–78, 84, 118–119, 381
Transsexual, 77–78, 115, 188
Transudation, 136
Tur-Kaspa, I., 162
Two-Spirited, 256

U

Uniform Crime Report, 296

V

Vaginismus, 269
Van der Kolk, B., 270, 300, 302, 304
van Lunsen, R., 161
Verdon, T., 3
Vestibularitis, 269
Viagra, 118, 137, 141, 143–144, 175, 241
von Sydow, K., 160

W

Wallace, A., 23–24, 138
Walling, W., 95, 112
Walters, A., 118, 164
Webster's Dictionary, 94, 97, 100
Weeks, D., 140, 164–165
Weiss, R., 313
Whipple, B., 9–10, 117, 140, 145, 156–157
Whiptail lizard, 254
Wilcox, A., 159
Williams, L., 139, 280, 302, 367, 375–376
Woolley, H., 112
Worchester, E., 112
World Association of Sexual Health, 360, 379, 382
World Health Organization, 32, 52, 117, 195, 379
World Professional Association for Transgender Health, 49, 77
Wright, O., xvii
Wright, S., 93
Wright State University School of Medicine, xvii
Writers Eclectic (WE), xvii

Y

Yarber, W., 6, 84, 97, 152, 194, 196, 205, 207, 223, 256
Young, B., 26, 45, 113, 130, 183, 249, 291, 294, 307, 382

Z

Zippe, C., 162

CPSIA information can be obtained
at www.ICGtesting.com
Printed in the USA
LVHW100116050619
620129LV00002B/2/P

9 781516 544530